PROBLEM SOLVING SURVIVAL GUIDE

to accompany

FINANCIAL ACCOUNTING

8th Edition

Jerry J. Weygandt, Ph.D., C.P.A.
Arthur Andersen Alumni Professor of Accounting
University of Wisconsin - Madison
Madison, Wisconsin

Donald E. Kieso, Ph.D., C.P.A.
KPMG Peat Marwick Emeritus Professor of Accountancy
Northern Illinois University
DeKalb, Illinois

Paul D. Kimmel, Ph.D., C.P.A.
Associate Professor of Accounting
University of Wisconsin - Milwaukee
Milwaukee, Wisconsin

Prepared By
Marilyn F. Hunt, M.A., C.P.A.
University of Central Florida
Orlando, Florida

WILEY
JOHN WILEY & SONS, INC.

COVER PHOTO: ©Pacific Stock / Superstock

Copyright © 2012 by John Wiley & Sons, Inc.

Founded in 1807, John Wiley & Sons, Inc. has been a valued source of knowledge and understanding for more than 200 years, helping people around the world meet their needs and fulfill their aspirations. Our company is built on a foundation of principles that include responsibility to the communities we serve and where we live and work. In 2008, we launched a Corporate Citizenship Initiative, a global effort to address the environmental, social, economic, and ethical challenges we face in our business. Among the issues we are addressing are carbon impact, paper specifications and procurement, ethical conduct within our business and among our vendors, and community and charitable support. For more information, please visit our website: www.wiley.com/go/citizenship.

No part of this publication may be reproduced, stored in a retrieval system, or transmitted in any form or by any means, electronic, mechanical, photocopying, recording, scanning, or otherwise, except as permitted under Sections 107 or 108 of the 1976 United States Copyright Act, without either the prior written permission of the Publisher, or authorization through payment of the appropriate per-copy fee to the Copyright Clearance Center, Inc., 222 Rosewood Drive, Danvers, MA 01923, (978)750-8400, fax (978)750-4470, or on the web at www.copyright.com. Requests to the Publisher for permission should be addressed to the Permissions Department, John Wiley & Sons, Inc., 111 River Street, Hoboken, NJ 07030-5774, (201)748-6011, fax (201)748-6008, or online at http://www.wiley.com/go/permissions.

Evaluation copies are provided to qualified academics and professionals for review purposes only, for use in their courses during the next academic year. These copies are licensed and may not be sold or transferred to a third party. Upon completion of the review period, please return the evaluation copy to Wiley. Return instructions and a free of charge return shipping label are available at www.wiley.com/go/returnlabel. If you have chosen to adopt this textbook for use in your course, please accept this book as your complimentary desk copy. Outside of the United States, please contact your local representative.

ISBN-13 978-1-118-10292-3

10 9 8 7 6 5 4 3 2 1

CONTENTS

PREFACE: To the Student

The purpose of this problem-solving tutorial is to help you to improve your success rate in solving accounting homework assignments and in answering accounting exam questions. For each chapter we provide you with:

OVERVIEW	To briefly introduce the chapter topics and their importance.
LEARNING OBJECTIVES	To provide you with a learning framework. Explanations of these objectives also provide you with a summary of the major points covered in the chapter.
TIPS	To alert you to common pitfalls and misconceptions and to remind you of important terminology, concepts, and relationships that are relevant to answering specific questions or solving certain problems. To help you to understand the intricacies of a problematic situation and to tell you what to do in similar circumstances.
EXERCISES	To provide you with a selection of problems which are representative of homework assignments which an introductory accounting student may encounter.
MULTIPLE CHOICE	To provide you with a selection of multiple-choice questions which are representative of common exam questions covering topics in the chapter.
PURPOSES	To identify the essence of each question or exercise and to link them to learning objectives.
SOLUTIONS	To show you the appropriate solution for each exercise and multiple choice question presented.
EXPLANATIONS	To give you the details of how selected solutions were derived and to explain why things are done as shown.
APPROACHES	To coach you on the particular model, computational format, or other strategy to be used to solve particular problems. To teach you how to analyze and solve multiple-choice questions.

This book will be a welcome teaching/learning aid because it provides you with the opportunity to solve accounting problems in addition to the ones assigned by your instructor without having to rely on your teacher for solutions. Many of the exercises and questions contained herein are very similar to items in your accounting principles textbook; the difference is, the ones in this book are accompanied with detailed clearly-laid out solutions.

The use of the multiple choice questions in this volume and the related suggestions on how to approach them can easily increase your ability (and confidence in your ability) to deal with exam questions of this variety.

We are grateful to James M. Emig, of Villanova University for his constructive suggestions and editorial comments. We give special thanks to Chelsea E. Hunt for her invaluable editorial work and other assistance with this project. Our appreciation goes to Mary Ann Benson who skillfully prepared the manuscript and performed the composition of this book.

<table>
<tr><td>Marilyn F. Hunt</td><td>Donald E. Kieso</td></tr>
<tr><td>Jerry J. Weygandt</td><td>Paul D. Kimmel</td></tr>
</table>

HOW TO STUDY ACCOUNTING

The successful study of accounting requires a different approach than most other subjects. In addition to reading a chapter, applying the material through the completion of exercises or problems is necessary to develop a true and lasting understanding of the concepts introduced in the text chapter. The study of accounting principles is a combination of theory and practice; theory describes what to do and why, and practice is the application of guidelines to actual situations. We use illustrations (practice) to demonstrate how theory works and we use theory to explain why something is done in practice. Therefore, it is impossible to separate the two in the study of accounting.

Learning accounting is a cumulative process. It is difficult to master Chapter 4 until you are thoroughly familiar with Chapters 1-3, and so on. Therefore, it is imperative that you keep up with class assignments. And because accounting is a technical subject, you must pay particular attention to terminology.

Accounting is the language of business. It is an exciting subject that provides a challenge for most business majors. Your ultimate success in life may well depend on your ability to grasp financial data. The effort you expend now will provide rewards for years to come.

We encourage you to follow the four steps for study outlined below to give yourself the best possible chance for a successful learning experience and to make the most efficient use of your time. These steps provide a system of study for each new chapter in your text.

Step 1
- Scan the learning objectives in the text.
- Read the concepts for review. Look up and review any items with which you are not thoroughly familiar.
- Scan the chapter (or chapter section) rather quickly.
- Glance over the questions at the end of the chapter.

This first step will give you an overview of the material to be mastered.

Step 2
- Read the assigned pages slowly.
- Use the marginal notes to review and to locate topics within each chapter.
- Study carefully and mark for later attention any portions not clearly understood.
- Pay particular attention to examples and illustrations.
- Use the Do it! exercise and Do it! comprehensive problem at the end of the text chapter.
- Try to formulate tentative answers to end-of-chapter questions.

During this phase, you will be filling in the "outline" you formed in Step 1. Most of the details will fall into place during this part of your study. The remaining steps are necessary, however, for a keen understanding of the subject.

Step 3
- Carefully read the **Overview, Learning Objectives,** and **Tips** sections of this *Problem-Solving Survival Guide* volume.
- Do the **Exercises** in the *Problem-Solving Survival Guide* that pertain to the same study objectives as your homework assignments. Review the relevant **Illustrations** in this book.
- Do the **Multiple-Choice Type Questions** in the *Problem-Solving Survival Guide* that pertain to the same learning objectives as your homework assignments. Also do the relevant Self-Study Questions (multiple choice) at the end of the chapter in the text.

- Refer back to the sections of the chapter in the text that you marked as unclear if any. It is likely that any confusion or questions on your part will have been cleared up through your work in the *Problem-Solving Survival Guide* book. If a section remains unclear, carefully reread it and rework relevant pages of the *Problem-Solving Survival Guide.*
- Repeat this process for each assigned topic area.

Step 4
- Write out formal answers to homework assignments in the text.
This step is crucial because you find out whether you can independently **apply** the material you have been studying to fresh situations. You may find it necessary to go back to the text and/or *Problem-Solving Survival Guide* to restudy certain sections. This is common and merely shows that the study assignments are working for you.

Additional comments pertaining to Step 3 and your usage of this *Problem-Solving Survival Guide* volume are as follows:

- The **Learning Objectives** and **Tips** sections along with **Illustrations** will aid your understanding and retention of the material. **Exercises** provide examples of application of the text material. These should be very valuable in giving you guidance in completing homework assignments which are often similar in nature and content.

- The **Approach** stated for an exercise or question is likely the most valuable feature of this *Problem-Solving Survival Guide* volume because it tells you how to **think** through the situation at hand. This thought process can then be used for similar situations. It is impossible to illustrate every situation you may encounter. You can, however, handle new situations by simply applying what you know and making modifications where appropriate. Many students make the mistake of attempting to memorize their way through an accounting book. That too is an impossible feat. **Do not rely on memorization.** If this material is going to be useful to you, you must **think** about what you are reading and always be thinking of **why** things are as they are. If you know the reasoning for a particular accounting treatment, it will be much easier to remember that treatment and reconstruct it even weeks after your initial study of it.

- **Explanations** are provided for exercise and questions. These are very detailed so that you will thoroughly understand what is being done and why. These details will serve you well when you complete your homework assignments.

- Always make an honest effort to solve the exercises and answer the questions contained in this *Problem-Solving Survival Guide* volume **before** you look at the solutions. Usage in this manner will maximize the benefits you can expect to reap from this book.

- The **Multiple-Choice Type Questions** are self-tests to give you immediate feedback on how well you understand the material. Study the **Approaches** suggested for answering these questions in the *Problem-Solving Survival Guide.* Practice them when answering the multiple choice questions in the text. Apply them when taking examinations. By doing so, you will learn to calmly, methodically, and successfully process examination questions. This will definitely improve your exam scores.

- When you work an **Exercise** in the *Problem-Solving Survival Guide* or in the text, always read the instructions **before** you read all of the given data. This allows you to determine what you are to accomplish. Therefore, as you now read through the data, you can begin to process it because you can determine its significance and relevance. If you read the data before the instructions, you are likely to waste your time because you will have to reread the facts once you find out what you are to do with them. Also, more importantly, you are likely to begin to anticipate what the problem is about, which will often cause you to do things other than what is requested in the question.

Good luck and best wishes for a positive learning experience!

HOW TO APPROACH A MULTIPLE CHOICE EXAMINATION

1. Work questions in the order in which they appear on the exam. If a question looks too long or difficult and you choose to skip over it, put a big question mark in the margin to remind yourself to return to that question after others are completed. Also put a mark in the margin for any question meriting additional review at the end of the exam period.

2. Do not look at the answer choices until you have thoroughly processed the question stem (see 3 and 4 below). The wrong answers are called "distracters". The manner in which these "distractors" are developed causes them to likely mislead you or cause you to misinterpret the question if you read them too early in the process.

3. Read each question very carefully. Start with the requirement or essence of the question first (this is usually the last sentence or last phrase of the stem of the question) so that you immediately focus on the question's intent. Now as you read through the rest of the stem and encounter data, you can tell which data are relevant. Underline keywords and important facts. Be especially careful to note exception words such as **not**. Prepare intermediary solutions as you read the question. Identify pertinent information with notations in the margin of the exam. If a set of data is the basis for two or more questions, read the requirements of each of the questions **before** reading the data and before beginning to work on the first question (sometimes the questions can be worked simultaneously or you may find it easier to work them out of order).

4. Anticipate the answer before looking at the alternative solutions. Recall the applicable definition, concept, principle, rule, model, or format. If the question deals with a computation, perform the computation. Use abbreviations to describe each component of your computation; this will greatly aid you in following your work and staying on target with the question.

5. Read the answers and select the best answer choice. For computational questions, if the answer you have computed is not among the choices, check your math and the logic of your solution.

6. When you have completed all questions, review each question again to verify your choices. Reread the question requirement, scan the data, look at your selected answer, scan your work, and determine the reasonableness of your choice.

· ·

CHAPTER 1

Accounting in Action

OVERVIEW

You and every other member of society depend on information to function efficiently and effectively. For example, people who invest in business enterprises use economic information to guide their decisions about future financial possibilities. Information about the effects of past actions is accumulated to serve as an aid in making better decisions in the future. Accounting is the system that provides relevant financial information to every person who owns or uses economic resources or otherwise engages in economic activity.

As a financial information system, accounting is the process of identifying, recording, and communicating the economic events of an organization. In this chapter, we: (1) introduce the subject of accounting and GAAP (generally accepted accounting principles), (2) discuss the basic accounting equation and the effects of transactions on its elements, and (3) examine the composition of the four general purpose financial statements required for business enterprises.

SUMMARY OF LEARNING OBJECTIVES

1. **Explain what accounting is.** Accounting is an information system that identifies, records, and communicates the economic events of an organization to interested users.

2. **Identify the users and uses of accounting.** The major users and uses of accounting are: (a) Management uses accounting information to plan, organize, and run the business. (b) Investors (owners) decide whether to buy, hold, or sell their financial interests on the basis of accounting data. (c) Creditors (suppliers and bankers) evaluate the risks of granting credit or lending money on the basis of the accounting information. Other groups that use accounting information are taxing authorities, regulatory agencies, customers, and labor unions.

3. **Understand why ethics is a fundamental business concept.** Ethics are the standards of conduct by which one's actions are judged as right or wrong. Effective financial reporting depends on sound ethical behavior.

4. **Explain the meaning of generally accepted accounting principles.** Generally accepted accounting principles are a common set of standards used by accountants.

5. **Explain the meaning of the monetary unit assumption and the economic entity assumption.** The monetary unit assumption requires that companies include in the accounting records only transaction data capable of being expressed in terms of money. The economic entity assumption requires that the activities of each economic entity be kept separate from the activities of its owners and other economic entities.

6. **State the basic accounting equation and explain the meaning of its components.** The basic accounting equation is:

    ## ASSETS = LIABILITIES + STOCKHOLDERS' EQUITY

    Assets are resources a business owns. Liabilities are creditorship claims on total assets. Stockholders' equity is the ownership claim on total assets and is often referred to as residual equity.

    The expanded accounting equation is:

    Assets = Liabilities + Common Stock + Revenues – Expenses – Dividends

    Common stock is affected when the company issues new shares of stock in exchange for cash. Revenues are increases in assets resulting from income-earning activities. Expenses are the costs of assets consumed or services used in the process of earning revenue. Dividends are payments the company makes to its stockholders.

7. **Analyze the effect of business transactions on the basic accounting equation.** Each business transaction must have a dual effect on the accounting equation. For example, if an individual asset increases, there must be a corresponding (1) decrease in another asset, (2) increase in a specific liability, or (3) increase in stockholders' equity.

8. **Understand the four financial statements and how they are prepared.** An income statement presents the revenues and expenses, and resulting net income or net loss for a specified period of time. A retained earnings statement summarizes the changes in retained earnings that have occurred during a given period of time. A balance sheet reports the assets, liabilities, and stockholders' equity of a business at a specific date. A statement of cash flows summarizes information concerning the cash inflows (receipts) and outflows (payments) for a specific period of time.

*9. **Explain the career opportunities in accounting.** Accounting offers many different jobs in fields such as public and private accounting, government, and forensic accounting. Accounting is a popular major because there are many different types of jobs with unlimited potential for career advancement.

*This material appears in the **Appendix to Chapter 1** in the text.

TIPS ON CHAPTER TOPICS

TIP: Accounting is the language of business. Thus, the more you learn and understand about accounting and its usefulness, the better you will be able to succeed in any business endeavor, regardless of what your major field of study and job title is.

TIP: **Transactions** are the economic events of an entity recorded by accountants. Some events (happenings of consequence to an entity) are not measurable in terms of money and thus do not get recorded in the accounting records. Hiring employees, placing an order for supplies, greeting a customer and quoting prices for products are examples of activities that do not by themselves constitute transactions. When an event is identified as a transaction, it must be measured (i.e., the appropriate dollar amount must be determined) before it can be recorded.

TIP: There are three types of business organizations: proprietorships, partnerships, and corporations. Ignoring the specific type of organization of a particular entity, we can express its basic accounting equation as follows:

ASSETS = LIABILITIES + OWNERS' EQUITY

If the entity is a corporation, the **owners' equity** is called **stockholders' equity**; if the entity is a partnership, the owners' equity is called **partners' equity**; if the entity is a proprietorship, the residual equity is called **owner's equity**. The emphasis in this textbook is on the corporate form of organization.

TIP: When you encounter a transaction, always analyze it in terms of its effects on the elements of the basic accounting equation (sometimes called the **balance sheet equation).** For your analysis to be complete, the transaction must maintain balance in the basic accounting equation. The **basic accounting equation** for a corporation is as follows:

ASSETS = LIABILITIES + STOCKHOLDERS' EQUITY

Assets are economic resources. Liabilities and stockholders' equity are sources of resources; liabilities are creditor sources, and stockholders' equity represents owner sources (owner investments and undistributed profits).

TIP: The balance of liabilities and the balance of stockholders' equity at a point in time simply serve as scorecards of the total amounts of unspecified assets which have come about from creditor sources (liabilities) and owner sources (stockholders' equity). Thus, you can **not** determine the amount of cash (or any other specific asset) held by an entity by looking at the balance of stockholders' equity or liabilities. You must look at the listing of individual assets on the balance sheet to determine the amount of cash owned.

TIP: The **cost principle** is often called the **historical cost principle.** Because of this principle, we typically report the cost of assets held, not their current market values. Generally, the balance sheet does not purport to reflect current market values. Cost is the value exchanged at the time something is acquired; thus cost equals the market value (sometimes called fair market value) at the date of acquisition.

TIP: A **revenue type transaction** will always cause an increase in stockholders' equity. In addition, it will cause either an increase in assets **OR** a decrease in liabilities (the former is the more common effect). An **expense type transaction** will always cause a decrease in stockholders' equity. In addition, it will cause either a decrease in assets **OR** an increase in liabilities (the former is the more common effect).

TIP:	Like any other discipline, accounting has its own vocabulary. In order for you to be able to understand what you read in subsequent chapters of this book, it is imperative that you master the new terms explained in this chapter. If you are not thoroughly familiar with the basic concepts used to explain more advanced material, you will likely have an erroneous interpretation of that later material. For each chapter in your text, make it a habit to study the glossary until you master the new terms being introduced.
TIP:	Accounting assumptions and principles are often referred to as accounting concepts.
TIP:	Generally, accounting is based on completed transactions. As a result, salaries which have been earned by employees (whether paid or not) must be accounted for presently; however, salaries to be earned by employees and paid by the entity in future periods are not reflected in the entity's statements until the future period in which they are incurred.
TIP:	Read the Preface and How to Study Accounting. These precede Chapter 1 of this self-study volume.

EXERCISE 1-1

Purpose: (L.O. 6, 7) This exercise will test your understanding of the components of the basic accounting equation.

Instructions
A list of **independent** situations appears below. Answer each question posed.

1.   The total assets of Mitzer Corporation at December 31, 2014 are $380,000 and its total liabilities are $150,000 at that same date. **Question:** What is the amount of Mitzer Corporation's total stockholders' equity at December 31, 2014?

    Answer: _____

2.   The total assets of Heidi Corporation are $400,000 at December 31, 2014, and its total stockholders' equity is $280,000 at the same date. **Question:** What is the amount of Heidi Corporation's total liabilities at December 31, 2014?

    Answer: _____

3.   The total liabilities of Aaron Corporation are $128,000 at December 31, 2014. Total stockholders' equity for the company is $220,000 at that same date. **Question:** What is the amount of total assets for the corporation at December 31, 2014?

    Answer: _____

4.   The total liabilities of Malcohm Corporation are $80,000. The total assets of the company are three times the amount of its total liabilities. **Question:** What is the amount of Malcohm Corporation's total stockholders' equity?

    Answer: _____

5.   At January 1, 2014, Molly Corporation had total assets of $600,000 and total liabilities of $340,000. During the calendar year of 2014, total assets increased $80,000, and total liabilities decreased $30,000. **Question 1:** What was the change in stockholders' equity during 2014?

Answer 1: _____

Question 2: What was the amount of stockholders' equity at December 31, 2014?

Answer 2: _____

6.   At January 1, 2014, Blackford Corporation had total assets of $500,000 and total stockholders' equity of $280,000. During 2014, total assets decreased $40,000, and total liabilities decreased $22,000. **Question 1:** What was the amount of total liabilities at January 1, 2014?

Answer 1: _____

Question 2: What was the change during 2014 in total stockholders' equity?

Answer 2: _____

Question 3: What was the total stockholders' equity at December 31, 2014?

Answer 3: _____

SOLUTION TO EXERCISE 1-1

Approach: Write down the basic accounting equation:

$$\text{ASSETS = LIABILITIES + STOCKHOLDERS' EQUITY}$$
$$\text{or}$$
$$\text{A = L + SE}$$

Fill in the amounts given and use your knowledge of algebra to solve for any unknown.

Explanation:
1.   Assets = Liabilities + Stockholders' Equity
     $380,000 = $150,000 + SE
     $380,000 - $150,000 = SE
     $230,000 = SE
     <u>$230,000</u> = Stockholders' Equity

TIP:	Recall that algebraic rules require the change in a number's sign when moved to the other side of the equals sign. Thus, a positive $150,000 becomes a negative $150,000 when moved from the right side of the equation to the left side of the equation.

2.   Assets = Liabilities + Stockholders' Equity
     $400,000 = L + $280,000
     $400,000 - $280,000 = L
     $120,000 = L
     <u>$120,000</u> = Liabilities

3. Assets = Liabilities + Stockholders' Equity
    A = $128,000 + $220,000
    A = $348,000
    Assets = $348,000

4. Assets = Liabilities + Stockholders' Equity
    3 (L) = L + SE
    3 ($80,000) = $80,000 + SE
    $240,000 = $80,000 + SE
    $240,000 - $80,000 = SE
    $160,000 = SE
    $160,000 = Stockholders' Equity

5. (1) $\Delta A = \Delta L + \Delta SE$
    $\uparrow\$80,000 = \downarrow\$30,000 + \Delta SE$
    $\uparrow\$80,000 + \uparrow\$30,000 = \Delta SE$
    $\uparrow\$110,000 = \Delta SE$
    Increase of $110,000 = Change in Stockholders' Equity

> **TIP:** When the ↓$30,000 is moved from the right side of the "=" to the left side of the equation, its sign changes so it becomes a ↑$30,000.
>
> **TIP:** The basic accounting equation is applied at a specific point in time. When you have the facts for the equation components at two different points in time for the same entity (such as amounts as of the beginning of a year and amounts as of the end of the year), you can modify the basic accounting equation to reflect that total changes in assets equals total changes in liabilities plus total changes in stockholders' equity. Using the symbol Δ to designate change, the following equation also holds true:
>
> $$\Delta A = \Delta L + \Delta SE$$

(2) Assets = Liabilities + Stockholders' Equity
    $600,000 = $340,000 + SE
    $600,000 - $340,000 = SE at January 1, 2014
    $260,000 = Stockholders' Equity at January 1, 2014

Stockholders' Equity at January 1, 2014	$260,000
Increase in Stockholders' Equity during 2014 (Answer 1)	110,000
Stockholders' Equity at December 31, 2014	$370,000

OR

Assets at January 1, 2014	$600,000
Increase in Assets during 2014	80,000
Total Assets at December 31, 2014	$680,000
Liabilities at January 1, 2014	$340,000
Decrease in Liabilities during 2014	(30,000)
Total Liabilities at December 31, 2014	$310,000

Assets = Liabilities + Stockholders' Equity
$680,000 = $310,000 + SE
$680,000 - $310,000 = SE
$370,000 = SE
$370,000 = Stockholders' Equity at December 31, 2014

6. (1) Assets = Liabilities + Stockholders' Equity
         $500,000 = L + $280,000
         $500,000 - $280,000 = L
         $220,000 = L
         $220,000 = Liabilities at January 1, 2014

    (2) $\Delta A = \Delta L + \Delta SE$
         $\downarrow$$40,000 = $\downarrow$$22,000 + ΔSE
         $\downarrow$$40,000 + $\uparrow$$22,000 = ΔSE
         $\downarrow$$18,000 = ΔSE
         Decrease of $18,000 = Change in Stockholders' Equity during 2014

    (3) Stockholders' Equity at January 1, 2014 $280,000
         Decrease in Stockholders' Equity during 2014 (Answer 2)   (18,000)
         Stockholders' Equity at December 31, 2014 $262,000

                                    OR

         Assets at January 1, 2014 $500,000
         Decrease in Assets during 2014   (40,000)
         Assets at December 31, 2014 $460,000

         Liabilities at January 1, 2014 (Answer 1) $220,000
         Decrease in Liabilities during 2014   (22,000)
         Liabilities at December 31, 2014 $198,000

         Assets = Liabilities + Stockholders' Equity
         $460,000 = $198,000 + SE
         $460,000 - $198,000 = SE
         $262,000 = Stockholders' Equity at December 31, 2014

EXERCISE 1-2

Purpose: (L.O. 7) This exercise illustrates that:
          (1) Each transaction has a dual effect on the basic accounting equation.
          (2) The basic accounting equation remains in balance after each transaction is
               properly analyzed and recorded.

Marc Anthony owns and operates the J. Lo Motorcycle Repair Shop, Inc. A list of the
transactions that take place in August 2014 follows:

1. August 1   Marc begins the business by investing $5,000 cash in the business in
                 exchange for $5,000 of common stock.

2. August 2   J. Lo Motorcycle Repair Shop, Inc. rents space for the shop behind a
                 strip mall and pays August rent of $800.

3.   August 3   J. Lo Motorcycle Repair Shop, Inc. purchases supplies for cash, $3,000.

4.   August 4   J. Lo Motorcycle Repair Shop, Inc. pays Cupboard News, a local newspaper, $300 for an ad appearing in the Sunday edition.

5.   August 5   J. Lo Motorcycle Repair Shop, Inc. repairs a cycle for a customer. The customer pays cash of $1,300 for services rendered.

6.   August 11   J. Lo Motorcycle Repair Shop, Inc. repairs a cycle for a customer, Ben Affleck, on credit, $500.

7.   August 13   J. Lo Motorcycle Repair Shop, Inc. purchases supplies for $900 by paying cash of $200 and charging the rest on account.

8.   August 14   J. Lo Motorcycle Repair Shop, Inc. repairs a Harley for Zonie Kinkennon, a champion rider, for $1,900. J. Lo Motorcycle Repair Shop, Inc. collects $1,000 in cash and puts the rest on account.

9.   August 24   J. Lo Motorcycle Repair Shop, Inc. collects cash of $400 from Ben Affleck.

10. August 28   J. Lo Motorcycle Repair Shop, Inc. pays $200 to Mini Maid for cleaning services for the month of August.

11. August 29   J. Lo Motorcycle Repair Shop, Inc. repairs a cycle for Burt Reynolds for $1,200 on account.

12. August 31   The board of directors of the corporation declared and paid a dividend of $400 in cash to its stockholders.

Instructions

Prepare a tabular analysis of the transactions above to indicate the effect of each of the transactions on the various balance sheet items. Use a "+" to indicate an increase and a "-" to indicate a decrease. Indicate the new balances after each transaction. In the stockholders' equity column, indicate the specific portion of stockholders' equity affected (common stock or retained earnings). Also, indicate the cause of each change in stockholders' equity. Use the following column headings:

| Transaction Number | ASSETS | | | = | LIABIL- ITIES | + | EQUITY | STOCKHOLDERS' | |
| | Cash + | Accounts Receivable + | Supplies | = | Accounts Payable | + | Common Stock | Retained Earnings | Explanation |

SOLUTION TO EXERCISE 1-2

Transaction Number	ASSETS Cash	+	Accounts Receivable	+	Supplies	=	LIABILITIES Accounts Payable	+	STOCKHOLDERS' EQUITY Common Stock	+	Retained Earnings	Explanation
(1)	+$5,000	+		+		=		+	$5,000	+		Owner Investment
(2)	-800					=					-$ 800	Rent Expense
Balances	4,200					=			5,000	+	(800)	
(3)	-3,000				+$3,000	=						
Balances	1,200	+		+	3,000	=		+	5,000	+	(800)	
(4)	-300					=					-300	Advertising Expense
Balances	900			+	3,000	=			5,000	+	(1,100)	
(5)	+1,300					=					+1,300	Service Revenue
Balances	2,200			+	3,000	=			5,000	+	200	
(6)			+$ 500			=					+500	Service Revenue
Balances	2,200	+	500	+	3,000	=		+	5,000	+	700	
(7)	-200				+900	=	+$700					
Balances	2,000	+	500	+	3,900	=	700	+	5,000	+	700	
(8)	+1,000		+900			=					+1,900	Service Revenue
Balances	3,000	+	1,400	+	3,900	=	700	+	5,000	+	2,600	
(9)	+400		-400			=						
Balances	3,400	+	1,000	+	3,900	=	700	+	5,000	+	2,600	
(10)	-200					=					-200	Cleaning Expense
Balances	3,200	+	1,000	+	3,900	=	700	+	5,000	+	2,400	
(11)			+1,200			=					+1,200	Service Revenue
Balances	3,200		2,200		3,900	=	700		5,000	+	3,600	
(12)	-400					=					-400	Dividends
Balances	$2,800	+	$2,200	+	$3,900	=	$700	+	$5,000	+	$3,200	

> **TIP:** Make sure the balances at any given point in time reflect equality in the components of the basic accounting equation. If equality does not exist, the work is incomplete or some error has been made. After all transactions are analyzed for J. Lo Motorcycle Repair Shop, Inc. total assets = $8,900, total liabilities = $700, and total stockholders' equity = $8,200. The equation is in balance.
>
> **TIP:** Notice transaction number 7. Even though there were three items affected (Cash, Supplies, and Accounts Payable), the analysis of the transaction maintains balance in the basic accounting equation. Total assets increased by $700 ($900 - $200), and liabilities increased by $700.
>
> **TIP:** Notice transaction number 8. Even though there were three items affected (Cash, Accounts Receivable, and Retained Earnings), the analysis of the transaction maintains balance in the equation. Total assets increased by $1,900 ($1,000 + $900), and stockholders' equity increased by $1,900.

Approach: Take each transaction and analyze it separately. Determine if the transaction involves the following:

Assets: Assets are resources owned or controlled by a business. Thus, they are the things of value used in carrying out such activities as production, consumption, and exchange. An asset represents a future economic benefit that will eventually result in an inflow of cash to the holder.

Liabilities: Liabilities are creditor sources of resources or creditors' claims on total assets. They are existing debts and obligations which will become due in the future and will normally require an outlay of cash in order to be liquidated.

Stockholders' Equity: The owners' claim on total assets of a corporation is known as stockholders' equity. Total assets minus total liabilities equals total stockholders' equity. The components of stockholders' equity are as follows:

(1) **Paid-in (contributed) capital**—the total amount paid in (invested) by stockholders. The amount of cash and other assets acquired by the corporation from stockholders in exchange for capital stock. Although some corporations issue more than one class of stock, each corporation has common stock.

(2) **Retained earnings**—business earnings retained for use in the business; net income since the inception of the business less total dividends (owner withdrawals) since the inception of the business. Often called **earned capital.**

    (a) **Net income** is the amount of excess of total revenues over total expenses for a particular period of time. (An excess of total expenses over total revenues for a particular period of time is referred to as **net loss.**)

    (b) **Revenues** are the gross increases in stockholders' equity resulting from business activities entered into for the purpose of earning income. Generally, revenues result from the sale of merchandise, the performance of services, the rental of property, or the lending of money.

    (c) **Expenses** are the costs of assets consumed or services used up in the process of earning revenue. Expenses are the decreases in stockholders' equity that result from operating the business. Expenses represent actual or expected cash outflows (payments).

    (d) **Dividends** occur when a corporation distributes cash or other assets to stockholders. Dividends cause a decrease in retained earnings; hence, dividends cause a decrease in total stockholders' equity.

> **TIP:**   A keen understanding of the definitions for the terms discussed above (especially assets, liabilities, stockholders' equity, revenues, and expenses) is vitally important for your study of accounting. Proceed with your reading **only** after you have mastered these terms. As you progress through the book, periodically return here to review these concepts.

If a transaction involves assets or liabilities, identify which particular asset or liability is affected and in what direction and by what amount. If a transaction involves stockholders' equity, identify the specific reason for that change—owner investment (common stock), owner withdrawal (dividends), revenue earned, or expense incurred. Be sure to classify each revenue and expense item by type (for example, salaries expense or rent expense). Also identify the amount and direction of each change in stockholders' equity.

ILLUSTRATION 1-1
MEASUREMENT PRINCIPLES (L.O. 4)

GAAP (generally accepted accounting principles) generally uses one of two measurement principles, the **cost principle** or the **fair value principle**. Selection of which principle to follow generally relates to trade-offs between relevance and faithful representation. **Relevance** means that financial information is capable of making a difference in a decision. **Faithful representation** means that the numbers and descriptions match what really existed or happened—it is factual.

The **cost principle** (or historical cost principle) dictates that companies record assets at their cost and continue to report assets at their cost over the time the assets are held. For example, if Office Depot purchases land for $60,000, the company initially reports it in its accounting records at $60,000. But what does Office Depot do if, by the end of the next year, the fair value of the land has increased to $80,000? Under the cost principle it continues to report the land at $60,000.

The **fair value principle** indicates that assets and liabilities should be reported at fair value (the price received to sell an asset or settle a liability). Fair value information may be more useful than historical cost for certain types of assets and liabilities. For example, certain investment securities are reported at fair value because market value information is often readily available for these types of assets. In choosing between cost and fair value, the FASB uses two qualities that make accounting information useful for decision making—relevance and faithful representation. In determining which measurement principle to use, the FASB weighs the factual nature of cost figures versus the relevance of fair value. In general, the FASB indicates that most assets must follow the cost principle because market values are not representationally faithful. Only in situations where assets are actively traded, such as investment securities, is the fair value principle applied.

> **TIP:**   The cost of an asset is measured by the fair value of the asset (or the fair value of the consideration given in the exchange) at the date the item is acquired. Therefore an asset is always recorded at cost (which is equal to fair value) at the acquisition date. It is reported at a later date at either its original cost or at its current fair value, depending on which measurement principle is employed.

ILLUSTRATION 1-2
DUAL EFFECT OF TRANSACTIONS ON THE BASIC ACCOUNTING EQUATION (L.O. 6, 7)

Each transaction affects items in the basic accounting equation in such a manner as to maintain equality in the basic accounting equation. The possible combinations of dual effects are illustrated below with examples of transactions that fit each category of combinations. Some examples are too advanced to be comprehended at this level in your accounting study so references are made to future chapters for those items. Do not attempt to research those items at this time—just accept the fact that in the future you will more readily understand those examples. These advanced examples are included here to show you that there are illustrations of every conceivable combination of dual effects on the basic accounting equation.

Effects of Transaction on Basic Equation

1. $A = L + SE$
    $\uparrow \ \uparrow$

2. $A = L + SE$
    $\downarrow \ \downarrow$

3. $A = L + SE$
    $\uparrow \ \uparrow$

4. $A = L + SE$
    $\downarrow \ \downarrow$

5. $A = L + SE$
    $\downarrow \uparrow$

6. $A = L + SE$
    $\uparrow \downarrow$

7. $A = L + SE$
    $\uparrow \downarrow$

Examples of Transactions

a. Owner investment of personal assets into the business (such as exchange of cash for stock in a corporation).
b. Sale of services for cash or on account.

a. Owner withdrawal of assets from the business for personal use (such as a cash dividend distributed to stockholders in a corporation).
b. Cash payment for various expenses, such as salaries expense and advertising expense. (Also, Chapter 3, consumption of noncash assets in operations, such as the consumption of supplies.)

a. Acquisition of any asset on credit. Borrowing money.

a. Payment of any debt.

a. Exchange of any asset for another asset, such as purchase of equipment for cash or collection of an account receivable.

a. Exchange of one liability for another, such as settling an account payable by issuing a note payable.

a. [Chapter 11—Corporation declares a stock dividend].

ILLUSTRATION 1-1 (Continued)

8. $A = L + SE$
    $\downarrow \uparrow$

    a.   Liquidation of a debt by giving an ownership interest in the entity (such as issuing stock to settle a liability).

    b.   [Chapter 3—Entity earns revenue after cash was previously received and recorded].

9. $A = L + SE$
    $\uparrow \downarrow$

    a.   [Chapter 11—Corporation declares cash dividends on stock and the dividends are to be distributed at a later date.]

    b.   [Chapter 3—Incurring expense (that is, consuming benefits in carrying out operations) before paying for the goods or services, (such as having an advertisement appear in a newspaper before paying for the advertisement.)]

TIP: Examine the examples. Some of them are preceded by an "a" and some are preceded by a "b." Notice that all of the "a" type examples have no impact on the income statement; whereas all of the "b" type examples do impact the income statement. All examples above impact the balance sheet.

TIP: A single transaction may affect more than two items in the basic accounting equation and still maintain equality in the equation. For example, assume a company receives a $700 bill for repairs to a copier. If the company pays $500 cash to the vendor and promises to pay the remaining $200 in one month, the transaction (receipt of services in exchange for cash and a promise to pay cash in the future) would affect the components of the basic accounting equation as follows:

$$A \quad = \quad L \quad + \quad SE$$
$$\downarrow \$500 \quad = \quad \uparrow \$200 \quad + \quad \downarrow \$700$$

The equation remains in balance.

TIP: As you progress through your accounting course(s) and possibly a career in business, you will constantly encounter new transactions and familiar transactions with a new twist. These unfamiliar situations can be addressed with confidence if you carefully analyze the effects of each transaction on the basic accounting equation.

EXERCISE 1-3

Purpose: (L.O. 8) This exercise will provide you with an illustration of an income statement, a retained earnings statement, a balance sheet, and a statement of cash flows.

The J. Lo Motorcycle Repair Shop, Inc. in Monrovia, California, prepares financial statements each month.

Instructions
Refer to the **Solution to Exercise 1-2** above. Use the information displayed to:
(a)   Prepare an income statement for the month of August 2014.
(b)   Prepare a retained earnings statement for the month of August 2014.
(c)   Prepare a balance sheet at August 31, 2014.
(d)   Prepare a statement of cash flows for the month of August 2014.

Approach: Think about what each statement is to report. A summary is as follows:
(a)   The **income statement** reports the results of operations for a period of time. Therefore, the income statement in this exercise reports revenues and expenses for August.
(b)   The **retained earnings statement** reports all changes in retained earnings for a period of time. It starts with the balance of retained earnings at the beginning of the period. Then, net income (or net loss, whichever is applicable) and dividends are identified in the statement. The retained earnings balance at the end of the period is the final amount on the statement.
(c)   The **balance sheet** reports on the financial position at a point in time (August 31 in this case). It reports assets, liabilities, and stockholders' equity. The balance of stockholders' equity used here includes the ending balance of common stock and the ending balance of retained earnings (the latter comes from the retained earnings statement).
(d)   The **statement of cash flows** reports the cash inflows and cash outflows during a period of time and classifies these flows into three activities: (1) operating, (2) investing, and (3) financing.

SOLUTION TO EXERCISE 1-3

(a)

J. LO MOTORCYCLE REPAIR SHOP, INC.
Income Statement
For the Month Ended August 31, 2014

Revenues		
Service revenue		$4,900*
Expenses		
Rent expense	$800	
Advertising expense	300	
Cleaning expense	200	
Total expenses		1,300
Net income		$3,600

*Computation: $1,300 + $500 + $1,900 + $1,200 = $4,900.

TIP:	Even though there were four separate revenue transactions, they are reported in the aggregate on the income statement. Also notice that there is no distinction made on the income statement between cash revenue transactions and revenue transactions that are on account.
TIP:	As you might be wondering, there are likely some other expenses incurred by the J. Lo Motorcycle Repair Shop, Inc. during August that have not yet been addressed. For example, some supplies were probably consumed in making repairs. Also, services such as power and telephone likely were consumed in August (for which payment will be made in September). These situations will be explained in **Chapter 3.**
TIP:	**Dividends** are a form of **owner withdrawals.** They do **not** appear on the income statement because they are not expenses—they have no impact on operations. Dividends are a distribution of company profits and not a determinant of profits (net income).

(b)

J. LO MOTORCYCLE REPAIR SHOP, INC.
Retained Earnings Statement
For the Month Ended August 31, 2014

Retained Earnings, August 1, 2014	$ 0
Add: Net income	3,600
	3,600
Less: Dividends	400
Retained Earnings, August 31, 2014	$3,200

TIP:	**Net income** for one particular period is often referred to as **earnings.** Net income for all periods since the corporation was formed less total dividends since the inception of the business is referred to as **retained earnings** or **accumulated earnings**.
TIP:	The **retained earnings statement** is often expanded to become the **statement of stockholders' equity** or the **statement of shareholders' equity** (as is the case with the PepsiCo, Inc. illustrated in **Appendix A** of your textbook and the Coca-Cola Company illustrated in **Appendix B** of your textbook). A statement of stockholders' equity will show all reasons for all changes in all stockholders' equity items during the period. Thus, it will include all of the information normally found on a statement of retained earnings as well as the reasons for changes in paid-in capital items (common stock) during the period.

(c)

J. LO MOTORCYCLE REPAIR SHOP, INC.
Balance Sheet
August 31, 2014

Assets

Cash		$2,800
Accounts receivable		2,200
Supplies		3,900
Total assets		$8,900

Liabilities and Stockholders' Equity

Liabilities		
Accounts payable		$ 700
Stockholders' Equity		
Common Stock	$5,000	
Retained Earnings	3,200	8,200
Total liabilities and stockholders' equity		$8,900

TIP: Supplies refers to supplies on hand. Therefore, this item is an asset.

TIP: Notice that although the total stockholders' equity balance is $8,200, the balance of cash is far less than that. Also notice what gave rise to that $8,200 balance of stockholders' equity: the owners invested $5,000, the company has operated at a profit of $3,600 (total revenues exceeded total expenses) since its inception, and total company earnings ($3,600) exceed total dividends ($400). Therefore, the ending stockholders' equity stems from owner investments of $5,000 and undistributed earnings of $3,200.

TIP: Think about the logical order in which the financial statements are prepared: the income statement then the retained earnings statement and then the balance sheet. That's because the income statement provides the net income figure used to compute the change in retained earnings. All changes in retained earnings are reported on the retained earnings statement to determine the ending balance for retained earnings. That ending retained earnings balance is then used as a necessary component of the balance sheet.

TIP: Notice that everything on the balance sheet in the liabilities and stockholders' equity section lacks physical existence. The balance of Accounts Payable represents the total amount owed at the balance sheet date to suppliers of goods and services because of past transactions. The balance of total stockholders' equity tells us the dollar amount of the entity's resources at the balance sheet date which have resulted from the owners' investments and the entity's profitable operations (i.e., profits that have not been distributed to the owners). Notice that in this particular situation the ending amount of stockholders' equity exceeds the amount of cash. Also, the amount of net income for the month of August exceeds the amount of cash at August 31, 2014.

(d)

J. LO MOTORCYCLE REPAIR SHOP, INC.
Statement of Cash Flows
For the Month Ended August 31, 2014

Cash flows from operating activities		
Cash receipts from customers		$2,700
Cash payments for expenses and supplies		(4,500)
Net cash used by operating activities		(1,800)
Cash flows from investing activities		
[None illustrated here]		
Net cash provided by investing activities		0
Cash flows from financing activities		
Sale of common stock	$5,000	
Payment of cash dividends	(400)	
Net cash provided by financing activities		4,600
Net increase in cash		2,800
Cash at the beginning of the period		0
Cash at the end of the period		$2,800

Computations:
Cash receipts from customers: $1,300 + $1,000 + $400 = $2,700.
Cash payments for expenses and supplies: $800 + $3,000 + $300 + $200 + $200 = $4,500.

EXERCISE 1-4

Purpose: (L.O. 8) This exercise will give you practice in classifying items on financial statements.

_____	1.	Cash	_____	21. Commission revenue
_____	2.	Accounts payable	_____	22. Insurance expense
_____	3.	Equipment	_____	23 Rent expense
_____	4.	Utilities expense	_____	24. Rent revenue
_____	5.	Common stock	_____	25. Interest expense
_____	6.	Salaries and wages payable	_____	26. Interest revenue
_____	7.	Salaries and wages expense	_____	27. Interest income
_____	8.	Advertising expense	_____	28. Office supplies expense
_____	9.	Advertising payable	_____	29. Audit fees incurred
_____	10.	Office supplies	_____	30. Service revenue
_____	11.	Note payable	_____	31. Legal fees earned
_____	12.	Note receivable	_____	32. Legal fees incurred
_____	13.	Dividends	_____	33. Prepaid insurance
_____	14.	Fees earned	_____	34. Property tax expense
_____	15.	Fees incurred	_____	35. Mortgage payable
_____	16.	Telephone expense	_____	36. Loan receivable
_____	17.	Cleaning supplies on hand	_____	37. Bank loan payable
_____	18.	Property taxes payable	_____	38. Royalty revenue
_____	19.	Cleaning expense	_____	39. Royalty expense
_____	20.	Commission expense	_____	40. Medical supplies

Instructions

Indicate how each of the above should be classified on a set of financial statements. Use the following abbreviations to communicate your responses.

A	Asset on the balance sheet
L	Liability on the balance sheet
SE	Stockholders' equity balance on the balance sheet
D	Dividends on the retained earnings statement
R	Revenue on the income statement
E	Expense on the income statement

SOLUTION TO EXERCISE 1-4

Approach: Look for the key word or words, if any, in each individual item. For examples, a list of key words or phrases follows along with the likely classifications:

Key word (phrases)	Classification
Revenue	Revenue on the income statement
Expense	Expense on the income statement
Earned	Revenue on the income statement
Incurred	Expense on the income statement
On hand	Asset on the balance sheet
Prepaid	Asset on the balance sheet
Receivable	Asset on the balance sheet
Payable	Liability on the balance sheet

1.	A	11.	L	21.	R	31.	R
2.	L	12.	A	22.	E	32.	E
3.	A	13.	D	23.	E	33.	A
4	E	14.	R	24.	R	34.	E
5.	SE	15.	E	25.	E	35.	L
6.	L	16.	E	26.	R	36.	A
7.	E	17.	A	27.	R[a]	37.	L
8.	E	18.	L	28.	E	38.	R
9.	L	19.	E	29.	E	39.	E
10.	A	20.	E	30.	R	40.	A

[a]The word income in an item is often used instead of the word revenue. Such as rent income, interest income, and commission income. This usage of the word income should not be confused with the term "net income" which is the excess of total revenues over total expenses.

TIP:	Keep in mind that an asset is an item that offers probable future economic benefits. If something will assist the revenue generating process of a future accounting period, it is an asset.
TIP:	You can determine the position of an entity in a particular transaction by the wording of the explanation. For example, we would use the item "bank loan payable" (a liability) if we had borrowed money from the bank. The bank would have a "loan receivable" (an asset) item on its balance sheet. As another example, we would have "legal fees incurred" (an expense) on our income statement if we had used legal services. The law firm which provided the services would report a corresponding "legal fees earned" (revenue) item on its income statement.

EXERCISE 1-5

Purpose: (L.O. 6, 7, 8) This exercise reviews the basic accounting equation (A = L + SE) and the connection between the income statement and the balance sheet. The connection is a change in stockholders' equity during a period due to the net income or net loss for the period.

The following data were extracted from the records of Handy Hernanco Corporation:

Total assets, beginning of the period	$250,000
Total liabilities, beginning of the period	90,000
Dividends declared and paid during the period	75,000
Total assets, end of the period	270,000
Total liabilities, end of the period	95,000
Sale of additional stock during the period	25,000

Instructions
Compute the amount of net income (or net loss) for the period. Show your computations.

SOLUTION TO EXERCISE 1-5

Approach: The question asks you to solve for net income; however, no information is given regarding revenues and expenses for the period. Only balance sheet data and transactions affecting stockholders' equity are given. Net income (or net loss) for a period is one reason for change in the balance of stockholders' equity. Write down the items that reconcile the beginning stockholders' equity balance with the ending stockholders' equity balance, enter the amounts known, compute beginning and ending stockholders' equity balances by use of the basic accounting equation, and then solve for the amount of net income.

Beginning stockholders' equity	$160,000[a]
Additional owner contributions (sale of stock)	25,000
Owner withdrawals (dividends) during the period	(75,000)
Subtotal	110,000
Net income (loss) for the period	+ X
Ending stockholders' equity	$175,000[b]
Solving for X, net income =	$65,000

[a]A = L + SE
$250,000 = $90,000 + ?
Beginning stockholders' equity = $160,000

[b]A = L + SE
$270,000 = $95,000 + ?
Ending stockholders' equity = $175,000

TIP:	Solving an exercise of this type requires a lot of thought and a clear understanding of the relationships of accounting data.

EXERCISE 1-6

Purpose: (L.O. 1 thru 9) This exercise will quiz you about terminology used in this chapter.

A list of accounting terms with which you should be familiar appears below.

Accounting	International Accounting Standards Board (IASB)
Assets	International Financial Reporting Standards (IFRS)
*Auditing	Liabilities
Balance sheet	*Management consulting
Basic accounting equation	Managerial accounting
Bookkeeping	Monetary unit assumption
Common stock	Net income
Corporation	Net loss
Cost principle	Owners' equity
Dividend	Partnership
Economic entity assumption	*Private (or managerial) accounting
Ethics	Proprietorship
Expanded accounting equation	*Public accounting
Expenses	Relevance
Fair value principle	Retained earnings statement
Faithful representation	Revenues
Financial accounting	Sarbanes-Oxley Act of 2002 (SOX)
Financial Accounting Standards Board (FASB)	Securities and Exchange Commission (SEC)
*Forensic accounting	Statement of cash flows
Generally accepted accounting principles (GAAP)	Stockholders' equity
	*Taxation
Income statement	Transactions

*These items appear in the **Appendix to Chapter 1** in the text.

Instructions
For each item below, enter in the blank the term that is described.

1. _____The information system that identifies, records, and communicates the economic events of an organization to interested users.

2. _____An accounting principle that states that assets should be recorded at their cost.

3. _____A financial statement that presents the revenues and expenses and resulting net income or net loss of a company for a specific period of time. It is sometimes called the **operating statement.**

4. _____The gross increase in stockholders' equity resulting from business activities entered into for the purpose of earning income.

5. _____The cost of assets consumed or services used in the process of earning revenue.

6. _____Assets = Liabilities + Stockholders' equity.

7. _____Resources owned by a business.

8. _____Creditors' claims on total assets.

9. _____The ownership claim on total assets; usually called stockholders' equity in a corporate form of organization.

10. _____A financial statement that reports the assets, liabilities, and stockholders' equity of a company at a specific date. It is sometimes called the **statement of financial position.**

11. _____Common standards that indicate how to report economic events.

12. _____A financial statement that summarizes the changes in retained earnings for a specific period of time.

13. _____An assumption stating that only transaction data that can be expressed in terms of money be included in the accounting records.

14. _____An assumption that requires that the activities of the entity be kept separate and distinct from the activities of its owners and all other economic entities.

15. _____The economic events of the enterprise that are recorded by accountants.

16. _____A distribution by a corporation to its stockholders (owners) on a pro rata (equal) basis.

17. _____A financial statement that provides information about the cash inflows (receipts) and cash outflows (payments) of an entity for a specific period of time.

18. _____The standards of conduct by which one's actions are judged as right or wrong, honest or dishonest, fair or not fair.

19. _____A private organization that establishes generally accepted accounting principles.

20. _____A governmental agency that requires companies to file financial reports in accordance with generally accepted accounting principles.

21. _____The amount by which revenues exceed expenses for a specific period of time.

22. _____The ownership claim on total assets of a corporation.

23. _____A business organized as a separate legal entity under state corporation law having ownership divided into transferable shares of stock.

24. _____An association of two or more persons to carry on as co-owners of a business for profit.

25. _____A business owned by one person.

26. _____A part of accounting that involves only the recording of economic events.

27. _____The amount by which expenses exceed revenues for a specific period of time.

28. _____The field of accounting that provides economic and accounting information for managers and other interenal users.

29. _____The field of accounting that provides economic and financial information for investors, creditors, and other external users.

30. _____An area of accounting in which the accountant offers expert service to the general public.

31. _____An area of public accounting involving financial planning and control and the development of accounting and computer systems.

32. _____An area of public accounting involving tax advice, tax planning, and preparation of tax returns.

33. _____An area of accounting within a company that involves such activities as cost accounting, budgeting, and accounting information systems.

34. _____The examination of financial statements by a certified public accountant in order to express an opinion as to the fairness of presentation.

35. _____An area of accounting that uses accounting, auditing, and investigative skills to conduct investigations into theft and fraud.

36. _____Term used to describe the total amount paid in by stockholders for the shares they purchase.

37. _____An accounting principle that states that companies should report assets at their fair value.

38. _____It means that the numbers and descriptions of financial information match what really existed or happened—it is factual.

39. _____An accounting standard-setting body that issues standards adopted by many countries outside of the United States.

40. _____It means that financial information is capable of making a difference in a decision.

41. _____Law passed by Congress in 2002 intended to reduce unethical corporate behavior.

42. _____Assets = Liabilities + Common Stock + Revenues – Expenses – Dividends.

43. _____International accounting standards set by the International Accounting Standards Board (IASB).

SOLUTION TO EXERCISE 1-6

1. Accounting
2. Cost principle
3. Income statement
4. Revenues
5. Expenses
6. Basic accounting equation
7. Assets
8. Liabilities
9. Owners' equity
10. Balance sheet
11. Generally accepted accounting principles
12. Retained earnings statement
13. Monetary unit assumption
14. Economic entity assumption
15. Transactions
16. Dividend
17. Statement of cash flows
18. Ethics
19. Financial Accounting Standards Board
20. Securities and Exchange Commission
21. Net income
22. Stockholders' equity
23. Corporation
24. Partnership
25. Proprietorship
26. Bookkeeping
27. Net loss
28. Managerial accounting
29. Financial accounting
30. Public accounting
31. Management consulting
32. Taxation
33. Private (or managerial) accounting
34. Auditing
35. Forensic accounting
36. Common stock
37. Fair value principle
38. Faithful representation
39. International Accounting Standards Board (IASB)
40. Relevance
41. Sarbanes-Oxley Act of 2002 (SOX)
42. Expanded accounting equation
43. International Financial Reporting Standards

ANALYSIS OF MULTIPLE-CHOICE TYPE QUESTIONS

1. **Question**
    (L.O. 4) The two organizations who are primarily responsible for establishing generally accepted accounting principles are:
    a. The FASB and the FBI.
    b. The SEC and the IRS.
    c. The SEC and the FASB.
    d. The IRS and the publisher of the <u>Wall Street Journal</u>.

    Explanation: The Financial Accounting Standards Board (FASB) is a private organization that establishes broad reporting standards of general applicability as well as specific accounting rules. The Securities and Exchange Commission (SEC) is a governmental agency that requires companies filing financial reports with it to follow generally accepted accounting principles. In situations where no principles exist, the SEC often mandates that certain guidelines be used. In general, the FASB and the SEC work hand in hand to assure that timely and useful accounting principles are developed. (Solution = c.)

2. **Question**
    (L.O. 5) Which accounting assumption or principle dictates that a business owner's personal expenses should not be recorded on the books of the business?
    a. Economic entity assumption.
    b. Monetary unit assumption.
    c. Cost principle.
    d. Basic accounting equation.

Approach and Explanation: Briefly explain each answer selection. Compare your explanations with the question. The economic entity assumption requires that the activities of the entity be kept separate and distinct from (1) the activities of its owners, and (2) all other economic entities. The monetary unit assumption requires that only transaction data that can be expressed in terms of money be included in the accounting records and provides that all transactions and events can be measured in terms of a common denominator—units of money. The cost principle states that assets should be recorded at cost and indicates that cost is measured by the value exchanged at the time something is acquired. The basic accounting equation provides that total assets at a point in time equals total liabilities plus total owner's equity at the same point in time. (Solution = a.)

3. **Question**
(L.O. 4) The Seller Company sold the Buyer Company a building on August 1, 2014. Buyer Company paid Seller Company $92,000 cash. The Seller Company had originally purchased the building in 2013 for $80,000. The county taxing authority showed an assessed valuation of $78,000 for the building for 2015 taxing purposes and an independent appraisal agency appraised it at $95,000 on July 15, 2014. The Buyer Company should record the building in their accounting books at:
a. $78,000.
b. $80,000.
c. $92,000.
d. $95,000.

Approach and Explanation: Read the last sentence first. You can tell by that last sentence the Buyer is acquiring a building (an asset). Think about the cost principle. It provides that all assets be recorded at cost. Cost is measured by the value exchanged at the time something is acquired. In any exchange transaction, cost is therefore measured by the fair market value (cash equivalent value) of the consideration given or by the fair market value of the consideration received, whichever is more clearly (objectively) determinable. When cash is paid, there is no question about the cash value of the consideration given. Read the rest of the question. In this case, the cash payment of $92,000 clearly determines the cost of the building to the Buyer Company. (Solution = c.)

4. **Question**
(L.O. 8) The balance sheet is sometimes called the:
a.   Earnings statement.
b.   Operating statement.
c.   Profit and loss statement.
d.   Statement of financial position.

Approach and Explanation: Read the question stem. Think of alternative names for the balance sheet. Then take each answer selection and see if it agrees with your response or not. Answer selections "a", "b", and "c" are all alternative names for the income statement. Statement of financial position is a name for the balance sheet because it reports on the entity's financial position at a point in time. Statement of assets and equities might be another (but not popular) alternative name for the balance sheet. (Solution = d.)

5. **Question**
    (L.O. 6, 7) Tully Company, a sole proprietorship, began business in 2013 At January 1, 2014, Tully Company's assets totaled $70,000, and its liabilities amounted to $40,000. Net income for 2014 was $24,000 and owner withdrawals amounted to $25,000. At December 31, 2014, assets totaled $90,000, and liabilities amounted to $57,000. The amount of additional owner investments during 2014 amounted to:
    a. $0.
    b. $2,000.
    c. $3,000.
    d. $4,000.

    Approach: Use your knowledge of the basic accounting equation and reasons for changes in owner's equity to solve.

    Explanation:

A	=	L	+	OE	
$70,000	=	$40,000	+	$30,000[a]	Balance at Jan. 1, 2014
				24,000	Net income for 2014
				(25,000)	Drawings for 2014
				+ X	Investments for 2014
$90,000	=	$57,000	+	$33,000[b]	Balance at Dec. 31, 2014

    [a]$70,000 - $40,000 = $30,000
    [b]$90,000 - $57,000 = $33,000

    Solving for X: $30,000 + $24,000 - $25,000 + X = $33,000
    $29,000 + X = $33,000
    X = $33,000 - $29,000
    X = $4,000 owner investments during 2014 (Solution = d.)

6. **Question**
    (L.O. 6, 7) At January 1, 2014, King Corporation's assets totaled $76,000, and its liabilities amounted to $42,000. Net income for 2014 was $17,000, and dividends amounted to $13,000. The amount of stockholders' equity at December 31, 2014 is:
    a. $38,000.
    b. $51,000.
    c. $80,000.
    d. $93,000.

    Approach: Use your knowledge of the basic accounting equation and reasons for changes in stockholders' equity to solve.

    Explanation:

A	=	L	+	SE
$76,000	=	$42,000	+	SE at 1/1/14

    $76,000 - $42,000 = $34,000 SE at 1/1/14

$34,000	Stockholders' equity at January 1, 2014
17,000	Net income for 2014
(13,000)	Dividends for 2014
0	Additional owner investments for 2014
$38,000	Stockholders' equity at December 31, 2014 (Solution = a.)

7. **Question**
    (L.O. 7) Which of the following phrases describes the effects of the purchase of an asset on account?
    a. Increase in assets and increase in expenses.
    b. Increase in assets and increase in liabilities.
    c. Increase in expenses and increase in liabilities.
    d. Increase in liabilities and decrease in stockholders' equity.

    Approach: Determine the effects of the transaction and write them down before you read the answer selections. Write down the basic accounting equation and analyze the effects of the transaction on the elements of the equation. If the transaction affects stockholders' equity, clearly state why and how.

    Explanation: $A = L + SE$
    $\uparrow \uparrow$ (Solution = b.)

8. **Question**
    (L.O. 6) Which of the following statements is **not** true about all expenses?
    a. They result in a decrease in stockholders' equity.
    b. They result from the consumption of goods and services.
    c. They occur in the process of generating revenue.
    d. They are the same thing as liabilities.

    Approach and Explanation: Write down the definition of expense and the possible effects of an expense type transaction on the basic accounting equation. Then take each answer selection and see if it is true or not true about all expenses. An expense is the cost of an asset or other goods or services consumed in the process of generating revenue. The possible effects of an expense on the basic accounting equation are as follows:

    $$A = L + SE$$
    $$\downarrow \downarrow$$
    OR $\uparrow \downarrow$

    Liabilities are debts or obligations. A liability may arise because an asset is acquired on credit or because money is borrowed. A liability may arise in an expense transaction but not all expense transactions involve liabilities. Liabilities and expenses are **not** synonymous terms. (Solution = d.)

9. **Question**
    (L.O. 7) Which of the following statements is true regarding the current period's consumption of office supplies which were purchased and recorded as an asset in a prior accounting period?
    a. Total assets remain unchanged.
    b. Total stockholders' equity decreases.
    c. Total liabilities increase.
    d. Total assets increase.

    Approach and Explanation: Write down the effects of the consumption of office supplies previously on hand. The supplies were an asset when they were on hand. Now, they are an expense because they have been consumed. Therefore, assets decrease, and stockholders' equity decreases. (Solution = b.)

10. **Question**
    (L.O. 7) Which of the following statements is true regarding the effect of the purchase of equipment for cash?
    a.   Total assets decrease.
    b.   Total liabilities increase.
    c.   Total assets remain unchanged.
    d.   Total stockholders' equity decreases.

    Approach and Explanation: Think about the transaction. Cash (an asset) decreases. Equipment (another asset) increases by the same amount. There is no effect on liabilities or stockholders' equity. Look for the answer selection that fits the effects described. (Solution = c.)

    $$A = L + SE$$
    $$\downarrow\uparrow$$

11. **Question**
    (L.O. 6) Which of the following items is an example of a liability?
    a.   Wages expense.
    b.   Mortgage payable.
    c.   Accounts receivable.
    d.   Stockholders' equity

    Approach and Explanation: Think about the definition of a liability. Key words often associated with a liability are "debt," "obligation," or "payable." Examine each answer selection and determine its classification on financial statements. Write down your responses. Wages expense is an expense item on the income statement. Mortgage payable is a liability (Bingo!). Accounts receivable is an asset (key word is receivable). Stockholders' equity is owner's equity on the balance sheet of a corporation. (Solution = b.)

12. **Question**
    (L.O. 7) The effects of a corporation distributing earnings to its stockholders are to:
    a.   Increase expenses and decrease net income.
    b.   Increase expenses and decrease stockholders' equity.
    c.   Decrease assets and decrease net income.
    d.   Decrease assets and decrease stockholders' equity.

    Approach and Explanation: Write down the basic accounting equation and use arrows to indicate the effects of an owner withdrawal (of cash or other assets).

    $$A = L + SE$$
    $$\downarrow \quad \downarrow$$

Examine each answer selection and see if it fits your description. Owner withdrawals from a corporation are usually in the form of dividend distributions. An owner withdrawal is not an expense because it does not have anything to do with carrying out operations and generating revenue; it is a distribution of profits to the owner. (Solution = d.)

*13. Question

(L.O. 9) Which of the following terms refers to the process of reviewing the accounting records and reports to evaluate the fairness of the presentations in the reports and their compliance with established guidelines and rules?

a.   Auditing.
b.   Tax return preparation.
c.   Management consulting work.
d.   Public accounting.

Approach and Explanation: Briefly define each answer selection. Compare your definitions with the question stem to determine your answer. Auditing services are provided by public accounting firms. An audit is an examination of the financial statements of a company by a CPA for the purpose of an expression of an opinion as to the fairness of presentation. Tax return preparation involves preparing tax returns, usually without any verification of the data to be used for completion. Management consulting work involves giving advice to management on various matters. Public accounting involves providing services to clients. As a public accountant, an individual may perform one or more of the following services: auditing, taxation, and management consulting. (Solution = a.)

CHAPTER 2

. . . .

*T*HE RECORDING PROCESS

OVERVIEW

Due to the great number of transactions that occur daily in most businesses, accountants do not find it practical to present the cumulative effects of these transactions on the basic accounting equation in tabular form as we did in Exercise 2 in Chapter 1. Instead, they have developed a system by which the effects of transactions and events may conveniently be recorded, sorted, summarized, and stored until financial statements are desired. That system is the focus of this chapter.

SUMMARY OF LEARNING OBJECTIVES

1. **Explain what an account is and how it helps in the recording process.** An account is a record of increases and decreases in specific asset, liability, and stockholders' equity items.

2. **Define debits and credits and explain their use in recording business transactions.** The terms debit and credit are synonymous with left and right. Assets, dividends, and expenses are increased by debits and decreased by credits. Liabilities, common stock, retained earnings, and revenues are increased by credits and decreased by debits.

3. **Identify the basic steps in the recording process.** The basic steps in the recording process are: (a) analyze each transaction in terms of its effect on the accounts, (b) enter the transaction information in a journal, (c) transfer the journal information to the appropriate accounts in the ledger.

4. **Explain what a journal is and how it helps in the recording process.** The initial accounting record of a transaction is entered in a journal before the data are entered in the accounts. A journal (a) discloses in one place the complete effect of a transaction, (b) provides a chronological record of transactions, and (c) prevents or locates errors because the debit and credit amounts for each entry can be readily compared.

5. **Explain what a ledger is and how it helps in the recording process.** The ledger is the entire group of accounts maintained by a company. The ledger keeps in one place all the information about changes in specific account balances.

6. **Explain what posting is and how it helps in the recording process.** Posting is the procedure of transferring journal entries to the ledger accounts. This phase of the recording process accumulates the effects of journalized transactions in the individual accounts.

7. **Prepare a trial balance and explain its purposes.** A trial balance is a list of accounts and their balances at a given time. The primary purpose of the trial balance is to prove the mathematical equality of debits and credits after posting. A trial balance also uncovers errors in journalizing and posting and is useful in preparing financial statements.

TIPS ON CHAPTER TOPICS

TIP: An **account** is an individual accounting record of increases and decreases in a specific asset, liability, owner's capital, revenue, or expense item. An account consists of three parts: (1) the title of the account, (2) a left or debit side, and (3) a right or credit side. In classrooms and in textbooks, we refer to this as a **T-account.** We need a separate account for each item reported in the company's financial statements. When we refer to a specific account (such as Cash or Accounts Payable or Service Revenue), we capitalize its name.

The basic form of any T-account is as follows:

Title of Account

" Left" side → Debit | Credit ← "Right" side

Periodically, the accounts are totaled to arrive at balances. For each account, the amounts entered on the debit side are totaled, and the amounts entered on the credit side are separately totaled. The difference between these two totals is the account's balance; the balance appears on the side that has the greater total.

TIP: **To journalize** or **journalizing** refers to the process of recording a transaction or event in a journal. **To post** or **posting** refers to the transferring of information from journal entries to the appropriate ledger accounts. The posting phase of the recording process accumulates the effects of journalized transactions in the individual accounts.

ILLUSTRATION 2-1
EXPANDED BASIC ACCOUNTING EQUATION AND DEBIT
AND CREDIT RULES (L.O. 2)

Basic Equation

Assets = Liabilities + Stockholders' Equity

Expanded Basic Equation Debit/Credit Rules

Assets		=	Liabilities		+	Common Stock		+	Retained Earnings		-	Dividends		+	Revenues		-	Expenses	
Dr.	Cr.		Dr.	Cr.		Dr.	Cr.		Dr.	Cr.		Dr.	Cr.		Dr.	Cr.		Dr.	Cr.
+	-		-	+		-	+		-	+		+	-		-	+		+	-

TIP: A "+" indicates an increase and a "-" indicates a decrease. Therefore, a transaction which causes an increase in an asset is recorded by a debit to the related asset account; a transaction which causes a decrease in the same asset is recorded by a credit to the same account.

TIP: Drill on the "debit and credit rules" until you can quickly and correctly repeat them. If you memorize the rules for an asset account, you can figure out the rules for all other types of accounts by knowing which rules are the opposite of the rules for assets and which are the same.

TIP: "Debit" is a term that simply refers to the left side of any account. Thus, the debit side of an account is always the left side. "Credit" is a word that simply refers to the right side of an account. Thus, the credit side of an account is always the right side of the account. The phrase "to debit an account" means to enter an amount on the debit side of an account.

TIP: Total Assets at December 31, 2014 = Total Liabilities at December 31, 2014 + Common Stock at December 31, 2014 + Retained Earnings balance at January 1, 2014 - Dividends during the year of 2014 + Total Revenues earned during 2014 - Total Expenses incurred during 2014. (Carefully notice the dates involved in the expanded equation.)

Retained earnings at January 1, 2014 - Dividends for 2014 + Revenues for 2014 - Expenses for 2014 = Retained Earnings balance at December 31, 2014. (Thus, Dividends, Revenues, and Expenses are components of the Retained Earnings account because they explain the changes in total retained earnings. Although all changes in retained earnings could be recorded in the Retained Earnings account, it is preferable to use separate accounts for each type of revenue, each type of expense, and for dividends so that detailed data on these items can be accumulated and reported.) Assets at December 31, 2014 = Liabilities at December 31, 2014 + Common Stock at December 31, 2014 + Retained Earnings at December 31, 2014. Common Stock + Retained Earnings = Total Stockholders' Equity. Thus, Assets at December 31, 2014 = Liabilities at December 31, 2014 + Stockholders' Equity at December 31, 2014.

EXERCISE 2-1

Purpose: (L.O. 2) This exercise will test your understanding of the debit and credit rules.

A list of accounts appears below:

		Debit	Credit
1.	Cash	✓	
2.	Sales Revenue		
3.	Commissions Expense		
4.	Advertising Expense		
5.	Salaries and Wages Payable		
6.	Prepaid Insurance		
7.	Property Taxes Payable		
8.	Property Tax Expense		
9.	Dividends		
10.	Interest Revenue		
11.	Salaries and Wages Expense		
12.	Commissions Revenue		
13.	Unearned Service Revenue		
14.	Equipment		
15.	Note Payable		
16.	Building		
17.	Accounts Payable		
18.	Land		
19.	Accounts Receivable		
20.	Common Stock		

Instructions
For each account, put a check mark (✓) in the appropriate column to indicate if it is increased by an entry in the debit (left) side of the account or by an entry in the credit (right) side of the account. The first one is done for you.

TIP: In essence, you are being asked to identify the normal balance of each of the accounts listed. The **normal balance** of an account is the side where increases are recorded.

SOLUTION TO EXERCISE 2-1

Approach: Determine the classification of the account (asset, liability, common stock, retained earnings, dividends, revenue or expense). Think about the debit and credit rules for that classification.

	Account	Debit	Credit	Classification
1.	Cash	✓		Asset
2.	Sales Revenue		✓	Revenue
3.	Commissions Expense	✓		Expense
4.	Advertising Expense	✓		Expense
5.	Salaries and Wages Payable		✓	Liability
6.	Prepaid Insurance	✓		Asset
7.	Property Taxes Payable		✓	Liability
8.	Property Tax Expense	✓		Expense
9.	Dividends	✓		Dividends
10.	Interest Revenue		✓	Revenue
11.	Salaries and Wages Expense	✓		Expense
12.	Commissions Revenue		✓	Revenue
13.	Unearned Service Revenue		✓	Liability
14.	Equipment	✓		Asset
15.	Note Payable		✓	Liability
16.	Building	✓		Asset
17.	Accounts Payable		✓	Liability
18.	Land	✓		Asset
19.	Accounts Receivable	✓		Asset
20.	Common Stock		✓	Common Stock (owners' equity)

TIP: Increases in assets are recorded by debits. Because liabilities and stockholders' equity are on the other side of the equals sign in the basic accounting equation, they must have debit and credit rules opposite of the rules for assets. Therefore, a liability or a stockholders' equity account such as Common Stock or Retained Earnings is increased by a credit entry. Revenues earned increase retained earnings so the rules to record increases in revenue are the same as the rules to record increases in the Retained Earnings account (increases are recorded by credits). Because expenses and dividends reduce retained earnings, they have debit/credit rules which are opposite of the rules for the Retained Earnings account.

TIP: A separate account should exist in the ledger for each item that will appear on the financial statements.

The debit and credit rules are summarized below:

Asset Accounts			Liability Accounts	
Debit	Credit		Debit	Credit
Increase	Decrease		Decrease	Increase
+	-		-	+

Dividends Accounts			Stockholders' Equity Accounts	
Debit	Credit		Debit	Credit
Increase	Decrease		Decrease	Increase
+	-		-	+

Expense Accounts			Revenue Accounts	
Debit	Credit		Debit	Credit
Increase	Decrease		Decrease	Increase
+	-		-	+

Notice that the accounts are arranged in such a way here that all of the increases ("+" signs) are on the outside and all of the decreases ("-" signs) are on the inside of this diagram.

EXERCISE 2-2

Purpose: (L.O. 2, 4) This exercise will give you practice in applying the debit and credit rules.

A list of transactions appears below:
1. Dan Harrier invested $1,000 cash in a new business, Luxury Detailing, in exchange for common stock.
2. Purchased equipment for $600 cash.
3. Purchased $300 of supplies on account.
4. Rented a vehicle for the month and paid $250.
5. Paid $100 for an ad in a local newspaper.
6. Purchased gas for $20 on credit.
7. Sold services for $200 cash.
8. Sold services for $300 on account.
9. Paid $90 wages for an assistant's work.
10. Declared and paid a cash dividend of $80.
11. Paid for use of beeper service, $30.
12. Borrowed $2,000 from the Cash-N-Carry Bank in anticipation of expanding the business.

Instructions
Indicate how you would record each transaction. What account would you debit and what account would you credit? Use the appropriate code designation. The first transaction is coded for you.

	Transaction	**Code**

1. _____D11, C31_____

2. _____

3. _____

4. _____

5. _____

6. _____

7. _____

8. _____

9. _____

10. _____

11. _____

12. _____

D—Debit
C—Credit

11—Cash
12—Accounts Receivable
14—Supplies
16—Equipment
21—Accounts Payable
22—Loan Payable
31—Common Stock
32—Retained Earnings
41—Dividends
51—Service Revenue
63—Beeper Expense
64—Gas Expense
65—Rent Expense
66—Advertising Expense
67—Salaries and Wages Expense

SOLUTION TO EXERCISE 2-2

Approach: Analyze each transaction to determine what items are increased or decreased. Translate that information into debit and credit language by applying the debit and credit rules (see **Illustration 2-1**). Visualize the resulting journal entry.

	Transaction		**Transaction**		**Transaction**
1.	D11, C31	6.	D64, C21	11.	D63, C11
2.	D16, C11	7.	D11, C51	12.	D11, C22
3.	D14, C21	8.	D12, C51		
4.	D65, C11	9.	D67, C11		
5.	D66, C11	10.	D41, C11		

TIP:	The account Supplies is sometimes called Supplies on Hand.
TIP:	The fourth transaction could be recorded by a debit to Prepaid Rent and a credit to Cash at the date the rent is paid (at the beginning of the rental month). Then, at the end of the rental month, the expired amount would be transferred to the expense account (this approach will be explained in **Chapter 3**).

EXERCISE 2-3

Purpose: (L.O. 4) This exercise will illustrate how to record transactions in the general journal.

Transactions for the J.Lo Motorcycle Repair Shop, Inc.. (from **Exercise 1-2**) for August 2014 are repeated below.

Marc Anthony owns and operates the J. Lo Motorcycle Repair Shop, Inc. A list of the transactions that take place in August 2014 follows:

1. August 1   Marc begins the business by investing $5,000 cash in the business in exchange for $5,000 of common stock.

2. August 2   J. Lo Motorcycle Repair Shop, Inc. rents space for the shop behind a strip mall and pays August rent of $800.

3. August 3   J. Lo Motorcycle Repair Shop, Inc. purchases supplies for cash, $3,000.

4. August 4   J. Lo Motorcycle Repair Shop, Inc. pays Cupboard News, a local newspaper, $300 for an ad appearing in the Sunday edition.

5. August 5   J. Lo Motorcycle Repair Shop, Inc. repairs a cycle for a customer. The customer pays cash of $1,300 for services rendered.

6. August 11   J. Lo Motorcycle Repair Shop, Inc. repairs a cycle for a customer, Ben Affleck, on credit, $500.

7. August 13   J. Lo Motorcycle Repair Shop, Inc. purchases supplies for $900 by paying cash of $200 and charging the rest on account.

8. August 14   J. Lo Motorcycle Repair Shop, Inc. repairs a Harley for Zonie Kinkennon, a champion rider, for $1,900. J. Lo Motorcycle Repair Shop, Inc. collects $1,000 in cash and puts the rest on account.

9. August 24   J. Lo Motorcycle Repair Shop, Inc. collects cash of $400 from Ben Affleck.

10. August 28   J. Lo Motorcycle Repair Shop, Inc. pays $200 to Mini Maid for cleaning services for the month of August.

11. August 29   J. Lo Motorcycle Repair Shop, Inc. repairs a cycle for Burt Reynolds for $1,200 on account.

12. August 31   The board of directors of the corporation declared and paid a dividend of $400 in cash to its stockholders.

Instructions
(a) Explain the impact of each transaction on the elements of the basic accounting equation and translate that into debit and credit terms.
(b) Journalize the transactions listed above. Include a brief explanation with each journal entry.

SOLUTION TO EXERCISE 2-3

Approach: Write down the effects of each transaction on the basic accounting equation. Think about the individual asset, liability, or stockholders' equity accounts involved. Apply the debit and credit rules to translate the effects into a journal entry.

TIP:	Refer to the Solution to **Exercise 1-2** for an analysis of the effects of the transaction on the individual components of the basic accounting equation. Refer to **Illustration 2-1** for the summary of the debit and the credit rules.

(a) 1.   Increase in Cash.   Debit Cash
           Increase in Common Stock.   Credit Common Stock

     2.   Increase in Rent Expense.   Debit Rent Expense
           Decrease in Cash.   Credit Cash

     3.   Increase in Supplies.   Debit Supplies
           Decrease in Cash.   Credit Cash

     4.   Increase in Advertising Expense.   Debit Advertising Expense
           Decrease in Cash.   Credit Cash

     5.   Increase in Cash.   Debit Cash
           Increase in Service Revenue   Credit Service Revenue

     6.   Increase in Accounts Receivable.   Debit Accounts Receivable
           Increase in Service Revenue.   Credit Service Revenue

     7.   Increase in Supplies.   Debit Supplies
           Decrease in Cash.   Credit Cash
           Increase in Accounts Payable.   Credit Accounts Payable

     8.   Increase in Cash.   Debit Cash
           Increase in Accounts Receivable.   Debit Accounts Receivable
           Increase in Service Revenue   Credit Service Revenue

     9.   Increase in Cash.   Debit Cash
           Decrease in Accounts Receivable.   Credit Accounts Receivable

     10. Increase in Cleaning Expense.   Debit Cleaning Expense
           Decrease in Cash.   Credit Cash

     11. Increase in Accounts Receivable.   Debit Accounts Receivable
           Increase in Service Revenue.   Credit Service Revenue

     12. Increase in Dividends.   Debit Dividends
           Decrease in Cash.   Credit Cash

(b)

GENERAL JOURNAL

J1

	Date		Account Titles and Explanations	Ref.	Debit	Credit
	2014					
1.	Aug.	1	Cash		5,000	
			Common Stock			5,000
			(Issued shares of stock for cash)			
2.		2	Rent Expense		800	
			Cash			800
			(Paid August rent)			
3.		3	Supplies		3,000	
			Cash			3,000
			(Purchased supplies for cash)			
4.		4	Advertising Expense		300	
			Cash			300
			(Paid Cupboard News for advertising)			
5.		5	Cash		1,300	
			Service Revenue			1,300
			(Received cash for service fees earned)			
6.		11	Accounts Receivable		500	
			Service Revenue			500
			(Performed services for Ben Affleck on account)			
7.		13	Supplies		900	
			Cash			200
			Accounts Payable			700
			(Purchased supplies for cash and on credit)			
8.		14	Cash		1,000	
			Accounts Receivable		900	
			Service Revenue			1,900
			(Performed services for Zonie Kinkennon for cash and on credit)			
9.		24	Cash		400	
			Accounts Receivable			400
			(Received cash from Ben Affleck on account)			

GENERAL JOURNAL J1

	Date	Account Titles and Explanations	Ref.	Debit	Credit
	2014				
10.	Aug. 28	Cleaning Expense		200	
		Cash			200
		(Paid Mini Maid for cleaning services)			
11.	29	Accounts Receivable		1,200	
		Service Revenue			1,200
		(Performed services for Burt Reynolds on account)			
12.	31	Dividends		400	
		Cash			400
		(Declared and paid a cash dividend)			

TIP: A journal entry must contain equal debits and credits. That is, the total amount debited to individual accounts in an entry **must equal** the total amount credited to individual accounts. Thus, the dual (two-sided) effect of each transaction is recorded in appropriate accounts. This **double-entry system** offers a means of proving the accuracy of the recorded amounts. If every transaction is recorded with equal debits and credits, then the sum of all the debits to the accounts must equal the sum of all the credits to the accounts.

TIP: A journal entry is either a **simple entry** (an entry that contains only one debit and one credit) or a **compound entry** (an entry that contains more than one debit and/or more than one credit). Entries 7 and 8 above are compound entries.

TIP: Unless otherwise indicated, the use of the term **journal** refers to the general journal. Companies may use various kinds of journals, but every entity has a general journal which is the most basic form of journal.

TIP: Unless otherwise indicated, the use of the term **ledger** refers to the **general ledger.** Companies may use various kinds of ledgers, but every company has a general ledger. The general ledger contains accounts for each of the assets, liabilities, and owner's equity of an entity.

TIP: When specific account titles are given in homework assignments such as this exercise, they should be used. When account titles are not given, you may select account titles that identify the nature and content of each account. The account titles are for specific items that appear on the balance sheet (for example, asset type accounts include Cash, Accounts Receivable, Land, and Equipment and liability accounts include Accounts Payable and Note Payable) and on the income statement (for example, revenue type accounts include Service Revenue and Fee Revenue and expense type accounts include Salaries and Wages Expense, Repairs Expense, and Utilities Expense). The account titles used in journalizing should not contain explanations such as Cash Paid or Cash Received. When cash is received, the account Cash is debited, when cash is paid, the account Cash is credited.

TIP: To correctly record a transaction, you must carefully analyze the event and translate that analysis into debt and credit language. First, determine what items in the expanded basic accounting equation are affected by the transaction. Second, determine if those items are increased or decreased and by how much. Third, translate the increases and decreases into debits and credits.

EXERCISE 2-4

Purpose: (L.O. 6) This exercise will illustrate how to post transactions from the general journal to the general ledger.

Journal entries to record transactions for the J. Lo Motorcycle Repair Shop, Inc.. for August 2014 appear in the **Solution to Exercise 2-3.**

Instructions
Post the entries referred to above from the general journal to the following T-accounts. In the reference column of the journal (using the **Solution to Exercise 2-3**), write the account number to which a debit or credit amount is posted.

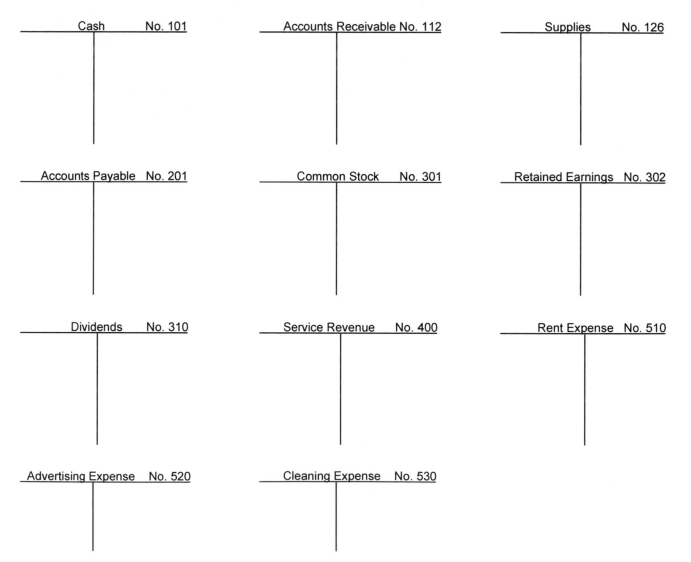

SOLUTION TO EXERCISE 2-4

Cash			No. 101
8/1	5,000	8/2	800
8/5	1,300	8/3	3,000
8/14	1,000	8/4	300
8/24	400	8/13	200
		8/28	200
		8/31	400

Accounts Receivable			No. 112
8/11	500	8/24	400
8/14	900		
8/29	1,200		

Supplies			No. 126
8/3	3,000		
8/13	900		

Accounts Payable			No. 201
		8/13	700

Common Stock			No. 301
		8/1	5,000

Retained Earnings			No. 302

Dividends			No. 310
8/31	400		

Service Revenue			No. 400
		8/5	1,300
		8/11	500
		8/14	1,900
		8/29	1,200

Rent Expense			No. 510
8/2	800		

Advertising Expense			No. 520
8/4	300		

Cleaning Expense			No. 530
8/28	200		

> **TIP:**   Notice that there are no amounts reflected yet in the Retained Earnings account. The process of getting amounts into that account is discussed in **Chapter 3.**

Explanation: Posting refers to the process of transferring journal entries to the ledger accounts. This phase of the recording process accumulates the effects of journalized transactions in the individual accounts. Posting involves the following steps:

1. In the ledger, enter, in the appropriate columns of the account(s) debited, the date, journal page, and debit amount shown in the journal.
2. In the reference column of the journal, write the account number to which the debit amount was posted.
3. In the ledger, enter, in the appropriate columns of the account(s) credited, the date, journal page, and credit amount shown in the journal.
4. In the reference column of the journal, write the account number to which the credit amount was posted.

The use of the reference column in the journal serves two purposes. It allows for:
(a) Cross referencing between the journal and the ledger which facilitates tracing of transactions from the journal to the ledger at a later date.
(b) A method of noting that the posting has been completed.

When T-accounts are used, such as in this exercise, the journal page of the debit or credit amount being posted is typically omitted in the ledger.

The general journal for the J.Lo Motorcycle Repair Shop, Inc.. should appear as follows when the posting process is completed:

		GENERAL JOURNAL			J1
	Date	Account Titles and Explanations	Ref.	Debit	Credit
1.	2014 Aug. 1	Cash Common Stock (Issued shares of stock for cash)	101 301	5,000	5,000
2.	2	Rent Expense Cash (Paid August rent)	510 101	800	800
3.	3	Supplies Cash (Purchased supplies for cash)	126 101	3,000	3,000
4.	4	Advertising Expense Cash (Paid Cupboard News for advertising)	520 101	300	300
5.	5	Cash Service Revenue (Received cash for service fees earned)	101 400	1,300	1,300
6.	11	Accounts Receivable Service Revenue (Performed services for Ben Affleck on account)	112 400	500	500
7.	13	Supplies Cash Accounts Payable (Purchased supplies for cash and on credit)	126 101 201	900	200 700

Date			Account Titles and Explanations	Ref.	Debit	Credit
2014						
8.	Aug.	14	Cash	101	1,000	
			Accounts Receivable	112	900	
			Service Revenue	400		1,900
			(Performed services for Zonie Kinkennon for cash and on credit)			
9.		24	Cash	101	400	
			Accounts Receivable	112		400
			(Received cash from Ben Affleck on account)			
10.		28	Cleaning Expense	530	200	
			Cash	101		200
			(Paid Mini Maid for cleaning services)			
11.		29	Accounts Receivable	112	1,200	
			Service Revenue	400		1,200
			(Performed services for Burt Reynolds on account)			
12.		31	Dividends	310	400	
			Cash	101		400
			(Declared and paid a cash dividend)			

GENERAL JOURNAL J1

EXERCISE 2-5

Purpose: (L.O. 7) This exercise will (1) illustrate how to prepare a trial balance, and (2) will discuss the reasons for preparing a trial balance.

A trial balance is prepared after all transactions have been posted from the journal to the ledger.

Instructions
Use the **Solution to Exercise 2-4** and do the following:
(a) Balance each account in the ledger.
(b) Prepare a trial balance.
(c) Describe a trial balance and list reasons why it is to be prepared.

TIP:	To balance a T-account, a balancing line is to be drawn in the T-account; the balance is entered beneath that line on the side of the account which has the largest total. (An account balance is determined by totaling the debits and totaling the credits and taking the difference between those two totals.) If an account has only one entry in it, no balancing line is needed because that one entry readily establishes the account's balance.

SOLUTION TO EXERCISE 2-5

(a)

```
          Cash      No. 101
8/1   5,000 | 8/2     800
8/5   1,300 | 8/3   3,000
8/14  1,000 | 8/4     300
8/24    400 | 8/13    200
            | 8/28    200
            | 8/31    400
Bal.  2,800 |
```

```
   Accounts Receivable No. 112
8/11    500 | 8/24    400
8/14    900 |
8/29  1,200 |
Bal.  2,200 |
```

```
        Supplies    No. 126
8/3   3,000 |
8/13    900 |
Bal.  3,900 |
```

```
   Accounts Payable  No. 201
            | 8/13    700
```

```
   Common Stock   No. 301
            | 8/1   5,000
```

```
   Retained Earnings  No. 302
```

```
      Dividends    No. 310
8/31    400 |
```

```
   Service Revenue  No. 400
            | 8/5   1,300
            | 8/11    500
            | 8/14  1,900
            | 8/29  1,200
            | Bal.  4,900
```

```
    Rent Expense  No. 510
8/2     800 |
```

```
 Advertising Expense No. 520
8/4     300 |
```

```
   Cleaning Expense  No. 530
8/28    200 |
```

(b)
J.Lo Motorcycle Repair Shop, Inc.
Trial Balance
August 31, 2014

	Debit	Credit
Cash	$ 2,800	
Accounts Receivable	2,200	
Supplies	3,900	
Accounts Payable		$ 700
Common Stock		5,000
Retained Earnings		0
Dividends	400	
Service Revenue...		4,900
Rent Expense	800	
Advertising Expense	300	
Cleaning Expense...	200	
	$10,600	$10,600

(c)   A **trial balance** is a list of the accounts and their balances at a given point in time. A trial balance serves several purposes, including:

1.   It proves that the ledger is in balance (that is, that total debits equal total credits in the ledger accounts). If errors are made in journalizing and posting, they may be detected in the process of preparing a trial balance.
2.   It is a starting point for organizing the information to be reported on a company's financial statements.

> **TIP:**   Scan over **Exercises 2-3, 2-4,** and **2-5.** Notice the logical progression of the steps in recording, classifying, and summarizing the transactions. In **Exercise 2-3,** each transaction had to be identified and analyzed in terms of its effects on various accounts. Then the transactions were recorded in the journal. In **Exercise 2-4,** the information in the journal is transferred (posted) to the ledger. Thus, all transactions that affect individual components of the basic accounting equation are summarized together. In **Exercise 2-5,** the accounts are balanced, and a trial balance is prepared which furthers the summarization process and checks for the maintenance of equality of debits and credits in the recording and posting phases.

EXERCISE 2-6

Purpose: (L.O. 7) This exercise will test your ability to identify the effects of errors that commonly occur in the process of recording and posting transactions. As you will see, some errors cause the accounts to be out of balance, thus quickly identifying the existence of an error. However, some errors do **not** cause an imbalance in the accounts and are more difficult to discover.

An inexperienced bookkeeper for Nip-N-Tuck Alteration Shop made the following errors in journalizing and posting the transactions that occurred during February 2014.

1.   The credit portion of a journal entry to record a $500 loan payment was posted to the ledger twice.
2.   A fictitious transaction was recorded in the journal for the amount of $300.
3.   A cash payment of $700 for rent was recorded in the journal by a debit of $700 to Rent Expense and a credit of $70 to Cash.

4. A debit entry of $50 to the Accounts Receivable account was incorrectly recorded as a debit entry of $50 to the Cash account.
5. A cash sale of $890 was incorrectly recorded in the journal as a cash sale of $980.
6. The debit portion of a journal entry to record a $60 credit sale was posted to the ledger, but the credit portion of this entry was not posted.
7. A $150 credit entry in the journal to the Accounts Payable account was posted as a credit to the Accounts Receivable account in the ledger.
8. An entire entry in the journal to record the $75 payment to the City of Orlando for an annual business license fee was omitted in the posting process.
9. A debit of $200 to the Equipment account was incorrectly posted as a $200 credit to the Equipment account.
10. The debit portion of a journal entry to record a $80 sale on account was posted to the ledger twice.
11. A $40 cash sale was completely omitted from the journal.
12. A $45 cash sale was recorded in the journal twice.
13. The balance in the Cash account was calculated incorrectly at $1,700. It should be $1,640.
14. A payment on account of $190 was journalized and posted as a debit to Repairs Expense and a credit to cash for $190.
15. A cash receipt of $80 from a customer on account was recorded twice in the journal.
16. The debit portion of a journal entry to record a cash sale was correctly posted to the ledger for $120. The credit portion of the same journal entry was posted to the Sales account in the ledger for $210.

Instructions

For each error, indicate (a) whether or not the resulting trial balance will balance. If the trial balance will not balance, indicate (b) the amount of the difference, and (c) the trial balance column that will have the larger total. Consider each error separately. Use the following form, in which error (1) is given as an example.

Error	(a) In Balance?	(b) $ Difference	(c) Larger Column
(1)	No	$500	Credit
(2)			
(3)			
(4)			
(5)			
(6)			
(7)			
(8)			
(9)			
(10)			
(11)			
(12)			
(13)			
(14)			
(15)			
(16)			

SOLUTION TO EXERCISE 2-6

Error	(a) In Balance?	(b) $ Difference	(c) Larger Column
(1)	No	$500	Credit
(2)	Yes		
(3)	No	$630	Debit
(4)	Yes		
(5)	Yes		
(6)	No	$60	Debit
(7)	Yes		
(8)	Yes		
(9)	No	$400	Credit
(10)	No	$80	Debit
(11)	Yes		
(12)	Yes		
(13)	No	$60	Debit
(14)	Yes		
(15)	Yes		
(16)	No	$90	Credit

Approach: For each error:

(a) Determine if total debits equal total credits in the journal and in the ledger. An imbalance in debits and credits in the journal and posting errors may cause an imbalance of total debits and credits in the ledger.

(b) Determine the amount of difference and larger column if the trial balance is not in balance. Errors that will cause an imbalance in the trial balance include:
1. Failure to record either the debit or credit portion (but not both portions) of a journal entry.
2. Recording the debit and credit portions of a journal entry but for unequal amounts.
3. Failure to post either the debit or credit portion of a journal entry.
4. Posting either the debit or credit portion (but not both portions) of a journal entry more than once.
5. Incorrect computation of a ledger account balance.

EXERCISE 2-7

Purpose: (L.O. 1 thru 7) This exercise will quiz you about terminology used in this chapter.

A list of accounting terms with which you should be familiar appears below:

Account	Journal
Chart of accounts	Journalizing
Common stock	Ledger
Compound entry	Normal balance
Credit	Posting
Debit	Retained earnings
Dividend	Simple-entry
Double-entry system	T-account
General journal	Three-column form of account
General ledger	Trial balance

Instructions
For each item below, enter in the blank the term that is described.

1. _____A record of increases and decreases in specific asset, liability, or stockholders' equity items.

2. _____The basic form of an account.

3. _____A form containing money columns for debit, credit, and balance amounts in an account.

4. _____A list of accounts and the account numbers which identify their relative location in the ledger.

5. _____The right side of an account.

6. _____The left side of an account.

7. _____An accounting record in which transactions are initially recorded in chronological order.

8. _____A journal entry that involves three or more accounts (more than one debit and/or more than one credit).

9. _____A journal entry that involves only two accounts (one debit and one credit).

10. _____The most basic form of journal.

11. _____The procedure of entering transaction data in the journal.

12. _____The entire group of accounts maintained by a company.

13. _____The procedure of transferring journal entries to the ledger accounts.

14. _____A list of accounts and their balance at a given time.

15. _____The ledger that contains all of the asset, liability, and stockholders' equity accounts.

16. _____A system that records the dual effect of each transaction in appropriate accounts.

17. _____Issued in exchange for the owners' investment paid in to the corporation.

18. _____A distribution by a corporation to its stockholders on a pro rata (equal) basis.

19. _____Net income that is retained in the business.

20. _____An account balance on the side where an increase in the account is recorded.

SOLUTION TO EXERCISE 2-7

1. Account
2. T-account
3. Three-column form of account
4. Chart of accounts
5. Credit
6. Debit
7. Journal
8. Compound entry
9. Simple entry
10. General journal
11. Journalizing
12. Ledger
13. Posting
14. Trial balance
15. General ledger
16. Double-entry system
17. Common stock
18. Dividend
19. Retained earnings
20. Normal balance

ANALYSIS OF MULTIPLE-CHOICE TYPE QUESTIONS

1. **Question**
   (L.O. 2) The left side of an account is called:
   a. debit.
   b. journal.
   c. credit.
   d. asset.

   Explanation: The left side of any account is the debit side; the right side of any account is the credit side. (Solution = a.)

2. **Question**
    (L.O. 2) Credits are used to record increases in:
    a. assets, revenues, liabilities, and common stock.
    b. expenses, liabilities, and common stock.
    c. revenues, dividends, and assets.
    d. revenues, liabilities, and common stock.

    Approach and Explanation: List the types of accounts which are increased by credits: liabilities, common stock, retained earnings, and revenues. Then look for the answer selection which matches your list. (Solution = d.)

3. **Question**
    (L.O. 2) Which of the following accounts is increased by credits?
    a. Cash.
    b. Supplies.
    c. Prepaid Rent.
    d. Accounts Payable.

    Approach and Explanation: List the types of accounts which are increased by credits: liabilities, common stock, retained earnings, and revenues. Identify each answer selection as an asset, liability, common stock, retained earnings, revenue or expense. Cash, supplies, and prepaid rent are all assets, and, thus, are increased by debits. Accounts payable is a liability and, thus, is increased by credits. (Solution = d.)

4. **Question**
    (L.O. 4) The Ref. column of the journal is used to:
    a. cross reference entries in the ledger and to indicate that posting has been completed.
    b. indicate that entries have been properly posted to the financial statements.
    c. test the equality of debits and credits in the journal.
    d. indicate the initials of the employee who performed the posting process.

    Explanation: The Ref. (Reference) column of the journal is left blank at the time a journal entry is made. At the time of posting, the ledger account number to which the amount is posted is placed in the Reference column to indicate what account received the posting. Thus, the Reference column in the journal is used to indicate whether posting has been completed and to what account an amount has been posted. (Solution = a.)

5. **Question**
    (L.O. 4) The payment of rent for office space solely for the current period is recorded in the accounts by a debit to:
    a. Rent Expense and a credit to Cash.
    b. Rent Expense and a credit to Stockholders' Equity.
    c. Cash and a credit to Accounts Payable.
    d. Cash and a credit to Rent Expense.

    Approach and Explanation: Do **not** read the answer selections until you analyze and journalize the transaction. Always start with the easiest part of the transaction. Cash was paid. Credit Cash to reduce its balance. Because the payment was for the rental of space for the current period, benefits do not extend beyond the current period; hence, an expense has been incurred. Debit Rent Expense to record the increase in expense. (Solution = a.)

6.   **Question**
     (L.O. 4) The journal entry to record the payment for three years' rent in advance involves a debit to:
     a.   Rent Expense and a credit to Prepaid Rent.
     b.   Common Stock and a credit to Cash.
     c.   Prepaid Rent and a credit to Cash.
     d.   Prepaid Rent and a credit to Retained Earnings.

     Approach and Explanation: Analyze and journalize the transaction **before** you read the answer selections. Match your written response with the appropriate answer choice. Start with the easiest part of the transaction: a cash payment was made. Credit Cash to decrease the balance of that account. The payment is for benefits which are to extend beyond the current period; hence, an asset account should be increased (by a debit). The particular asset in this case is Prepaid Rent. (Solution = c.)

7.   **Question**
     (L.O. 4) The "book of original entry" is the:
     a.   journal.
     b.   ledger.
     c.   trial balance.
     d.   transactions book.

     Approach: Complete the statement in the question stem **before** you look at the answer selections. Choose the selection which corresponds to your response. (Solution = a.)

8.   **Question**
     (L.O. 4) The receipt of cash from a customer for services to be provided in a future accounting period is recorded by a:
     a.   debit to Cash and a credit to Unearned Service Revenue.
     b.   debit to Cash and a credit to Service Revenue.
     c.   debit to Unearned Service Revenue and a credit to Cash.
     d.   debit to Service Revenue and a credit to Cash.

     Approach: Analyze the transaction and prepare the journal entry to record that transaction before you read the answer selections. The receipt of cash from a customer in advance of the earning of revenue causes the asset cash to increase and a liability (unearned service revenue) to increase. At a later time, the revenue will be earned; then the liability (unearned service revenue) will decrease and revenue will increase. (Solution = a.)

9.   **Question**
     (L.O. 5) Which statement is true regarding posting?
     a.   Posting must be done at the end of each week.
     b.   Posting must be done after the financial statements are prepared.
     c.   Posting must be done immediately after the transaction is recorded in the journal.
     d.   Posting may be done at any time but must be completed before financial statements are prepared.

     Explanation: There is no set time to perform the posting process; however, financial statements cannot be prepared until all transactions are reflected in the accounts. Transactions are recorded in the accounts via the process of posting from the journal to the ledger. (Solution = d.)

10. **Question**
    (L.O. 7) The debit column of a trial balance amounts to $78,000; the credit column also amounts to $78,000. Which error may still exist?
    a. A journal entry contains a correct debit amount and an incorrect credit amount.
    b. A debit entry to the Accounts Receivable account in the journal is incorrectly posted as a credit to the Accounts Receivable account in the ledger.
    c. The debit portion of a journal entry is posted to the ledger twice.
    d. A cash payment on account of $240 is incorrectly recorded as a cash payment of $420.

    Approach and Explanation: Analyze each error (answer selection) and write down whether or not the error will cause the trial balance to be out of balance. Look for the selection which will not cause an imbalance in the trial balance (selection "d"). Both the debit and credit amounts recorded in the journal entry in selection "d" are in error. Selections "a", "b", and "c" all cause an imbalance in the trial balance. (Solution = d.)

11. **Question**
    (L.O. 7) A transposition error in entering one ledger account balance on the trial balance will cause a difference figure in the trial balance totals that will be evenly divisible by:
    a. 2.
    b. 7.
    c. 9.
    d. 10.

    Approach and Explanation: Set up an example for yourself to prove how this works. For instance, assume a $240 account balance is listed on the trial balance as $420. That error causes a difference of $180 which is divisible by 2, 9, and 10. Another example would be 9 entered for 90. The difference is 81 which is divisible by 9. Thus, the answer is narrowed down to the digit of 9. (Solution = c.)

12. **Question**
    (L.O. 7) Which of the following errors will cause an **imbalance** in the trial balance?
    a. Omission of a transaction in the journal.
    b. Posting an entire journal entry twice to the ledger.
    c. Posting a credit of $720 to Accounts Payable as a credit of $720 to Accounts Receivable.
    d. Listing the balance of an account with a debit balance in the credit column of the trial balance.

    Approach and Explanation: Analyze each error (answer selection) and write down whether or not the error will cause the trial balance to be out of balance. Look for the selection which will cause an imbalance (selection "d"). Selections "a", "b", and "c", do not cause an imbalance in the trial balance. (Solution = d.)

13. **Question**
    (L.O. 7) A trial balance that is in balance proves that:
    a. all entries have been entered in the journal correctly.
    b. total debits equal total credits in the ledger accounts.
    c. all entries have been posted from the journal to the ledger correctly.
    d. no significant errors exist in the ledger accounts.

    Explanation: A number of errors can still exist even though a trial balance is in balance. A trial balance that balances only proves that there are equal amounts of debits and credits in the ledger accounts. (Solution = b.)

CHAPTER 3

. . . .

ADJUSTING THE ACCOUNTS

OVERVIEW

In accordance with the **revenue recognition principle,** revenue is to be recognized (reported) in the period in which the performance obligation is satisfied. In accordance with the **expense recognition (matching principle),** the expenses incurred in generating revenues should be recognized in the same period as the revenues they helped to generate. Adjusting entries are often required so that revenues and expenses are reflected on an accrual-basis of accounting (revenues recognized when services are performed and expenses recognized when incurred) rather than on a cash basis of accounting. Therefore, adjusting entries reflect the accruals and deferrals of revenues and expenses. Adjusting entries are simply entries required to bring account balances up to date before financial statements can be prepared. The failure to record proper adjustments will cause errors in both the income statement and the balance sheet.

SUMMARY OF LEARNING OBJECTIVES

1. **Explain the time period assumption.** The time period assumption assumes that the economic life of a business can be divided into artificial time periods of equal length.

2. **Explain the accrual-basis of accounting.** Accrual-basis accounting means that companies record events that change a company's financial statements in the periods in which those events occur, rather than in the periods in which the company receives or pays cash.

3. **Explain the reasons for adjusting entries.** Companies make adjusting entries at the end of an accounting period. Such entries ensure that companies recognize revenues in the period in which the performance obligation is satisfied, and that they recognize expenses in the period in which they are incurred.

4. **Identify the major types of adjusting entries.** The major types of adjusting entries are deferrals (prepaid expenses and unearned revenues), and accruals (accrued revenues and accrued expenses).

5. **Prepare adjusting entries for deferrals.** Deferrals are either prepaid expenses or unearned revenues. Companies make adjusting entries for deferrals to record the portion of the prepayment that represents the expense incurred or the revenue earned (for services performed) in the current accounting period.

6.   **Prepare adjusting entries for accruals.** Accruals are either accrued revenues or accrued expenses. Companies make adjusting entries for accruals to record revenues for services performed and expenses incurred in the current accounting period that have not been recognized through daily entries.

7.   **Describe the nature and purpose of an adjusted trial balance.** An adjusted trial balance is a trial balance that shows the balances of all accounts, including those that have been adjusted, at the end of an accounting period. Its purpose is to prove the equality of the total debit balances and total credit balances in the ledger after all adjustments.

*8.   **Prepare adjusting entries for the alternative treatment of deferrals.** Companies may initially debit prepayments to an expense account. Likewise, they may credit unearned revenues to a revenue account. At the end of the period, these accounts may be overstated. The adjusting entries for prepaid expenses are a debit to an asset account and a credit to an expense account. Adjusting entries for unearned revenues are a debit to a revenue account and a credit to a liability account..

*This material appears in the **Appendix to Chapter 3** in the text.

TIPS ON CHAPTER TOPICS

TIP:	**This chapter is an extremely important one.** A good understanding of this chapter and an ability to think and work quickly with the concepts incorporated herein are necessary for comprehending subsequent chapters. Pay close attention when studying this chapter.
TIP:	Notice that **each adjusting entry** discussed in this chapter **involves a balance sheet account and an income statement account.**
TIP:	Notice that **none** of the adjusting entries discussed in Chapter 3 involve the **Cash** account. Therefore, if you are instructed to record **adjusting entries,** double check your work when it is completed. If you have used the Cash account in any adjusting entry, it is very likely in error. (The only time Cash belongs in an adjusting entry is when a bank reconciliation discloses a need to adjust the Cash account—this will be explained in **Chapter 7**—or when an error has been made that involves the Cash account, in which case a correcting entry is required.)
TIP:	Keep in mind that for accrued items (accrued revenues and accrued expenses), the related cash flow **follows** the period in which the relevant revenue or expense is recognized; whereas, with prepayment type items (unearned revenues and prepaid expenses), the related cash flow **precedes** the period in which the relevant revenue or expense is recognized. For example, assume the accounting period is the calendar year. Consider an accrued expense such as accrued salaries at the end of 2014 An adjusting entry will be recorded at the end of 2014 so the expense will get reported on the 2014 income statement. The related cash payment to employees will take place in the following accounting period (2015, in this case). For another example, consider a prepaid expense such as the prepayment of rent in December 2014 for January 2015 occupancy. The cash payment occurs in December 2014. The expense is incurred and recognized in the following accounting period (January 2015).

TIP: Revenue is to be recognized in the period the performance obligation is satisfied and an expense is to be recognized in the period the expense is incurred. **Recognition** is the process of formally recording an item as an asset, liability, revenue, expense or the like. A **revenue meets the criteria to be recognized** in the period the related product or service is provided to the customer. The performance obligation associated with some revenues is satisfied with the passage of time; such as interest revenue which is earned as the borrower has use of the lender's funds and rent revenue which is earned as the tenant has use of a landlord's property. An **expense is incurred** (sustained) in the period in which the benefits of goods and services are consumed in the process of generating revenue. Some expenses are incurred with the passage of time; such as interest expense which is incurred as the borrower has use of a lender's funds and insurance expense which is incurred as the time period lapses for which insurance coverage has been obtained.

TIP: If cash is **received** in a rental situation, the amount will be recorded in either a rent revenue account or an unearned rent revenue account, not in an expense or a prepaid expense account. Cash received for rent relates to revenue or unearned revenue. If cash is **paid** in a rental situation, the amount will be recorded in either an expense or a prepaid expense account.

TIP: You should be able to define the following four terms and describe the related adjusting entry for each. They are:
1. **Prepaid expense** is an expense that has been paid but has not been incurred. An adjusting entry for a deferred expense involves an EXPENSE account and an ASSET (prepaid expense) account.
2. **Unearned revenue** is revenue for which cash has been collected but the related services have not been performed. An adjusting entry for unearned revenue involves a LIABILITY (unearned revenue) account and a REVENUE account.
3. **Accrued revenue** is revenue for which services have been performed but cash has not been received. An adjusting entry for accrued revenue involves an ASSET (receivable) account and a REVENUE account.
4. **Accrued expense** is an expense that has been incurred but has not been paid. An adjusting entry for an accrued expense involves an EXPENSE account and a LIABILITY (payable) account.

TIP: A **prepaid expense** may be called a **deferred expense.** A deferred expense is so named because the recognition of expense is being deferred (put-off) to a future period; thus, an asset is carried on the balance sheet now and will be released to the income statement in a future period when the related benefits are consumed (expense is incurred).

TIP: An **unearned revenue** is often called **deferred revenue** because the recognition of revenue is being deferred to a future period; thus, a credit (liability in this case) is carried on the balance sheet now and will be released to the income statement in a future period when the related performance obligation has been satisfied.

TIP: An **adjusting entry for prepaid insurance expense** (expense paid but not incurred) involves an expense account and an asset account. The expense account is often called Insurance Expense or Expired Insurance. Possible titles for the asset account include Prepaid Insurance, Deferred Insurance Expense, Prepaid Insurance Expense, Deferred Insurance, and Unexpired Insurance.

TIP: An **adjusting entry for deferred rent revenue** (revenue collected but related services not yet performed) involves a liability account and a revenue account. Possible titles for the liability account include Unearned Rent Revenue, Unearned Rent, Deferred Rent Revenue, Rent Revenue Received in Advance, and Rental Income Collected in Advance. The use of Prepaid Rent Revenue as an account title is **not** appropriate because the term prepaid usually refers to the payment of cash in advance, **not** the receipt of cash in advance. The revenue account is often called Rent Revenue or Rental Income or Rent Earned.

TIP: In an **adjusting entry to record accrued interest revenue** (revenue services performed but related cash not yet received), the debit is to an asset account and the credit is to a revenue account. Possible names for that asset account are Interest Receivable and Accrued Interest Receivable. Possible names for the revenue account include Interest Revenue, Interest Income, and Interest Earned.

TIP: In an **adjusting entry to record accrued salaries and wages expense** (expense incurred, but not paid) the debit is to an expense account and the credit is to a liability account. The expense account is usually titled Salaries and Wages Expense. Possible names for the liability account include Salaries and Wages Payable and Accrued Salaries and Wages Payable.

TIP: In an **adjusting entry for an accrual** (accrued revenue or accrued expense), the word "accrued" is not needed in either account title. If you choose to use the word "accrued" in an account title, it is appropriate to do so only in the balance sheet account title. For example, accrued salaries of $1,000 may be recorded as follows:

Salaries and Wages Expense...	1,000	
Salaries and Wages Payable		1,000

The word "accrued" is not needed in either account title, but it could be used in the liability account title if desired (the account title would then be Accrued Salaries and Wages Payable). It would be wrong to insert the word "accrued" in the expense account title. Some people simply call the credit account "Accrued Salaries and Wages" but we advise that you include the key word "Payable" and omit the unnecessary "Accrued."

TIP: The **revenue recognition principle** is applied to determine in what period(s) to recognize revenue. Then, the **expense recognition (matching principle)** is applied to determine in what period(s) to recognize expense.

TIP: An **unadjusted trial balance** is referred to as either "unadjusted trial balance" or simply "trial balance." An adjusted trial balance is referred to as either "adjusted trial balance" or the "adjusted trial."

EXERCISE 3-1

Purpose: (L.O. 6) This exercise will provide you with examples of adjusting entries for the accrual of expenses and revenues.

The following information relates to the Yuppy Clothing Sales Corporation at the end of 2014. The accounting period is the calendar year. This is the company's first year of operations.

1. Employees are paid every Monday for the five-day work week ending on the prior Friday. Salaries amount to $2,400 per week. The accounting period ends on a Monday.
2. On October 1, 2014, Yuppy borrowed $16,000 cash by signing a note payable due in one year at 8% interest. Interest is due when the principal is due.
3. A note for $2,000 was received from a customer in a sales transaction on May 1, 2014. The note matures in one year and bears 12% interest per annum. Interest is due when the principal is due.
4. A portion of Yuppy's parking lot is used by executives of a neighboring company. A person pays $6 per day for each day's use. The parking fees are due by the fifth business day following the month of use. The fees for December 2014 amount to $2,904.

Instructions
Prepare the necessary adjusting entries at December 31, 2014.

SOLUTION TO EXERCISE 3-1

1. Salaries and Wages Expense.. 480
        Salaries and Wages Payable.. 480
        (To record accrued salaries)
        ($2,400 ÷ 5 = $480); ($480 X 1 = $480)

2. Interest Expense.. 320
        Interest Payable.. 320
        (To record accrued interest on note payable)
        ($16,000 X 8% X 3/12 = $320)

3. Interest Receivable.. 160
        Interest Revenue.. 160
        (To record accrued interest on note receivable)
        ($2,000 X 12% X 8/12 = $160)

> **TIP:** An **interest rate** is an annual rate unless otherwise indicated. For preparing an adjusting entry involving interest, compute interest assuming the rate given is for a whole year, unless it is evident that this is not the case. Also, assume a 360 day year, unless otherwise indicated.

4. Parking Fees Receivable.. 2,904
        Parking Fees Revenue.. 2,904
        (To accrue fees for services performed but not billed or collected)

Explanation: An accrued expense is an expense that has been incurred but not paid. The "incurred" part results in an increase in Expense (debit) and the "not paid" part results in an increase in Payable (credit). An accrued revenue is a revenue for which services have been performed but the related cash has not been received. The "performed" part results in an increase in Revenue (credit) and the "not received" part results in an increase in Receivable (debit).

EXERCISE 3-2

Purpose: (L.O. 2) This exercise illustrates the different results that are obtained when the accrual and the cash methods of accounting are used.

Annabelle's Specialty Service Shop, Inc. conducted the following transactions during the first week in March.
1. Purchased supplies for $1,800. Paid 20% down; remaining 80% to be paid in 10 days.
2. Paid $30 for newspaper advertising to appear this week.
3. Collected $1,400 from customers on account.
4. Performed services at a $1,620 charge to a customer's account.
5. Paid $600 rent for the month of March.
6. Performed services for $280 cash.
7. Paid part-time sales clerk $40 wages for the week.
8. Declared and paid dividends of $100 to stockholders.
9. Consumed supplies of $1,400.

Instructions
(a)   Compute the net income for the week, using the cash method of accounting.
(b)   Compute the net income for the week, using the accrual method of accounting.
Show your computations in good form.

SOLUTION TO EXERCISE 3-2

(a)   **Cash Method**

Cash received from customers ($1,400 + $280).............................		$1,680
Less: Payment for supplies ($1,800 X 20%)	$360	
Payment for advertising..	30	
Payment for rent	600	
Payment to employee	40	1,030
Net income (cash method)...		$ 650

> **TIP:** Using the **cash basis (method) of accounting,** revenues are recognized (recorded and reported) in the period in which they are **received** and expenses are recognized in the period in which they are **paid.** The cash basis is **not** a generally accepted accounting method for income statement reporting. However, the cash basis income figure does appear on the statement of cash flows by the caption "net cash provided (used) by operating activities."

(b)   **Accrual Method**

Service revenue ($1,620 + $280)....................................		$1,900
Less: Operating expenses		
Supplies expense...	$1,400	
Advertising expense..	30	
Rent expense ($600 ÷ 4)...	150	
Wages expense...	40	1,620
Net income (accrual method)...		$ 280

> **TIP:** Dividends ($100) do **not** enter into the income computations. Dividends are a distribution of income, not a component of income.
>
> **TIP:** Using **accrual-basis (method) of accounting,** revenues are recognized in the period in which the related services are performed and expenses are recognized in the period in which they are **incurred.**

EXERCISE 3-3

Purpose: (L.O. 5, 6, 7) This exercise will allow you to practice doing simple adjusting entries.

The unadjusted trial balance for the J. Lo Motorcycle Repair Shop, Inc. appears below (copied from the **Solution to Exercise 2-5**). Information needed for adjusting entries follows the trial balance.

J. LO MOTORCYCLE REPAIR SHOP, INC.
Trial Balance
August 31, 2014

	Debit	Credit
Cash	$ 2,800	
Accounts Receivable	2,200	
Supplies	3,900	
Accounts Payable		$ 700
Common Stock		5,000
Retained Earnings		0
Dividends	400	
Service Revenue		4,900
Rent Expense	800	
Advertising Expense	300	
Cleaning Expense	200	
	$10,600	$10,600

Additional Information:
1.   An observation and count of supplies at August 31 shows $2,100 of unused items on hand.
2.   The shop received an utility bill of $80 for August. Payment is due by September 20. Roxy and Malcom decided to wait until September to make payment.

Instructions
Using the trial balance above:
(a)   Prepare the appropriate adjusting entries.
(b)   Prepare an adjusted trial balance at August 31, 2014.

SOLUTION TO EXERCISE 3-3

Approach: From the facts given, determine the adjustments needed to report the financial statements in accordance with generally accepted accounting principles. Look at the existing account balances. Make the appropriate entries to adjust the trial balance.

(a)	1.	Supplies Expense	1,800	
		Supplies		1,800
		(To record supplies used: $3,900 - $2,100 = $1,800)		
	2.	Utilities Expense	80	
		Utilities Payable		80
		(To record accrued utilities)		

(b)

J. LO MOTORCYCLE REPAIR SHOP, INC.
Adjusted Trial Balance
August 31, 2014

	Debit	Credit
Cash	$ 2,800	
Accounts Receivable	2,200	
Supplies	2,100	
Accounts Payable		$ 700
Common Stock		5,000
Retained Earnings		0
Dividends	400	
Service Revenue		4,900
Rent Expense	800	
Advertising Expense	300	
Cleaning Expense	200	
Supplies Expense	1,800	
Utilities Expense	80	
Utilities Payable		80
	$10,680	$10,680

TIP: Notice the account balances that are different on the adjusted trial when compared to the unadjusted trial balance. They are: Supplies, Supplies Expense, Utilities Expense, and Utilities Payable.

TIP: Notice that the balance of the Retained Earnings account on the adjusted trial balance represents the balance of retained earnings at the beginning of the period (August 1). That is, the balance here does not yet reflect the effect of this period's results of operations (revenues and expenses) on owners' equity. Also, the balance here does not yet reflect the effect of dividends declared during this period.

TIP: Refer to the **Solution to Exercise 1-3.** The financial statements shown in that exercise were prepared **before** considering the information for the adjusting entries for supplies consumed during the period and accrued utilities expense. Those financial statements did not reflect the two necessary adjustments because the subject of financial statements was introduced in **Chapter 1** but, for purposes of simplicity, the subject of adjusting entries was **not** introduced until **Chapter 3.** Be aware now that financial statements for the J. Lo Motorcycle Repair Shop, Inc. for August 31, 2014, should reflect the balances shown on the "Adjusted Trial Balance" above in this exercise. Thus, the correct net income figure is $1,720 ($3,600 - $1,800 - $80 = $1,720) for the income statement and the ending balance for Retained Earnings for the balance sheet is $1,220 ($0 beginning balance + $1,720 net income - $400 dividends = $1,320 ending balance).

EXERCISE 3-4

Purpose: (L.O. 5) This exercise will provide you with examples of adjusting entries for prepaid expenses and unearned revenues (that is, for the deferral of expenses and revenues).

The following information relates to the Brittany Spears Magazine Company at the end of 2014. The accounting period is the calendar year.

1.   An insurance premium of $8,000 was paid on April 1, 2014, and was charged to Prepaid Insurance. The premium covers a 24-month period beginning April 1, 2014.

2. The Office Supplies On Hand account showed a balance of $3,500 at the beginning of 2014. Supplies costing $12,000 were purchased during 2014 and debited to the asset account. Supplies of $2,200 were on hand at December 31, 2014.

3. On July 1, 2014, cash of $48,000 was received from subscribers (customers) for a 36-month subscription period beginning on that date. The receipt was recorded by a debit to Cash and a credit to Unearned Subscription Revenue.

4. At the beginning of 2014, the Unearned Advertising Revenue account had a balance of $75,000. During 2014, collections from advertisers of $800,000 were recorded by credits to Unearned Advertising Revenue. At the end of 2014, revenues received but not earned are computed to be $51,000.

Instructions
Using the information given above, prepare the necessary adjusting entries at December 31, 2014.

SOLUTION TO EXERCISE 3-4

1. Insurance Expense   3,000
        Prepaid Insurance   3,000
        ($8,000 X 9/24 = $3,000 expired cost)

2. Supplies Expense   13,300
        Office Supplies on Hand.......................................   13,300
        ($3,500 + $12,000 - $2,200 = $13,300
            supplies consumed)

3. Unearned Subscription Revenue   8,000
        Subscription Revenue   8,000
        ($48,000 X 6/36 = $8,000 earned revenue)

4. Unearned Advertising Revenue   824,000
        Advertising Revenue   824,000
        ($75,000 + $800,000 - $51,000 = $824,000
            earned revenue)

Approach and Explanation: Write down the definitions for prepaid expense and unearned revenue. Think about what is to be accomplished by each of the adjustments required in this exercise. A **prepaid expense** is an expense that has been paid but not incurred. In a case where the prepayment was recorded as an increase in an asset account (such as Prepaid Expense or Supplies on Hand), the adjusting entry will record the increase in Expense (debit) and a decrease in the recorded Asset (credit) due to the consumption of the benefits yielded by the earlier prepayment. An **unearned revenue** is a revenue that has been received but not performed. In a case where the cash receipt was recorded as an increase in a liability account (such as Unearned Revenue or Deferred Revenue), the adjusting entry will record a decrease in the recorded liability Unearned Revenue (debit) and an increase in Earned Revenue (credit) due to the earning of all or a portion of the revenue represented by the earlier cash receipt.

It is helpful to sketch a T-account for the related asset or liability account. Enter the amounts reflected in that account before adjustment, enter the desired ending balance, and notice how the required adjustment is then obvious from facts reflected in your T-account. The T-accounts would appear as follows:

1.

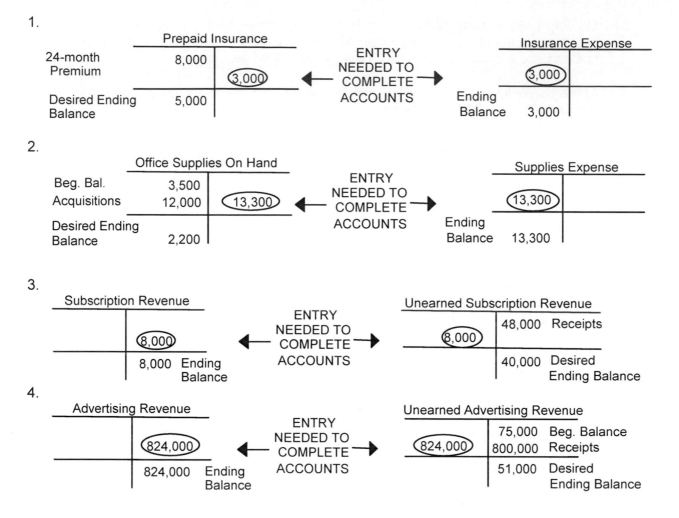

ILLUSTRATION 3-1
SUMMARY OF ADJUSTMENT RELATIONSHIPS
AND EXPLANATIONS (L. O. 4, 5, 6, 8)

Type of Adjustment		Reason for Adjustment	Account Balances Before Adjustment	Adjusting Entry	Examples
1. Prepaid Expenses	(a)	Prepaid expenses initially recorded in asset accounts have been used.	Assets overstated Expenses understated	Dr. Expenses Cr. Assets	Insurance, Rent, Supplies
	*(b)	Prepaid expenses initially recorded in expense accounts have not been used.	Assets understated Expenses overstated	Dr. Assets Cr. Expenses	
2. Unearned Revenues	(a)	Unearned revenues initially recorded in liability accounts have been earned.	Liabilities overstated Revenues understated	Dr. Liabilities Cr. Revenues	Subscriptions, deposits, rent
	*(b)	Unearned revenues initially recorded in revenue accounts have not been earned.	Liabilities understated Revenues overstated	Dr. Revenues Cr. Liabilities	
3. Accrued Revenues		Revenues earned have not been billed nor collected nor recorded.	Assets understated Revenues understated	Dr. Assets Cr. Revenues	Interest, rent
4. Accrued Expenses		Expenses incurred have not been billed nor paid nor recorded.	Expenses understated Liabilities understated	Dr. Expenses Cr. Liabilities	Salaries, wages, interest, taxes

*This situation is addressed in the **Appendix to Chapter 3** in the text.

Explanation:

1.   When expenses are paid for before they are incurred, the payment may either be recorded by a debit to an asset account (prepaid expense) or by a debit to an expense account. At the end of the accounting period, the accounts are adjusted as needed. If the prepayment was initially recorded by use of a prepaid (asset) account, the consumed portion is transferred to an expense account in the adjusting entry. Whereas, if the prepayment was initially recorded by use of an expense account, an adjusting entry is required only if a portion of the expense remains prepaid at the end of the accounting period. (The latter case is discussed in the **Appendix to Chapter 3** in the text.)

2.   When revenues are received before they are earned (performed), the receipt may either be recorded by a credit to a liability account (unearned revenue) or by a credit to a revenue account. At the end of the accounting period, the accounts are adjusted as needed. If the collection was initially recorded by a credit to a liability account (unearned revenue), the earned portion is transferred to a revenue account in the adjusting entry. Whereas, if the collection was initially recorded by use of a revenue account, an adjusting entry is required only if a portion of the revenue remains unearned at the end of the accounting period.. (The latter case is discussed in the **Appendix to Chapter 3** in the text.)

3.   Revenues are often earned (performed) before they are collected. A revenue earned but not received is called an accrued revenue. If at the end of an accounting period this accrued revenue has not been recorded (which is often the case because it usually has not been billed yet), it must be recorded by way of an adjusting entry. Revenue that accrues with the passage of time (such as interest revenue) is a good example of a reason to need an accrued revenue type of adjusting entry.

4.   Expenses are often incurred before they are paid. An expense incurred but not yet paid is called an accrued expense. If at the end of an accounting period this accrued expense has not been recorded (which is often the case because it usually has not been billed yet by the vendor), it must be recorded by way of an adjusting entry. Expense that accrues with the passage of time (such as interest expense) is a good example of a reason to need an accrued expense type adjusting entry.

TIP:	Examine each type of adjustment explained above and notice the logic of the resulting entry. For example, an adjustment to recognize supplies used (when the supplies were recorded in an asset account when purchased) should reduce assets and increase expenses.

*ILLUSTRATION 3-2
ALTERNATIVE TREATMENTS OF PREPAID EXPENSES AND UNEARNED REVENUES (L.O. 5, *8)

*This material is covered in the **Appendix to Chapter 3** in the text.

PREPAID EXPENSES

When a company writes a check to pay for an item that affects expense in at least two different time periods (such as for an insurance premium or a license or dues), the bookkeeper may record the payment in one of two ways; either as a prepaid expense (asset) or as an expense. The first way is used most often in introductory accounting textbooks; the second is used most often in the real world. Regardless of the way the payment is recorded, an appropriate adjusting entry should be made at the end of the accounting period so that correct balances appear on the income statement and the balance sheet.

For example, a $1,200 payment is made on April 1, 2014, for a twelve-month insurance premium covering the time between April 1, 2014 and March 31, 2015. (Assume a calendar year reporting period.) A comparison of the two possible approaches appears below:

Prepayment (Cash Paid) Initially Debited to Asset Account			OR	Prepayment (Cash Paid) Initially Debited to Expense Account		
Apr. 1 Prepaid Insurance	1,200		Apr. 1	Insurance Expense	1,200	
Cash		1,200		Cash		1,200
Dec. 31 Insurance Expense	900		Dec. 31	Prepaid Insurance	300	
Prepaid Insurance		900		Insurance Expense		300

After posting the entries, the accounts appear as follows:

Prepaid Insurance					Prepaid Insurance		
4/1	1,200	12/31 Adj.	900		12/31 Adj.	300	
12/31 Bal.	300						

Insurance Expense					Insurance Expense		
12/31 Adj.	900				4/1	1,200	12/31 Adj.	300
					12/31 Bal.	900	

Notice that regardless of the path, you end up at the same place—with a balance of $300 in Prepaid Insurance and a balance of $900 in Insurance Expense. That was your objective—to report balances in accordance with accrual-basis accounting.

UNEARNED REVENUES

When a company receives cash from a customer in advance of performing the services to earn the related revenue, the bookkeeper may record the receipt in one of two ways: either as an unearned revenue (liability) or as an earned (performed) revenue. The first way is used most often in introductory accounting textbooks; the second is used most often in the real world. Regardless of the way the receipt is recorded, an appropriate adjusting entry should be made at the end of the accounting period so that correct balances appear on the income statement and the balance sheet.

For example, $1,200 is received on May 1, 2014, for a twelve-month magazine subscription covering the time between May 1, 2014 and April 30, 2015. (Assume a calendar year reporting period.) A comparison of the two possible approaches appears below:

Unearned Revenue (Cash Received) Initially Credited to Liability Account			OR	Unearned Revenue (Cash Received) Initially Credited to Revenue Account		
May 1	Cash	1,200		May 1	Cash	1,200
	Unearned Sub-scription Revenue	1,200			Subscription Revenue	1,200
Dec. 31	Unearned Subscription Revenue	800		Dec. 31	Subscription Revenue 400	
	Subscription Revenue	800			Unearned Subscrip-tion Revenue	400

After posting the entries, the accounts appear as follows:

Unearned Subscription Revenue					Unearned Subscription Revenue		
12/31 Adj.	800	5/1	1,200			12/31 Adj.	400
		12/31 Bal.	400				

Subscription Revenue					Subscription Revenue		
		12/31 Adj.	800		12/31 Adj. 400	5/1	1,200
						12/31 Bal.	800

Notice that the account balances are the same regardless of the approach used; that is, Unearned Subscription Revenue is $400, and Subscription Revenue is $800 at December 31.

EXERCISE 3-5

Purpose: (L.O. 5, 6, 7) This exercise will illustrate the preparation of adjusting entries from an unadjusted trial balance and additional data.

Tammy Equipment Rentals, Inc. began business in 2010. The following list of accounts and their balances represents the unadjusted trial balance of Tammy's Equipment Rentals, Inc. at December 31, 2014, the end of the annual accounting period.

TAMMY'S EQUIPMENT RENTALS, INC.
Trial Balance
December 31, 2014

	Debit	Credit
Cash	$ 16,500	
Prepaid Insurance	4,320	
Supplies	13,200	
Land	62,000	
Building	50,000	
Equipment	130,000	
Accumulated Depreciation—Building		$ 10,000
Accumulated Depreciation—Equipment		52,000
Note Payable		50,000
Accounts Payable		9,310
Unearned Rent Revenue		10,200
Common Stock		30,000
Retained Earnings		60,660
Dividends	31,000	
Rent Revenue		161,960
Salaries and Wages Expense	70,600	
Interest Expense	3,500	
Miscellaneous Expense	3,010	
	$384,130	$384,130

Additional data:

1. On November 1, 2014, Tammy received $10,200 rent from a lessee for a 12-month equipment lease beginning on that date and credited Unearned Rent Revenue for the entire collection.
2. Per a physical inventory at December 31, 2014, Tammy determines that supplies costing $2,200 were on hand at the balance sheet date. The cost of supplies is debited to an asset account when purchased.
3. Prepaid Insurance contains the premium cost of a policy that is for a 3-year term and was taken out on May 1, 2014.
4. The cost of the building is being depreciated at a rate of 5% per year.
5. The cost of the equipment is being depreciated at a rate of 10% per year.
6. The note payable bears interest at 12% per year. Interest is payable each August 1. The $50,000 principal is due in full on August 1, 2017.
7. At December 31, 2014, Tammy has some equipment in the hands of renters who have used the equipment but have not yet been billed. They will make payment of $1,400 on January 2, 2015.
8. Employees are paid total salaries of $6,400 every other Friday for a two-week period ending on that payday. December 31, 2014 falls on a Monday. The last payday of the year is the last Friday in the year. The work week is Monday through Friday.

Instructions

(a) Prepare the year-end adjusting entries in general journal form using the information above.
(b) Prepare an adjusted trial balance at December 31, 2014.

SOLUTION TO EXERCISE 3-5

(a) 1.   Unearned Rent Revenue   1,700

           Rent Revenue   1,700

           (To record rent revenue earned: $10,200 X 2/12 = $1,700)

     2.   Supplies Expense   11,000

           Supplies...   11,000

           (To record supplies used: $13,200 - $2,200 = $11,000)

     3.   Insurance Expense   960

           Prepaid Insurance   960

           (To record insurance expired: $4,320 X 8/36 = $960)

     4.   Depreciation Expense—Building   2,500

           Accumulated Depreciation—Building   2,500

           (To record annual depreciation on building:
             $50,000 X 5% = $2,500)

     5.   Depreciation Expense—Equipment   13,000

           Accumulated Depreciation—Equipment   13,000

           (To record annual depreciation on equipment:
             $130,000 X 10% = $13,000)

6. Interest Expense..   2,500
        Interest Payable   2,500
        (To record interest accrued on note:
        $50,000 X 12% X 5/12 = $2,500)

7. Accounts Receivable (or Rent Receivable)   1,400
        Rent Revenue   1,400
        (To record accrued revenue)

8. Salaries and Wages Expense...   640
        Salaries and Wages Payable   640
        (To record accrued salaries: $6,400 X 1/10 = $640)

Approach and Explanation: Identify each item as involving: (1) a prepaid expense, (2) an unearned revenue, (3) an accrued revenue, or (4) an accrued expense. From the facts, determine the existing account balances. Read the facts carefully to determine the desired account balances for financial statements in accordance with generally accepted accounting principles (cost principle, revenue recognition principle, expense recognition (matching) principle, etc.). Determine the adjusting entries necessary to bring existing account balances to the appropriate account balances.

1. On November 1, 2014, cash was received and recorded as follows:
        Cash   10,200
            Unearned Rent Revenue..   10,200

    This situation involves unearned revenue. At December 31, 2014, before adjustment, there is an Unearned Rent Revenue account with a balance of $10,200. The amount unearned at that date is $10,200 X 10/12 = $8,500. Therefore, an adjusting entry is necessary to transfer the $1,700 earned from the Unearned Rent Revenue account to an earned revenue account.

2. This situation involves a prepaid expense. All supplies are charged to an asset account, Supplies, when purchased. Therefore, Supplies has an unadjusted balance of $13,200, which reflects the balance at the beginning of the year plus the cost of all supplies acquired during the year. Supplies on hand of $2,200 are to appear on the balance sheet. Thus, $11,000 of consumed supplies must be transferred from the asset account to an expense account in an adjusting entry.

3. This item involves a prepaid expense. The Prepaid Insurance account reflects a $4,320 balance which represents the cost of a three-year premium. That three-year period began on May 1, 2014. Therefore, eight of the total 36 months have gone by and the cost of the eight month's coverage ($960) has expired. The expired portion must be transferred from the asset account to an expense account. This will leave 28 months of coverage ($4,320 X 28/36 = $3,360 or $4,320 - $960 = $3,360) in the asset account, Prepaid Insurance.

4. This item involves a long-term prepaid expense. A long-lived tangible item such as building or equipment represents a bundle of benefits when it is acquired. These benefits are to be used up (consumed) over the course of the asset's estimated service life.

Depreciation is a term that refers to the process of allocating the cost of a long-lived tangible asset to the periods benefited from its use. The process of depreciation is necessary to comply with the expense recognition (matching) principle. The building or equipment is used to generate revenue during the period. Consequently, a portion of the bundle of benefits represented by the asset is consumed. There is a cost associated with those consumed benefits. This cost is to be matched with the revenues it helped generate. Thus, an expense is recorded (Depreciation Expense), and an asset is reduced. It is customary, however, to make use of a contra asset account, Accumulated Depreciation, rather than to credit the asset account itself.

5.   See the explanation for 4. above. Notice that a credit to Accumulated Depreciation has the same impact as a credit to the account being depreciated (Equipment, for example). Thus, total assets are reduced by the journal entry to record depreciation.

6.   This situation involves an accrued expense. Interest is a function of debt balance, interest rate, and time. Interest is due and payable at the end of an interest period. The last interest payment date was August 1, 2014. Thus, interest incurred and not yet paid or payable amounts to five months worth or $2,500 ($50,000 X 12% X 5/12 = $2,500). The accrued interest is recorded by an increase to the Interest Expense account and a credit to a liability account, Interest Payable. (Note the balance before adjustment in the Interest Expense account represents seven months of interest. On August 1, 2014, an interest payment of $6,000 was made and $3,500 of that represented the interest from January 1, 2014 through July 31, 2014. The other $2,500 paid for interest would have been accrued earlier at the end of 2013.)

7.   This situation involves an accrual of revenue. Revenue has been earned (related services have been performed) but has not yet been billed or recorded or received. The "earned" part is recorded in the adjusting entry by a credit to Rent Revenue. The "not received" part is recorded by a debit to Accounts Receivable or Rent Receivable. Thus, the appropriate adjusting entry increases assets and revenues earned.

8.   This item involves an accrued expense. An accrued expense is an expense incurred but not yet paid. The salary for the last two work days of the year has been incurred because the employees have contributed their labor services for a period of time that has passed. The employees will not be paid until eleven calendar days after the balance sheet date. The accrued expense is recorded at the balance sheet date by a debit to an expense account and a credit to a liability account.

TIP:	Scan down Tammy's unadjusted trial balance again. Think about what you would expect to see on an adjusted trial balance. The adjusted trial appears below for your study. Verify that the balances are what you would expect them to be.

(b)

TAMMY'S EQUIPMENT RENTALS, INC.
Adjusted Trial Balance
December 31, 2014

	Debit	Credit
Cash...	$ 16,500	
* Accounts Receivable..	1,400	
Prepaid Insurance	3,360	
Supplies	2,200	
Land..	62,000	
Building	50,000	
Equipment..	130,000	
Accumulated Depreciation—Building...................................		$ 12,500
Accumulated Depreciation—Equipment		65,000
Note Payable..		50,000
Accounts Payable		9,310
* Interest Payable		2,500
* Salaries and Wages Payable..		640
Unearned Rent Revenue		8,500
Common Stock..		30,000
Retained Earnings..		60,660
Dividends	31,000	
Rent Revenue		165,060
Salaries and Wages Expense...	71,240	
Interest Expense	6,000	
* Supplies Expense	11,000	
* Insurance Expense	960	
* Depreciation Expense—Building..	2,500	
* Depreciation Expense—Equipment	13,000	
* Miscellaneous Expense	3,010	
	$404,170	$404,170

* Although these accounts are listed in a logical order on this adjusted trial balance when you consider the item's position on financial statements (see the discussion that follows), account titles which are used in adjusting entries but that do **not** appear on the unadjusted trial balance are typically listed on the adjusted trial at the end of the listing of accounts which appeared on the unadjusted trial.

TIP: Now that the adjusted trial balance is complete, think about where the account balances are to go in the preparation of financial statements. Study the following diagrams to verify your conclusions.

TAMMY'S EQUIPMENT RENTALS, INC.
Adjusted Trial Balance
December 31, 2014

Account	Debit	Credit
Cash	$ 16,500	
Accounts Receivable	1,400	
Prepaid Insurance	3,360	
Supplies	2,200	
Land	62,000	
Building	50,000	
Equipment	130,000	
Accumulated Depreciation—Building		$ 12,500
Accumulated Depreciation—Equipment		65,000
Note Payable		50,000
Accounts Payable		9,310
Interest Payable		2,500
Salaries and Wages Payable		640
Unearned Rent Revenue		8,500
Common Stock		30,000
Retained Earnings		60,660
Dividends	31,000	
Rent Revenue		165,060
Salaries and Wages Exp.	71,240	
Interest Expense	6,000	
Supplies Expense	11,000	
Insurance Expense	960	
Depreciation Expense—Building	2,500	
Depreciation Expense—Equipment	13,000	
Miscellaneous Expense	3,010	
	$404,170	$404,170

TAMMY'S EQUIPMENT RENTALS, INC.
Income Statement
For the Year Ended December 31, 2014

Revenues		
Rent revenue		$165,060
Expenses:		
Salaries and wages expense	$71,240	
Interest expense	6,000	
Supplies expense	11,000	
Insurance expense	960	
Depreciation expense—building	2,500	
Depreciation expense—equipment	13,000	
Miscellaneous expense	3,010	
Total expenses		107,710
Net income		$ 57,350

TAMMY'S EQUIPMENT RENTALS, INC.
Retained Earnings Statement
For the Year Ended December 31, 2014

Retained earnings, January 1	$60,660
Add: Net income	57,350
	118,010
Less: Dividends	31,000
Retained earnings, December 31	$87,010

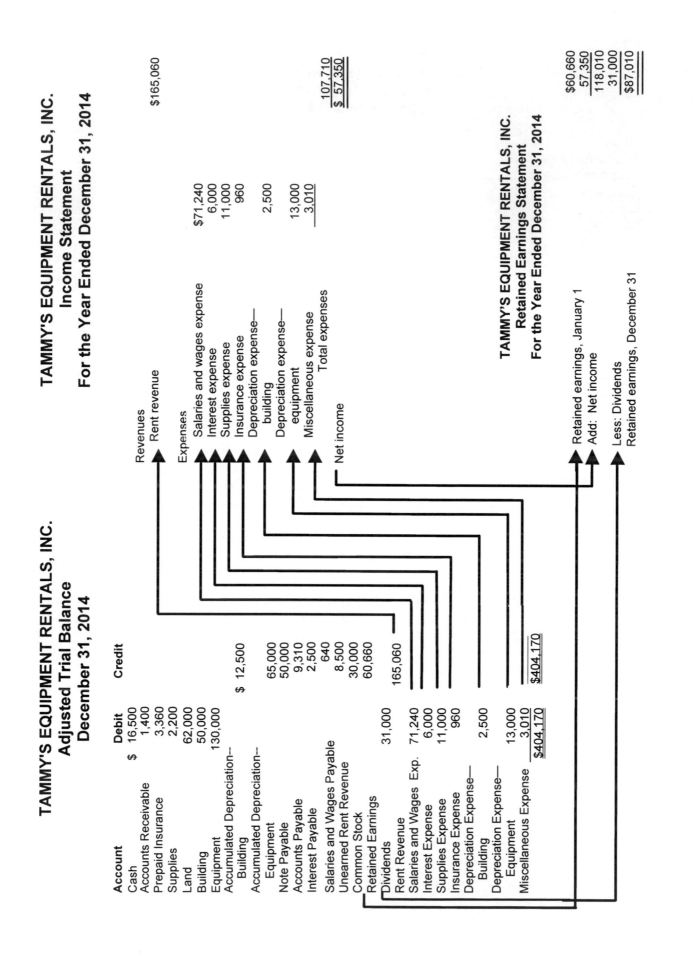

TAMMY'S EQUIPMENT RENTALS, INC.
Adjusted Trial Balance
December 31, 2014

Account	Debit	Credit
Cash	$16,500	
Accounts Receivable	1,400	
Prepaid Insurance	3,360	
Supplies	2,200	
Land	62,000	
Building	50,000	
Equipment	130,000	
Accumulated Depreciation—Building		$12,500
Accumulated Depreciation—Equipment		65,000
Note Payable		50,000
Accounts Payable		9,310
Interest Payable		2,500
Salaries and Wages Payable		640
Unearned Rent Revenue		8,500
Common Stock		30,000
Retained Earnings		60,660
Dividends	31,000	
Rent Revenue		165,060
Salaries and Wages Exp.	71,240	
Interest Expense	6,000	
Supplies Expense	11,000	
Insurance Expense	960	
Depreciation Expense—Building	2,500	
Depreciation Expense—Equipment	13,000	
Miscellaneous Expense	3,010	
	$404,170	$404,170

TAMMY'S EQUIPMENT RENTALS, INC.
Balance Sheet
December 31, 2014

ASSETS

Cash		$ 16,500
Accounts receivable		1,400
Prepaid insurance		3,360
Supplies		2,200
Land		62,000
Building	$ 50,000	
Less: Accumulated depreciation	12,500	37,500
Equipment	130,000	
Less: Accumulated depreciation	65,000	65,000
Total assets		$187,960

LIABILITIES AND STOCKHOLDERS' EQUITY

Liabilities		
Note payable		$ 50,000
Accounts payable		9,310
Interest payable		2,500
Salaries and wages payable		640
Unearned rent revenue		8,500
Total liabilities		70,950
Stockholders' equity		
Common stock		30,000
Retained earnings		87,010
Total liabilities and stockholders' equity		$187,960

Balance at Dec. 31 from Retained Earnings Statement

EXERCISE 3-6

Purpose: (L.O. 4) This exercise will help you develop skill in recognizing circumstances involving accrual of revenue, accrual of expense, unearned revenue, and prepaid expense.

Instructions

Assume it is now Saturday, December 31, 2014. For each of the situations below, indicate whether (a) An accrued revenue, or (b) An accrued expense, or (c) An unearned revenue, or (d) A prepaid expense or (e) neither an accrual nor a prepayment is involved. You may use the designated letters (a), (b), (c), (d), and (e) to indicate your answers. The accounting period is the calendar year of 2014.

Answers   **Situations**

_____ 1. A check was written on June 2, 2014, for $6,000 to pay for an insurance policy which covers the period June 1, 2014 through May 31, 2015. An asset was debited.

_____ 2. At December 31, 2014, the company reviews tenants' records and notes that rent of $3,000 has been earned but not received.

_____ 3. The company has some revenue that has been received but has not been earned as of December 31, 2014.

_____ 4. Property taxes for the period July 1, 2014 through June 30, 2015 amount to $9,000 and are due by July 31, 2015.

_____ 5. $1,200 was received from a tenant on December 20, 2014, to cover the months of December 2014, January 2015, and February 2015.

_____ 6. At Jan. 1, 2014, office supplies on hand were valued at $220. During the year, purchases of office supplies amounted to $800. On Dec. 31, a count of supplies discloses $230 worth to be on hand.

_____ 7. The company wrote a check on Dec. 14 for $100 to pay for an ad which appeared in the Dec. 10 newspaper.

_____ 8. The company employs an office clerk and pays him $300 every Friday for the week ending on that payday. December 31, 2014 falls on a Saturday.

_____ 9. Charges for local telephone service were paid on Dec. 1 for the month of December. Another payment is due on Jan. 1 for local telephone service for January.

_____ 10. An employee was hired on December 31, 2014, and is to begin work on Jan. 2.

SOLUTION TO EXERCISE 3-6

1.	d	6.	d
2.	a	7.	e
3.	c	8.	e
4.	b	9.	e
5.	c	10.	e

EXERCISE 3-7

Purpose: (L.O. 5, 6, 7) This exercise will test your ability to detect adjusting entries by comparing an adjusted trial balance with an unadjusted trial balance.

The trial balance and the subsequent adjusted trial balance at December 31, 2014, for the Bradley Company appear below. The accounting period coincides with the calendar year.

BRADLEY COMPANY
Trial Balance
December 31, 2014

	Before Adjustment		After Adjustment	
	Debit	**Credit**	**Debit**	**Credit**
Cash	$30,000		$30,000	
Accounts Receivable	8,000		8,700	
Note Receivable (8%)	10,000		10,000	
Interest Receivable	0		200	
Prepaid Rent	8,400		1,200	
Prepaid Licenses	3,200		800	
Office Supplies	2,000		300	
Office Equipment	12,000		12,000	
Accumulated Depreciation—Equipment		$ 3,000		$ 4,000
Accounts Payable		3,400		3,400
Unearned Service Fees		5,000		1,300
Salaries and Wages Payable		0		1,800
Common Stock		20,000		20,000
Retained Earnings		42,000		42,000
Dividends	36,000		36,000	
Fees Earned		82,100		86,500
Interest Earned		0		200
Salaries and Wages Expense	45,900		47,700	
Rent Expense	0		7,200	
Licenses Expense	0		2,400	
Office Supplies Expense	0		1,700	
Depreciation Expense	0		1,000	
	$155,500	$155,500	$159,200	$159,200

Instructions

(a)   Journalize the adjusting entries recorded on December 31, 2014.

(b)   Answer the following questions:

1.   How many months was the note receivable outstanding during 2014?

2.   If the rent is a constant amount each month, how many months rent is prepaid as of December 31, 2014?

3.   How much is the monthly license fee assuming the monthly amount has remained unchanged during the whole year?

4.   If the depreciation is a constant amount each year, for how many years has the office equipment been in use?

5.   Assuming the balance of Salaries and Wages Payable at January 1, 2014 was $0, how much cash was paid to employees during 2014?

SOLUTION TO EXERCISE 3-7

(a) 1. Accounts Receivable.. 700

Fees Earned 700

(To record fees earned but not yet billed or collected)

2. Interest Receivable 200

Interest Earned 200

(To accrue interest revenue on a note receivable)

3. Rent Expense... 7,200

Prepaid Rent... 7,200

(To record rent expired)

4. Licenses Expense.. 2,400

Prepaid Licenses 2,400

(To record licenses expired)

5. Office Supplies Expense 1,700

Office Supplies.. 1,700

(To record supplies consumed)

6. Depreciation Expense 1,000

Accumulated Depreciation—Equipment 1,000

(To record depreciation on Equipment)

7. Unearned Service Fees 3,700

Fees Earned 3,700

(To record fees earned)

8. Salaries and Wages Expense 1,800

Salaries and Wages Payable... 1,800

(To accrue salaries incurred but not paid or recorded)

TIP: Watch that your journal entries utilize the exact account titles appearing in the adjusted trial balance.

(b) 1. 3 months.   4. 4 years.
    2. 2 months prepaid rent.   5. $45,900.
    3. $200 per month.

Explanations:

1. Face   X   Rate   X   Time   =   Interest Earned
    $10,000   X   8%   X   T/12   = $200
    $800   X   T/12   = $200
    T/12 = $200/$800
    T = 3 months

2. Rent Expense = $7,200
    $7,200 ÷ 12 months = $600 expense per month
    Prepaid Rent = $1,200
    $1,200 ÷ $600 = 2 months prepaid rent

3. Licenses Expense = $2,400
    $2,400 ÷ 12 months = $200 per month

4. Depreciation Expense for 2008 = $1,000
    Accumulated Depreciation = $4,000
    $4,000 ÷ $1,000 = 4 years of service thus far

5.

Salaries and Wages Expense			Salaries and Wages Payable		
Paid	45,900			1/1/14	0
Adj.	1,800			Adj.	1,800
Total Sal.	47,700			12/31/14 Bal.	1,800

$47,700 - $1,800 = $45,900 cash paid.

EXERCISE 3-8

Purpose: (L.O. 5, 8) This exercise will provide you with examples of adjusting entries for:
   (1)   Prepaid expenses when cash payments are recorded in an asset account.
   (2)   Prepaid expenses when cash payments are recorded in an expense account.
   (3)   Unearned revenues when cash receipts are recorded in a liability account.
   (4)   Unearned revenues when cash receipts are recorded in a revenue account.
   Thus, this exercise will compare the approach explained in the **Appendix to Chapter 3** in your text with the approach explained in the chapter.

Each situation described below is **independent** of the others.

(1)   Office supplies are recorded in an asset account when acquired. There were no supplies on hand at the beginning of the period. Cash purchases of office supplies during the period amounted to $900. A count of supplies at the end of the period shows $320 worth to be on hand. The asset account is titled Office Supplies on Hand.

(2)   Office supplies are recorded in an expense account when acquired. There were no supplies on hand at the beginning of the period. Cash purchases of office supplies during the period amount to $900. A count of supplies at the end of the period shows $320 worth to be on hand.

(3)   Office supplies are recorded in an asset account when acquired. There were $400 of supplies on hand at the beginning of the period. Cash purchases of office supplies during the period amount to $900. A count of supplies at the end of the period shows $320 worth to be on hand.

(4)   Office supplies are recorded in an expense account when acquired. There were $400 of supplies on hand at the beginning of the period. Cash purchases of office supplies during the period amount to $900. A count of supplies at the end of the period shows $320 worth to be on hand.

(5)   Receipts from customers for magazine subscriptions are recorded as a liability when cash is collected in advance of delivery. There was no beginning balance in the liability account. During the period, $54,000 was received for subscriptions. At the end of the period, it was determined that the balance of the Unearned Subscription Revenue account should be $8,000.

(6)   Receipts from customers for magazine subscriptions are recorded as revenue when cash is collected in advance of delivery. There was no balance in the Unearned Subscription Revenue account at the beginning of the period. During the period, $54,000 was received for subscriptions. At the end of the period, it was determined that the balance of the Unearned Subscription Revenue account should be $8,000.

(7)   Receipts from customers for magazine subscriptions are recorded as a liability when cash is collected in advance of delivery. The beginning balance in the liability account was $6,700. During the period, $54,000 was received for subscriptions. At the end of the period, it was determined that the balance of the Unearned Subscription Revenue account should be $8,000.

(8)   Receipts from customers for magazine subscriptions are recorded as revenue when cash is collected in advance of delivery. The beginning balance in the liability account was $6,700. During the period, $54,000 was received for subscriptions. At the end of the period, it was determined that the balance of the Unearned Subscription Revenue account should be $8,000.

Instructions
For each of the **independent** situations above:
(a)   Prepare the appropriate adjusting entry in general journal form.
(b)   Indicate the amount of revenue or expense which will appear on the income statement for the period.
(c)   Indicate the balance of the applicable asset or liability account at the end of the period.
(d)   Indicate the amount of cash received or paid during the period.
(e)   Indicate the change in the applicable asset or liability account from the beginning of the period to the end of the period.

TIP:	It would be helpful to draw T-accounts for each situation. Enter the information given as it would be, or needs to be, reflected in the accounts. Solve for the adjusting entry that would be necessary to "reconcile" the facts given.
TIP:	Situations (1), (3), (5), and (7) above involve the approach discussed in the text chapter whereas situations (2), (4), (6), and (8) above involve the alternative approach to handling prepayments which is discussed in the **Appendix to Chapter 3** in your text.

SOLUTION TO EXERCISE 3-8

(1) (a) Office Supplies Expense 580
              Office Supplies on Hand   580
    (b) Office Supplies Expense $580
    (c) Office Supplies on Hand $320
    (d) Cash paid $900
    (e) Increase in Office Supplies on Hand $320

Approach:

Office Supplies on Hand			Office Supplies Expense	
Beg. Bal.	0	(580) ◄— ENTRY NEEDED TO COMPLETE ACCOUNTS —► (580)		
Acquisitions	900			
Desired Ending			Ending	
Balance	320		Balance	580

(2) (a) Office Supplies on Hand... 320
              Office Supplies Expense   320
    (b) Office Supplies Expense $580
    (c) Office Supplies on Hand $320
    (d) Cash paid $900
    (e) Increase in Office Supplies on Hand $320

Approach:

Office Supplies Expense			Office Supplies on Hand	
			Beg. Bal.	0
Acquisitions	900	(320) ◄— ENTRY NEEDED TO COMPLETE ACCOUNTS —► (320)		
Ending Bal.	580		Desired Ending	
			Balance	320

> **TIP:** Compare situation (2) with situation (1). Notice the facts are the same **except** for the account debited for acquisitions of office supplies. The solution is the same **except** for the adjusting entry required.

(3) (a) Office Supplies Expense 980
              Office Supplies on Hand   980
    (b) Office Supplies Expense $980
    (c) Office Supplies on Hand $320
    (d) Cash paid $900
    (e) Decrease in Office Supplies on Hand $ 80

Approach:

Office Supplies on Hand			Office Supplies Expense	
Beg. Bal.	400	(980) ◄— ENTRY NEEDED TO COMPLETE ACCOUNTS —► (980)		
Acquisitions	900			
Desired Ending			Ending	
Balance	320		Balance	980

(4) (a) Office Supplies Expense 80
          Office Supplies on Hand...   80
     (b) Office Supplies Expense $980
     (c) Office Supplies on Hand $320
     (d) Cash paid $900
     (e) Decrease in Office Supplies on Hand $ 80

Approach:

Office Supplies on Hand			Office Supplies Expense		
Beg. Bal.	400		Acquisitions	900	
		(80) ◄—— ENTRY NEEDED TO COMPLETE ACCOUNTS ——► (80)			
Desired Ending Balance	320		Ending Bal.	980	

> **TIP:** Compare situation (4) with situation (3). Notice the facts are the same **except** for the account debited for acquisitions of office supplies. The solution is the same **except** for the adjusting entry required.

(5) (a) Unearned Subscription Revenue 46,000
          Subscription Revenue   46,000
     (b) Subscription Revenue $46,000
     (c) Unearned Subscription Revenue $ 8,000
     (d) Cash received $54,000
     (e) Increase in Unearned Subscription Revenue $ 8,000

Approach:

Subscription Revenue			Unearned Subscription Revenue		
	(46,000) ◄——ENTRY NEEDED TO COMPLETE ACCOUNTS——► (46,000)		Beg. Bal.	0	
			Receipts	54,000	
Ending Balance	46,000		Desired End Bal.	8,000	

(6) (a) Subscription Revenue 8,000
          Unearned Subscription Revenue   8,000
     (b) Subscription Revenue $46,000
     (c) Unearned Subscription Revenue $ 8,000
     (d) Cash received $54,000
     (e) Increase in Unearned Subscription Revenue $ 8,000

Approach:

Unearned Subscription Revenue			Subscription Revenue		
	Beg. Bal.	0		Receipts	54,000
	(8,000) ◄—— ENTRY NEEDED TO COMPLETE ACCOUNTS ——► (8,000)				
	Desired End. Bal.	8,000		Ending Balance	46,000

> **TIP:** Compare situation (6) with situation (5). Notice the facts are the same **except** for the account credited for receipt of revenue in advance of the period in which the revenue is earned. The solution is the same **except** for the adjusting entry required.

(7)   (a)   Unearned Subscription Revenue   52,700
               Subscription Revenue...   52,700
     (b)   Subscription Revenue $52,700
     (c)   Unearned Subscription Revenue $ 8,000
     (d)   Cash received $54,000
     (e)   Increase in Unearned Subscription Revenue $ 1,300

Approach:

Subscription Revenue	Unearned Subscription Revenue
	Beg. Bal. 6,700
(52,700) ◄—ENTRY NEEDED TO COMPLETE ACCOUNTS—► (52,700)	Receipts 54,000
Ending Bal. 52,700	Desired End. Bal. 8,000

(8)   (a)   Subscription Revenue   1,300
               Unearned Subscription Revenue   1,300
     (b)   Subscription Revenue $52,700
     (c)   Unearned Subscription Revenue $ 8,000
     (d)   Cash received $54,000
     (e)   Increase in Unearned Subscription Revenue $ 1,300

Approach:

Unearned Subscription Revenue	Subscription Revenue
Beg. Bal. 6,700	
(1,300) ◄— ENTRY NEEDED TO COMPLETE ACCOUNTS—► (1,300)	Receipts 54,000
Desired Ending Bal. 8,000	End. Bal. 52,700

TIP: Compare situation (8) with situation (7). Notice the facts are the same **except** for the account credited for receipt of revenue in advance of the period in which the revenue is earned. The solution is the same **except** for the adjusting entry required.

EXERCISE 3-9

Purpose: (L.O. 1 thru 8) This exercise will quiz you about terminology used in this chapter.

A list of accounting terms with which you should be familiar appears below:

Accrual-basis accounting

Accruals

Accrued expenses

Accrued revenues

Adjusted trial balance

Adjusting entries

Book value

Calendar year

Cash-basis accounting

Contra asset account

Deferrals

Depreciation

Expense recognition principle (matching principle)

Fiscal year

Interim periods

Prepaid expenses

Revenue recognition principle

Time period assumption

Unearned revenues

Useful life

Instructions

For each item below, enter in the blank the term that is described.

1. _____Accounting basis in which events that change a company's financial statements are recorded in the periods in which the events occur, rather than in the periods in which the company receives or pays cash. Thus, revenues are recognized when earned and expenses are recognized when incurred, regardless of when the related cash is received or paid.

2. _____Revenue is recorded only when cash is received, and an expense is recorded only when cash is paid.

3. _____An assumption that the economic life of a business can be divided into artificial time periods of equal length. Another name for this assumption is the periodicity assumption.

4. _____The principle that dictates revenue be recognized in the accounting period in which the performance obligation is satisfied.

5. _____The principle that dictates efforts (expenses) be matched with accomplishments (revenues).

6. _____Expenses incurred but not yet paid in cash or recorded. They result in accrued liabilities.

7. _____Revenues for services performed but not yet received in cash or recorded. They result in accrued receivables.

8. _____Expenses paid in cash and reported as assets before the related goods and services are used up or consumed (often called **deferred expenses).**

9. _____Revenues received in cash and reported as liabilities before the related services are performed (often called **deferred revenues).**

10. _____Entries made at the end of an accounting period to ensure that the revenue recognition and matching principles are followed.

11. _____Adjusting entries for either accrued revenues or accrued expenses.

12. _____Adjusting entries for either prepaid expenses or unearned revenues.

13. _____A list of accounts and their balances after all adjustments have been made.

14. _____The difference between the cost of a depreciable asset and its related accumulated depreciation (often called **carrying value** or **carrying amount).**

15. _____An accounting period that extends from January 1 to December 31.

16. _____An account that is offset against an asset account on the balance sheet.

17. _____The length of service of a productive facility (often called **estimated service life).**

18. _____The process of allocating the cost of a plant asset to expense over its useful life in a rational and systematic manner.

19. _____An accounting period that is one year in length.

20. _____Monthly or quarterly accounting time periods.

SOLUTION TO EXERCISE 3-9

1.	Accrual-basis accounting	11.	Accruals
2.	Cash-basis of accounting	12.	Deferrals
3.	Time period assumption	13.	Adjusted trial balance
4.	Revenue recognition principle	14.	Book value
5.	Expense recognition principle (matching principle)	15.	Calendar year
6.	Accrued expenses	16.	Contra asset account
7.	Accrued revenues	17.	Useful life
8.	Prepaid expenses	18.	Depreciation
9.	Unearned revenues	19.	Fiscal year
10.	Adjusting entries	20.	Interim periods

ANALYSIS OF MULTIPLE-CHOICE TYPE QUESTIONS

1. **Question**
    (L.O. 2) Which of the following statements best describes the matching principle?
    a. Total debits to expense accounts should equal total credits to revenue accounts.
    b. Total debits must be matched with total credits in the ledger accounts.
    c. Amounts on the balance sheet must be matched with amounts reported on the income statement.

d. Expenses should be recognized in the same period that the related revenues are recognized.

Approach and Explanation: Mentally define the matching principle **before** you read the answer selections. Jot down the key words of your definition. The **revenue recognition principle** gives us guidance to determine when to recognize (record and report) revenue. The **expense recognition (matching) principle** then dictates that the expenses incurred in generating the revenue earned during the current period should be recognized in the same period as the revenue it helped to create. Answer selections "a" and "c" are nonsensical responses. Answer selection "b" refers to the fact that there is an equality of debits and credits in the ledger but that equality is due to the basic accounting equation and the double-entry accounting system, not the matching principle. (Solution = d.)

2. **Question**
(L.O. 2) Which of the following statements is associated with the accrual-basis of accounting?
a. The timing of cash receipts and disbursements is emphasized.
b. A minimum amount of record keeping is required.
c. This method is used less frequently by businesses than the cash method of accounting.
d. Revenues are recognized in the period they are earned (when the related services are performed), regardless of the time period the cash is received.

Approach and Explanation: Mentally define the accrual-basis of accounting. Write down the key words and phrases of your definition. Compare each answer selection with your definition and choose the one that best matches. Using the **accrual-basis of accounting,** events that change a company's financial statements are recorded in the periods in which the events occur. Thus, revenues are recognized in the period in which they are earned, and expenses are recognized in the period in which they are incurred, regardless of when the related cash is received or paid. Answer selections "a" and "b" refer to the cash basis of accounting which is not GAAP. (Solution = d.)

3. **Question**
(L.O. 2) The McKiernan Company made cash sales of services of $5,000 and credit sales of services of $4,200 during the month of July. The company incurred expenses of $6,000 during July of which $2,000 was paid in cash and the remainder was expected to be paid in August. Using the accrual method of accounting, net income for July amounts to:
a. $7,200.
b. $5,200.
c. $3,200.
d. $200.

Approach and Explanation: Write down the essence of the accrual method: revenues are recorded when earned and expenses are recorded when incurred. Look for the figures to fit the description. Cash sales of $5,000 plus credit sales of $4,200 equals $9,200 total revenue earned during July. Revenues earned of $9,200 minus expenses incurred of $6,000 equals net income of $3,200. (Solution = c.)

4. **Question**
    (L.O. 2, 3) Accruals of expenses are often necessary to:
    a. comply with the matching principle.
    b. comply with the cost principle.
    c. make the balance sheet balance.
    d. ensure that revenues exceed expenses.

    Explanation: Accruals of expenses are often necessary to comply with the accrual-basis of accounting which stems from the revenue recognition and expense recognition (matching) principles. (Solution = a.)

5. **Question**
    (L.O. 4) Which of the following adjusting entries will cause an increase in revenues and a decrease in liabilities?
    a. Entry to record an accrued expense.
    b. Entry to record an accrued revenue.
    c. Entry to record the consumed portion of an expense paid in advance and initially recorded as an asset.
    d. Entry to record the earned portion of revenue received in advance and initially recorded as unearned revenue.

    Approach and Explanation: For each answer selection, write down the sketch of the adjusting entry described and the effects of each half of the entry. Compare the stem of the question with your analyses to determine the correct answer. (Solution = d.)

    The entry to record an accrued expense:
    >   Dr.   Expenses
    >   Cr.   Liabilities
    The effects of the entry are to increase expenses and to increase liabilities.

    The entry to record an accrued revenue:
    >   Dr.   Assets
    >   Cr.   Revenues
    The effects of the entry are to increase assets and to increase revenues.

    The entry to record the consumed portion of a prepaid expense initially recorded as an asset is:
    >   Dr.   Expenses
    >   Cr.   Assets
    The effects of the entry are to increase expenses and to decrease assets.

    The entry to record the earned portion of unearned revenue initially recorded as a liability is:
    >   Dr.   Liabilities
    >   Cr.   Revenues
    The effects of the entry are to decrease liabilities and to increase revenues.

6. **Question**
    (L.O. 5) An adjusting entry to allocate a previously recorded asset to expense involves a debit to an:
    a. asset account and a credit to Cash.
    b. expense account and a credit to Cash.
    c. expense account and a credit to an asset account.
    d. asset account and a credit to an expense account.

Approach and Explanation: Write down the sketch of an adjusting entry to transfer an asset to expense. Compare each answer selection with your entry and choose the one that matches.

        Dr.   Expenses
                Cr.   Assets

(Solution = c.)

7. **Question**
   (L.O. 6) An accrued expense is an expense that:
   a.   has been incurred but has not been paid.
   b.   has been paid but has not been incurred.
   c.   has been incurred for which payment is to be made in installments.
   d.   will never be paid.

   Approach and Explanation: Write down a definition for accrued expense. Compare each answer selection with your definition and choose the best match. Expenses may be paid for in the same period in which they are incurred or they may be paid for in the period before or in the period after the one in which they are incurred. An **accrued expense** refers to an expense that has been incurred but has not yet been paid. It will be paid for in a period subsequent to the period in which it was incurred. (Solution = a.)

8. **Question**
   (L.O. 6) An adjusting entry to record an accrued expense involves a debit to a(an):
   a.   expense account and a credit to a prepaid account.
   b.   expense account and a credit to Cash.
   c.   expense account and a credit to a liability account.
   d.   liability account and a credit to an expense account.

   Approach and Explanation: Write down a definition for accrued expense and the types of accounts involved in an adjusting entry to accrue an expense. Find the answer selection that describes your entry.

        Dr.   Expenses
                Cr.   Liabilities

   Notice the logic of the entry. An **accrued expense** is an expense incurred but not yet paid. Thus, you record the incurrence by increasing an expense account and you record the "not paid" aspect by increasing a liability account. (Solution = c.)

9. **Question**
   (L.O. 6) The failure to properly record an adjusting entry to accrue an expense will result in an:
   a.   understatement of expenses and an understatement of liabilities.
   b.   understatement of expenses and an overstatement of liabilities.
   c.   understatement of expenses and an overstatement of assets.
   d.   overstatement of expenses and an understatement of assets.

   Approach and Explanation: Write down the adjusting entry to record an accrued expense. Analyze the effects of the entry. This will help you to determine the effects of the failure to properly make that entry.

Dr.   Expenses
        Cr.   Liabilities

This entry increases expenses and liabilities. Therefore, the failure to make this entry would result in an understatement of expenses and an understatement of liabilities. (Solution = a.)

10. **Question**
(L.O. 5) The term "book value" of an asset refers to:
a.   the market value of a used asset.
b.   the original cost of an asset minus the amount of depreciation accumulated to date.
c.   an asset's original cost.
d.   an asset's assessed value for tax purposes.

Explanation: Book value is the difference between the cost of a depreciable asset and its related accumulated depreciation. (Solution = b.)

11. **Question**
(L.O. 5) The balance in the Accumulated Depreciation account that relates to a building represents the amount of:
a.   the asset's remaining unallocated cost.
b.   depreciation expense for the building for the current period.
c.   total depreciation recorded to date for the building.
d.   reduction in market value experienced to date on the building.

Explanation: Depreciation is the process of allocating the cost of a long-lived asset to expense over the periods benefited by use of the asset. This cost allocation process is performed to comply with the matching principle. The depreciation recorded for a single period (for example, the current period) is referred to as **depreciation expense.** The total depreciation recorded on the asset since its acquisition is referred to as **accumulated depreciation.** (Solution = c.)

12. **Question**
(L.O. 5) Which of the following accounts is a contra account?
a.   Accounts Payable.
b.   Building.
c.   Unearned Revenue.
d.   Accumulated Depreciation.

Explanation: A **contra account** is one whose normal balance is opposite of the normal balance of the account to which it relates. A contra account is offset against the account to which it relates in order to properly value that item for financial reporting purposes. In recording depreciation, the account Accumulated Depreciation is used instead of crediting the asset account itself in order to permit disclosure of both the original cost of the asset and the total cost that has expired to date. (Solution = d.)

*13. Question

(L.O. 8) An adjusting entry contains a debit to Prepaid Advertising and a credit to Advertising Expense. The purpose of this entry is to:

a. defer advertising cost to a future period in which it will be incurred.
b. accrue advertising expense to the current period.
c. reduce a prepaid item.
d. report a revenue item.

Approach and Explanation: Think about the impact of the entry described. A debit to a prepaid account increases assets; a credit to an expense reduces expenses. Thus, the entry reduces expenses this period and increases prepaids so that an expense is deferred to a future period. Apparently, when the cash payment was made earlier, it was recorded by the alternative treatment; whereby, a debit was recorded to Advertising Expense and a credit was made to Cash. Thus, the adjusting entry will put the appropriate amount of asset on the books for the amount of expense to be deferred to a future period. (Solution = a.)

CHAPTER 4

. . . .

COMPLETING THE ACCOUNTING CYCLE

OVERVIEW

During the accounting period, transactions are recorded daily in the journal. At convenient times, information is posted from the journal to the ledger. At the end of the accounting period, the accountant summarizes the effects of the many recorded transactions, adjusts the accounts, and prepares financial statements. To help organize the information, the accountant uses an organized piece of scratch paper called a worksheet. The worksheet is a simple tool and is an optional step in the accounting cycle. Its preparation and uses are discussed in this chapter. After financial statements are drafted, the nominal (or temporary) accounts must be prepared for the accumulation of data pertaining to transactions in the following accounting period. Closing entries are journalized and posted to do just that; they are a required step in the accounting cycle and are discussed in this chapter. At the beginning of the subsequent (new) accounting period, reversing entries may be prepared in order to facilitate the recording of cash receipts and disbursements that relate to adjusting entries of the prior period. Reversing entries are an optional step in the accounting cycle and are discussed in the appendix to this chapter.

SUMMARY OF LEARNING OBJECTIVES

1. **Prepare a worksheet.** The steps in preparing a worksheet are as follows: (a) Prepare a trial balance on the worksheet. (b) Enter the adjustments in the adjustment columns. (c) Enter adjusted balances in the adjusted trial balance columns. (d) Extend adjusted trial balance amounts to appropriate financial statement columns. (e) Total the statement columns, compute net income (or net loss), and complete the worksheet.

2. **Explain the process of closing the books.** Closing the books occurs at the end of an accounting period. The process is to journalize and post closing entries and then rule and balance all accounts. In closing the books, companies make separate entries to close revenues and expenses to Income Summary, Income Summary to Retained Earnings, and Dividends to Retained Earnings. Only temporary accounts are closed.

3. **Describe the content and purpose of a post-closing trial balance.** A post-closing trial balance contains the balances in permanent accounts that are carried forward to the next accounting period. The purpose of this trial balance is to prove the equality of these balances.

4.   **State the required steps in the accounting cycle.** The required steps in the accounting cycle are: (1) analyze business transactions, (2) journalize the transactions, (3) post to ledger accounts, (4) prepare a trial balance, (5) journalize and post adjusting entries, (6) prepare an adjusted trial balance, (7) prepare financial statements, (8) journalize and post closing entries, and (9) prepare a post-closing trial balance.

5.   **Explain the approaches to preparing correcting entries.** One way to determine the correcting entry is to compare the incorrect entry with the correct entry. After comparison, a correcting entry is made to correct the accounts. An alternative to a correcting entry is to reverse the incorrect entry and then prepare the correct entry.

6.   **Identify the sections of a classified balance sheet.** A classified balance sheet, categorizes assets as current assets; long-term investments; property, plant, and equipment; and intangibles. Liabilities are classified as either current or long-term. There is also an owners' equity section, which varies with the form of business organization (in a corporation it is called the stockholders' equity section).

*7.   **Prepare reversing entries.** Reversing entries are the opposite of the adjusting entries made in the preceding period. Some companies choose to make reversing entries at the beginning of a new accounting period to simplify the recording of later transactions related to the adjusting entries. In most cases, only accrual-type adjusting entries are reversed.

*This material appears in the **Appendix to Chapter 4** in the text.

EXERCISE 4-1

Purpose: (L.O. 1) This exercise will allow you to quickly check your knowledge of how items are extended on a worksheet.

A partial jumbled worksheet for the Piper Wood Investigative Services Corporation appears below. (The accounts are **not** listed in their usual order, the worksheet is only partially illustrated, and the Trial Balance and Adjustments columns have been omitted.)

PIPER WOOD INVESTIGATIVE SERVICES CORPORATION
Worksheet
For the Year Ended December 31, 2014

Account	Adjusted Trial Balance		Income Statement		Balance Sheet	
	Debit	Credit	Debit	Credit	Debit	Credit
Salaries and Wages Payable		X				X
Prepaid Insurance						
Accumulated Depreciation—Equipment						
Unearned Revenue						
Rent Expense						
Service Revenue						
Prepaid Rent						
Dividends						
Repairs Expense						
Utilities Payable						
Interest Receivable						
Accounts Receivable						
Advertising Expense						
Depreciation Expense						
Land						
Equipment						
Salaries and Wages Expense						
Mortgage Payable						
Cash						
Net Income						

Instructions
For each account, place an "X" in the appropriate Adjusted Trial Balance column pair to indicate whether the account balance will appear in the Debit or Credit column (assume a normal balance in each account) on the worksheet. Also for each account, place an "X" in the appropriate Income Statement or Balance Sheet column to indicate the column to which the balance should be extended. The first one is done for you.

TIP:	Because the accounts are in a jumbled order, you must first identify for each item the type of account and then determine where the related amounts will fall column-wise on the worksheet.

SOLUTION TO EXERCISE 4-1

PIPER WOOD INVESTIGATIVE SERVICES CORPORATION
Worksheet
For the Year Ended December 31, 2014

Account	Adjusted Trial Balance Debit	Adjusted Trial Balance Credit	Income Statement Debit	Income Statement Credit	Balance Sheet Debit	Balance Sheet Credit
Salaries and Wages Payable		X				X
Prepaid Insurance	X				X	
Accumulated Depreciation—Equipment		X				X
Unearned Revenue		X				X
Rent Expense	X		X			
Service Revenue		X		X		
Prepaid Rent	X				X	
Dividends	X				X	
Repairs Expense	X		X			
Utilities Payable		X				X
Interest Receivable	X				X	
Accounts Receivable	X				X	
Advertising Expense	X		X			
Depreciation Expense	X		X			
Land	X				X	
Equipment	X				X	
Salaries and Wages Expense	X		X			
Mortgage Payable		X				X
Cash	X				X	
Net Income[a]			X			X

[a]In the process of completing a worksheet, each of the statement columns must be totaled. The net income or loss for the period is then found by computing the difference between the totals of the two income statement columns. If total credits exceed total debits, net income has resulted. In such a case, the words "net income" are inserted in the account title space. The amount then is entered in the income statement debit column and the balance sheet credit column. The debit amount balances the income statement columns and the credit amount balances the balance sheet columns. In addition, the credit in the balance sheet column indicates the increase in owners' (stockholders') equity resulting from net income. Conversely, if total debits in the income statement columns exceed total credits, a net loss has occurred. The amount of the net loss is entered in the income statement credit column and the balance sheet debit column.

EXERCISE 4-2

Purpose: (L.O. 1) This exercise illustrates the function of a worksheet.

Carl's Video Service, Inc. has a fiscal year ending on April 30. The following information is available at the end of the corporation's first year of operations:

(a)   Parts and supplies on hand at April 30, 2014, amount to $1,600.
(b)   Wages incurred but not paid at April 30, 2014, amount to $320.
(c)   The $540 balance in the Prepaid Insurance account represents a payment for 12 months that began on August 1, 2013.
(d)   The note payable bears interest of 6% per year and was issued on December 1, 2013.
(e)   The estimated amount of utilities consumed but unpaid as of year end amounts to $400.
(f)   Depreciation on equipment for the year amounts to $3,000.

Instructions
Complete the worksheet for Carl's Video Service, Inc. for the year ended April 30, 2014. The trial balance has already been put on the worksheet for you.

TIP:	Remember to cross-reference (key) your adjustments by use of the appropriate letters.
TIP:	Before beginning a worksheet, think about the steps involved in its completion: Step 1: Prepare a trial balance on the worksheet. Step 2: Enter the adjustments in the adjustments columns. Step 3: Enter adjusted balances in the adjusted trial balance columns. Step 4: Extend adjusted trial balance amounts to appropriate financial statement columns. Step 5: Total the statement columns, compute the net income (or net loss), and complete the worksheet.
TIP:	The debit and credit columns for every column pair must be equal before you can proceed to the next column pair on a worksheet. (This pertains to the first three column pairs.)
TIP:	Every amount appearing in the adjusted trial balance column pair on a worksheet must be extended to one of the four statement columns. Debit amounts go to a debit column further to the right and credit amounts go to a credit column further to the right of the adjusted trial balance column pair.
TIP:	When a dollar amount is added to balance the income statement column pair of columns on a worksheet, the same amount must be added in an opposite debit or credit column in the balance sheet column pair. This amount in a balance sheet column indicates the impact of net income (or net loss) on stockholders' equity.

CARL'S VIDEO SERVICE, INC.
Worksheet
For the Year Ended April 30, 2014

Account Titles	Trial Balance Dr.	Trial Balance Cr.	Adjustments Dr.	Adjustments Cr.	Adjusted Trial Balance Dr.	Adjusted Trial Balance Cr.	Income Statement Dr.	Income Statement Cr.	Balance Sheet Dr.	Balance Sheet Cr.
Cash	21,000									
Accounts Receivable	1,800									
Parts and Supplies	9,100									
Prepaid Insurance	540									
Lab Equipment	24,000									
Accum. Depreciation—Equip.		6,000								
Accounts Payable		2,000								
Note Payable (due 11/30/17)		4,000								
Common Stock		20,560								
Retained Earnings		0								
Dividends	1,700									
Service Revenue Earned		43,500								
Salaries and Wages Exp.	10,380									
Rent Expense	4,800									
Utilities Expense	2,170									
Advertising Expense	490									
Miscellaneous Expense	80									
Totals	76,060	76,060								

SOLUTION TO EXERCISE 4-2

CARL'S VIDEO SERVICE, INC.
Worksheet
For the Year Ended April 30, 2014

Account Titles	Trial Balance Dr.	Trial Balance Cr.	Adjustments Dr.	Adjustments Cr.	Adjusted Trial Balance Dr.	Adjusted Trial Balance Cr.	Income Statement Dr.	Income Statement Cr.	Balance Sheet Dr.	Balance Sheet Cr.
Cash	21,000				21,000				21,000	
Accounts Receivable	1,800				1,800				1,800	
Parts and Supplies	9,100			(a) 7,500	1,600				1,600	
Prepaid Insurance	540			(c) 405	135				135	
Lab Equipment	24,000				24,000				24,000	
Accum. Depreciation—Equip.		6,000		(f) 3,000		9,000				9,000
Accounts Payable		2,000				2,000				2,000
Note Payable (due 11/30/17)		4,000				4,000				4,000
Common Stock		20,560				20,560				20,560
Retained Earnings		0				0				0
Dividends	1,700				1,700				1,700	
Service Revenue Earned		43,500				43,500		43,500		
Salaries and Wages Exp.	10,380		(b) 320		10,700		10,700			
Rent Expense	4,800				4,800		4,800			
Utilities Expense	2,170		(e) 400		2,570		2,570			
Advertising Expense	490				490		490			
Miscellaneous Expense	80				80		80			
Totals	76,060	76,060								
Parts and Supplies Exp.			(a) 7,500		7,500		7,500			
Salaries and Wages Payable				(b) 320		320				320
Insurance Expense			(c) 405		405		405			
Interest Expense			(d) 100		100		100			
Interest Payable				(d) 100		100				100
Utilities Payable				(e) 400		400				400
Depreciation Expense			(f) 3,000		3,000		3,000			
			11,725	11,725	79,880	79,880	29,645	43,500	50,235	36,380
Net Income							13,855			13,855
							43,500	43,500	50,235	50,235

TIP:	All five pairs of columns must balance for a worksheet to be complete.
TIP:	The amount shown for Retained Earnings on the completed worksheet is the account balance **before** considering dividends and net income (or net loss) for the current accounting period. In this case, it is the corporation's first year of operations; hence, the balance of retained earnings on the worksheet is zero.

EXERCISE 4-3

Purpose: (L.O. 1, 6) This exercise will illustrate the preparation of financial statements from information contained in the worksheet.

A worksheet is a tool used by most accountants to aid in the organization of data for the preparation of financial statements.

Instructions
Refer to the **Solution to Exercise 4-2.** Use the completed worksheet for Carl's Video Service, Inc. to:
(a)   Prepare an income statement for the year ending April 30, 2014.
(b)   Prepare a retained earnings statement for the year ending April 30, 2014.
(c)   Prepare a classified balance sheet at April 30, 2014.

SOLUTION TO EXERCISE 4-3

(a)

CARL'S VIDEO SERVICE, INC.
Income Statement
For the Year Ended April 30, 2014

Revenues		
Service revenue earned		$43,500
Expenses		
Salaries and Wages	$10,700	
Parts and supplies expense	7,500	
Rent expense	4,800	
Depreciation expense	3,000	
Utilities expense	2,570	
Advertising expense	490	
Insurance expense	405	
Interest expense	100	
Miscellaneous expense	80	
Total expenses		29,645
Net income		$13,855

(b)

CARL'S VIDEO SERVICE, INC.
Retained Earnings Statement
For the Year Ending April 30, 2014

Retained Earnings, May 1, 2013	$ 0
Add: Net income	13,855
	13,855
Less: Dividends	1,700
Retained Earnings, April 30, 2014	$12,155

(c)

CARL'S VIDEO SERVICE, INC.
Balance Sheet
April 30, 2014

Assets

Current assets		
Cash		$21,000
Accounts receivable		1,800
Parts and supplies		1,600
Prepaid insurance		135
Total current assets		24,535
Property, plant, and equipment		
Lab equipment	$24,000	
Less: Accumulated depreciation	9,000	
Total property, plant, and equipment		15,000
Total assets		$39,535

Liabilities and Stockholders' Equity

Current liabilities	
Accounts payable	$ 2,000
Salaries and Wages payable	320
Utilities payable	400
Interest payable	100
Total current liabilities	2,820
Long-term liabilities	
Note payable	4,000
Total liabilities	6,820
Stockholders' equity	
Common stock	20,560
Retained earnings	12,155
Total liabilities and stockholders' equity	$39,535

TIP: Recall the order of items listed within categories on the financial statements. Although not mandatory, expenses are usually listed in descending order of amounts (with miscellaneous expenses always being the last in the list). Current assets are to be listed in order of liquidity. Current liabilities have no certain order but typically notes payable (short-term notes payable or current portion of long-term notes payable) and accounts payable are listed first and the rest are often listed in descending order.

TIP: Total stockholders' equity for Carl's Video Service, Inc. at April 30, 2014 is $32,715 ($20,560 + $12,155).

EXERCISE 4-4

Purpose: (L.O. 2) This exercise will give you practice in identifying those accounts which are closed at the end of the accounting period and those accounts which are not closed.

Instructions

Indicate whether the following accounts would or would not be closed at the end of the accounting period by placing an "X" in the appropriate column.

TIP:	Remember the general rule: All nominal accounts (revenues, expenses, and dividends) are closed and all real accounts (assets, liabilities, common stock, and retained earnings) are **not** closed. Therefore to determine if an account will be closed or not closed, analyze the classification of the account.
TIP:	Nine of the following are nominal or temporary accounts; eleven are real or permanent accounts.

Accounts	Closed	Not Closed
1. Accounts Receivable		
2. Rental Revenue		
3. Repairs Expense		
4. Building		
5. Depreciation Expense		
6. Accumulated Depreciation		
7. Notes Payable		
8. Interest Payable		
9. Sales Revenue		
10. Salaries and Wages Expense		
11. Revenue Received in Advance[a]		
12. Furniture		
13. Prepaid Insurance		
14. Insurance Expense		
15. Advertising Expense		
16. Retained Earnings		
17. Dividends		
18. Interest Revenue		
19. Common Stock		
20. Cash		

[a]Another title for Unearned Revenue.

SOLUTION TO EXERCISE 4-4

Accounts	Closed	Not Closed
1. Accounts Receivable		X
2. Rental Revenue	X	
3. Repairs Expense	X	
4. Building		X
5. Depreciation Expense	X	
6. Accumulated Depreciation		X
7. Notes Payable		X
8. Interest Payable		X
9. Sales Revenue	X	
10. Salaries and Wages Expense	X	
11. Revenue Received in Advance		X
12. Furniture		X
13. Prepaid Insurance		X
14. Insurance Expense	X	
15. Advertising Expense	X	
16. Retained Earnings		X
17. Dividends	X	
18. Interest Revenue	X	
19. Common Stock		X
20. Cash		X

EXERCISE 4-5

Purpose: (L.O. 2, 3) This exercise illustrates the preparation of closing entries and discusses their importance.

The recording and posting of closing entries is a required step in the accounting cycle.

Instructions
Refer to the **Solution to Exercise 4-2.**
(a)   Prepare the closing entries for Carl's Video Service, Inc. at April 30, 2014.
(b)   Discuss the two reasons why closing entries are prepared.

(c)   Prepare a post-closing trial balance for Carl's Video Service, Inc.
(d)   Explain why a post-closing trial balance is prepared and indicate what type of accounts will appear on the post-closing trial.

SOLUTION TO EXERCISE 4-5

(a)   Service Revenue Earned 43,500
        Income Summary   43,500
            (To close revenue account)

Income Summary 29,645
        Salaries and Wages Expense 10,700
        Rent Expense 4,800
        Utilities Expense 2,570
        Advertising Expense   490
        Miscellaneous Expense   80
        Parts and Supplies Expense 7,500
        Insurance Expense   405
        Interest Expense   100
        Depreciation Expense 3,000
            (To close expense accounts)

Income Summary 13,855
        Retained Earnings 13,855
            (To close net income to retained earnings)

Retained Earnings 1,700
        Dividends 1,700
            (To close dividends to retained earnings)

TIP: The Income Summary account is used only in the closing process. Before it is closed, the balance in this account must equal the net income or net loss figure for the period.

The amounts above would be reflected in the Income Summary account as follows:

Income Summary	
29,645	43,500
	13,855 Balance
To close 13,855	

TIP: Where do you look for the accounts (and their amounts) to be closed? If a worksheet is used, you can use the amounts listed in the Income Statement column pair and the balance of the Dividends account. If a worksheet is not used, you must refer to the temporary accounts (after adjustment) in the ledger to determine the balances to be closed.

(b)   The major reason closing entries are needed is that they prepare the temporary (nominal) accounts for the recording of transactions of the next accounting period. Closing entries produce a zero balance in each of the temporary accounts so that they can be used to accumulate data pertaining to the next accounting period. Because of closing entries, the revenues of 2014 are not commingled with the revenues of the prior period (2013). A second reason closing entries are needed is that the Retained Earnings account will reflect a true balance only after closing entries have been completed. Closing entries formally recognize in the ledger the transfer of net income (or loss) and dividends to retained earnings as shown in the retained earnings statement.

(c)

CARL'S VIDEO SERVICE, INC.
Post-Closing Trial Balance
April 30, 2014

	Debit	Credit
Cash	$21,000	
Accounts Receivable	1,800	
Parts and Supplies	1,600	
Prepaid Insurance	135	
Lab Equipment	24,000	
Accumulated Depreciation—Equipment		$ 9,000
Accounts Payable		2,000
Salaries and Wages Payable		320
Utilities Payable		400
Interest Payable		100
Note Payable		4,000
Common Stock		20,560
Retained Earnings		12,155
Totals	$48,535	$48,535

TIP:	Notice that although all of the balance sheet accounts appear on this post-closing trial balance, the total asset figure does not correspond to the total of the debit column on this trial. The reason for the difference is the placement of the Accumulated Depreciation account. Although its balance appears in the credit column of the trial balance, its balance is a reduction within the asset section of the balance sheet.

(d)   The purpose of a post-closing trial balance is to prove the equality of the permanent (real) accounts after the closing entries have been recorded and posted. The accounts appearing on a post-closing trial are the ones having balances that are carried forward into the next accounting period which can be described as the **real accounts** or the **permanent accounts** or the **balance sheet accounts.**

EXERCISE 4-6

Purpose: (L.O. 4) This exercise will review the proper sequence of the required steps in the accounting cycle.

The required steps in the accounting cycle are listed in random order below.

_____   a.   Prepare an adjusted trial balance.

_____   b.   Analyze business transactions.

_____   c.   Prepare a post-closing trial balance.

_____   d.   Prepare a trial balance.

_____   e.   Prepare financial statements.

_____   f.   Post to ledger accounts.

_____   g.   Journalize and post adjusting entries.

_____   h.   Journalize and post closing entries.

_____   i.   Journalize the transactions.

Instructions
Indicate the proper sequence of the steps by numbering them "1," "2," and so forth in the spaces provided.

TIP:	As you work through this exercise, concentrate on the logical step progression and the flow of information in the data gathering process.

SOLUTION TO EXERCISE 4-6

a.	6	d.	4	g.	5
b.	1	e.	7	h.	8
c.	9	f.	3	i.	2

EXERCISE 4-7

Purpose: (L.O. 1, 4) This exercise reviews the procedures involved in the accounting cycle when the two optional steps, a worksheet and reversing entries, are employed.

Ten steps in the accounting cycle for a company which uses a worksheet and reversing entries are listed in random order below.

_____   a.   Journalize and post closing entries.

_____   b.   Prepare financial statements from the worksheet.

_____   c.   Prepare a post-closing trial balance.

_____   d.   Balance the ledger accounts and prepare a trial balance on the worksheet.

_____   e.   Journalize and post adjustments made on the worksheet.

_____   f.   Record transactions in the journal.

_____   g.   Journalize and post reversing entries.

_____   h.   Post from journal to the ledger.

_____   i.   Complete the worksheet (adjusting entries, adjusted trial balance and extend amounts to financial statement columns).

_____   j.   Analyze business transactions.

Instructions
Arrange the ten procedures carried out in the accounting cycle in the order in which they should be performed by numbering them "1," "2," and so forth in the spaces provided.

TIP:	As you work through this exercise, concentrate on the logical progression and the flow of information in the data gathering process.

SOLUTION TO EXERCISE 4-7

a.	8	e.	7	h.	3
b.	6	f.	2	i.	5
c.	9	g.	10	j.	1
d.	4				

ILLUSTRATION 4-1
BALANCE SHEET CLASSIFICATIONS (L.O. 6)

Current assets—includes cash and items which are expected to be converted to cash or sold or consumed within the next year or operating cycle, whichever is longer.

Long-term investments—includes assets such as investments in stocks and bonds of other companies which can be realized in cash, but conversion into cash is not expected within the next year or operating cycle, whichever is longer.

Property, plant, and equipment—includes long-lived tangible assets (land, building, equipment, and machinery) that are currently being used in operations (used to produce goods and services for customers). Assets in this category are often referred to as **plant assets** or **fixed assets.** They are not held for resale.

Intangible assets—includes assets that lack physical substance, such as patent, copyright, trademark, or trade names that give the holder exclusive right of use for a specified period of time. Their value to a company is generally derived from the rights or privileges granted by governmental authority.

Current liabilities—includes obligations that are due within a year **and** are expected to require the use of existing current assets or the creation of other current liabilities to liquidate them such as accounts payable, short-term notes payable, accrued liabilities, and unearned revenue.

Long-term liabilities—includes obligations that do not meet the criteria to be classified as current liabilities such as bonds payable, mortgages payable, long-term notes payable, lease liabilities, and obligations under employee pension plans.

Owner's equity—includes the owner's contributions and profits retained for use in the business. For a proprietorship, there is one capital account. For a partnership, there is a capital account for each partner. For a corporation, owner's equity is called **stockholders' equity** and includes two sub classifications—Paid-in Capital and Retained Earnings. Paid-in Capital includes Common Stock and Additional Paid-in Capital (to be discussed in **Chapter 11).**

TIP: Memorize the definition of current assets. **Current assets** are cash and other assets that are expected to be converted into cash, sold, or consumed within the year or operating cycle that immediately follows the balance sheet date, whichever is longer. Think about how various examples of current assets meet this definition. Accounts receivable are current assets because they will be converted to cash shortly after the balance sheet date; inventory (to be discussed in the next chapter) is a current asset because it will be sold within the year that follows the balance sheet date; prepaid insurance is a current asset because it will be consumed (used up) within the next year.

ILLUSTRATION 4-1 (Continued)

TIP:	A normal **operating cycle** is the length of time required to go from cash and then back to cash. That is, for an entity which sells products, the operating cycle is the time required to take cash out to buy inventory then sell the inventory and receive cash (either from a cash sale or the collection of an account receivable stemming from a credit sale). Unless otherwise indicated, always assume the operating cycle is less than a year so the one-year test is used as the cutoff between current and noncurrent.
TIP:	Memorize the definition of current liabilities. **Current liabilities** are obligations which are expected to require the use of current assets or the incurrence of other current liabilities. A liability may be due within a year of the balance sheet date and not be a current liability. An example is a debt due in six months that will be liquidated by use of a noncurrent asset.
TIP:	In a classified balance sheet, any asset that is not classified as a current asset is a **noncurrent asset.** There are three noncurrent asset classifications: long-term investments; property, plant and equipment; and intangible assets. Some entities add another noncurrent section titled "other assets" to use for assets that don't fit well into other classifications.
TIP:	In a classified balance sheet, liabilities are classified either as current or noncurrent liabilities. The noncurrent liabilities are usually titled "long-term liabilities."
TIP:	It is extremely important that items are properly classified on a balance sheet. Errors in classification can result in incorrect ratio analyses (to be discussed in **Chapter 14**) which may lead to misrepresentations of the meaning of the information conveyed and can affect decisions that are based on those analyses.
TIP:	Current assets are listed in the order of their liquidity, with the most liquid ones being listed first. (**Liquidity** refers to the ease with which an asset can be converted to cash.) Current liabilities are not listed in any prescribed order; however, notes payable (short-term) is usually listed first followed by accounts payable (and the remainder of the current liabilities are often listed in descending order of amount).
TIP:	**"Short-term"** is synonymous with **"current"** and **"long-term"** is synonymous with **"noncurrent."** Therefore, "short-term debt" can be used to refer to "current liabilities". Asset classifications are typically titled current and noncurrent; whereas, liability classifications are typically titled current and long-term.
TIP:	All **noncurrent assets** (assets in classifications other than "current assets") are resources that are not expected to be converted into cash or fully consumed in operations within one year or the operating cycle, whichever is longer.
TIP:	Long-term investments are investments made by the business; they are **not** investments by the owners of the business. Investments by the owner in the business are reported as part of owners' equity on the balance sheet of the business.

EXERCISE 4-8

Purpose: (L.O. 6) This exercise will allow you to practice identifying the classification of accounts on a classified balance sheet.

A list of the balance sheet classifications appears below along with a list of account titles for the Steve Martin Corporation.

Classifications

CA	Current Assets	CL	Current Liabilities
INV	Long-Term Investments	LTL	Long-Term Liabilities
PPE	Property, Plant and Equipment	SE	Shareholders' Equity
ITG	Intangible Assets	NRBS	Not Reported on the Balance Sheet

Accounts

_____ 1. Accounts Receivable

_____ 2. Wages and Salaries Payable

_____ 3. Notes Payable (due in 4 years)

_____ 4. Office Equipment

_____ 5. Bank Loan Payable (due in 6 months)

_____ 6. Patent

_____ 7. Notes Payable (due in 4 mos.)

_____ 8. Bonds Payable (due in 20 years)

_____ 9. Notes Receivable (due in 3 years)

_____ 10. Mortgages Payable (due in 5 years)

_____ 11. Salaries and Wages Expense

_____ 12. Prepaid Insurance

_____ 13. Delivery Trucks

_____ 14. Copyright

_____ 15. Cash

_____ 16. Utilities Expense

_____ 17. Depreciation Expense

_____ 18. Rent Revenue Received in Advance (to be earned in 6 mos.)

_____ 19. Interest Receivable

_____ 20. Rent Revenue

_____ 21. Common Stock

_____ 22. Building

_____ 23. Prepaid Advertising

_____ 24. Prepaid Property Taxes

_____ 25. Investment in Orlando Aviation Authority Bonds

_____ 26. Property Taxes Payable

_____ 27. Investment in Stock of ABC Corporation

_____ 28. Land

_____ 29. Parking Lots & Driveways

_____ 30. Trademark

_____ 31.   Unearned Subscription Revenue

_____ 32.   Retained Earnings

Instructions

Indicate which balance sheet classification is the most appropriate for reporting each account listed above by selecting the abbreviation of the corresponding section. If the account is not a real (permanent) account, use the abbreviation NRBS for Not Reported on the Balance Sheet.

Approach: Mentally review the brief descriptions of each classification. (See **Illustration 4-1.**) Use these descriptions to aid your analysis.

SOLUTION TO EXERCISE 4-8

Item #	Solution	Item #	Solution	Item #	Solution	Item #	Solution
1.	CA	9.	INV	17.	NRBS	25.	INV
2.	CL	10.	LTL	18.	CL	26.	CL
3.	LTL	11.	NRBS	19.	CA	27.	INV
4.	PPE	12.	CA	20.	NRBS	28.	PPE
5.	CL	13.	PPE	21.	SE	29.	PPE
6.	ITG	14.	ITG	22.	PPE	30.	ITG
7.	CL	15.	CA	23.	CA	31.	CL
8.	LTL	16.	NRBS	24.	CA	32.	SE

Selected Explanations:

a.   Salaries and Wages Expense (Item #11), Utilities Expense (Item #16), Depreciation Expense (Item #17), and Rent Revenue (Item #20) are all income statement accounts. Hence, they are nominal or temporary accounts and do **not** belong on the balance sheet.

b.   Prepaid items such as Prepaid Insurance (Item #12), Prepaid Advertising (Item #23), and Prepaid Property Taxes (Item #24) are generally expected to be consumed within the next year or operating cycle, whichever is longer; hence, they are current assets.

c.   Rent Revenue Received in Advance (Item #18) is an alternate title for Unearned Rent Revenue. Unless otherwise indicated, you should assume the unearned amount will be earned within the year following the balance sheet date; hence, it is a current liability. If evidence existed to show the unearned amount was not expected to be earned in the next year, it would be classified as a long-term (noncurrent) liability. The same reasoning applies to Unearned Subscription Revenue (Item #31).

d.   Interest payments are typically due monthly, quarterly, semiannually, or at least annually. Hence, we expect to collect the amount in Interest Receivable (Item #19) within the next year (unless evidence exists to the contrary).

e. Investments such as Investment in Orlando Aviation Authority Bonds (Item #25) and Investment in Stock of ABC Corporation (Item #27) are assumed to be held for a long-term purpose (unless there is evidence to the contrary); hence, they are classified as long-term investments. If an investment is held for sale and is expected to be sold within the next year, it is to be classified as a current asset.

EXERCISE 4-9

Purpose: (L.O. 5) This exercise will illustrate how to correct errors made in the recording process.

The following errors were discovered in the books of the Cool Way AC Repair Shop.

1. A cash payment of $120 for repairs on a typewriter was recorded by a debit to Office Equipment and a credit to Cash.

2. A cash payment of $70 for office supplies was recorded by a debit to Office Supplies and a credit to Accounts Payable.

3. The declaration and distribution of a cash dividend was recorded by a debit to Salaries and Wages Expense and a credit to Cash for $700.

4. A cash payment of $150 for an ad appearing in Sunday's edition of the local newspaper was recorded by a debit to Utilities Expense and a credit to Cash for $150.

5. A $500 cash receipt from a customer on account was recorded by a debit to Cash for $50 and a credit to Service Revenue for $50.

6. The first interest payment made this accounting period (on a note payable) was for $1,000, which included $300 of interest accrued at the end of the last accounting period. The payment was recorded by a debit to Interest Expense for $1,000 and a credit to Cash for $1,000. (No reversing entries were made at the beginning of this accounting period.)

7. A $300 cash sale of services was recorded by a debit to Accounts Receivable for $300 and a credit to Service Revenue for $300.

8. A cash payment of $2,000 for some new tools was recorded by a debit to Tools for $200 and a credit to Cash for $200.

Instructions
Prepare an analysis of each error showing the
(a) incorrect entry,
(b) correct entry, and
(c) correcting entry.

SOLUTION TO EXERCISE 4-9

1. (a) **Incorrect entry:**

    Office Equipment 120

    Cash 120

    (b) **Correct entry:**

    Repairs Expense.. 120

    Cash 120

    (c) **Correcting entry:**

    Repairs Expense.. 120

    Office Equipment 120

2. (a) **Incorrect entry:**

    Office Supplies.. 70

    Accounts Payable.. 70

    (b) **Correct entry:**

    Office Supplies.. 70

    Cash 70

    (c) **Correcting entry:**

    Accounts Payable 70

    Cash 70

3. (a) **Incorrect entry:**

    Salaries and Wages Expense.. 700

    Cash 700

    (b) **Correct entry:**

    Dividends 700

    Cash 700

    (c) **Correcting entry:**

    Dividends 700

    Salaries and Wages Expense 700

4. (a) **Incorrect entry:**

    Utilities Expense 150

    Cash 150

    (b) **Correct entry:**

    Advertising Expense 150

    Cash 150

    (c) **Correcting entry:**

    Advertising Expense 150

    Utilities Expense 150

5. (a) **Incorrect entry:**
        Cash 50
            Service Revenue   50

    (b) **Correct entry:**
        Cash 500
            Accounts Receivable   500

    (c) **Correcting entry:**
        Service Revenue... 50
        Cash 450
            Accounts Receivable   500

TIP:	This one is tricky because both the amount and an account were in error in the original entry.

6. (a) **Incorrect entry:**
        Interest Expense... 1,000
            Cash   1,000

    (b) **Correct entry:**
        Interest Payable... 300
        Interest Expense... 700
            Cash   1,000

    (c) **Correcting entry:**
        Interest Payable... 300
            Interest Expense...   300

7. (a) **Incorrect entry:**
        Accounts Receivable 300
            Service Revenue   300

    (b) **Correct entry:**
        Cash 300
            Service Revenue   300

    (c) **Correcting entry:**
        Cash 300
            Accounts Receivable   300

8. (a) **Incorrect entry:**
        Tools... 200
            Cash   200

(b) **Correct entry:**

Tools	2,000	
Cash		2,000

(c) **Correcting entry:**

Tools	1,800	
Cash		1,800

Approach: Compare the correct entry with the incorrect entry to determine the accounts which need to be increased or decreased in the correcting entry to arrive at their correct balances.

Alternate Approach: If you are not usually successful in identifying the appropriate correcting entry by using the approach above, a simpler approach may be to reverse the incorrect entry and prepare the correct entry. These two entries together constitute the correction. For example, refer to error number 1. The correction could be made by the following:

Reversal of the erroneous entry:

Cash	120	
Office Equipment		120

Correct entry:

Repairs Expense	120	
Cash		120

Notice that these two entries are the equivalent to the single correcting entry given earlier in the solution as:

Repairs Expense	120	
Office Equipment		120

You can readily tell this because in the two entry (second) approach, the debit to Cash for $120 offsets the credit to Cash for $120 which leaves only the remainder of the entries having an impact on account balances. That remainder is a debit to Repairs Expense a credit to Office Equipment for $120.

EXERCISE 4-10

Purpose: (L.O. 1 thru 7) This exercise will quiz you about terminology used in this chapter.

A list of accounting terms with which you should be familiar appears below:

Classified balance sheet	Long-term liabilities (long-term debt)
Closing entries	Operating cycle
Correcting entries	Permanent (real) accounts
Current assets	Post-closing trial balance
Current liabilities	Property, plant, and equipment
Income Summary	Reversing entry
Intangible assets	Stockholders' equity
Liquidity	Temporary (nominal) accounts
Long-term investments	Worksheet

Instructions
For each item below, enter in the blank the term that is described.

1. _____A multiple-column form that may be used in the adjustment process and in preparing financial statements.

2. _____Entries made at the end of an accounting period to transfer the balances of temporary accounts to a permanent stockholders' equity account. For a corporation, the temporary accounts are closed to Retained Earnings.

3. _____A list of permanent accounts and their balances after closing entries have been journalized and posted.

4. _____Revenue, expense, and dividend accounts whose balances are transferred to retained earnings at the end of an accounting period.

5. _____Accounts whose balances are carried forward to the next accounting period. Balance sheet accounts.

6. _____A temporary account used in closing revenue and expense accounts.

7. _____An entry made at the beginning of a new accounting period that is the exact opposite of the related adjusting entry made in the previous period.

8. _____The average time required to go from cash to cash in producing revenues.

9. _____Cash and other resources that are reasonably expected to be realized in cash or sold or consumed in the business within the next year or the operating cycle, whichever is longer.

10. _____Resources such as stocks and bonds of other entities not expected to be realized in cash within the next year or operating cycle.

11. _____Assets of a relatively permanent nature that are being used in the business and not intended for resale.

12. _____Noncurrent resources that do not have physical substance.

13. _____Obligations reasonably expected to be paid from existing current assets or through the creation of other current liabilities within the next year or operating cycle, whichever is longer.

14. _____Obligations expected to be paid after one year or to be settled by the use of assets other than current assets or by the incurrence of long-term debt.

15. _____Owners' equity of a corporation; the owner-ship claim of shareholders on total assets.

16. _____The ability of a company to pay obligations that are expected to become due within the next year or operating cycle.

17. _____Entries to correct errors made in recording transactions.

18. _____A balance sheet that contains a number of standard classifications or sections.

SOLUTION TO EXERCISE 4-10

1. Worksheet
2. Closing entries
3. Post-closing trial balance
4. Temporary accounts (or nominal accounts)
5. Permanent accounts (or real accounts)
6. Income Summary
7. Reversing entry
8. Operating cycle
9. Current assets
10. Long-term investments
11. Property, plant and equipment
12. Intangible assets
13. Current liabilities
14. Long-term liabilities (or long-term debt)
15. Stockholders' equity
16. Liquidity
17. Correcting entries
18. Classified balance sheet

ILLUSTRATION 4-2
USE OF REVERSING ENTRIES VERSUS
NO REVERSING ENTRIES USED* (L.O. 7)

---

*This material is covered in the **Appendix to Chapter 4** in the text.

Reversing entries are most often used to reverse two types of adjusting entries: accrued revenues and accrued expenses.

As an example of the flow of information through the accounts when using reversing entries versus the flow when no reversing entries are used, consider the following information and the resulting entries and account balances. Notice that you arrive at the same account balances, regardless of your path, by the time financial statements are to be prepared.

Data:
A three-year note receivable for $12,000 was accepted on May 1, 2014. It carries a 10% interest rate. The interest is to be collected every 6 months so the first interest receipt was on November 1, 2014 and the second interest receipt is scheduled for May 1, 2015. The annual accounting period ends on December 31, 2014. Two months of accrued interest exists at year end.

Entries:

When Reversing Entries Are Not Used			When Reversing Entries Are Used		

Receipt Entry--Nov. 1, 2014

Cash	600		Cash	600	
Interest Revenue		600	Interest Revenue		600

Adjusting Entry--Dec. 31, 2014

Interest Receivable	200		Interest Receivable	200	
Interest Revenue		200	Interest Revenue		200

Closing Entry--Dec. 31, 2014 / **Closing Entry--December 31, 2014**

Interest Revenue	800		Interest Revenue	800	
Income Summary		800	Income Summary		800

Reversing Entry--Jan. 1, 2015

None			Interest Revenue	200	
			Interest Receivable		200

ILLUSTRATION 4-2 (Continued)

When Reversing Entries Are Not Used			When Reversing Entries Are Used		
Receipt Entry--May 1, 2015			**Receipt Entry--May 1, 2015**		
Cash	600		Cash	600	
Interest Receivable		200	Interest Revenue		600
Interest Revenue		400			
Receipt Entry--Nov. 1, 2015			**Receipt Entry--Nov. 1, 2015**		
Cash	600		Cash	600	
Interest Revenue		600	Interest Revenue		600

The posting of the entries through Nov. 1, 2015 is reflected as follows:

Interest Receivable			Interest Receivable	
12/31/14 Adj. 200	**5/1/15 Rec.** **200**		12/31/14 Adj. 200	**1/1/15 Rev.** **200**

Interest Revenue			Interest Revenue	
12/31/14 Closing 800	11/1/14 Rec. 600		12/31/14 Closing 800	11/1/14 Rec. 600
	12/31/14 Adj. 200			12/31/14 Adj. 200
800	800		800	800
	5/1/15 Rec. **400**	**1/1/15 Rev.** **200**	**5/1/15 Rec.** **600**
	11/1/15 Rec. 600			11/1/15 Rec. 600

TIP:	The differences are highlighted in bold print. Notice that by the end of the day on December 31, 2014, the account balances are the same regardless of which alternative is chosen. Also, by the end of the day on May 1, 2015, the account balances are once again the same under both approaches. (Abbreviations are: Rec. = Receipt; Rev. = Reversing; Adj. = Adjusting.)
TIP:	Notice how reversing entries allowed the bookkeeper to record the receipt of $600 on May 1, expediently like the November 1, 2014 receipt (debit to Cash for $600 and a credit to Interest Revenue for $600) without looking in the records to determine if the receipt is partially for revenue earned in a prior period or not. (Think of the time savings if you collect varying amounts of accrued interest from hundreds of different sources.)

EXERCISE 4-11

Purpose: (L.O. 7) This exercise will provide practice in determining which adjusting entries may be reversed.

The following represent adjusting entries prepared for the Office Furniture Design Company.

_____	1.	Interest Expense	700	
		Interest Payable		700
_____	2.	Depreciation Expense	1,100	
		Accumulated Depreciation		1,100
_____	3.	Rent Receivable	600	
		Rent Revenue		600
_____	4.	Insurance Expense	400	
		Prepaid Insurance		400
_____	5.	Accounts Receivable (or Fees Receivable)	300	
		Fees Revenue		300
_____	6.	Supplies Expense	200	
		Prepaid Supplies		200
_____	7.	Salaries and Wages Expense	1,000	
		Salaries and Wages Payable		1,000
_____	8.	Unearned Subscription Revenue	1,200	
		Subscription Revenue		1,200

Instructions
For each adjusting entry above (prepared at December 31, 2014), indicate if it would be appropriate to reverse the entry at the beginning of 2015. Indicate your answer by writing **yes** or **no** in the space provided.

SOLUTION TO EXERCISE 4-11

1.	Yes	5.	Yes
2.	No	6.	No
3.	Yes	7.	Yes
4.	No	8.	No

Explanation:

1. An expense accrual type adjustment can always be reversed. The reversing entry will eliminate the payable balance established by the adjustment and create a credit balance (an abnormal balance) in the expense account at the beginning of the new period. Thus, when the related cash is paid for the interest, the payment can be recorded by a credit to Cash and a debit to Interest Expense for the entire amount paid. (The abnormal balance in the expense account which was created by the reversing entry is eliminated with the posting of the cash payment entry.) This entry to record the cash payment is simpler than the alternate route of using no reversal and recording a portion of the payment (representing the accrued amount) by a debit to a payable account and the remainder (incurred in the new period) by a debit to the expense account.

2. An adjusting entry to record depreciation should **never** be reversed. It would not make sense to reverse this adjustment because to do so would reduce the depreciation to date (accumulated depreciation).

3. A revenue accrual type adjustment can always be reversed. The reversing entry will eliminate the receivable balance established by the adjustment and create a debit balance (an abnormal balance) in the revenue account at the beginning of the new period. Thus, when the related cash is collected from the tenant, the receipt can be recorded by a debit to Cash and a credit to Rent Revenue for the entire amount received. (The abnormal balance in the revenue account is eliminated with the posting of the cash collection entry.) This entry to record the cash receipt is simpler than the alternate route of using no reversal and recording a portion of the collection (representing the accrued amount) by a credit to the receivable account and the remainder (earned in the new period) by a credit to the revenue account.

4. An adjusting entry to transfer the expired portion of the insurance premium from an asset account (prepaid) to an expense account should **never** be reversed. A reversing entry would put the expired portion back into an asset account.

5. An adjusting entry to record accrued revenue can always be reversed. Refer to the logic explained for item 3. above.

6. An adjusting entry to transfer the cost of consumed supplies from an asset account to an expense account should never be reversed. Refer to the logic explained for item 4. above.

7. An adjusting entry to record accrued expense can always be reversed. Refer to the logic explained for item 1. above.

8. An adjusting entry to transfer the earned portion of the revenue collected in advance from the unearned account to an earned revenue account should **never** be reversed. A reversing entry would put the earned portion back into an unearned (liability) account, which would not make sense because that portion of the cash received has been earned and no liability remains for that portion.

ANALYSIS OF MULTIPLE-CHOICE QUESTIONS

1.   **Question**
     (L.O. 2) Which of the following accounts is a nominal (temporary) account?
     a.   Cash.
     b.   Prepaid Rent.
     c.   Accumulated Depreciation.
     d.   Advertising Expense.

     Approach and Explanation: Write down the definition of a nominal (or temporary) account. A **nominal account** is an account which is closed at the end of an accounting period. Think of what types of accounts get closed—revenues, expenses, and dividends. Think of what types of accounts never get closed—asset, liability, common stock, and retained earnings. Identify the classification of each of the accounts mentioned:

Cash	Asset
Prepaid Rent	Asset
Accumulated Depreciation	Contra Asset
Advertising Expense	Expense

     When judging if an account is temporary or permanent (real), a contra account is classified in the same manner (temporary or permanent) as the account to which it relates. Hence, a contra asset account is a real account. (Solution = d.)

2.   **Question**
     (L.O. 2) Certain accounts are closed at the end of an accounting period in order to:
     a.   reduce the number of items that get reported in the general purpose financial statements.
     b.   prepare those accounts for recording of transactions of the subsequent accounting period.
     c.   reduce the number of accounts that appear in the ledger.
     d.   transfer the effect of transactions recorded in real accounts to owners' equity.

     Approach and Explanation: Review the two reasons for preparing closing entries: (1) closing entries prepare the temporary accounts for the recording of transactions of the succeeding accounting period, and (2) closing entries transfer the net income (or net loss) amount and dividends to retained earnings as shown in the retained earnings statement. Net income is determined by the balances in revenue and expense accounts (collectively called nominal or temporary accounts). (Solution = b.)

3.   **Question**
     (L.O. 2) A journal entry to close the Service Revenue account in the closing process will involve a debit to:
     a.   Service Revenue and a credit to Income Summary.
     b.   Income Summary and a credit to Service Revenue.
     c.   Retained Earnings and a credit to Service Revenue.
     d.   Service Revenue and a credit to Cash.

     Approach and Explanation: Think of the normal balance of the account to be closed. Revenue accounts have a normal credit balance. A closing entry will involve the opposite action to that account; therefore, debit the Service Revenue account. All closing entries for income statement accounts involve the Income Summary account; therefore, credit Income Summary. (Solution = a.)

4.   **Question**
     (L.O. 2) If a corporation has profitable operations for the period, the balance of the Income Summary account will be closed by:
     a.   a debit to Income Summary and a credit to Retained Earnings.
     b.   a debit to Retained Earnings and a credit to Income Summary.
     c.   debits to the expense accounts, credits to the revenue accounts, and a credit to the Income Summary account.
     d.   debits to the revenue accounts, credits to the expense accounts, and a credit to the Income Summary account.

     Approach and Explanation: Keep in mind that assets have normal debit balances and owners' equity has the opposite (credit) normal balance. Revenues increase retained earnings (a component of owners' equity) so revenue accounts have normal credit balances and expense accounts have normal debit balances. Revenue accounts are closed by debits to those revenue accounts and credits to Income Summary; expense accounts are closed by credits to those expense accounts and debits to Income Summary. When revenues exceed expenses, the entity is profitable and the Income Summary account therefore has a credit balance before closing. The Income Summary account is closed, in those conditions, by a debit to Income Summary (for its balance) and a credit to the Retained Earnings account. (Solution = a.)

5.   **Question**
     (L.O. 3) Which of the following groups of accounts have balances after the books have been closed at the end of an accounting period?
     a.   All asset and revenue accounts.
     b.   All expense and liability accounts.
     c.   All asset, liability, capital stock, retained earnings, revenue, and expense accounts.
     d.   All asset, liability, capital stock, and retained earnings accounts.

Approach and Explanation: Think of which accounts get closed. They are the temporary or nominal accounts (which include all revenue, expense and dividend accounts). The real accounts are not closed (asset, liability, capital stock, and retained earnings accounts). (Solution = d.)

6. **Question**
   (L.O. 1) Before computing the net income figure for the period, the total of the income statement debit column of a worksheet is $42,000 and the total of the income statement credit column is $40,000. This indicates that:
   a. there was a net loss of $2,000 for the period.
   b. there was a net income of $2,000 for the period.
   c. the Income Summary account will be closed by a debit to that Income Summary account.
   d. an error has been made in preparing the worksheet.

   Explanation: Debits on the income statement reduce net income; credits on the income statement increase income. An excess of debits over credits on the income statement results in a net loss. A net loss will cause a debit balance in the Income Summary account so that account will be closed by a credit. (Solution = a.)

7. **Question**
   (L.O. 1) The preparation of a worksheet at the end of an accounting period will:
   a. eliminate the need for journalizing and posting adjusting entries.
   b. replace the preparation of individual financial statements.
   c. eliminate the need for preparing closing entries and a post-closing trial balance.
   d. serve as an aid to the accountant in organizing the data required for the preparation of financial statements.

   Explanation: The worksheet is an optional step in the accounting cycle. It does **not** eliminate the need for adjusting entries, financial statements, or closing entries. These are prepared in the same manner whether or not a worksheet is prepared. (Solution = d.)

8. **Question**
   (L.O. 1) In completing a worksheet, the account Depreciation Expense requires an amount in the adjusted trial balance debit column and also an amount in the:
   a. Income Statement debit column.
   b. Income Statement credit column.
   c. Balance Sheet debit column.
   d. Balance Sheet credit column.

   Explanation: Depreciation expense is to appear on the income statement as a reduction in net income (debit). (Solution = a.)

9. **Question**
   (L.O. 1) In completing a worksheet, the account Prepaid Insurance requires an amount in the adjusted trial balance debit column and also an amount in the:
   a.   Income Statement debit column.
   b.   Income Statement credit column.
   c.   Balance Sheet debit column.
   d.   Balance Sheet credit column.

   Approach and Explanation: Think about the statement on which the Prepaid Insurance account will appear and where. Prepaid Insurance will appear on the balance sheet as an asset (debit). (Solution = c.)

10. **Question**
    (L.O. 1) When revenues exceed expenses for a period, the worksheet will require the net income figure to be entered in the following columns to properly complete the worksheet.
    a.   income statement debit column and balance sheet credit column.
    b.   income statement credit column and balance sheet debit column.
    c.   income statement debit column and balance sheet debit column.
    d.   income statement credit column and balance sheet credit column.

    Explanation: Revenue accounts have credit balances; expense accounts have debit balances. Due to worksheet technique, when revenues exceed expenses (credits in income statement column exceed debits in income statement column on worksheet), a debit is needed in the income statement column pair to balance that pair. That debit is the net income figure. Debits have to equal credits. The corresponding credit is to the balance sheet column pair. (Solution = a.)

11. **Question**
    (L.O. 5) A piece of office equipment was acquired for cash this period and was **incorrectly** recorded by a debit to Repairs Expense. The correcting entry should:
    a.   increase assets and reduce expenses.
    b.   increase expenses and reduce assets.
    c.   increase liabilities and increase assets.
    d.   reduce assets and reduce expenses.

    Approach and Explanation: Write down the incorrect entry (debit to Repairs Expense and a credit to Cash) and the correct entry (debit to Office Equipment and a credit to Cash). Compare the two entries and identify the errors (Repairs Expense is overstated and Office Equipment is understated). Prepare the correcting entry (debit to Office Equipment and a credit to Repairs Expense). Notice that the effect of the correcting entry is to reduce expenses and to increase assets. (This solution ignores the depreciation that should also be recorded for the period.) (Solution = a.)

12. **Question**

(L.O. 7) Which of the following adjusting entries could be reversed at the beginning of the following accounting period?
a.   The entry to record depreciation for the period.
b.   The entry to record accrued revenue.
c.   The entry to transfer the expired portion of the office supplies from an asset account to an expense account.
d.   The entry to transfer the earned portion of revenue received in advance from a liability account to a revenue account.

Approach and Explanation: Think about the adjusting entries that can be reversed. Accrual type adjusting entries can always be reversed (the procedure is optional). Prepayment type adjusting entries are usually not reversed. Selection "a" is incorrect because depreciation entries are never reversed. Selection "c" is incorrect because a reversing entry would put expired costs back into an asset account. Selection "d" is incorrect because a reversing entry would put earned revenue back into a liability account. (Solution = b.)

13. **Question**

(L.O. 6) McSwain Clothiers has an obligation coming due on July 1, 2015, which will be settled by transferring assets which are properly classified as a long-term investment. The obligation should be classified on the company's December 31, 2014 balance sheet as:
a.   a current liability.
b.   a long-term liability.
c.   a contra current liability item.
d.   a contra current asset item.

Approach and Explanation: Write down the definition of current liability and determine if the obligation described meets the criteria contained in that definition. A **current liability** is an obligation which will come due within a year of the balance sheet date and is expected to require the use of assets properly classifiable as current assets or the creation of other current liabilities to liquidate it. The obligation described in the question is coming due within a year of the balance sheet date, but a noncurrent asset will be used to settle the debt; thus the obligation is properly classifiable as a long-term liability. (Solution = b.)

. . . .

CHAPTER 5

ACCOUNTING FOR MERCHANDISING OPERATIONS

OVERVIEW

A service entity performs services for its customers to earn service revenue. A merchandising entity sells products to its customers to earn sales revenue. Both types of entities incur expenses in generating revenue. Thus, expenses incurred must be matched with revenues earned. This chapter will acquaint you with the income statement for a merchandising entity. The major differences between the income statement for a service type firm and the income statement for a merchandising firm lie with the data reported for net sales revenue and cost of goods sold expense for the merchandiser. Both the single-step and the multiple-step formats for the income statement are discussed in this chapter.

A merchandiser must account for the purchase and sale of its inventory items. Both the periodic and perpetual inventory systems are also explained in this chapter.

SUMMARY OF LEARNING OBJECTIVES

1. **Identify the differences between service and merchandising companies.** Because of inventory, a merchandising company has sales revenue, cost of goods sold, and gross profit. To account for inventory, a merchandising company must choose between a perpetual inventory system and a periodic inventory system.

2. **Explain the recording of purchases under a perpetual inventory system.** The company debits the Inventory account for all purchases of merchandise and freight-in, and credits it for purchase discounts and purchase returns and allowances.

3. **Explain the recording of sales revenues under a perpetual inventory system.** When a merchandising company sells inventory, it debits Accounts Receivable (or Cash), and credits Sales for the **selling price** of the merchandise. At the same time, it debits Cost of Goods Sold, and credits Inventory for the **cost** of the inventory items sold.

4. **Explain the steps in the accounting cycle for a merchandiser.** Each of the required steps in the accounting cycle for a service company applies to a merchandising company. A worksheet is again an optional step. Under a perpetual inventory system, the Inventory account must be adjusted to agree with the physical count.

5. **Distinguish between a multiple-step and a single-step income statement.** A multiple-step income statement shows numerous steps in determining net income, including nonoperating activities sections. A single-step income statement classifies all data under two categories, revenues or expenses, and determines net income in one step.

*6.   **Explain the recording of purchases and sales of inventory under a periodic inventory system.** In recording purchases under a periodic system, companies must make entries for (a) cash and credit purchases, (b) purchase returns and allowances, (c) purchase discounts, and (d) freight costs. In recording sales, companies must make entries for (a) cash and credit sales, (b) sales returns and allowances, and (c) sales discounts.

7.   **Prepare a worksheet for a merchandising company. The steps in preparing a worksheet for a merchandising company are the same as they are for a service company. The unique accounts for a merchandiser are Inventory, Sales, Sales Returns and Allowances, Sales Discounts, and Cost of Goods Sold.

*This material is covered in **Appendix 5-A** in the text.

This material is covered in **Appendix 5-B in the text.

TIPS ON CHAPTER TOPICS

TIP: Sales revenue is recorded and reported in the period that it is earned. Sales revenue is earned in the period in which the related products are sold (which satisfies the performance obligation associated with a revenue transaction). For a given sales transaction, the related cash may or may not be received in the same time period as the sale. If the sale occurs before the cash is received, the business has an account receivable until the point of collection. If the cash receipt occurs before the sale, the business has a liability (which is often called unearned revenue) until the point in time when the revenue is earned.

TIP: Be careful to distinguish between a purchase type transaction and a sales type transaction. When one entity has a purchase, another entity has a sale. **Always describe the transaction from the viewpoint of the party for whom you are accounting.** For example, if Intel sells a computer chip to IBM, Intel has a sale and IBM has a purchase. When IBM sells a computer to Ray Sturm, IBM has a sale and Ray Sturm has a purchase.

TIP: Purchases of merchandise inventory are recorded by debiting the Inventory account (assuming the perpetual inventory system is used). Purchases of equipment are recorded by debits to Equipment. Purchases of office supplies are recorded by debits to the Office Supplies on Hand account.

TIP: **Freight-in** is often called **Transportation-in.** Freight-in refers to freight charges incurred to transport merchandise from the supplier's location to the merchandiser's warehouse. Freight-out refers to transportation charges incurred to transport merchandise from the merchandiser's warehouse to the customer's (consumer's) location. **Freight-out** is often called **Transportation-out.** Freight-in is a component of the cost of goods sold computation, while Freight-out is classified as a selling expense (which is part of operating expenses).

TIP: One of the two basic systems may be used to keep tract of inventory costs: (1) the perpetual inventory system, or (2) the periodic inventory system.

Under a **perpetual inventory system,** the cost of each inventory item is debited to the Inventory account when it is purchased. **At the time of sale,** the cost of an item is transferred from the Inventory account to the Cost of Goods Sold account. Thus, the Cost of Goods Sold account is continually updated **so at all times,** it reflects the cost of merchandise sold during the period and the balance of the Inventory account **at all times** reflects the cost of merchandise on hand. (The perpetual system is discussed in this chapter.)

Under a **periodic inventory system,** no attempt is made to keep detailed inventory records of the goods on hand throughout the accounting period. The cost of goods sold is determined **only** at the end of the period when a physical inventory count is taken to determine the quantity of goods on hand and their related cost. (The details of the periodic system are discussed in **Appendix 5-A** in the text).

TIP: When a perpetual inventory system is used, the balance of the Inventory account at the end of the accounting period reflects the cost of inventory on hand at the balance sheet date. This balance is verified by physically counting the merchandise and identifying its historical cost. If shrinkage or theft has occurred, an adjustment of the ending Inventory balance is necessary.

TIP: The following T-account displays the information which is reflected in the Inventory account when the **perpetual inventory system** is used:

Inventory	
Beginning Balance	
Purchases	Purchase Discounts
Freight-in	Purchase Returns and
	Allowances
	Cost of Goods Sold
Ending Balance	

By looking at the entries in the T-account above, we can see that the net cost of goods purchased during a period is added to the balance of the Inventory account. (That is, purchases are added, returns and discounts related to purchases are deducted, and freight-in is added.) The cost of goods sold during a period is removed from the Inventory account so that the cost of the inventory on hand at the end of the accounting period is the balance that remains in the Inventory account. That balance is called ending inventory.

Thus, the following relationships exist:

	Purchases
-	Purchase Returns and Allowances
-	Purchase Discounts
=	Net Purchases
+	Freight-In
=	Cost of Goods Purchased

	Beginning Inventory Balance
+	Cost of Goods Purchased
=	Cost of Goods Available for Sale
-	Cost of Goods Sold
=	Ending Inventory Balance

TIP: The cost of an inventory item is to include all costs necessary to acquire the item and get it ready for resale. Thus, if inventory is purchased FOB shipping point, freight-in is recorded by a debit to Inventory (assuming the perpetual inventory system is in use). Thus, when the inventory item is ultimately sold, the freight-in is included in the cost of goods sold figure on the income statement. Any freight-out is an operating expense.

TIP: An **invoice** is a document prepared by the seller that shows the relevant information about a sale. From the seller's perspective, this document is a **sales invoice;** from the buyer's perspective, it is a **purchase invoice.**

ILLUSTRATION 5-1
COMPUTATION MODELS FOR COMPONENTS OF
A MULTIPLE-STEP INCOME STATEMENT (L.O. 1, 5, 6)

	Sales
-	**Sales Returns and Allowances**
-	**Sales Discounts**
=	**Net Sales**

	Net Sales
-	**Cost of Goods Sold**
=	**Gross Profit**

	Gross Profit
-	**Operating Expenses**
=	**Income (Loss) from Operations**

	Income (Loss) from Operations
+	**Other Revenues and Gains**
-	**Other Expenses and Losses**
=	**Net Income (Loss)**

TIP: An entity often has two types of sales: cash sales and credit sales. **Credit sales** are often called **sales on account** or **charge sales** or **sales on credit**. Both cash sales and credit sales are recorded in the Sales account and are reported by the caption Sales on the income statement.

TIP: Even if a credit customer has paid the balance of his account, there are several reasons why the amount of cash collected from the customer may not equal the amount of the related sales revenue. Three of these reasons are discussed in this chapter; they are sales returns, sales allowances, and sales discounts.

TIP: The normal balance of the **Sales Returns and Allowances account** is a debit balance. It is **not** an expense account. Its balance is reported as a deduction from the sales revenue figure on the income statement; hence, it is classified as a **contra revenue** account. Although the amounts of sales returns and allowances could be directly debited to the Sales account, most businesses prefer to use a separate Sales Returns and Allowances account in order for management to readily notice if these items get unreasonably large. Similarly, the **Sales Discounts** account is a **contra revenue** account.

TIP: **Cost of goods sold** is an expense item. For most retail companies, it is the largest expense displayed on the income statement.

TIP: **Gross profit** is often called **gross margin.**

TIP: The Sales account (sometimes titled Sales Revenue) is used only to record the sale of goods held for resale (inventory). The sale of an asset not held for sale in the ordinary course of business does not affect the Sales account. For example, assume two items are sold for cash of $10,000 each. The first item is an inventory item with a cost of $6,000. The second item is a plot of land which was purchased years ago for $6,000 and held as a future store site. Assuming a **perpetual inventory system** (rather than a periodic inventory system) is used, the sale of the inventory item would be recorded as follows:

Cash	10,000	
Sales Revenue		10,000
Cost of Goods Sold	6,000	
Inventory		6,000

A gross profit of $4,000 would be reflected on the income statement because of the sales figure of $10,000 and the expense (cost of goods sold) of $6,000.

The sale of the land would be recorded as follows:

Cash	10,000	
Land..		6,000
Gain on Sale of Land...		4,000

The gain would be reflected as a nonoperating item on the income statement; thus it is included under the Other Revenues and Gains caption.

TIP: The transactions related to a company's primary operating activities are summarized by the caption "Income (Loss) from Operations." Nonoperating activities consist of (1) revenues and expenses from auxiliary operations and (2) gains and losses that are unrelated to the company's operations. The results of nonoperating activities are shown in two sections: **"Other revenues and gains"** and **"Other expenses and losses."**

EXERCISE 5-1

Purpose: (L.O. 1) This exercise will help you to identify the relationships among the components involved in measuring net income for a merchandising company.

The following information applies to The Sports Shop for 2014:

Sales	$748,000
Sales returns	10,000
Sales discounts	7,000
Cost of goods sold	388,000
Sales commissions expense	107,700
Advertising expense	16,800
Executive salaries expense	100,000
Utilities expense	25,000
Insurance expense	6,000
Freight-out	8,000
Interest revenue	5,500
Interest expense	7,200

Instructions
(a)   Compute net sales for 2014.
(b)   Compute gross profit for 2014.
(c)   Compute total operating expenses for 2014.
(d)   Compute net income for 2014.

SOLUTION TO EXERCISE 5-1

Explanations:

(a)	Sales	$748,000
	Sales returns	(10,000)
	Sales discounts	(7,000)
	Net sales	$731,000
(b)	Net sales	$731,000
	Cost of goods sold	(388,000)
	Gross profit	$343,000
(c)	Sales commissions expense	$107,700
	Advertising expense	16,800
	Freight-out	8,000
	Executive salaries expense	100,000
	Utilities expense	25,000
	Insurance expense	6,000
	Total operating expenses	$ 263,500

(d)	Gross profit	$343,000
	Total operating expenses	(263,500)
	Other revenue—interest revenue	5,500
	Other expense—interest expense	(7,200)
	Net income	$ 77,800

Approach for parts (a), (b) and (d): Write down the elements of the computations for net sales, gross profit, and net income. **Refer to Illustration 5-1.** Enter the data given and solve.

TIP: Some companies subdivide the operating expenses into the two major subclassifications of selling expenses and administrative expenses. **Administrative expenses** are often called general and administrative expenses. **Selling expenses** include expenses associated with the making of sales, such as salaries for the sales force, sales commissions, advertising, freight, delivery, and depreciation of sales counters, showroom, and store equipment. **General and administrative expenses** include expenses relating to general operating activities such as rent, officer salaries, personnel management, insurance, accounting, and store security.

TIP: **Nonoperating items** include other revenues, other gains, other expenses, and other losses.

ILLUSTRATION 5-2
DAILY RECURRING AND ADJUSTING AND CLOSING ENTRIES FOR A MERCHANDISING ENTITY USING A PERPETUAL INVENTORY SYSTEM (L.O. 2, 3, 4)

The following are the typical entries for a merchandising entity employing a perpetual inventory system:

Transactions	Daily Recurring Entries	Dr.	Cr.	Effect on A = L + OE
Selling merchandise to customers	Cash or Accounts Receivable	XX		↑
	Sales		XX	↑
	Cost of Goods Sold	XX		↓
	Inventory		XX ↓	
Paying freight costs on sales FOB destination	Freight-Out	XX		↓
	Cash		XX ↓	
Granting sales returns (or allowances) to customers	Sales Returns and Allowances	XX		↓
	Cash or Accounts Receivable		XX ↓	
	Inventory	XX		↑
	Cost of Goods Sold		XX	↑
Receiving payment from customers within discount period	Cash	XX		↑
	Sales Discounts	XX		↓
	Accounts Receivable		XX ↓	
Receiving payment from customers after discount period	Cash	XX		↑
	Accounts Receivable		XX ↓	
Purchasing merchandise for resale	Inventory	XX		↑
	Cash (or Accounts Payable)		XX ↓ or ↑	
Paying freight costs on merchandise purchased; FOB shipping point	Inventory	XX		↑
	Cash		XX ↓	
Receiving purchase returns or allowances from suppliers	Cash (or Accounts Payable)	XX		↑ or ↓
	Inventory		XX ↓	
Paying suppliers within discount period	Accounts Payable	XX		↓
	Inventory		XX ↓	
	Cash		XX ↓	
Paying suppliers after discount period	Accounts Payable	XX		↓
	Cash		XX ↓	

ILLUSTRATION 5-2 (Continued)

Events	Adjusting Entry	Dr.	Cr.	Effect on A = L + OE
Adjust because booked amount is higher than the inventory amount determined to be on hand	Cost of Goods Sold	XX		↓
	Inventory		XX	↓
	Closing Entries			
Closing accounts with credit balances	Sales	XX		↓
	Income Summary		XX	↑
Closing accounts with debit balances	Income Summary	XX		↓
	Sales Returns and Allowances		XX	↑
	Sales Discounts		XX	↑
	Cost of Goods Sold		XX	↑
	Freight-Out		XX	↑
	Expenses (various operating expenses)		XX	↑

TIP: Notice that the first five transactions in this Illustration involve activities related to the sale of merchandise inventory; whereas, each of the second group of five transactions involves activities related to the purchase of merchandise inventory.

EXERCISE 5-2

Purpose: (L.O. 2) This exercise reviews the journal entries to record purchases of merchandise inventory under a perpetual inventory system.

A list of transactions for the Garth Brooks Memorabilia Sales Company appears below. A perpetual inventory system is used.

July	1	Purchased merchandise from Oliver Company for $3,000 cash.
	2	Purchased merchandise from Medlin Company, $5,000, FOB shipping point, terms 2/10, n/30.
	6	Paid freight on July 2 purchase, $125.
	10	Paid Medlin Company the amount owed.
	11	Purchased merchandise from McBride Company, $7,000, FOB destination, terms 1/10, n/30.
	23	Paid McBride Company the amount owed.
Aug.	7	Purchased merchandise from Dun Company, $4,000, FOB destination, terms 2/10, n/30.
	9	Returned one-fourth of the merchandise acquired in the August 7 transaction to Dun Company because of detected defects.
	16	Paid Dun Company the balance owed.

Instructions

Prepare the journal entries to record these transactions on the books of the Garth Brooks Memorabilia Sales Company.

SOLUTION TO EXERCISE 5-2

July	1	Inventory	3,000	
		Cash		3,000
		(To record cash purchases)		
	2	Inventory	5,000	
		Accounts Payable...		5,000
		(To record goods purchased on account, terms 2/10, n/30)		
	6	Inventory	125	
		Cash		125
		(To record payment of freight, terms FOB shipping point)		
	10	Accounts Payable	5,000	
		Inventory..		100
		Cash		4,900
		(To record payment within discount period) ($5,000 X .02 = $100; $5,000 - $100 = $4,900)		
	11	Inventory	7,000	
		Accounts Payable...		7,000
		(To record goods purchased on account, terms 1/10, n/30)		
	23	Accounts Payable	7,000	
		Cash		7,000
		(To record payment with no discount taken)		
Aug.	7	Inventory	4,000	
		Accounts Payable...		4,000
		(To record goods purchased on account, terms 2/10, n/30)		
	9	Accounts Payable	1,000	
		Inventory..		1,000
		(To record allowance for damaged goods) (1/4 X $4,000 = $1,000)		
	16	Accounts Payable	3,000	
		Inventory..		60
		Cash		2,940
		(To record payment within discount period) ($4,000 - $1,000 returned = $3,000; $3,000 X .02 = $60 discount; $3,000 - $60 = $2,940 payment)		

TIP:	Freight terms are expressed as either FOB shipping point or FOB destination. The letters **FOB** mean **free on board.** Thus, **FOB shipping point** means that goods are placed free on board the carrier by the seller, and the buyer pays the freight. Conversely, **FOB destination** means that the goods are placed free on board for the buyer's place of business, and the seller pays the freight.
TIP:	A purchase discount is computed on the amount purchased less any purchase returns or purchase allowances.

EXERCISE 5-3

Purpose: (L.O. 3) This exercise reviews the journal entries to record sales of merchandise inventory under a perpetual inventory system.

A list of transactions for the Garth Brooks Memorabilia Sales Company appears below. A perpetual inventory system is used.

July	17	Sold merchandise with a cost of $300 to Eric Nelson for $520 cash.
	18	Sold merchandise with a cost of $340 to Guy Sellars for $580, terms 2/10, n/30.
	23	Issued a credit memo for $80 to Guy Sellars because of a sales allowance granted to him due to the inferior quality of goods sold to him on July 18.
	26	Received payment from Guy Sellars for amount due for sale of July 18.
	27	Sold merchandise to Jason Zahner, $200, terms n/30. The merchandise cost $120.
Aug.	25	Received payment in full from Jason Zahner.
	26	Sold merchandise with a cost of $460 to Michele Blackburn for $800, terms 2/10, n/30.
	28	Issued a credit memo for $150 to Michele Blackburn because she returned a portion of the goods sold to her on Aug. 26; the returned merchandise had a cost of $90.
Sept.	4	Collected balance of account from Michele Blackburn.
	5	Sold merchandise to Andrea Brotherly, $600, terms 2/10, n/30. The merchandise cost $350.
	22	Received payment from Andrea Brotherly for amount due for sale of Sept. 5.
	23	Sold merchandise costing $220 to Herman Ichner for $400, terms 2/10, n/30.
Oct.	10	Received payment from Herman Ichner for sale of September 23.

Instructions
Prepare the journal entries to record these transactions on the books of the Garth Brooks Memorabilia Sales Company.

SOLUTION TO EXERCISE 5-3

July	17	Cash...	520	
		Sales...		520
		(To record cash sales)		
		Cost of Goods Sold..	300	
		Inventory..		300
		(To record cost of merchandise sold)		
	18	Accounts Receivable......................................	580	
		Sales...		580
		(To record sales on account, terms 2/10, n/30)		
		Cost of Goods Sold..	340	
		Inventory..		340
		(To record cost of merchandise sold)		
	23	Sales Returns and Allowances........................	80	
		Accounts Receivable		80
		(To record allowance because of inferior goods)		

TIP: There is no entry affecting the Inventory account because there was no return of merchandise; there was a sales allowance granted.

	26	Cash...	490	
		Sales Discounts..	10	
		Accounts Receivable		500
		(To record collection within discount period)		
		($580 - $80 allowance = $500; $500 X .02 = $10; $500 - $10 = $490)		
	27	Accounts Receivable......................................	200	
		Sales...		200
		(To record sales on account, terms n/30)		
		Cost of Goods Sold..	120	
		Inventory..		120
		(To record cost of merchandise sold)		
Aug.	25	Cash...	200	
		Accounts Receivable		200
		(To record collection on account)		
	26	Accounts Receivable......................................	800	
		Sales...		800
		(To record sales on account, terms 2/10, n/30)		
		Cost of Goods Sold..	460	
		Inventory..		460
		(To record cost of merchandise sold)		

Aug. 28	Sales Returns and Allowances	150
	Accounts Receivable	150
	(To record return of goods)	
	Inventory..	90
	Cost of Goods Sold...	90
	(To record cost of goods returned)	

TIP: This entry assumes the goods returned were still in good condition.

Sept. 4	Cash..	637
	Sales Discounts	13
	Accounts Receivable	650
	(To record collection within discount period)	
	($800 - $150 = $650)	
	($650 X .02 = $13; $650 - $13 = $637)	
5	Accounts Receivable..	600
	Sales..	600
	(To record sales on account, terms 2/10, n/30)	
	Cost of Goods Sold	350
	Inventory	350
	(To record cost of merchandise sold)	
22	Cash..	600
	Accounts Receivable	600
	(To record collection, not within the discount period)	

TIP: The amount was collected after the end of discount period so no discount is allowed.

23	Accounts Receivable..	400
	Sales..	400
	(To record sales on account, terms 2/10, n/30)	
	Cost of Goods Sold	220
	Inventory	220
	(To record cost of merchandise sold)	
Oct. 10	Cash..	400
	Accounts Receivable	400
	(To record collection with no discount taken)	

TIP: The terms of a credit sale may include an offer for a cash discount, called a sales discount, to the customer for prompt payment of the balance due. Credit terms of 2/10, n/30, which is read "two-ten, net thirty" means that a 2% cash discount may be taken on the invoice price (less any returns or allowances) if payment is made within 10 days of the invoice date (the discount period); otherwise, the invoice price less any returns or allowances is due 30 days from the invoice date. Alternatively, the discount period may extend to a specified number of days following the month in which the sale occurs. For example, 1/10 EOM (end-of-month) means that a 1% discount is available if the invoice is paid within the first 10 days of the next month. Payment terms of n/30 means no discount is offered and the invoice price is due within 30 days of the invoice date.

EXERCISE 5-4

Purpose: (L.O. 1, 2, 3, 5, and 6) This exercise reviews the elements of the net sales, cost of goods sold, gross profit, total operating expenses, and net income computations for a merchandising company.

Instructions

Compute the missing amounts for each of the independent situations below.

(a)		
Beginning inventory	$22,000	
Purchases	79,000	
Purchase returns	3,000	
Sales allowances	2,000	
Ending inventory	23,500	
Cost of goods sold	_____	

(b)		
Net sales	$140,000	
Beginning inventory	20,000	
Purchases	80,000	
Purchase returns	2,000	
Cost of goods sold	83,500	
Ending inventory	_____	

(c)		
Cost of goods available for sale	$42,000	
Beginning inventory	12,000	
Purchase returns and allowances	1,100	
Purchases (gross)	_____	

(d)		
Beginning inventory	$ 14,000	
Ending inventory	17,000	
Net sales	105,000	
Gross profit	41,000	
Cost of goods purchased	_____	

(e)		
Cost of goods purchased	$82,000	
Ending inventory	21,000	
Net income	8,000	
Total operating expenses	44,000	
Net sales	140,000	
Gross profit	_____	
Cost of goods sold	_____	
Beginning inventory	_____	

(f)		
Beginning inventory	$10,000	
Purchases	62,000	
Freight-out	2,100	
Freight-in	1,800	
Purchase returns	3,100	
Ending inventory	13,500	
Cost of goods purchased	_____	

(g)		
Sales	$100,000	
Sales returns	7,000	
Net sales	90,000	
Sales discounts	_____	

TIP: Be careful to distinguish between purchase allowances and sales allowances. **Sales allowances** are reductions in sales prices allowed to customers. **Purchase allowances** are reductions in the purchase prices of merchandise from suppliers. Sales allowances are a contra revenue item; purchase allowances reduce the balance of the Inventory account (when the perpetual system is used to record inventory purchases). Likewise, be careful to distinguish between (a) sales returns and purchase returns, and (b) sales discounts and purchase discounts. Returns and discounts processed for customers are related to sales; returns and discounts honored by suppliers of merchandise inventory are related to purchases.

SOLUTION TO EXERCISE 5-4

Approach: Use the computation models in **Illustration 5-1** and the data that flows through the Inventory account. Fill in the information given. Solve for the unknown.

(a)

Beginning inventory		$22,000
Purchases	$79,000	
Purchase returns and allowances	(3,000)	
Purchase discounts	(-0-)	
Net purchases	76,000	
Freight-in	-0-	
Cost of goods purchased		76,000
Cost of goods available for sale		98,000
Cost of goods sold		(X)
Ending inventory		$23,500

Solving for X: $98,000 - X = $23,500
$98,000 - $23,500 = $74,500
X = **$74,500** **Cost of goods sold**

TIP: Sales allowances have **no** impact on the balance of the Inventory account or the cost of goods sold computation.

(b)

Beginning inventory		$20,000
Purchases	$80,000	
Purchase returns and allowances	(2,000)	
Purchase discounts	(-0-)	
Net purchases	78,000	
Freight-in	-0-	
Cost of goods purchased		78,000
Cost of goods available for sale		98,000
Cost of goods sold		83,500
Ending inventory		$ (X)

Solving for X: $98,000 - $83,500 = X
X = **$14,500** = **Ending Inventory**

TIP: Net sales is irrelevant information for the question at hand.

(c)

Beginning inventory		$12,000
Purchases	$ X	
Purchase returns and allowances	(1,100)	
Purchase discounts	(-0-)	
Net purchases	Y	
Freight-in	-0-	
Cost of goods purchased		Z
Cost of goods available for sale		$42,000

Solving for Z: $12,000 + Z = $42,000
                   Z = $42,000 - $12,000
                   Z = $30,000 = Cost of goods purchased

Solving for Y: Y + $0 = $30,000
                   Y = $30,000 = Net purchases

Solving for X: X - $1,100 - $0 = $30,000
                   X = $30,000 + $1,100
                   X = **$31,100** = **Purchases**

(d) Beginning inventory $14,000
     Cost of goods purchased   X
     Cost of goods available for sale   Y
     Cost of goods sold   (Z)
     Ending inventory   17,000

     Net sales   105,000
     Cost of goods sold   (Z)
     Gross profit $ 41,000

Solving for Z: $105,000 - Z = $41,000
                   Z = $105,000 - $41,000
                   Z = $64,000 = Cost of goods sold

Solving for Y: Y - $64,000 = $17,000
                   Y = $17,000 + $64,000
                   Y = $81,000 = Cost of goods available for sale

Solving for X: $14,000 + X = $81,000
                   X = $81,000 - $14,000
                   X = **$67,000** = **Cost of goods purchased**

(e) Net sales $140,000
     Cost of goods sold   (W)
     Gross profit   X
     Operating expenses   (44,000)
     Net income $ 8,000

     Beginning inventory $ Y
     Cost of goods purchased   82,000
     Cost of goods available for sale   Z
     Cost of goods sold   (W)
     Ending inventory $21,000

Solving for X: X - $44,000 = $8,000
$$X = \$8,000 + \$44,000$$
X = **$52,000** = **Gross profit**

Solving for W: $140,000 - W = $52,000
$$\$140,000 - \$52,000 = W$$
W = **$88,000** = **Cost of goods sold**

Solving for Z: Z - $88,000 = $21,000
$$Z = \$21,000 + \$88,000$$
Z = **$109,000** = Cost of goods available for sale

Solving for Y: Y + $82,000 = $109,000
$$Y = \$109,000 - \$82,000$$
Y = **$27,000** = **Beginning Inventory**

(f)

Purchases	$62,000
Purchase returns and allowances	(3,100)
Purchase discounts	(-0-)
Net purchases	58,900
Freight-in	1,800
Cost of goods purchased	$ X

Solving for X: $58,900 + $1,800 = X
$$X = \textbf{\$60,700} = \textbf{Cost of goods purchased}$$

TIP: The beginning and ending inventory amounts have no effect on the computation of the cost of goods purchased. Freight-out is a selling expense and, therefore, does not affect the computation of the cost of goods purchased.

(g)

Sales	$100,000
Sales returns and allowances	(7,000)
Sales discounts	(X)
Net sales	$ 90,000

Solving for X: $100,000 - $7,000 - X = $90,000
$$\$100,000 - \$7,000 - \$90,000 = X$$
X = **$3,000** = **Sales discounts**

EXERCISE 5-5

Purpose: (L.O. 5) This exercise will allow you to practice preparing an income statement and to contrast the multiple-step format and the single-step format for this statement.

The accountant for Steve Bradley Golf Products, Inc. has compiled the following information from the company's records as a basis for an income statement for the year ended December 31, 2014.

Rental revenue	$ 29,000
Interest expense	18,000
Salaries and wages	151,700
Supplies	10,000
Sales	970,000
Freight-out	7,600
Advertising expense	15,800
Depreciation on store equipment	65,000
Sales returns and allowances	9,000
Rent expense	154,900
Cost of goods sold	446,000
Dividends	40,000

Instructions
(a) Prepare a multiple-step income statement.
(b) Prepare a single-step income statement.

SOLUTION TO EXERCISE 5-5

(a)

STEVE BRADLEY GOLF PRODUCTS, INC.
Income Statement
For the Year Ended December 31, 2014

Sales revenues		
Sales		$970,000
Less: Sales returns and allowances		9,000
Net sales		961,000
Cost of goods sold		446,000
Gross profit		515,000
Operating expenses		
Rent	154,900	
Salaries and wages	151,700	
Depreciation	65,000	
Advertising	15,800	
Supplies	10,000	
Freight-out	7,600	
Total operating expenses		405,000
Income from operations		110,000
Other revenues and gains		
Rental revenue	29,000	
Other expenses and losses		
Interest expense	18,000	11,000
Net income		$121,000

(b)

STEVE BRADLEY GOLF PRODUCTS, INC.
Income Statement
For the Year Ended December 31, 2014

Net sales		$ 961,000
Rental revenue		29,000
Total revenues		990,000
Expenses		
Cost of goods sold	$446,000	
Operating expenses	405,000	
Interest expense	18,000	
Total expenses		869,000
Net income		$121,000

TIP:	A merchandising business has various types of expenses. Common expense categories are as follows: (1) cost of goods sold, (2) selling, (3) administrative, (4) interest, and (5) income taxes. Collectively, selling expenses and administrative expenses are usually called operating expenses. Refer to the multiple-step income statement [part (a) above]. Notice where each of these types of expenses appear on a multiple-step income statement. (Income tax expense will be illustrated in a later chapter.)
TIP:	Nonoperating activities consist of (1) revenues and expenses that result from secondary or auxiliary operations and (2) gains and losses that are unrelated to the company's operations. The results of nonoperating activities are shown in two sections on a multiple-step income statement: Other Revenues and Gains and Other Expenses and Losses. Items classified in the **Other Revenues and Gains** section of a multiple-step income statement include rent revenue, investment revenues (interest revenue and dividend revenue), unusual inflows (such as prizes received), and gains on the sale of assets **not** classified as inventory. Items classified in the **Other Expenses and Losses** section of a multiple-step income statement include financing expenses (interest expense), unusual outflows (such as casualty losses and litigation losses), and losses on the sale or abandonment of assets **not** classified as inventory (such as loss on the sale of property, plant and equipment).
TIP:	The term **revenue** is a gross concept and the term **income** is usually used as a net concept. Thus, net income results after expenses are offset against revenues. Sometimes the word income is used interchangeably with revenue in describing other types of revenues (such as interest income and rental income); it is best, however, if the term "revenue" instead of "income" is used in those contexts.
TIP:	Dividends are **not** a component of earnings and, therefore, do **not** appear on the income statement. Dividends represent a distribution of earnings to owners.

EXERCISE 5-6

Purpose: (L.O. 4) This exercise will review closing entries for a merchandising enterprise.

Closing entries are recorded at the end of an accounting period to prepare the temporary accounts for the subsequent accounting period. For example, assume the calendar year is the accounting period for a company. At the end of 2014, the Sales account balance is closed so that the Sales account begins the year of 2015 with a zero balance. Therefore, at the end of 2015, the balance in the Sales account will reflect sales that took place in that single year (2015).

Closing entries also update the balance of the Retained Earnings account.

Instructions
Refer to the facts in **Exercise 5-5** and its Solution. Prepare the closing entries for Steve Bradley Golf Products, Inc. for the year ending December 31, 2014.

SOLUTION TO EXERCISE 5-6

Sales	970,000	
Rental Revenue	29,000	
Income Summary		999,000
(To close temporary accounts with credit balances)		
Income Summary	878,000	
Sales Returns and Allowances		9,000
Cost of Goods Sold		446,000
Rent Expense		154,900
Salaries and Wages Expense		151,700
Depreciation Expense		65,000
Advertising Expense		15,800
Supplies Expense		10,000
Freight-Out		7,600
Interest Expense		18,000
(To close income statement accounts with debit balances)		
Income Summary	121,000	
Retained Earnings		121,000
(To transfer net income to retained earnings)		
Retained Earnings	40,000	
Dividends		40,000

TIP:	The closing process for a merchandiser includes the following:
	(1) entry to (a) debit Sales for its ending balance, debit any other revenue or gain accounts for their ending balances, and (b) credit Income Summary. This entry closes the temporary account(s) with credit balance(s).
	(2) entry to (a) credit contra sales items (Sales Returns and Allowances and Sales Discounts) for their ending balances, (b) credit operating expense accounts for their ending balances, and (c) credit interest expense and any other expense or loss accounts for their ending balances, and (d) debit Income Summary.
	(3) entry to close the balance of the Income Summary account to the owner's capital account.
	(4) entry to credit the owner's drawing account for its ending balance and debit the owner's capital account. This entry closes the owner's drawing account to the owner's capital account.

*EXERCISE 5-7

Purpose: (L.O. *6) This exercise reviews the journal entries to record purchases of merchandise inventory under a periodic inventory system.

A list of transactions for the Randy Travis Sales Company appears below. A periodic inventory system is used.

July   1   Purchased merchandise from Oliver Company for $3,000 cash.

        2   Purchased merchandise from Medlin Company, $5,000, FOB shipping point, terms 2/10, n/30.

        6   Paid freight on July 2 purchase, $125.

      10   Paid Medlin Company the amount owed.

      11   Purchased merchandise from McBride Company, $7,000, FOB destination, terms 1/10, n/30.

      23   Paid McBride Company the amount owed.

Aug.   7   Purchased merchandise from Dun Company, $4,000, FOB destination, terms 2/10, n/30.

        9   Returned one-fourth of the merchandise acquired in the August 7 transaction to Dun Company because of detected defects.

      16   Paid Dun Company the balance owed.

Instructions
Prepare the journal entries to record these transactions on the books of the Randy Travis Sales Company.

SOLUTION TO EXERCISE 5-7

July	1	Purchases..	3,000	
		Cash..		3,000
		(To record cash purchases)		
	2	Purchases..	5,000	
		Accounts Payable..		5,000
		(To record goods purchased on account, terms 2/10, n/30)		
	6	Freight-In	125	
		Cash..		125
		(To record payment of freight, terms FOB shipping point)		
	10	Accounts Payable..	5,000	
		Purchase Discounts		100
		Cash..		4,900
		(To record payment within discount period) ($5,000 X .02 = $100; $5,000 - $100 = $4,900)		
	11	Purchases..	7,000	
		Accounts Payable..		7,000
		(To record goods purchased on account, terms 1/10, n/30)		
	23	Accounts Payable..	7,000	
		Cash..		7,000
		(To record payment with no discount taken)		
Aug.	7	Purchases..	4,000	
		Accounts Payable..		4,000
		(To record goods purchased on account, terms 2/10, n/30)		
	9	Accounts Payable..	1,000	
		Purchase Returns and Allowances		1,000
		(To record allowance for damaged goods) (1/4 X $4,000 = $1,000)		
	16	Accounts Payable..	3,000	
		Purchase Discounts		60
		Cash..		2,940
		(To record payment within discount period) ($4,000 - $1,000 returned = $3,000; $3,000 X .02 = $60 discount; $3,000 - $60 = $2,940 payment)		

TIP:	A **periodic inventory system** is characterized by no entries being made to the Inventory account during the period. Acquisitions are recorded in a Purchases account. The cost of inventory withdrawals is computed and reflected in the accounts **only** at the end of the period.

*EXERCISE 5-8

Purpose: (L.O. *6) This exercise reviews the journal entries to record sales of merchandise inventory under a periodic inventory system.

A list of transactions for the Randy Travis Sales Company appears below. A periodic inventory system is used.

July   17   Sold merchandise with a cost of $300 to Eric Nelson for cash, $520.
18   Sold merchandise with a cost of $340 to Guy Sellars for $580, terms 2/10, n/30.
23   Issued a credit memo for $80 to Guy Sellars because of a sales allowance granted to him due to the inferior quality of goods sold to him on July 18.
26   Received payment from Guy Sellars for amount due for sale of July 18.
27   Sold merchandise to Jason Zahner, $200, terms n/30. The merchandise cost $120.
Aug.   25   Received payment in full from Jason Zahner.
Sept.   5   Sold merchandise to Andrea Brotherly, $600, terms 2/10, n/30. The merchandise cost $350.
22   Received payment from Andrea Brotherly for amount due for sale of Sept. 5.

Instructions
Prepare the journal entries to record these transactions on the books of the Randy Travis Sales Company.

SOLUTION TO EXERCISE 5-8

July	17	Cash	520	
		Sales		520
		(To record cash sales)		
	18	Accounts Receivable	580	
		Sales		580
		(To record sales on account, terms 2/10, n/30)		

TIP:	When the periodic inventory system is used, withdrawals from inventory are not recorded as cost of goods sold until the end of the accounting period.

	23	Sales Returns and Allowances	80	
		Accounts Receivable		80
		(To record allowance because of inferior goods)		

July	26	Cash...	490	
		Sales Discounts	10	
		Accounts Receivable		500
		(To record collection within discount period)		
		($580 - $80 allowance = $500; $500 X .02 = $10;		
		$500 - $10 = $490)		
	27	Accounts Receivable..	200	
		Sales...		200
		(To record sales on account, terms n/30)		
Aug.	25	Cash...	200	
		Accounts Receivable		200
		(To record collection on account)		
Sept.	5	Accounts Receivable..	600	
		Sales...		600
		(To record sales on account, terms 2/10, n/30)		
	22	Cash...	600	
		Accounts Receivable		600
		(To record collection, not within the discount period)		

TIP: The amount was collected after the end of discount period so no discount is allowed.

**EXERCISE 5-9

Purpose: (L.O. **7) This exercise will give you practice in completing a worksheet for a business engaged in merchandising activity.

The trial balance of the Heron Foliage Sales Company at December 31, 2014, has already been entered on the worksheet on the following page.

Adjustment data:
    a.   A count of store supplies shows $300 worth to be on hand.
    b.   A count of office supplies shows $100 worth to be on hand.
    c.   Accrued salaries at year end amount to $150 for office salaries and $600 for sales salaries.
    d.   Depreciation on the building amounts to $1,500 for the year. Two-thirds of the building is used to display the merchandise for purposes of making sales and the other one-third is used as office space.

Instructions
Complete the worksheet for the Heron Foliage Sales Company for the year ended December 31, 2014.

HERON FOLIAGE SALES COMPANY
Worksheet
For the Year Ended December 31, 2014

Account Titles	Trial Balance Dr.	Trial Balance Cr.	Adjustments Dr.	Adjustments Cr.	Adjusted Trial Balance Dr.	Adjusted Trial Balance Cr.	Income Statement Dr.	Income Statement Cr.	Balance Sheet Dr.	Balance Sheet Cr.
Cash	4,150									
Accounts Receivable	4,000									
Inventory	14,000									
Store Supplies	1,000									
Office Supplies	500									
Building	30,000									
Accumulated Deprecia-tion—Building		4,500								
Accounts Payable		15,000								
Common Stock		5,000								
Retained Earnings		21,000								
Dividends	15,000									
Sales		78,000								
Sales Returns & Allow.	2,000									
Sales Discounts	500									
Cost of Goods Sold	37,300									
Sales Salaries Expense	11,400									
Advertising Expense	800									
Office Salaries Expense	2,850									
Totals	123,500	123,500								

HERON FOLIAGE SALES COMPANY
Worksheet
For the Year Ended December 31, 2014

Account Titles	Trial Balance Dr.	Trial Balance Cr.	Adjustments Dr.	Adjustments Cr.	Adjusted Trial Balance Dr.	Adjusted Trial Balance Cr.	Income Statement Dr.	Income Statement Cr.	Balance Sheet Dr.	Balance Sheet Cr.
Cash	4,150				4,150				4,150	
Accounts Receivable	4,000				4,000				4,000	
Inventory	14,000				14,000				14,000	
Store Supplies	1,000			(a) 700	300				300	
Office Supplies	500			(b) 400	100				100	
Building	30,000				30,000				30,000	
Accumulated Deprecia-tion—Building		4,500		(d) 1,500		6,000				6,000
Accounts Payable		15,000				15,000				15,000
Common Stock		5,000				5,000				5,000
Retained Earnings		21,000				21,000				21,000
Dividends	15,000				15,000				15,000	
Sales		78,000				78,000		78,000		
Sales Returns & Allow.	2,000				2,000		2,000			
Sales Discounts	500				500		500			
Cost of Goods Sold	37,300				37,300		37,300			
Sales Salaries Expense	11,400		(c) 600		12,000		12,000			
Advertising Expense	800				800		800			
Office Salaries Expense	2,850		(c) 150		3,000		3,000			
Totals	123,500	123,500								
Store Supplies Expense			(a) 700		700		700			
Office Supplies Expense			(b) 400		400		400			
Salaries Payable				(c) 750		750				750
Depreciation Expense—Store			(d) 1,000		1,000		1,000			
Depreciation Expense—Office			(d) 500		500		500			
Totals			3,350	3,350	125,750	125,750	58,200	78,000	67,550	47,750
Net Income							19,800			19,800
Totals							78,000	78,000	67,550	67,550

**EXERCISE 5-10

Purpose: (L.O. 5, **7) This exercise will give you practice in preparing a multiple-step income statement.

A worksheet is a tool to organize accounting data to be reported in external financial statements.

Instructions
Refer to the worksheet in the **Solution for Exercise 5-9** above.

a. Prepare a multiple-step income statement for Heron Foliage Sales Company for the year ended December 31, 2014.
b. Prepare a retained earnings statement for Heron Foliage Sales Company for the year ended December 31, 2014.

SOLUTION TO EXERCISE 5-10

a.
HERON FOLIAGE SALES COMPANY
Income Statement
For the Year Ended December 31, 2014

Sales revenues			
Sales			$78,000
Less: Sales returns and allowances		$ 2,000	
Sales discounts		500	2,500
Net sales			75,500
Cost of goods sold			37,300
Gross profit			38,200
Operating expenses			
Selling expenses			
Sales salaries expense	12,000		
Advertising expense	800		
Store supplies expense	700		
Depreciation expense—store	1,000		
Total selling expenses		14,500	
Administrative expenses			
Office salaries expense	3,000		
Office supplies expense	400		
Depreciation expense—office	500		
Total administrative expenses		3,900	
Total operating expenses			18,400
Net income			$19,800

b.

HERON FOLIAGE SALES COMPANY
Retained Earnings Statement
For the Year Ended December 31, 2014

Retained Earnings, January 1	$21,000
Add: Net income	19,800
	40,800
Less: Dividends	15,000
Retained Earnings, December 31	$25,800

---

*ILLUSTRATION 5-3
COMPUTATION MODELS FOR COMPONENTS OF A MULTIPLE-STEP INCOME STATEMENT WHEN THE PERIODIC INVENTORY SYSTEM IS USED (L.O. *6)

	Net Sales			Sales
-	Cost of Goods Sold		-	Sales Returns and Allowances
=	Gross Profit		-	Sales Discounts
			=	Net Sales

	Gross Profit			Beginning Inventory
-	Operating Expenses		+	Cost of Goods Purchased
=	Income (Loss) from Operations		=	Cost of Goods Available for Sale
			-	Ending Inventory
			=	Cost of Goods Sold

	Income (Loss) from Operations			Purchases
+	Other Revenues and Gains		-	Purchase Returns and Allowances
-	Other Expenses and Losses		-	Purchase Discounts
=	Net Income (Loss)		=	Net Purchases
			+	Freight-In
			=	Cost of Goods Purchased

TIP: You should memorize all of the models in this Illustration. Think about the logic of each computation. Visualize the transactions that give rise to the account balances used in these computations. This should make the memorization process easier and more effective.

TIP: The **Freight-In** account is often called **Transportation-In.** Freight-In is used to record freight charges incurred to transport merchandise from the supplier's location to the merchandiser's warehouse. Freight-Out is used to record transportation charges incurred to transport merchandise from the merchandiser's warehouse to the customer's (consumer's) location. **Freight-Out** is often called **Transportation-Out.** Freight-In is a component of the cost of goods sold computation, while Freight-Out is classified as a selling expense (which is part of operating expenses).

TIP: **Ending Inventory** refers to the inventory balance reported at a balance sheet date (for example, December 31, 2014). The ending inventory for 2014 is the beginning inventory for 2015.

TIP: The **cost of goods purchased** is to include all costs necessary to acquire merchandise during the period and get it to the place and condition for its intended purpose (resale). Thus, freight charges borne by the purchasing entity are added to the invoice price of purchases, and purchase discounts and purchase returns and allowances are deducted in arriving at the net cost of merchandise acquisitions for the period. Purchase Discounts and Purchase Returns and Allowances are thus contra accounts to Purchases.

TIP: Think about the components of the **cost of goods sold computation** before you attempt to memorize them; it will make it much easier to recall these items in the future. A merchandiser will begin a period (the year of 2014, for example) with some merchandise inventory on hand (beginning inventory). Add to that the merchandise purchased during the period (to arrive at total goods available for sale). Deduct from that total the goods that are still on hand at the end of the period (ending inventory) to arrive at the goods that are gone (goods sold). This calculation can be done in terms of units (quantity) or cost. To do it in terms of cost: cost of the beginning inventory plus the cost of goods purchased minus the cost of the ending inventory equals the cost of goods sold. The cost of goods purchased is determined by taking the cost of gross purchases (purchases) and deducting the merchandise that was returned to the supplier (purchase returns) and any reductions in price allowed by the supplier for defective items (purchase allowances) or for prompt payment (purchase discounts) and adding the cost of transporting it from the supplier to the merchandiser's location (freight-in). The cost of the ending inventory is determined by a physical count of goods on hand and applying unit costs to those goods.

*ILLUSTRATION 5-4
PERPETUAL VS. PERIODIC INVENTORY SYSTEMS (L.O. 2, *6)

Features of
A Periodic System

1. Purchases of merchandise for resale are debited to Purchases.
2. The Freight-In, Purchase Returns and Allowances, and Purchase Discounts accounts are separate accounts which are used to record information about inventory acquisitions during the accounting period.
3. Cost of goods sold is recognized only at the end of the accounting period when the (1) ending inventory amount (determined by physical count, pricing, and extensions) is recorded in the Inventory account, (2) the Purchases, Freight-In, Purchase Returns and Allowances, and Purchase Discounts account balances are closed to the Cost of Goods Sold account, and (3) the beginning inventory amount is transferred from the Inventory account to the Cost of Goods Sold account.
4. All during the accounting period, the Inventory account reflects the cost of the inventory items on hand at the beginning of the accounting period (beginning inventory). The Inventory account is **not** updated for acquisitions and withdrawals of inventory during the period; it is updated only at the end of the period to reflect the cost of the items on hand at the balance sheet date.

Features of
A Perpetual System

1. Purchases of merchandise for resale are debited to Inventory rather than to Purchases.
2. Freight-in, purchase returns and allowances, and purchase discounts are recorded in the Inventory account rather than in separate accounts.
3. Cost of goods sold is recognized for each sale by debiting the account, Cost of Goods Sold, and crediting Inventory at the time of sale.
4. The Cost of Goods Sold account and the Inventory account are continuously updated for acquisitions and withdrawal of inventory during the period. Thus, at any point during the accounting period (assuming all postings are up to date), the balance of the Inventory account reflects the cost of the items that should be on hand at that point in time, and the Cost of Goods Sold account reflects the cost of the goods sold during the period.
5. Inventory is a control account that is supported by a subsidiary ledger of individual inventory records. The subsidiary records show the quantity and cost of each type of inventory on hand.

TIP: When the perpetual system is used, purchases of merchandise inventory are charged to the Inventory account. When the periodic system is used, four temporary accounts are used to record the net cost of purchases (Purchases, Purchase Returns and Allowances, Purchase Discounts, and Freight-In); the balances in these temporary accounts must be closed (reduced to zero at the end of the accounting period) so that information about the cost of goods sold in the next accounting period can be properly accumulated.

EXAMPLE

Periodic System	Perpetual System

1. Start with 8 units in beginning inventory at a cost of $2,000 each.

The inventory account shows the inventory on hand at $16,000.	The inventory accounts shows the inventory on hand at $16,000.

2. Purchase 12 items on account at $2,000 each.

Periodic			Perpetual		
Purchases	24,000		Inventory	24,000	
Accounts Payable		24,000	Accounts Payable		24,000

3. Return 1 defective item for $2,000 credit.

Periodic			Perpetual		
Accounts Payable	2,000		Accounts Payable	2,000	
Purchase Returns and Allowances		2,000	Inventory		2,000

4. Sell 16 items on account for $3,000 each.

Periodic			Perpetual		
Accounts Receivable	48,000		Accounts Receivable	48,000	
Sales		48,000	Sales		48,000
			Cost of Goods Sold	32,000	
			Inventory		32,000

5. Receive 1 item back from customer as a sales return. Give customer credit on his account.

Periodic			Perpetual		
Sales Returns and Allowances	3,000		Sales Returns and Allowances	3,000	
Accounts Receivable		3,000	Accounts Receivable		3,000
			Inventory	2,000	
			Cost of Goods Sold		2,000

6. Prepare end of period entries for inventory related accounts (4 units on hand at $2,000 each).

Closing entries are necessary:

Cost of Goods Sold	16,000	
Inventory (Beginning)		16,000
Inventory (Ending)	8,000	
Cost of Goods Sold		8,000
Cost of Goods Sold	24,000	
Purchases		24,000
Purchases Returns and Allowances	2,000	
Cost of Goods Sold		2,000

No entries are necessary:
The account, Inventory, shows the ending balance, $8,000 ($16,000 + $24,000 - $2,000 - $32,000 + $2,000). If the ending inventory on hand did not agree with the book balance for Inventory, an adjusting entry would be used to bring the book balance into agreement with the actual inventory on hand (as determined by a physical count).

---

*ILLUSTRATION 5-5
DAILY RECURRING AND CLOSING ENTRIES FOR A MERCHANDISING ENTITY USING A PERIODIC INVENTORY SYSTEM (L.O. *7)

Transactions	Daily Recurring Entries	Dr.	Cr.	Effect on A = L + OE		
Selling merchandise to customers	Cash or Accounts Receivable	XX		↑		
	Sales		XX			↑
Paying freight costs on sales FOB destination	Freight-Out	XX				↓
	Cash		XX	↓		
Granting sales returns or allowances to customers	Sales Returns and Allowances	XX				↓
	Cash or Accounts Receivable		XX	↓		
Receiving payment from customers within discount period	Cash	XX		↑		
	Sales Discounts	XX				↓
	Accounts Receivable		XX	↓		
Receiving payment from customers after discount period	Cash	XX		↑		
	Accounts Receivable		XX	↓		
Purchasing merchandise for resale	Purchases	XX				↓*
	Cash (or Accounts Payable)		XX	↓ or ↑		
Paying freight costs on merchandise purchased; FOB shipping point	Freight-In	XX				↓*
	Cash		XX	↓		
Receiving purchase returns or allowances from suppliers	Cash (or Accounts Payable)	XX		↑ or ↓		
	Purchase Returns and Allowances		XX			↑
Paying suppliers within discount period	Accounts Payable	XX			↓	
	Purchase Discounts		XX			↑
	Cash		XX	↓		
Paying suppliers after discount period	Accounts Payable	XX			↓	
	Cash		XX	↓		

*Increases in Purchases and Freight-In cause decreases in owner's equity because purchases and freight-in are positive components of the cost of goods sold computation. Cost of goods sold is an expense; therefore, an increase in cost of goods sold will cause a decrease in owner's equity. If the goods purchased have not been sold by the end of the accounting period, the journal entry to establish the amount of the ending inventory in the Inventory account will include the relevant freight charges and will be a debit to Inventory and a credit to Cost of Goods Sold. This latter entry causes an increase in assets and an increase in owner's equity.

ILLUSTRATION 5-5 (Continued)

Event	Closing Entries	Dr.	Cr.	Effect on A = L + OE
Recording ending inventory and transferring components of cost of good sold to the Cost of Goods Sold account	Inventory (End.)	XX		↑
	Purchase Returns and Allow- ances	XX		↓
	Purchase Discounts	XX		↓
	Cost of Goods Sold		XX	↑
	Cost of Goods Sold	XX		↓
	Inventory (Beg.)		XX	↑
	Purchases		XX	↑
	Freight-in		XX	↑

TIP:	Compare **Illustration 5-5** (entries for a periodic system) with **Illustration 5-2** (entries for a perpetual system). Note the differences and think about the reasons for the differences.

EXERCISE 5-11

Purpose: (L.O. 1 thru 7) This exercise will quiz you about terminology used in this chapter.

A list of accounting terms with which you should be familiar appear below.

Contra revenue account	Other revenues and gains
Cost of goods sold	Periodic inventory system
FOB destination	Perpetual inventory system
FOB shipping point	Purchase allowance
Gross profit	Purchase discount
Gross profit rate	Purchase invoice
Income from operations	Purchase return
Multiple-step income statement	Sales discount
Net sales	Sales invoice
Nonoperating activities	Sales returns and allowances
Operating expenses	Sales revenue (Sales)
Other expenses and losses	Single-step income statement

Instructions
For each item below, enter in the blank the term that is described.

1. _____Freight terms indicating that the goods will be placed free on board for the buyer's place of business, and the seller pays the freight costs.

2. _____Freight terms indicating that goods are placed free on board the carrier by the seller, and the buyer pays the freight costs.

3. _____Primary source of revenue in a merchandising company.

4. _____Sales less sales returns and allowances and sales discounts.

5. _____The total cost of merchandise sold during the period. A synonymous term is **cost of sales.**

6. _____The excess of net sales over the cost of goods sold. A synonymous term is **gross margin.**

7. _____Expenses incurred in the process of earning sales revenues that are deducted from gross profit in the income statement. Includes selling expenses and administrative expenses.

8. _____Gross profit expressed as a percentage by dividing the amount of gross profit by net sales.

9. _____Various revenues, expenses, gains, and losses that are unrelated to a company's main line of operations.

10. _____A nonoperating section of the income statement that shows expenses from auxiliary operations and losses unrelated to the company's operations.

11. _____A nonoperating section of the income statement that shows revenues from auxiliary operations and gains unrelated to the company's operations.

12. _____Income from a company's principal operating activity, determined by subtracting cost of goods sold and operating expenses from net sales.

13. _____An income statement that shows numerous steps in determining net income or net loss, including operating and nonoperating sections.

14. _____An income statement that shows only one step in determining net income (or net loss).

15. _____An inventory system in which detailed inventory records are **not** maintained and the cost of goods sold is determined only at the end of an accounting period.

16. _____An inventory system in which the cost of each inventory item is maintained throughout the accounting period, and detailed records continuously show the quantity and cost of the inventory that should be on hand.

17. _____A reduction given by a seller for prompt payment of a credit sale.

18. _____A document that supports each credit sale.

19. _____A document that supports each credit purchase.

20. _____A cash discount claimed by a buyer for prompt payment of a balance due.

21. _____An account that is offset against a revenue account on the income statement.

22. _____A deduction made to the price of merchandise allowed to a buyer so that the buyer will keep the merchandise.

23. _____A return of goods from the buyer to a seller for a cash or credit refund.

24. _____A return of goods to the seller by the buyer and a deduction made to the price of merchandise granted by the seller so that the buyer will keep the merchandise.

SOLUTION TO EXERCISE 5-11

1.	FOB destination	13.	Multiple-step income statement
2.	FOB shipping point	14.	Single-step income statement
3.	Sales revenue	15.	Periodic inventory system
4.	Net sales	16.	Perpetual inventory system
5.	Cost of goods sold	17.	Sales discount
6.	Gross profit	18.	Sales invoice
7.	Operating expenses	19.	Purchase invoice
8.	Gross profit rate	20.	Purchase discount
9.	Nonoperating activities	21.	Contra revenue account
10.	Other expenses and losses	22.	Purchase allowance
11.	Other revenues and gains	23.	Purchase return
12.	Income from operations	24.	Sales returns and allowances

ANALYSIS OF MULTIPLE-CHOICE TYPE QUESTIONS

1. **Question**
   (L.O. 1) Which of the following formulas will yield the net income figure for a merchandising firm?
   a. Gross profit minus cost of goods sold.
   b. Net sales minus cost of goods sold.
   c. Gross profit minus operating expenses.
   d. Net sales minus operating expenses.

Approach and Explanation: Before you look at the alternative answers, write down the components in the net income computation. Abbreviations for these components will suffice.

	Net Sales
-	**Cost of Goods Sold**
=	**Gross Profit**
-	**Operating Expenses**
=	**Income from Operations**
+/-	**Other Revenues, Gains, Losses, & Expenses**
=	**Net Income**

Then take each answer selection and see if it describes your model. (Solution = c.)

2.   **Question**

(L.O. 2) The following amounts relate to the current year for the Ira Company:

Beginning inventory	$ 20,000
Ending inventory	28,000
Purchases	166,000
Purchase returns	4,800
Freight-out	6,000

The amount of cost of goods sold for the period is:

a. $169,200.
b. $162,800.
c. $153,200.
d. $147,200.

Approach and Explanation: Write down the components of the cost of goods sold. Enter the amounts given and solve for the unknown.

	$ 20,000		**Beginning Inventory**
+	166,000	+	**Purchases**
-	4,800	-	**Purchase Returns and Allowances**
		-	**Purchase Discounts**
		+	**Freight-In**
	181,200	=	**Cost of Goods Available for Sale**
-	X	-	**Cost of Goods Sold**
	$ 28,000	=	**Ending Inventory**

Solving for Cost of Goods Sold: $181,200 - $28,000 = X; X = $153,200

(Solution = c.)

TIP: Freight-out is classified as a selling expense, not a component of cost of goods sold.

3.   **Question**
      (L.O. 1, 2) The following amounts relate to the Crown Sales Company:

Beginning inventory	$12,500
Purchases	42,500
Net sales	45,000
Gross profit	15,000

The amount of ending inventory is:
a. $40,000.
b. $25,000.
c. $30,000.
d. $15,000.

Approach and Explanation: Write down the models for the net sales and cost of goods sold computations. Fill in the amounts given.

$ 45,000		Net Sales
- _____	-	Cost of Goods Sold
15,000	=	Gross Profit
12,500		Beginning Inventory
+ 42,500	+	Cost of Goods Purchased
55,000	=	Cost of Goods Available for Sale
- _____	-	Cost of Goods Sold
X	=	Ending Inventory

Solving for Cost of Goods Sold: $45,000 - $15,000 = $30,000 Cost of Goods Sold. $55,000 - $30,000 Cost of Goods Sold = X. Solving for X: $55,000 - $30,000 = $25,000 Ending Inventory. (Solution = b.)

4.   **Question**
      (L.O. 2) Abraham Company sold a product to Walsh Company. Abraham finds reason to prepare a credit memorandum related to the sale to Walsh. Abraham will record the credit memorandum by a credit to:
a.   Accounts Receivable.
b.   Sales Returns and Allowances.
c.   Purchase Returns and Allowances.
d.   Accounts Payable.

Explanation: A credit memorandum is prepared by a seller to grant a customer a sales return or allowance. This document informs a customer that a credit has been made to the customer's account receivable for a return or allowance. The document is recorded on the seller's (Abraham) books by a debit to Sales Returns and Allowances and a credit to Accounts Receivable. This credit reduces the balance of the Accounts Receivable account. There is an accompanying entry to record the return of the goods to the Inventory account and a reduction of the Cost of Goods Sold account on the seller's books. The credit memorandum is recorded on the buyer's (Walsh) books by a debit to Accounts Payable and a credit to Inventory. (Solution = a.)

5. **Question**
(L.O. 3) The balance in the Sales Discounts account is to be reported on the income statement as a(n):
a. contra account to Sales.
b. expense account.
c. reduction of the cost of goods sold.
d. addition to Sales.

Approach and Explanation: Write down a sketch of the portion of the income statement that includes sales discounts.

Sales
Less: Sales returns and allowances
            Sales discounts
_____
Net sales

Then examine each answer solution to see if it describes what you know about sales discounts. The items which are deducted from sales are called contra revenue items; they are contra type valuation accounts. They are **not** to be called expenses even though they have debit balances and reduce net income in the same fashion as expense accounts. (Solution = a.)

6. **Question**
(L.O. 3) The purchaser is responsible for the transportation charges on goods that are sold and shipped on terms of:
a. FOB destination.
b. FOB shipping point.
c. FOB common carrier.
d. FOB buyer.

Approach and Explanation: Before you look at the alternative answers, write down the two shipping terms and describe who bears the freight cost:

FOB shipping point = Buyer bears freight cost
FOB destination = Seller bears freight cost

The question asks for the terms where the purchaser bears the cost, which is FOB shipping point. Look for that answer. (Solution = b.)

TIP: FOB buyer is another name for FOB destination. FOB common carrier is a nonsense type answer selection.

7. **Question**
   (L.O. 3) The following information pertains to the Boot Sales Company:

Sales	$100,000
Sales returns and allowances	4,500
Sales discounts	500
Purchase returns	2,000
Transportation-out	3,200

   The amount of net sales for the period is:
   a. $100,000.
   b. $95,000.
   c. $93,000.
   d. $89,800.

   Approach and Explanation: Write down the computation model for net sales. Enter the data given and solve for the unknown.

$100,000		**Sales**
- 4,500	-	**Sales Returns and Allowances**
- 500	-	**Sales Discounts**
$ 95,000	=	**Net Sales**

   (Solution = b.)

TIP:	Purchase returns are a contra purchases (therefore contra cost of goods sold) item, not a contra sales item. Transportation-out (or freight-out) is a selling expense, not a contra sales item, for classification purposes.

8. **Question**
   (L.O. 5) Which of the following is **not** a selling expense?
   a. Advertising expense.
   b. Office salaries expense.
   c. Freight-out.
   d. Store supplies expense.

   Approach and Explanation: Take each account and determine its classification. Items "a", "c", and "d" are selling expenses because they are associated with the sales function. Office salaries are related to normal operations, but they are not related to the sales function of the business. Therefore, they are not classified as a selling expense. They are not associated with the cost of merchandise sold; therefore, they are not part of cost of goods sold expense. By the process of elimination, they are classified as an administrative expense (which is one classification of operating expenses). (Solution = b.)

9. **Question**

(L.O. 5) The following expenses and loss were among those incurred by Mitzer Corporation during 2014:

Rent for office space	$660,000
Loss on sale of office furniture	55,000
Interest	132,000
Accounting and legal fees	352,000
Freight-out	70,000

One-half of the rented premises is occupied by the sales department. How much of the items listed above should be classified as administrative expenses in Mitzer's income statement for 2014?

a. $682,000.
b. $869,000.
c. $884,000.
d. $939,000.

Explanation:

One-half of office space (.5 X $660,000)	$330,000
Accounting and legal fees	352,000
Total administrative expenses	$682,000

Approach: For each item listed, identify where it is reported. Then collect together the ones that you identify as administrative expenses.

Rent for office space	—	One-half selling; one-half administrative
Loss on sale of equipment	—	Other expenses and losses
Interest	—	Other expenses and losses
Accounting and legal fees	—	Administrative expenses
Freight-out	—	Selling expenses

(Solution = a.)

10. **Question**

(L.O. 1, 2, 3, *6) The net cost of goods purchased is affected by:

a. Sales returns.
b. Purchase discounts.
c. Freight-out.
d. Sales allowances.

Explanation: The net cost of goods purchased is computed as follows:

	Purchases
-	Purchase discounts
-	Purchase returns and allowances
=	Net purchases
+	Freight-in
=	Net cost of goods purchased

Sales returns and sales allowances reduce net sales revenue. Freight-out is classified as an operating expense. (Solution = b.)

*11. Question

(L.O. *6) The following amounts relate to the current year for the Rod Buckley Company:

Beginning inventory	$ 40,000
Ending inventory	56,000
Purchases	332,000
Purchase returns	9,600
Freight-out	12,000

The amount of cost of goods sold for the period is:

a. $338,400.
b. $325,600.
c. $306,400.
d. $294,400.

Approach and Explanation: Write down the computation model for cost of goods sold. Enter the amounts given and solve for the unknown.

	$ 40,000		Beginning Inventory	
+	332,000	+	Purchases	
-	9,600	-	Purchase Returns and Allowances	
	0	-	Purchase Discounts	
	0	+	Freight-in	
	362,400	=	Cost of Goods Available for Sale	
-	56,000	-	Ending Inventory	
	$306,400	=	Cost of Goods Sold	(Solution = c.)

TIP: Freight-out is classified as a selling expense, not a component of cost of goods sold.

*12. Question

(L.O. *6) The following amounts relate to the Rachael's Sales Company:

Beginning inventory	$25,000
Purchases	85,000
Net sales	90,000
Gross profit	30,000

The amount of ending inventory is:

a. $80,000.
b. $50,000.
c. $60,000.
d. $30,000.

Approach and Explanation: Write down the models for the net sales and cost of goods sold computations. Fill in the amounts given.

	$ 90,000		Net Sales
-		-	Cost of Goods Sold
	30,000	=	Gross Profit
	25,000		Beginning Inventory
+	85,000	+	Cost of Goods Purchased
	110,000	=	Cost of Goods Available for Sale
-	X	-	Ending Inventory
		=	Cost of Goods Sold

Solving for Cost of Goods Sold: $90,000 - $30,000 = $60,000 Cost of Goods Sold. $110,000 - X = $60,000 Cost of Goods Sold. Solving for X: $110,000 - $60,000 = X = $50,000 Ending Inventory. (Solution = b.)

*13. **Question**

(L.O. *6) The accountant for the Orion Sales Company is preparing the income statement for 2014 and the balance sheet at December 31, 2014. Orion uses the periodic inventory system. The January 1, 2014 merchandise inventory balance will appear:

a. only as an asset on the balance sheet.
b. only in the cost of goods sold section of the income statement.
c. as a deduction in the cost of goods sold section of the income statement and as a current asset on the balance sheet.
d. as an addition in the cost of goods sold section of the income statement and as a current asset on the balance sheet.

Explanation: The January 1, 2014 inventory amount is the beginning inventory figure. Beginning inventory is a component of the cost of goods available for sale for the period which is a component of cost of goods sold. (Solution = b.)

TIP:	If the question asked about the December 31, 2014 merchandise inventory balance (ending inventory) rather than the beginning inventory balance, the correct answer would have been "c" (as a deduction in computing cost of sales and as a current asset).

CHAPTER 6

· ·

*I*NVENTORIES

OVERVIEW

In accounting, the term inventory refers to a stock of goods held for sale in the ordinary course of business or goods that will be used or consumed in the production of goods to be sold. A number of questions regarding inventory are addressed in this chapter. These include: (1) What goods should be included in inventory? (2) How will the selection of a particular cost flow assumption affect the income statement and balance sheet? (3) What is the LCM rule for inventory valuation? (4) How do you compute an estimate of the cost of ending inventory using the gross-profit method? (5) How do you determine the cost of ending inventory using the retail method? (6) How do inventory errors affect the financial statements?

SUMMARY OF LEARNING OBJECTIVES

1. **Describe the steps in determining inventory quantities.** The steps are: (1) take a physical inventory of goods on hand, and (2) determine the ownership of goods in transit or on consignment.

2. **Explain the accounting for inventories and apply the inventory cost flow methods.** The primary basis of accounting for inventories is cost. Cost of goods available for sale include (a) the cost of beginning inventory and (b) the cost of goods purchased. The inventory cost flow methods are: specific identification, and three assumed cost flow methods--FIFO, LIFO, and average cost.

3. **Explain the financial effects of the inventory cost flow methods.** Companies may allocate the cost of goods available for sale to cost of goods sold and ending inventory by specific identification or by a method based on an assumed cost flow. These methods have different effects on financial statements during periods of changing prices. When prices are rising, the first-in, first-out method (FIFO) results in lower cost of goods sold and higher net income than the other methods. The reverse is true when prices are falling. In the balance sheet, FIFO results in an ending inventory that is closest to current value, whereas the inventory under LIFO is the farthest from the current value. In a period of rising prices, LIFO results in the lowest income taxes.

4. **Explain the lower-of-cost-or-market basis of accounting for inventories.** Companies may use the lower-of-cost-or-market (LCM) basis when the current replacement cost (market) is less than cost. Under LCM, companies recognize the loss in the period in which the price decline occurs.

5. **Indicate the effects of inventory errors on the financial statements.** *In the income statement of the current year* : (a) an error in beginning inventory will have an opposite effect on net income (i.e. the overstatement of beginning inventory will result in an understatement of net income, and vice versa) and, (b) an error in ending inventory will have a similar effect on net income (i.e. the overstatement of ending inventory will result in an overstatement of net income, and vice versa). If ending inventory errors are not corrected in the next period, their effect on net income for that period is reversed (i.e., opposite of the impact that the error had on the period the error originated), and total net income for the two years will be correct. *In the balance sheet*: Ending inventory errors will have the same effect on total assets and total stockholders' equity and no effect on liabilities on the balance sheet at the end of the year an error originates; the error's impact "reverses" in the following period and thus, does not affect the balance sheet at the end of the following period.

6. **Compute and interpret the inventory turnover ratio.** The inventory turnover ratio is cost of goods sold divided by average inventory. To convert it to average days in inventory, divide 365 days by the inventory turnover ratio

*7. **Apply the inventory cost flow methods to perpetual inventory records.** Under FIFO and a perpetual inventory system, companies charge to cost of goods sold the cost of the earliest goods on hand prior to each sale. Under LIFO and a perpetual system, companies charge to cost of goods sold the cost of the most recent purchase prior to sale. Under the moving average (average cost) method and a perpetual system, companies compute a new average cost after each purchase.

8. **Describe the two methods of estimating inventories. The two methods of estimating inventories are the gross profit method and the retail inventory method. Under the gross profit method, companies apply a gross profit rate to net sales to determine estimated gross profit. Estimated gross profit is deducted from net sales to determine estimated cost of goods sold. Estimated cost of goods sold is then subtracted from cost of goods available for sale to determine the estimated cost of the ending inventory. Under the retail inventory method, a cost-to-retail ratio is computed by dividing the cost of goods available for sale by the retail value of the goods available for sale. They then apply this ratio to the ending inventory at retail to determine the estimated cost of the ending inventory.

*This material appears in Appendix 6A in the text.
**This material appears in Appendix 6B in the text.

TIPS ON CHAPTER TOPICS

TIP:	**The cost of an inventory item (inventoriable costs)** includes all costs necessary to acquire the item and bring it to the location and condition for its intended purpose. The cost would include the item's purchase price, freight-in, and any special handling charges. However, freight-out is **not** included in the cost of inventory; it is classified as a selling expense on the income statement for the period in which the expense was incurred.
TIP:	FOB terms designate the time that title passes. **FOB (free on board) shipping point** or seller means the title passes to the buyer when it leaves the seller's dock. **FOB destination** or buyer means the title passes to the buyer when it arrives at the buyer's dock. FOB terms also designate which party is to bear the cost of the freight. If goods are shipped FOB shipping point, the buyer bears the cost; if goods are shipped FOB destination, the seller bears the cost.

EXERCISE 6-1

Purpose: (L.O. 1) This exercise will review how to determine (1) the owner of goods in transit and (2) the owner of goods on consignment at a balance sheet date.

As an auditor for Ryan's Art Company, you discover the following facts when auditing the client's inventory balance as of December 31, 2014.

1.   Ryan's Art received goods on January 2, 2015. The goods had been shipped FOB shipping point on December 27, by Wells Company.
2.   Ryan's Art received goods on January 4, 2015. The goods had been shipped FOB destination on December 28 by Nanula Company.
3.   Ryan's Art sold goods to O'Toole Company on December 29, 2014. The goods were picked up by the common carrier on that same date and shipped FOB shipping point. They were expected to arrive at the buyer's business as early as January 3, 2015.
4.   Ryan's Art sold goods to Matheson Company on December 31, 2014. The goods were picked up by the common carrier on that same date and shipped FOB destination. They were expected to arrive at the buyer's store as early as January 2, 2015.
5.   Ryan's Art is the consignor for a collection of prints. The prints are hanging in the showroom of Decorator's Den.
6.   Ryan's Art is the consignee for some goods on consignment from European Collectibles.

Instructions
For each situation above, indicate whether or not the goods being described should be **Included In** or **Excluded From** the amount to be reported for inventory on the balance sheet for Ryan's Art at December 31, 2014. Also, briefly explain your reason for each answer.

SOLUTION TO EXERCISE 6-1

1.   **Included In**   When the terms of sale are FOB shipping point, ownership of the goods passes to the buyer when the public carrier accepts the goods from the seller. Therefore, title passed to Ryan's Art on December 27, 2014.

2.   **Excluded From**   When the terms of sale are FOB destination, legal title to the goods remains with the seller until the goods reach the buyer. Therefore, title did not pass to Ryan's Art until January 4, 2015.

3.   **Excluded From**   With shipping terms of FOB shipping point, title passed to O'Toole when the goods were picked up by the common carrier on December 29, 2014.

4.   **Included In**   With shipping terms of FOB destination, title did not pass to Matheson (the buyer) until the goods were received by the buyer which was expected to be January 2, 2015, or later.

5. **Included In** Under a consignment arrangement, the holder of the goods (called the **consignee)** does not own the goods. Ownership remains with the shipper of the goods (called the **consignor)** until the goods are sold to a customer. Ryan's Art, the consignor, should include merchandise held by the consignee as part of its inventory.

6. **Excluded From** Ryan's Art does not own the goods which it holds on consignment. Therefore, these goods should be included in the inventory of the consignor, European Collectibles.

EXERCISE 6-2

Purpose: (L.O. 2, 3) This exercise reviews the characteristics and the effects of using various cost flow methods to determine inventory costs.

The selection of an inventory cost flow method is an important one. It affects the computation of net income (and thus the resulting amount of income taxes) as well as the amount of total assets and owners' equity.

Instructions
Answer each of the following questions by inserting one of these abbreviations in the space provided:

SI	(specific identification)	**FIFO**	(first-in-first-out)
A	(average cost)	**LIFO**	(last-in-first-out)

_____ 1. Which inventory cost flow method **best** matches current costs with current revenues on the income statement?

_____ 2. Which inventory cost flow method yields the most realistic amount for inventory, compared to replacement cost, on the balance sheet?

_____ 3. Which method results in the most exact ending inventory valuation when inventory items of the same type are **not** homogeneous?

_____ 4. Which method is based on the assumption that inventory flow is "mixed" and therefore "mixes" all acquisition prices?

During a period of **rising prices,** which method yields the:

_____ 5. lowest net income figure?

_____ 6. lowest amount for inventory on the balance sheet?

_____ 7. lowest cost of goods sold figure?

_____ 8. lowest owner's equity figure?

_____ 9. lowest income tax bill for the current year?

During a period of **declining prices,** which method yields the:

_____ 10. lowest net income figure?

_____ 11. lowest amount for inventory on the balance sheet?

_____ 12. lowest cost of goods sold figure?

_____ 13. lowest owner's equity figure?

_____ 14. lowest income tax bill for the current year?

SOLUTION TO EXERCISE 6-2

1. LIFO	5. LIFO	9. LIFO	12. LIFO
2. FIFO	6. LIFO	10. FIFO	13. FIFO
3. SI	7. FIFO	11. FIFO	14. FIFO
4. A	8. LIFO		

TIP: Inventory **pricing method, inventory costing method,** and **inventory cost** method are synonymous terms for **inventory cost flow method.**

TIP: **FIFO (first-in, first-out)** means the cost of the first items put into inventory are used to price the first items out to cost of goods sold. Thus, the earliest acquisition prices are used to price cost of goods sold for the period, and the latest (most current) acquisition prices are used to price items in the ending inventory. **LIFO (last-in, first-out)** uses the most recent costs to price the units sold during the period, and it uses the oldest prices to cost the items in ending inventory. Thus, in a period of rising prices, the method that will yield the lowest net income on the income statement and the lowest ending inventory on the balance sheet is the LIFO method.

TIP: Some corporations prefer to use the LIFO method for purposes of determining taxable income on the entity's tax return because in periods of inflation, LIFO yields a lower taxable income figure than other inventory costing methods. LIFO is said to defer holding gains; therefore, the payment of related income taxes is deferred also. For example, assume two inventory items are purchased for $50. One is sold for $75 and the other is held for awhile. In the meantime, the supplier raises his price to $60. One more item is purchased to keep the inventory quantity at two. Then the old item is sold at a new selling price of $90. There is a $10 gain experienced because an item was purchased at $50 and held while prices (both acquisition and selling) increased. Using the FIFO method, that holding gain will be recognized in the current period as a part of the gross profit figure (Sales of $75 + $90 minus cost of goods sold of $50 + $50 = gross profit of $25 + $40). Whereas if the LIFO method is used, that holding gain is deferred to a future period when the LIFO base inventory is liquidated. Thus, the gross profit would only amount to $55 under LIFO (Sales of $75 + $90 minus cost of goods sold of $50 + $60 = gross profit of $25 + $30). The difference between $65 gross profit under FIFO and $55 gross profit under LIFO is the $10 deferral of holding gain under LIFO.

EXERCISE 6-3

Purpose: (L.O. 2, 3) This exercise reviews the computations that you must make when you use the LIFO, FIFO, and average cost methods to determine inventory cost.

The following information pertains to the inventory of the Jeff Wilson Sales Company:

Jan. 1	Balance on hand	200 units	@ $26.....................	$ 5,200
Mar. 3	Purchase	300 units	@ 27.....................	8,100
July 2	Purchase	200 units	@ 28.....................	5,600
Sept. 21	Purchase	100 units	@ 30.....................	3,000
Oct. 31	Purchase	200 units	@ 31.....................	6,200
	Total Goods Available for Sale	1,000 units		$28,100

The selling price of Wilson's product was $48 for the first six months of the year and $50 for the last six months of the year. Total sales amounted to $29,300. A physical count of the inventory on December 31, 2014 revealed that 400 units were on hand.

Instructions
Compute the amount of (1) ending inventory for the December 31, 2014 balance sheet, (2) cost of goods sold for the 2014 income statement, and (3) gross profit for the 2014 income statement using each of the following inventory cost flow methods:
(a)   FIFO.
(b)   LIFO.
(c)   Average cost.

SOLUTION TO EXERCISE 6-3

(a)   (1)

100	@ $28	$ 2,800
100	@ 30	3,000
200	@ 31	6,200
400	units	$12,000 Ending Inventory

   (2) $28,100 CGAS - $12,000 EI = $16,100 Cost of Goods Sold

   (3) $29,300 NS - $16,100 CGS = $13,200 Gross Profit

(b)   (1)

200	@ $26	$ 5,200
200	@ 27	5,400
400	units	$10,600 Ending Inventory

   (2) $28,100 CGAS - $10,600 EI = $17,500 Cost of Goods Sold

   (3) $29,300 NS - $17,500 CGS = $11,800 Gross Profit

(c)   (1) $\dfrac{\$28,100}{1,000}$ = $28.10   Average Unit Cost

         $28.10 X 400   =   <u>$11,240</u>   Ending Inventory

   (2) $28,100 CGAS - $11,240 EI   =   <u>$16,860</u>   Cost of Goods Sold

   (3) $29,300 NS - $16,860 CGS   =   <u>$12,440</u>   Gross Profit

Abbreviations:
   CGAS   = Cost of Goods Available for Sale
      EI   = Ending Inventory
     NS   = Net Sales Revenue
   CGS   = Cost of Goods Sold

TIP: Examine your solution to the exercise above and judge the reasonableness of your answers. What do you expect the relationship of the answers to be?
     (1)   Because the trend of the acquisition costs was upward, the ending inventory and gross profit figures computed under LIFO should be lower than the ending inventory and gross profit figures computed under FIFO.
     (2)   The cost of the ending inventory determined by using the average cost method should be between the amount of the ending inventory determined by using the LIFO method and the amount of the ending inventory determined by using the FIFO method.

TIP: When working a problem which requires the computation of either ending inventory or cost of goods sold, remember that the total of the ending inventory and the cost of goods sold should equal the total cost of goods available for sale during the period (beginning inventory plus the net cost of the purchases).

TIP: Sales revenue represents the **selling prices** of goods sold; whereas, cost of goods sold expense represents the **cost** of items sold.

TIP: The inventory cost flow method selected by an entity does **not** have to correspond to the actual physical flow of goods. Thus, a company can use the LIFO method to determine the cost of ending inventory even though the first goods purchased are the first to be sold.

TIP: In this exercise you can only compute amounts that would pertain to a company using the periodic system because to compute amounts that result from use of the perpetual inventory system, you would have to have information about the dates and quantities of the **individual** sales transactions.

EXERCISE 6-4

Purpose: (L.O. 4) This exercise will review the lower of cost or market rule for inventory valuation.

Electronics Galore had net cost of purchases of $5,000,000 and net sales revenue of $7,200,000 for 2014, its first year of operations. The following information pertains to its inventory at December 31, 2014:

         Historical cost (using FIFO) $420,000
         Current replacement cost $340,000

Instructions

Answer the following questions:

(a) What amount should appear for inventory on the company's balance sheet at December 31, 2014? Why?

(b) What amount should appear for cost of goods sold on the income statement for the year ending December 31, 2014?

(c) What is the theory behind the use of the lower of cost or market (LCM) rule?

SOLUTION TO EXERCISE 6-4

(a) $340,000   The current replacement cost of $340,000 should be used to value the ending inventory for purposes of reporting the asset on the balance sheet because market (replacement cost) is lower than cost.

(b)
Beginning inventory	$ 0
Net cost of purchases	5,000,000
Cost of goods available for sale	5,000,000
Ending inventory	(340,000)
Cost of goods sold	$4,660,000

(c) The **lower of cost of market (LCM) rule** is based on the accounting concept of **conservatism** which dictates that when choosing among accounting alternatives, the best choice is the treatment that is the least likely to overstate assets and net income. Or to state it another way, in matters of doubt and uncertainty, take the conservative approach (the approach that has the **least** favorable effect on net income and owner's equity).

The current replacement cost (cost of purchasing the same goods at the present time from the usual suppliers in the usual quantities) is lower than original cost. This indicates the supplier has been lowering prices. The same economic forces that caused the supplier to lower its prices are likely to cause Electronics Galore (EG) to lower its selling prices so that EG will end up selling them at a price lower than cost or at a price that cuts down on the normal gross profit experienced by EG. There has been a loss in the utility (value) of the inventory. The LCM rule provides that the loss should be recognized in the period of the decline in utility rather than be deferred and recognized in the period of sale.

By reporting a lower amount for inventory on the December 31, 2014 balance sheet (replacement cost of $340,000 rather than original cost of $420,000), the gross profit figure for 2014 will be $2,540,000 rather than $2,620,000. By using $340,000 for the beginning inventory of 2015 rather than $420,000, cost of goods sold for 2015 will be lower, and gross profit for 2015 will be relatively higher. The loss thus reduces net income for 2014 rather than net income for 2015.

EXERCISE 6-5

Purpose: (L.O. 5) This exercise will test your skill in analyzing inventory errors and determining their effects on the financial statements.

Four separate situations are described below:

1.   An error in the physical count on December 31, 20XA caused the inventory to be overstated.
2.   An error in the physical count on December 31, 20XA caused the inventory to be understated.
3.   An error in the physical count on December 31, 20XB caused the inventory to be overstated.
4.   An error in the physical count on December 31, 20XB caused the inventory to be understated.

Instructions

For each of the **independent** situations, explain the effect of each error by filling in the matrix with the proper code letters.

O = Overstatement   **U** = Understatement   **NE** = No Effect

	Income Statement for 20XA		Balance Sheet at Dec. 31, 20XA		Income Statement for 20XB		Balance Sheet at Dec. 31, 20XB		Income Statement for 20XC		Balance Sheet at Dec. 31, 20XC	
	Cost of Goods Sold	Net Income	Assets	Owner's Equity	Cost of Goods Sold	Net Income	Assets	Owner's Equity	Cost of Goods Sold	Net Income	Assets	Owner's Equity
1												
2												
3												
4												

SOLUTION TO EXERCISE 6-5

	Income Statement for 20XA		Balance Sheet at Dec. 31, 20XA		Income Statement for 20XB		Balance Sheet at Dec. 31, 20XB		Income Statement for 20XC		Balance Sheet at Dec. 31, 20XC	
	Cost of Goods Sold	Net Income	Assets	Owner's Equity	Cost of Goods Sold	Net Income	Assets	Owner's Equity	Cost of Goods Sold	Net Income	Assets	Owner's Equity
1	U	O	O	O	O	U	NE	NE	NE	NE	NE	NE
2	O	U	U	U	U	O	NE	NE	NE	NE	NE	NE
3	NE	NE	NE	NE	U	O	O	O	O	U	NE	NE
4	NE	NE	NE	NE	O	U	U	U	U	O	NE	NE

Explanation: The following points are relevant:

1. The proper determination of the amount to report for inventory is vital to the preparation of both the balance sheet and the income statement. Any misstatement of the ending inventory value has a direct impact on the total of current assets (and total assets) on the balance sheet. This misstatement of inventory will cause a similar misstatement (overstatement or understatement) of the net income calculation on the income statement. The misstated net income figure will cause a similar misstatement of the amount of owner's equity on the balance sheet (because net income is closed to the owner's capital account which is an owner's equity account).

2. Due to the manner in which the inventory balance at the balance sheet date is used in the calculation of the cost of goods sold, an inventory error will result in errors in the cost of goods sold, gross profit, and net income figures. As a review, the cost of goods sold and net income computations are:

	Beginning inventory		Net sales
+	<u>Cost of goods purchased</u>	-	<u>Cost of goods sold</u>
=	Cost of goods available for sale	=	Gross profit
-	<u>Ending inventory</u>	-	<u>Operating expenses</u>
=	Cost of goods sold	=	Net income

3. If **ending inventory for Year A is overstated,** the following effects on **Year A** will result:
    (a) Cost of goods sold for Year A will be understated.
    (b) Gross profit for Year A will be overstated.
    (c) Net income for Year A will be overstated.
    (d) Inventory on the balance sheet at the end of Year A will be overstated.
    (e) Owner's equity on the balance sheet at the end of Year A will be overstated.

4. The ending inventory for Year A is the beginning inventory for Year B; thus, if Year A's ending inventory **(Year B's beginning inventory) is overstated,** the following effects on **Year B** will result:
    (a) Cost of goods sold for Year B will be overstated.
    (b) Gross profit for Year B will be understated.
    (c) Net income for Year B will be understated.
    (d) The inventory on the balance sheet at the end of Year B should be correct, as it is determined by a new physical count at that date. If errors are made in this count or in the pricing of this count, additional misstatements will result.
    (e) The owner's equity on the balance sheet at the end of Year B should be correct, as the understated net income for Year B, which was closed to the owner's capital account, counterbalances (offsets) the effect of the overstated net income for Year A (which had previously been closed to the owner's capital account).

5. On the other hand, if the **ending inventory for Year A is understated** the effects on the balance sheet at the end of Year A and on the income statements for Years A and B would be **opposite** of the effects listed in Points 3 and 4 above. The owner's equity on the balance sheet at the end of Year B should be correct, as the overstated net income for Year B—which was closed to the owner's capital account—counterbalances the effect of the understated net income for Year A (which had previously been closed to the owner's capital account). The inventory on the balance sheet at the end of Year B should be correct unless additional errors are made in the new determination of inventory value at that date.

EXERCISE 6-6

Purpose: (L.O. 5) This exercise will enable you to practice identifying the effects of inventory errors on the financial statements.

The net income per books was determined without knowledge of the errors indicated.

Year	Net Income Per Books	Error in Ending Inventory	
2011	$100,000	Overstated	$ 6,000
2012	104,000	Overstated	14,000
2013	108,000	Understated	22,000
2014	112,000	No error	
Total	$424,000		

Instructions
Compute the corrected net income figure for each of the four years for the Red Bliss Company after taking into account the inventory errors.

SOLUTION TO EXERCISE 6-6

Year	Net Income Per Books	Add Overstate-ment Jan. 1	Deduct Understate-ment Jan. 1	Deduct Overstate-ment Dec. 31	Add Understate-ment Dec. 31	Corrected Net Income
2011	$100,000			$ 6,000		$ 94,000
2012	104,000	$ 6,000		14,000		96,000
2013	108,000	14,000			$22,000	144,000
2014	112,000		$22,000			90,000
Total						$424,000

Approach and Explanation: When more than one error affects a given year (such as in 2012), analyze each error separately then combine the effects of each analysis to get the net impact of the errors. The beginning inventory for 2012 (ending inventory for 2011) was overstated by $6,000. Therefore, cost of goods sold was overstated by $6,000, and net income for 2012 was understated by $6,000. The ending inventory for 2012 was overstated by $14,000. Therefore, cost of goods sold was understated, and net income for 2012 was overstated by $14,000. An understatement in net income of $6,000 and an overstatement of $14,000 in 2012 net to an overstatement of $8,000 for the net income figure reported for 2012. This overstatement of $8,000 combined with the $104,000 amount reported yields a corrected net income figure of $96,000 for 2012.

Another way of analyzing the effects of an individual error is illustrated below for the $14,000 overstatement of inventory at the end of 2012.

		Effect on 2012	Effect on 2013
	Beginning inventory		Overstated 14,000
+	Cost of goods purchased		
=	Cost of goods available for sale		Overstated 14,000
-	Ending inventory	Overstated 14,000	
=	Cost of goods sold	Understated 14,000	Overstated 14,000

		Effect on 2012	Effect on 2013
	Sales		
-	<u>Cost of goods sold</u>	Understated 14,000	Overstated 14,000
=	Gross profit	Overstated 14,000	Understated 14,000
-	<u>Operating expenses</u>		
=	Net income	Overstated 14,000	Understated 14,000

Thus, the previously computed net income figure for 2012 must be reduced by $14,000 to correct for this error. Also, the net income figure for 2013 must be increased by $14,000 to correct for the same error.

*EXERCISE 6-7

Purpose: (L.O. 2, 7) This exercise will allow you to practice performing calculations to determine inventory cost under each of three cost flow methods, using both the periodic and the perpetual systems.

The Griggs Company is a multi-product firm. Presented below is information concerning one of their products, Infusion-39.

Date	Transaction	Quantity	Cost
1/1	Beginning inventory	1,000	$12
2/4	Purchase	2,000	18
2/20	Sale	2,500	
4/2	Purchase	3,000	22
11/4	Sale	2,000	

Instructions
Compute the cost of the ending inventory, assuming Griggs uses:
(a) Periodic system, FIFO cost method.
(b) Perpetual system, FIFO cost method.
(c) Periodic system, LIFO cost method.
(d) Perpetual system, LIFO cost method.
(e) Periodic system, average cost method.
(f) Perpetual system, moving-average cost method.

SOLUTION TO EXERCISE 6-7

(a) **Periodic-FIFO:**

	Units	
Beginning inventory	1,000	
Purchases (2,000 + 3,000)	<u>5,000</u>	
Units available for sale	6,000	
Sold (2,500 + 2,000)	<u>4,500</u>	
Goods on hand (assumed)	1,500	1,500 units X $22 = **$33,000**

(b) **Perpetual-FIFO:** Same as periodic: **$33,000**

TIP: The use of FIFO with a perpetual system always yields the same results as the use of FIFO with a periodic system. The same does **not** hold true with the LIFO or average cost methods.

(c) **Periodic-LIFO:**

1,000 units X $12	=	$12,000	
500 units X $18	=	9,000	
1,500 units		**$21,000**	

(d) **Perpetual-LIFO:**

Date	Purchased	Sold	Balance	
1/1			1,000 X $12 =	$12,000
2/4	2,000 X $18 = $36,000		(2,000 X $18) + (1,000 X $12) =	$48,000
2/20		(2,000 X $18) + (500 X $12) = $42,000	500 X $12 =	$ 6,000
4/2	3,000 X $22 = $66,000		(3,000 X $22) + (500 X $12) =	$72,000
11/4		2,000 X $22 = $44,000	(1,000 X $22) + (500 X $12) =	**$28,000**

(e) **Periodic-average:**

1,000 X $12 =	$ 12,000			
2,000 X $18 =	36,000			
3,000 X $22 =	66,000		1,500 units	
6,000	$114,000 ÷ 6,000 = $19 each		X $19	
			$28,500	

(f) **Perpetual-average:**

Date	Purchased	Sold	Balance	
1/1			1,000 X $12 =	$12,000
2/4	2,000 X $18 = $36,000		3,000 X $16[a] =	$48,000
2/20		2,500 X $16 = $40,000	500 X $16 =	$ 8,000
4/2	3,000 X $22 = $66,000		3,500 X $21.14[b] =	$73,990
11/4		2,000 X $21.14 = $42,280	1,500 X $21.14 =	**$31,710**

[a]1,000 X $12 =	$12,000	[b] 500 X $16 =	$ 8,000
2,000 X $18 =	36,000	3,000 X $22 =	66,000
3,000	$48,000	3,500	$74,000

$48,000 ÷ 3,000 = $16.00 average unit cost $74,000 ÷ 3,500 = $21.14 average unit cost

TIP: When using the average method and a perpetual system, a new average unit cost must be computed **only** after each new purchase; a sale will **not** affect the average unit cost.

TIP: Examine your solution to the exercise above and judge the reasonableness of your answers. What do you expect the relationship of the answers to be for the **periodic system?**

(1)   Because the trend of the acquisition costs was upward, the ending inventory computed under LIFO should be lower than the ending inventory figure computed under FIFO.

(2)   The cost of the ending inventory determined by using the average cost method should be between the amount of the ending inventory determined by using the LIFO method and the amount of ending inventory determined by using the FIFO method.

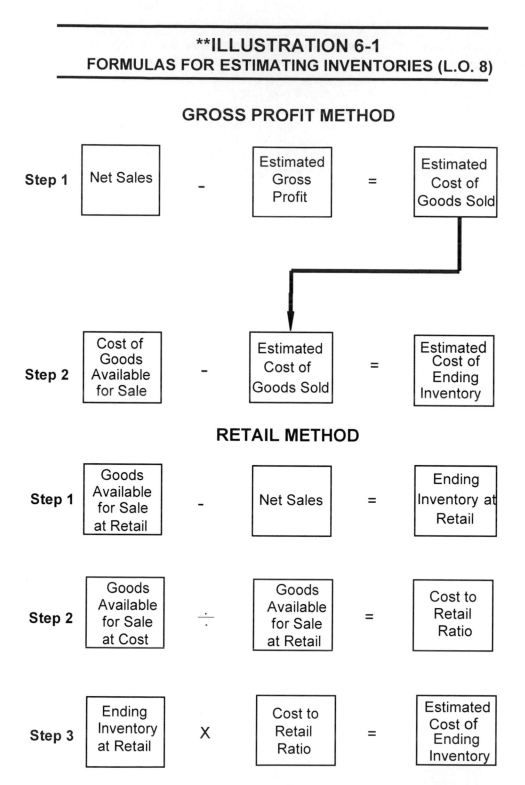

**ILLUSTRATION 6-1
FORMULAS FOR ESTIMATING INVENTORIES (L.O. 8)

GROSS PROFIT METHOD

Step 1 | Net Sales | − | Estimated Gross Profit | = | Estimated Cost of Goods Sold

Step 2 | Cost of Goods Available for Sale | − | Estimated Cost of Goods Sold | = | Estimated Cost of Ending Inventory

RETAIL METHOD

Step 1 | Goods Available for Sale at Retail | − | Net Sales | = | Ending Inventory at Retail

Step 2 | Goods Available for Sale at Cost | ÷ | Goods Available for Sale at Retail | = | Cost to Retail Ratio

Step 3 | Ending Inventory at Retail | X | Cost to Retail Ratio | = | Estimated Cost of Ending Inventory

The retail method can be used as a cost (pricing) method (rather than an estimating technique) if the ending inventory at retail is actually observed rather than estimated. This means a physical count of inventory is taken at the balance sheet date and that actual quantity is priced at selling prices (retail). Then steps 2 and 3 above are applied to determine the actual cost of the inventory at the count date.

**EXERCISE 6-8

Purpose: (L.O. 8) This exercise reviews the relationships and computations involved with methods of estimating inventory.

Information relating to five different situations is as follows:

1.	Net sales	$132,000
	Gross profit	52,800
	Gross profit rate	_____
2.	Net sales	$ 80,000
	Cost of goods sold	52,000
	Net income	12,000
	Gross profit rate	_____
3.	Cost of goods available for sale	$ 74,000
	Estimated cost of goods sold	60,000
	Estimated ending inventory at cost	_____
4.	Beginning inventory at cost	$ 20,000
	Purchases at cost	112,000
	Purchases returns at cost	4,000
	Net sales	200,000
	Gross profit rate	45%
	Estimated cost of goods sold	_____
	Estimated ending inventory at cost	_____
5.	Cost of goods available for sale	$ 52,000
	Selling prices of goods for sale	78,000
	Cost to retail ratio	_____
6.	Beginning inventory at cost	$ 12,000
	Beginning inventory at retail	20,000
	Purchases at cost	62,100
	Purchases at retail	94,000
	Ending inventory at retail	17,200
	Operating expenses	38,000
	Cost to retail ratio	_____
	Estimated ending inventory at cost	_____

Instructions
Fill in the missing figure(s) for each of the **independent** situations above.

SOLUTION TO EXERCISE 6-8

1. Gross profit, $52,800 ÷ Net sales, $132,000 = **Gross profit rate, 40%.**

2. | | |
    |---|---:|
    | Net sales | $ 80,000 |
    | Cost of goods sold | (52,000) |
    | Gross profit | $28,000 |

    Gross profit, $28,000 ÷ Net sales, $80,000 = **Gross profit rate, 35%.**

3. | | |
    |---|---:|
    | Cost of goods available for sale | $74,000 |
    | Estimated cost of goods sold | (60,000) |
    | **Estimated ending inventory at cost** | **$14,000** |

4. | | |
    |---|---:|
    | Net sales | $200,000 |
    | Gross profit rate | 45% |
    | Estimated gross profit | $ 90,000 |

Net sales	$200,000
Estimated gross profit	(90,000)
Estimated cost of goods sold	**$110,000**

Purchases at cost	$112,000
Purchase returns at cost	(4,000)
Net purchases	108,000
Freight-in	0
Cost of goods purchased	$108,000

Beginning inventory at cost	$ 20,000
Cost of goods purchased	108,000
Cost of goods available for sale	128,000
Estimated cost of goods sold	(110,000)
Estimated ending inventory at cost	**$ 18,000**

5. Cost of goods available for sale, $52,000 ÷ Selling price of goods available for sale, $78,000 = **Cost to retail ratio, 66.67%.**

6. | | |
    |---|---:|
    | Beginning inventory at cost | $12,000 |
    | Cost of goods purchased | 62,100 |
    | Cost of goods available for sale | $74,100 |

Beginning inventory at retail	$ 20,000
Net purchases at retail	94,000
Goods available for sale at retail	$114,000

    Cost of goods available for sale, $74,100 ÷ Goods available for sale at retail, $114,000 = **Cost to retail ratio, 65%.**

Ending inventory at retail	$17,200
Cost to retail ratio	65%
Estimated ending inventory at cost	**$11,180**

TIP:	The ending inventory at retail was probably determined by a physical inventory count.
TIP:	Operating expenses are not used in any of the computations requested in this exercise.

**EXERCISE 6-9

Purpose: (L.O. 8) This exercise will illustrate the use of the gross profit method of inventory estimation.

Carol Morlan requires an estimate of the cost of goods lost by fire on March 9. Merchandise on hand on January 1, was $38,000. Purchases since January 1 were $72,000; freight-in, $3,400; purchase returns and allowances, $2,400. Net sales totaled $100,000 to March 9. All goods on hand on March 9 were destroyed. Prior experience shows that the gross profit rate is 25% of sales.

Instructions
Compute the cost of goods destroyed.

SOLUTION TO EXERCISE 6-9

$36,000 is the estimated cost of goods destroyed.

Computations:
Step 1   Net Sales - Estimated Gross Profit = Estimated Cost of Goods Sold.

$100,000   - $25,000[1]   = $75,000

Step 2

Cost of Goods Available for Sale		Estimated Cost of Goods Sold		Estimated Cost of Ending Inventory
$111,000[2]	-	$75,000	=	**$36,000** Goods Destroyed

[1]Net sales	$100,000
Gross profit rate	25%
Estimated gross profit	$ 25,000

[2]Inventory, January 1	$ 38,000
Purchases	72,000
Purchase returns and allowances	(2,400)
Freight-in	3,400
Cost of goods available for sale	$111,000

Approach: Follow the two steps as illustrated above (these steps are diagrammed in **Illustration 6-1**). Plug in the amounts known and solve.

OR

If you cannot recall the steps diagrammed in **Illustration 6-1** or do not want to memorize more formulas, write down the basic formulas or equations to compute the cost of goods sold and gross profit. Enter the amounts given and solve for the rest. For example:

	Net sales	$100,000	
-	CGS	(X)	
=	GP	$ 25,000	100,000 X 25%

	Beginning inventory	$38,000	
+	Cost of goods purchased	73,000	(72,000 - $2,400 + $3,400)
=	Cost of goods available for sale	111,000	
-	Ending inventory	(Y)	
=	Cost of goods sold	X	

Solving for X: X = $100,000 Sales - $25,000 Gross profit = $75,000 Estimated cost of goods sold

Solving for Y: $111,000 - X = Y
$111,000 CGAS - $75,000 CGS = $36,000 Estimated ending inventory

**EXERCISE 6-10

Purpose: (L.O. 8) This exercise illustrates the use of the retail inventory method to estimate ending inventory.

The records of Petite Clothiers report the following figures for the month of September:

Sales	$79,000
Sales returns	1,000
Freight on purchases	2,400
Purchases (at cost)	48,000
Purchases (at sales price)	92,000
Purchase returns (at cost)	2,000
Purchase returns (at sales price)	3,000
Beginning inventory (at cost)	30,000
Beginning inventory (at sales price)	51,000

Instructions

Compute an estimate of the cost of ending inventory by using the retail inventory method.

SOLUTION TO EXERCISE 6-10

		Cost	Retail
Beginning inventory		$30,000	$ 51,000
Purchases		48,000	92,000
Purchase returns		(2,000)	(3,000)
Freight on purchases		2,400	
Goods available for sale		78,400	140,000
Net sales ($79,000 - $1,000)			(78,000)
Step 1	Ending inventory at retail		$ 62,000

Step 2   Cost to retail ratio = $\dfrac{\$78,400}{\$140,000}$ = <u>56%</u>

Step 3   Estimated cost of ending inventory = $62,000 X 56% = **$34,720**

Approach and Explanation:
Refer to the steps diagrammed in **Illustration 6-1.**

(a)   **Step 1:**   **Compute the ending inventory at retail.** This is done by determining the retail value of goods available for sale and deducting the retail value of goods no longer on hand (sales, estimated theft, etc.).

Step 2:   **Compute the cost to retail ratio.** This is done by dividing the cost of goods available for sale by the retail value of the goods available for sale. The retail method approximates an average cost amount so both beginning inventory and net purchases information is used in the ratio.

Step 3:   **Determine the estimated cost of ending inventory.** Apply the appropriate cost to retail ratio (Step 2) to the ending inventory at retail (Step 1).

TIP: The retail inventory method can be used only if sufficient information is accumulated and maintained. Purchases are recorded in the accounts at cost. Although not recorded in the accounts, the retail value of purchases must be recorded in supplemental records for use in inventory calculations utilizing the retail inventory method.

EXERCISE 6-11

Purpose: (L.O. 1 thru 8) This exercise will quiz you about terminology used in this chapter.

A list of accounting terms with which you should be familiar appears below.

Average-cost method
Conservatism
Consigned goods
Consistency principle
Current replacement cost
Days in inventory
Finished goods inventory
First-in, first-out (FIFO) method
FOB (free on board) destination
FOB (free on board) shipping point

**Gross profit method
Inventory turnover
Just-in time (JIT) inventory method
Last-in, first out (LIFO) method
Lower of cost or market (LCM) basis
Raw materials
**Retail inventory method
Specific identification method
Weighted-average unit cost
Work in process

These items appear in **Appendix 6B in the text.

Instructions
For each item below, enter in the blank the term that is described.

1. _____An actual inventory physical flow costing method in which items still in inventory are specifically costed to arrive at the total cost of the ending inventory.

2. _____An inventory cost flow method that assumes that the goods available for sale have the same (average) cost per unit; generally they are identical.

3. _____An inventory cost flow method that assumes that the costs of the earliest goods acquired are the first to be recognized as cost of goods sold.

4. _____An inventory cost flow method that assumes that the costs of the latest units purchased are the first to be allocated to cost of goods sold.

5. _____A method of valuing inventory that recognizes the decline in the value of inventory when the current purchase price (market) is less than cost.

6. _____The amount that would be paid at the present time to acquire an identical item.

7. _____A method for estimating the cost of the ending inventory by applying a gross profit rate to net sales to compute the estimated gross profit.

8. _____A method used to estimate the cost of the ending inventory by applying a cost to retail ratio to the ending inventory at retail.

9. _____Goods shipped by a consignor (who retains ownership) to another party called the consignee.

10. _____A measure of the number of times the average amount of inventory on hand is sold during the period; computed by dividing cost of goods sold by the average inventory balance during the period.

11. _____A concept that dictates that when in doubt, choose the method that will be least likely to overstate assets and net income.

12. _____A concept that dictates that a company use the same accounting principles and methods from year to year.

13. _____A measure of the average number of days inventory is held; calculated as 365 divided by inventory turnover ratio.

14. _____Manufactured items that are completed and ready for sale.

15. _____An inventory system in which companies manufacture or purchase goods just in time for use.

16. _____Freight terms indicating that ownership of the goods remains with the seller until the goods reach the buyer.

17. _____Freight terms indicating that ownership of the goods passes to the buyer when the public carrier accepts the goods from the seller.

18. _____Basic goods that will be used in production but have not yet been placed into production.

19. _____Average cost that is weighted by the number of units purchased at each unit cost.

20. _____That portion of manufactured inventory that has been placed into the production process but is not yet complete.

SOLUTION TO EXERCISE 6-11

1. Specific identification method
2. Average-cost method
3. First-in, first-out method (FIFO)
4. Last-in, first-out method (LIFO)
5. Lower of cost or market basis (LCM)
6. Current replacement cost
7. Gross profit method
8. Retail inventory method
9. Consigned goods
10. Inventory turnover

11. Conservatism
12. Consistency principle
13. Days in inventory
14. Finished goods inventory
15. Just-in-time (JIT) inventory method
16. FOB (free-on-board) destination
17. FOB (free-on-board) shipping point
18. Raw materials
19. Weighted-average unit cost
20. Work in process

ANALYSIS OF MULTIPLE-CHOICE TYPE QUESTIONS

1.   **Question**
     (L.O. 1) At December 31, 2014, a physical count of merchandise inventory belonging to Klintworth Corp. showed $500,000 to be on hand. The $500,000 was calculated before any potential necessary adjustments related to the following:
     - Excluded from the $500,000 was $80,000 of goods shipped FOB shipping point by a vendor to Klintworth on December 30, 2014 and received on January 3, 2015.
     - Excluded from the $500,000 was $72,000 of goods shipped FOB destination to Klintworth on December 30, 2014 and received on January 3, 2015.
     - Excluded from the $500,000 was $95,000 of goods shipped FOB destination by Klintworth to a customer on December 28, 2014. The customer received the goods on January 4, 2015.

     The correct amount to report for inventory on Klintworth's balance sheet at December 31, 2014 is:
     a. $572,000.
     b. $595,000.
     c. $675,000.
     d. $747,000.

     Explanation: (1) The $80,000 should be added to the $500,000 because FOB shipping point means the title transferred when the goods left the seller's dock on December 30, 2014.
     (2) The $72,000 is properly excluded from the ending inventory because title did not pass to Klintworth until Klintworth received the goods on January 3, 2015.
     (3) The $95,000 should be added to the $500,000 because the goods belong to Klintworth until they are received by the customer (in 2015)
     $500,000
     + 80,000
     + 95,000
     $675,000   Amount to report for ending inventory at December 31, 2014. (Solution = c.)

2.   **Question**
     (L.O. 3) Which inventory cost flow method most closely approximates current cost for each of the following?

	Ending inventory	Cost of Goods Sold
a.	FIFO	FIFO
b.	FIFO	LIFO
c.	LIFO	FIFO
d.	LIFO	LIFO

     Approach and Explanation: Write down which inventory method (LIFO or FIFO) reports current cost for ending inventory and which uses current cost to price cost of goods sold and then look for your answer combination. FIFO uses the first cost in as the first cost out, so the last (more current) costs are used to price the ending inventory. Therefore, FIFO is the answer for the first column. In contrast, LIFO uses the last cost in (current cost) as the first cost out (to cost of goods sold), so LIFO reflects current costs in cost of goods sold. Therefore, LIFO is the answer for the second column. Answer "b" is the determined combination. (Solution = b.)

3. **Question**
(L.O. 3) For 2014, Selma Co. had beginning inventory of $75,000, ending inventory of $90,000 and net income of $120,000 using the LIFO inventory method. If the FIFO method had been used, beginning inventory would have been $85,000, ending inventory would have been $105,000, and net income would have been:
   a. $125,000.
   b. $115,000.
   c. $145,000.
   d. $95,000.

Approach and Explanation: Develop the answer by analyzing the effects on the cost of goods sold computation and resulting effects on net income.

		LIFO	FIFO	Effect on Cost of Goods Sold		Effect on Net Income	
	Beginning inventory	$ 75,000	$ 85,000	Increase	$10,000	Decrease	$10,000
+	Cost of goods purchased						
=	Cost of goods available for sale						
-	Ending inventory	90,000	105,000	Decrease	15,000	Increase	15,000
=	Cost of goods sold						
	Net income	120,000	?	Decrease	5,000	Increase	5,000

Net income using LIFO $120,000
Net increase in net income using FIFO   5,000
Net income using FIFO $125,000   (Solution = a.)

4. **Question**
(L.O. 3) The following facts pertain to the cost of one product carried in the merchandise inventory of the Herara Store:

Inventory on hand, January 1	200 units @ $20 =	$ 4,000
Purchase, March 18	600 units @ $24 =	14,400
Purchase, July 20	800 units @ $26 =	20,800
Purchase, October 31	400 units @ $30 =	12,000

A physical count of the inventory on December 31 reveals that 500 units are on hand. If the FIFO cost method is used, the inventory should be reported on the balance sheet at:
   a. $40,000.
   b. $36,600.
   c. $14,600.
   d. $11,200.

Approach and Explanation: Think about what FIFO stands for: the first cost in is the first out to cost of goods sold. Therefore, ending inventory is comprised of the latest costs experienced.

400 units @ $30 =	$12,000	
100 units @ $26 =	2,600	
Ending inventory at FIFO	$14,600	(Solution = c.)

5.   **Question**
(L.O. 3) Refer to the data in **Question 4** above.

If the average cost method is used, the cost of goods sold for the year amounts to:
a. $38,400.
b. $37,500
c. $12,800.
d. $12,500.

Approach and Explanation: Read the question carefully. Notice it asks for the cost of goods sold and **not** for the ending inventory as you might expect.

Total cost of all units available for sale:

Beginning inventory	$ 4,000
Purchases ($14,400 + $20,800 + $12,000)	47,200
Cost of goods available for sale	$51,200

$51,200 Cost of goods available for sale $\div$ 2,000[1]
Units available for sale = $25.60 Average unit cost

$25.60 Average unit cost X 500 units = $12,800 Ending inventory
$25.60 Average unit cost X 1,500[2] units = $38,400 Cost of goods sold

[1]200 + 600 + 800 + 400 = 2,000 units available.
[2]2,000 units available - 500 units in ending inventory = 1,500 units sold.   (Solution = a.)

6.   **Question**
(L.O. 3) Refer to the data in **Question 4** above.

If the LIFO cost method is used, the cost of goods sold for the year amounts to:
a. $40,000.
b. $36,600.
c. $14,600.
d. $11,200.

Approach and Explanation: Notice the question asks for the cost of goods sold rather than the cost of the ending inventory. You may approach the solution one of two ways: You may cost the items sold or compute the cost of the ending inventory and deduct that cost from the cost of goods available for sale. Using the first of these two approaches, think of what LIFO stands for: the last cost in is the first cost out to cost of goods sold.

	Units available	2,000
	Units on hand at end of period	(500)
	Units sold	1,500

400	@ $30	=	$12,000		
800	@ $26	=	20,800		
300	@ $24	=	7,200		
1,500 units		=	$40,000	cost of goods sold	(Solution = a.)

TIP:	The cost of the ending inventory using LIFO would be:	
	200 @ $20 =	$ 4,000	
	300 @ $24 =	7,200	
	500	$11,200	ending inventory

7. **Question**

(L.O. 3) In a period of rising prices, which of the following inventory cost flow methods will yield the largest reported amount for cost of goods sold?
a.   Specific identification.
b.   FIFO.
c.   LIFO.
d.   Average.

Explanation: In a period of rising prices, the most recent purchase prices are the highest ones experienced by the entity. Using LIFO, the latest costs (the highest ones, in this instance) are used to price cost of goods sold and the earliest ones are used to price ending inventory. FIFO would give the lowest cost of goods sold in a period of rising prices. The results of the average method would fall between the results of the LIFO and FIFO methods. The specific identification method would likely yield a cost of goods sold figure similar to FIFO (but not more than LIFO) because specific identification would use the cost of the specific items sold to price the cost of the goods sold, and the specific items sold usually follow a first-in, first-out physical flow. (Solution = c.)

8. **Question**

(L.O. 3) Which of the following statements is **false** regarding an assumption of inventory cost flow?
a.   The cost flow assumption need not correspond to the actual physical flow of goods.
b.   The assumption selected may be changed each accounting period.
c.   The FIFO assumption uses the earliest acquired prices to cost the items sold during a period.
d.   The LIFO assumption uses the earliest acquired prices to cost the items on hand at the end of an accounting period.

Explanation: Once a method is selected from acceptable alternative methods, the entity must consistently apply that method for successive periods. The reason for this **consistency concept** is that **comparability** of financial statements for the entity for successive periods is reduced or lost if methods are changed from period to period. However, an entity may change a method if it becomes evident that there is a more appropriate method and proper disclosure of the change is made. (Solution = b.)

9.   **Question**
(L.O. 4) In applying the lower-of-cost or market (LCM) basis for inventories, the most conservative valuation will be derived when LCM is applied to:
a.   each individual item in the inventory.
b.   categories of inventory.
c.   the total inventory.
d.   the beginning inventory

Explanation: When categories or total inventory is used, situations caused by products whose replacement cost is higher than original cost are allowed to offset situations where replacement cost is lower than original cost. When an item-by-item approach is used, all possible declines in utility are recognized and not offset by inventory items whose replacement cost exceeds original cost. (Solution = a.)

10.   **Question**
(L.O. 4) Peachy Products has an item in inventory with a cost of $85. Current replacement cost is $75. The expected selling price is $100 and estimated selling costs are $18. Using the lower of cost or market rule, the item should be included in the inventory at:
a. $100.
b. $85.
c. $82.
d. $75.

Approach and Explanation: Write down the two steps in determining LCM and follow them:
(1)   **Find market:** Replacement cost = $75
(2)   **Compare market with cost and choose the lower:**
Market of $75 versus cost of $85. Lower = $75   (Solution = d.)

11.   **Question**
(L.O. 5) If the beginning inventory for 2014 is overstated, the effects of this error on cost of goods sold for 2014, net income for 2014, and assets at December 31, 2015, respectively are:
a.   overstatement, understatement, overstatement.
b.   overstatement, understatement, no effect.
c.   understatement, overstatement, overstatement.
d.   understatement, overstatement, no effect.

Approach and Explanation: For questions dealing with inventory errors, assume a periodic system unless otherwise indicated. Write down the components of the cost of goods sold computation and analyze the resulting effects on net income.

		2014	**2015**
	Beginning inventory	Overstated	No effect
+	Cost of goods purchased		↓
=	Cost of goods available for sale	Overstated	
-	Ending inventory		
=	Cost of goods sold	Overstated	
	Net income	Understated	

The inventory at the end of 2014 and the inventory at the end of 2015 are both apparently free of error because the inventory at a balance sheet date is determined by a physical count and pricing process. Assume there are no errors in this process unless otherwise indicated. (Solution = b.)

TIP:	The fact that the inventory at the beginning of 2014 was in error indicates that the inventory at the end of 2013 was in error because the ending inventory of one period is the beginning inventory of the next period.

12. **Question**
(L.O. 5) If beginning inventory is understated by $8,000 and ending inventory is overstated by $3,000, net income for the period will be:
a. overstated by $11,000.
b. overstated by $5,000.
c. understated by $5,000.
d. understated by $11,000.

Approach and Explanation: The effect on net income is dependent on the effect on the computation of cost of goods sold (which is an expense affecting net income). Each error's effect on net income should be determined separately. The effects are then combined to compute the **total** effect on net income for the period.

		Effect on Net Income		
		First Error	**Second Error**	**Total (Net) Effect**
	Beginning inventory	Understated $8,000		Understated $ 8,000
+	Purchases			
=	Goods available	Understated $8,000		Understated $ 8,000
-	Ending inventory		Overstated $3,000	Overstated $ 3,000
=	Cost of goods sold	Understated $8,000	Understated $3,000	Understated $11,000
	Net income	Overstated $8,000	Overstated $3,000	Overstated $11,000

(Solution = a.)

TIP:	When analyzing a question like this one, it is often helpful to create an example with numbers.

13. Question
(L.O. 6) The inventory turnover is computed by dividing:
a.   net sales by cost of goods sold.
b.   cost of goods sold by net sales.
c.   cost of goods sold by average inventory.
d.   average inventory by cost of goods sold.

Explanation: The inventory turnover ratio measures the number of times on average the inventory balance was sold during the period. Its purpose is to measure the liquidity of the inventory. The inventory turnover is computed by dividing cost of goods sold by the average inventory during the period. Unless seasonal factors are significant, average inventory can be computed from the beginning and ending inventory balances rather than from monthly inventory balances. (Solution = c.)

14. Question
(L.O. 6) The **average days to sell inventory** is computed by dividing:
a.   365 days by the inventory turnover ratio.
b.   the inventory turnover ratio by 365 days.
c.   net sales by the inventory turnover ratio.
d.   365 days by cost of goods sold.

Explanation: The average days to sell inventory is a variant of the inventory turnover ratio. It is computed by dividing 365 days by the inventory turnover ratio. It measures the average number of days an item remains in inventory before it is sold. (Solution = a.)

*15. (L.O. 7) The average-cost method used in a perpetual inventory system is called the moving-average method. Under this method, the company computes a new average
a.   after each purchase.
b.   after each sale.
c.   after each purchase and after each sale.

Explanation: A new average is computed after each new purchase (assuming the new purchase is at a price different than the existing weighted-average cost). A withdrawal of inventory due to a sale is recorded at the weighted-average cost existing at the moment of sale. (Solution = a.)

**16. Question
(L.O. 8) The following data relate to the merchandise inventory of the Hofma Company:
Beginning inventory at cost	$13,800
Beginning inventory at selling price	20,000
Purchases at cost	31,000
Purchases at selling price	50,000

The cost to retail percentage (ratio) to be used in calculating an estimate of ending inventory by use of the retail method is:
a.   156%.
b.   145%.
c.   69%.
d.   64%.

Explanation: $\dfrac{\text{Cost} = \$13,800 + \$31,000}{\text{Retail} = \$20,000 + \$50,000} = \dfrac{\$44,800}{\$70,000} = \underline{64\%}$ (Solution = d.)

**17. Question

(L.O. 8) The following information pertains to the Godfrey Company for the six months ended June 30 of the current year:

Merchandise inventory, January 1	$ 700,000
Purchases	5,000,000
Freight-in	400,000
Net sales	6,000,000

Gross profit is normally 25% of sales. What is the estimated amount of inventory on hand at June 30?
a. $100,000.
b. $1,600,000.
c. $2,100,000.
d. $4,600,000.

Approach and Explanation: Use the following steps to solve a gross profit inventory method question:

(1) Determine the **estimated cost of goods sold** during the period:

Net sales	$6,000,000
Estimated gross profit (25%)	(1,500,000)
Estimated cost of goods sold	$4,500,000

(2) Compute the **estimated cost of inventory on hand** at the end of the period:

Beginning inventory	$ 700,000
Purchases	5,000,000
Freight-in	400,000
Cost of goods available for sale	6,100,000
Estimated cost of goods sold	(4,500,000)
Estimated ending inventory	$1,600,000

(Solution = b.)

**18. Question

(L.O. 8) The Ruffier Department Store uses the retail inventory method. The following information is available at December 31, 2014:

	Cost	Retail
Beginning inventory	$ 37,800	$ 60,000
Purchases	200,000	290,000
Freight-in	7,200	
Net sales		275,000

What is the estimated cost of the ending inventory?
a. $47,250.
b. $52,500.
c. $53,586.
d. $192,500.

Computations:

	Cost	Retail
Beginning inventory	$ 37,800	$ 60,000
Purchases	200,000	290,000
Freight-in	7,200	
Cost of goods available for sale	$245,000	350,000
Net sales		(275,000)

Step 1:   Ending inventory at retail $ 75,000

Step 2:   Cost to retail ratio = $245,000 ÷ $350,000 = 70%

Step 3:   Estimated cost of ending inventory = $75,000 X 70% = $52,500

(Solution = b.)

CHAPTER 7

. . . .

*F*RAUD, INTERNAL CONTROL AND CASH

OVERVIEW

In previous chapters, you learned the basic formats for general purpose financial statements. In this chapter, you begin your in-depth study of accounting for items reported on the balance sheet: (1) what is to be included in an item classification, (2) related internal control procedures, (3) rules for determining the dollar amount to be reported, (4) disclosure requirements, and (5) special accounting procedures which may be required. In this chapter, you will learn what is to be included with the cash caption on the balance sheet and some key internal controls which should be employed for business activities involving cash.

At the end of an accounting period, after all transactions have been recorded and posted, the balance of the Cash account usually does not reflect the amount of cash available in the checking account per the bank statement. A bank reconciliation should be prepared as one control feature over cash disbursements to determine whether errors have been made or if any unrecorded transactions exist. The adjusted cash balance as determined by the bank reconciliation will be the amount used to report for cash on the balance sheet. (The Cash account in the general ledger often includes cash on hand and cash in the bank, although separate ledger accounts such as Cash in Bank and Cash on Hand may be used. The balance of this account and any other unrestricted cash accounts, such as the Petty Cash account, are added together to report cash on the balance sheet.) Bank reconciliations and petty cash funds are discussed in this chapter.

SUMMARY OF LEARNING OBJECTIVES

1. **Define fraud and internal control.** A fraud is a dishonest act by an employee that results in personal benefit to the employee at a cost to the employer. The fraud triangle refers to the three factors that contribute to fraudulent activity by employees: opportunity, financial pressure, and rationalization. Internal control consists of all the related methods and measures adopted within an organization to safeguard its assets, enhance the reliability of its accounting records, increase efficiency of operations, and ensure compliance with laws and regulations.

2. **Identify the principles of internal control activities.** The principles of internal control are: establishment of responsibility; segregation of duties; documentation procedures; physical controls; independent internal verification; and human resource controls such as bonding and requiring employees to take vacations.

3. **Explain the applications of internal control principles to cash receipts.** Internal controls over cash receipts include: (a) designating personnel to handle cash; (b) assigning different individuals to receive cash, record cash, and maintain custody of cash; (c) using remittance advices for mail receipts, cash register tapes for over-the-counter receipts, and deposit slips for bank deposits; (d) using company safes and bank vaults to store cash with access limited to authorized personnel, and using cash registers in executing over-the-counter receipts; (e) making independent daily counts of register receipts and daily comparing total receipts with total deposits; and (f) bonding personnel that handle cash and requiring them to take vacations.

4. **Explain the applications of internal control principles to cash disbursements.** Internal controls over cash disbursements include: (a) having specific individuals, such as the treasurer, authorized to sign checks and approve invoices; (b) assigning different individuals to approve items for payment, pay the items, and record the payment; (c) using prenumbered checks and accounting for all checks, with each check supported by an approved invoice; (d) storing blank checks in a safe or vault with access restricted to authorized personnel, and using a checkwriting machine to imprint amounts on checks; (e) comparing each check with the approved invoice before issuing the check, and making monthly reconciliations of bank and book balances; and (f) bonding personnel who handle cash, require employees to take vacations, and conduct background checks.

5. **Describe the operation of a petty cash fund.** Companies operate a petty cash fund to pay relatively small amounts of cash. They must establish the fund, make payments from the fund, and replenish the fund when the cash in the fund reaches a minimum level.

6. **Indicate the control features of a bank account.** A bank account contributes to good internal control by providing physical controls for the storage of cash. It minimizes the amount of currency that a company must keep on hand, and it creates a double record of a depositor's bank transactions.

7. **Prepare a bank reconciliation.** It is customary to reconcile the balance per books and balance per bank to their adjusted balances. The steps in the reconciling process are to determine deposits in transit, outstanding checks, errors by the depositor or the bank, and unrecorded bank memoranda.

8. **Explain the reporting of cash.** Companies list cash first in the current assets section of the balance sheet. In some cases, they report cash together with cash equivalents. Cash restricted for a special purpose is reported separately as a current asset or as a noncurrent asset, depending on when the cash is expected to be used.

TIPS ON CHAPTER TOPICS

TIP: A **bank memorandum** is often called a **bank memo.** A depositor's checking account is a liability on the bank's books, so a bank debit memo decreases the depositor's cash balance and a bank credit memo increases the depositor's cash balance.

TIP: If you have a checking account, look at the back of your bank statement. A bank often provides a form there to assist you in reconciling your bank account. Very often that form reconciles the cash balance per bank to the cash balance per books rather than reconciling both the bank cash balance and the book cash balance to the adjusted (correct) cash balance. Use of that alternative format is not illustrated in this book.

TIP: The "Adjusted cash balance" caption on a bank reconciliation is often replaced with "Correct cash balance" or "True cash balance."

TIP: Total receipts per bank for a month include all deposits made by the depositor during the month plus any bank credit memos (such as for interest credited by the bank or a customer's note receivable collected by the bank).

TIP:	Total disbursements per bank for a month include all depositor's checks that cleared the banking system during the month plus any bank debit memos originating during the month (such as for bank service charges or a customer's NSF check).
TIP:	Beginning cash balance per bank plus total receipts for the month per bank minus total disbursements for the month per bank equals ending cash balance per bank.
TIP:	Beginning cash balance per books plus total receipts for the month per books minus total disbursements for the month per books equals ending cash balance per books.

EXERCISE 7-1

Purpose: (L.O. 4) This exercise will test your knowledge of internal control procedures related to cash disbursements. The following procedures pertain to cash disbursements for Jon Ron's Surf Shop in Daytona Beach.

1. The company checks come in books of twenty-five each and are unnumbered.
2. The company checks are stored in an unlocked drawer in the manager's office.
3. The assistant manager approves all payments, signs all checks, and distributes all checks.
4. A bank reconciliation is prepared once every six months.
5. Employees are allowed two weeks of vacation after they have been with the company for one full year. An employee can then take the vacation time earned or choose to work continuously and receive regular pay as well as vacation pay for the two "vacation weeks."

Instructions
For each procedure, explain the weakness in internal control and identify the internal control principle that is violated.

SOLUTION TO EXERCISE 7-1

Weakness	Principle
1. Checks are not prenumbered. (Checks should be prenumbered and subsequently accounted for.)	Documentation procedures.
2. Checks are not stored in a secure area. (Checks should be stored in a safe or locked file drawer.)	Physical controls.
3. The approval and payment of bills is done by the same individual. (One person, such as the store manager, should approve bills for payment and another person, possibly the assistant manager, should sign and issue checks.)	Segregation of duties.
4. The bank reconciliation is not prepared on a timely basis. (It should be prepared monthly soon after the bank statement is received.)	Independent internal verification (also called independent check).
5. Employees who handle cash are allowed to work continuously. A company should rotate employees' duties and require employees to take vacations. These measures deter employees from attempting thefts since they will not be able to permanently conceal their improper actions.	Human resource controls.

EXERCISE 7-2

Purpose: (L.O. 2, 3, 4) This exercise will illustrate the need for certain internal control procedures.

Four independent situations appear below:

Situation 1: The Broadway Cinema Company operates six movie screens in a local mall. Although the cashier gives a ticket to each customer upon payment of the movie price, no one collects the ticket as the customer enters the theater.

Situation 2: Home Gadgets sells a multitude of housewares. Although there is a register at the check out counter, it has been situated so that the customer cannot see the display and thus has no evidence of what the clerk rings up. (No scanning equipment is used.)

Receipts are allowed to remain on the cash register in a continuous strip unless a customer requests that their receipt be torn from the register.

Situation 3: Better Bath Wear Company hires people based solely on an interview with the store manager.

Situation 4: The individual who is responsible for writing the checks to pay bills for Seafin Seafoods is also the employee who prepares the monthly bank reconciliation.

Instructions
For each situation, identify the internal control principle being violated and briefly describe the risk inherent in the existing circumstances.

SOLUTION TO EXERCISE 7-2

Situation 1: The independent internal verification principle is being violated. The cashier may collect the ticket price from a customer and pocket the cash then not give the customer a ticket. Because sales are tracked by tickets, the theft will most likely occur undetected. On the other hand, the cashier may collect the price of an adult ticket, ring up the price of a child's ticket and pocket the difference in price. Because no one independently verifies the sale, the theft can easily go unnoticed.

Situation 2: The documentation procedures principle is being violated. If the customer cannot see the display and receives no written evidence of the amount rung into the register, the clerk can easily tell the customer the correct total but ring up less than that amount. The difference can be pocketed by the employee and go undetected.

Situation 3: The human resource controls principle is being violated. The company should conduct a thorough background check on the prospective employee before hiring them.

Situation 4: The segregation of duties principle is being violated. The employee can make improper disbursements and have them go undetected because the employee has access to the records and can "doctor" them.

EXERCISE 7-3

Purpose: (L.O. 2, 3, 4) This exercise will help you understand the reasons for implementing a system of internal control. This exercise focuses on the one component of an internal control system—the **control activities.**

Family Grub, a large grocery store in Louisiana has a policy manual which contains the following guidelines:

_____   1. Customers who pay by check must be identified via a store I.D. card or other means.

_____   2. Store personnel are prohibited from accepting checks for anything **except** merchandise sales plus a nominal cash amount.

_____   3. For each sale, a receipt is to be produced by the cash register and is to be given to the customer.

_____   4. A reading of each cash register is to be taken periodically by an employee who is independent of the handling of cash receipts.

_____   5. Cash counts are to be made on a surprise basis by an individual who is independent of the handling of cash receipts.

_____   6. The reading of each cash register is to be compared regularly to the cash received.

_____   7. A summary listing of cash register readings is to be prepared by an employee who is independent of personnel physically handling cash receipts.

_____   8. Receipts are to be forwarded to an independent employee who makes the bank deposits.

_____   9. Cash receipts are to be deposited in the company's bank account daily.

_____   10. The summary listing of cash register receipts is to be reconciled to the duplicate deposit slips authenticated by the bank.

_____   11. Entries to the cash receipts journal are to be prepared from duplicate deposit slips or the summary listing of cash register readings.

_____   12. The entries to the cash receipts journal are compared to the deposits per bank statement.

_____   13. Areas involving the physical handling of cash are to be reasonably safeguarded.

_____   14. Employees who handle cash receipts are to be bonded.

_____   15. Customer checks charged back by the bank (NSF checks) are to be directed to an employee who does **not** physically handle cash receipts or have access to the books.

_____ 16. Each cashier works out of a separate cash drawer and begins each shift with a two-hundred dollar change fund.

_____17. When a prospective employee completes a job application and lists the phone number of a previous employer, the manager is to search for and independently obtain the phone number of that entity.

_____18. Duties for employees are to be rotated periodically.

These policies were designed to comply with the following principles of internal control:

a. Establishment of responsibility.
b. Segregation of duties.
c. Documentation procedures.
d. Physical controls.
e. Independent internal verification.
f. Human resource controls.

Instructions
For each policy listed above, indicate to which principle of internal control the procedure is most closely related.

SOLUTION TO EXERCISE 7-3

1.	c	6.	e	11.	c	15.	b
2.	d	7.	b	12.	e	16.	a
3.	c	8.	b	13.	d	17.	f
4.	e	9.	d	14.	f	18.	f
5.	e	10.	e				

TIP:	**Internal control** consists of all the related methods and measures adopted within an organization to safeguard its assets, enhance the reliability of its accounting records, increase efficiency of operations, and ensure compliance with laws and regulations. Internal control systems have five primary components as listed below:

- **A control environment.** It is the responsibility of top management to make it clear that the organization values integrity and that unethical activity will not be tolerated. This component is often referred to as the "tone at the top"

- **Risk assessment.** Companies must identify and analyze the various factors that create risk for the business and must determine how to manage these risks.

- **Control activities.** To reduce the occurrence of fraud, management must design policies and procedures to address the specific risks faced by the company.

- **Information and communication.** The internal control system must capture and communicate all pertinent information both down and up the organization, as well as communicate information to appropriate external parties.

- **Monitoring.** Internal control systems must be monitored periodically for their adequacy. Significant deficiencies need to be reported to top management and/or the board of directors.

ILLUSTRATION 7-1
BANK RECONCILIATION FORMAT (L.O. 7)

Balance per bank
- Add positive items per books not on bank's records.
- Deduct negative items per books not on bank's records.
- Add or deduct, whichever is applicable, bank error in recording receipts or disbursements.

Adjusted cash balance per bank.

Balance per books
- Add positive items per bank not on books.
- Deduct negative items per bank not on books.
- Add or deduct, whichever is applicable, depositor error in recording receipts or disbursements.

Adjusted cash balance per books.

Examples of reconciling items:
Positive item per books not on bank's records:
    Deposit in transit
Negative item per books not on bank's records:
    Outstanding check
Positive item per bank not on books:
    Note collected by bank
    Interest paid by bank to depositor on account balance
Negative item per bank not on books:
    Bank service charge
    Customer's NSF check returned by bank
Error by bank:
    In recording receipt
    In recording disbursement
Error by depositor:
    In recording receipt
    In recording disbursement

TIP: The objective of a bank reconciliation is to explain all reasons why the bank balance differs from the book balance and to identify the errors and omissions in the bank's records and in the depositor's records.

TIP: In the context of a bank reconciliation, "per bank" refers to the records of the bank pertaining to the depositor's account and "per books" refers to the depositor's records of the same bank account.

TIP:	Some items in a bank reconciliation will require adjustments either on the depositor's books or in the bank's records while others will not. Using the reconciliation format above, all of the reconciling items appearing in the lower half of the reconciliation (balance per books to adjusted cash balance) require adjustment on the depositor's books. All of the reconciling items appearing in the upper half of the reconciliation **except** for deposits in transit and outstanding checks require adjustment on the bank's books.
TIP:	Unless otherwise indicated, an NSF (nonsufficient funds) check is assumed to be a customer's NSF check; that is, an NSF check from a customer of the depositor rather than a depositor's NSF check.

EXERCISE 7-4

Purpose: (L.O. 5) This exercise reviews the journal entries involved with establishing and maintaining a petty cash fund.

The Kirmani Corporation makes most expenditures by check. The following transactions relate to an imprest fund established by the Kirmani Corporation to handle small expenditures on an expedient basis.

Transactions

May	4	Wrote a $100 check to establish the petty cash fund.
	6	Paid taxi $10 to deliver papers to a branch office.
	6	Purchased stamps, $19.
	8	Paid $15 for advertising posters.
	12	Paid $8 for coffee supplies.
	13	Paid $17 for office supplies.
	14	Paid bus charges of $18 to ship goods to a customer.
	15	Counted the remaining coins and currency in the fund, $12. Wrote a check to replenish the fund.

Instructions
(a)   Record the transactions in general journal form.
(b)   Answer the questions that follow.

Questions

1. How much coin and currency should have been in the petty cash box at the end of the day on May 12? $_____

2. How much coin and currency should have been in the petty cash box on May 15 before replenishment? $_____

3. What was the balance in the Petty Cash ledger account on May 12?
   $_____

4. What was the balance in the Petty Cash ledger account at the end of the day, May 15?
   $_____

TIP:	In order to answer the last two questions, it would be helpful to post the journal entries to a T-account for Petty Cash.

SOLUTION TO EXERCISE 7-4

(a) May   4   Petty Cash..   100
                    Cash   100
                    (To establish a petty cash fund)

       May   15   Miscellaneous Expense ($10 + $8)   18
                   Postage Expense   19
                   Advertising Expense...   15
                   Office Supplies   17
                   Freight-out...   18
                   Cash Over and Short..   1
                    Cash   88
                    (To replenish the petty cash fund)

(b) 1. There should have been $48 in coin and currency in the fund at the end of the day on May 12. ($100 - $10 - $19 - $15 - $6 - $8 = $48)
      2. There should have been $13 in coin and currency in the fund on May 15 before replenishment. ($100 - $10 - $19 - $15 - $6 - $8 - $17 - $18 = $13)

TIP:	Because only $12 was found in the fund on May 15, there was a shortage of $1 which must be recorded by a debit to the Cash Over and Short account.

   3. $100
   4. $100

TIP:	The balance of the Petty Cash account changes only when the fund is established or the size of the fund is increased or decreased. The Petty Cash account balance is **not** affected by expenditures from the fund nor by replenishments. (No journal entry is made at the time an expenditure is made. Expenditures from the fund are accounted for at the date of replenishment.)
TIP:	Petty Cash is not normally reported separately on the balance sheet. The balance of the Petty Cash account is generally lumped together with all other cash items when a balance sheet is prepared.

EXERCISE 7-5

Purpose: (L.O. 7) This exercise will help you review situations that give rise to reconciling items on a bank reconciliation and identify those which require adjusting entries on the depositor's books.

A sketch of the bank reconciliation at July 31, 20XX for the Ace Electric Company and a list of possible reconciling items appear below.

Ace Electric Co.
BANK RECONCILIATION
July 31, 20XX

Balance per bank statement, July 31		$X,XXX
A. Add	$XXX	
	XXX	X,XXX
		X,XXX
B. Deduct		X,XXX
Adjusted cash balance, July 31, per bank		$X,XXX
Balance per books, July 31		$X,XXX
C. Add	$XXX	
	XXX	X,XXX
		X,XXX
D. Deduct:	XXX	
	XXX	
	XXX	
	XXX	X,XXX
Adjusted cash balance, July 31, per books		$X,XXX

(a)   **Items**

_____   1. Deposits of July 30 amounting to $1,582 have **not** reached the bank as of July 31.

_____   2. A customer's check for $140 that was deposited on July 20 was returned NSF by the bank; return has not been recorded by Ace.

_____   3. Bank service charge for July amounts to $3.

_____   4. Included with the bank statement was check No. 422 for $702 as payment of an account payable. In comparing the check with the cash disbursement records, it was discovered that the check was incorrectly entered in the cash disbursements journal for $720.

_____   5. Outstanding checks at July 31 amount to $1,927.

_____   6. The bank improperly charged a check of the Ace Plumbing Co. for $25 to Ace Electric Co.'s account.

_____   7. The bank charged $8 during July for printing checks.

_____   8. During July, the bank collected a customer's note receivable for the Ace Electric Co.; face amount $1,000, interest $20, and the bank charged a $2 collection fee. This transaction has not been recorded by Ace.

_____   9. A check written by Ace in June for $180 cleared the bank during July.

_____   10. Deposits of June 30 for $1,200 were recorded by the company on June 30 but were not recorded by the bank until July 2.

Instructions
(a) Indicate how each of the 10 items listed above would be handled on the bank reconciliation by placing the proper code letter in the space provided. The applicable code letters appear in the sketch of the bank reconciliation. Use the code "NR" for any item which is not a reconciling item on July 31.
(b) Assume that the July 31 balance per bank statement was $4,232. Complete the bank reconciliation using the items given and answer the questions that follow:

1. What is the adjusted (correct) cash balance at July 31?
    $_____

2. What is the balance per books **before** adjustment at July 31?
    $_____

3. What reconciling items require an adjusting entry on Ace Electric Company's books? (Identify by item numbers.) _____

4. What item(s) requires a special entry on the bank's records to correct an error(s)?
    _____

SOLUTION TO EXERCISE 7-5

(a) 1. A   6. A
     2. D   7. D
     3. D   8. C, D
     4. C   9. NR
     5. B   10. NR

| TIP: | Items 9 and 10 would have been reconciling items of cash balances on the June 30 bank reconciliation (the prior month). |

(b) 1. $3,912* ($4,232 + $1,582 + $25 - $1,927 = $3,912)
     2. $3,027* [X + $18 + $1,020 - $140 - $3 - $8 - $2 = $3,912 (answer to question 1)]
         X = $3,027
     3. 2; 3; 4; 7; 8
     4. 6
     *See the completed bank reconciliation on the following page.

Approach to part (b) 2: You can compute the correct cash balance by completing the top half of the bank reconciliation (balance per bank to correct cash balance). The correct cash balance can then be entered on the last line of the bottom half of the reconciliation and used along with certain reconciling items to "work backwards" to compute the $3,027 cash balance per books before adjustment.

Ace Electric Co.
BANK RECONCILIATION
July 31, 20XX

Balance per bank statement, July 31		$4,232
Add: Deposits in transit on July 31	$1,582	
Check improperly charged by bank	25	1,607
		5,839
Deduct: Checks outstanding as of July 31		1,927
Adjusted cash balance per bank at July 31		$3,912
Balance per books, July 31		$3,027
Add: Error in recording check No. 422	$ 18	
Collection of customer's note receivable and interest		
by bank	1,020	1,038
		4,065
Deduct: Customer's NSF check	140	
Bank service charge for July	3	
Cost of printing checks	8	
Bank collection fee	2	153
Adjusted cash balance per books at July 31		$3,912

TIP:	The required adjusting entries on the depositor's books would be:		
Cash	....	18	
	Accounts Payable		18
	(To correct error in recording check No. 422)		
Cash	....	1,020	
	Note Receivable...		1,000
	Interest Revenue..		20
	(To record collection of note receivable by bank)		
Accounts Receivable...		140	
	Cash..		140
	(To record customer's NSF check)		
Miscellaneous Expense..		13	
	Cash..		13
	(To record bank service charges); ($3 + $8 + $2 = $13)		

EXERCISE 7-6

Purpose: (L.O. 7) This exercise will illustrate how to determine the amount of deposits in transit and outstanding checks at a given date.

Shown below for Molly's Folly are the
    (1)   bank reconciliation at September 30, 2014.
    (2)   listing of deposits for October per the bank statement.
    (3)   listing of deposits for October per the books.
    (4)   listing of checks paid by the bank during October.
    (5)   listing of checks written by the depositor during October.

Molly's Folly
BANK RECONCILIATION
September 30, 2014

Cash balance per bank statement		$15,000
Add: Deposits in transit		
September 29	$2,000	
September 30	1,600	3,600
		18,600
Deduct: Outstanding checks		
No. 514	650	
No. 516	410	
No. 520	560	
No. 521	740	
No. 522	1,000	3,360
Adjusted cash balance per bank		$15,240
Cash balance per books		$15,690
Deduct: Customer's NSF check	$400	
Bank service charge	50	450
Adjusted cash balance per books		$15,240

Bank Statement for October—Deposits

Date	Amount	Date	Amount
10/1	$2,000	10/21	$ 700
10/2	1,600	10/22	900
10/3	500	10/25	100
10/5	300	10/27	600
10/11	1,100	10/28	800
10/11	1,200	10/29	1,300
10/15	200	Total	$11,700
10/18	400		

Cash Receipts Journal

Date	Amount	Date	Amount
10/1	$ 500	10/21	$ 900
10/4	300	10/23	100
10/8	1,100	10/25	600
10/10	1,200	10/27	800
10/13	200	10/28	1,300
10/16	400	10/30	1,400
10/20	700	10/31	2,050
		Total	$11,550

Bank Statement for October—Checks Paid and Debit Memos

Date	Check No.	Amount	Date	Check No.	Amount
10/1	514	$ 650	10/12	533	$ 190
10/1	520	560	10/13	534	220
10/4	521	740	10/14	535	240
10/4	522	1,000	10/18	538	380
10/5	525	120	10/18	536	250
10/5	526	140	10/18	537	320
10/6	528	230	10/18	539	430
10/8	529	310	10/19	540	510
10/8	527	210	10/23	541	330
10/8	530	420	10/25	542	340
10/11	532	160	10/29	545	540
10/11	531	130	10/29	546	470
			10/31	DM	30
			Total		$8,920

Cash Payments Journal—Checks Issued

Date	Check No.	Amount	Date	Check No.	Amount
10/1	525	$120	10/14	538	$ 380
10/1	526	140	10/15	539	430
10/3	527	210	10/17	540	510
10/4	528	230	10/20	541	330
10/5	529	310	10/23	542	340
10/5	530	420	10/25	543	110
10/7	531	130	10/26	544	160
10/7	532	106	10/27	545	540
10/7	533	190	10/28	546	470
10/11	534	220	10/31	547	590
10/11	535	240	10/31	548	640
10/12	536	250	Total		$7,386
10/14	537	320			

Instructions

(a) Prepare a list of deposits in transit at October 31, 2014.
(b) Prepare a list of outstanding checks at October 31, 2014.
(c) Locate any errors per books assuming information recorded in the bank's records is correct.
(d) Locate any bank memoranda that will need to be recorded on the books.

SOLUTION TO EXERCISE 7-6

(a) Deposits in transit at October 31, 2014:

October 30	$1,400
October 31	2,050
Total	$3,450

(b) Outstanding checks at October 31, 2014:

No.	Amount
516	$ 410
543	110
544	160
547	590
548	640
	$1,910

(c) Check No. 532 was recorded on the depositor's books for $106 when it should have been recorded for the correct amount of $160.

(d) The DM for $30 on October 31 will need to be recorded on the depositor's books. (The DM is likely for bank service charges for October.)

Approach and Explanation:

(a) To identify the deposits in transit at October 31:

(1) Compare the deposits in transit at September 30 (per the company's bank reconciliation at that date) with the October bank statement. If the deposit did not get recorded by the bank during October, it is to be considered a deposit in transit at October 31. (It would be extremely rare for a particular deposit to be listed as a deposit in transit on two successive bank reconciliations because it would indicate the deposit was lost in the mail or lost in the bank's facilities or a victim of some strange fate or possibly related to an irregularity.)

For Molly's Folly, the $2,000 and $1,600 items deposited at the end of September (deposits in transit at September 30, 2014) both were recorded by the bank in early October as expected.

(2) Compare the deposits made during October per company records with the October deposits per the bank's records. Deposits not recorded by the bank represent **deposits in transit.** As can be expected, the items deposited at the very end of October have not had enough time to be processed by the bank by the end of the day on October 31. These include the deposits made by Molly's Folly on October 30 ($1,400) and October 31 ($2,050).

(b) To identify the outstanding checks at October 31, 2014:

  (1) Compare the checks outstanding at September 30, 2014 (per the September 30th bank reconciliation) with the paid checks shown on the October bank statement. If a September check remains unpaid at the end of October, it is an outstanding check at October 31. For Molly's Folly, check numbers 514, 520, 521, and 522 all cleared the bank during October but check number 516 ($410) remains unpaid at October 31, 2014. (The check could be lost in the mail or lost in the banking system. More likely, the check is still in the hands of the payee who, for some reason, has not yet deposited it to his account.)

  (2) Compare the checks written by Molly's Folly during October with the checks paid by the bank. Issued checks that have not been paid by the bank represent **outstanding checks.**

  For Molly's Folly, October check numbers 543 ($110), 544 ($160), 547 ($590) and 548 ($640) were written during October and are outstanding at October 31.

(c) To identify errors on either the bank's records or the depositor's books, compare all of the figures on the October bank statement with their source on the depositor's records. If there are any discrepancies, determine which is in error. For Molly's Folly, check number 532 correctly cleared the bank for $160 but was entered in the cash payments journal as $106 (the facts of the problem state that the bank's records are correct). This transposition type error caused the depositor's bank balance per ledger to be overstated by $54 ($160 - $106 = $54).

TIP:	Recall that a transposition error (reversing the order of numbers) will cause a difference that is divisible by 9.

EXERCISE 7-7

Purpose: (L. O. 7) This exercise will allow you to practice preparing a bank reconciliation.

A bank reconciliation should be prepared by a depositor every month.

The cash balance per bank at October 31 is $17,780, and the cash balance per Molly's Folly books at October 31 is $19,404.

Instructions
(a) Using the data in **Exercise 7-6** and the solution to that exercise, prepare a bank reconciliation for Molly's Folly at October 31, 2014.
(b) Prepare the adjusting entries at October 31 for the depositor's books. Assume check No. 532 was issued to the power company for utilities.

SOLUTION TO EXERCISE 7-7

(a)

**Molly's Folly
BANK RECONCILIATION
October 31, 2014**

Cash balance per bank statement		$17,780*
Add: Deposits in transit (Answer (a) **Exercise 7-6**)		3,450
		21,230
Deduct: Outstanding checks (Answer (b) **Exercise 7-6**)		1,910
Adjusted cash balance per bank		$19,320
Cash balance per books		$19,404**
Deduct: Bank service charge	$30	
Error in recording check No. 532	54	84
Adjusted cash balance per books		$19,320

*To add to the complexity of this exercise, you could be asked to solve for the $17,780 cash balance per bank statement. The computation would be as follows:

Balance per bank statement at September 30, 2014	$15,000
Add: Deposits recorded during October and credit memoranda	11,700
Deduct: Checks paid during October and debit memoranda	8,920
Balance per bank statement at October 30, 2014	$17,780

**To add to the complexity of this exercise, you could be asked to solve for the $19,404 cash balance per books at October 31, 2014. The computation would be as follows:

Balance per books at September 30, 2014, before adjustment	$15,690
Deduct: NSF check recorded by an adjusting entry	400
Deduct: Bank service charge for September recorded by an adjusting entry	50
Adjusted cash balance at September 30	15,240
Add: Deposits made during October	11,550
Deduct: Checks written (issued) during October	7,386
Balance per books at October 31, 2014	$19,404

An alternate approach to solving for the balance per books before adjustment is illustrated in the **Solution to Exercise 7-5** part (b) 2.

TIP: Keep in mind that deposits in transit and outstanding checks are reconciling items but do **not** require adjusting entries on either the bank's books or the depositor's books.

(b) Oct. 31	Miscellaneous Expense...	30	
	Cash..		30
	(To record the bank service charges for October)		
Oct. 31	Utilities Expense..	54	
	Cash..		54
	(To correct error in recording check no 532)		

EXERCISE 7-8

Purpose: (L.O. 1 thru 8) This exercise will quiz you about terminology used in this chapter.

A list of accounting terms with which you should be familiar appears below:

Bank reconciliation	Fraud triangle
Bank service charge	Internal auditors
Bank statement	Internal control
Bonding	NSF check
Cash	Outstanding checks
Cash equivalents	Petty cash fund
Check	Restricted cash
Compensating balances	Sarbanes-Oxley Act
Deposits in transit	Voucher
Electronic funds transfer (EFT)	Voucher system
Fraud	

Instructions
For each item below, enter in the blank the term that is described.

1. _____Resources that consist of coins, currency, checks, money orders, and money on hand or on deposit in a bank or similar depository.

2. _____Short-term, highly liquid investments that can be converted to a specific amount of cash.

3. _____A cash fund used to pay relatively small amounts.

4. _____All of the related methods and measures adopted within an organization to safeguard its assets and enhance the accuracy and reliability of its accounting records.

5. _____A fee charged by a bank for the use of its services.

6. _____A monthly statement from the bank that shows the depositor's bank transactions and balances.

7. _____A written order signed by a bank depositor directing the bank to pay a specified sum of money to a designated recipient.

8. _____Minimum cash balances required by a bank in support of bank loans.

9. _____Checks issued and recorded by a company **not** yet paid by the bank.

10. _____Deposits recorded by the depositor but **not** yet recorded by the bank.

11. _____A check that is **not** paid by a bank because of insufficient funds in a customer's bank account.

12. _____A disbursement system that uses wire, telephone, telegraph, or computer to transfer funds from one location to another.

13. _____Company employees who continually evaluate the effectiveness of the company's internal control system.

14. _____An extensive network of approvals by authorized individuals acting independently to ensure that all disbursements by check are proper.

15. _____An authorization form prepared for each payment in a voucher system.

16. _____Obtaining insurance protection against misappropriation of assets by employees.

17. _____The process of comparing the bank's balance of an account with the company's recorded cash balance and explaining any differences to make them agree.

18. _____Cash that must be used for a special purpose.

19. _____Regulations passed by Congress to try to reduce unethical corporate behavior.

20. _____A dishonest act by an employee that results in personal benefit to the employee at a cost to the employer.

21. _____The three factors that contribute to fraudulent activity by employees: opportunity, financial pressure, and rationalization.

SOLUTION TO EXERCISE 7-8

1.	Cash	8.	Compensating balances	15.	Voucher
2.	Cash equivalents	9.	Outstanding checks	16.	Bonding
3.	Petty cash fund	10.	Deposits in transit	17.	Bank reconciliation
4.	Internal control	11.	NSF check	18.	Restricted cash
5.	Bank service charge	12.	Electronic funds transfer (EFT)	19.	Sarbanes-Oxley Act
6.	Bank statement	13.	Internal auditors	20.	Fraud
7.	Check	14.	Voucher system	21.	Fraud triangle

ANALYSIS OF MULTIPLE-CHOICE TYPE QUESTIONS

1.   (L.O. 1) One of the main objectives of a good system of internal control is to:
a.   increase sales.
b.   provide a means of gathering information about competitors.
c.   prevent errors and irregularities in the accounting records.
d.   prosecute employees who embezzle from the company.

Approach and Explanation: Mentally define internal control before you look at the answer selections. **Internal control** consists of the plan of organization and all the related methods and measures adopted within a business to:
1.   Safeguard its assets from employee theft, robbery, and unauthorized used.
2.   Enhance the accuracy and reliability of its accounting records by reducing the risks of errors (unintentional mistakes) and irregularities (intentional mistakes and misrepresentations) in the accounting process.
3.   Increase efficiency of operations.
4.   Ensure compliance with laws and regulations. (Solution = c.)

2.   (L.O. 1) Irregularities are also known as:
a.   errors.
b.   unintentional mistakes.
c.   fraud.
d.   defects in internal control.

Explanation: Errors are unintentional mistakes. Irregularities are intentional mistakes and misrepresentations; irregularities are also called fraud. Irregularities can occur even in a company with adequate internal control when a situation such as collusion exists. (Solution = c.)

3.   (L.O. 2) The basic internal control principle that is being applied when the work assignment for one employee is designed to check on the work of another employee is:
a.   independent internal verification.
b.   documentation procedures.
c.   separation of duties.
d.   double duties.

Explanation: Independent internal verification (or independent check) involves the review, comparison, and reconciliation of data prepared by one or several employees. To be effective, the verification should (1) be made periodically or on a surprise basis, (2) be done by an employee who is independent of the personnel responsible for the information, and (3) have discrepancies reported to a management level that can take appropriate corrective action. (Solution = a.)

4.   (L.O. 3) The best way to discourage a sales clerk from using a sales invoice to make a cash sale to a customer and then pocketing the cash and destroying the company's copy of the sales invoice is to require:
a.   verification of sales invoices.
b.   authorization of sales invoices.
c.   serialization of sales invoices.
d.   separation of duties for making the sale and recording the sale in the journal.

Explanation: Whenever possible, documents should be prenumbered, and all documents should be accounted for. Prenumbering helps to prevent a transaction from being recorded more than once, or conversely, to prevent the transaction from not being recorded. Serialization of sales invoices refers to prenumbering. (Solution = c.)

5. (L.O. 4) An extensive network of approvals by authorized individuals acting independently to ensure that all disbursements by check are proper is called a(n):
   a. electronic funds transfer system.
   b. computerized system.
   c. verifiable system.
   d. voucher system.

   Explanation: A voucher system is an extensive network of approvals by authorized individuals acting independently to ensure that all disbursements by check are proper. A voucher system may or may not include electronic transfer of fund as a mode of disbursement. A computerized system for cash disbursements may or may not be a voucher system. (Solution = d.)

6. (L.O. 5) The journal entry to record the replenishment of a petty cash fund that was established at $200 and is replenished at a date when petty cash vouchers in the fund amount to $172 and coins and currency in the fund amount to $30 will contain:
   a. debits to various expense accounts, a debit to Cash Over and Short, and a credit to Cash.
   b. debits to various expense accounts, a credit to Cash Over and Short, and a credit to Cash.
   c. a debit to Petty Cash, a credit to Cash Over and Short, and a credit to Cash.
   d. a debit to Cash and a credit to Petty Cash.

   Approach and Explanation: Reconstruct the journal entry in question:

Miscellaneous Expenses...	172	
Cash Over and Short..		2
Cash..		170

   The amount of expense receipts ($172) and the amount of coins and currency ($30) exceed the fund balance ($200) which indicates there is $2 too much in the fund. This $2 overage is recorded in the Cash Over and Short account. A credit balance in the Cash Over and Short account is classified as a revenue item on the income statement. (Solution = b.)

7.   (L.O. 6) A debit memorandum issued by a bank will:
     a.   not affect the depositor's account balance.
     b.   increase the depositor's account balance.
     c.   decrease the depositor's account balance.
     d.   be recorded as a debit to Cash on the depositor's books.

Approach and Explanation: Think about what a bank debit memorandum is used for. Think about how it affects the bank's books and the depositor's books. A depositor's bank account balance is a liability on the bank's books. Therefore, the bank uses a debit memorandum (memo), often abbreviated as DM on a bank statement, to indicate the bank has reason to debit the depositor's account. This debit reduces the bank's liability. Therefore, the bank debit memorandum reduces the depositor's bank balance and is recorded by the depositor as a credit to Cash. (Solution = c.)

8.   **Question**
     (L.O. 6) Which of the following items would **not** accompany a monthly bank statement?
     a.   Depositor's checks paid by the bank during the month (or copies thereof).
     b.   Copies of outstanding checks at the end of the month.
     c.   Copies of bank debit memos issued during the month.
     d.   Copies of bank credit memos issued during the month.

Explanation: A bank statement is usually accompanied by the paid checks (checks which were paid by the bank during the month), bank debit memoranda, and bank credit memoranda. Copies of outstanding checks would **never** be included because the bank is unaware of any information related to checks outstanding at the date a bank statement is prepared. (Solution = b.)

9.   (L.O. 7) Which of the following would most likely **not** appear as a reconciling item on a bank reconciliation prepared at the end of August?
     a.   Deposits in transit at August 31.
     b.   Checks which were disbursed and recorded by the depositor in July and were paid by the bank during August.
     c.   Bank service charges for the month of August.
     d.   Error in the depositor's account made by the bank during August and discovered by the depositor when examining the bank statement.

Approach and Explanation: Think about the possible reconciling items (refer to **Illustration 7-1**): deposits in transit, outstanding checks, bank debit memoranda, bank credit memoranda, bank errors, and depositor errors. Bank debit memoranda are issued for items such as bank service charges, customers' NSF checks deposited, and wire transfers. Checks disbursed in July and paid by the bank in August would be outstanding checks at July 31, but they are not outstanding at August 31; thus, they are not a reconciling item at August 31. (Solution = b.)

10. (L.O. 7) The term "outstanding checks" refers to
  a. checks that have been lost in the mail or for some other reason have been misplaced.
  b. depositor checks which have been processed by the bank but have not yet been recorded by the depositor.
  c. customer checks which have been returned by the bank because the customer's bank would not honor them.
  d. depositor checks which have not yet cleared the banking system.

Explanation: There is a lag in time between the date a check is issued and the date the check clears the banking system. During the time between these two dates, the checks are referred to as "outstanding checks." (Solution = d.)

11. (L.O. 7) The following information pertains to Honeybee Co. at December 31, 2014

Bank statement balance	$40,000
Checkbook balance	56,400
Deposits in transit	20,000
Outstanding checks	4,000
Bank service charges for December	400

In Honeybee's balance sheet at December 31, 2014 cash should be reported as:
  a. $36,000.
  b. $40,000.
  c. $56,000.
  d. $60,000.

Approach and Explanation: When a question relates to data used in a bank reconciliation, you should sketch out the format for a bank reconciliation, put in the information given, and solve for the unknown piece.

Cash balance per bank statement	$40,000
Deposits in transit	20,000
Outstanding checks	(4,000)
Adjusted cash balance per bank	$56,000
Cash balance per books	$56,400
Bank service charges	(400)
Adjusted cash balance per books	$56,000

In this particular question, the completion of either the top half or the bottom half of the reconciliation using the bank-to-adjusted balance format would be enough to solve for the answer requested. (Solution = c.)

12. (L.O. 7) The following information pertains to the Berry Bear Corporation at December 31, 2014

Balance per bank	$20,000
Deposits in transit	6,000
Outstanding checks	16,000
Bank service charges for December	400
Bank erroneously charged Berry Bear's account for Sonny-Bear's check written for $1,400. As of December 31, the bank had not corrected this error	1,400

Berry Bear's cash balance per ledger (books) before adjustment at December 31, 2014 is
a. $28,200.
b. $11,800.
c. $11,000.
d. $8,200.

Approach and Explanation: The balance per books (before adjustment) can easily be computed by putting the data into the format for a bank reconciliation. Solve for the unknown.

Cash balance per bank statement	$20,000
Deposits in transit	6,000
Outstanding checks	(16,000)
Bank error in charge for check	1,400
Adjusted cash balance per bank	$11,400
Cash balance per books	$ X
Bank service charges	(400)
Adjusted cash balance per books	$11,400

X = $11,800 (Solution = b.)

13. (L.O. 7) The following data relate to the bank account of Springfield Cleaners:

Cash balance, September 30 per bank	$10,000
Cash balance, October 31 per bank	21,500
Checks paid during October by bank	5,900
Checks written during October per books	6,800
Cash balance, October 31 per books	22,200
Bank service charge for October, not recorded on books	100
Deposits per books for October	19,000

The amount of deposits recorded by the bank in October is
a. $19,000.
b. $17,500.
c. $11,500.
d. $5,700.

Approach and Explanation: Think about how deposits recorded by the bank affect the cash balance per bank and other items that cause that balance to change. Plug in the figures given and solve for the unknown.

Balance per bank, September 30	$10,000
Deposits per bank during October	X
Bank credit memoranda	-0-
Checks paid by bank during October	(5,900)
Bank service charge for October and other bank debit memoranda	(100)
Balance per bank, October 31	$21,500

Solving for X: $10,000 + X - $5,900 - $100 = $21,500
  X = $21,500 - $10,000 + $5,900 + $100

  X = $17,500 (Solution = b.)

14. (L.O. 8) When financial statements are prepared, the balance of the Petty Cash account is:
   a.   not reflected in the financial statements.
   b.   reported along with other unrestricted cash items in the current asset section of the balance sheet.
   c.   reported as restricted cash in the balance sheet.
   d.   reported as a miscellaneous expense item on the income statement.

   Explanation: Cash on hand, cash in banks, and petty cash are usually combined and reported simply as Cash in the current asset section of the balance sheet. (Solution = b.)

15. (L.O. 8) Which of the following items should **not** be included in the Cash caption on the balance sheet?
   a.   Coins and currency in the cash register.
   b.   Checks from other parties presently in the cash register.
   c.   Amounts on deposit in checking account at the bank.
   d.   Postage stamps on hand.

   Explanation: Cash on hand, unrestricted cash in banks, and petty cash are usually combined and reported simply as Cash. Postage stamps on hand are classified as office supplies (a prepaid expense). Cash on hand consists of coins, currency (paper money), checks, and money orders. The general rule is that if a bank will accept it for deposit, it is cash. (Solution = d.)

CHAPTER 8

· ·

Accounting for Receivables

OVERVIEW

Receivables are claims that are expected to be collected in cash. Three major types of receivables are usually recognized; they are accounts, notes, and other receivables. Receivables can be (a) held until they are collected, (b) sold before they are collected, or (c) held and never collected. Many businesses grant credit to customers; hence, they have accounts receivable. They know that, when making sales "on account," a risk exists because some accounts will never be collected. However, the cost of these bad debts is more than offset by the profit from the extra sales made because of the attraction of granting credit. The collections department may make many attempts to collect an account before "writing-off" a bad debtor. Frequently an account is deemed to be uncollectible a year or more after the date of the credit sale. In this chapter, we will discuss the allowance method of accounting for bad debts. The allowance method permits the accountant to estimate the amount of bad debt expense that should be matched with revenues rather than waiting to book expense at the time of an actual write-off.

SUMMARY OF LEARNING OBJECTIVES

1. **Identity the different types of receivables.** Receivables are frequently classified as (1) accounts, (2) notes, and (3) other. Accounts receivable are amounts customers owe on account. Notes receivable are claims for which lenders issue formal instruments of credit as proof of the debt. Other receivables include nontrade receivables such as interest receivable, loans to company officers, advances to employees, and income taxes refundable.

2. **Explain how companies recognize accounts receivable in the accounts.** Companies record accounts receivable at invoice price (i.e. sales price). They are reduced by sales returns and allowances. Cash discounts also reduce the amount received on accounts receivable. When interest is charged on a past due receivable, the company adds this interest to the accounts receivable balance and recognizes it as interest revenue.

3. **Distinguish between the methods and bases companies use to value accounts receivable.** There are two methods of accounting for uncollectible accounts: the allowance method and the direct write-off method. The allowance method is required for financial reporting purposes when bad debts are material (significant) in size. Companies may use either the percentage-of-sales or the percentage-of-receivables basis to estimate uncollectible accounts using the allowance method. The percentage-of-sales basis emphasizes the expense recognition (matching) principle. The percentage-of-receivables basis emphasizes the cash realizable value of the accounts receivable. An aging schedule is often used with this basis.

4. **Describe the entries to record the disposition of accounts receivable.** When a company collects an account receivable, it credits Accounts Receivable. When a company (factors) an account receivable, a service charge expense reduces the amount of cash received.

5. **Compute the maturity date of and interest on notes receivable.** For a note stated in months, the maturity date is found by counting the months from the date of issue. For a note stated in days, the actual number of days is counted, omitting the issue date and counting the due date. The formula for computing interest is: Face value X Interest rate X Time.

6. **Explain how companies recognize notes receivable in the accounts.** Companies record notes receivable at face value. In some cases, it is necessary to record accrued interest prior to maturity. In this case, companies debit Interest Receivable and credit Interest Revenue.

7. **Describe how companies value notes receivable.** As with accounts receivable, companies report notes receivable at their cash (net) realizable value. The notes receivable allowance account is the Allowance for Doubtful Accounts. The computation and estimations involved in valuing notes receivables at cash realizable value, and in recording the proper amount of bad debt expense and related allowance are similar to those for accounts receivable.

8. **Describe the entries to record the disposition of notes receivable.** Notes can be held to maturity. At that time the face value plus accrued interest is due, and the note is removed from the accounts. In many cases, the holder of the note speeds up the conversion to cash by selling the receivable to another party (a factor). In some situations, the maker of the note dishonors the note (defaults), in which case the company transfers the note and accrued interest to an account receivable or writes off the note.

9. **Explain the financial statement presentation and analysis of receivables.** Companies should identify in the balance sheet or in the notes to the financial statements each major type of receivable. Short-term receivables are reported as current assets. Companies report the gross amount of receivables and the allowance for doubtful accounts. They report bad debt expense and service charge expense in the multiple-step income statement as operating (selling) expenses; interest revenue appears under other revenues and gains in the nonoperating activities section of the income statement. Managers and investors evaluate accounts receivable for liquidity by computing a turnover ratio and an average collection period.

TIPS ON CHAPTER TOPICS

TIP: **Trade accounts receivable** result from the sale of products or services to customers. **Non-trade accounts receivable** (amounts that are due from nontrade customers who do not buy goods or services in the normal course of the company's main business activity) should be listed separately on the balance sheet from the trade accounts receivable balance.

TIP: Notice how the subjects of this chapter affect the balance sheet and the income statement. The balance of the Accounts Receivable account and its contra account—Allowance for Doubtful Accounts—are reported in the current asset section of the balance sheet. The balance of Notes Receivable (assuming the notes are due within one year of the balance sheet date) is also classified in the current asset section of the balance sheet. The balance of Bad Debt Expense is usually reported in the operating expense section of the multiple-step income statement.

TIP: Assets such as current receivables and inventories should never be reported at more than their net (cash) realizable value. Thus, if some uncollectible accounts are expected, receivables are reduced by these uncollectible amounts when presented on the balance sheet.

TIP: The **carrying value** (or **book value** or **carrying amount**) of accounts receivable is equal to the balance of the Accounts Receivable account less the balance of the related valuation account (Allowance for Doubtful Accounts). The carrying value of accounts receivable is also referred to as **net (cash) realizable value** of accounts receivable.

TIP: In the event that a customer's account has a credit balance on the balance sheet date, it should be classified as a current liability and **not** be offset against other accounts receivable with debit balances.

ILLUSTRATION 8-1
ENTRIES FOR THE ALLOWANCE METHOD (L.O. 3)

Journal Entry			Effect on Net Income	Effect on Current Assets	Effect on Allowance Account	Effect on Net Receivables
Entry to record bad debt expense, $1,000						
Bad Debt Expense	1,000		Decrease $1,000	No effect	No effect	No effect
Allowance for Doubtful Accounts		1,000	No effect	Decrease $1,000	Increase $1,000	Decrease $1,000
Net effect of entry			Decrease $1,000	Decrease $1,000	Increase $1,000	Decrease $1,000
Entry to write-off a customer's account, $200						
Allowance for Doubtful Accounts	200		No effect	Increase $200	Decrease $200	Increase $200
Accounts Receivable		200	No effect	Decrease $200	No effect	Decrease $200
Net effect of entry			No effect	No effect	Decrease $200	No effect
Entries to record collection of account receivable previously written off, $120						
Accounts Receivable	120		No effect	Increase $120	No effect	Increase $120
Allowance for Doubtful Accounts		120	No effect	Decrease $120	Increase $120	Decrease $120
Cash	120		No effect	Increase $120	No effect	No effect
Accounts Receivable		120	No effect	Decrease $120	No effect	Decrease $120
Net effect of entries			No effect	No effect	Increase $120	Decrease $120

TIP: Study the effects of the journal entries related to accounting for accounts receivable using the allowance method. Those entries and their effects are clearly shown above. Notice that the entry to record bad debts reduces current assets and reduces net income. The entry to record the write off of an individual account has no net effect on the amount of current assets nor does it affect income. It merely reduces Accounts Receivable and the Allowance for Doubtful Accounts account (which is a contra item); thus, the entry has no net effect on the carrying value of the accounts receivable. Thus, it is the entry to record the bad debt expense that impacts **both** the balance sheet and the income statement.

TIP: Bad Debt Expense is often called Uncollectible Accounts Expense or Doubtful Accounts Expense or Provision for Bad Debts. Allowance for Doubtful Accounts is often called Allowance for Uncollectible Accounts or Allowance for Bad Debts. Notice that these account titles all start with "Allowance for" which typically indicates a contra type balance sheet account.

EXERCISE 8-1

Purpose: (L.O. 3) This exercise will identify the two approaches of applying the allowance method of accounting for uncollectible accounts receivable.

Howell's Department Store offers a store credit card for the convenience of its customers. Even though the store follows up on delinquent accounts, past experience indicates that a predictable amount of credit sales will ultimately result in uncollectible accounts. Howell uses the allowance method of accounting for uncollectible accounts. Bad debts are a material amount.

Instructions
(a)   Describe the two methods available for determining the amount of the adjusting entry to record bad debt expense and to adjust the allowance account. Also discuss the emphasis of each method.
(b)   Explain why the direct write-off method is not a generally accepted accounting method for Howell's Department Store.

SOLUTION TO EXERCISE 8-1

(a)   When using the allowance method of accounting for bad debts, there are two methods available for determining the amount of the adjusting entry to record bad debt expense and to adjust the allowance account. They are:

   (1)   **The percentage-of-sales basis:** This method focuses on estimating bad debt expense. The average percentage relationship between actual bad debt losses and net credit sales (or total credit sales) of the period is used to determine the amount of expense for the period. That is, this method focuses on the matching of current bad debt expense with revenues of the current period and thus emphasizes the income statement. The amount of bad debt expense is simply calculated and recorded; a by-product of this approach is the increase in the allowance account.

> **TIP:**   The allowance method calls for the recognition of bad debt expense in the same period as the revenues that were recognized when the receivables originated rather than waiting to recognize expense until the period the receivables are deemed to definitely be uncollectible. This exercise is looking at two different approaches (methods) of applying this method.

   (2)   **The percentage-of-receivables basis:** This method focuses on estimating the cash (net) realizable value of the current receivables and thus emphasizes the balance sheet. It only incidentally measures bad debt expense; the expense reported may not be the best figure to match with the amount of credit sales of the current period. If this method is to be used, the aging technique is preferable to the use of a simple percentage times total accounts receivable. An aging analysis takes into consideration the age of a receivable. The older the age, the lower the probability of collection.

(b)   Under the direct write-off method, bad debt losses are not estimated and no allowance account is used. No entry regarding bad debts is made until a specific account has definitely been established as uncollectible. Then the loss is recorded by a debit to Bad Debt Expense and a credit to Accounts Receivable.

When the direct write-off method is used, Accounts Receivable will be reported at its gross amount and bad debt expense is often recorded in a period different from the period in which the revenue was recorded. Thus, no attempt is made to match bad debt expense to sales revenues in the income statement or to show the cash (net) realizable value of the accounts receivable in the balance sheet. Consequently, unless bad debt losses are insignificant, the direct write-off method is **not** acceptable for financial reporting purposes. Howell's bad debts are material (significant) in amount so the allowance method must be used for financial reporting purposes. The direct write-off method is, however, used for tax purposes.

EXERCISE 8-2

Purpose: (L.O. 3) This exercise will review the two bases for determining the dollar amount of the adjusting entry to recognize bad debt expense and to adjust the Allowance for Doubtful Accounts account.

The trial balance before adjustment at December 31, 2014 for the Liz Company shows the following balances:

	Debit	**Credit**
Accounts Receivable	$82,000	
Allowance for Doubtful Accounts	2,120	
Sales (all on credit)		$410,000
Sales Returns and Allowances	7,600	

Instructions
Using the data above, give the journal entries to record each of the following cases (each situation is **independent**):
(a)   The company expects bad debts to be 1 3/4% of net credit sales.
(b)   Liz performs an aging analysis at December 31, 2014 which indicates an estimate of $6,000 uncollectible accounts.

SOLUTION TO EXERCISE 8-2

(a)	Bad Debt Expense	7,042	
	Allowance for Doubtful Accounts [($410,000 - $7,600) X 1.75%]..		7,042
(b)	Bad Debt Expense	8,120	
	Allowance for Doubtful Accounts ($6,000 + $2,120).................		8,120

Explanation

(a)   The percentage-of-net-credit-sales approach to applying the allowance method of accounting for bad debts focuses on determining an appropriate expense figure. The existing balance in the allowance account is **not** relevant in the computation.

(b)   An aging analysis provides the best estimate of the net realizable value of accounts receivable. By using the results of the aging to adjust the allowance account, the amount reported for net receivables on the balance sheet is the cash (net) realizable value of accounts receivable. It is important to notice that the balance of the allowance account before adjustment is a determinant in the adjustment required. The following T-account reflects the facts used to determine the necessary adjustment.

Allowance for Doubtful Accounts

Unadjusted balance	2,120	**Adjustment needed**	**8,120**
		Desired balance at 12/31/14	6,000

TIP:	Notice that in this particular instance, the allowance account has an **abnormal** balance before adjustment. The normal balance of the Allowance for Doubtful Accounts is a credit. Therefore, a debit balance in this account indicates an abnormal balance. It is **not** uncommon to have a debit balance in the allowance account before adjusting entries are prepared because individual accounts may be written off at various times during a period, and the entry to adjust the allowance account is made at the end of the period before financial statements are prepared. After adjustment, the allowance account must have a credit balance.
TIP:	Refer to the **Solution to Exercise 8-1** (a) to review the emphasis of both the percentage of sales basis and the percentage of receivables basis for estimating uncollectible accounts using the allowance method.

> **TIP:** When it is time to prepare the adjusting entry for bad debts (at the end of an accounting period), the existing balance in the Allowance for Doubtful Accounts account (that is, the balance before adjustment) is **NOT** considered in determining the amount of the adjusting entry **IF** the percentage-of-sales-basis is used. However, the balance of the allowance account before adjustment **IS** used in determining the amount of the adjusting entry when the percentage-of-receivables-basis is used to implement the allowance method of accounting for bad debts. The use of an aging analysis is one approach to using the percentage-of-receivables basis.

EXERCISE 8-3

Purpose: (L.O. 4) This exercise will illustrate the journal entries related to credit card sales.

Bubba's Bed & Bath Shop accepts MasterCard, VISA, and its own Bubba's Bed & Bath Shop (BB&BS) credit cards. MasterCard and VISA sales slips are deposited in the bank daily; the bank charges a 3% fee. The following transactions occurred on May 3, 2014.

1. Made sales of $7,200 to customers who presented MasterCard and VISA cards.
2. Made sales to the following who used their BB&BS cards:
   a. Nadine Adam, $120
   b. Connie Dawson, $240
   c. Dale Bandy, $500

Instructions
(a) Prepare the journal entries to record the transactions above for Bubba's Bed and Bath Shop.
(b) Prepare the journal entry to record collections of $120, $40, and $100 from Nadine Adam, Connie Dawson, and Dale Bandy, respectively.
(c) Prepare the journal entry to record interest charged to customer accounts at the rate of 1.5% per month as follows: Connie Dawson, $3; Dale Bandy, $6.

SOLUTION TO EXERCISE 8-3

(a) 1.
Cash	6,984	
Service Charge Expense (3% X $7,200)	216	
Sales		7,200
(To record MasterCard and VISA sales)		

2.
Accounts Receivable—Nadine Adam	120	
Accounts Receivable—Connie Dawson	240	
Accounts Receivable—Dale Bandy	500	
Sales		860
(To record company credit card sales)		

(b)
Cash	260	
Accounts Receivable—Nadine Adam		120
Accounts Receivable—Connie Dawson		40
Accounts Receivable—Dale Bandy		100
(To record collections on account)		

(c)	Accounts Receivable—Connie Dawson	3	
	Accounts Receivable—Dale Bandy	6	
	Interest Revenue		9
	(To record interest on amounts due)		

EXERCISE 8-4

Purpose: (L.O. 4) This exercise will illustrate the factoring of accounts receivable.

The Tuscawilla Tailgate Company often factors its accounts receivable. On May 1, 2014, the company factored $250,000 of customer accounts receivable to Fagan Factors, Inc. which charged a 3% service charge.

Instructions
(a)   Prepare the journal entry to record the sale of the accounts receivable to the factor.
(b)   Explain how the service charge will affect Tuscawilla Tailgates' financial statements.

SOLUTION TO EXERCISE 8-4

(a)	Cash	242,500	
	Service Charge Expense	7,500	
	Accounts Receivable		250,000
	(To record the sale of accounts receivable)		

(b)   The service charge expense incurred should be reported as a selling expense (operating expense) on the income statement because the company often sells its receivables. If receivables were sold infrequently, the service charge expense may be classified in the Other Expenses and Losses section of the income statement.

EXERCISE 8-5

Purpose: (L.O. 6) This exercise reviews the journal entries for various transactions involving notes receivable.

The following transactions occurred during 2014 and pertain to the Aaron Retail Company.

June 1   Accepted a note from R. Greenblatt in settlement of his $2,000 account. The note is due in six months and bears interest at 12%.
July 1   Sold merchandise to C. Lynn for $5,000. Accepted a note due in nine months at 10%.
Oct. 1   Accepted a note from D. Gioia for $6,000 in settlement of his account receivable. The 10% note is due in 180 days.

Instructions
(a)   Prepare the journal entries to record the receipt of each of the three notes.
(b)   Indicate the due date of each note.
(c)   Assume the first note is collected on its due date. Prepare the appropriate journal entry to record its collection.
(d)   Assume the accounting period ends on December 31. Prepare the appropriate adjusting entry(s) at December 31, 2014, to record accrued interest on the second and third notes.
(e)   Assume the second note is honored on its maturity date. Prepare the journal entry to record this transaction.
(f)   Assume the third note is dishonored on its due date. Aaron expects eventual collection. Prepare the appropriate journal entry.

SOLUTION TO EXERCISE 8-5

(a)   2014
     June   1   Notes Receivable—R. Greenblatt 2,000
                  Accounts Receivable—R. Greenblatt............... 2,000
                  (To record acceptance of R. Greenblatt note)

     July   1   Notes Receivable—C. Lynn 5,000
                  Sales 5,000
                  (To record sale of merchandise and
                  acceptance of C. Lynn note)

     Oct.   1   Notes Receivable—D. Gioia.................................... 6,000
                  Accounts Receivable—D. Gioia 6,000
                  (To record acceptance of D. Gioia note)

(b)   R. Greenblatt note is due on December 1, 2014.
       C. Lynn note is due on April 1, 2015.
       D. Gioia note is due on March 30, 2015.
              Computations for due date of D. Gioia note:

October (31 - 1 = 30)	30
November	30
December	31
January	31
February	28
Subtotal	150
March	30
Total	180

TIP: When the life of a note is expressed in terms of months, the due date is found by counting the months from the date of issue. A note drawn on the last day of a month matures on the last day of a subsequent month. When the due date is stated in terms of days, it is necessary to count the exact number of days to determine the maturity date. In counting, the day the note was issued is omitted but the due date is included.

(c)   Dec. 1   Cash...   2,120
                      Notes Receivable—R. Greenblatt.........................   2,000
                      Interest Revenue..   120
                      (To record collection of note at maturity);
                      ($2,000 X 12% X 6/12 = $120)

TIP: The formula for computing interest on an interest-bearing note is:

Face Value of Note	X	Annual Interest Rate	X	Time in Terms of One Year	= Interest

---

(d)   Dec.31   Interest Receivable...   400
                      Interest Revenue..   400
                      (To record six months of accrued interest on
                      the Lynn note and three months interest on the
                      Gioia note) ($5,000 X 10% X 6/12 = $250);
                      ($6,000 X 10% X 3/12 = $150); ($250 + $150
                      = $400)

TIP: An interest rate is always stated in terms of an annual basis, unless otherwise indicated.

(e)   2015
       Apr. 1   Cash...   5,375
                      Notes Receivable—C. Lynn   5,000
                      Interest Receivable   250
                      Interest Revenue..   125
                      (To record collection of note at maturity);
                      ($5,000 X 10% X 9/12 = $375 interest for
                      9 mos.); ($5,000 + $375 = $5,375 total
                      cash collected); ($375 - $250 accrued
                      last year = $125 interest earned this year)

TIP: A note is said to be **honored** when it is paid in full at its maturity date.

(f)   2015

Mar. 30	Accounts Receivable—D. Gioia	6,300	
	Notes Receivable...		6,000
	Interest Revenue..		150
	Interest Receivable		150

          (To record the dishonor of the D. Gioia
          note);
          ($6,000 X 10% X 180/360 = $300);
          ($300 - $150 = $150)

TIP: A **dishonored note** is a note that is **not** paid in full at its maturity date.

TIP: No interest revenue would be recorded at this date if collection of the note was **not** expected.

TIP: Review the terminology related to notes receivable:

Promissory note	is a written promise to pay a specified amount of money on demand or at a definite time.
Face value	is the principal amount of a note.
Maker	is the person who promises to pay money later.
Payee	is the person to whom the money is owed.

TIP: **Interest** is always a function of time, rate, and balance. Always assume a 360-day year when computing interest (unless a 365-day year is specified). This assumption makes computations easier.

EXERCISE 8-6

Purpose: (L.O. 9) This exercise will review the measures used to evaluate the liquidity of accounts receivable.

The management of M. F. Specie Company is analyzing the entity's recent financial statements to determine the efficiency of the company's credit policies for customers. The following information is extracted from the statements:

Sales	$930,000
Sales returns	30,000
Accounts receivable, 12/31/14	85,000
Accounts receivable, 12/31/13	60,000

Instructions

1. Assuming all sales are credit sales (on account), compute the receivables turnover for 2014.
2. Assuming the company's policy is to require payment within 30 days of invoicing a customer and invoices are sent within two days of a sale, explain whether the company's average collection period suggests that the company has weak or strong controls surrounding its credit-granting activity.

SOLUTION TO EXERCISE 8-6

1. Receivables turnover ratio = $\dfrac{\text{Net credit sales}}{\text{Average accounts receivable}}$

    Receivables turnover ratio = $\dfrac{\$930,000 - \$30,000}{1/2(\$85,000 + \$60,000)}$ = 12.41 times

2. The average collection period of 29.41 days when compared to the typical 32 days between a sale date and the payment due date suggests that the company has adequate to strong controls surrounding its credit-granting activity.

    The average number of days to collect an account receivable is computed as follows:

    $$\frac{365 \text{ days}}{\substack{\text{Accounts receivable} \\ \text{turnover ratio}}} = \frac{365}{12.41 \text{ times}} = 29.41 \text{ days}$$

TIP: A **ratio** is an expression of the relationship of one item (or group of items) to a second item (or group of items). It is determined by dividing the first item (amount) by the second item (amount). The relationship may be expressed either as a percentage, a rate, or a simple proportion.

For example: If A is $100,000 and B is $25,000 the ratio of A to B can be expressed in several ways, such as the following:

A:B	A/B
4:1	4.00
4 to 1	$4.00
4 times	400%

The way in which the ratio is expressed depends on the particular ratio. If it is the current ratio, it would likely be expressed as a proportion (4:1 or 4 to 1) or as a rate (4 times). If it is the debt to stockholders' equity ratio, it would likely be expressed as a percentage (400%).

TIP: In this chapter we look at the financial ratio used to assess the liquidity of receivables--the receivables turnover ratio. In the remaining chapters of this book, be alert for discussions of other financial ratios.

TIP: The **average collection period** is not very meaningful until it is compared with the company's credit terms.

TIP: The denominator of a turnover ratio (such as for receivables) always involves an **average** balance. That average can be determined by adding the balance at the end of the period to the balance at the beginning of the period and dividing by 2. However, if seasonal variances are significant, the annual average should be determined by adding together the balances at the end of each month and dividing by 12.

EXERCISE 8-7

Purpose: (L.O. 1 thru 9) This exercise will quiz you about terminology used in this chapter.

A list of accounting terms with which you should be familiar appears below.

Accounts receivable	Factor
Accounts receivable turnover ratio	Maker
Aging the accounts receivable	Notes receivable
Allowance for doubtful accounts	Other receivables
Allowance method	Payee
Average collection period	Percentage-of-receivables basis
Bad Debt Expense	Percentage-of-sales basis
Cash (net) realizable value	Promissory note
Direct write-off method	Receivables
Dishonored note	Trade receivables

Instructions
For each item below, enter in the blank the term that is described.

1. _____Amounts due from individuals and other companies.

2. _____Amounts owed by customers on account.

3. _____Claims for which formal instruments of credit are issued as proof of the debt.

4. _____Various forms of nontrade receivables, such as interest receivable and income taxes refundable.

5. _____The analysis of customer balances by the length of time they have been unpaid.

6. _____Management establishes a percentage relationship between the expected losses from uncollectible accounts and the amount of receivables.

7. _____Management establishes a percentage relationship between expected losses from uncollectible accounts and the amount of credit sales.

8. _____The net amount expected to be received in cash.

9. _____A written promise to pay a specified amount of money on demand or at a definite time.

10. _____The party in a promissory note who is making the promise to pay.

11. _____The party to whom payment of a promissory note to be made.

12. _____A note that is **not** paid in full at maturity.

13. _____A finance company or bank that buys receivables from businesses and then collects the payments directly from the customers.

14. _____Notes and accounts receivable that result from sales transactions.

15. _____A measure of the liquidity of accounts receivables, computed by dividing net credit sales by average net accounts receivables.

16. _____The average amount of time that a receivable is outstanding, calculated by dividing 365 days by the accounts receivable turnover ratio.

17. _____An expense account used to record the cost of uncollectible receivables.

18. _____A method of accounting for bad debts that involves expensing accounts at the time they are determined to be uncollectible.

19. _____A method of accounting for bad debts that involves estimating uncollectible accounts at the end of each period.

20. _____An account that shows the estimated amount of claims on customers that the company expects will become uncollectible in the future.

SOLUTION TO EXERCISE 8-7

1. Receivables
2. Accounts receivable
3. Notes receivable
4. Other receivables
5. Aging the accounts receivable
6. Percentage-of-receivables basis
7. Percentage-of-sales basis
8. Cash (net) realizable value
9. Promissory note
10. Maker
11. Payee
12. Dishonored note
13. Factor
14. Trade receivables
15. Accounts receivable turnover ratio
16. Average collection period
17. Bad Debt Expense
18. Direct write-off method
19. Allowance method
20. Allowance for Doubtful Accounts

ANALYSIS OF MULTIPLE-CHOICE TYPE QUESTIONS

1.   (L.O. 3) The journal entry to record the write-off of an individual customer's account receivable using the allowance method involves a debit to:
     a.   Allowance for Doubtful Accounts and a credit to Accounts Receivable.
     b.   Bad Debt Expense and a credit to Accounts Receivable.
     c.   Accounts Receivable and a credit to Allowance for Doubtful Accounts.
     d.   Bad Debt Expense and a credit to Allowance for Doubtful Accounts.

     Approach and Explanation: Write down the journal entry to record the write-off of an individual customer's account:

     Allowance for Doubtful Accounts... XXX
            Accounts Receivable... XXX

     Find the answer selection that describes this entry. Answer selection "d" describes the journal entry to record bad debt expense and to adjust the allowance account. (Solution = a.)

2.   (L.O. 3) The balances of the Accounts Receivable account and Allowance for Doubtful Accounts account, before adjustment, are $60,000 and $1,200 respectively. Bad debt expense for the period is estimated to be $3,100. What amount should be reported for net accounts receivable on the balance sheet?
     a. $58,100.
     b. $58,800.
     c. $56,900.
     d. $55,700.

     Approach and Explanation: One approach is to draw T-accounts, enter the balances before adjustment, reflect in the accounts the entry to record bad debt expense, balance the accounts, and deduct the balance of the contra account from the balance of the Accounts Receivable account to determine net accounts receivable at the balance sheet date.

Accounts Receivable	Allowance for Doubtful Accounts	Bad Debt Expense
60,000	1,200	Adjust. 3,100
	Adjust. 3,100	
	Bal. 4,300	

     $60,000 Accounts receivable - $4,300 Allowance = $55,700 Net accounts receivable. (Solution = d.)

3.   (L.O. 3) The journal entry to record uncollectible accounts expense using the allowance method will:
     a.   reduce net income and total current assets.
     b.   reduce net income but will not affect total current assets.
     c.   not affect net income but will reduce total current assets.
     d.   not affect net income or total current assets.

     Approach and Explanation: Before you read all of the answer choices, write down the journal entry to record bad debt expense (uncollectible accounts expense is synonymous to bad debt expense). Analyze both parts of the entry (one part at a time) to determine the impact on (1) net income and (2) current assets.

			Effect on Net Income	Effect on Current Assets
Bad Debt Expense	5,000		Decrease $5,000	No Effect
Allowance for Doubtful Accounts	5,000		No Effect	Decrease $5,000
Net effect of entry			Decrease $5,000	Decrease $5,000

The amount used in the entry can be any assumed amount since no amount was specified. (Solution = a.)

4. (L.O. 3) The journal entry to write off an individual customer's account receivable using the allowance method will:
    a. reduce net income and total current assets.
    b. reduce net income but will not affect total current assets.
    c. not affect net income but will reduce total current assets.
    d. not affect net income or total current assets.

    Approach and Explanation: Write down the journal entry to write off an individual customer's account. Analyze each part of the entry to determine its impact on (1) net income and (2) current assets. Summarize the effects and locate the correct answer selection. Assume any amount you want for the entry since no amount was specified in the question.

			Effect on Net Income	Effect on Current Assets
Allowance for Doubtful Accounts	5,000		No Effect	Increase $5,000
Accounts Receivable		5,000	No Effect	Decrease $5,000
Net effect of entry			No Effect	No Effect

(Solution = d.)

5. (L.O. 3) The balance of the Allowance for Doubtful Accounts account represents the:
    a. total amount of uncollectible accounts written off to date.
    b. amount of credit sales made this period that has not been collected.
    c. amount of cash that has been set aside in a special fund to make up for bad debt losses.
    d. portion of total accounts receivable that is not expected to be converted to cash.

    Approach and Explanation: Think about what prompts entries to the valuation (allowance) account for accounts receivable. The allowance is increased when the provision for bad debt (expense) is recorded. The allowance is decreased when an individual account is ultimately deemed to be uncollectible. The provision is recorded because some yet unidentified portion of receivables arising from credit sales will never be collected (hence, will never be converted to cash). Selection "c" is false because cash is not involved in the entry to set up the allowance; no fund is set aside for this purpose. (Solution = d.)

6. (L.O. 3) The balance of the Allowance for Doubtful Accounts account at January 1, 2014 was $5,900. During 2014, accounts receivable amounting to $8,000 were written off. Estimated uncollectible accounts expense for 2014 amounts to $7,100. The balance of the Allowance for Doubtful Accounts account to be reported on the balance sheet at December 31, 2014 is:
    a. $13,000.
    b. $ 7,100.
    c. $ 6,800.
    d. $ 5,000.

    Approach and Explanation: Draw a T-account for the account in question. Visualize the journal entries to write off accounts and to estimate bad debt expense. Enter the resulting postings as they would be reflected in the allowance account.

Allowance for Doubtful Accounts			
Write-offs, 2014	8,000	Balance, 1/1/14	5,900
		Expense, 2014	7,100
		Balance, 12/31/14	5,000

    It is evident that the company is using the percentage-of-sales basis of applying the allowance method because its entry to the allowance account is based on the amount of bad debt expense rather than an appropriate ending balance for the allowance account. (Solution = d.)

7. (L.O. 3) The following data are available for 2014:

Sales, cash	$200,000
Sales, credit	500,000
Accounts Receivable, January 1	80,000
Accounts Receivable, December 31	72,000
Allowance for Doubtful Accounts, January 1	4,000
Accounts written off during 2014	4,600

    The journal entry to record bad debt expense for the period and to adjust the allowance account is to be based on an estimate of 1% of credit sales. The entry to record the uncollectible accounts expense for 2014 would include a debit to the Bad Debt Expense account for:
    a. $7,200.
    b. $5,600.
    c. $4,400.
    d. $5,000.

    Approach and Explanation: Think about the emphasis of the entry when the percentage-of-sales basis is used. This basis emphasizes the income statement. Therefore, 1% times credit sales equals expense. $500,000 X 1% = $5,000. The balance of the allowance account before adjustment does **not** affect this computation or entry. (Solution = d.)

8. (L.O. 3) The following data are available for 2014:

Sales, cash	$200,000
Sales, credit	500,000
Accounts Receivable, January 1	80,000
Accounts Receivable, December 31	72,000
Allowance for Doubtful Accounts, January 1	4,000
Accounts written off during 2014	4,600

The journal entry to record bad debt expense for the period and to adjust the allowance account is to be based on an aging analysis of accounts receivable. The aging analysis of accounts receivable at December 31, 2014, reveals that $5,200 of existing accounts receivable are estimated to be uncollectible. The entry to record the uncollectible accounts expense for 2014 will involve a debit to the Bad Debt Expense account for:
a. $9,800.
b. $5,800.
c. $5,200.
d. $4,600.

Approach and Explanation: An aging analysis is performed to determine the best figure to represent the cash (net) realizable value for accounts receivable in the balance sheet. Thus, $5,200 is the desirable balance for the allowance account at the reporting date. Determine the existing balance in the allowance account and the adjusting entry needed to arrive at the predetermined balance.

Allowance for Doubtful Accounts

Write-offs, 2014	4,600	Balance, 1/1/14	4,000	
				Entry
Balance before adjustment	600	Adjustment needed	X	←needed.
		Desired bal. at 12/31/14	5,200	

Solving for X: X - $600 = $5,200
$\qquad$ X = $5,200 + $600
$\qquad$ X = $\underline{$5,800}$ (Solution = b.)

9. (L.O. 3) Gatorland recorded bad debt expense of $30,000 and wrote off accounts receivable of $25,000 during 2014. The net effect of these two transactions on net income was a decrease of:
a. $55,000.
b. $30,000.
c. $25,000.
d. $5,000.

Approach and Explanation: Reconstruct both entries referred to in the question. Then analyze each debit and each credit separately as to its effect on net income.

			Effect on Net Income
Bad Debt Expense	30,000		Decrease $30,000
Allowance for Doubtful Accounts		30,000	No Effect
Allowance for Doubtful Accounts	25,000		No Effect
Accounts Receivable		25,000	No Effect
Net effect of entries			Decrease $30,000

(Solution = b.)

10. (L.O. 3) Chelser Corporation performed an analysis and an aging of its accounts receivable at December 31, 2014 which disclosed the following:

Accounts receivable balance	$100,000
Allowance for doubtful accounts balance	5,000
Accounts deemed uncollectible	7,400

The cash (net) realizable value of the accounts receivable at December 31 is:
a. $87,600.
b. $92,600.
c. $95,000.
d. $97,600.

Approach and Explanation: Read the last sentence of the question. "The cash (net) realizable value of the accounts receivable at December 31 is." Underline cash (net) realizable value of accounts receivable. Write down the definition of cash (net) realizable value of accounts receivable—amount of accounts receivable ultimately expected to be converted into cash. Read the details of the question. If an aging shows $7,400 of the $100,000 accounts receivable are deemed uncollectible, then the remaining $92,600 are expected to be converted into cash. (Because the balance of the allowance account does not agree with the amount of uncollectibles per the aging, the allowance for doubtful accounts balance must be the unadjusted balance or the percentage of sales method is being used to determine the amount to record as bad debt expense.) (Solution = b.)

11. (L.O. 5) The term "maker" as it applies to a promissory note refers to the:
a. payee.
b. lender.
c. borrower.
d. seller.

Approach and Explanation: Think about the terminology related to a promissory note:
Face value or face amount: Denomination of note. Principal.
Maker or borrower: Entity promising to pay face amount plus interest.
Payee: Entity to receive face value plus interest.
(Solution = c.)

12. (L.O. 5) A note receivable with a face value of $20,000 was received from a customer. The note was dated April 1, 2014 and becomes due on April 1, 2015. Interest of 12% is payable at the maturity date. The income statement for the calendar year of 2014 should report interest income (or interest revenue) for this note of:

a. $0.
b. $600.
c. $1,800.
d. $2,400.

Approach and Explanation: Write down the formula for the computation of interest. Fill in the amounts known and solve for the unknown.

$$\text{Face Value X Rate X Time} = \text{Interest}$$
$$\$20,000 \ X \ 12\% \ X \ 9/12 = \$1,800$$

Interest would be accrued for the time between April 1, 2013 and December 31, 2014, which is nine months. (Solution = c.)

13. (L.O. 6) The journal entry to adjust for the accrued interest on a note receivable involves:

a. a debit to Interest Revenue and a credit to Notes Receivable.
b. a debit to Interest Receivable and a credit to Notes Receivable.
c. a debit to Interest Receivable and a credit to Interest Revenue.
d. a debit to Interest Expense and a credit to Interest Payable.

Approach and Explanation: Recall that an accrued revenue is revenue that has been earned but not received. The adjusting entry to record an accrued revenue will increase revenue (record earned revenue) and increase a receivable (record the fact that the earned revenue has not been received.) Therefore, debit a receivable account and credit a revenue account. (Solution = c.)

14. (L.O. 8) If a maker of a note fails to pay the amount due on the due date, the note is said to be:

a. uncollectible.
b. discounted.
c. dishonored.
d. due on demand.

Explanation: A note is said to be honored when it is paid in full at the maturity date. A dishonored note is a note that is not paid in full at maturity. (Solution = c.)

15. (L.O. 8) A note receivable with a face value of $10,000 was received from a customer in connection with a sale of merchandise on October 1, 2014. The note has a stated interest rate of 12% and the principal and interest are both due on October 1, 2015. An appropriate adjusting entry was made on December 31, 2014, the end of the annual accounting period. No reversing entry was recorded on January 1, 2015. The journal entry to record the collection of the principal plus interest on October 1, 2015 will involve a credit to:
   a. Notes Receivable for $11,200.
   b. Interest Revenue for $1,200.
   c. Interest Revenue for $900.
   d. Cash for $11,200.

   Approach and Explanation: Prepare the journal entry to record the collection of the principal plus interest on October 1, 2015. That entry is as follows:

Cash	11,200	
Notes Receivable		10,000
Interest Receivable..		300
Interest Revenue		900

   $10,000 X 12% X 3/12 = $300 interest accrued at December 31, 2014:
   $10,000 X 12% X 9/12 = $900 interest earned in 2012.
   $10,000 + ($10,000 X 12%) = $11,200 total cash collected.
   (Solution = c.)

TIP:	If a reversing entry had been made on January 1, 2015, to reverse the prior period's accrual, the entry on October 1, 2015, would include a credit to Interest Revenue for $1,200 and no credit to Interest Receivable.

16. (L.O. 9) When the multiple-step format is used by Petite Clothiers Company for the income statement, bad debt expense (arising from sales to customers using the Petite Clothiers credit card) and service charge expense (arising from sales to customers using the VISA credit card) are to be:
   a. included with cost of goods sold.
   b. reported as selling expenses.
   c. reported as contra sales revenue items.
   d. reported as "other expenses" in the nonoperating section.

   Explanation: Bad debt expense and service charge expense are to be classified as selling expenses; the "selling expenses" classification is a subsclassification of operating expenses. Thus, bad debt expense and service charge expense are **not** included with cost of goods sold expense or with nonoperating expenses and losses. (Solution = b.)

17. (L.O. 9) Zollo Corporation's net accounts receivable were $500,000 at December 31, 2013 and $600,000 at December 31, 2014. The accounts receivable turnover was 5.0 for 2014 and net cash sales for 2014 were $200,000. Zollo's total net sales for 2014 were:
  a. $2,950,000.
  b. $3,000,000.
  c. $3,200,000.
  d. $5,000,000.

Approach and Explanation: Write down the formula for computing the accounts receivable turnover. Enter the data given and solve for the unknown (net credit sales). Add net cash sales ($200,000) to net credit sales ($2,750,000) to obtain total net sales ($2,950,000). The formula for the accounts receivable turnover ratio is:

$$\frac{\text{Net credit sales}}{\text{Average accounts receivable}} = \frac{X}{1/2(\$500,000 + \$600,000)} = 5.0$$

$$\frac{X}{\$550,000} = 5.0 \qquad X = \$2,750,000$$

(Solution = a.)

CHAPTER 9

· ·

*P*LANT ASSETS, NATURAL RESOURCES, AND INTANGIBLE ASSETS

OVERVIEW

Assets that have physical existence and that are expected to be used in revenue-generating operations for more than one year or operating cycle, whichever is longer, are classified as plant assets. Some problems may arise in determining the acquisition cost of a plant asset. For example, the initial acquisition may be the result of several expenditures or additional expenditures may be involved subsequent to acquisition.

Expenses arise from the cost of goods or services that are consumed in the process of generating revenue. When a long-term tangible asset (plant asset) is acquired, it actually represents a bundle of future asset services. The total cost of these services equals the acquisition cost of the asset minus the asset's expected market value at the end of its useful life. As a productive asset is used, services (benefits) are consumed; therefore, a portion of the original asset cost should be charged to expense, in order to comply with the expense recognition (matching) principle. The process of allocating (expensing) the cost of long-term tangible assets over the accounting periods during which the asset is used is called depreciation.

An entity commonly disposes of plant assets before or at the end of their estimated service lives. The disposal may be by retirement, sale or exchange. The asset's fair value will usually differ from its book value at the date of disposal, and this difference usually results in recognizing a gain or loss on disposal.

Companies which extract natural resources from the earth must account for the acquisition cost of the wasting assets and determine the cost of units extracted and sold during the period.

Intangible means "lack of physical substance." The balance sheet classification for intangible assets is used to report assets which lack physical existence and are not properly classifiable elsewhere. For instance (1) bank deposits and accounts receivable both are intangible by a legal definition but they are properly classifiable as current assets for accounting purposes, and (2) investment in stock is intangible in nature but should be classified as either a current asset or a long-term investment for accounting purposes. Assets such as patents, trademarks, copyrights, franchises, licenses, and goodwill are intangible in nature and are classified in the intangible asset section of a balance sheet.

The subjects mentioned above along with other issues involved in accounting for plant assets, natural resources, and intangible assets are discussed in this chapter.

SUMMARY OF LEARNING OBJECTIVES

1.   **Describe how the cost principle applies to plant assets.** The cost of a plant asset includes all expenditures necessary to acquire the asset and make it ready for its intended use. Cost is measured by the cash or cash equivalent price paid.

2.   **Explain the concept of depreciation and how to compute it. Depreciation** is the allocation of the cost of a plant asset to expense over its limited useful (service) life in a rational and systematic manner. Depreciation is **not** a process of valuation, nor is it a process that results in an accumulation of cash.

    Three depreciation methods are:

Method	Effect on Annual Depreciation	Formula
Straight-line	Constant amount	Depreciable cost ÷ Useful life (in years)
Units-of-activity	Varying amount	Depreciation cost per unit X Units of activity during the year
Declining-balance	Decreasing amount	Book value at beginning of year X Declining-balance rate

    Companies make revisions of periodic depreciation in present and future periods, not retroactively. When the straight-line depreciation method is used, they determine the new annual depreciation by dividing the depreciable cost at the time of the revision by the remaining useful life.

3.   **Distinguish between revenue and capital expenditures, and explain the entries for each.** Companies incur **revenue expenditures** to maintain the operating efficiency and expected productive life of an asset. They debit these expenditures to Maintenance and Repairs Expense as incurred. **Capital expenditures** add new asset services or increase the operating efficiency, productive capacity, or expected useful life of the asset. Companies generally debit these expenditures to the plant asset affected.

4.   **Explain how to account for the disposal of a plant asset.** The accounting for disposal of a plant asset through retirement or sale is as follows:
    (a)   Eliminate the book value of the plant asset at the date of disposal.
    (b)   Record cash proceeds, if any.
    (c)   Account for the difference between the book value and the cash proceeds as a gain or loss on disposal.

5.   **Compute periodic depletion of natural resources.** Companies compute depletion cost per unit by dividing the total cost of the natural resources minus salvage value by the number of units estimated to be in the tract of natural resources. They then multiply the depletion cost per unit by the number of units extracted and sold.

6.   **Explain the basic issues related to accounting for intangible assets.** The process of allocating the cost of an intangible asset to expense is referred to as **amortization.** The cost of an intangible asset with an indefinite service life is not amortized. Companies normally use the straight-line method for amortizing intangible assets.

7.   **Indicate how plant assets, natural resources, and intangible assets are reported.** Companies usually combine plant assets and natural resources under the property, plant, and equipment classification; they show intangibles separately under intangible assets. Either within the balance sheet or in the notes, companies should disclose: (1) the balances of the major classes of assets, such as land, buildings, and equipment, and (2) accumulated depreciation by major classes or in total. They should also describe the depreciation and amortization methods used and the amount of depreciation and amortization expense for the period. The asset turnover ratio measures the productivity of a company's assets in generating sales.

*8.   **Explain how to account for the exchange of plant assets.** Ordinarily companies record a gain or loss on the exchange of plant assets. The rationale for recognizing a gain or loss is that most exchanges have commercial substance. An exchange has commercial substance if the future cash flows change significantly as a result of the exchange.

*This material appears in **Appendix to Chapter 9A** in the text.

TIPS ON CHAPTER TOPICS

TIP:	**Plant assets** is a balance sheet classification that is often referred to as **fixed assets** or **property, plant and equipment.** Included in this section should be long-lived tangible assets that are currently being used in operations (to generate goods and services for customers). Examples include land, buildings, and equipment.
TIP:	In determining the cost of a plant asset, keep in mind the same guideline we used for inventory: the asset's **cost** includes all costs necessary to get the item to the condition and location for its intended use.
TIP:	In determining the cost of a plant asset, keep in mind the cost principle. **Cost** of an asset is measured by the cash paid or the cash equivalent price paid. Thus, the recorded cost of an asset is determined by the fair market value of the asset(s) or other consideration given or by the fair market value of the asset(s) or other consideration received, whichever is the more objectively determinable. Fair market value refers to cash equivalent value. When cash is given to acquire an asset, it is a relatively simple matter to determine the asset's cost. However, when a noncash asset is given in exchange, more thought is required to determine the newly acquired asset's cost.
TIP:	The cost of tearing down an old building should be charged (debited) to the Land account if the building was someone else's old building and was acquired along with a parcel of land in a case where the land was intended to be used as a site for another structure. This cost is charged to Land because it was necessary to get the land in the condition for its intended purpose—to provide space upon which to erect a new building. (Any proceeds from material salvaged in the removal is considered to be a recovery of land cost.) The cost of tearing down an old building is **never** charged to the Building account.
TIP:	In the context of accounting for property, plant, and equipment, the term **"to capitalize"** means to record and carryforward into one or more periods expenditures from which benefits or proceeds will be realized; thus, a balance sheet account is debited for capital expenditures.
TIP:	**Salvage value** is often referred to as **residual value,** and sometimes it is called **estimated scrap value.**
TIP:	Salvage value is used in the computation of depreciation for each year of life of an asset whenever the straight-line method or the units-of-activity method is used. Salvage value is **not** a factor in determining depreciation for the early years of life if a declining-balance method is used; however, salvage value can affect the amount computed for depreciation in the last year(s) of an asset's life because an asset should **not** be depreciated below its salvage value.
TIP:	Most plant assets have a limited service (useful) life because the asset will lose its utility or usefulness over time due to wear and tear and/or obsolescence. Land does not lose its utility; thus, it has an unlimited life and is **not** depreciated.

TIP: The **units-of-activity method** is often called the **units-of-output method** or the **units-of-production method.**

TIP: The **book value** of a plant asset is determined by deducting the balance of accumulated depreciation from the balance of the related asset account. The balance in the related asset account is generally the asset's original cost. Thus, the estimated salvage value does not directly affect the book value computation. Book value for a plant asset is often called **carrying value** or **carrying amount** or **undepreciated cost.** An asset's book value at a given date may be far different than its market value at the same date.

TIP: Depreciable cost or depreciation base is a term that refers to the total amount to be depreciated over the useful life of the asset. It is determined by deducting the estimated salvage value from the cost of the asset.

TIP: The **declining-balance depreciation method** applies a constant rate to a declining book value to calculate depreciation. The rate used is often twice the straight-line rate in which case the method is then referred to as the **200% declining-balance method** or the **double-declining-balance method.** Sometimes the rate is one and one-half times the straight-line rate in which case the method is called the **150% declining-balance method.**

TIP: For each class of depreciable plant assets, an entity must select the most appropriate depreciation method. The same method should then be used for subsequent periods of financial reporting purposes in order to comply with the **consistency concept.** However, a different method may be used for the same assets for tax purposes.

TIP: The annual rate of depreciation using the straight-line method can be determined by dividing 100% of the estimated service life. For example, an asset with a 5 year life will be depreciated 20% (100% ÷ 5 = 20%) per year.

TIP: If a company uses the straight-line method of depreciation, a rough estimate of the **average life** of the company's plant assets can be made by dividing the cost of property, plant, and equipment by the current period's depreciation expense. Likewise, a rough estimate of the **average age** of the plant assets can be determined by dividing accumulated depreciation by depreciation expense. This analysis is usually performed by asset class; that is, a separate computation is made for each type of plant assets.

TIP: When a plant asset is retired from service or sold, it must be removed from the accounts; hence, the appropriate asset account is credited for the amount of the asset's original cost, and the related accumulated depreciation account is debited for the total depreciation recorded on that asset to date. Cash is debited for the amount of net proceeds, if any, from the disposal. An excess of book value over cash proceeds is recorded by a debit to a loss account; an excess of cash proceeds over book value is recorded by a credit to a gain account.

TIP: Depreciation must be updated before an asset disposal can be properly recorded. Additional depreciation recorded in such an update impacts the determination of the amount of gain or loss experienced on disposal.

TIP: Most plant assets have a limited service life. A limited service life (and the resulting depreciation) is caused by wear and tear or by obsolescence.

TIP: A gain on disposal of plant assets is reported in the Other Revenues and Gains section of the income statement. A loss on disposal of plant assets is reported in the Other Expenses and Losses section of the income statement.

TIP: **Fair market value** is a term that refers to an item's current value; the price at which a seller who is willing to sell at a fair price and a buyer who is willing to buy at a fair price will trade, assuming both parties have knowledge of the facts and bargain in his or her own self-interest. The terms **market value** or **fair value** are often used to indicate fair market value.

TIP: The cost of an intangible asset should be allocated to expense over its useful life, assuming the useful life is limited. If the life of the intangible is indefinite, the cost of the intangible should **not** be amortized until its life is determined to be limited. At that time, the intangible asset should be amortized.

TIP: Trademarks, trade names, and copyrights have indefinite lives; therefore, they are not amortized. Goodwill is **not** amortized. Patents are amortized over their useful lives.

TIP: **Natural resources** are often called **wasting assets.** They include tracts of resources still attached to the earth, such as oil in an oil well, minerals in a mine, and trees in a forest.

TIP: Research and development (R & D) costs are to be expensed in the period incurred. The Financial Accounting Standards Board established this guideline after a study revealed that very few R & D projects ever culminate in a successfully marketed product. When great uncertainty exists, the **concept of conservatism** dictates that we choose the alternative with the least favorable effect on net income and on assets.

TIP: The rate of turnover of assets may be used in analyzing the productivity of a company's assets. The **asset turnover ratio** is computed by dividing net sales by average total assets; it gauges how efficiently a company uses its assets to generate sales. If the asset turnover ratio is 5, it means that for the period in question, there was $5 of sales generated by each $1 invested in assets.

ILLUSTRATION 9-1
CAPITAL EXPENDITURES VS. REVENUE EXPENDITURES (L.O. 3)

The terms, capital expenditure and revenue expenditure, are used in the context of accounting for property, plant, and equipment. A **capital expenditure** is one which is expected to benefit two or more accounting periods. A **revenue expenditure** is one whose benefits are not expected to extend beyond the current period. Thus a revenue expenditure benefits only the current period or no period at all.

Capital expenditures are recorded by increasing an asset account (or by decreasing the balance of the Accumulated Depreciation account). If an asset is of limited life, its cost is depreciated (expensed) over the periods which will be benefited (to comply with the matching principle). Because a revenue expenditure does not yield benefits beyond the current period, it is recorded as an expense in the period it is made.

The distinction between capital and revenue expenditures is of significance because it involves the timing of the recognition of expense and, consequently, the determination of periodic net income. This distinction also affects the costs reflected in asset accounts which will be recovered from future periods' revenues.

Examples of capital expenditures include the acquisition of land, building and/or equipment. Examples of revenue expenditures include outlays for maintenance and repair services.

The **acquisition cost for a plant asset** includes all costs necessary to acquire the item and get it in the location and condition for its intended use.

The **acquisition cost of land** may include costs such as:
  (1) purchase price.
  (2) survey fees.
  (3) attorney fees and escrow fees.
  (4) delinquent property taxes and interest assumed by buyer.
  (5) real estate broker's commission.
  (6) title search fees and recording fees.
  (7) cost of clearing, grading, landscaping and subdividing (less salvage).
  (8) cost of removing old building (less salvage).
  (9) landscaping of a permanent nature.

TIP: Typically, the cost of land includes the cost of elements that occur prior to excavation for a new building. Costs related to the foundation of the building are elements of building cost.

The **acquisition cost of a building** may include costs such as:
  (1) construction costs.
  (2) excavation fees.
  (3) architectural fees and building permit fees.
  (4) cost of insurance during construction (if paid by property owner).
  (5) property taxes and interest during construction.
  (6) cost of temporary buildings.

The **acquisition cost of equipment** may include costs such as:
  (1) purchase price (less discounts allowed).
  (2) sales tax.
  (3) freight charges and installation charges.
  (4) insurance during transit.
  (5) cost of labor and materials for test runs (breaking-in costs).
  (6) cost of special platforms.

An expenditure that relates to property, plant, and equipment already in use (often called an **expenditure subsequent to acquisition**) should be capitalized (recorded by a debit to a balance sheet account rather than an income statement account) if the expenditure is:
(1) Material in nature and
(2) Nonrecurring in nature and
(3) Of benefit to future periods by doing one of the following:
  a. Extending the useful life of an existing plant asset.
  b. Enhancing the quality of existing services or increasing the productive capacity of an existing asset.
  c. Adding new asset services.
  d. Reducing the operating costs of existing assets thereby increasing operating efficiency.

Examples of expenditures subsequent to acquisition that should be capitalized are additions, improvements, and betterments. These expenditures should be charged to an asset account unless they extend the life of an existing asset (in which case they should debited to Accumulated Depreciation).

EXERCISE 9-1

Purpose: (L.O. 1, 3) This exercise will help you identify which expenditures should be capitalized (debited to a balance sheet account) and which should be expensed (charged to an income statement account).

TIP:	Remember that expenditures which benefit the company for more than the current accounting period should be capitalized in order to properly match expenses with revenues over successive accounting periods. Expenditures for items that do **not** yield benefits beyond the current accounting period should be expensed.

Instructions
Assume all amounts are material (significant). For each of the following independent items, indicate by use of the appropriate letter if it should be:

C for Capitalized

or

E for Expensed

_____   1.   Invoice price of drill press.

_____   2.   Sales tax on computer.

_____   3.   Costs of permanent partitions constructed in office building.

_____   4.   Installation charges for new conveyer system.

_____   5.   Costs of trees and shrubs planted in front of office building.

_____   6.   Cost of surveying new land site to determine property boundaries.

_____   7.   Costs of major overhaul of delivery truck which extends the life of the truck.

_____   8.   Costs of constructing new counters for show room.

_____   9.   Costs of powders, soaps, and wax for office floors.

_____   10.   Cost of janitorial services for office and show room.

_____   11.   Costs of carpets in a new office building.

_____   12.   Costs of annual termite inspection of warehouse.

_____   13.   Insurance charged for new equipment while in transit.

_____ 14. Property taxes on land used for parking lot.

_____ 15. Cost of a fan installed to help cool an old factory machine.

_____ 16. Cost of exterminator's services.

_____ 17. Costs of major redecorating of executive's offices.

_____ 18. Cost of fertilizers for shrubs and trees.

_____ 19. Cost of labor services for self-constructed machine.

_____ 20. Costs of materials used and labor services expended during trial runs of new machine.

SOLUTION TO EXERCISE 9-1

1.	C	6.	C	11.	C	16.	E
2.	C	7.	C	12.	E	17.	C
3.	C	8.	C	13.	C	18.	E*
4.	C	9.	E*	14.	E	19.	C
5.	C	10.	E	15.	C	20.	C

*This answer assumes the products were consumed during the current period. Material (significant) amounts of unused supplies on hand at the balance sheet date should be reported as a prepaid expense on the balance sheet.

Approach: Refer to **Illustration 9-1** for a discussion of capital expenditures versus revenue expenditures.

EXERCISE 9-2

Purpose: (L.O. 1, 3) This exercise will give you practice in identifying capital expenditures and revenue expenditures.

Sellen Supply Company, a newly formed corporation, incurred the following expenditures related to Land, Buildings, and Equipment.

Abstract company's fee for title search		$ 520
Architect's fees		10,200
Cash paid for land and dilapidated building thereon		100,000
Removal of old building	$20,000	
Less salvage	5,500	14,500
Surveying before construction		370
Excavation before construction for basement		19,000
Machinery purchased		55,000
Freight on machinery purchased		1,340
New building constructed		500,000
Assessment by city for drainage project		1,600
Installation of machinery		2,000
Trees, shrubs, and other landscaping after completion of building		
(permanent in nature)		5,400

Instructions
(a)   Identify the amounts that should be debited to Land.
(b)   Identify the amounts that should be debited to Buildings.
(c)   Identify the amounts that should be debited to Equipment.

SOLUTION TO EXERCISE 9-2

	(a) Land	(b) Buildings	(c) Equipment
Abstract fees	$ 520		
Architect's fees		$ 10,200	
Cash paid for land and old building	100,000		
Removal of old building ($20,000 - $5,500)	14,500		
Surveying before construction		370	
Excavation before construction		19,000	
Machinery purchased			$55,000
Freight on machinery			1,340
New building		500,000	
Assessment by city	1,600		
Installation—machinery			2,000
Landscaping	5,400		
Totals	$122,020	$529,570	$58,340

Approach: Refer to **Illustration 9-1** and review the common cost elements for land, building, and equipment.

EXERCISE 9-3

Purpose: (L.O. 2) This exercise will allow you to practice using various depreciation methods and it will also give you the opportunity to compare the results of using one method to the results of using another method.

On January 1, 2014, Kinka Company, a manufacturer, acquires for $230,000 a piece of new equipment. The new equipment has a useful life of five years and the salvage value is estimated to be $30,000. Kinka estimates that the new equipment can produce a total of 80,000 units. Kinka expects it to produce 20,000 units in its first year, 18,000 units in its second year, 32,000 units in its third year, and 5,000 units each in its last two years.

The following depreciation methods are being considered:
- Straight-line
- Declining-balance using double the straight-line rate
- Units-of-activity

Instructions
(a) Prepare depreciation schedules for the equipment using the following methods:
   (1) straight-line
   (2) double-declining-balance
   (3) units-of-activity
   Each schedule should display the annual depreciation expense for each year of service life and the resulting amounts of accumulated depreciation and book value. Round to the nearest dollar.

(b) Identify the depreciation method which would result in the maximization of profits for financial reporting for the three-year period ending December 31, 2016. Explain why.

(c) Identify the depreciation method which would result in the highest book value at the end of the third year of service life.

(d) Identify the depreciation method which would result in the lowest book value at the end of the third year of service life.

SOLUTION TO EXERCISE 9-3

(a)   (1)

KINKA COMPANY
Depreciation Schedule Using Straight-Line Method

	Computation				End of Year	
				Annual		
	Depreciable	**X**	**Depreciation**	**= Depreciation**	**Accumulated**	**Book**
Year	**Cost[a]**		**Rate[b]**	**Expense**	**Depreciation[c]**	**Value[d]**
2014	$200,000		20%	$ 40,000	$ 40,000	$190,000
2015	200,000		20%	40,000	80,000	150,000
2016	200,000		20%	40,000	120,000	110,000
2017	200,000		20%	40,000	160,000	70,000
2018	200,000		20%	40,000	200,000	30,000
				$200,000		

[a]Depreciable cost is original cost ($230,000) less estimated salvage ($30,000).
[b]Depreciation rate (straight-line) equals 100% divided by the estimated service life (5 years).
[c]Accumulated depreciation is the total depreciation expense reported to date. Thus, the accumulated depreciation at the end of the first year is equal to the depreciation expense for that first year. The accumulated depreciation at the end of the second year is equal to the total of the depreciation expense figures for the first and second years.
[d]Book value is determined by the original cost less the depreciation taken to date (accumulated depreciation). Thus, book value at the end of the first year is $230,000 - $40,000 = $190,000. Book value at the end of 2018 is $230,000 - $200,000 = $30,000 (the $30,000 is the estimated salvage value).

(2)

KINKA COMPANY
Depreciation Schedule Using Double-Declining-Balance Method

	Computation				End of Year	
	Book Value			**Annual**		
	Beginning	**X**	**Depreciation**	**= Depreciation**	**Accumulated**	**Book**
Year	**of Year[a]**		**Rate[b]**	**Expense**	**Depreciation**	**Value**
2014	$230,000		40%	$ 92,000	$ 92,000	$138,000
2015	138,000		40%	55,200	147,200	82,800
2016	82,800		40%	33,120	180,320	49,680
2017	49,680		40%	19,680[c]	200,000	30,000
2018	30,000			-0- [c]	200,000	30,000
				$200,000		

[a]Book value is original cost less accumulated depreciation. The book value of the asset at the beginning of the asset's first year is the asset's acquisition cost.
[b]The depreciation rate is a multiple of the straight-line rate. The straight-line rate is 100% divided by the 5-year service life which is 20%. The depreciation rate for the double declining-balance method is twice the straight-line rate. 2 X 20% = 40%.
[c]An asset is not to be depreciated below its residual value.

> **TIP:** An asset is not depreciated below its residual (salvage) value. Because of the relatively high salvage value in this case, use of the double-declining-balance method resulted in reaching a book value equal to the residual value by the end of the fourth year of service. Because it makes good accounting sense to match some cost with every year of service, it is a common practice (in cases such as this) to use the double-declining-balance method to the mid-point in the asset's life (through 2016 in this case) and then spread the remaining depreciable cost equally (straight-line) over the remaining useful life. This procedure applied to the asset in question would result in depreciation of $9,840 for 2017 and $9,840 for year 2018.

(3)

KINKA COMPANY
Depreciation Schedule Using Units-of-Activity Method

	Computation			End of Year	
Year	Units of Activity	X	Depreciation Cost Per Unit[a] =	Annual Depreciation Expense	Accumulated Depreciation	Book Value
2014	20,000		$2.50	$ 50,000	$ 50,000	$180,000
2015	18,000		2.50	45,000	95,000	135,000
2016	32,000		2.50	80,000	175,000	55,000
2017	5,000		2.50	12,500	187,500	42,500
2018	5,000		2.50	12,500	200,000	30,000
	80,000			$200,000		

[a]Depreciation per unit = Depreciable cost of $200,000 (cost of $230,000 less salvage of $30,000) divided by the 80,000 total estimated units to be produced during the total service life of the asset.

> **TIP:** Notice that none of the depreciation methods depreciate the asset below the amount recoverable through sale of the asset at the end of the asset's estimated economic service life. That recoverable amount is called **salvage value** or **residual value.**

(b) The **straight-line method** will report the most net income for the three years (2014-2016) combined because the straight-line method results in the lowest amount of accumulated depreciation at the end of 2016. Total depreciation expense for the three year period is summarized as follows:

Straight-line method	$120,000
Double-declining-balance method	180,320
Units-of-activity method	175,000

(c) The **straight-line method** will result in reporting the highest book value at the end of 2016 because it is the method that yields the lowest total depreciation expense over the first three years of the asset's life.

(d) The **double-declining-balance method** will result in the lowest book value at the end of 2016 because it is the method that yields the greatest total depreciation expense over the first three years of the asset's life.

EXERCISE 9-4

Purpose: (L.O. 2) This exercise will provide an illustration of the computations for depreciation of partial periods using two common methods.

Scanlan Company purchased a new plant asset on April 1, 2014, at a cost of $690,000. It was estimated to have a service life of 20 years and a salvage value of $60,000. Scanlan's accounting period is the calendar year.

Instructions
(a) Compute the amount of depreciation for this asset for 2014 and 2015 using the straight-line method.
(b) Compute the amount of depreciation for this asset for 2014 and 2015 using the double-declining-balance method.
(c) Briefly define depreciation as the term is used in accounting.

SOLUTION TO EXERCISE 9-4

(a) $\dfrac{\$690,000 - \$60,000}{20 \text{ years}} \times \dfrac{9}{12} = \underline{\$23,625}$ depreciation for 2014

$\dfrac{\$690,000 - \$60,000}{20 \text{ years}} = \underline{\$31,500}$ depreciation for 2015

(b) Straight - line rate $= \dfrac{100\%}{20} = 5\%$; 5% X 2 = 10% double the straight-line rate.

$690,000 X 10% X 9/12 = \underline{\$51,750}$ depreciation for 2014

($690,000 - $51,750) X 10% = $\underline{\$63,825}$ depreciation for 2015

(c) Depreciation is the accounting process of allocating an asset's historical cost (recorded amount) to the accounting periods benefited by the use of the asset. It is a process of cost allocation, **not** valuation. Depreciation is **not** intended to provide funds for an asset's replacement; it is merely an application of the matching principle.

Approach and Explanation:

(a) Write down and apply the formula for straight-line depreciation. Then multiply the annual depreciation amount by the portion of the asset's year of service that falls in the given accounting period.

$$\frac{\text{Cost - Salvage Value}}{\text{Estimated Service Life}} = \text{Depreciation Expense for Full Asset Year}$$

Only nine months of the first asset year falls in 2014 so the fraction 9/12 (or 3/4) must be applied to the annual depreciation amount calculated to arrive at the depreciation expense for the income statement for 2014.

(b) Write down and apply the formula for the declining-balance method.

Book Value
at Beginning X Constant Percentage = Depreciation for Asset Year
of Asset Year

Only nine months of the first asset year falls in 2014 so the fraction of 3/4 must be applied to the annual depreciation amount calculated to arrive at the depreciation for the income statement for 2014.

After the first partial year, depreciation can be calculated for a full **accounting year** by multiplying the constant percentage by the **book value of the asset at the beginning of the accounting period.** Thus, the computation for 2015 for this asset is as follows: ($690,000 - $51,750) X 10% = $63,825.

EXERCISE 9-5

Purpose: (L.O. 2, 3) This exercise will provide you with an illustration of how to handle a change in the estimated service life and salvage value of a plant asset due to an expenditure subsequent to acquisition.

The Royal Company purchased a machine at the very end of 2001 for $210,000. The machine was being depreciated using the straight-line method over an estimated life of 20 years, with a $30,000 salvage value. At the beginning of 2012, the company paid $50,000 to overhaul the machine. As a result of this improvement, the company estimated that the useful life of the machine would be extended an additional 5 years, and the salvage value would be reduced to $20,000.

Instructions
Compute the depreciation charge for 2012.

SOLUTION TO EXERCISE 9-5

Approach: Whenever you have a situation that involves a change in the estimated service life and/or salvage value of a depreciable asset, use the format shown below to compute the remaining depreciable cost and allocate that amount over the remaining useful life using the given depreciation method.

Cost	$210,000
Accumulated depreciation	(90,000)[a]
Book value (before overhaul)	120,000
Additional expenditure capitalized[c] (if any)	50,000
Revised book value (after overhaul)	170,000
Current estimate of salvage	(20,000)
Remaining depreciable cost	150,000
Remaining years of useful life at 1/1/12	÷ 15[b]
Depreciation expense for 2012	$ 10,000

[a]Cost	$210,000
Original estimate of salvage	(30,000)
Original depreciable cost	180,000
Original service life in years	÷ 20
Original depreciation per year	9,000
Number of years used	X 10
Accumulated depreciation at 1/1/12	$ 90,000

[b]Original estimate of life in years	20
Number of years used	(10)
Additional years	5
Remaining years of useful life at 1/1/12	15

[c]The term capitalized refers to being recorded by a debit to a balance sheet account—Accumulated Depreciation in this case.

TIP:	**A change in the estimated useful life and/or salvage value** of an existing depreciable asset is to be accounted for prospectively; that is, there is no correction of previously recorded depreciation expense. Therefore, the book value at the beginning of the period of change, less the current estimate of salvage, is to be allocated over the remaining periods of life using the appropriate depreciation method. The book value at the beginning of the period of change is calculated using the original estimates of service life and salvage value. Using the straight-line method, the new annual depreciation is determined by dividing the remaining depreciable cost by the remaining useful life.
TIP:	The $50,000 cost of overhaul is capitalized in this case because the cost benefits the future periods by extending the useful life of the machine.

TIP:	Be careful when computing the length of time between two dates. The length of time between the **end** of 2001 and the **beginning** of 2012 is 10 years; whereas, the length of time between the **beginning** of 2001 and the **beginning** of 2012 is 11 years and the length of time between the **beginning** of 2001 and the **end** of 2012 is 12 years. It is a common mistake to deduct one year from the other (2012 - 2001 = 11 years). As you can see from the foregoing, that will not always work. It is wise to write down the years that fall between the two dates and then count those years on your list. For example, the length of time between the **end** of 2008 and the **beginning** of 2012 is three years and is determined as follows:

	2009	1
	2010	2
	2011	3

EXERCISE 9-6

Purpose: (L.O. 4) This exercise will help you to understand how the sale of a plant asset compares with the sale of inventory.

Houston Merchandising Company sold two items. The following facts pertain:

	Item 1	**Item 2**
Sales price	$10,000	$10,000
Cost/book value	5,200	5,200
Sales commission	400	400

Item 1 is an inventory item. Item 2 is a plant asset.

Instructions
Explain the manner of reporting each item on a multiple-step income statement.

SOLUTION TO EXERCISE 9-6

Item 1: Sale of an inventory item:
The sale of inventory is Houston's main line of business. The $10,000 sales price is included in sales revenue on the income statement. The cost, $5,200, is included in cost of goods sold. Therefore, this transaction causes $4,800 to be reflected in the gross profit figure for the period. The $400 commission is reported as a selling expense (operating expense) on the income statement. The net impact is a $4,400 increase in the net income amount for the period.

Item 2: Sale of a plant asset:
The sale of a plant asset is incidental to the main focus of Houston's business (to sell goods to customers). Therefore, the $10,000 sales price, $5,200 book value, and $400 commission are all netted off of the income statement; one line item, a gain of $4,400, is reported in the Other Revenues and Gains section of the income statement.

TIP:	Notice both transactions have the same net impact on net income.

EXERCISE 9-7

Purpose: (L.O. 4) This exercise will (1) illustrate several different ways in which you may dispose of property, and (2) discuss the appropriate accounting procedures for each.

Presented below is a schedule of property dispositions for Barbara Steiner Co. during 2014:

SCHEDULE OF PROPERTY DISPOSITIONS

	Cost	Accumulated Depreciation at 12/31/13	Cash Proceeds	Fair Market Value	Nature of Disposition
Furniture	$10,000	$ 8,800	--	--	Abandonment
Automobile	8,000	3,500	3,100	3,100	Sale
Land	40,000	--	92,000	100,000	Sale

The following additional information is available:

Furniture. On January 1, 2014, furniture was tossed out in the dumpster because it was no longer adequate to serve the company's needs. It cost $10,000 when it was acquired. Depreciation of $8,800 was taken in prior years.

Automobile. On January 2, 2014, an automobile was sold for $3,100 cash. It had a cost of $8,000, and total depreciation recorded prior to the sale date amounted to $3,500.

Land. On February 15, 2014, land previously used in operations was subdivided and a section was sold for $100,000. A commission of $8,000 went to a real estate agent. The original cost of that land segment was $40,000.

Instructions
Prepare the appropriate journal entry for each of the dispositions. Show computations where appropriate.

TIP: The **disposal of property, plant, and equipment** should be accounted for as follows:
(1) The book (carrying) value at the date of the disposal (cost of the property, plant, and equipment less the accumulated depreciation) should be removed from the accounts.
(2) The cash (or other assets), if any, recovered should be recorded.
(3) The difference between (1) and (2) should be recorded:
    (a) An excess of cash (or other dissimilar assets) over the book value removed is accounted for as a gain on the disposal.
    (b) An excess of book value removed over the cash (or other assets) from the disposal is accounted for as a loss on the disposal.

SOLUTION TO EXERCISE 9-7

Jan.	1	Loss on Disposal of Plant Assets	1,200	
		Accumulated Depreciation...	8,800	
		Furniture		10,000
		(To record abandonment of furniture)		
Jan.	2	Cash	3,100	
		Accumulated Depreciation...	3,500	
		Loss on Disposal of Plant Assets	1,400	
		Automobile..		8,000
		(To record the sale of an automobile at a loss)		
Feb.	15	Cash	92,000	
		Land...		40,000
		Gain on Disposal of Plant Assets		52,000[a]
		(To record sale of land at a gain)		

[a]Sales price of land	$100,000
Commission	(8,000)
Net proceeds	92,000
Book value of land	(40,000)
Gain on sale	$ 52,000

Explanations:

Furniture. There is no salvage (residual) value; hence, the book value ($1,200) is written off as a loss.

Automobile. The book value ($8,000 - $3,500 = $4,500) is removed from the accounts. The cash recovered ($3,100) is recorded. The book value exceeds the cash; therefore, a loss is recorded for the difference.

Land. The book value ($40,000) is removed from the accounts. The net proceeds ($100,000 - $8,000 = $92,000) is recorded. The commission is a cost of the disposal rather than an operating expense; hence, it is a reduction of the gain or increase in the loss on disposal. (In this case, it is a decrease in gain.) The excess of the net proceeds ($92,000) over the book value ($40,000) is recorded as a gain.

EXERCISE 9-8

Purpose: (L.O. 5) This exercise will give you practice in computing depletion.

During 2014, Alston Corporation acquired a mineral mine for $2,000,000 of which $450,000 is attributable to the land value after the mineral has been removed. Alston spent $700,000 to prepare the mine for removal of the minerals. Engineers estimate that 15 million units of mineral can be recovered from this mine. During 2014, 1,200,000 units were extracted and sold.

Instructions
Compute the depletion for 2014.

SOLUTION TO EXERCISE 9-8

$$\frac{\$2,000,000 \ + \ \$700,000 \ - \ \$450,000}{15,000,000} = \$.15 \text{ per unit}$$

$.15 X 1,200,000 = $180,000 Depletion for 2014

Approach and Explanation: Write down the formulas to compute depletion, enter the data given, and solve.

$$\frac{\text{Acquisition Cost + Costs to Explore and Develop - Residual Value of Land}}{\text{Number of Units to be Extracted}} = \text{Depletion Cost Per Recoverable Unit}$$

$$\begin{array}{ccccc} \text{Depletion Cost} & & \text{Units Extracted} & & \text{Depletion} \\ \text{Per Recoverable} & X & \text{During} & = & \text{for the} \\ \text{Unit} & & \text{Period} & & \text{Period} \end{array}$$

TIP: The depletion cost is the amount to be removed from the property, plant, and equipment classification ($180,000 in this case). It is based on the units extracted from the earth during the period. The portion of this $180,000 which appears on the income statement is dependent upon the number of units sold. The depletion costs related to units sold—depletion expense—is classified as part of cost of goods sold expense on the income statement. When the number of units extracted exceed the number sold, a portion of the depletion costs goes into the inventory account on the balance sheet.

EXERCISE 9-9

Purpose: (L.O. 6) This exercise illustrates the steps in estimating the value of goodwill.

Mr. Judski is contemplating the sale of his business, Classic Vettes. The following data are available.

Book value of tangible & identifiable intangible assets less liabilities	$135,000
Fair market value of tangible & identifiable intangible assets less liabilities	200,000
Estimated fair market value of the business as a whole	240,000

Instructions
(a)   Compute the estimated value of goodwill.
(b)   Assume Tom Benyon Enterprises purchases the business for $240,000 cash. Explain how Tom Benyon Enterprises should account for the goodwill at the purchase date and in the future as well as the reasons why.

> **TIP:**   Companies record goodwill **only** when an entire business is purchased (that is, what some people call "internally generated" goodwill cannot be recorded). When an entire business is purchased, **goodwill** is the excess of cost over the fair market value of the net identifiable assets acquired. Net identifiable assets are determined by deducting total liabilities from total identifiable (tangible and intangible) assets.

SOLUTION TO EXERCISE 9-9

(a)   Purchase price (cost) $240,000
         Fair market value of net assets acquired other than goodwill   (200,000)
         Goodwill $ 40,000

(b)   Tom Benyon would record a credit to Cash for $240,000, debits to individual asset accounts for the inventory, plant assets, identifiable intangible assets and other assets acquired for their fair market values, credits to liability accounts (at market value) for any liabilities assumed, and a debit to Goodwill for $40,000.

Goodwill is **not** to be amortized (written off) because it is considered to have an indefinite life, but goodwill must be written down if its value is determined to have declined (been permanently impaired). Goodwill appears on the balance sheet under Intangible Assets.

---

*ILLUSTRATION 9-2
SUMMARY OF REQUIREMENTS FOR RECORDING GAINS AND LOSSES ON EXCHANGES OF PLANT ASSETS (When the Exchange has Commercial Substance) (L.O. 8)

1. Eliminate the book value of the asset given up.

2. Record the cost of the asset acquired. The cost is equal to the fair value of the asset given up plus the cash (if any) given in the exchange or minus any cash received in the exchange. (This should equal the fair value of the asset received in the exchange.)

3. Recognize the gain or loss on disposal. The total gain or loss experienced on the transaction is equal to the difference between the fair market value of the asset given up and the book value of the asset given up. An excess of fair market value over book value indicates a **gain**; an excess of book value over fair market value indicates a **loss.**

TIP:	An exchange has commercial substance if the future cash flows expected to be generated by use of the asset being acquired (referred to as the new asset) are significantly different than the future cash flows that would be expected to be generated by use of the asset being relinquished (the old asset).
TIP:	An asset exchange may be one of similar or dissimilar assets. An exchange of dissimilar assets is almost sure to be one of commercial substance. An exchange of similar assets may or may not be one of commercial substance. Examples of a dissimilar asset exchange are the exchange of land for equipment and the exchange of office equipment for manufacturing equipment. An example of a similar asset exchange is the exchange of an old delivery truck for a new delivery truck. Most exchanges have commercial substance even those of similar assets.
TIP:	Accounting for an exchange of plant assets becomes more complex if the transaction does **not** have commercial substance (especially if cash is **received** rather than **given** in the exchange). These issues are discussed in more advanced accounting texts.

*EXERCISE 9-10

Purpose: (L.O. 8) This exercise will allow you to practice recording the exchange of plant assets when the exchange has commercial substance.

Soon Yoon Company exchanged equipment used in its manufacturing operations plus $5,000 in cash for delivery equipment used in the operations of Peggy Gunshanan Company. The exchange is determined to have commercial substance because the timing and the amount of the cash flows arising from the delivery equipment will likely differ significantly from the cash flows arising from the manufacturing equipment. The following information pertains to the exchange.

	Soon Yoon Co.	Peggy Gunshanan Co.
Equipment (cost)	$28,000	$28,000
Accumulated depreciation	22,000	10,000
Fair market value of equipment	10,500	15,500
Cash given up	5,000	

Instructions
(a)   Prepare the journal entries to record the exchange on the books of Soon Yoon Co.
(b)   Prepare the journal entries to record the exchange on the books of Soon Yoon Co. assuming the fair value of Soon Yoon Co.'s old asset is $5,500 (rather than $10,500) and the fair value of Peggy Gunshanan's old equipment is $10,500 (rather than $15,500). (Assume the rest of the facts are unchanged.)

SOLUTION TO EXERCISE 9-10

(a)   **Soon Yoon Company:**

Delivery Equipment (New)	15,500	
Accumulated Depreciation (Old)	22,000	
Manufacturing Equipment (Old)...		28,000
Cash		5,000
Gain on Disposal of Equipment		4,500
(To record exchange of manufacturing equipment		
for delivery equipment)		

Computation of book value:

Cost of old asset	$28,000
Accumulated depreciation	(22,000)
Book value of old asset	$ 6,000

Computation of gain:

Fair market value of equipment given	$10,500
Book value of equipment given	(6,000)
Gain experienced on old asset	$ 4,500

Valuation of new equipment:

Fair market value of equipment given	$10,500
Cash given	5,000
Cost of new equipment	$15,500

TIP: When plant assets are exchanged where the exchange has commercial substance and cash is given and a gain is experienced on disposal of the old asset, there are two other ways of computing the cost of the new equipment. They are as follows:

Book value of equipment given	$ 6,000		Fair value of equip. received is	
Cash given	5,000	**OR**	Cost of new equipment	$15,500
Gain on old asset	4,500			
Cost of new equipment	$15,500			

Approach and Explanation: Refer to **Illustration 9-2** which summarizes the rules for recognizing gains and losses on exchanges of plant assets where the exchange has commercial substance.

Soon Yoon has experienced a gain of $4,500 on the exchange of its old asset. It is an exchange of plant assets where cash is given and the exchange has commercial substance. This is an application of the cost principle in determining the cost of the new asset.

TIP: The parties will bargain so that the total fair value given equals the total fair value received. Therefore, since Peggy Gunshanan is giving up equipment worth $15,500 but Soon Yoon's equipment is only worth $10,500, Soon Yoon is also giving $5,000 cash to Peggy Gunshanan.

(b) **Soon Yoon Company:**

Delivery Equipment (New)	10,500	
Accumulated Depreciation (Old)	22,000	
Loss on Disposal of Plant Asset	500	
Manufacturing Equipment (Old)...		28,000
Cash		5,000

Computation of loss:

Fair market value of equipment given	$5,500
Book value of equipment given	6,000
Loss on disposal	$ (500)

Valuation of new equipment:

Fair market value of equipment given	$ 5,500
Cash given	5,000
Cost of new equipment	$10,500

OR

Book value of equipment given	$ 6,000
Loss recognized on old asset	(500)
Cash given	5,000
Cost of new equipment	$10,500

Explanation: Soon Yoon has experienced a loss on the disposal of the old plant asset; the loss is to be recognized. The cost principle is followed in determining the cost of the new plant asset.

TIP:	The rules for recording the exchange of **plant** assets where the exchange does **not** have commercial substance are not illustrated in this book or your text. They are complex and are reserved for a more advanced accounting course.
TIP:	Peggy Gunshanan Company would also have to record the exchange. The guidelines to be followed when cash is **received** in a transaction involving the exchange of plant assets are not discussed in this book or your text. They are reserved for a more advanced accounting course.

EXERCISE 9-11

Purpose: (L.O. 1 thru 8) This exercise will quiz you about terminology used in this chapter.

A list of accounting terms with which you should be familiar appears below:

Accelerated-depreciation method
Additions and improvements
Amortization
Asset turnover ratio
Capital expenditures
Copyright
Declining-balance method
Depletion
Depreciation
Depreciable cost
Franchise (license)
Going-concern assumption
Goodwill
Intangible assets

Licenses
Materiality principle
Natural resources
Ordinary repairs
Patent
Plant assets
Research and development (R & D) costs
Revenue expenditures
Salvage value
Straight-line method
Trademark (trade name)
Units-of-activity method
Useful life

Instructions
For each item below, enter in the blank the term that is described.

1. _____Expenditures that increase the company's investment in productive facilities. Expenditures that relate to plant assets and benefit more than the current period.

2. _____Expenditures related to plant assets that are immediately charged against revenues as expense.

3. _____An estimate of an asset's value at the end of its useful life.

4. _____Tangible resources that are used in the operations of the business and are not intended for sale to customers.

5. _____Costs incurred to increase the operating efficiency, productive capacity, or expected useful life of a plant asset.

6. _____The process of allocating to expense the cost of a plant asset over its useful (service) life in a rational and systematic manner.

7. _____The cost of a plant asset less its salvage value.

8. _____A depreciation method in which periodic depreciation is the same for each year of the asset's useful life.

9. _____A depreciation method that produces higher depreciation expense in the early years than in the later years of an asset's useful life.

10. _____A depreciation method that applies a constant rate to the declining book value of the asset and produces a decreasing annual depreciation expense over the useful life of the asset.

11. _____A depreciation method in which useful life is expressed in terms of the total units of production or use expected from an asset.

12. _____Expenditures to maintain the operating efficiency and productive life of the plant asset.

13. _____Rights, privileges, and competitive advantages that result from the ownership of long-lived assets that do not posses physical substance.

14. _____An exclusive right granted from the federal government that allows the owner to reproduce and sell an artistic or published work.

15. _____The value of all favorable attributes that relate to a business enterprise.

16. _____An exclusive right issued by the U.S. Patent Office that enables the recipient to manufacture, sell or otherwise control his or her invention for a period of 20 years from the date of the grant.

17. _____A work, phrase, jingle, or symbol that identifies a particular enterprise or product.

18. _____A contractual arrangement under which the franchisor grants the franchisee the right to sell certain products, render specific services, or use certain trademarks or trade names, usually within a designated geographical area.

19. _____The allocation of the cost of an intangible asset to expense over its useful life in a systematic and rational manner.

20. _____Expenditures that may lead to patents, copyrights, new processes, and new products.

21. _____Assets that consist of standing timber and underground deposits of oil, gas, and minerals.

22. _____The process of allocation of the cost of a natural resource to expense in a rational and systematic manner over the resource's useful life.

23. _____An estimate of the expected productive life, also called service life, of an asset.

24. _____Operating rights to use public property, granted to a business enterprise by a governmental agency.

25. _____A measure of how efficiently a company uses its assets to generate sales, calculated as net sales divided by average total assets.

26. _____States that the company will continue in operation for the foreseeable future.

27. _____If an item would **not** make a difference in decision making, a company does **not** have to follow GAAP in reporting it.

SOLUTION TO EXERCISE 9-11

1. Capital expenditures
2. Revenue expenditures
3. Salvage value
4. Plant assets
5. Additions and improvements
6. Depreciation
7. Depreciable cost
8. Straight-line method
9. Accelerated-depreciation method
10. Declining-balance method
11. Units-of-activity method
12. Ordinary repairs
13. Intangible assets
14. Copyright
15. Goodwill
16. Patent
17. Trademark (trade name)
18. Franchise (license)
19. Amortization
20. Research and development (R & D) costs
21. Natural resources
22. Depletion
23. Useful life
24. Licenses
25. Asset turnover ratio
26. Going concern assumption
27. Materiality principle

ANALYSIS OF MULTIPLE-CHOICE TYPE QUESTIONS

1. (L.O. 1) The Jupiter Company purchased a parcel of land to be used as the site of a new office complex. The following data pertain to the purchase of the land and the beginning of construction for the new building:

Purchase price of land	$200,000
Attorney's fees for land transaction	1,000
Title insurance cost	2,000
Survey fees to determine the boundaries of the lot	800
Excavation costs for the building's foundation	8,000
Costs of clearing and grading the land	1,400

The total acquisition cost of the land is:
a. $213,200.
b. $205,200.
c. $203,800.
d. $202,400.
e. $200,000.

Approach and Explanation: Think about how the cost of land is determined: an asset's cost includes all costs necessary to acquire the asset and get it to the location and condition for its intended purpose. When land has been purchased for the purpose of constructing a building, all costs incurred up to the excavation for the new building are considered land costs. Think of the common components of land cost (refer to the listing in **Illustration 9-1).** The cost is computed as follows:

Purchase price	$200,000
Attorney's fees	1,000
Title insurance	2,000
Survey fees	800
Costs of clearing and grading	1,400
Total cost of land	$205,200

The $8,000 excavation costs for the building's foundation should be charged (debited) to the Building account. (Solution = b.)

2. (L.O. 1) The Venus Company hired an architect to design plans and a construction firm to build a new office building on a parcel of land it owns. The following data relates to the building:

Price paid to the construction firm	$320,000
Architect fees	18,000
Permit fees	1,200
Property taxes during the construction period	800
Insurance premium for first year of operations	3,000
Property taxes during the first year of operations	6,000

The total acquisition cost of the new building is:
a. $349,000.
b. $340,000.
c. $338,000.
d. $320,000.

Approach and Explanation: Think about how the cost of a building is determined: an asset's cost includes all costs necessary to acquire the asset and get it to the location and condition for its intended purpose. Think of the common components of building cost (refer to the listing in **Illustration 9-1**). The cost is computed as follows:

Price paid to construction firm	$320,000
Architect fees	18,000
Permit fees	1,200
Property taxes during construction	800
Total cost of building	$340,000 (Solution = b.)

3.   (L.O. 1) The Patty Company purchased a piece of office equipment to be used in operations. The following expenditures and other data relate to the equipment:

Invoice price excluding sales tax	$12,000
Sales tax	600
Delivery charges	200
Installation costs	300
Cost of a special platform	400
Cost of supplies used in testing	80
Insurance premium for first year of use	60

The total acquisition cost of this piece of equipment is:
a. $13,640.
b. $13,580.
c. $13,100.
d. $12,700.

Approach and Explanation: Apply the cost principle: the cost of equipment includes all costs necessary to acquire the equipment, transport it to the place where it will be used, and prepare it for use. Thus, all costs related to equipment incurred prior to use in regular operations are charged to the Equipment account. Recurring costs (such as for insurance and maintenance) incurred after the equipment is ready for use should be expensed in the period incurred. Refer to the list of common elements of equipment cost in **Illustration 9-1.** The cost of the equipment is determined as follows:

Invoice price	$12,000
Sales tax	600
Delivery charges	200
Installation costs	300
Costs of special platform	400
Costs of supplies used in testing	80
	$13,580 (Solution = b.)

4.   (L.O. 3) In accounting for plant assets, which of the following subsequent outlays should be fully expensed in the period the expenditure is made?
a.   Expenditure made to increase the efficiency or effectiveness of an existing asset.
b.   Expenditure made to extend the useful life of an existing asset beyond the time frame originally anticipated.
c.   Expenditure made to maintain an existing asset so that it can function in the manner intended.
d.   Expenditure made to add new asset services.

Explanation: If an expenditure benefits future periods, it should be capitalized (debited to a balance sheet account); if the expenditure does not yield benefits to a future period, it should be recorded by a debit to an income statement account. An expenditure made to maintain an existing asset in good working condition does not provide any benefits other than those that were in potential when the original asset was acquired. Hence, it should be expensed. Answer selections "a", "b", and "d", all represent future economic benefits; hence, they should be debited to an asset account or to an accumulated depreciation account, depending on whether or not an asset's life is increased by the expenditure subsequent to acquisition. (Solution = c.)

5.   (L.O. 2) The term depreciable cost, as it is used in accounting for a plant asset, refers to:
   a.   the total amount to be charged (debited) to expense over the asset's useful life.
   b.   cost of the asset less the related depreciation recorded to date.
   c.   the estimated market value of the asset at the end of its useful life.
   d.   the acquisition cost of the asset.

Approach and Explanation: Write down a definition of depreciable cost **before** you read any of the answer selections. **Depreciable cost** is the total amount of asset cost that can be expensed over the useful life of the asset; thus, it is original cost less estimated residual (salvage) value. Answer selection "b" describes the term book value. Answer "c" describes salvage value or residual value. Selection "d" represents total cost of the asset. (Solution = a.)

6.   (L.O. 2) The book value of a plant asset is:
   a.   the fair market value of the asset at a balance sheet date.
   b.   the asset's acquisition cost less the total related depreciation recorded to date.
   c.   equal to the balance of the related accumulated depreciation account.
   d.   the assessed value of the asset for property tax purposes.

Approach and Explanation: Write down the definition for the term book value: **book value** is the asset's original cost (acquisition cost) less accumulated depreciation. Look for the answer selection that agrees with your definition. Book value is often called **carrying value** or **carrying amount.** (Solution = b.)

7.   (L.O. 2) A machine is purchased by the Dunnagin Company for $18,000. Dunnagin pays $6,000 in cash and gives a note payable for $12,000 that is payable in installments over a four-year period. Dunnagin estimates that the machine could physically last for 12 years even though Dunnagin expects to use it in its business for only 9 years. The period of time to be used by Dunnagin for depreciation purposes is:
   a.   4 years.
   b.   5 years.
   c.   9 years.
   d.   12 years.

Approach and Explanation: Think about the objective of the depreciation process—to comply with the matching principle. The process of depreciation serves to allocate an asset's cost to the periods benefited in order to match the cost of asset services consumed with the revenues the asset services helped to generate. The asset should be depreciated over its useful life, which is the length of time the asset will be of service to the entity using it in operations. (Solution = c.)

8.   (L.O. 2) A machine was purchased for $8,000,000 on January 1, 2014. It has an estimated useful life of 8 years and a residual value of $800,000. Depreciation is being computed using the straight-line method. What amount should be shown for this machine, net of accumulated depreciation, in the company's December 31, 2015 balance sheet?
a. $5,400,000.
b. $6,200,000.
c. $7,100,000.
d. $7,200,000.

Approach and Explanation: Write down the formula to compute book value and the formula to compute depreciation using the straight-line method. Fill in the data from the scenario at hand and solve. Be careful that you don't get so involved with the computation of depreciation that you lose sight of the question—and that is, to compute the book value of the equipment. It would be helpful to underline the middle of the last sentence of the stem of the question in order to keep your focus on what is being asked.

Cost - Accumulated Depreciation = Book Value

$$\frac{\text{Cost - Salvage Value}}{\text{Estimated Service Life}} = \text{Depreciation for Full Asset Year}$$

($8,000,000 - $800,000) ÷ 8 = $900,000 depreciation for one year.

Depreciation for 2014	$ 900,000
Depreciation for 2015	900,000
Accumulated depreciation	$1,800,000

Cost	$8,000,000
Accumulated depreciation	(1,800,000)
Book value	$6,200,000

(Solution = b.)

9.   (L.O. 2) Tammy Company purchased a machine on July 1, 2014 for $900,000. The machine has an estimated life of five years and a salvage value of $120,000. The machine is being depreciated by the declining-balance method using double the straight-line rate. What amount of depreciation should be recorded for the year ended December 31, 2015?
a. $360,000.
b. $288,000.
c. $249,600.
d. $180,000.

Approach and Explanation: Write down the formula to use for the declining-balance approach. (Notice the facts indicate there is a partial period for the first year (2014) and the question asks for the depreciation for the 2015 reporting period.) Compute the rate that is double the straight-line rate. Apply the formula to the facts given. Remember that salvage value is **not** used with this method in computing depreciation in the early years of the asset's life.

Book Value at Beginning of Year X Declining-Balance Rate = Depreciation

$$\frac{100\%}{\text{Life}} = \frac{100\%}{5 \text{ years}} = 20\% \qquad 20\% \times 2 = 40\% \text{ constant percentage}$$

$900,000 \times 40\% \times 1/2 = \$180,000$ for 2014
($900,000 - $180,000) \times 40\% = \underline{\$288,000 \text{ for } 2015}$ (Solution = b.)

10. (L.O. 2) A machine was purchased at the beginning of 2012 for $68,000. At the time of its purchase, the machine was estimated to have a useful life of six years and a salvage value of $8,000. The machine was depreciated using the straight-line method of depreciation through 2014. At the beginning of 2015, the estimate of useful life was revised to a total life of eight years and the expected salvage value was changed to $5,000. The amount to be recorded for depreciation for year 2015, reflecting these changes in estimates, is:
   a. $7,875.
   b. $7,600.
   c. $6,600.
   d. $4,125.

Approach and Explanation: Write down the model to compute depreciation whenever there has been a change in the estimated service life and/or salvage value of a plant asset. Fill in the data of the case at hand and solve:

Cost	$68,000
Accumulated depreciation	(30,000)[a]
Book value	38,000
Additional expenditure capitalized	-0-
Revised book value	38,000
Current estimate of salvage	(5,000)
Remaining depreciable cost	33,000
Remaining years of useful life at 1/1/15	÷ 5[b]
Depreciation expense for 2015	$ 6,600 (Solution = c.)

[a]Cost	$68,000
Original estimate of salvage	(8,000)
Original depreciable cost	60,000
Original service life in years	÷ 6
Original depreciation per year	10,000
Number of years used	3
Accumulated depreciation—1/1/15	$30,000

[b]Total life as revised	8
Number of years used	(3)
Remaining part of useful life at 1/1/15	5

11. **(L.O. 4)** A van has an original cost of $42,000 and accumulated depreciation of $11,000. It is sold for $27,000 cash. The journal entry to record the sale will include a:
a. debit to Loss on Disposal of Plant Assets for $4,000.
b. credit to Gain on Disposal of Plant Assets for $4,000.
c. credit to Vans for $27,000.
d. debit to Loss on Disposal of Plant Assets for $15,000.

Approach and Explanation: Prepare the journal entry to record the sale. Begin with the cash received so debit Cash. Remove the old asset from the books; credit Vans for $42,000 and debit Accumulated Depreciation for $11,000. Examine the entry and determine what is needed to balance the entry; a debit balancing figure represents a loss or a credit balancing figure represents a gain.

In this case, a debit of $4,000 is needed to balance; hence, a loss of $4,000 is recorded. (Solution = a.)

Cash	27,000	
Accumulated Depreciation—Vans..	11,000	
Loss on Disposal of Plant Assets	4,000	
Vans..		42,000

12. **(L.O. 6)** Which of the following items would **not** be classified as an intangible asset for accounting purposes:
a. Patent.
b. Goodwill.
c. Trade name.
d. Advertising to promote long-term relationship with customers.

Explanation: Patent, trade name (or trademark) and goodwill are all examples of intangible assets. Advertising and other costs to promote goodwill must be expensed in the period incurred. (Solution = d.)

13. **Question**
(L.O. 6) A company has recorded purchased goodwill at a cost of $200,000. What is the maximum amount which may be recorded as amortization expense for the full year immediately following its acquisition?
a. $0.
b. $4,000.
c. $5,000.
d. $20,000.

Approach and Explanation: Goodwill is considered to have an indefinite life; therefore, it is not to be amortized. In the case where a permanent impairment is determined to have occurred, a write down is required. (Solution = a.)

14. (L.O. 6) Which of the following items conveys the legal right to perform a service or to sell a product in a defined geographical area?
    a. Copyright.
    b. Trademark.
    c. Patent.
    d. Franchise.

    Explanation: A **copyright** gives the owner the exclusive right to reproduce and sell an artistic or published work. A **trademark** or **trade name** is a word, phrase, jingle, or symbol that distinguishes a particular enterprise or product. A **patent** is an exclusive right that enables the recipient to manufacture, sell, or otherwise control his or her invention. A **franchise** is a contractual arrangement under which the franchisor grants the **franchisee** the right to sell certain products, to render specific services, or to use certain trademarks or trade names, usually within a designated geographical area. (Solution = d.)

15. (L.O. 6) In 2014, Barry Sanders Corporation incurred $600,000 of research and development costs. The costs relate to a product that will be marketed beginning in 2015 when the patent is obtained. It is estimated that these costs will be recouped by December 31, 2016. What is the amount of research and development costs that should be charged to income in 2014?
    a. $0.
    b. $150,000.
    c. $200,000.
    d. $600,000.

    Explanation: All R & D costs are to be expensed in the period incurred. (Solution = d.)

16. (L.O. 6) Paws Inn is for sale. The following facts pertain:

	Book Value	Fair Market Value
Current assets	$100,000	$170,000
Plant assets	400,000	700,000
Intangible assets	60,000	90,000
Liabilities	300,000	300,000

    Cousin Vinnie Resorts purchases Paws Inn for $825,000. The value of goodwill amounts to:
    a. $30,000.
    b. $165,000.
    c. $300,000.
    d. $370,000.

    Approach and Explanation:
    (1) **Compute the total fair market value of the identifiable assets:**
    $170,000 + $700,000 + $90,000 = $960,000
    (2) **Compute the fair market value of the net identifiable assets:**
    $960,000 - $300,000 liabilities = $660,000
    (3) **Compute the excess of cost over the fair market value of the net identifiable assets.** That excess represents goodwill.
    $825,000 - $660,000 = $165,000 goodwill   (Solution = b.)

17. (L.O. 6) A patent was acquired in early 2010. Its useful life was determined to be 12 years even though its legal life is 20 years. At the beginning of 2014, a large sum was spent for legal costs to successfully defend the patent rights. Those legal costs should be:
    a. expensed in 2013.
    b. amortized over 20 years.
    c. amortized over 12 years.
    d. amortized over 8 years.

    Explanation: The legal costs are necessary to establish the validity of the patent. They should be amortized over the periods benefited which are the remaining years of the useful life of the patent (12 - 4 = 8). (Solution = d.)

18. (L.O. 7) All of the following must be disclosed **except:**
    a. depreciation method(s) used.
    b. amount of depreciation expense for the period.
    c. balances of the major classes of plant assets.
    d. service lives of plant assets.

    Explanation: Either within the balance sheet or in the notes to the financial statements, there should be disclosure of the balances of the major classes of assets, such as land, buildings, and equipment, and accumulated depreciation by major classes or in total. In addition, the depreciation and amortization methods used should be described, and the amount of depreciation and amortization expense for the period should be disclosed. (Solution = d.)

19. (L.O. 7) The asset turnover ratio may be used to determine:
    a. the average service life of plant assets.
    b. the average age of plant assets.
    c. the dollars of sales produced for each dollar invested in assets.
    d. the number of times you can divide depreciation expense into total assets.

    Explanation: The asset turnover ratio is computed by dividing average assets into net sales; it measures the productivity of a company's total assets. (Solution = c.)

*20. (L.O. 8) The King-Kong Corporation exchanges one plant asset for another plant asset and gives cash in the exchange. If a gain on the disposal of the old asset is indicated, and the exchange has commercial substance, the gain will:
    a. be reported in the Other Revenues and Gains section of the income statement.
    b. effectively reduce the amount to be recorded as the cost of the new asset.
    c. be credited directly to the owner's capital account.
    d. be ignored.

    Explanation: The gain results from an excess of fair value over book value of the asset relinquished. The gain is reported like other gains from nonoperating sources. (Solution = a.)

*21. (L.O. 8) Two home builders agree to exchange plant assets. The exchange has commercial substance.. An appraiser was hired and the following information is available.

	Batson	**Beamer**
Book value of asset given up	$50,000	$108,000
Fair market value of asset given up	80,000	100,000
Cash paid	20,000	

In recording this exchange, Batson should recognize:
a.   a loss of $20,000.
b.   a gain of $20,000.
c.   a gain of $30,000.
d.   no gain or loss.

Approach and Explanation:
Determine if a gain or loss is experienced. Fair market value ($80,000) exceeds book value ($50,000) for Batson's old asset so Batson has experienced a gain of $30,000. The gain is recognized in an exchange that has commercial substance. (Solution = c.)

*22. (L.O. 8) Refer to the facts of **Question 21.** The amount to be recorded by Batson for the acquisition cost of the new plant asset is:
a. $50,000.
b. $70,000.
c. $80,000.
d. $100,000.
e. $108,000.

Approach and Explanation:

The cost of the new asset can be determined as follows:

Fair market value of asset given	$ 80,000
Cash given	20,000
Cost of new asset	$100,000 (Solution = d.)

A journal entry approach can also be used (the debit to the new asset account is a plug figure):

Plant Asset (New)	100,000		**Plug last.**
Plant Asset (Old)		50,000	**Do second.**
Cash		20,000	**Do first.**
Gain on Disposal of Plant Asset		30,000	**Do third.**

CHAPTER 10

. . . .

*L*IABILITIES

OVERVIEW

Initially, the resources (assets) of a business have to come from an entity outside of the particular organization. Two main sources of resources are creditor sources (liabilities) and owners' sources (owners' equity). Liabilities are considered "temporary" sources of assets; whereas, stockholders' equity is a more "permanent" source of assets. When a company borrows money, it does so with the expectation of using the borrowed funds to acquire assets that can be used to generate more income. The objective is to generate an amount of additional income which exceeds the cost of borrowing the funds (interest).

Due to the nature of some business activities, an entity will commonly receive goods and services and not pay for them until days or weeks later. Therefore, at a specific point in time, such as a balance sheet date, we may find that a business has obligations for merchandise received from suppliers (accounts payable), for money it has borrowed (notes payable), for interest incurred (interest payable), for sales tax charged to customers which has not yet been remitted to the government (sales taxes payable), for salaries and wages (salaries and wages payable), and for amounts due to government agencies in connection with employee compensation (Federal Income Tax Withholdings Payable, FICA Taxes Payable, Federal Unemployment Taxes Payable, and State Unemployment Taxes Payable). Such payables are reported as current (short-term) liabilities because they will fall due within the next 12 months and will require the use of current assets (cash, in most cases) to liquidate them. Accounting for current liabilities is discussed in this chapter.

Long-term debt consists of probable future sacrifices of economic benefits arising from present obligations that are not payable within a year or the operating cycle of the business, whichever is longer. Bonds payable, long-term notes payable, mortgages payable, pension liabilities, and lease obligations are examples of long-term liabilities. This chapter will focus on the first three of these.

SUMMARY OF LEARNING OBJECTIVES

1. **Explain a current liability and identify the major types of current liabilities.** A current liability is a debt that a company can reasonably expect to pay (1) from existing current assets or through the creation of other current liabilities, and (2) within one year or the operating cycle, whichever is longer. The major types of current liabilities are notes payable, accounts payable, sales taxes payable, unearned revenues, and accrued liabilities such as taxes, salaries and wages, and interest payable.

2.   **Describe the accounting for notes payable.** When a promissory note is interest-bearing, the amount of assets received upon the issuance of the note is generally equal to the face value of the note. Interest expense accrues over the life of the note. At maturity, the amount paid equals the face value of the note plus accrued interest.

3.   **Explain the accounting for other current liabilities.** Companies record sales taxes payable at the time the related sales occur. The company serves as a collection agent for the taxing authority. Sales taxes are **not** an expense to the company. Companies initially record unearned revenues in an Unearned Revenue account. As the company earns the revenue (that is, as the performance obligation is satisfied), a transfer from unearned revenue to earned revenue occurs. Companies report the current maturities of long-term debt as a current liability in the balance sheet.

4.   **Explain why bonds are issued, and identify the types of bonds.** Companies may sell bonds to many investors to raise long-term capital. Bonds offer the following advantages over common stock: (a) stockholder control is **not** affected, (b) tax savings result, (c) earnings per share of stock may be higher. The following different type of bonds may be issued: secured and unsecured bonds, term and serial bonds, registered and bearer bonds, convertible, and callable bonds.

5.   **Prepare the entries for the issuance of bonds and interest expense.** When companies issue bonds, they debit Cash for the cash proceeds, and credit Bonds Payable for the face value of the bonds. The account Premium on Bonds Payable is used to show a bond premium; Discount on Bonds Payable is used to show a bond discount.

6.   **Describe the entries when bonds are redeemed or converted.** When bondholders redeem bonds at maturity, the issuing company credits Cash and debits Bonds Payable for the face value of the bonds. When bonds are redeemed before maturity, the issuing company (a) eliminates the carrying value of the bonds at the redemption date, (b) records the cash paid, and (c) recognizes the gain or loss on redemption. When bonds are converted to common stock, the issuing company transfers the carrying (or book) value of the bonds to appropriate paid-in capital accounts; no gain or loss is recognized.

7.   **Describe the accounting for long-term notes payable.** Each payment consists of (1) interest on the unpaid balances of the loan and (2) a reduction of loan principal. The interest decreases each period, while the portion applied to the loan principal increases.

8.   **Identify the methods for the presentation and analysis of long-term liabilities.** Companies should report the nature and amount of each long-term debt in the balance sheet or in the notes accompanying the financial statements. Stockholders and long-term creditors are interested in a company's long-run solvency. Debt to total assets and times interest earned are two ratios that provide information about debt-paying ability and long-run solvency.

*9.   **Compute the market price of a bond.** Time value of money concepts are useful for pricing bonds. The present value (or market price) of a bond is a function of three variables: (1) the payment amounts, (2) the length of time until the amounts are paid, and (3) the interest rate.
*This material is covered in **Appendix 10A** in the text.

10.   **Apply the effective-interest method of amortizing bond discount and bond premium. The effective-interest method results in varying amounts of amortization and interest expense per period but a *constant percentage rate* of interest. When the difference between the straight-line and effective-interest method is material, GAAP requires the use of the effective-interest method.
This material is covered in **Appendix 10B in the text.

***11.   **Apply the straight-line method of amortization.** A method of amortizing bond discount or bond premium that results in allocating the same amount to interest expense in each interest period.
***This material is covered in **Appendix 10C** in the text.

TIPS ON CHAPTER TOPICS

TIP: **Current liabilities** are often called **short-term liabilities** or **short-term debt. Non-current liabilities** are often called **long-term liabilities** or **long-term debt.**

TIP: **Current liabilities** are obligations which come due within one year and whose liquidation is reasonably expected to require the use of existing resources properly classifiable as current assets, or the creation of other current liabilities. **Noncurrent liabilities** (or **long-term liabilities**) are obligations which do **not** meet the criteria to be classified as current.

TIP: Companies often have a portion of long-term debt that is due each year. At a balance sheet date, any portion of long-term debt that is due within one year of that balance sheet date is referred to as "current maturities of long-term debt" or "current portion of long-term debt" or "long-term debt due within one year" and is classified as a current liability.

TIP: A liability is recognized (recorded) when a legally binding obligation is incurred. Examples include:
    (a)   When cash is received from a creditor as a loan.
    (b)   When cash is received from a customer in advance of the date that goods or services are provided to the customer.
    (c)   When legal title to some asset other than cash is received (change in legal title usually occurs at the point that the asset is delivered to the buyer) and payment is deferred.
    (d)   When services are received and payment is deferred.
    (e)   As time passes (for example, interest accrues with passage of time).

TIP: The amount of a liability is determined in one of three ways:
    (a)   By the amount of cash when cash is exchanged (for example, when money is borrowed from a bank).
    (b)   By the negotiated or fair market value of noncash assets or services involved in a transaction.
    (c)   By estimate.

TIP: Computing the weekly, biweekly, or monthly payroll involves four basic steps:
    (a)   Determining the amount of employee compensation.
    (b)   Calculating deductions from employee compensation.
    (c)   Calculating employer tax liabilities based on employee compensation.
    (d)   Maintaining proper employee payroll records.

TIP: Current liabilities are presented before long-term liabilities on the balance sheet. The individual current liabilities are often listed by order of magnitude, with the largest obligations first. As a matter of custom, many companies show current maturities of long-term debt first, regardless of amount.

TIP: Classifying both assets and liabilities as current or noncurrent (long-term) items allows a company's liquidity to be analyzed and evaluated. Liquidity refers to the ability of a company to pay its maturing obligations and meet unexpected needs for cash. The relationship of current assets and current liabilities is critical in analyzing liquidity. When expressed as a dollar amount, this relationship is referred to as **working capital** (i.e., current assets minus current liabilities equals working capital). When expressed as a ratio, this relationship is referred to as the **current ratio** (i.e., current assets divided by current liabilities equals the current ratio).

TIP: The denomination of a bond is called the **face value.** Synonymous terms are **par value, principal amount, maturity value,** and **face amount.** Although most textbook illustrations use a face value of $1,000, other denominations such as $100, $400, and $10,000 are also commonly used in practice.

TIP: Bond prices are quoted in terms of percentage of face value. Thus a bond with a face value of $4,000 and a price quote of 102 is currently selling for a price of $4,080 (102% of $4,000). A bond with a quote of 100 is selling for its face (par) value.

TIP: The bond contract is called an **indenture.** This term is often confused with the term debenture. A **debenture** bond is an unsecured bond.

TIP: The interest rate written in the bond indenture and ordinarily appearing on the bond certificate is known as the **contractual interest rate.** Synonymous terms are **stated interest rate, coupon interest rate, nominal interest rate,** and **contract interest rate.**

TIP: The rate of interest actually incurred by an issuer of bonds and the rate actually earned by bondholders is called the **effective interest rate, yield rate,** or **market interest rate.**

TIP: If a bond is issued at a price above its face value, it is said to be issued at a **premium.** An excess of face value over a bond's issuance price is called a **discount.**

TIP: A bond's **issuance price** is determined by the present value of all of the future cash flows promised by the bond indenture. The future cash flows include the face value and interest payments. The bond's present value is determined by using the market interest rate at the date of issuance to discount all of the related future cash flows.

TIP: Bond prices vary inversely with changes in the market interest rate. This means that as the market interest rate goes down, bond prices go up; and as the market interest rate goes up, bond prices go down. It also means that at the date of issuance, if the market interest rate is below the contractual interest rate, the price will be above face value (that is, the bond will be issued at a premium); likewise, if the market interest rate is above the contractual interest rate, the issuance price will be below face value (that is, the bond will be issued at a discount). Hence, a **premium or a discount is an adjustment to interest via an adjustment to price.**

TIP: Interest payments on notes payable are generally made on a monthly or quarterly basis. Interest payments on bonds payable are usually made semiannually. Despite these common practices, **interest rates generally are expressed on an annual basis.** Therefore, care must be taken that the annual rate be converted to a "rate per period" before other computations are performed.

TIP: A bond's **carrying value (book value or carrying amount)** is equal to the (1) face value plus any unamortized bond premium, or (2) face value minus any unamortized bond discount.

TIP: An **interest payment** promised by a bond is computed by multiplying the bond's face value by its contractual interest rate. This amount is often referred to as the **cash interest** or **stated interest** or **interest to be paid.**

TIP: The **life** of a bond is measured by the time between the date of issuance and the date of maturity. The bond's life is shorter than the term of the bond if the bond is issued on a date later than the date appearing on the indenture.

TIP: The Discount on Bonds Payable account is a contra liability account so its balance should be deducted from Bonds Payable on the balance sheet. The Premium on Bonds Payable account is an adjunct type valuation account so its balance should be added to the balance of Bonds Payable on the balance sheet. The balance of the Bonds Payable account is always equal to the face value of the bonds issued. At a balance sheet date (after adjusting entries have been made), the balance of a Discount on Bonds Payable account or a Premium on Bonds Payable account represents the unamortized amount of discount or premium at that date.

*TIP: (Appendix 10A) In computing the present value of a bond's (1) maturity value and (2) interest payments, the **same** interest rate is used. That rate is the effective-interest rate on a per interest period basis. As an example, if a ten-year bond has a stated rate of 10%, pays interest semiannually, and is issued to yield 12%, a 6% rate is used to perform all of the present value calculations. (Also see Appendix C near the very end of your text for more material on the subject of present value.)

**TIP: (Appendix 10B) A bond premium or discount must be amortized (allocated to interest expense) over the bond's life; the amortization of a bond premium will reduce the amount to be reported as interest expense; whereas, the amortization of a bond discount will increase interest expense. There are two amortization methods—the straight-line method and the effective interest method. The effective interest method is required when there is a material difference in the results yielded by the two methods. The effective interest method is discussed in Appendix 10B in the text and the straight-line method is explained in Appendix 10C.

**TIP: (Appendix 10B) If the effective-interest method of amortization is used, the following relationships will exist:
1. The interest rate is constant each period.
2. The interest expense is an increasing amount each period if the bond is issued at a discount (because a constant rate is applied to an increasing carrying value each period).
3. The interest expense is a decreasing amount each period if the bond is issued at a premium (because a constant rate is applied to a decreasing carrying value each period).
4. The amount of amortization increases each period because the difference between the effective interest expense and the cash interest widens each period.

TIP: (Appendix 10B) The **effective-interest method of amortization is sometimes called the **interest method** or the **present value method** or the **effective method.**

TIP: (Appendix 10B) The **effective interest expense (interest expense using the effective-interest method of amortization) for an interest period is determined by multiplying the bond's carrying value at the beginning of the period by the effective-interest rate at the date of issuance (this rate never changes). The difference between the interest payment (cash interest) and the effective interest expense for a period is the amount of premium or discount amortization for the period. The amount of amortization for a period causes the carrying value to change.

**TIP: (Appendix 10B) When the effective-interest method of amortization is used, the bond's carrying value will equal its present value (assuming the amortization is up to date).

**TIP: (Appendix 10B and Appendix 10C) Regardless of whether the straight-line method of amortization or the effective-interest method of amortization is used, the following will occur:
1. The amount of cash interest (stated interest) is a constant amount each period.
2. The bond's carrying value increases over the bond's life if it is issued at a discount, due to the amortization of the discount.
3. The bond's carrying value decreases over the bond's life if it is issued at a premium, due to the amortization of the premium.

***TIP: (Appendix 10C) Using the **straight-line method of amortization,** interest expense is determined by either adding the amount of discount amortization for the period to the cash (stated) interest or deducting the amount of premium amortization from the cash (stated) interest for the period. The periodic amount of amortization is determined by dividing the issuance premium or discount by the number of periods in the bond's life.

***TIP: (Appendix 10C) If the straight-line method of amortization is used, the following relationships will exist:
1. The amount of amortization is a constant amount each period.
2. The amount of interest expense is a constant amount each period.

EXERCISE 10-1

Purpose: (L.O. 1) This exercise tests your ability to distinguish between current and long-term liabilities.

_____ 1. Obligation to supplier for merchandise purchased on credit. (Terms 2/10, n/30).

_____ 2. Note payable to bank maturing 90 days after balance sheet date.

_____ 3. Note payable due January 1, 2017.

_____ 4. Property taxes payable.

_____ 5. Interest payable on note payable.

_____ 6. Sales taxes payable.

_____ 7. Portion of mortgage obligation due in years 2016 through 2020.

_____ 8. Revenue received in advance, to be earned over the next six months.

_____ 9. Wages and salaries payable.

_____ 10. Rent payable.

_____ 11. Short-term notes payable.

_____ 12. Pension obligations maturing in ten years.

_____ 13. Installment loan payments due three months after the balance sheet date.

_____ 14. Installment loan payments due more than one year after the balance sheet date.

_____ 15. Portion of mortgage obligation due within a year after the December 31, 2014 balance sheet date.

_____ 16. Note payable maturing March 1, 2015.

Instructions:
Indicate whether each of the above items would be reported as a current liability (C) or a long-term liability (LT) on a balance sheet prepared at December 31, 2014.

Approach: Review the definition of a current liability. Analyze each situation above and determine if the liability will fall due within a year (or operating cycle) of the balance sheet date and whether it will require the use of current assets or the incurrence of another current liability to liquidate. If so, it is current; if not, it is long-term.

SOLUTION TO EXERCISE 10-1

1.	C	5.	C	9.	C	13.	C
2.	C	6.	C	10.	C	14.	LT
3.	LT	7.	LT	11.	C	15.	C
4.	C	8.	C	12.	LT	16.	C

EXERCISE 10-2

Purpose: (L.O. 2) This exercise will review the journal entries involved for an interest-bearing note payable.

On November 1, 2014, Bono Company borrowed $80,000 from National Bank and signed a note stipulating that $80,000 was to be repaid in 6 months with interest at 12%. Bono Company adjusts its accounts and prepares financial statements annually on December 31. (Reversing entries discussed in the **Appendix to Chapter 4** are **not** used.)

Instructions
(a)   Prepare the journal entry on November 1, 2014, to record the loan.
(b)   Prepare the adjusting entry on December 31, 2014.
(c)   Prepare the journal entry at maturity (May 1, 2015).
(d)   Determine the total financing cost (interest expense) for the six-month period.

SOLUTION TO EXERCISE 10-2

(a)	2014	Cash	80,000	
	Nov. 1	Notes Payable		80,000
		(To record issuance of 12%, six-month note		
		to National Bank)		
(b)	2014	Interest Expense..	1,600	
	Dec. 31	Interest Payable..		1,600
		(To accrue interest for two months on		
		National Bank note)		
		($80,000 X 12% X 2/12 = $1,600)		
(c)	2015	Notes Payable	80,000	
	May 1	Interest Payable...	1,600	
		Interest Expense..	3,200	
		Cash		84,800
		(To record payment of National Bank interest-		
		bearing note and accrued interest at maturity)		
		($80,000 X 12% X 4/12 = $3,200 interest expense)		

(d) $1,600 + $3,200 = $4,800

TIP:	Interest rates are stated on an annual basis (per annum) unless otherwise indicated. Thus, the 12% rate in this exercise is an annual rate.

EXERCISE 10-3

Purpose: (L.O. 3) This exercise will provide an example of the proper accounting for an obligation to an agency of the state government—unremitted sales taxes.

During the month of June, Chelsea's Boutique had cash sales of $234,000 and credit sales of $137,000, both of which include the 6% sales tax that must be remitted to the state by July 15. Sales taxes on June sales were lumped with the sales price and recorded as a credit to the Sales Revenue account.

During the month of July, Chelsea's Boutique set up a new cash register that rings up sales and the 6% sales tax separately. The register totals for July were cash sales of $220,000 and credit sales of $110,000. The related sales tax is not due to be paid until August 15.

Instructions
(a) Prepare the journal entry to record June's sales at June 30 (assuming the total sales for June are recorded at June 30).
(b) Prepare the adjusting entry that should be recorded to fairly present the financial statements at June 30.
(c) Prepare the journal entry to record the remittance of the sales taxes on July 12.
(d) Prepare the journal entry to record July's sales at July 31.

SOLUTION TO EXERCISE 10-3

(a)	June 30	Cash..	234,000	
		Accounts Receivable...	137,000	
		Sales..		371,000
		(To record sales revenue including sales taxes)		
(b)	June 30	Sales	21,000	
		Sales Taxes Payable..		21,000
		(To record the sales tax liability on June sales)		

Computation:

Sales plus sales tax ($234,000 + $137,000)	$371,000	
Sales exclusive of tax ($371,000 ÷ 1.06)	(350,000)	
Sales tax	$ 21,000	

(c)	July 12	Sales Taxes Payable..	21,000	
		Cash		21,000
		(To record payment of sales taxes collected in June)		
(d)	July 31	Cash ($220,000 X 1.06)	233,200	
		Accounts Receivable ($110,000 X 1.06)	116,600	
		Sales..		330,000
		Sales Taxes Payable..		19,800
		(To record sales revenue and sales taxes)		

EXERCISE 10-4

Purpose: (L.O. 3) This exercise will illustrate the accounting for unearned revenue.

Soap Opera Summarized is published by Viewer Publishers. Subscriptions to the magazine are sold for a one-year, two-year, or three-year period. Cash receipts from subscribers are credited to Unearned Subscription Revenue, and this account had a balance of $3,000,000 at December 31, 2014, before adjustment. Outstanding subscriptions at December 31, 2014, expire as follows:

During 2015	$ 600,000
During 2016	400,000
During 2017	300,000
Total	$1,300,000

Instructions
(a)   Prepare the journal entry to adjust the Unearned Subscription Revenue account at December 31, 2014.
(b)   Explain how relevant amounts will be reported on the annual financial statements prepared at the end of 2014.

SOLUTION TO EXERCISE 10-4

(a)   Unearned Subscription Revenue 1,700,000
          Subscription Revenue   1,700,000
             (To record subscription revenues earned)

(b)   Subscription revenue of $1,700,000 will appear on the income statement for the year ending December 31, 2014.

Unearned subscription revenue of $600,000 will appear as a current liability on the December 31, 2014, balance sheet because Viewer Publishers has an obligation to deliver magazines (or refund $600,000) to subscribers within one year of the balance sheet date because of revenues collected in advance.

Unearned subscription revenue of $700,000 will appear as a long-term liability on the December 31, 2014, balance sheet because of collections from customers for revenue to be earned in periods beyond one year from the balance sheet date.

Approach and Explanation: Draw a T-account. Enter the information given. Solve for the missing link.

Unearned Subscription Revenue

		12/31/14 Bal. before adjustment	3,000,000
Adjustment required	1,700,000		
		12/31/14 Desired balance	1,300,000

A magazine company often collects cash from subscribers before it provides magazines to them. Thus, at the point of receipt of cash, the company has an obligation to publish and deliver magazines for a number of months that follow the cash receipts.

Revenue is to be recognized in the period it is earned. If cash collections of $3,000,000 have been received and credited to the unearned revenue account during the period and the only unearned amount at the end of the period is $1,300,000, $1,700,000 must be removed from the liability account (unearned revenue) and transferred to an earned revenue account.

TIP:	Synonymous terms for **unearned revenue** are **deferred revenue, revenue collected in advance,** and **revenue received in advance.** Unearned revenue is a liability until the point in time when the revenue is earned or a refund is made.

EXERCISE 10-5

Purpose: (L.O. 4) This exercise will compare and contrast the effects of debt financing with the effects of stock financing.

The Siuda Specialty Corporation has the following items on its financial statements at December 31, 2014:

Assets	$1,000,000
Stockholders' equity	$1,000,000
Number of common stock shares outstanding	60,000

Management is considering two alternatives to finance the acquisition of $500,000 of new assets:
(1)   Issuance of 50,000 shares of $1 par value common stock at the market price of $10 per share.
(2)   Issuance of $500,000, 10% bonds at par.

The income tax rate is 30%.

Instructions
(a)   If income before interest and income taxes is estimated to be $180,000 in 2015, compute the projected earnings per share figure for 2015 for each alternative. (Round to the nearest cent.)
(b)   Explain the advantages that bonds offer over common stock to a corporation seeking long-term financing.

SOLUTION TO EXERCISE 10-5

(a)	(1) Issue Stock	(2) Issue Debt
Income before interest and taxes	$180,000	$180,000
Interest expense from bonds ($500,000 X 10%)		50,000
Income before income taxes	180,000	130,000
Income tax expense (30%)	54,000	39,000
Net income	$126,000	$ 91,000
Outstanding shares of stock	110,000	60,000
Earnings per share	$1.15	$1.52

TIP:	This analysis shows that if the company issues debt securities and can operate at the estimated income level, it will be using leverage successfully (that is, favorable trading on the equity).
TIP:	Notice the difference between the two net income figures ($126,000 - $91,000) is the net-of-tax interest amount (70% X $50,000 = $35,000).

(b) From the standpoint of the corporation seeking long-term financing, bonds offer the following advantages over common stock:

1. **Stockholder control is not affected.** Bondholders do not have voting rights, so current stockholders retain full control of the company.

2. **Tax savings result.** Bond interest is deductible for tax purposes; dividends on stock are not. For example, if a bond pays 10% interest and the corporation is in the 30% tax bracket, the net cash cost to the corporation is only 7%. If a corporation pays a 10% cash dividend, the cash resources of the company are reduced by the full 10%.

3. **Earnings per share of common stock may be higher.** Although bond interest expense will reduce net income, earnings per share of common stock will often be higher under bond financing because no additional shares of common stock are issued.

ILLUSTRATION 10-1
FORMATS FOR COMMON COMPUTATIONS
INVOLVING BONDS PAYABLE (L.O. 5, 6, 10, 11)

1.   Cash Interest Per Period.
     Face value
     X <u>Contractual interest rate per period</u>
     = Cash (stated) interest per period

Cash interest is always a constant amount each period.

2.   Carrying Value.
     Face value
     - Unamortized discount
     OR + <u>Unamortized premium</u>
     = Carrying value

The process of amortization decreases the unamortized amount of discount or premium; hence the carrying value moves toward the face value.

3.   Gain or Loss on Bond Redemption.
     Carrying value
     - <u>Redemption price</u>
     = Gain if positive, that is, if carrying value is the greater.
     = Loss if negative, that is, if redemption price is the greater.

**4. Interest Expense Using the Effective-Interest Method.
     Carrying value at the beginning of the period
     X <u>Effective-interest rate per interest period</u>
     = Interest expense for the interest period

The carrying value changes each interest period so the interest expense changes each period.

**5. Amortization Amount Using the Effective-Interest Method.
     Interest expense for the interest period
     - <u>Cash interest for the interest period</u>
     = Amortization of discount for the interest period

Interest expense is greater than cash interest for bonds issued at a discount.

OR

     Cash interest for the interest period
     - <u>Interest expense for the interest period</u>
     = Amortization of premium for the interest period

Cash interest is greater than interest expense for bonds issued at a premium.

***6. Interest Expense Using Straight-line Amortization Method.
     Cash interest for the period
     + Discount amortization for the period
     OR - <u>Premium amortization for the period</u>
     = Interest expense for the period

Interest expense is a constant amount each period using this method.

***7. Amortization Amount Using the Straight-line Method.
     Issuance premium or discount ÷ Periods in bond's life = Amortization per period

This material is covered in **Appendix 10B in the text.
***This material is covered in **Appendix 10C** in the text.

EXERCISE 10-6

Purpose: (L.O. 5) This exercise will illustrate the journal entries required to record the issuance of bonds at face value and the entries to account for the related interest expense.

The Hale Corporation issued bonds dated April 1, 2014. These bonds are 5-year term bonds with a face value of $1,000 each and a stated interest rate of 7%. Interest is payable semiannually on October 1 and April 1.

Instructions
(a)   Prepare the journal entry to record the sale of 5,000 of these bonds on April 1, 2014 at 100.
(b)   Prepare the journal entry to record the first interest payment on October 1, 2014, assuming no previous accrual of interest.
(c)   Prepare the adjusting entry on December 31, 2014, to record interest expense, assuming a calendar year reporting period.

SOLUTION TO EXERCISE 10-6

(a)	Cash	5,000,000	
	Bonds Payable		5,000,000
	(5,000 X $1,000 X 100% = $5,000,000)		
(b)	Interest Expense	175,000	
	Cash		175,000
	($5,000,000 X 7% X 6/12 = $175,000)		
(c)	Interest Expense	87,500	
	Interest Payable		87,500
	($5,000,000 X 7% X 3/12 = $87,500)		

Explanation:
(a)   The 5,000 bonds each have a face (par) value of $1,000. Each bond is issued at a price of 100 which means 100% of the face value (100% X $1,000 = $1,000 each). Therefore, cash of $5,000,000 is received and the company records a liability called Bonds Payable.

(b)   Interest is a function of balance (face value in this case), interest rate, and time. The amount of time that lapsed between the issuance date of April 1, 2014 and the interest payment date of October 1, 2014 is six months. The interest rate is the stated rate of 7%. The interest paid is recorded as a credit to Cash and a debit to Interest Expense (because none of the interest was previously accrued).

(c)   When an accounting period ends on a date other than an interest payment date, the interest accrued since the last interest payment date is recorded by a debit to Interest Expense and a credit to Interest Payable. This adjustment is necessary to get interest expense recorded in the proper time period (matching principle). The number of months between July 1 and October 1 is 3.

EXERCISE 10-7

Purpose: (L.O. 5) This exercise will illustrate the journal entry required to record the issuance of bonds at a price other than par.

The Russell Corporation issued 4,000 bonds dated May 1, 2014. These bonds are 10-year term bonds with a face value of $1,000 each and a stated interest rate of 8%. Interest is payable semiannually on November 1 and May 1.

Instructions
(a) Prepare the journal entry to record the sale of these bonds on May 1, 2014. Assuming the bonds are sold for a total of $4,055,000.
(b) Ignore the assumption in part (a) above. Prepare the journal entry to record the sale of these bonds on May 1, 2014, assuming the bonds are sold on May 1, 2014, and the proceeds amount to $3,950,000.

SOLUTION TO EXERCISE 10-7

(a)	Cash	4,055,000	
	Bonds Payable		4,000,000
	Premium on Bonds Payable		55,000
	($4,055,000 - $4,000,000 = $55,000)		
(b)	Cash	3,950,000	
	Discount on Bonds Payable	50,000	
	Bonds Payable		4,000,000

Explanation:
(a) The face value of bonds issued is always recorded in the Bonds Payable (liability) account. The amount by which the proceeds ($4,055,000) exceed the face value ($4,000,000) is recorded in a separate liability account called Premium on Bonds Payable.

(b) The face value of bonds payable is always recorded in the liability account called Bonds Payable. The amount by which the par value ($4,000,000) exceeds the issuance proceeds ($3,950,000) represents a discount and is recorded in a contra liability account called Discount on Bonds Payable.

EXERCISE 10-8

Purpose: (L.O. 5, 8) This exercise will illustrate how account balances involved in accounting for bonds payable are to be reported in the financial statements.

When a company borrows money by issuing long-term debt instruments such as bonds, the entity is obligated to repay the principal plus interest on the outstanding debt. A balance sheet should properly reflect the amounts owed at the statement date. An income statement must report the interest (cost of borrowing) for the period that precedes the related balance sheet date.

The following amounts pertain to a bond issue of the Arnie Howell Corporation (they use a calendar year reporting period):

Face amount of 3-year term bonds issued on January 1, 2014	$100,000.00
Discount on bonds payable at issuance date	$7,460.05
Stated interest rate	7%
Interest payment date is annually on January 1	
Maturity date is January 1, 2017	
Unamortized discount as of December 31, 2015	$2,486.69
Interest paid during 2015	$7,000.00
Interest expense for the year ending Dec. 31, 2015	$9,486.68
Interest payable at December 31, 2015	$7,000.00

Instructions

Explain what amount(s) would appear on Arnie's multiple-step income statement for the year ended December 31, 2015 and identify the appropriate classification. Also explain what amount(s) would appear on Arnie's balance sheet at December 31, 2015 and identify the appropriate classification.

SOLUTION TO EXERCISE 10-8

ARNIE HOWELL CORPORATION
Partial Income Statement
For the Year Ended December 31, 2015

Other expenses and losses	
Interest expense	$9,486.68

ARNIE HOWELL CORPORATION
Partial Balance Sheet
December 31, 2015

Current liabilities		
Bond interest payable		$ 7,000.00
Long-term liabilities		
Bonds payable	$100,000.00	
Less: Discount on Bonds Payable	2,486.69	97,513.31

Explanation: The interest expense is reported as an other expense near the bottom of a multiple-step income statement. The total expense incurred appears on the income statement; which in Arnie's case is the stated (cash) interest for the year plus the amortization of the discount for the year. On the balance sheet, interest for a full interest period ($7,000.00) appears under current liabilities because a cash payment of $7,000.00 is due to be made to bondholders on January 1, 2016, which is the day that follows the balance sheet date. This $7,000.00 results from accrued interest expense (that is, expense that has been incurred but has not yet been paid).

Bonds payable is classified in the long-term liabilities section of the balance sheet because the bonds are due at a date that is beyond one year of the balance sheet date. The balance of the Discount on Bonds Payable account appears as a contra liability item; thus, it is deducted from bonds payable on the balance sheet. In Arnie's situation, the $2,486.69 balance in the discount account at December 31, 2015, is the amount that relates to future interest periods (interest period 3 in this case).

> **TIP:**   After you have studied Appendix 10C, refer to **Exercise 10-13** for an expanded exercise using the same facts as this exercise.

EXERCISE 10-9

Purpose: (L.O. 6) This exercise will illustrate how to account for (1) the redemption of bonds by cash payment prior to maturity, and (2) the conversion of bonds to stock.

The balance sheet for Sea Willy Corporation reports the following information on June 30, 2014:

<u>Long-term liabilities</u>

9% Convertible bonds payable	$1,000,000	
Less: Discount on bonds payable	50,000	$950,000

A semiannual interest payment was made and recorded on June 30, 2014.

Instructions

Prepare the appropriate journal entry for each of the **independent** situations below:

(a)   Interest rates have declined in the market place. Sea Willy decides to borrow money from another source at a lower interest rate to lower its annual interest charges. Therefore, on July 1, 2014, Sea Willy redeems all of the outstanding bonds at 102 (bond prices vary inversely with changes in the market rate of interest).

(b)   Holders of one-half of the bonds exercise the conversion feature. Thus, each of 500 bonds is converted into 12 shares of Sea Willy $50 par common stock on July 1, 2014. At this date, the market price of a bond was $984 and the market value of a share of stock was $82.

SOLUTION TO EXERCISE 10-9

(a)	Bonds Payable	1,000,000	
	Loss on Bond Redemption	70,000	
	Discount on Bonds Payable		50,000
	Cash ($1,000,000 X 1.02)		1,020,000

Approach and Explanation: (1) Always begin with the easiest part of the journal entry. Credit Cash to record the payment of the redemption price which is 102% of the face value of the bonds. (2) Remove the carrying value of the bonds from the accounts by debiting Bonds Payable for the face value of the bonds and crediting Discount on Bonds Payable for the balance of the related unamortized discount. The difference between the redemption (retirement) price and the carrying value of the bonds represents a gain or loss on redemption. An excess of redemption price over carrying value results in a loss; an excess of carrying value over redemption price results in a gain. In the case at hand, the redemption price ($1,020,000) exceeds the carrying value of the bonds ($950,000). When it costs $1,020,000 to eliminate a debt that appears on the books at only $950,000, a loss results.

> **TIP:**   Gains or losses on extinguishment of debt are classified as other revenue or gain or other expense or loss on the income statement.

(b)	Bonds Payable	500,000	
	Discount on Bonds Payable		25,000
	Common Stock (500 X 12 X $50)		300,000
	Paid-in Capital in Excess of Par—Common Stock...		175,000

Approach and Explanation: The carrying value of the bonds being converted ($500,000 face value less the related unamortized bond discount of $25,000 equals the carrying value of $475,000) is transferred to paid-in capital accounts, and no gain or loss is recognized. The journal entry for the conversion (1) removes the carrying value of these bonds from the accounts, (2) records the par value of the related shares of stock in the capital stock account, and (3) records the excess of the bonds' carrying value over the stocks' par value in an additional paid-in capital account.

> **TIP:** This method of recording the bond conversion is often referred to as the **book (or carrying value method.** Notice that with this method the current market price of the bonds (500 X $984 = $492,000) and the current market price of the stocks (500 X 12 X $82 = $492,000) are **not** considered in making this entry.

EXERCISE 10-10

Purpose: (L.O. 7) This exercise will illustrate the accounting entries for a long-term note payable.

The Agron Feelgood Clinic issued a $400,000, 10%, 10-year mortgage note on December 31, 2013. The terms provide for semiannual installment payments of $32,097.03 on June 30 and December 31. The note along with $80,000 cash was given in exchange for a new building.

Instructions
Prepare the journal entries to record:
(a) The acquisition of the building and inception of the mortgage loan payable.
(b) The first mortgage payment on June 30, 2014.
(c) The second mortgage payment on December 31, 2014.

SOLUTION TO EXERCISE 10-10

December 31, 2013

(a)	Building	480,000.00	
	Cash		80,000.00
	Mortgage Notes Payable		400,000.00

June 30, 2014

(b)	Interest Expense	20,000.00*	
	Mortgage Notes Payable	12,097.03**	
	Cash		32,097.03

*Principal balance at December 31, 2013	$400,000.00
Semiannual interest rate	X .05
Interest expense for first 6 months	$ 20,000.00
**First payment	$32,097.03
Interest portion of first payment	(20,000.00)
Reduction in principal - first installment payment	$12,097.03

December 31, 2014

(c) Interest Expense 19,395.15*
     Mortgage Notes Payable..   12,701.88**
          Cash...   32,097.03

*Principal balance at December 31, 2013	$400,000.00
Reduction in principal - first installment payment	(12,097.03)
Principal balance at June 30, 2014	387,902.97
Semiannual interest rate	.05
Interest expense for second 6 months	$ 19,395.15
**Second payment	$32,097.03
Interest portion of second payment	(19,395.15)
Reduction in principal - second installment payment	$12,701.88

Explanation to part (a): The cost of the building is determined by the fair market value of the consideration given which is the $80,000 cash plus the $400,000 present value of the note payable.

Explanation to parts (b) and (c): The mortgage note payable is recorded initially at its face value [see part (a)], which is often referred to as the note's beginning principal, and each installment payment reduces the outstanding principal amount. The installment payments are an equal amount each interest period; however, the portion of the payment going to cover interest charges and the portion going to reduce the outstanding principal varies each period. In this exercise, the installment payments are due semiannually; thus, the length of an interest period is six months and the annual interest rate (10%) must be expressed on a semiannual basis (5%) to perform the interest computation. Interest is a function of outstanding balance, interest rate, and time. Thus, the interest sustained for the first six months is determined by the note's initial carrying value (the face value of $400,000), the annual rate of 10%, and a six-month time period. The interest sustained for the second six months cannot be determined until the outstanding principal balance is updated for the portion of the first installment payment that is to be applied to the principal balance. The updated principal balance (carrying value) is used to compute the interest charges for the second interest period. Although the exercise does not require a complete payment schedule (often called an amortization schedule) for this note, one is presented below for your observation and study. Notice that as subsequent installment payments are made, a decreasing portion of each payment goes to cover interest and an increasing portion is applied to the principal balance. The reason for this is the fact that interest is computed by a constant interest rate (5% each interest period) multiplied by a decreasing principal balance (carrying value).

Mortgage Installment Payment Schedule

Semiannual Interest Period	(A) Cash Payment	(B) Interest Expense (D) X 5%	(C) Reduction of Principal (A) - (B)	(D) Principal Balance (D) - (C)
Issue date				$400,000.00
1	$ 32,097.03	$ 20,000.00	$ 12,097.03	387,902.97
2	32,097.03	19,395.15	12,701.88	375,201.09
3	32,097.03	18,760.05	13,336.98	361,864.11
4	32,097.03	18,093.21	14,003.82	347,860.29
5	32,097.03	17,393.01	14,704.02	333,156.27
6	32,097.03	16,657.81	15,439.22	317.717.05
7	32,097.03	15,885.85	16,211.18	301,505.87
8	32,097.03	15,075.29	17,021.74	284,484.13
9	32,097.03	14,224.21	17,872.82	266,611.31
10	32,097.03	13,330.57	18,766.46	247,844.85
11	32,097.03	12,392.24	19,704.79	228,140.06
12	32,097.03	11,407.00	20,690.03	207,450.03
13	32,097.03	10,372.50	21,724.53	185,725.50
14	32,097.03	9,286.28	22,810.75	162,914.75
15	32,097.03	8,145.74	23,951.29	138,963.46
16	32,097.03	6,948.17	25,148.86	113,814.60
17	32,097.03	5,690.73	26,406.30	87,408.30
18	32,097.93	4,370.42	27,726.61	59,681.69
19	32,097.03	2,984.08	29,112.95	30,568.74
20	32,097.03	1,528.29[a]	30,568.74	0.00
Totals	$641,940.60	$241,940.60	$400,000.00	

[a]Includes rounding error of 15¢.

> **TIP:** The balance of the Mortgage Note Payable account is reported as a liability in the balance sheet. The portion of the installment payments to be made within the next year that represents the reduction of the principal balance is to be reported in the current liability section; the remaining unpaid principal balance is classified in the long-term liability section. For example, the total unpaid balance of this mortgage note payable is $375,201.09 at December 31, 2014 (the end of the second semi-annual interest period). Of that amount, $27,340.80 ($13,336.98 + $14,003.82 = $27,340.80) should be reported as a current liability and $347,860.29 ($375,201.09 - $27,340.80 = $347,860.29) should be reported as a long-term liability.

EXERCISE 10-11

Purpose: (L.O. 3, 8) This exercise will review the computation of the current ratio, debt to total assets ratio, and the times interest earned ratio.

The balance sheets at December 31, 2014 and December 31, 2013 and the income statement for 2014 for the M.F. Specie Corporation are presented below:

M.F. SPECIE CORPORATION
Balance Sheet
December 31

Assets

	2014	2013
Cash	$ 75,000	$ 70,000
Accounts receivable (net)	85,000	60,000
Inventory	170,000	150,000
Plant and equipment (net)	470,000	500,000
Total assets	$800,000	$780,000

Liabilities and stockholders' equity

	2014	2013
Accounts payable	$ 95,000	$130,000
Accrued liabilities	8,000	10,000
Notes payable	100,000	100,000
Common stock, $10 par	300,000	300,000
Retained earnings	297,000	240,000
Total liabilities and stockholders' equity	$800,000	$780,000

M.F. SPECIE CORPORATION
Income Statement
For the Year Ending December 31, 2014

Net sales		$900,000
Cost of goods sold		
Inventory, January 1	$150,000	
Purchases	570,000	
Goods available for sale	720,000	
Inventory, December 31	170,000	550,000
Gross profit		350,000
Operating expenses		
Depreciation	40,000	
Other	184,000	224,000
Income from operations		126,000
Interest expense		6,000
Income before income taxes		120,000
Income tax expense		48,000
Net income		$ 72,000

Additional information: Dividends of $.50 per share were paid in 2014 to common stockholders. The notes payable have a maturity date in 2017. All sales during 2014 were on credit. The market value per share of common stock was $30 at December 31, 2014.

Instructions

A creditor of M.F. Specie Corporation is analyzing recent financial statements to determine the company's short-term liquidity, long run solvency, and ability to pay interest as it comes due.

Refer to the financial statements and compute the following:

(a) Working capital ratio at December 31, 2014.
(b) Debt to total assets ratio at December 31, 2014.
(c) Times interest earned ratio for 2014.

SOLUTION TO EXERCISE 10-11

(a) Current ratio $= \dfrac{\text{Current assets}}{\text{Current liabilities}}$

Current ratio $= \dfrac{\$75,000 \ + \ \$85,000 \ + \ \$170,000}{\$95,000 \ + \ \$8,000} = 3.20:1$

(b) Debt to total assets ratio $= \dfrac{\text{Total liabilities}}{\text{Total assets}}$

Debt to total assets ratio $= \dfrac{\$95,000 \ + \ \$8,000 \ + \ \$100,000}{\$800,000} = 25.38\%$

(c) Times interest earned ratio $= \dfrac{\begin{array}{c}\text{Income before income taxes}\\\text{and interest expense}\end{array}}{\text{Interest expense}}$

Times interest earned ratio $= \dfrac{\$72,000 \ + \ \$48,000 \ + \ \$6,000}{\$6,000} = 21 \text{ times}$

TIP:	By reviewing these calculations, M.F. Specie's creditor can tell that the company has a low credit risk. The company's liquid assets are three times greater than its current obligations, i.e. the company does not have to struggle to meet monthly payments. Total debt is relatively low when compared to the total assets the company has access to, and interest expense represents only a small portion of the company's income.

*EXERCISE 10-12

Purpose: (L.O. 10) This exercise will illustrate the computations and journal entries for a bond when the effective-interest method of amortization is used.

The Jan Larsen Corporation issued bonds with the following details:

Face value	$100,000.00
Contractual interest rate	7%
Market interest rate	10%
Maturity date	January 1, 2017
Date of issuance	January 1, 2014
Issuance price	$92,539.95
Interest payments due	Annually on January 1
Method of amortization	Effective-interest
End of annual reporting period	December 31

Instructions
(a) Complete the amortization schedule for these bonds which appears below.
(b) Prepare the journal entries to record:
   (1) The issuance of the bonds on January 1, 2014.
   (2) The adjusting entry(s) at December 31, 2014.
   (3) The payment entry on January 1, 2015. (Assume reversing entries are not used.)

Amortization Schedule

Annual Interest Periods	(A) Interest to be Paid (7% X ___?___)	(B) Interest Expense to be Recorded (10% X Preceding Bond Carrying Value)	(C) Discount Amortization (B) - (A)	(D) Unamortized Discount (D) - (C)	(E) Bond Carrying Value ($ ___?___ - D)
Issue date			$		$92,539.95
1	$	$	$		
2					
3					
	$_____	$_____	$_____		

SOLUTION TO EXERCISE 10-12

(a)

Amortization Schedule

Annual Interest Periods	(A) Interest to be Paid (7% X $100,000)	(B) Interest Expense to be Recorded (10% X Pre- ceding Bond Carrying Value)	(C) Discount Amortization (B) - (A)	(D) Unamortized Discount (D) - (C)	(E) Bond Carrying Value ($100,000 - D)
Issue date				$7,460.05	$ 92,539.95
1	$ 7,000.00	$ 9,254.00	$2,254.00	5,206.05	94,793.95
2	7,000.00	9,479.40	2,479.40	2,726.65	97,273.35
3	7,000.00	9,726.65*	2,726.65	-0-	100,000.00
	$21,000.00	$28,460.05	$7,460.05		

*Includes rounding error of 69¢.

Explanation: Interest to be paid (stated interest) is determined by multiplying the face value ($100,000) by the contractual interest rate (7%). Interest expense is computed by multiplying the carrying value at the beginning of the interest period by the effective-interest rate (10%). The amount of discount amortization for the period is the excess of the interest expense over the stated interest (cash interest) amount. The carrying value at an interest payment date is the carrying value at the beginning of the interest period plus the discount amortization for the period.

TIP:	The amount of interest expense of $9,479.40 appearing on the 2nd interest period (or second payment line) is the amount of interest expense for the interest period ending on that date. Thus, in this case, $9,479.40 is the interest expense for the twelve months preceding the second interest payment date (January 1, 2016) which would be the calendar year of 2015.
TIP:	Any rounding error should be plugged to (included in) the interest expense amount for the last period. Otherwise, there would forever be a small balance left in the Discount on Bonds Payable account long after the bonds were extinguished.
TIP:	Notice that the total interest expense ($28,460.05) over the three-year period equals the total cash interest ($21,000.00) plus the total issuance discount ($7,460.05). Thus, you can see that the issuance discount represents an additional amount of interest to be recognized over the life of the bonds.
TIP:	Instead of just memorizing what goes on an amortization schedule, think about the reason the amounts have been included. That will help you to construct a schedule without much effort. In the interest period (or date) column, start with the issuance date, followed by each interest period (or date). The cash (stated) interest amount is computed by multiplying the face value of the instrument by the contractual interest rate per period. Interest expense is computed by multiplying the carrying value at the beginning of the period (end of the previous line on the amortization schedule) by the effective-interest rate per period. The difference between the stated interest and the interest expense for the period is the amount of the amortization for the period. Discount amortization is added to the previous carrying value (or premium amortization is deducted from the previous carrying value) to arrive at the carrying value at the end of the interest period (interest payment date).

> **TIP:** The amortization schedule displays amounts according to bond periods. If one interest period overlaps into two different accounting periods, the amount of expense and amortization for that interest period must be appropriately allocated to the respective accounting periods. Thus, when the accounting period ends on a date other than an interest date, the amortization schedule for a bond or a note payable is unaffected by this fact. That is, the schedule is prepared and computations are made according to the bond periods, ignoring the details of the accounting period. The interest expense amounts shown in the amortization schedule are then apportioned to the appropriate accounting period(s). As an example, if the interest expense for the six months ending April 30, 2015 is $120,000, then $40,000 of that amount would go on the income statement for the 2014 calendar year and $80,000 of it should be reflected on the income statement for the 2015 calendar year.
>
> **TIP:** Notice that when the effective-interest method is used for bonds issued at a discount, the interest expense amount increases each period because interest is computed by multiplying a constant rate (effective-interest rate) times an increasing carrying value (the carrying value is increasing due to the amortization of the discount).

(b)   (1)

January 1, 2014

Cash	92,539.95	
Discount on Bonds Payable	7,460.05	
Bonds Payable		100,000.00
(To record the issuance of bonds payable)		

(2)

December 31, 2014

Bond Interest Expense	9,254.00	
Interest Payable		7,000.00
Discount on Bonds Payable		2,254.00
(To record accrued interest and amortization of bond discount)		

(3)

January 1, 2015

Bond Interest Payable	7,000.00	
Cash		7,000.00
(To record payment of bond interest)		

*EXERCISE 10-13

Purpose: (L.O. 5, 11) This exercise will illustrate the computations and journal entries made throughout a bond's life when the straight-line method of amortization is used.

Arnie Howell Corporation issued bonds with the following details:

Face value	$100,000.00
Contractual interest rate	7%
Market interest rate	10%
Maturity date	January 1, 2017
Date of issuance	January 1, 2014
Issuance price	$92,539.95
Interest payments due	Annually on January 1
Method of amortization	Straight-line
End of annual reporting period	December 31

Instructions
(a)   Compute the amount of issuance premium or discount.
(b)   Prepare the journal entry for the issuance of the bonds.
(c)   Complete the amortization schedule (for these bonds) which appears below. Also supply the missing amount in the heading for columns (A), (C), and (E).
(d)   Prepare all of the journal entries (subsequent to the issuance date) for 2014, 2015, and 2016. (Assume reversing entries are not used.)
(e)   Prepare the journal entry to record the payment of the face value at the maturity date. Also prepare the journal entry to record the final interest payment due on January 1, 2017.

Amortization Schedule

Annual Interest Periods	(A) Interest to be Paid (7% X $?)	(B) Interest Expense to be Recorded (A) + (C)	(C) Discount Amortization ($? ÷ 3)	(D) Unamortized Discount (D) - (C)	(E) Bond Carrying Value ($? - D)
Issue date				$	$92,539.95
1	$	$	$		
2					
3					
	$_____	$_____	$_____		

SOLUTION TO EXERCISE 10-13

(a)
Face value of bonds	$100,000.00
Issuance price of bonds	92,539.95
Discount on bonds payable	$ 7,460.05

TIP: An excess of face value over issuance price results in a **discount.**

January 1, 2014

(b)
Cash	92,539.95	
Discount on Bonds Payable	7,460.05	
Bonds Payable...		100,000.00
(To record sale of bonds at a discount)		

Approach and Explanation: Always start with the easiest part of a journal entry. The issuance of a bond is **always** recorded by a credit to the Bonds Payable account for the face value of the bonds ($100,000 in this case). Because the issuance price is less than face, a contra type valuation account must be established; it is titled Discount on Bonds Payable and is debited for the issuance discount of $7,460.05. Cash was received for the issuance price so debit Cash for the proceeds of $92,539.95.

TIP: The Discount on Bonds Payable account is sometimes called Unamortized Bond Discount. Regardless of whether the word unamortized appears in the account title or not, the balance of this account at a balance sheet date (after adjustments) represents the unamortized amount.

(c)

Amortization Schedule

Annual Interest Periods	(A) Interest to be Paid (7% X $100,000.00)	(B) Interest Expense to be Recorded (A) + (C)	(C) Discount Amortization ($7,460.05 ÷ 3)	(D) Unamortized Discount (D) - (C)	(E) Bond Carrying Value ($100,000.00 - D)
Issue date				$7,460.05[1]	$ 92,539.95
1	$ 7,000.00	$ 9,486.68	$2,486.68	4,973.37	95,026.63
2	7,000.00	9,486.68	2,486.68	2,486.69	97,513.31
3	7,000.00	9,486.69[2]	2,486.69[2]	-0-	100,000.00
	$21,000.00	$28,460.05	$7,460.05		

[1]Face value ($100,000.00) minus the issuance price ($92,539.95) = Discount on issuance ($7,460.05).
[2]Any rounding errors are plugged to (included in) the interest expense amount for the last period. Otherwise, there would forever be a small balance left in the Discount on Bonds Payable account long after the bonds were extinguished. Hence, interest expense increased by a penny in interest period 3 due to a rounding difference.

TIP: Column (A) remains constant because the face value of the bonds ($100,000) is multiplied by the annual contractual interest rate (7.0%) to compute the interest to be paid each period. Column (B) is computed as the interest paid (Column A) plus the discount amortization (Column C). Column (C) indicates the discount amortization each period. Column (D) decreases each period by the same amount of amortization until it reaches zero at maturity.

Column (E) increases each period by the amount of discount amortization until it equals the face value at maturity.

The straight-line method of amortization is used in this exercise. This method causes (1) the amounts in Column (B) to be equal each period, (2) the balance in Column (D) to change by an equal amount each period, and (3) the amount in Column (E) to change by an equal amount each period.

TIP: An amount in the "Bond Carrying Value" column (Column E) represents the carrying value at the end of the related interest period. Thus, $95,026.63 is the carrying value at December 31, 2014. (The first interest period is the calendar year of 2014). The carrying value at an interest payment date is the carrying value at the beginning of the interest period plus the discount amortization for the period.

TIP: Although most homework assignments call for rounding to the nearest dollar, the amounts in this exercise are rounded to the nearest cent.

TIP: Notice that the total interest expense ($28,460.05) over the three-year period equals the total cash interest ($21,000.00) plus the total issuance discount ($7,460.05). Thus, you can see that the issuance discount represents an additional amount of interest to be recognized over the life of the bonds.

(d)

December 31, 2014

Bond Interest Expense	9,486.68	
Discount on Bonds Payable		2,486.68
Bond Interest Payable		7,000.00
(To record accrued bond interest and amortization of bond discount)		

January 1, 2015

Bond Interest Payable	7,000.00	
Cash		7,000.00
(To record payment of bond interest)		

December 31, 2015

Bond Interest Expense	9,486.68	
Discount on Bonds Payable		2,486.68
Bond Interest payable		7,000.00
(To record accrued bond interest and amortization of bond discount)		

January 1, 2016

Bond Interest Payable	7,000.00	
Cash		7,000.00
(To record payment of bond interest)		

December 31, 2016

Bond Interest Expense	9,468.69	
Discount on Bonds Payable		2,486.69
Bond Interest Payable		7,000.00
(To record accrued bond interest and amortization of bond discount)		

(e)   <u>**January 1, 2017**</u>

Bonds Payable	100,000.00	
Cash..		100,000.00
(To record payment of face value of bonds at maturity)		
Bond Interest Payable	7,000.00	
Cash..		7,000.00
(To record payment of bond interest)		

> TIP: Refer to the **Solution to Exercise 10-8** to review how these bonds would affect the financial statements for the second year of the bond's life.

EXERCISE 10-14

Purpose: (L.O. 1 thru 11) This exercise will quiz you about terminology used in this chapter.

A list of accounting terms with which you should be familiar appears below:

Bearer (coupon) bonds	Long-term liabilities
Bond certificate	Market interest rate
Bond indenture	Mortgage bond
Bonds	Mortgage note payable
Callable bonds	Notes payable
Contractual interest rate	Premium (on a bond)
Convertible bonds	Registered bonds
Current liabilities	Secured bonds
Current ratio	Serial bonds
Debenture bonds	Sinking fund bonds
Debt to total assets ratio	**Straight-line method of amortization
Discount (on a bond)	Term bonds
*Effective-interest method	Times interest earned ratio
of amortization	Unsecured bonds
*Effective-interest rate	Working capital
Face value (par value)	

*This material is covered in Appendix 10B in the text.
**This material is covered in Appendix 10C in the text.

Instructions
For each item below, enter in the blank the term that is described.

1. _____ Obligations expected to be paid more than one year in the future.

2. _____ Bonds **not** registered.

3. _____ A form of interest bearing notes payable issued by corporations, universities, and governmental entities.

4. _____ Bonds issued in the name of the owner.

5. _____ Bonds that are subject to call and retirement at a stated dollar amount prior to maturity at the option of the issuer.

6. _____ Bonds that permit bondholders to convert them into common stock at their option.

7. _____ Bonds issued against the general credit of the borrower. Also called **unsecured bonds.**

8. _____ Bonds issued against the general credit of the borrower. Also called **debenture bonds.**

9. _____ Bonds that have specific assets of the issuer pledged as collateral.

10. _____ Bonds that mature at a single specified future date.

11. _____ Bonds that mature in installments.

12. _____ Amount of principal due at the maturity date of the bond.

13. _____ Rate used to determine the amount of interest the borrower pays and the investor receives.

14. _____ Rate established when the bonds are issued and remains constant in each interest period.

15. _____ The rate investors demand for loaning funds to the corporation.

16. _____ A method of amortizing bond discount or bond premium that results in periodic interest expense that is the same amount each interest period.

17. _____ A method of amortizing bond discount or bond premium that results in periodic interest expense equal to a constant percentage of the carrying value of the bonds.

18. _____ A legal document that sets forth the terms of the bond issue.

19. _____ A bond secured by real estate.

20. _____ A legal document that indicates the name of the issuer, the face value of the bonds, and other data such as the contractual interest rate and maturity date of the bonds.

21. _____ Bonds secured by specific assets set aside to retire them.

22. _____ A long-term note secured by a mortgage that pledges title to specific units of property as security for the loan.

23. _____A measure of a company's liquidity, computed as the difference between current assets and current liabilities.

24. _____A measure of a company's liquidity, computed as current assets divided by current liabilities.

25. _____A solvency measure that indicates the percentage of total assets provided by creditors, computed as total debt divided by total assets.

26. _____A solvency measure that indicates a company's ability to meet interest payments, computed by dividing income before income taxes and interest expense by interest expense.

27. _____The amount by which a bond sells at less than its face value.

28. _____The amount by which a bond sells above its face value.

29. _____Obligations in the form of promissory notes.

30. _____Debts that a company reasonably expects to pay from existing current assets within the next year or operating cycle.

SOLUTION TO EXERCISE 10-14

1. Long-term liabilities
2. Bearer (coupon) bonds
3. Bonds
4. Registered bonds
5. Callable bonds
6. Convertible bonds
7. Debenture bonds
8. Unsecured bonds
9. Secured bonds
10. Term bonds
11. Serial bonds
12. Face value (par value)
13. Contractual interest rate
14. Effective-interest rate
15. Market interest rate
16. Straight-line method of amortization
17. Effective-interest method of amortization
18. Bond indenture
19. Mortgage bond
20. Bond certificate
21. Sinking fund bonds
22. Mortgage note payable
23. Working capital
24. Current ratio
25. Debt to total assets ratio
26. Times interest earned ratio
27. Discount (on a bond)
28. Premium (on a bond)
29. Notes payable
30. Current liabilities

ANALYSIS OF MULTIPLE-CHOICE TYPE QUESTIONS

1. **Question**
    (L.O. 1) A current liability is an obligation that:
    a. was paid during the current period.
    b. will be reported as an expense within the year or operating cycle that follows the balance sheet date, whichever is longer.
    c. will be converted to a long-term liability within the next year.
    d. is expected to require the use of current assets or the creation of another current liability to liquidate it.

    Approach and Explanation: Before you read the answer selections, write down the definition for current liability. Compare each answer selection with your definition. A **current liability** is an obligation which will come due within one year and whose liquidation is reasonably expected to require the use of existing resources properly classifiable as current assets or the creation of other current liabilities. (Solution = d.)

2. **Question**
    (L.O. 1) Included in Jurassick Company's liability accounts at December 31, 2014, was the following:

12% note payable issued in 2004 for cash and due in May 2015	$200,000
Sales taxes payable	16,000
Interest payable	11,000
Federal income tax withholdings	6,000

    How much of the above should be included in the current liability section of Jurassick's balance sheet at December 31, 2014?
    a. $27,000.
    b. $33,000.
    c. $227,000.
    d. $233,000.

    Explanation: All of the obligations will become due within a year of the balance sheet date and will require the use of current assets to liquidate them ($200,000 + $16,000 + $11,000 + $6,000 = $233,000). (Solution = d.)

3. **Question**
    (L.O. 1, 3) Which of the following should be reported as a current liability at December 31, 2014?
    a. Revenue received in advance to be earned in 2015.
    b. Installment loan payments due after December 31, 2015.
    c. Pension obligations estimated to mature in ten years.
    d. Note payable due in 2016.

    Approach and Explanation: Define current liability. A **current liability** is an obligation that comes due within one year of the balance sheet date and is expected to require the use of current assets or the incurrence of another current liability to liquidate it. Analyze each answer selection to see if it meets the definition. Revenue received in advance represents an obligation to perform services or to deliver goods or to provide a refund to the customer. If the revenue will be earned in the period that immediately follows the balance sheet date, it is a current liability; if it will be earned beyond that one year mark, it is to be classified as a long-term liability. Selections "b", "c", and "d", are all incorrect because they do not meet the definition. (Solution = a.)

4.   **Question**

(L.O. 2) Which of the following is true regarding a situation where the accounting period ends on a date that does **not** coincide with an interest payment date for a note payable that is outstanding?

a.   No adjusting entry is required. The interest expense will be recorded in the period it is paid.

b.   An adjusting entry is required and it contains a debit to Interest Expense and a credit to Interest Payable.

c.   An adjusting entry is required and it contains a debit to Note Payable and a credit to Interest Expense.

d.   An adjusting entry is required and it contains a debit to Income Summary and a credit to Interest Expense.

Explanation: An adjusting entry is required to properly match the interest expense with the time period for which the interest was incurred. Interest is payment for use of someone else's money. The cost of that use should be matched with the period to which the interest pertains. (Solution = b.)

5.   **Question**

(L.O. 2) A note payable dated October 1, 2014 has a face value of $10,000, an interest rate stipulated at 10%, and a maturity date of April 1, 2015. Interest expense (pertaining to this note) to appear on the income statement for the year ending December 31, 2014 amounts to:

a. $0.

b. $125.00.

c. $166.67.

d. $250.00.

Approach and Explanation: Write down the formula for computing interest. Plug in the amounts given and solve.

$$\frac{\text{Face}}{\text{Value}} \times \frac{\text{Interest}}{\text{Rate}} \times \text{Time} = \text{Interest}$$

$10,000 X   10%   X 3/12 = $250.00   (Solution = d.)

6.   **Question**

(L.O. 3) McGuire Company sells a product on credit for $200. The sale is subject to a 5% state sales tax which is **not** included in the $200. The entry to record the sale would include a:

a.   debit to Accounts Receivable for $200.

b.   credit to Sales for $210.

c.   credit to Sales Taxes Payable for $10.

d.   debit to Sales Taxes for $10.

Approach and Explanation: Before looking at the alternative answers, prepare the journal entry on paper (or mentally). Then find the solution that agrees with your entry. The entry is:

Accounts Receivable	210	
Sales		200
Sales Taxes Payable		10

The sales tax is levied by the state government. The company making the sale acts as an agent for the state government as it collects the tax and remits it to the taxing authority. (Solution = c.)

7. **Question**
   (L.O. 3) Working capital is computed by the formula:
   a. assets - liabilities.
   b. current assets - current liabilities
   c. assets - stockholders' equity
   d. current assets - inventories

   Explanation: Working capital is the excess of current assets over current liabilities. It is a measure of short-term liquidity of the entity. (Solution = b.)

8. **Question**
   (L.O. 3) The current ratio is computed by the formula:
   a. current assets minus current liabilities.
   b. current assets divided by current liabilities.
   c. cash divided by current liabilities.
   d. total assets divided by total liabilities.

   Approach and Explanation: Write down the formula for the current ratio **before** you read the answer selections. Choose the answer that matches the formula.

   $$\text{Current ratio} = \frac{\text{Current assets}}{\text{Current liabilities}}$$

   Answer selection "a" is the formula for computing the amount of working capital. Answer selections "c" and "d" do not describe any useful ratio computations. (Solution = b.)

9. **Question**
   (L.O. 4) Bonds which contain a provision that permits the issuing corporation to redeem the bonds prior to the regularly scheduled maturity date are called:
   a. convertible bonds.
   b. debenture bonds.
   c. callable bonds.
   d. secured bonds.

   Approach and Explanation: Briefly define each of the answer selections. Choose the one that agrees with the stem of the question. **Convertible bonds** permit bondholders to convert them into common stock at the option of the investor. **Debenture bonds** are **unsecured bonds;** hence, they are issued with only the general credit rating of the borrower to back them up. **Callable bonds** are bonds subject to retirement at a stated dollar amount prior to maturity at the option of the issuer. **Secured bonds** have specific assets of the issuer pledged as collateral for the bonds. For example, a bond secured by real estate is called a **mortgage bond.** (Solution = c.)

10. **Question**
(L.O. 4) Bonds for which the owners' names are **not** registered with the issuing corporation are called:
a. bearer bonds.
b. term bonds.
c. debenture bonds.
d. secured bonds.

Approach and Explanation: Briefly define each answer selection. Choose the one that is described in the question's stem. **Bearer (or coupon) bonds** are bonds for which the name of the owner is not registered with the issuer; bondholders are required to send in coupons to receive interest payments and the bonds may be transferred directly to another party. **Registered bonds** are bonds registered in the name of the owner. **Term bonds** are bonds that mature (become due for payment) at a single specified future date. **Debenture bonds** are unsecured bonds. **Secured bonds** are bonds having specific assets pledged as collateral by the issuer. (Solution = a.)

11. **Question**
(L.O. 4) Term bonds are bonds which:
a. may be redeemed by the issuing corporation prior to the scheduled maturity date.
b. may be exchanged by the bondholders for common stock at the end of the bond term.
c. mature in one lump sum at the maturity date.
d. cannot be sold by the bondholders because they are required to be held by one owner for the entire term of the bond.

Explanation: Term bonds are bonds that are due for payment (mature) at a single specified future date. In contrast, bonds that mature in installments are called **serial bonds.** Answer selection "a" describes **callable bonds.** Answer selection "b" hints at the description of **convertible bonds;** however, the conversion can take place during the term. Answer selection "d" is a nonsense type response. (Solution = c.)

12. **Question**
(L.O. 5) Assume the face value of a bond is $1,000. If the bond's current price is quoted at 102 3/4, the bond price is:
a. $1,000.
b. $1,002.75.
c. $1,020.75.
d. $1,027.50.

Approach and Explanation: Convert the fraction (3/4) to a decimal (.75). Now take 102.75% of the bonds face value to determine its current price of $1,027.50. (Solution = d.)

13. **Question**

(L.O. 5) A large department store issues bonds with a maturity date that is twenty years after the issuance date. If the bonds are issued at a discount, this indicates that at the date of issuance, the:
a. contractual rate of interest and the stated rate of interest coincide.
b. contractual rate of interest exceeds the market rate.
c. market rate exceeds the stated rate of interest.
d. stated rate of interest exceeds the effective rate.

Approach and Explanation: Before reading the answer selections, write down the relationship that causes a bond to be issued at a discount: market interest rate exceeds the contractual (stated) interest rate. Then list the synonymous terms for market interest rate and for contractual (stated) interest rate: (1) market rate and effective rate; (2) contractual rate, stated rate, and contract rate. Selection "a" is incorrect because the contractual rate and the stated rate are just different names for the same thing. Selections "b" and "d" are incorrect because an excess of stated rate over the effective rate will result in a premium, not a discount. When the market rate (effective rate) exceeds the stated rate (contractual rate), an issuance discount will result. (Solution = c.)

14. **Question**

(L.O. 5) If the market interest rate at the date of issuance is lower than the contractual interest rate, bonds will:
a. not sell until the issuer changes the contractual interest rate.
b. be sold at a discount.
c. be sold at a premium.
d. be sold at face (par) value.

Approach and Explanation: Think about what happens to a bond price when the market interest rate changes. Bond prices vary inversely with changes in the market interest rate. Thus, as the market interest rate increases, a bond price decreases. If at the date of issuance, the market interest rate equals the contractual interest rate, the bond's price will equal the bond's face (par) value. However, if the market interest rate declines below the contractual interest rate, then the price rises above the bond's face (par) value. (Solution = c.)

15. **Question**

(L.O. 5) The market interest rate for a particular bond issue is:
a. always equal to the stated interest rate.
b. the rate that the issuer will actually bear and the rate that the investor will actually earn over the bond's life.
c. used to calculate the dollar amount of cash interest payments to be made by the issuer.
d. always higher than the stated interest rate.

Explanation: The market interest rate is the rate investors demand for loaning funds to the corporation. A premium or a discount results when the market interest rate differs from the bond's contractual interest rate. A premium or a discount is an adjustment to interest via an adjustment to price. Thus, the market interest rate is the rate the investor actually yields (earns) and the rate the issuer effectively bears (incurs). Answer selection "a" is incorrect because the market interest rate may be equal to, below, or above the stated interest rate. Answer selection "c" is incorrect because the contractual (or stated) interest rate is used to compute the amount of each cash interest payment. Answer selection "d" is incorrect because the market interest rate can be less than the stated interest rate. (Solution = b.)

16. **Question**

    (L.O. 5) The amount of cash to be paid for interest on bonds payable for any given year is calculated by multiplying the:
    a. face value by the stated interest rate.
    b. face value by the market interest rate at the date of issuance.
    c. carrying value at the beginning of the year by the market interest rate in existence at the date of issuance.
    d. carrying value at the beginning of the year by the stated interest rate.

    Explanation: The amount of cash interest to be paid is the amount promised by the bond contract (indenture) which is the contractual (stated) interest rate multiplied by the face value of the bond. (Solution = a.)

17. **Question**

    (L.O. 6) At a balance sheet date, the carrying value of bonds payable which were initially issued at a premium is determined by:
    a. the face value of the bonds without any adjustment.
    b. the market value of the bonds at the balance sheet date.
    c. adding the unamortized premium to the face value.
    d. deducting the unamortized premium from the face value.

    Explanation: A Premium on Bonds Payable account is an adjunct type valuation account; thus the balance of the account is added to the item to which it relates in order to properly value that item on the financial statements. The carrying value (book value) of bonds payable represents the net amount to be reported for bonds payable on the balance sheet. (Solution = c.)

18. **Question**

    (L.O. 6) At December 31, 2014, the following balances existed on the books of the Malloy Corporation:

Bonds Payable	$500,000
Discount on Bonds Payable	70,000
Interest Payable	12,500

    If the bonds are retired on January 1, 2015, at 102, what will Malloy report as a loss on bond redemption?
    a. $92,500.
    b. $80,000.
    c. $67,500.
    d. $10,000.

Approach and Explanation: Write down the format for the computation of the gain or loss on redemption and plug in the amounts from this question.

	Face value	$500,000
-	Unamortized discount	(70,000)
	Carrying value	430,000
-	Redemption price	(510,000)*
=	Gain (Loss) on redemption	$ (80,000)

*$500,000 X 102% = $510,000 redemption price. (Solution = b.)

> **TIP:** The Interest Payable balance also needs to be settled in the retirement process and therefore requires an additional cash outlay; however, it does **not** affect the gain or loss computation.

19. Question

(L.O. 7) A corporation borrowed money from a bank to build a building. The long-term note signed by the corporation is secured by a mortgage that pledges title to the building as security for the loan. The corporation is to pay the bank $80,000 each year for 10 years to repay the loan. Which of the following relationships can you expect to apply to the situation?
a. The balance of mortgage payable at a given balance sheet date will be reported as a long-term liability.
b. The balance of mortgage payable will remain a constant amount over the 10-year period.
c. The amount of interest expense will decrease each period the loan is outstanding, while the portion of the annual payment applied to the loan principal will increase each period.
d. The amount of interest expense will remain constant over the 10-year period.

Explanation: Mortgage notes payable are recorded initially at face value, and entries are required subsequently for each installment payment. Each payment consists of (1) interest on the unpaid principal balance of the loan, and (2) a reduction of loan principal. Because a portion of each payment is applied to the principal, the principal balance decreases each period. Interest for a period of time is computed by multiplying the stated (contract) rate of interest by the principal balance outstanding at the beginning of the period. Thus, the amount of each payment required to cover interest decreases while the portion of the payment applied to the loan principal balance will increase each period. (Solution = c.)

20. Question

(L.O. 8) The debt to total assets ratio measures the:
a. relationship between interest expense and income.
b. portion of assets financed through creditor sources.
c. portion of debt used to acquire assets.
d. relationship between debt and interest expense.

Approach and Explanation: Write down the computation for the debt to total assets ratio and think about its components and their relationship. The debt to total assets ratio is computed by dividing total debt by total assets. This ratio measures the percentage of the total assets provided by creditors. The higher the percentage of debt to total assets, the greater the risk that the company may be unable to meet its maturing obligations. (Solution = b.)

21. Question

(L.O. 8) The times interest earned ratio provides an indication of the:
a. company's ability to meet interest payments as they become due.
b. relationship between current liabilities and current assets.
c. percentage of assets financed by debt.
d. relationship between debt and interest expense.

Approach and Explanation: Write down the computation for the interest earned ratio and think about the relationship of the components of the ratio. The interest earned ratio is computed by dividing interest before income taxes and interest expense by interest expense. This ratio provides an indication of the relationship between income (before taxes and interest expense have been deducted) and the amount of interest expense for the period. It is an indication of the company's ability to meet interest payments as they become due. (Solution = a.)

*22. Question

(L.O. 9) The selling price of a bond will be equal to the:
a. future amount of the bond's face value, calculated by using the market interest rate
b. present value of all interest payments to be made over the bond's remaining life, calculated by using the contractual interest rate.
c. present value of the face value using the contractual interest rate for discounting plus the present value of all remaining interest payments using the market interest rate for discounting.
d. present value of the bond's face value plus the present value of all interest payments to be made over the bond's remaining life, both calculated by using the market interest rate for all present value computations.

Explanation: At any point in time, a bond is worth the present (discounted) value of all of the future cash flows associated with the bond. The bond promises periodic interest payments and the face value at maturity. Thus, the selling price of a bond is determined by the present value of the bond's face (par) value plus the present value of the remaining interest payments. All discounted values are calculated using the market interest rate. (Solution = d.)

*23. Question

(L.O. 10 or 11) The amortization of a discount on bonds payable results in reporting an amount of interest expense for the period which:
a. exceeds the amount of cash interest for the period.
b. equals the amount of cash interest for the period.
c. is less than the amount of cash interest for the period.
d. bears no predictable relationship to the amount of cash interest for the period.

Approach and Explanation: Think about the process of amortizing a discount on bonds payable and how it affects interest expense. The Discount on Bonds Payable has a normal debit balance. Thus, to amortize it, you credit Discount on Bonds Payable and debit Bond Interest Expense. A debit to the expense account increases its balance. Thus, interest expense is comprised of the amount to be paid in cash for interest for the period plus the amount of discount amortization for the period. Another way of viewing this situation is as follows: a discount is an additional amount of interest to be paid at maturity but is recognized (charged to expense) over the periods benefited (which would be the periods the bonds are to be outstanding). (Solution = a.)

*24. Question
(L.O. 10 or 11) The periodic amortization of a premium on bonds payable will:
a. cause the carrying value of the bonds to increase each period.
b. cause the carrying value of the bonds to decrease each period.
c. have no effect on the carrying value of the bonds.
d. cause the carrying value always to be less than the par value of the bonds.

Approach and Explanation: Think about the process of amortizing a premium on bonds payable and how it affects the carrying value of the bonds. The Premium on Bonds Payable account has a normal credit balance. A premium is an adjustment to interest via an adjustment to price. Therefore, the entry to amortize the premium involves a debit to Premium on Bonds Payable and a credit to Bond Interest Expense. The amortization process reduces the balance of the unamortized premium. The carrying value of a bond issued at a premium is calculated by adding the unamortized premium balance to the face (par) value of the bond. Thus, the carrying value of bonds payable issued at a premium will decrease each period until the maturity date (at which time the carrying value will equal the face value). (Solution = b.)

*25. Question
(L.O. 10) At the beginning of 2014, the Alston Corporation issued 10% bonds with a face value of $400,000. These bonds mature in five years, and interest is paid semiannually on June 30 and December 31. The bonds were sold for $370,560 to yield 12%. Alston uses a calendar-year reporting period. Using the effective-interest method of amortization, what amount of interest expense should be reported for 2014? (Round all computations to the nearest dollar.)
a. $44,333.
b. $44,467.
c. $44,601.
d. $45,888.

Approach and Explanation: Write down the formula for computing interest using the effective-interest method of amortization. Use the data in the question to work through the formula. (Solution = c.)

	Carrying value at the beginning of the period	$370,560.00
X	Effective interest rate per interest period	6%
	Interest expense for the first interest period	22,233.60
-	Cash interest for the interest period	20,000.00*
	Amortization of discount for the first interest period	2,233.60
+	Carrying value at the beginning of the first period	370,560.00
	Carrying value at the beginning of the second period	372,793.60
X	Effective interest rate per interest period	6%
	Interest expense for the second interest period	22,367.62
+	Interest expense for the first interest period	22,233.60
=	Interest expense for the calendar year of 2014	$ 44,601.22

*$400,000 X (10% / 2) = $20,000.

TIP: The interest must be computed on a per interest period basis. In this question, the interest period is six months. The interest for 2014 is comprised of the interest for the bond's first two interest periods.

*26. Question

(L.O. 10, 11) If bonds are initially sold at a discount and the straight-line method of amortization is used, interest expense in the earlier years of the bond's life will:

a.   be less than the amount of interest actually paid.

b.   be less than it will be in the latter years of the bond's life.

c.   be the same as what it would have been had the effective-interest method of amortization been used.

d.   exceed what it would have been had the effective-interest method of amortization been used.

Approach and Explanation: Quickly sketch a graph that shows the patterns of and relationships between interest paid, interest expense using the straight-line method, and interest expense using the effective-interest method. The graph appears below. Treat each of the possible answer selections as a True-False question. Look at the graph after reading each of the answer selections to determine if it is a correct statement.

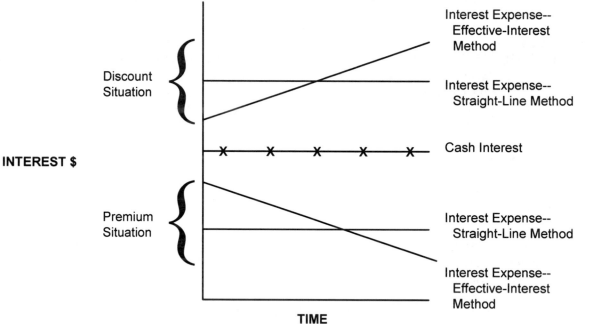

Selection "a" is false because interest expense for a bond issued at a discount will be greater than interest actually paid throughout the bond's entire life, regardless of the amortization method used. Selection "b" is false because interest expense is a constant amount each period when the straight-line method is used; hence, interest expense will be the same amount in the latter years as it is in the earlier years. Selection "c" is false because in the earlier years of life for a bond issued at a discount, interest expense computed using the straight-line method is greater than interest expense computed using the effective-interest method. Selection "d" is true. The interest expense will increase over a bond's life when the bond is issued at a discount and the effective-interest method of amortization is used because the expense is computed by multiplying an increasing carrying value times a constant effective-interest rate. In the earlier years of life that expense amount is less than interest expense computed using the straight-line method, and in the latter years of life, that expense amount is more than interest expense computed using the straight-line method. (Solution = d.)

*27. **Question**

(L.O. 10) Using the effective-interest method, the amount of bond discount to be amortized for a given period is calculated by:

a.   deducting the amount of cash interest for the period from the amount of interest expense for the period.

b.   adding the amount of cash interest for the period and the amount of interest expense for the period.

c.   deducting the amount of interest expense for the period from the carrying value of the liability.

d.   multiplying the carrying value of the bond at the beginning of the period by the stated interest rate.

Approach and Explanation: Think about the manner in which interest expense and the discount amortization are computed when the effective-interest method is used.

Interest Expense Using Effective-Interest Method:

       Carrying value of the bond at the beginning of the period

  X <u>Effective interest rate per interest period   </u>

  = Interest expense for the interest period

Amortization Amount Using Effective-Interest Method:

       Interest expense for the interest period

  - <u>Cash interest for the interest period   </u>

  = Amortization of discount for the interest period

Refer to the graph in the **Explanation to Question 26** above. The amount of amortization for a period is the difference between the appropriate "Interest Expense" line and the "Cash Interest" line. (Solution = a.)

· ·

CHAPTER 11

Corporations: Organization, Stock Transactions, Dividends, and Retained Earnings

OVERVIEW

A major source of assets of an entity is owners' equity. Owner's equity of a corporation is called **stockholders' equity** or **shareholders' equity** because the owners of the business hold shares of stock as evidence of their ownership claims. Stockholders' equity typically has two major classifications for reporting purposes: **paid-in capital (contributed capital)** and **retained earnings (earned capital).** Paid-in capital includes the subclassifications of **capital stock** and **additional paid-in capital.** This chapter discusses the issuance of stock and the reacquisition of shares.

The term **earnings** refers to net income for a period. The term **retained earnings** refers to accumulated earnings. That is, retained earnings is the total of all amounts reported as net income since the inception of the corporation less the sum of any amounts reported as net losses and dividends declared since the inception of the corporation. Thus, distributions of corporate profits to stockholders reduce retained earnings. A corporation may distribute cash, noncash assets, or additional shares of the corporation's own stock to its owners in the form of dividends. A distribution of a corporation's own stock results in capitalizing retained earnings. Cash dividends and stock dividends are discussed in this chapter.

SUMMARY OF LEARNING OBJECTIVES

1. **Identify the major characteristics of a corporation.** The major characteristics of a corporation are separate legal existence, limited liability of stockholders, transferable ownership rights, ability to acquire capital, continuous life, corporation management, government regulations, and additional taxes.

2. **Record the issuance of common stock.** When companies record the issuance of common stock for cash, they credit the par value of the shares to Common Stock. They record in a separate paid-in capital account the portion of the proceeds that is above or, below par value. When no-par common stock has a stated value, the entries are similar to those for par value stock. When no-par stock does **not** have a stated value, the entire proceeds are credited to Common Stock.

3. **Explain the accounting for treasury stock.** The cost method is generally used in accounting for treasury stock. Under this approach, Treasury Stock is debited at the price paid to reacquire the shares. The same amount is credited to Treasury Stock when the shares are sold. The difference

between the sales price and cost is recorded in stockholders' equity accounts, not in income statement accounts.

4. **Differentiate preferred stock from common stock.** Preferred stock has contractual provisions that give it priority over common stock in certain areas. Typically, preferred stockholders have a preference as to (1) dividends and (2) assets in the event of liquidation. They usually do not have voting rights.

5. **Prepare the entries for cash dividends and stock dividends.** Entries for both cash and stock dividends are required at the declaration date and at the payment date. At the **declaration date** the entries are: Cash dividend—debit Cash Dividends and credit Dividends Payable; small stock dividend—debit Stock Dividends, credit Common Stock Dividends Distributable and credit Paid-in Capital in Excess of Par (or Stated) Value. On the **payment date**, the entries for cash and stock dividends, respectively, are: debit Dividends Payable and credit Cash; and debit Common Stock Dividends Distributable and credit Common Stock.

6. **Identify the items that are reported in a retained earnings statement.** Each of the individual debits and credits to retained earnings should be reported in the retained earnings statement. Additions consist of net income and prior period adjustments to correct understatements of prior years' net income. Deductions consist of net loss, adjustments to correct overstatements of prior years' net income, cash and stock dividends, and some disposals of treasury stock.

7. **Prepare and analyze a comprehensive stockholders' equity section.** In the stockholders' equity section, paid-in capital and retained earnings are reported and specific sources of paid-in capital are identified. Within paid-in capital, two classifications are shown: capital stock and additional paid-in capital. If a corporation has treasury stock, the cost of treasury stock is deducted from total of paid-in capital and retained earnings to obtain total stockholders' equity. One measure of profitability is the return on common stockholders' equity ratio. It is calculated by dividing net income minus preferred stock dividends by average common stockholders' equity.

*8. **Describe the use and content of the stockholders' equity statement.** Corporations must disclose changes in stockholders' equity accounts and may choose to do so by issuing a separate stockholders' equity statement. This statement, prepared in columnar form, shows changes in each stockholders' equity account and in total stockholders' equity during the accounting period. When this statement is presented, a retained earnings statement is not necessary.

*This material is covered in **Appendix 11A** in the text.

9. **Compute book value per share. Book value per share represents the equity a common stockholder has in the net assets of a corporation from owning one share of stock. When there is only common stock outstanding, the formula for computing book value is: Total Stockholders' Equity ÷ Number of Common Shares Outstanding = Book Value per Share.

This material is covered in **Appendix 11B in the text.

TIPS ON CHAPTER TOPICS

TIP: **Paid-in capital** is often called **contributed capital. Additional paid-in capital** is often called **additional contributed capital. Stockholders** are often called **shareholders. Retained earnings** is sometimes called **earned capital.**

TIP: Make sure you understand the components of **total paid-in capital** which include the capital stock accounts plus additional paid-in capital accounts. **Capital stock** accounts include Common Stock and Preferred Stock. Additional paid-in capital accounts include Paid-in Capital in Excess of Par Value and Paid-in Capital from Treasury Stock.

TIP: As you progress through this chapter, pay particular attention to the effect of the various transactions on total paid-in capital, retained earnings, and total stockholders' equity.

TIP: Additional paid-in capital can arise from many situations which include the following: the issuance of capital stock at a price above par, some treasury stock transactions and the retirement of stock.

TIP: There is a considerable amount of terminology relating to capital stock. You should have a clear understanding of all of the terms mentioned in this chapter before going on to subsequent chapters.

TIP: The **par value** of a stock is an arbitrary value assigned to a share of stock at the time of incorporation and is printed on the stock certificate. Par value usually has **no** direct relationship to the stock's issuance price or to its market value at any date subsequent to the issuance date. The **par value** of a stock has legal significance because it establishes the amount of **legal capital,** which is an amount of owners' equity that must be maintained by the corporation for the protection of creditors.

TIP: The **market value** of a share of stock at a given point in time is the value at which the stock can be bought or sold.

TIP: **Premium** on capital stock is defined as an excess of issuance price over par for newly issued stock. In recording the issuance, this excess is usually credited to an account called Paid-in Capital in Excess of Par Value (which is an adjunct type valuation account). The premium amount is often reported on the balance sheet by the caption Additional Paid-in Capital.

TIP: When a corporation issues more than one class of capital stock (i.e., preferred stock and common stock), each additional paid-in capital account should specify the class of stock to which it relates.

TIP: When stock is issued in a noncash exchange, the cost principle is used to determine the issuance price. Thus, the exchange price is the fair market value (cash equivalent) of the consideration given or the fair market value of the consideration received, whichever is the more objectively determinable.

TIP: Memorize the definition of treasury stock: **Treasury stock** is a corporation's own stock that has been issued, fully paid for, and subsequently reacquired, but not cancelled. Thus treasury shares are **issued shares but are not outstanding shares.** Treasury stock is **not** an asset; rather, it is a contraction of owners' equity. The Treasury Stock account is a **contra equity** account. The **purchase** of treasury stock will cause owners' equity to **decrease** by the cost of the shares acquired; the **sale** of treasury stock will cause owners' equity to **increase** by the selling price of the shares sold.

TIP: The **cost method** is generally used in accounting for **treasury stock**. This method derives its name from the fact that the Treasury Stock account is maintained at the cost of shares purchased. Under the cost method, Treasury Stock is debited at the price paid to reacquire the shares, and the same amount is credited to Treasury Stock when the shares are sold. The Treasury Stock account is classified contra to the sum of all of the other stockholder equity accounts, and its balance is the cost of the treasury shares held.

TIP:	When the cost method is used to account for treasury stock transactions, a "gain on the sale of treasury stock" is an expression used to indicate that treasury stock was sold for a price in excess of the treasury stock's cost; a "loss on the sale of treasury stock" refers to treasury stock which is sold for a price that is less than the cost of the treasury shares.
TIP:	When a corporation engages in treasury stock transactions, a gain or loss is **never** reported on the income statement because a corporation cannot have an accounting gain or loss when dealing with the owners of the business in their capacity of being owners of the business. The purchase and sale of treasury stock are capital transactions; there is no element of income in a capital transaction. Treasury stock transactions can sometimes reduce retained earnings but they can **never** increase retained earnings.
TIP:	Once a share of stock is issued by a corporation, any subsequent sale of that share by one investor to another investor is not journalized by the corporation (although the company does keep records of the names of stockholders for dividend and voting purposes). A corporation makes journal entries only when it issues or buys back shares of its stock.
TIP:	Retained earnings represents a source of corporate assets. The balance of the Retained Earnings account at any point in time reflects the total unspecified assets which have been obtained through profitable operations of the reporting entity. The balance of the Retained Earnings account has **no** direct relationship to the amount of cash held by the entity; a corporation can have a large balance in the Cash account and a small balance in Retained Earnings or a small balance in Cash and a large balance in Retained Earnings.
TIP:	**Stockholders' equity** is often referred to as **capital.** In accounting for stockholders' equity, the emphasis is on the source. **Retained earnings** is sometimes called **earned capital** because it is the portion of stockholders' equity which has been generated by the entity's operations. **Paid-in capital** is often called **contributed capital** or **invested capital** because it arises from owner contributions.

EXERCISE 11-1

Purpose: (L.O. 1) This exercise will review the major characteristics of a corporation.

Twenty-two businessmen in the local community have a plan to start a new business. They have decided to use the corporate form of organization.

Instructions
List and briefly describe the most important characteristics of a corporation that distinguish it from a proprietorship or partnership form of organization.

SOLUTION TO EXERCISE 11-1

The most important characteristics of a corporation that distinguish it from a proprietorship or partnership are as follows:

1. **Separate legal existence.**

    As an entity separate and distinct from its owners, the corporation acts under its own name rather than in the name of its stockholders. A corporation may buy, own, and sell property, borrow money, and enter into legally binding contracts in its own name. It may also sue or be sued, and it pays its own taxes.

    In contrast to a partnership, in which the acts of the owners (partners) bind the partnership, the acts of the owners (stockholders) do not bind the corporation unless such owners are duly appointed agents of the corporation.

2. **Limited liability of stockholders.**

    Since a corporation is a separate legal entity, creditors ordinarily have recourse only to corporate assets to satisfy their claims. The liability of stockholders is normally limited to their investment in the corporation, and creditors have no legal claim on the personal assets of the owners unless fraud has occurred. Thus, even in the event of bankruptcy of the corporation, stockholders' losses are generally limited to their capital investment in the corporation.

3. **Transferable ownership rights.**

    Ownership of a corporation is shown in shares of capital stock, which are transferable units. Stockholders may dispose of part or all of their interest in a corporation simply by selling their stock. In contrast to the transfer of an ownership interest in a partnership, which requires the consent of each owner, the transfer of stock is entirely at the discretion of the stockholder. It does not require the approval of either the corporation or other stockholders. The transfer of ownership rights between stockholders normally has no effect on the operating activities of the corporation or on a corporation's assets, liabilities, and total ownership equity. That is, the enterprise does not participate in the transfer of these ownership rights after it issues the capital stock.

4. **Ability to acquire capital.**

    It generally is relatively easy for a corporation to obtain capital through the issuance of stock. Buying stock in a corporation is often more attractive to an investor than investing in a partnership. A stockholder has limited liability, and shares of stock are readily transferable. Moreover, many individuals can become stockholders by investing small amounts of money. In sum, the ability of a successful corporation to obtain capital is virtually unlimited.

5. **Continuous life.**

    The life of a corporation is stated in its charter; it may be perpetual or it may be limited to a specific number of years. If it is limited, the period of existence can be extended through renewal of the charter. Since a corporation is a separate legal entity, the life of a corporation and its continuance as a going concern are not affected by the withdrawal, death, or incapacity of a stockholder, employee, or officer. As a result, a successful enterprise can have a continuous and perpetual life.

6. **Corporation management.**

   Although stockholders legally own the corporation, they manage the corporation indirectly through a board of directors they elect. The board, in turn, formulates the operating policies for the company and selects officers, such as a president and one or more vice-presidents, to execute policy and to perform daily management functions. The organizational structure of a corporation enables a company to hire professional managers to run the business. On the other hand, the separation of ownership and management prevents owners from having an active role in managing the company.

7. **Government regulations.**

   A corporation is subject to numerous state and federal regulations. For example, state laws usually prescribe the requirements for issuing stock, the distributions permitted to stockholders, and the effects of retiring stock, as well as other procedures and restrictions. Similarly, federal securities laws govern the sale of capital stock to the general public, and most publicly held corporations are required to make extensive disclosure of their financial affairs to the Securities and Exchange Commission through quarterly and annual reports. In addition, when a corporate stock is listed and traded on organized securities markets, the corporation must comply with the reporting requirements of these exchanges.

   Government regulations are designed to protect the owners of the corporation. Unlike the owners of unincorporated entities, most stockholders do not participate in the day-to-day management of the company.

8. **Additional taxes.**

   Neither proprietorships nor partnerships pay income taxes. The owner's share of these organizations' earnings is reported on his or her personal income tax return. Taxes are then paid by the individual on this amount. Corporations, on the other hand, must pay federal and state income taxes. These taxes are substantial; they can amount to as much as 40% of taxable income. In addition, stockholders are required to pay taxes on cash dividends, which are pro rata distributions of net income. Thus, many argue that corporate income is **taxed twice (double taxation),** once at the corporate level, and again at the individual level.

EXERCISE 11-2

Purpose: (L.O. 1, 7) This exercise will review the meaning of some important terminology related to the area of stockholders' equity.

A corporation's common stock may have a par value or it may be a no-par stock. A no-par stock may or may not have a stated value.

The five different situations described below are examples of the various ways stockholders' equity may be structured:

1. Zollo Corporation has 100,000 authorized shares of $10 par value common stock. 60,000 shares were issued at an average price of $33 each. The balance of retained earnings at December 31, 2014 is $630,000.

2. Oiler Corporation has 50,000 authorized shares of no-par common stock. The stock has a stated value of $1 per share. 10,000 shares were issued at an average price of $25 each. The balance of retained earnings at December 31, 2014 is $140,000.

3. Kelly Corporation has 100,000 authorized shares of no-par common stock with no stated value. All of the 40,000 issued shares were sold for $24 each. The balance of retained earnings at December 31, 2014 is $300,000.

4. Scotty Corporation has 100,000 authorized shares of $40 par common stock. 70,000 shares were issued at an average price of $68. 6,000 of these shares were reacquired and are currently held in the treasury; they were purchased for $60 each. The balance of retained earnings at December 31, 2014 is $1,500,000.

5. Grennan Corporation has 200,000 authorized shares of $10 par common stock and 100,000 authorized shares of $100 par preferred stock. Over the years, 150,000 shares of common were issued at an average price of $40 per share and 50,000 shares of preferred were issued at average price of $102. There are 2,000 shares of treasury—common which were acquired at $30 per share. The balance of retained earnings at December 31, 2014 is $2,515,000.

Instructions
Assume it is December 31, 2014. For each of the **independent** situations above, determine the following:
(a)   Total paid-in capital.
(b)   Total stockholders' equity.
(c)   Number of common stock shares outstanding.

SOLUTION TO EXERCISE 11-2

1. (a) Balance of Common Stock account .... $ 600,000*
      Balance of Paid-in Capital in Excess of Par
        Value account 1,380,000**
      Total paid-in capital $1,980,000

   *60,000 shares issued X $10 par value per share = $600,000.
   **60,000 shares issued X ($33 issuance price - $10 par value per share) = $1,380,000
   additional paid-in capital.

   (b) Total paid-in capital [part (b) above] $1,980,000
      Retained earnings 630,000
      Total stockholders' equity at December 31, 2014 .... $2,610,000

   (c) Shares issued 60,000
      Treasury shares held .... (0)
      Shares outstanding 60,000

2. (a) Balance of Common Stock account .... $ 10,000*
      Balance of Paid-in Capital in Excess of Stated
        Value account 240,000**
      Total paid-in capital $250,000

   *10,000 shares issued X $1 stated value per share = $10,000.
   **10,000 shares issued X ($25 issuance price - $1 stated value per share) =
     $240,000 additional paid-in capital.

   (b) Total paid-in capital [part (b) above] $250,000
      Retained earnings 140,000
      Total stockholders' equity at December 31, 2014 .... $390,000

   (c) Shares issued 10,000
      Treasury shares held .... (0)
      Shares outstanding 10,000

3. (a) Balance of Common Stock account $960,000*
      Total paid-in capital $960,000

   *40,000 shares X $24 issuance price = $960,000.

   (b) Total paid-in capital [part (b) above] .... $ 960,000
      Retained earnings 300,000
      Total stockholders' equity at December 31, 2014 .... $1,260,000

   (c) Shares issued 40,000
      Treasury shares held .... (0)
      Shares outstanding 40,000

4. (a) Balance of Common Stock account $2,800,000*
         Balance of Paid-in Capital in Excess of Par Value
           account   1,960,000**
         Total paid-in capital $4,760,000

    *70,000 shares issued X $40 par value per share = $2,800,000.
    **70,000 shares issued X ($68 issuance price - $40 par value per share) = $1,960,000
    additional paid-in capital.

    (b) Total paid-in capital [part (b) above] $4,760,000
         Retained earnings   1,500,000
         Total paid-in capital plus retained earnings   6,260,000
         Balance of Treasury Stock account   (360,000)*
         Total stockholders' equity at December 31, 2014 $5,900,000

    *6,000 treasury shares X $60 cost each = $360,000 balance of treasury stock.

    (c) Shares issued   70,000
         Treasury shares held   (6,000)
         Shares outstanding   64,000

5. (a) Balance of Preferred Stock account   5,000,000*
         Balance of Common Stock account   1,500,000**
         Balance of Paid-in Capital in Excess of Par Value—
           Preferred account   100,000***
         Balance of Paid-in Capital in Excess of Par Value—
           Common account   4,500,000****
         Total paid-in capital $11,100,000

    *50,000 shares issued X $100 par value per share = $5,000,000.
    **150,000 shares issued X $10 par value per share = $1,500,000.
    ***50,000 shares issued X ($102 issuance price - $100 par value per share) =
         $100,000.
    ****150,000 shares issued X ($40 issuance price - $10 par value per share) =
         $4,500,000.

    (b) Total paid-in capital [part (b) above] $11,100,000
         Retained earnings   2,515,000
         Total paid-in capital plus retained earnings   13,615,000
         Balance of Treasury—Common Stock account   (60,000)*
         Total stockholders' equity at December 31, 2014 $13,555,000

    *2,000 treasury—common shares X $30 cost per share = $60,000.

    (c) Shares of common stock issued   150,000
         Shares of treasury—common stock held   (2,000)
         Shares of common stock outstanding   148,000

Explanation:

(a) **Total paid-in capital** is determined by the sum of the balances of the capital stock account(s) and any additional paid-in capital accounts (such as Paid-in Capital in Excess of Par or Stated Value and Paid-in Capital from Treasury Stock). When a par value stock (or a no-par stock with a stated value) is issued at a price above par (stated value), the par value (stated value) is recorded in the appropriate capital stock account (Common Stock or Preferred Stock) and the excess of issuance price over par (stated) value is recorded in an additional paid-in capital account (Paid-in Capital in Excess of Par [Stated] Value).

(b) **Total stockholders' equity** is the sum of the balances of the paid-in capital accounts and the Retained Earnings account less the balance of the Treasury Stock account.

(c) The **number of common stock shares outstanding** is the number of common stock shares in the hands of shareholders; it is determined by deducting the number of treasury common stock shares from the number of issued common shares.

EXERCISE 11-3

Purpose: (L.O. 2, 3) This exercise will point out the relationship between authorized, issued, outstanding, and subscribed shares.

The following data are available regarding the common stock of the Daffy Corporation at December 31, 2014:

Authorized shares	200,000
Unissued shares	60,000
Treasury shares	12,000

Instructions
Compute the number of outstanding shares.

SOLUTION TO EXERCISE 11-3

Authorized shares	200,000
Unissued shares	(60,000)
Issued shares	140,000
Treasury shares	(12,000)
Outstanding shares	128,000

Approach and Explanation: Write down the formula for determining the number of outstanding shares:

Issued Shares - Treasury Shares = Outstanding Shares

Fill in the data given. Authorized shares are either issued or unissued. The number of issued shares can readily be computed in this situation. Treasury shares are issued shares but are not outstanding (in the hands of shareholders).

EXERCISE 11-4

Purpose: (L.O. 2, 4, 7) This exercise will illustrate how to record selected transactions related to the issuance of capital stock.

On March 1, 2014, Aladdin Corporation received authorization to issue 400,000 shares of $10 par value common stock and 100,000 shares of $50 par value 6% preferred stock. The following transactions occurred during 2014:

March 24   Issued 100,000 shares of common stock for cash at a price of $22 per share.

March 28   Issued 50,000 shares of common stock in exchange for a group of modular warehouses.

June   5   Sold 20,000 shares of preferred stock at $52 each.

Instructions
(a) Prepare the journal entries to record the transactions listed above.
(b) Assuming no other stock transactions occurred during 2014, prepare the stockholders' equity section of the balance sheet at December 31, 2014. Assume the balance of the Retained Earnings account is $820,000 at the balance sheet date.

SOLUTION TO EXERCISE 11-4

(a)

March 24

Cash (100,000 X $22)...	2,200,000	
Common Stock (100,000 X $10)		1,000,000
Paid-in Capital in Excess of Par—Common Stock		1,200,000
(100,000 X $12)		

March 28

Warehouses (50,000 X $22)......................................	1,100,000	
Common Stock (50,000 X $10)		500,000
Paid-in Capital in Excess of Par—Common Stock		600,000
(50,000 X $12)		

June 5

Cash (20,000 X $52)..	1,040,000	
Preferred Stock (20,000 X $50).......................................		1,000,000
Paid-in Capital in Excess of Par—Preferred Stock...........		40,000
(20,000 X $2)		

Explanation:
March 24 The issuance of stock in exchange for cash is recorded by crediting stockholder equity accounts for the amount of the cash consideration received ($2,200,000). The par value ($10) per share is put into the related capital stock account, and the excess of the issuance price over par per share ($12) is recorded in the related additional paid-in capital account. When more than one class of stock is authorized, any additional paid-in capital amounts are properly identified to indicate the related class of stock.

March 28 The issuance of stock in exchange for noncash assets requires an application of the cost principle. The asset and the stock are to be recorded at the fair market value of the consideration given (the stock) or the fair market value of the consideration received (warehouses), whichever is the more clearly determinable. Because some shares of common were issued only four days earlier at $22 per share, the March 24 transaction provides good evidence of the fair value (cash equivalent value) of the stock issued on March 28.

June 5 In recording the issuance of preferred shares for cash, the par value of the preferred shares issued is placed in a capital stock account for that class of stock. The amount received in excess of par is an element of additional paid-in capital; the account title clearly indicates the related class of stock.

(b) Stockholders' equity
    Paid-in capital
        Capital stock
            6% preferred stock, $50 par value, 100,000 shares
                authorized, 20,000 shares issued and outstanding $1,000,000
            Common stock, $10 par value, 400,000 shares
                authorized, 150,000 shares issued and outstanding   1,500,000
            Total capital stock   2,500,000
        Additional paid-in capital
            In excess of par—preferred stock $ 40,000
            In excess of par—common stock   1,800,000
            Total additional paid-in capital   1,840,000
            Total paid-in capital   4,340,000
    Retained earnings   820,000
        Total stockholders' equity $5,160,000

Explanation: When there is more than one class of stock issued, the preferred stock is usually listed first in the stockholders' equity section of the balance sheet. The first two transactions affected the Common Stock account ($1,000,000 + $500,000 = $1,500,000) and its related additional paid-in capital account ($1,200,000 + $600,000 = $1,800,000). Therefore, their effects must be added together to obtain the balances to be reported on the balance sheet.

ILLUSTRATION 11-1
COST METHOD OF ACCOUNTING FOR TREASURY STOCK (L.O. 3)

When treasury stock is purchased:
1. Cash is credited for the cost of the treasury shares acquired.
2. Treasury Stock is debited for the cost of the treasury shares acquired.

When treasury stock is sold:
1. Cash is debited for the selling price of the treasury shares sold.
2. Treasury Stock is credited for the cost of the treasury shares sold.
3. The selling (reissuance) price of the treasury shares is compared with the cost of those shares:
   a. An excess of selling price over cost is credited to Paid-in Capital from Treasury Stock.
   b. An excess of cost over selling price is debited to an additional paid-in capital account related to previous treasury stock transactions of the same class of stock. When the balance of that Paid-in Capital from Treasury Stock account is exhausted, Retained Earnings is debited for the remainder.

When treasury stock is retired:
1. Common Stock is debited for the par (or stated) value of the shares being retired.
2. Paid-in Capital in Excess of Par (or Stated) Value is debited for the pro rata (per share) amount of any excess of original issuance price over par (or stated) value.

> **TIP:** These first two steps in effect remove the amounts from the accounts that were recorded on the day the stock was first issued.

3. Treasury Stock is credited for the cost of the treasury shares being returned.
4. The acquisition cost of the treasury shares is compared with the original issuance price (amount received at the time of their original issuance):
   a. An excess of the original issuance price over the acquisition price of the treasury stock is credited to Paid-in Capital from Treasury Stock.
   b. An excess of the acquisition cost over the original issuance price is charged (debited) to Paid-in Capital from Treasury Stock to the extent of its balance; any deficiency is then charged (debited) to Retained Earnings.

ILLUSTRATION 11-2
JOURNAL ENTRIES FOR RECORDING
TREASURY STOCK TRANSACTIONS (L.O. 3)

1. 1,000 shares of $10 par stock are sold for $13.

Cash	13,000	
Common Stock		10,000
Paid-in Capital in Excess of Par—Common Stock		3,000

2. 100 shares are reacquired for $11 each.

Treasury Stock	1,100	
Cash		1,100

3. 10 treasury shares are sold at $14 each.

Cash	140	
Treasury Stock		110
Paid-in Capital from Treasury Stock		30

4. 10 treasury shares are sold at $6 each.

Cash	60	
Paid-in Capital from Treasury Stock	30	
Retained Earnings	20	
Treasury Stock		110

5. 10 treasury shares are sold at $7 each.

Cash	70	
Retained Earnings	40	
Treasury Stock		110

6. All 70 remaining treasury shares are retired.

Common Stock	700	
Paid-in Capital in Excess of Par Value—Common Stock	210	
Treasury Stock		770
Paid-in Capital from Treasury Stock		140

7. 100 shares are reacquired for $14 each.

Treasury Stock	1,400	
Cash		1,400

8. All 100 shares of treasury stock are retired.

Common Stock	1,000	
Paid-in Capital in Excess of Par Value—Common Stock	300	
Retained Earnings	100	
Treasury Stock		1,400

ILLUSTRATION 11-2 (Continued)

TIP: Assume the transactions take place in the order listed.

Explanation: Refer to the guidelines in **Illustration 11-1** and notice how they are applied in recording the following transactions:

1. **Stock is originally sold for $13 a share.** Assets increase and total stockholders' equity increases. The par value per share is recorded in the capital stock account and the $3 excess of the issuance price ($13) over the par value ($10) per share is recorded in an additional paid-in capital account (Paid-in Capital in Excess of Par).

2. **Treasury shares are acquired at a cost of $11 each.** When the cost method is used to account for treasury stock, the cost of the treasury shares is simply recorded by a debit to Treasury Stock and a credit to Cash for the amount of cash expended. The relationship between the original issuance price ($13 per share) and the cost of the treasury stock ($11 per share) is not a relevant fact.

3. **Treasury shares are sold for a price ($14) above the cost ($11) of these shares.** Therefore, the debit to Cash for the proceeds (selling price of the stock) exceeds the credit to Treasury Stock (for the cost of the shares). This $30 excess is often referred to as a "gain", but it is **not** recorded as a true accounting gain; rather, it is recorded as an increase in additional paid-in capital.

4. **Treasury shares are sold for a price ($6) below the cost ($11) of these shares.** Therefore, the debit to Cash for the proceeds (selling price of the stock) is less than the credit to Treasury Stock (for the cost of the reacquired shares). This difference is first charged to Paid-in Capital from Treasury Stock, if that account has a balance. If and when the credit balance of the account Paid-in Capital from Treasury Stock ($30) is exhausted, any additional excess of cost over selling price ($20) is debited to Retained Earnings. This situation is one where we say there is a $50 "loss" on the sale of treasury stock. Because there can never be an accounting gain or loss in a capital transaction, the charge must be to one or more stockholder equity accounts.

5. **Treasury shares are sold for a price ($7) below the cost ($11) of these shares.** Therefore, the debit to Cash for the proceeds from sale is less than the credit to Treasury Stock for the cost of the treasury shares sold. Because there is no remaining balance in the Paid-in Capital from Treasury Stock account (a previous balance of $30 was eliminated in the transaction immediately prior to this one), the difference is debited to the Retained Earnings account.

6. **Treasury shares are retired at a price ($11) below the stock's original issuance price ($13).** By definition, treasury shares are issued but not outstanding shares. If treasury shares are formally cancelled (retired), they revert to an unissued status. Therefore, the amounts originally recorded in stockholder equity accounts upon issuance are now removed from the relevant accounts. Therefore, Common Stock is debited for $10 per share and Paid-in Capital in Excess of Par—Common Stock is debited for $3 per share because the common stock was originally issued for $13 per share. The cost of the Treasury Stock ($11 per share) is removed from the Treasury Stock account.

ILLUSTRATION 11-2 (Continued)

The excess of the original issuance price over the cost of the treasury shares is credited to Paid-in Capital from Treasury Stock.

7. **Treasury shares are acquired at a cost of $14 each.** Treasury Stock is debited and Cash is credited for the cost of the shares purchased for the treasury.

8. **Treasury shares are retired at a price ($14) above the stock's original issuance price ($13).** The amounts that were recorded in stockholder equity accounts when the stock was first issued (transaction number 1) are removed from those same accounts by a debit to Common Stock for $10 per share and a debit to Paid-in Capital in Excess of Par—Common Stock for $3 per share. The cost of the treasury stock ($14 per share) is removed from the Treasury Stock account. The excess of the cost of the treasury stock ($14 per share) over the original issuance price ($13 per share) is to be debited to Paid-in capital from Treasury Stock to the extent that this account has a balance. Since there is no balance in this account, the charge must go to the Retained Earnings account.

EXERCISE 11-5

Purpose: (L.O. 7) This exercise will illustrate how the components of stockholders' equity should be reported in the balance sheet.

Al Gore Corporation's charter authorizes 200,000 shares of $20 par value common stock, and 50,000 shares of 6% cumulative preferred stock, par value $100 per share. The preferred stock has a call price of $105.

The corporation engaged in the following stock transactions between the date of incorporation and December 31, 2014:
1. Issued 40,000 shares of common stock for $1,920,000 cash.
2. Issued 10,000 shares of preferred stock in exchange for machinery valued at $1,120,000.
3. Sold 1,500 shares of common stock at a price of $50 per share.
4. Purchased 2,000 shares of common stock at $46 per share for the treasury. The cost method was used to record the transaction.
5. Sold 500 shares of treasury stock for $51 per share.

At December 31, 2014, Gore's retained earnings balance was $2,200,000.

Instructions
Prepare the stockholders' equity section of the balance sheet at December 31, 2014, in good form.

SOLUTION TO EXERCISE 11-5

AL GORE CORPORATION
Partial Balance Sheet
December 31, 2014

Stockholders' equity		
Paid-in capital		
Capital stock		
6% preferred stock, $100 par value, cumulative, call price $105, 50,000 shares authorized, 10,000 shares issued and outstanding		$1,000,000
Common stock, $20 par, 200,000 shares authorized 41,500 shares issued, 40,000 shares outstanding		830,000
Total capital stock		1,830,000
Additional paid-in capital		
In excess of par value—preferred stock	$ 120,000	
In excess of par value—common stock	1,165,000	
From treasury stock—common	2,500	
Total additional paid-in capital		1,287,500
Total paid-in capital		3,117,500
Retained earnings		2,200,000
Total paid-in capital and retained earnings		5,317,500
Less: Treasury stock—common (1,500 shares)		69,000
Total stockholders' equity		$5,248,500

Approach and Explanation: Reconstruct the journal entries for the transactions and post those entries to T-accounts. Use the resulting balances in the accounts to prepare the stockholders' equity section of the balance sheet at December 31, 2014.

1.	Cash	1,920,000	
	Common Stock (40,000 X $20)		800,000
	Paid-in Capital in Excess of Par—Common Stock		1,120,000
	($1,920,000 - $800,000 = $1,120,000)		
2.	Machinery	1,120,000	
	Preferred Stock (10,000 x $100)................................		1,000,000
	Paid-in Capital in Excess of Par—Preferred Stock		120,000
	($1,120,000 - $1,000,000 = $120,000)		

3. Cash (1,500 X $50) 75,000
       Common Stock (1,500 X $20) 30,000
       Paid-in Capital in Excess of Par—Common Stock
         (1,500 X $30).. 45,000

4. Treasury Stock—Common (2,000 X $46) 92,000
       Cash 92,000

5. Cash (500 X $51) 25,500
       Treasury Stock—Common (500 X $46)........................ 23,000
       Paid-in Capital from Treasury Stock
         ($25,500 - $23,000) 2,500

Preferred Stock	
	(2) 1,000,000

Common Stock	
	(1) 800,000
	(3) 30,000
	Bal. 830,000

Paid in Capital in Excess of Par—Preferred Stock	
	(2) 120,000

Paid-in Capital in Excess of Par—Common Stock	
	(1) 1,120,000
	(3) 45,000
	Bal. 1,165,000

Treasury Stock—Common	
(4) 92,000	(5) 23,000
Bal. 69,000	

Paid-in Capital from Treasury Stock	
	(5) 2,500

Number of common stock shares issued and outstanding:

			Issued	Outstanding
Transaction 1: Issue	40,000 shares		40,000	40,000
Transaction 3: Issue	1,500 shares		1,500	1,500
Subtotal	41,500		41,500	41,500
Transaction 4: Buy treasury stock	(2,000)			(2,000)
Transaction 5: Sell treasury stock	500			500
Subtotal			41,500	40,000

EXERCISE 11-6

Purpose: (L.O. 3) This exercise will illustrate the use of the cost method of accounting for treasury stock transactions under a variety of price relationships.

Cheers Corporation reported the following stockholders' equity items at December 31, 2013. Each share of stock was issued in a prior year for $12 each.

Common Stock, $10 par	$ 350,000
Paid-in Capital in Excess of Par Value	70,000
Retained Earnings	710,000
Total stockholders' equity	$1,130,000

During 2014, Cheers had the following treasury stock transactions:
1. Purchased 1,000 shares at $15 per share.
2. Purchased 1,000 shares at $13 per share.
3. Sold 1,000 treasury shares at $11 per share.
4. Sold 1,000 treasury shares at $14 per share.
5. Purchased and retired 1,000 shares at $16 per share.

Instructions
Prepare the journal entries for the treasury stock transactions listed above. Apply a FIFO (first-in, first-out) approach in determining the cost of treasury shares sold.

SOLUTION TO EXERCISE 11-6

1.	Treasury Stock (1,000 x $15)	15,000	
	Cash		15,000
2.	Treasury Stock (1,000 X $13)..	13,000	
	Cash		13,000
3.	Cash (1,000 X $11)	11,000	
	Retained Earnings	4,000	
	Treasury Stock (1,000 X $15)...		15,000
4.	Cash (1,000 X $14)	14,000	
	Treasury Stock (1,000 X $13)...		13,000
	Paid-in Capital from Treasury Stock		1,000

5. Treasury Stock	16,000	
Cash		16,000
Common Stock (1,000 X $10)	10,000	
Paid-in Capital in Excess of Par—Common Stock (1,000 X $2)	2,000*	
Paid-in Capital from Treasury Stock..	1,000	
Retained Earnings..	3,000	
Cash (1,000 X $16)		16,000

*$12 original issuance price - $10 par = $2 paid-in capital in excess of par per share from original issuance.

Approach: Follow the guidelines listed in **Illustration 11-1.**

Explanation:
1. Treasury Stock is debited for the cost of the treasury shares acquired.

2. Treasury Stock is debited for the cost of the treasury shares acquired.

3. Cash is debited for the selling price of the treasury shares sold ($11 per share). Treasury Stock is credited for the cost of the treasury shares sold ($15 per share). The excess of the cost over the selling price of the treasury shares is to be charged to Paid-in Capital from Treasury Stock to the extent that this account has a balance that came from previous transactions involving stock of the same class. In this scenario, there is no balance in this account so the entire excess ($4 per share) is charged to Retained Earnings.

4. Cash is debited for the selling price of the treasury shares sold ($14 per share). Treasury Stock is credited for the cost of the treasury shares sold ($13 per share). The excess of the selling price over the cost of the treasury shares ($1 per share) is to be credited to Paid-in Capital from Treasury Stock.

5. The acquisition of treasury stock is recorded first, and then the retirement of the shares is recorded. In the entry to record the retirement, the amounts recorded for the original issuance of the stock are removed from the accounts (debit Common Stock for $10 per share and debit Paid-in Capital in Excess of Par Value for $2 per share). The excess of the retirement price ($16 per share) over the original issuance price ($12 per share) is debited (charged) to the Paid-in Capital from Treasury Stock account to the extent of the balance of that account (which is $1,000 in this case). Because the Paid-in Capital from Treasury Stock account balance ($1,000) is insufficient to absorb the $4,000 excess in this situation, the remainder ($3,000) is charged to Retained Earnings.

ILLUSTRATION 11-3
DETERMINING HOW TO RECORD A
DISTRIBUTION OF STOCK TO STOCKHOLDERS (L.O. 5)

When a corporation distributes additional shares of its own stock to its existing stockholders for no consideration, the corporation must record the distribution as one of the following, whichever is appropriate: (1) a small stock dividend, (2) a large stock dividend, or (3) a stock split. The following flowchart will provide guidance in determining the proper treatment.

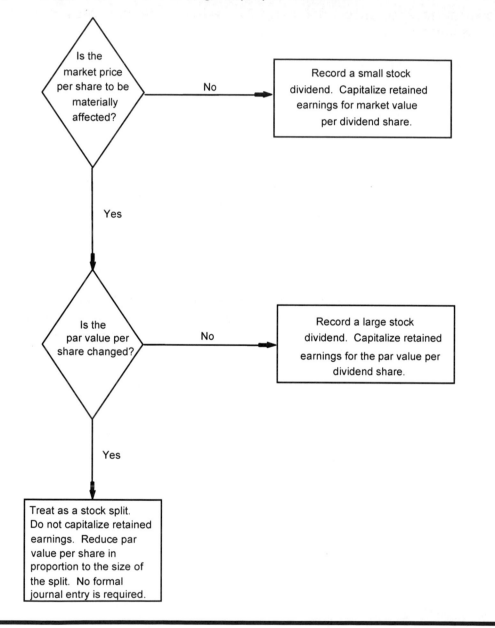

ILLUSTRATION 11-4
JOURNAL ENTRIES FOR RECORDING DIVIDENDS AND A STOCK SPLIT (L.O. 5)

Cash Dividend

Data: The board of directors declares a cash dividend of $100,000

Date of Declaration	Retained Earnings	100,000	
	Dividends Payable..		100,000
Date of Record	No entry.		
Date of Payment	Dividends Payable	100,000	
	Cash		100,000

> **TIP:** There are three dates associated with the declaration of any dividend: (1) the declaration date, (2) the date of record, and (3) the date of payment (or distribution). A journal entry is required at the date of declaration and at the date of payment.
>
> **TIP:** Dividends declared by a corporation are **not** an expense; they do not meet the definition of expense. (Recall from **Chapter 1** that an expense is the cost of an asset consumed or a service used up in the process of earning revenue; an expense is a decrease in owners' equity that results from operating the business.) Dividends are a distribution of income, not a determinant of income.
>
> **TIP:** The declaration of a cash dividend reduces total stockholders' equity; the payment of a previously declared (and recorded) cash dividend has no effect on total stockholders' equity.
>
> **TIP:** In recording the declaration of cash dividends, the accountant may use a temporary account called Dividends (or Dividends Declared), rather than debiting the Retained Earnings account directly. If this temporary account is used, the balance of the Dividends (or Dividends Declared) account is closed directly to the Retained Earnings account at the end of the period in the closing process.
>
> **TIP:** Dividends Payable is classified as a current liability because it will require a cash payment to settle the obligation within a year of the balance sheet date.
>
> **TIP:** Notice that the **declaration** of a cash dividend reduces retained earnings and increases current liabilities. The **payment** of the cash dividend reduces both current assets and current liabilities but has no effect on stockholders' equity. The net effect of the **declaration and payment** of a cash dividend on a company's balance sheet is to decrease both stockholders' equity and total assets.

Small Stock Dividend

Data: D & E Henry Corporation has 100,000 shares of $10 par common stock outstanding on March 2, 2014. On March 2, the board of directors declares a 10% stock dividend distributable on April 4 to stockholders of record on March 16. The market price per share of common is $24 on March 2, $23 on March 16, and $25 on April 4.

ILLUSTRATION 11-4 (Continued)

Date of Declaration	Retained Earnings	240,000	
	Common Stock Dividends Distributable		100,000
	Paid-in Capital in Excess of Par—Common Stock		140,000
	(10% X 100,000 = 10,000 dividend shares)		
	(10,000 shares X $24 = $240,000)		
	(10,000 shares X $10 par = $100,000)		
	($240,000 - $100,000 = $140,000)		
Date of Record	No entry.		
Date of Distribution	Common Stock Dividends Distributable.......................	100,000	
	Common Stock		100,000

TIP: Stock Dividends Distributable is a capital stock account and, therefore, is to be reported as an element of paid-in capital. It is **not** a liability because no associated debt must later be paid by the use of cash or other assets or services. This account only has a balance for a few weeks between the date of declaration and the date of distribution of a stock dividend.

TIP: Although a stock dividend results in a reduction in retained earnings, it also causes an increase in paid-in capital by the same amount; thus, there is **no change in total stockholders' equity** when a stock dividend is declared and distributed.

TIP: The term **capitalization of retained earnings** refers to the process of transferring an amount from retained earnings to paid-in capital. Stock dividends result in the capitalization of retained earnings. Thus, stock dividends are declared as a means of informing stockholders that assets arising from past income will be retained in the business rather than distributed as dividends to the stockholders.

Large Stock Dividend

Data: JJH Corporation has 100,000 shares of $10 par common stock outstanding on March 2, 2014. On March 2, the board of directors declares a 40% stock split-up effected in the form of a dividend. The par value per share is unchanged. The dividend shares are to be distributed on April 3 to stockholders of record on March 15. The market price per share of common stock is $24 on March 2, $15 on March 5, and $16 on April 3.

Date of Declaration	Retained Earnings	400,000	
	Common Stock Dividends Distributable		400,000
	(40% X 100,000 = 40,000 dividend shares)		
	(40,000 X $10 par = $400,000)		
Date of Record	No entry.		
Date of Distribution	Common Stock Dividends Distributable.......................	400,000	
	Common Stock		400,000

> **TIP:** The amount of retained earnings to be **capitalized** (transferred from retained earnings to paid-in capital) for a stock dividend depends on whether or not the issuance of the dividend shares is expected to have a material effect on the market price per share of stock. If a material effect is **not** expected, the market price at the date of declaration is used; if a material effect is expected, the par value is used. Generally, when the number of shares in the dividend is equal to 20% or less of the number of shares currently outstanding, the dividend is called a **small or ordinary stock dividend,** and no material effect on the market price per share is expected. When the number of shares in the dividend is equal to 25% or more of the number of shares currently outstanding, the dividend is called a **large stock dividend** and a material effect on the market price per share will likely occur.

Stock Split

Data: Howell Cove Corporation has 100,000 shares of $10.00 par common stock outstanding on March 2, 2014. On March 2, the board of directors declares a 4-for-1 stock split. The par value per share is to be reduced to $2.50. The split is to be effective April 2 for shareholders of record on March 13.

Date of Declaration   No entry.

Date of Record   No entry.

Date of Distribution   No entry. The par value per share is reduced from $10.00 to $2.50. The number of shares outstanding is increased from 100,000 to 400,000. The balance of Common Stock remains at $1,000,000.

EXERCISE 11-7

Purpose: (L.O. 5) This exercise will review the effects of various types of distributions to stockholders.

Instructions

For each transaction listed across the top of the following matrix, indicate the effect on each of the items listed down the left side of the matrix. Use an "I" to indicate an increase, a "D" to indicate a decrease, and a "NE" for no effect.

Item	Declaration of a cash dividend	Payment of a previously recorded cash dividend	Declaration and distribution of a small stock dividend	Declaration and distribution of a large stock dividend	Stock split
Assets					
Total capital stock					
Total additional Paid-in capital					
Retained earnings					
Total stockholders' equity					
Par value per share					
Total number of shares outstanding					

SOLUTION TO EXERCISE 11-7

Item	Declaration of a cash dividend	Payment of a previously recorded cash dividend	Declaration and distribution of a small stock dividend	Declaration and distribution of a large stock dividend	Stock split
Assets	NE	D	NE	NE	NE
Total capital stock	NE	NE	I	I	NE
Total additional paid-in capital	NE	NE	I	NE	NE
Retained earnings	D	NE	D	D	NE
Total stockholders' equity	D	NE	NE	NE	NE
Par value per share	NE	NE	NE	NE	D
Total number of shares outstanding	NE	NE	I	I	I

Approach: Write down the journal entry(ies) associated with each situation (refer to **Illustration 11-2**). Take the accounts in each entry and examine their individual effects on the items listed.

TIP: Study the solution and carefully notice the similarities and differences in the effects of the various distributions.

EXERCISE 11-8

Purpose: (L.O. 5) This exercise will allow you to practice recording various types of dividends.

A corporation has the following stockholder equity items at December 31, 2013:

Common stock, $10 par, 200,000 shares authorized, 80,000 shares issued	$ 800,000
Paid-in capital in excess of par value	2,400,000
Retained earnings	28,500,000
Total paid-in capital and retained earnings	31,700,000
Less: Treasury stock, 2,000 shares at cost	24,000
Total stockholders' equity	$31,676,000

Instructions

Assume each of the transactions listed below is **independent** of the others unless otherwise indicated. Dividends are distributed only on outstanding shares of stock. Record the following transactions at the beginning of 2014:

1.   Declared a cash dividend of $.50 per share.
2.   Paid the dividend declared in 1 above.
3.   Declared a 5% stock dividend when the market value was $14 per share.
4.   Distributed the shares for the stock dividend described in 3 above.
5.   Declared a 2:1 stock split.

SOLUTION TO EXERCISE 11-8

1.	Retained Earnings..	39,000	
	Dividends Payable...		39,000
	(80,000 issued - 2,000 treasury shares = 78,000 out-standing shares) (78,000 outstanding shares X $.50 = $39,000)		
2.	Dividends Payable	39,000	
	Cash...		39,000
3.	Retained Earnings..	54,600	
	Common Stock Dividends Distributable...........................		39,000
	Paid-in Capital in Excess of Par—Common Stock............		15,600
	(5% X 78,000 outstanding shares = 3,900 dividend shares)		
	(3,900 shares X $14 market value = $54,600)		
	(3,900 shares X $10 par value = $39,000)		
4.	Common Stock Dividends Distributable................................	39,000	
	Common Stock..		39,000

5.   No entry required except for a memorandum type entry. The par value per share is reduced to one-half of what it was (from $10 per share to $5 per share) and the number of shares are doubled. Thus, the authorized number increases to 400,000, the issued number increases to 160,000, and the number of treasury shares increases to 4,000 shares.

ILLUSTRATION 11-5
STEPS IN ALLOCATING DIVIDENDS TO PREFERRED
AND COMMON STOCKHOLDERS (L.O. 1)

Step 1: Assign arrearage to preferred, if any.
If there are any dividends in arrears, the amount of arrearage is first allocated to the preferred stockholders. The remaining amount of dividends to be allocated is computed. (If the amount declared is not enough to cover the arrearage, all dividends declared go to preferred holders, the remaining arrearage is computed for disclosure, and the rest of the steps are not performed.)

Step 2: Assign current period preference to preferred.
The amount of the preferred stockholders' current year preference is computed and that amount is allocated to the preferred holders. The remaining amount of dividends to be allocated is computed. (If the dividends declared are not enough to cover the preferred's current year preference, all of the dividends declared are allocated to the preferred holders, the remaining arrearage is computed for disclosure, and the next step is not performed).

Step 3: Assign the remaining dividends to common.
After the preferred stockholders have received dividends to cover any arrearage plus their current year preference, any remaining dividends declared are allocated on a pro rata basis to common stockholders.

TIP:	A preferred stock's preference as to dividends is usually expressed as a percentage of the par or stated value; sometimes, the preference is expressed in terms of dollars.

EXERCISE 11-9

Purpose: (L.O. 5) This exercise will illustrate the allocation of dividends when a corporation has both preferred stock and common stock.

Charlie B. Daly Corporation has the following stock outstanding without any changes for years 2013, 2014, and 2015.

50,000 shares of $10 par, 4% preferred	$ 500,000
200,000 shares of $5 par common	1,000,000
	$1,500,000

Dividends are declared as follows:

2013	$15,000
2014	$50,000
2015	$72,000

Instructions

Compute the amount of dividends (total and per share) to be allocated to the preferred stockholders and the common stockholders for each of the three years under the **independent** assumptions below.

(a)   The preferred stock is noncumulative.

(b)   The preferred stock is cumulative.

SOLUTION TO EXERCISE 11-9

Approach: Compute the preferred's current year preference (50,000 shares X $10 par X 4% = $20,000). Then use the steps listed in **Illustration 11-5** to solve.

		Preferred	Common	Total
(a)				
2013:	Total to distribute			$15,000
	Step 1: Not relevant for noncumulative stock			
	Step 2: Current year's preference (partial)	$15,000		$15,000
	Step 3: No remainder			
		$15,000	$ -0-	$15,000
	÷ by	50,000	200,000	
	=	$ .30	$ .00	
2014:	Total to distribute			$50,000
	Step 1: Not relevant for noncumulative stock			
	Step 2: Current year's preference	$20,000		$20,000
	Step 3: Remainder		$ 30,000	30,000
		$20,000	$ 30,000	$50,000
	÷ by	50,000	200,000	
	=	$ .40	$ .15	
2015:	Total to distribute			$72,000
	Step 1: Not relevant for noncumulative stock			
	Step 2: Current year's preference	$20,000		$20,000
	Step 3: Remainder		$ 52,000	52,000
		$20,000	$ 52,000	$72,000
	÷ by	50,000	200,000	
	=	$ .40	$ .26	

TIP: A preferred stockholder is entitled to receive his current year preference as to dividends ($10 X 4% = $.40 per share in this case) before common stockholders receive any dividends. If the preferred stock is cumulative, any preferred's preference not declared is said to be "in arrears." In a future year when dividends are declared, any dividends in arrears must be paid to preferred before common stockholders can receive any dividends. Dividends in arrears are **not** a liability because by definition, they have not been declared; dividends become a liability at the declaration date.

		Preferred	Common	Total
(b)				
2013:	Total to distribute			$15,000
	Step 1: No arrearage			
	Step 2: Current year's preference (partial)	$15,000		$15,000
	Step 3: No remainder			
		$15,000	$ -0-	$15,000
	÷ by	50,000	200,000	
	=	$ .30	$ .00	
2014:	Total to distribute			$50,000
	Step 1: Arrearage--$20,000 - $15,000	$ 5,000		5,000
	Step 2: Current year's preference	20,000		20,000
	Step 3: Remainder		$ 25,000	25,000
		$25,000	$ 25,000	$50,000
	÷ by	50,000	200,000	
	=	$ .50	$ .125	
2015:	Total to distribute			$72,000
	Step 1: No arrearage			
	Step 2: Current year's preference	$20,000		$20,000
	Step 3: Remainder		$ 52,000	52,000
		$20,000	$ 52,000	$72,000
	÷ by	50,000	200,000	
	=	$ .40	$ .26	

EXERCISE 11-10

Purpose: (L.O. 6) This exercise will illustrate the preparation of a retained earnings statement.

On January 1, 2014, Kimmie Corporation had a balance of $300,000 in its Retained Earnings account. During 2014, Kimmie had the following selected transactions:
1.   Declared cash dividends of $40,000.
2.   Declared stock dividends of $60,000.
3.   Corrected understatement of 2013 net income because of an error in computing depreciation expense, $32,000.
4.   Earned net income of $50,000.
5.   Sold treasury stock for a price that was $6,000 below its cost. There were no previous sales of treasury stock. The cost method is used to account for treasury stock.

Instructions
Prepare the retained earnings statement for Kimmie Corporation for the year ending December 31, 2014.

SOLUTION TO EXERCISE 11-10

KIMMIE CORPORATION
Retained Earnings Statement
For the Year Ended December 31, 2014

Balance, January 1, as reported...		$300,000
Correction for understatement of 2013 net income........................		32,000
Balance, January 1, as adjusted..		332,000
Add: Net income		50,000
		382,000
Less: Cash dividends...	$40,000	
Stock dividends..	60,000	
Excess cost over selling price of treasury stock	6,000	106,000
Balance, December 31		$276,000

TIP: The **retained earnings statement** is a required general purpose financial statement. It is frequently called the **statement of retained earnings.** Its purpose is to explain all of the reasons why the balance of the Retained Earnings account changed during the reporting period. Transactions and events that affect retained earnings are tabulated in account form as follows:

Retained Earnings

1. Net loss	1. Net income
2. Prior period adjustments for overstatement of net income	2. Prior period adjustments for understatement of net income
3. Cash dividends and stock dividends	
4. Some disposals of treasury stock	

As indicated, net income increases retained earnings and a net loss decreases retained earnings. Prior period adjustments may either increase or decrease retained earnings, whereas both cash and stock dividends decrease retained earnings. Some treasury stock transactions decrease retained earnings. One of those situations involves the sale of treasury stock for a price below cost when the cost method of accounting is used for treasury stock transactions and no balance exists in a Paid-in Capital from Treasury Stock account.

EXERCISE 11-11

Purpose: (L.O. 7) This exercise will allow you to practice preparing the stockholders' equity section of a corporation's balance sheet and the accompanying note disclosures.

The following accounts appear in the ledger of Zippadeedoda, Inc. after the books are closed at December 31, 2014.

Common Stock, $10 par, 700,000 shares authorized; 400,000 shares issued	$4,000,000
Common Stock Dividends Distributable	400,000
Paid-in Capital in Excess of Par Value—Common Stock	5,450,000
Preferred Stock, $50 par, 6% cumulative, 60,000 shares authorized; 40,000 shares issued	2,000,000
Paid-in Capital in Excess of Par Value—Preferred Stock	160,000
Paid-in Capital from Treasury Common Stock	30,000
Treasury Stock (20,000 common shares) (at cost)	380,000
Retained Earnings	990,000

Instructions
Prepare the stockholders' equity section of the balance sheet at December 31, 2014, assuming retained earnings is restricted for two reasons: (1) the cost of the treasury shares held, and (2) $175,000 for future plant expansion.

SOLUTION TO EXERCISE 11-11

ZIPPADEEDODA INC.
Partial Balance Sheet
December 31, 2014

Stockholders' equity		
Paid-in capital		
Capital stock		
6% preferred stock, $50 par value, cumulative, 60,000 shares authorized, 40,000 shares issued		$2,000,000
Common stock, $10 par, 700,000 shares authorized, 400,000 shares issued and 380,000 outstanding...	$4,000,000	
Common stock dividends distributable..............................	400,000	4,400,000
Total capital stock...		6,400,000
Additional paid-in capital		
In excess of par value—preferred stock..............................	160,000	
In excess of par value—common stock	5,450,000	
From treasury common stock.......................................	30,000	
Total additional paid-in capital..		5,640,000
Total paid-in capital		12,040,000
Retained earnings (See Note X)		990,000
Total paid-in capital and retained earnings		13,030,000
Less: Treasury stock (20,000 common shares).............................		380,000
Total stockholders' equity...		$12,650,000

Note X: Retained earnings is restricted for the cost of treasury stock, $380,000, and for future plant expansion, $175,000.

*EXERCISE 11-12

Purpose: (L.O. 8) This exercise will illustrate the preparation of a stockholders' equity statement.

On January 1, 2014, Huseman Corporation had the following stockholders' equity balances:

Common Stock ($1 stated value)	$300,000
Paid-in Capital in Excess of Stated Value	710,000
Retained Earnings	390,000
Treasury Stock (3,000 shares)	6,000

During 2014, the following occurred:

Issued 50,000 shares of common stock at $3 per share.
Declared a $70,000 cash dividend.
Purchased 1,000 shares of treasury stock at $2 per share.
Declared and distributed a 5% stock dividend when the market value
was $3 per share and there were 346,000 shares outstanding.
Earned net income for the year of $200,000.

Instructions
Prepare a stockholders' equity statement for the year ending December 31, 2014.

SOLUTION TO EXERCISE 11-12

HUSEMAN CORPORATION
Stockholders' Equity Statement
For the Year Ended December 31, 2014

	Common Stock ($1 Stated Value)	Paid-in Capital in Excess of Stated Value	Retained Earnings	Treasury Stock	Total
Balance January 1	$300,000	$710,000	$390,000	$(6,000)	$1,394,000
Issued 50,000 shares of common stock at $3	50,000	100,000			150,000
Declared a $70,000 cash dividend			(70,000)		(70,000)
Purchased 1,000 shares for treasury at $2				(2,000)	(2,000)
Declared a 5% stock dividend	17,300	34,600	(51,900)		
Net income for year			200,000		200,000
Balance December 31	$367,300	$844,600	$468,100	$(8,000)	$1,672,000

TIP: Notice how the columns on this statement foot and crossfoot.

Explanation: A corporation is to disclose all changes that took place in all stockholder equity items during the reporting period. A convenient and effective way of meeting that requirement is to present a stockholders' equity statement (sometimes called a statement of stockholders' equity). When this statement is presented, it replaces the retained earnings statement because it contains all the information that a retained earnings statement would contain plus data regarding changes in other components of stockholders' equity.

The computations for the stock dividend are as follows:
   346,000 shares outstanding X 5% = 17,300 dividend shares.
   17,300 shares X $3 = $51,900 decrease in Retained Earnings.
   17,300 shares X $1 stated value = $17,300 increase in Common Stock.
   17,300 shares X ($3 - $1) = $34,600 increase in additional paid-in capital.

**EXERCISE 11-13

Purpose: (L.O. 9) This exercise will illustrate the computation of book value per share when more than one class of stock is outstanding.

Book value per share of stock refers to the amount of stockholders' equity applicable to a share of stock.

Instructions
Refer to the facts of **Exercise 11-5** and the **Solution to Exercise 11-5.**
(a)   Determine the book value per share of preferred stock.
(b)   Determine the book value per share of common stock.

SOLUTION TO EXERCISE 11-13

(a)   The book value per share of preferred stock is $105—the call price per share.

Explanation: The preferred stock equity per share consists of the call price of the stock plus any dividends in arrears. If the preferred stock does not have a call price, the book value of one share of preferred is equal to the preferred's par value plus any dividends in arrears.

TIP:	Notice that **none** of the paid-in capital in excess of par value arising from the issuance of preferred stock at a price above par ($120,000) is directly allocated to preferred stock in the book value per share of preferred stock computation.
TIP:	There is no mention of any dividends in arrears for this entity at the specified balance sheet date.

(b) Total stockholders' equity $5,248,500
     Less: Preferred stock equity:
     Call price (10,000 X $105) $1,050,000
     Dividends in arrears   0   1,050,000
     Common stock equity $4,198,500

     Shares of common stock outstanding   40,000

     Book value per share of common stock ($4,198,500 ÷ 40,000) $104.96

TIP:	If only one class of stock is outstanding, the book value of common is computed simply by dividing total stockholders' equity by the total number of shares outstanding.

EXERCISE 11-14

Purpose: (L.O. 1 thru 9) This exercise will quiz you about terminology used in this chapter.

A list of accounting terms with which you should be familiar appears below:

Authorized stock	Par value stock
**Book value per share	Payment date
Cash dividend	Preferred stock
Charter	Prior period adjustment
Corporate capital	Privately held corporation
Corporation	Publicly held corporation
Cumulative dividend	Record date
Declaration date	Retained earnings
Deficit	Retained earnings restrictions
Dividend	Retained earnings statement
Legal capital	Return on common stockholders' equity ratio
Liquidating dividend	Stated value
No-par value stock	Stock dividend
Organization costs	Stock split
Outstanding stock	Stockholders' equity statement
Paid-in capital	Treasury stock

**This material is covered in Appendix 11B in the text.

Instructions
For each item below, enter in the blank the term that is described.

1. _____A corporation that may have thousands of
    stockholders and whose stock is regularly traded on a national securities market.

2. _____A corporation that has only a few stockholders
    and whose stock is **not** available for sale to the general public.

3. _____The amount of stock that a corporation is
    authorized to sell as indicated in its charter.

4. _____Costs incurred in the formation of a corporation.

5. _____Capital stock that has been issued and is being held by stockholders.

6. _____The amount per share of stock that must be retained in the business for the protection of corporate creditors.

7. _____Total amount of cash and other assets paid in to the corporation by stockholders in exchange for capital stock.

8. _____Net income that is retained in the business.

9. _____Capital stock that has been assigned a value per share in the corporate charter.

10. _____The amount per share assigned by the board of directors to no-par stock that becomes legal capital per share.

11. _____Capital stock that has **not** been assigned a value in the corporate charter.

12. _____Capital stock that has contractual preferences over common stock in certain areas.

13. _____The equity a common stockholder has in the net assets of the corporation from owning one share of stock.

14. _____A feature of preferred stock entitling the stockholder to receive current and unpaid prior-year dividends before common stockholders receive any dividends.

15. _____A corporation's own stock that has been issued, fully paid for, and reacquired by the corporation but **not** retired.

16. _____A corporation's distribution of cash or stock to its stockholders on a pro rata (equal) basis.

17. _____ A pro rata distribution of cash to stockholders.

18. _____ A pro rata distribution of the corporation's own stock to stockholders.

19. _____ The issuance of additional shares of stock to stockholders (according to their percentage ownership) accompanied by a reduction in the par or stated value per share.

20. _____ The date the board of directors formally declares the dividend and announces it to stockholders.

21. _____ The date when ownership of outstanding shares is determined for dividend purposes.

22. _____ The date dividend checks are mailed to stockholders.

23. _____ A dividend declared out of paid-in capital.

24. _____ A financial statement that shows the changes in retained earnings during the year.

25. _____ Circumstances that make a portion of retained earnings currently **unavailable** to serve as the basis for dividend declaration.

26. _____ The correction of an error in previously issued financial statements.

27. _____ A debit balance in retained earnings.

28. _____ A statement that shows the changes in each stockholders' equity account and in total stockholders' equity during the year.

29. _____A document that creates a corporation.

30. _____A business organized as a legal entity separate and distinct from its owners under state corporation law.

31. _____The owners' equity in a corporation. Also called **stockholders' equity** or **shareholders' equity.**

32. _____ A ratio that measures profitability from the stockholders' point of view. It is computed by dividing net income by average common stockholders' equity.

SOLUTION TO EXERCISE 11-14

1.	Publicly held corporation	18.	Stock dividend
2.	Privately held corporation	19.	Stock split
3.	Authorized stock	20.	Declaration date
4.	Organization costs	21.	Record date
5.	Outstanding stock	22.	Payment date
6.	Legal capital	23.	Liquidating dividend
7.	Paid-in capital	24.	Retained earnings statement
8.	Retained earnings	25.	Retained earnings restrictions
9.	Par value stock	26.	Prior period adjustment
10.	Stated value	27.	Deficit
11.	No-par value stock	28.	Stockholders' equity statement
12.	Preferred stock	29.	Charter
13.	Book value per share	30.	Corporation
14.	Cumulative dividend	31.	Corporate capital
15.	Treasury stock	32.	Return on common stockholders' equity ratio
16.	Dividend		
17.	Cash dividend		

ANALYSIS OF MULTIPLE-CHOICE TYPE QUESTIONS

1. **Question**
    (L.O. 1) Which of the following is **not** a characteristic of a corporation?
    a. Separate legal entity.
    b. Limited liability of owners.
    c. Flexible ownership.
    d. Nontaxable entity.

    Approach and Explanation: Mentally review the list of the most important characteristics of a corporation. Compare the answer selections with that list. The list includes: (1) separate legal existence, (2) limited liability of stockholders, (3) transferable ownership rights, (4) ability to acquire capital, (5) continuous life, and (6) corporation management. As an entity separate and distinct from its owners, the corporation acts under its own name rather than in the name of its stockholders. A corporation may buy, own, and sell property, borrow money, and enter into legally binding contracts in its own name. It may also sue or be sued, and it pays its own taxes. (Solution = d.)

2. **Question**
    (L.O. 1) Which of the following is true with regard to a corporation?
    a. Revenues and expenses do not affect owners' equity.
    b. Retained earnings, which is an element of owners' equity, is increased by revenues and is decreased by expenses.
    c. Revenues and expenses are ultimately closed to the Paid-in Capital in Excess of Par Value account.
    d. Revenue and expense accounts are never closed.

Explanation: Retained earnings is net income retained in a corporation. A corporation with net income of $52,000 will close the Income Summary account by the following closing entry:

Income Summary	52,000	
Retained Earnings		52,000
(To close Income Summary and transfer net income		
to retained earnings)		

Thus, revenues (reflected as a credit in the Income Summary account) increase Retained Earnings and expenses decrease the balance of the Retained Earnings account. (Solution = b.)

3. **Question**
   (L.O. 1) Which of the following represents the total number of shares that a corporation may issue under the terms of its charter?
   a. Authorized shares.
   b. Issued shares.
   c. Treasury shares.
   d. Outstanding shares.

   Approach and Explanation: Explain the meaning of each of the terms used as answer selections. Choose the one that matches the stem of the question. Issued shares (ones the corporation has issued to date) **plus** unissued shares (shares that have not been issued yet but may be issued in the future in accordance with the terms of the charter) **equals** total authorized (approved) shares. Outstanding shares are the issued shares which are now in the hands of the public. Treasury shares are issued shares which are not outstanding at the present time. (Solution = a.)

4. **Question**
   (L.O. 2, 3) Treasury shares are:
   a. shares held as an investment by the treasurer of the corporation.
   b. shares held as an investment of the corporation.
   c. issued and outstanding shares.
   d. unissued shares.
   e. issued but not outstanding shares.

   Approach and Explanation: Write down the definition of treasury stock. Treasury stock is a corporation's own stock that has been issued, fully paid for, and reacquired by the corporation but not retired. Treasury shares are shares that have been issued previously (so are not unissued) but are not outstanding now, as they have been subsequently reacquired by the company. Treasury shares refer to a company's own shares so they cannot be an investment. A company cannot own itself. The acquisition of treasury stock represents a contraction of capital (owners' equity) rather than the acquisition of an asset. (Solution = e.)

5. **Question**
   (L.O. 2) If common stock with a par value is issued for noncash assets, the amount to be recorded as paid-in capital related to this transaction is determined by the:
   a.   fair market value of the noncash assets received.
   b.   par value of the stock issued.
   c.   legal value of the stock issued.
   d.   book value of the noncash assets on the seller's books.

   Approach and Explanation: Recall that any time assets are acquired, the cost principle is applied; that is, the assets are to be recorded at historical cost. Cost is measured by the fair market value (cash equivalent value) of the consideration received or the fair market value of the consideration given, whichever is the more objectively determinable. Assuming equipment with a fair value of $70,000 is received in exchange for stock of a closely-held corporation with a par value of $20,000, the journal entry to record the transaction would be as follows:

Equipment...	70,000	
Common Stock		20,000
Paid-in Capital in Excess of Par—Common Stock		50,000

   Notice that two paid-in capital accounts (one capital stock account and one additional paid-in capital account) are affected. The increase in total paid-in capital is $70,000. (Solution = a.)

6. **Question**
   (L.O. 2) The value at which a stock could be bought or sold at a given point in time is called:
   a.   book value.
   b.   par value.
   c.   stated value.
   d.   market value.

   Approach and Explanation: Briefly define each of the answer selections. **Book value** is stockholders' equity per share of stock (stockholders' equity divided by number of shares outstanding). **Par value** is an arbitrary value which does not have much significance except in establishing legal capital and in determining the amount to appear in the Common Stock account for each share issued. **Stated value** refers to an arbitrary value that may be placed on a stock by the board of directors. Stated value has about the same significance as par value. **Market value** refers to the price for which a stock is currently being bought and sold in the open market. (Solution = d.)

7. **Question**
   (L.O. 2, 7) For a par value common stock issued at a price above par, the amount to appear on the balance sheet with the caption "common stock" is the:
   a.   amount of assets received by the corporation when the stock was sold.
   b.   total amount invested by the shareholder.
   c.   par value of the stock.
   d.   market value of the stock at the balance sheet date.

   Approach and Explanation: Reconstruct the journal entry to record the issuance of a par value stock for a price in excess of par. Notice the amount recorded in the capital stock account. (Assume a $10 par common stock is issued in exchange for $18 cash.) The entry to record the transaction is as follows:

Cash..	18	
Common Stock		10
Paid-in Capital in Excess of Par—Common Stock		8

(Solution = c.)

8. **Question**
    (L.O. 2, 7) Assume only one class of stock exists in the Janice Johnson Corporation. Total invested (contributed) capital of owners would most likely be found by:
    a. the amount appearing in the Common Stock account.
    b. adding the balance of the Common Stock account and the balance of the Paid-In Capital in Excess of Par—Common Stock account.
    c. multiplying the par value per share by the number of shares issued.
    d. adding the balance of the Common Stock account, the balance of the Paid-in Capital in Excess of Par—Common Stock account, and the balance of the Retained Earnings account.

    Explanation: An amount equal to the par value of stock is recorded in the Common Stock account (and hence, is reported on the balance sheet by the caption "Common Stock") when a share of common stock is issued. If the sales price is above par, the excess of the issuance price over par is recorded in another stockholders' equity account called Paid-in Capital in Excess of Par—Common Stock. Answer "a" would be correct only for a no-par common stock with no stated value or a par-value stock sold at par. Answer "c" would be correct only if the stock was sold for an amount equal to its par value. Answer "d" is not correct for any situation. (Solution = b.)

9. **Question**
    (L.O. 2, 7) The Tom Powell Corporation has 10,000 shares of $10 par common stock authorized. The following transactions took place during the first year of the corporation's existence:

    Sold 1,000 shares of common stock for $18 per share.
    Issued 1,000 shares of common stock in exchange for a patent valued at $20,000.
    Reported net income of $7,000.

    At the end of Tom Powell's first year, total paid-in capital amounted to:
    a. $8,000.
    b. $18,000.
    c. $20,000.
    d. $45,000.
    e. $38,000.

    Approach and Explanation: (1) Write down the components of paid-in capital: (a) balances of capital stock accounts, and (b) balances of additional paid-in capital accounts. (2) Reconstruct the journal entries for the transactions listed and post those entries to T-accounts. (3) Compute the balances of the relevant accounts. (4) Sum the relevant account balances.

Cash	18,000	
Common Stock...		10,000
Paid-in Capital in Excess of Par—Common Stock................		8,000
Patent...	20,000	
Common Stock...		10,000
Paid-in Capital in Excess of Par—Common Stock................		10,000
Income Summary...	7,000	
Retained Earnings..		7,000

Common Stock		Paid-in Capital In Excess of Par—Common Stock	
	10,000		8,000
	10,000		10,000
	20,000		18,000

Common stock	$20,000	
Additional paid-in capital	18,000	
Total paid-in capital	$38,000	(Solution = e.)

10. Question

(L.O. 2) Organization costs are to be recorded by a debit to:
a. an intangible asset account.
b. the Paid-in Capital in Excess of Par—Common Stock.
c. the Retained Earnings account.
d. an expense account.

Approach and Explanation: The costs of organizing a business in the corporate form include such costs as promotional expenditures involved in the organization of the business and fees paid to attorneys and to the state for obtaining the charter. They are called **organization costs.** In theory, these costs will benefit the corporation indefinitely which gives us good justification for deferring these costs to future periods. However, generally accepted accounting principles requires that these costs be expensed immediately in the period incurred because it is difficult to determine the amount and timing of the future benefits. (Solution = d.)

11. Question

(L.O. 3) The Jones Corporation uses the cost method of accounting for treasury stock. Which of the following transactions will cause a net decrease in total additional paid-in capital?
a. Sale of treasury stock at a price in excess of cost.
b. Retirement of treasury stock whose cost is in excess of par value but less than the original issuance price.
c. Purchase of treasury stock at a price in excess of par value but less than the original issuance price.
d. Purchase of treasury stock at a price in excess of par and in excess of the original issuance price.

Approach and Explanation: Write down the entry for each transaction described. Carefully analyze the debits and credits within each entry to determine the entry's net effect on total additional paid-in capital. The entries and analyses would be as follows:

a. Cash .... Selling Price
      Treasury Stock .... Cost
      Paid-in Capital from Treasury Stock.................. Difference

Additional paid-in capital is increased by the excess of the selling price over the cost of the treasury shares.

b. Common Stock .... Par
    Paid-in Capital in Excess of Par—Common Stock .... Issuance Premium
      Treasury Stock.. Cost
      Paid-in Capital from Treasury Stock .... Difference

The journal entry must balance (have total debits equal total credits). Because the cost is in excess of par, the debit to Paid-in Capital in Excess of Par—Common Stock is greater than the credit to Paid-in Capital from Treasury Stock. Additional paid-in capital is decreased by the "issuance premium" and increased by the "difference". Thus, the net effect on additional paid-in capital is a decrease.

c. Treasury Stock... Cost
      Cash.. Cost

This transaction has no effect on additional paid-in capital.

d. Treasury Stock... Cost
      Cash.. Cost

This transaction has no effect on additional paid-in capital.
(Solution = b.)

12. Question
(L.O. 3) Assume the cost method is used to account for treasury stock. A "gain " on the sale of treasury stock should be classified as an:
a. extraordinary item on the income statement.
b. element of other income on the income statement.
c. increase in additional paid-in capital.
d. increase in retained earnings.

Explanation: When the cost method is used, a "gain" on the sale of treasury stock refers to the disposition of treasury stock at a price in excess of cost. This excess is recorded as a credit to Paid-in Capital from Treasury Stock. Selections "a" and "b" are incorrect because treasury stock transactions are capital transactions, and capital transactions do not give rise to components of income determination. Answer selection "d" is incorrect because treasury stock transactions can sometimes reduce retained earnings but may **never** increase retained earnings. (Solution = c.)

13. **Question**
    (L.O. 4) "Dividends in arrears" are:
    a. dividends on common stock that have not been declared.
    b. the dividends of cumulative preferred stockholders that has not been declared for some given period of time.
    c. the dividends of noncumulative preferred stock that has not been declared for some given period of time.
    d. dividends on preferred stock which have been declared but not paid.

    Explanation: By definition of the term, "dividends in arrears," selection "b" is correct. There is no special term used to describe dividends on noncumulative preferred stock or on common stock that have not been declared. Dividends on preferred stock which have been declared but not paid are referred to as "dividends payable" (a liability). (Solution = b.)

14. **Question**
    (L.O. 4) Which of the following rights does a preferred shareholder normally posses?
    a. Right to vote.
    b. Right to receive a dividend before a common shareholder.
    c. Preemptive right.
    d. Right to participate in management.

    Explanation: A preferred stockholder usually has a preference over common stockholders as to dividends and as to distribution of assets upon liquidation. A preferred stockholder normally has to forego other rights because of the preference described above. The rights the preferred stockholder normally foregoes are the right to participate in management (right to vote on operational and financial decisions) and the preemptive right. A common stockholder normally has the right to vote and the preemptive right (right to maintain the same percentage ownership when additional shares of common stock are issued). (Solution = b.)

15. **Question**
    (L.O. 5) The declaration and payment of cash dividends by a corporation will result in a(an):
    a. increase in Cash and an increase in Retained Earnings.
    b. increase in Cash and a decrease in Retained Earnings.
    c. decrease in Cash and an increase in Retained Earnings.
    d. decrease in Cash and a decrease in Retained Earnings.

    Approach and Explanation: Prepare the journal entries required to record the declaration and payment of a cash dividend. Separately analyze each debit and credit to determine the effect on the balance of Cash and on the Retained Earnings account. Assuming cash dividends of $10,000 are declared, the entries and analysis are as follows:

At the date of declaration: **Effect**
Retained Earnings   10,000   Decrease in Retained Earnings
    Dividends Payable   10,000   Increase in current liabilities

At the date of payment:
Dividends Payable   10,000   Decrease in current liabilities
    Cash   10,000   Decrease in Cash

The net effect of the declaration and payment of a cash dividend is to reduce retained earnings (and, thus, total stockholders' equity) and Cash (and, thus, total assets). (Solution = d.)

16. **Question**

    (L.O. 5) The date that determines who is to be considered a stockholder for the purpose of receiving a dividend is the:
    a. declaration date.
    b. record date.
    c. payment date.
    d. distribution date.

    Explanation: The date the board of directors formally declares (authorizes) a dividend and announces it to stockholders is called the **declaration date.** The **record date** marks the time when ownership of the outstanding shares is determined for dividend purposes from the stockholders' records maintained by the corporation. On the **payment date,** the dividend checks are mailed to the stockholders. (Solution = b.)

17. **Question**

    (L.O. 5) What effect does the declaration and distribution of a 10% stock dividend have on the following?

	Retained Earnings	Total Paid-in Capital	Total Stockholders' Equity
a.	Decrease	Increase	No Effect
b.	Decrease	No Effect	No Effect
c.	Decrease	No Effect	Decrease
d.	No Effect	No Effect	No Effect

    Approach: Write down the journal entries for the declaration and distribution of a (small) stock dividend. Analyze the accounts in each entry separately to determine the impact on the three items requested.

    Explanation: The journal entry to record the declaration will (1) reduce retained earnings by the market value per share multiplied by the number of shares to be distributed in the dividend, (2) increase stock dividend distributable (a component of total capital stock and, therefore, a component of total paid-in capital) by the par value multiplied by the number of shares to be distributed in the dividend, and (3) increase additional paid-in capital by the excess of market value over par value per share multiplied by the number of dividend shares. Thus, the entry to record the declaration of the small stock dividend will **decrease retained earnings, increase total paid-in capital, and have no effect on total stockholders' equity.** The entry to record the distribution will reduce the dividend distributable balance (one capital stock account) and increase the common stock account (another capital stock account). Thus, the distribution entry will have **no effect** on any total within the major classifications of stockholders' equity. (Solution = a.)

18. **Question**
(L.O. 5) A 300% stock dividend will have the same impact on the number of shares outstanding as a:
a. 2-for-1 stock split.
b. 3-for-1 stock split.
c. 4-for-1 stock split.
d. 5-for-1 stock split.

Approach and Explanation: Set up an example with numbers. For instance, assume we begin with 10,000 shares outstanding. A 300% stock dividend will mean 30,000 new shares will be distributed and there will then be 40,000 total shares outstanding. A 2-for-1 split will cause 10,000 shares to be replaced by 20,000. A 3-for-1 split will result in 30,000 total shares. A 4-for-1 split will cause the 10,000 shares to be replaced by 40,000 shares. The example proves that a 300% stock dividend (shares are increased **by** 300%) has the same effect on the number of shares outstanding as does a 4-for-1 split (each share is replaced with four shares). (Solution = c.)

19. **Question**
(L.O. 5) Rosanne Barr Corporation declared a stock dividend of 10,000 shares when the par value was $1 per share, the market value was $5 per share, and the number of shares outstanding was 200,000. How does the entry to record this transaction affect retained earnings?
a. No effect.
b. $10,000 decrease.
c. $40,000 decrease.
d. $50,000 decrease.

Approach: Analyze the data to determine the size of the stock dividend. Prepare the journal entry to record the declaration of the stock dividend and analyze the entry's effect on retained earnings.

Explanation: Comparing the 10,000 dividend shares to the 200,000 outstanding shares, prior to the dividend, yields a 5% relationship; thus, the stock dividend is an ordinary (small) stock dividend. An ordinary stock dividend is recorded by transferring retained earnings equal to the market value of the dividend shares to paid-in capital. Therefore, 10,000 shares multiplied by $5 means retained earnings is to be charged for $50,000. (Solution = d.)

20. **Question**
(L.O. 5) The net effect of the declaration and payment of a liquidating dividend is a decrease in:
a. retained earnings and a decrease in total assets.
b. total paid-in capital and a decrease in total assets.
c. total paid-in capital and an increase in retained earnings.
d. total stockholders' equity and an increase in liabilities.

Explanation: A dividend based on paid-in capital (rather than retained earnings) is termed a **liquidating dividend,** because the amount originally paid in by stockholders is being reduced or "liquidated." (Solution = b.)

21. **Question**
    (L.O. 5) A 4-for-1 stock split will cause a decrease in:
    a. total assets.
    b. total stockholders' equity.
    c. retained earnings.
    d. the par value per share.

    Explanation: A stock split involves the issuance of additional shares of stock to existing stockholders according to the number of shares presently owned. A stock split does **not** result in the capitalization of any retained earnings; rather, the par value per share is reduced in proportion to the increase in shares. Thus, in a 2-for-1 split, the number of shares are doubled and the par value per share is cut in half. Whereas with a 4-for-1 stock split, the number of total shares is four times what the number was before the split and the par value per share after the spit is 1/4 of the par value per share before the split. Assets are not affected. (Solution = d.)

22. **Question**
    (L.O. 6) The balance of the Retained Earnings account represents:
    a. cash set aside for specific purposes.
    b. the earnings for the most recent accounting period.
    c. the balance of unrestricted cash on hand.
    d. the total of all amounts reported as net income since the inception of the corporation minus the sum of any amounts reported as net loss and dividends declared since the inception of the corporation.

    Approach and Explanation: Define retained earnings and select the answer that most closely matches that definition. Retained earnings is net income retained in a corporation. Retained earnings is often referred to as earnings retained for use in the business. Thus, net income (earnings for a period) increases the balance of retained earnings. Distributions of earnings to stockholders (owners) are called dividends; they reduce the balance of retained earnings. (Solution = d.)

23. **Question**
    (L.O. 6) Which of the following items is reported on a retained earnings statement?
    a. Unrestricted cash on hand.
    b. Restricted cash on hand.
    c. Dividends declared.
    d. Treasury stock on hand.

    Approach and Explanation: Think about the things that cause the balance of retained earnings to change. The retained earnings statement reports the reasons for all changes in retained earnings during the reporting period. Refer to the **TIP** in the **Solution to Exercise 11-10** and review the various reasons for changes in retained earnings. Restrictions on retained earnings are **not** the same thing as restricted cash on hand; retained earnings are not cash. Restrictions on retained earnings refer to amounts of retained earnings which may not be used as the basis of dividend declarations. The three reasons for restrictions on retained earnings are: (1) legal restrictions, (2) contractual restrictions, and (3) voluntary restrictions. These restrictions do not reduce total retained earnings. (Solution = c.)

*24. Question

(L.O. 8) Selected information for the Bradley Corporation is as follows:

	Dec. 31 2013	Dec. 31 2014
Preferred stock, 8%, par $100, noncumulative	$250,000	$250,000
Common stock	600,000	800,000
Retained earnings	150,000	370,000
Dividends paid on preferred stock for the year	20,000	20,000
Net income for the year	120,000	240,000

Bradley's return on common stockholders' equity, (rounded to the nearest percentage) for 2014 is:

a.   25%.
b.   23%.
c.   19%.
d.   17%.

Explanation: A widely used ratio that measures profitability from the common stockholders' viewpoint is **return on common stockholders' equity.** This ratio shows how many dollars of net income were earned for each dollar invested by the owners. It is computed by dividing net income applicable to common stockholders (net income - preferred dividends) by average common stockholders' equity. Thus, in this case, the formula is:

$$\frac{\text{Return on common}}{\text{stockholders' equity}} = \frac{\text{Net income - Preferred dividends}}{\text{Average common stockholders' equity}}$$

$$\frac{\$240,000 - \$20,000}{1/2\ (\$750,000^1 + \$1,170,000^2)} = \frac{\$220,000}{\$960,000} = 23\%$$

(Solution = b.)

[1]Beginning total stockholders' equity ($250,000 + $600,000 + $150,000) - par value of preferred stock ($250,000) = $750,000 beginning common stockholders' equity.

[2]Ending total stockholders' equity ($250,000 + $800,000 + $370,000) - par value of preferred stock ($250,000) = $1,170,000 ending common stockholders' equity.

**25. Question

(L.O. 9) Assume common stock is the only class of stock outstanding in the B-Bar-B Corporation. Total stockholders' equity divided by the number of common stock shares outstanding is called:

a.   book value per share.
b.   par value per share.
c.   stated value per share.
d.   market value per share.

Approach and Explanation: Briefly define each of the answer selections. **Book value** per common stock share represents the equity a common stockholder has in the net assets of the corporation. When only one class of stock is outstanding, book value per share is determined by dividing total stockholders' equity by the number of shares outstanding. **Par value** is an arbitrary value which does not have much significance except in establishing legal capital and in determining the amount to appear in the Common Stock account for each share issued. **Stated value** refers to an arbitrary value that may be placed on a stock by the board of directors. Stated value has about the same significance as par value. **Market value** refers to the price for which a stock is currently being bought and sold in the open market. (Solution = a.)

CHAPTER 12

*I*NVESTMENTS

OVERVIEW

Oftentimes an entity has cash that is temporarily in excess of its immediate needs. That cash should be invested wisely so that it produces income while being a ready source of funds. Sometimes an entity invests in the stocks and bonds of other entities for investment purposes. Accounting for both short-term (temporary) and long-term investments is discussed in this chapter.

SUMMARY OF LEARNING OBJECTIVES

1. **Discuss why corporations invest in debt and stock securities.** Corporations invest for three primary reasons: (a) They have excess cash; (b) They view investments as a significant revenue source; or (c) They have strategic goals such as gaining control of a competitor or moving into a new line of business.

2. **Explain the accounting for debt investments.** Companies record investments in debt securities when they purchase bonds, receive or accrue interest, and sell the bonds. They report gains or losses on the sale of bonds are reported in the "Other revenues and gains" or "Other expenses and losses" sections of the income statement.

3. **Explain the accounting for stock investments.** Companies record investments in common stock when they purchase the stock, receive dividends, and sell the stock. When ownership is less than 20%, the cost method is used. When ownership is between 20% and 50%, the equity method should be used. When ownership is more than 50%, companies prepare consolidated financial statements.

4. **Describe the use of consolidated financial statements.** When a company owns more than 50% of the common stock of another company, it usually prepares consolidated financial statements. These statements indicate the magnitude and scope of operations of the companies under common control.

5. **Indicate how debt and stock investments are valued and reported on the financial statements.** Investments in debt securities are classified as trading or held-for-collection securities for valuation and reporting purposes. Stock investments are classified either as trading or non-trading. Stock investments have no maturity date and therefore are never classified as held-for-collection. Trading securities are reported in current assets at fair value with changes from cost reported in net income. Non-trading securities are also reported at fair value with the changes from cost reported separately in stockholders' equity. Non-trading securities are classified as temporary (short-term) or long-term depending on their expected realization (i.e. future sale date).

6. **Distinguish between short-term and long-term investments.** Short-term investments are securities that are (a) readily marketable and (b) intended to be converted to cash within the next year or operating cycle, whichever is longer. Investments that do not meet both criteria are classified as long-term investments.

**7. Describe the form and content of consolidated financial statements as well as how to prepare them. Consolidated financial statements are similar in form and content to the financial statements of an individual corporation. A consolidated balance sheet shows the assets and liabilities controlled by the parent company. A consolidated income statement shows the results of operations of affiliated companies as though they are one economic unit. The worksheet for a consolidated balance sheet contains columns for (a) the balance sheet data for the separate entities, (b) intercompany eliminations, and (c) consolidated data.

*This material is discussed in the **Appendix 12A** in the text.

TIPS ON CHAPTER TOPICS

TIP: An investment may be classified as a current asset (if it is a short-term or temporary investment) or as a noncurrent asset (if it is a long-term investment). For an investment to be classified as a **current asset:** (1) it should be readily marketable, and (2) there should be a lack of management intent to hold it for long-term purposes. Thus, investments are listed on the balance sheet either under the caption "Current assets" or "Investments."

TIP: The cost of an investment includes its purchase price and all other costs necessary to acquire the investment. Thus, the cost of an investment in stocks or bonds is likely to include broker commissions and incidental fees.

TIP: When an investment is sold, broker commissions are deducted from the sales price to arrive at the net proceeds from sale. An excess of net proceeds over carrying value of the investment is recorded as a **gain on sale** of investment; an excess of carrying value over net proceeds is recorded as a **loss on sale** of investment. Gains and losses on the sale of investments are **realized gains and losses.**

TIP: Most of the terminology and computations involving bond investments are the same as those used by the issuer of bonds (which was a subject discussed in **Chapter 10**). A major difference is that a separate discount or premium account is normally **not** used by the investor; rather, a premium or discount on bond investment is netted against the face value of the investment and this net amount is reflected in the investment account.

TIP: An investor who owns only a small percentage of the outstanding shares of stock of an investee should use the cost method to account for the investment and report it at fair value. When an investor owns enough shares of common stock to exert significant influence over the financial and operating activities of the investee, the investor should use the equity method of accounting. It is generally presumed that the investor has that significant influence when the level of ownership is 20% or greater. When ownership is more than 50%, consolidated financial statements should be prepared.

TIP: Included in the noncurrent investment classification are the following: (1) long-term investments in stocks and bonds of other entities, (2) bond sinking funds, and (3) long-term receivables and advances (loans) to other companies.

ILLUSTRATION 12-1
SUMMARY OF REPORTING GUIDELINES FOR INVEST-MENTS IN DEBT AND EQUITY SECURITIES (L.O. 3, 5)

The major categories for investments in debt and equity securities and their reporting treatments are summarized below.

Category	Balance Sheet	Income Statement
Trading (debt and equity securities)	Investments shown at fair value. Current assets.	Interest and dividends received are recognized as revenue. Unrealized holding gains and losses are included in income. Gains and losses from sale (realized gains and losses) are included in income.
Non-trading (equity securities)	Investments shown at fair value. Current or long-term assets. Unrealized holding gains and losses are a separate component of stockholders' equity.	Dividends are recognized as revenue. Unrealized holding gains and losses are included as a **separate** component of stockholders' equity (that is, they are **not** included in net income). Gains and losses from sale are included in income.
Held-for-collection (debt securities)	Investments shown at amortized cost (unrealized holding gains and losses are not recognized). Current or long-term assets.	Interest is recognized as revenue. Gains and losses from sale are included in income.
Equity method and/or Consolidation (equity securities)	Investments are carried at cost, are periodically adjusted by the investor's share of the investee's earnings or losses, and are decreased by all dividends received from the investee. Classified in long-term assets.	Revenue is recognized to the extent of the investee's earnings or losses reported subsequent to the date of investment. Gains and losses from sale are included in income.

TIP: A current market price of a stock is usually used as a measure of the fair value of that stock.

TIP: Investments in the stocks of other companies are often referred to as investments in **equity securities** or stock investments. Investments in the bonds of other companies are often referred to as investments in **debt securities** or debt investments.

TIP: Investments in debt securities and investments in equity securities that are accounted for by the cost method (as opposed to the equity method) are categorized as follows:

Trading securities: Debt and equity securities held with the intention of selling them in a short period of time (generally less than a month); held to generate income on short-term price swings.

Held-for-collection securities: Debt securities that the investor has the intent and ability to hold to maturity.

Non-Trading securities: Equity securities that are held with the intent of selling them sometime in the future.

TIP: If an investor purchases a security and later sells it for less than the security's cost, the investor has a **realized loss** (loss on sale of investment). If the market price of a security changes while an investor holds the security, changes in the market price (fair value) are referred to as **unrealized holding gains and losses.** Thus, if an investor purchased a security for $1,000 and the fair value is $700 at the balance sheet date, the investor has an unrealized holding loss of $300. If the security is one which is to be reported at fair value on the balance sheet, the write-down of the investment is accomplished by the use of a valuation account (Fair Value Adjustment); thus, original cost information is preserved in the investment account.

The journal entry to record the decline in the fair value of the investment if the security is classified as trading is as follows:

Unrealized Loss—Income..	XX	
Fair Value Adjustment—Trading		XX

The effects of this entry on the basic accounting equation and on net income are as follows;

$$A = L + SE \quad NI$$
$$\downarrow \qquad \quad \downarrow \quad \downarrow$$

The journal entry to record the decline in fair value if the security is classified as non-trading is as follows:

Unrealized Gain or Loss—Equity..	XX	
Fair Value Adjustment—Non-Trading...................................		XX

The effects of this entry on the basic accounting equation and on net income are as follows:

$$A = L + SE \quad NI$$
$$\downarrow \qquad \quad \downarrow \quad NE$$

A = Assets	L = Liabilities	SE = Owners' Equity
NI = Net Income	NE = No Effect	

From the above, you can see that changes in the valuation account (Fair Value Adjustment) for investment securities classified as trading are included in the determination of net income of the period

In which they occur. Accumulated changes in the valuation account for investment securities classified as non-trading are included in the stockholders' equity section of the balance sheet and shown separately.

TIP: The only time an accountant records an entry affecting the Fair Value Adjustment—Trading account or the Fair Value Adjustment—Non-Trading account is in the adjusting process at the end of an accounting period. Thus, when securities are purchased and/or sold during the period, the accountant **ignores** the related valuation account and its contents. The balance of a valuation account should be adjusted as needed at the end of the period by performing the following three steps for the related portfolio:

Step 1: **Determine the total fair value:** Determine the aggregate fair value of the portfolio. This amount gets reported as the carrying value of the asset in the balance sheet.

Step 2: **Determine the desired balance in the related valuation account:** Compute the difference between the aggregate cost and the aggregate fair value of the portfolio.

Step 3: **Determine the amount of adjustment required:** Compare the result of Step 2 with the existing balance in the valuation account (which is the result of entries in previous periods, if any). The difference is the required adjustment (either increase or decrease in the valuation account).

TIP: The balance of an investment account and its related valuation account are often combined and reported net on a balance sheet.

TIP: The accounts Fair Value Adjustment—Trading and Fair Value Adjustment—Non-Trading are both real accounts (and are never closed). The Unrealized Gain—Income and Unrealized Loss—Income accounts are nominal accounts (and are closed at the end of an accounting period). The Unrealized Gain or Loss—Equity is a real account (and is **not** involved in the closing process).

TIP: The accounts Interest Revenue, Gain from Sale of Investment, Dividend Revenue, Revenue from Investment in X Company, and Unrealized Gain—Income are reported under Other Revenues and Gains in the income statement. The accounts Loss on Sale of Investment and Unrealized Loss—Income are reported under Other Expenses and Losses in the income statement.

EXERCISE 12-1

Purpose: (L.O. 2, 5) This exercise will illustrate how to record transactions related to an investment in bonds.

The Humpty Dumpty Company had the following transactions and events pertaining to an investment in bonds:

April 1, 2014   Acquired 100 King, Inc. 10%, 10-year, $1,000 bonds for $100,000. The bonds pay interest semiannually on April 1 and October 1; they mature on April 1, 2024.

Oct. 1, 2014   Received interest on the bonds.

Dec. 31, 2014   Adjusted the accounts in preparation of the financial statements.

April 1, 2015   Received interest on the bonds.

July 31, 2015   Sold all of the bonds for a price of $98,000 plus accrued interest. Incurred brokerage fees of $1,170.

Instructions
Prepare all of the relevant journal entries to record the transactions and events listed above.

SOLUTION TO EXERCISE 12-1

<u>2014</u>
April 1   Debt Investments   100,000
           Cash..   100,000
           (To record purchase of 100 King Inc. bonds)

Oct. 1   Cash (100 X $1,000 X 10% X 6/12)   5,000
           Interest Revenue..   5,000
           (To record receipt of interest on King Inc.
             bonds)

Dec. 31   Interest Receivable (100 X $1,000 X 10% X 3/12).........   2,500
           Interest Revenue..   2,500
           (To accrue interest on King Inc. bonds)

<u>2015</u>
April 1   Cash..   5,000
           Interest Receivable   2,500
           Interest Revenue..   2,500
           (To record receipt of interest of which
             half was previously accrued)

> **TIP:** In this entry, the credit to Interest Receivable is made under the assumption that reversing entries are **not** used by the investor.

July 31   Cash..   100,163[b]
          Loss on Sale of Debt Investments................................   3,170[d]
           Debt Investments ....   100,000[c]
           Interest Revenue..   3,333[a]
           (To record sale of King Inc. bonds)

       [a]100 X $1,000 X 10% X 4/12 = <u>$3,333</u>

[b]Sales price	$ 98,000
Brokerage fees	(1,170)
Net sales price	96,830
Accrued interest	3,333
Net cash collected	$100,163

[c]Cost of bonds being sold; balance of the investment account.

[d]Sales price	$98,000
Brokerage fees	(1,170)
Net sales price	96,830
Cost of investment	(100,000)
Loss on sale of investment	$ 3,170

> **TIP:** Accounting and reporting of debt investments acquired at a premium or discount is **not** covered in this text. Also, the accounting and valuation issues related to held-for-collection securities are discussed in more advanced accounting courses.

EXERCISE 12-2

Purpose: (L.O. 3, 5) This exercise will illustrate how to record and report transactions related to an investment in stock classified as non-trading securities.

The Jan Larson Corporation had the following transactions pertaining to a temporary investment in equity securities classified as non-trading (transactions are listed in chronological order):

1. Purchased 1,000 shares of PW Corporation common stock for $25,000 cash plus $370 in brokerage fees.
2. Received cash dividends of $2 per share on PW common stock.
3. Sold 400 shares of PW common stock for $11,000 less brokerage fees of $170.
4. Received cash dividends of $2 per share on PW common stock.
5. Sold 300 shares of PW common stock for $7,200 less brokerage fees of $100.
6. Adjusted the accounts and prepared financial statements. The market price of PW common stock at the balance sheet date was $26 per share.

Instructions
(a) Prepare all of the relevant journal entries to record the transactions and events listed above.
(b) List the resulting account balances at December 31 and also indicate the classification of each of the accounts (other than Cash) used in the journal entries.
(c) Explain how your answers to (a) and (b) above would change if the Jan Larson Corporation classifies the PW common stock as a long-term investment. (The investor does **not** have significant influence over the investee).

SOLUTION TO EXERCISE 12-2

(a)   1.   Stock Investments—Non-Trading   25,370

            Cash ($25,000 + $370)   25,370

            (To record purchase of 1,000 shares of PW Corporation common stock)

TIP:	The cost of an investment includes the acquisition price and any incidental costs to acquire the investment.

    2.   Cash ($2 X 1,000 shares)   2,000

          Dividend Revenue...   2,000

          (To record receipt of a cash dividend)

3. Cash ($11,000 - $170) 10,830
        Stock Investments—Non-Trading
            (400/1,000 X $25,370) 10,148
        Gain on Sale of Stock Investments .... 682[a]
            (To record sale of 400 shares of PW
            common stock)

    [a]Selling price of investment $11,000
    Cost of selling investment .... (170)
    Net proceeds from sale 10,830
    Carrying value (cost) of shares sold
        (400 shares / 1,000 shares X $25,370 total cost) ... (10,148)
    Gain on sale of investment .... $ 682

4. Cash ($2 X 600 shares) 1,200
        Dividend Revenue 1,200
            (To record receipt of a cash dividend)

5. Cash ($7,200 - $100) 7,100
    Loss on Sale of Stock Investments .... 511[a]
        Stock Investments—Non-Trading
            (300/1,000 X $25,370) 7,611
            (To record sale of 300 shares of PW
            common stock)

    [a]Selling price of investment $7,200
    Cost of selling investment .... (100)
    Net proceeds from sale 7,100
    Carrying value (cost) of shares sold
        (300 shares/1,000 shares X $25,370 total cost) ... (7,611)
    Loss on sale of investment .... $(511)

6. Fair Value Adjustment—Non-Trading .... 189[a]
        Unrealized Gain or Loss—Equity 189
            (To record unrealized gain on
            non-trading securities)

    [a]Market value of stock at Dec. 31 (300 shares X $26) ... $7,800
    Carrying value (cost) of shares held .... (7,611)
    Unrealized gain .... $ 189

Account	Balance	Classification
(b) Stock Investments—Non-Trading	$7,611 Dr.	Current Assets on the balance sheet (temporary investment)
Fair Value Adjustment—Non-Trading	$189 Dr.	Current Assets on the balance sheet—added to balance of Stock Investments—Non-Trading
Dividend Revenue	$3,200 Cr.	Other Revenues and Gains on the income statement
Gain on Sale of Stock Investments	$682 Cr.	Other Revenues and Gains on the income statement
Loss on Sale of Stock Investments	$511 Dr.	Other Expenses and Losses on the income statement
Unrealized Gain or Loss—Equity	$189 Cr.	Stockholders' Equity on balance sheet—positive component

TIP: When more than one investment is sold during the period, the resulting realized gains and losses are usually netted on the income statement; thus, the gain of $682 and the loss of $511 above would net to a gain of $171 for reporting purposes.

Approach and Explanation: Draw T-accounts, post the journal entries and balance the relevant accounts as follows:

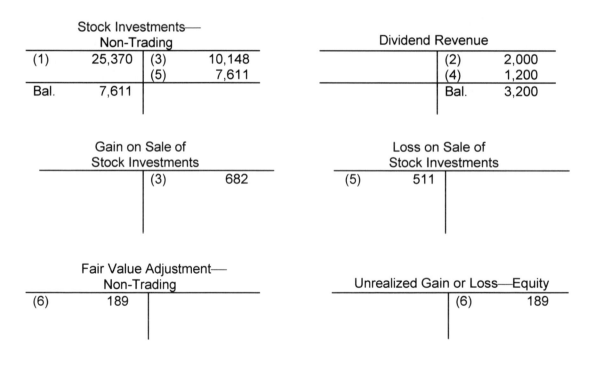

TIP: For non-trading securities, the unrealized gain or loss account is carried forward to future periods (that is, it is not closed); thus, at each future balance sheet date, it is adjusted with the fair value adjustment account to show the difference between cost and fair value at that time.

(c)   If the stock was classified as a long-term investment and the cost method was used to account for it (because Jan Larson does **not** have significant influence over PW), the answers to (a) and (b) would be exactly as they are above except for the classification of the Stock Investments account; it would be classified in the noncurrent asset section titled Investments rather than in the Current Assets section of the balance sheet.

EXERCISE 12-3

Purpose: (L.O. 3, 5) This exercise will illustrate how to record and report transactions related to an investment in stock classified as trading securities.

The Charlie Daley Corporation had the following transactions pertaining to a temporary investment in equity securities classified as trading (transactions are listed in chronological order):

1. Purchased 1,000 shares of PW Corporation common stock for $25,000 cash plus $370 in brokerage fees.
2. Received cash dividends of $2 per share on PW common stock.
3. Sold 400 shares of PW common stock for $11,000 less brokerage fees of $170.
4. Received cash dividends of $2 per share on PW common stock.
5. Sold 300 shares of PW common stock for $7,200 less brokerage fees of $100.
6. Adjusted the accounts and prepared financial statements. The market price of PW common stock at the balance sheet date was $26 per share.

Instructions
(a)   Prepare all of the relevant journal entries to record the transactions and events listed above.
(b)   List the resulting account balances at December 31 and also indicate the classification of each of the accounts (other than Cash) used in the journal entries.

TIP: In this exercise, the Fair Value Adjustment—Non Trading account has a debit balance at the balance sheet date so its balance is added in the asset classification. In cases where that account has a credit balance at a reporting date, its balance is a negative component in the asset classification.

TIP: In this exercise, the Unrealized Gain or Loss—Equity account has a credit balance at the balance sheet date so its balance is added in the stockholders' equity section. In cases where that account has a debit balance at a reporting date (indicating a net unrealized loss situation), its balance is deducted in the stockholders' equity section.

SOLUTION TO EXERCISE 12-3

(a) 1.   Stock Investments—Trading   25,370
              Cash ($25,000 + $370)   25,370
              (To record purchase of 1,000 shares of
              PW Corporation common stock)

     2.   Cash ($2 X 1,000 shares)   2,000
              Dividend Revenue...   2,000
              (To record receipt of a cash dividend)

     3.   Cash ($11,000 - $170)   10,830
              Stock Investments—Trading (400/1,000 X
              $25,370)..   10,148
              Gain on Sale of Stock Investments...............   682[a]
              (To record sale of 400 shares of PW
              common stock)

          [a]Selling price of investment $11,000
          Cost of selling investment   (170)
          Net proceeds from sale   10,830
          Carrying value (cost) of shares sold
            (400 shares / 1,000 shares X $25,370 total cost)   (10,148)
          Gain on sale of investment $ 682

     4.   Cash ($2 X 600 shares)   1,200
              Dividend Revenue...   1,200
              (To record receipt of a cash dividend)

     5.   Cash ($7,200 - $100)   7,100
          Loss on Sale of Stock Investments ....   511[a]
              Stock Investments—Trading (300/1,000 X
              $25,370)..   7,611
              (To record sale of 300 shares of PW
              common stock)

          [a]Selling price of investment $7,200
          Cost of selling investment   (100)
          Net proceeds from sale   7,100
          Carrying value (cost) of shares sold
            (300 shares/1,000 shares X $25,370 total cost)   (7,611)
          Loss on sale of investment $(511)

6. Fair Value Adjustment—Trading ....   189[a]
        Unrealized Gain—Income   189
        (To record unrealized gain on trading
        securities)

[a]Market value of stock at Dec. 31 (300 shares X $26) $7,800
Carrying value (cost) of shares held   (7,611)
Unrealized gain $ 189

	Account	Balance	Classification
(b)	Stock Investments—Trading	$7,611 Dr.	Current Assets on the balance sheet
	Fair Value Adjustment—Trading	$189 Dr.	Current Assets on the balance sheet—added to balance of Stock Investments—Trading
	Dividend Revenue	$3,200 Cr.	Other Revenues and Gains on the income statement
	Gain on Sale of Stock Investments	$682 Cr.	Other Revenues and Gains on the income statement
	Loss on Sale of Stock Investments	$511 Dr.	Other Expenses and Losses on the income statement
	Unrealized Gain—Income	$189 Cr.	Other Revenues and Gains on the income statement

TIP: When more than one investment is sold during the period, the resulting realized gains and losses are usually netted on the income statement; thus, the gain of $682 and the loss of $511 above would net to a gain of $171 for reporting purposes.

Approach and Explanation: Draw T-accounts, post the journal entries and balance the relevant accounts as follows:

Stock Investments—Trading			
(1)	25,370	(3)	10,148
		(5)	7,611
Bal.	7,611		

Dividend Revenue			
		(2)	2,000
		(4)	1,200
		Bal.	3,200

Gain on Sale of Stock Investments			
		(3)	682

Loss on Sale of Stock Investments			
(5)	511		

Fair Value Adjustment—Trading			
(6)	189		

Unrealized Gain—Income			
		(6)	189

> **TIP:** The facts for **Exercise 12-3** are the same as the facts for **Exercise 12-2** except for the fact that the stock is classified as trading securities in **Exercise 12-3** rather than as non-trading securities as in **Exercise 12-2.** Compare the **Solution to Exercise 12-3** with the **Solution to Exercise 12-2** and notice that although both situations report the investment at fair value on the balance sheet, the changes in fair value while the security is held (unrealized holding gains and losses) for the trading portfolio go through the income statement (and therefore affect retained earnings) whereas the changes in fair value for the non-trading portfolio bypass the income statement and go straight to a separate component of stockholders' equity. Thus, both situations have the same **net** impact on stockholders' equity but they affect different accounts within stockholders' equity.

EXERCISE 12-4

Purpose: (L.O. 2, 3, 5) This exercise will illustrate how to account for investments in trading and non-trading securities.

Accolades Cruise Company has two investment portfolios at the December 31, 2014 balance sheet date. The securities contained in these portfolios are all equity securities and were purchased during 2014, Accolades' first year of operations. None of the investments are accounted for by the equity method. No investments were sold during 2014. Details are as follows:

Trading Portfolio

	December 31, 2014		
	Cost	**Market**	**Difference**
Stock of ABC Co.	$100,000	$ 80,000	$(20,000)
Stock of DEF Co.	70,000	92,000	22,000
Stock of GHI Co.	60,000	50,000	(10,000)
Total	$230,000	$222,000	$(8,000)

Non-Trading Portfolio--Long-term

	December 31, 2014		
	Cost	**Market**	**Difference**
Stock of JKL Co.	$140,000	$153,000	$13,000
Stock of MNO Co.	120,000	135,000	15,000
Stock of PQR Co.	150,000	121,000	(29,000)
Stock of STU Co.	160,000	136,000	(24,000)
Total	$570,000	$545,000	$(25,000)

Instructions

(a) Prepare the appropriate adjusting entry(s) at December 31, 2014.

(b) Explain how the data will be displayed on the balance sheet. Compute total stockholders' equity. (Assume at the balance sheet date, Accolades has a balance of $400,000 in its Common Stock account and $600,000 in its Retained Earnings account.) Also, explain what will appear and where on the income statement for the year ending December 31, 2014.

(c) Assuming the stock of DEF Co. is sold for $94,000 on January 7, 2015 and the stock of STU Co. is sold for $141,000 on January 8, 2015, prepare the journal entries to record these sales and explain where realized gains and losses will appear in the income statement for the year ending December 31, 2015.

SOLUTION TO EXERCISE 12-4

(a) Unrealized Loss—Income   8,000
        Fair Value Adjustment—Trading.....................................   8,000

     Unrealized Loss—Equity   25,000
        Fair Value Adjustment—Non-Trading.............................   25,000

Explanation: Investments in marketable equity securities are to be accounted for by the equity method if the investor has significant influence over the investee. When the equity method is inappropriate, the securities are accounted for by the cost method and are reported at fair value. With this latter method, the securities are first grouped into one of two portfolios: the trading portfolio or the non-trading portfolio. Each portfolio is to be reported at fair value. Thus, the total market value of the trading portfolio at the balance sheet date ($222,000) is compared with the total cost of the trading portfolio ($230,000) to determine the balance needed in the related valuation (fair value adjustment) account. If market value is lower than cost, a credit balance is needed in the valuation account for the excess of cost over market ($8,000 in this case). Thus, the fair value adjustment account is credited and an unrealized loss account is debited. The same comparison is made for the non-trading portfolio. The journal entry to establish a valuation account for the non-trading portfolio looks very similar to the journal entry to establish a valuation account for the trading portfolio but a major difference lies in the reporting of the unrealized loss (or gain) account [see part (b) of this exercise].

(b)
Balance Sheet
    Current assets
        Temporary investments, at fair value $222,000

    Investments
        Investments in stock, at fair value $545,000

    Stockholders' equity
        Common stock $ 400,000
        Retained earnings   600,000
            Total paid-in capital and retained earnings   1,000,000
        Less: Unrealized loss on valuation of non-
                    trading securities   25,000
            Total stockholders' equity $ 975,000

Income Statement
    Other expenses and losses:
        Unrealized loss on valuation of trading
            securities $ 8,000

Explanation: Changes in the valuation account for the trading portfolio of marketable securities go through income but changes in the valuation account for a non-trading portfolio are reflected in a separate component in stockholders' equity (i.e. in a contra stockholders' equity account in this case).

(c)

January 7, 2015

Cash	94,000	
Stock Investments—Trading		70,000
Gain on Sale of Stock Investments		24,000

January 8, 2015

Cash	141,000	
Loss on Sale of Stock Investments..	19,000	
Stock Investments—Non-Trading		160,000

The sale of an investment (short-term or long-term) at a price other than its cost will result in a realized gain or loss to be reported in the Other Revenues and Gains or Other Expenses and Losses section of a multiple-step income statement. Thus, the $24,000 gain will be reported in the Other Revenues and Gains section and the $19,000 loss will be reported in the Other Expenses and Losses section of Accolades' 2015 income statement. It is permissible to net the realized gains and losses for a period in which case Accolades would report a gain of $5,000 in the Other Revenues and Gains classification on its 2015 income statement.

TIP: The valuation account is not involved in recording the purchase or sale of securities during the period. The valuation account is adjusted **only** at the end of an accounting period.

EXERCISE 12-5

Purpose: (L.O. 3, 5) This exercise will allow you to compare the results of using the cost method with the results of using the equity method of accounting for an investment in stock.

The F. Sanderlin Corporation purchased 2,000 shares of common stock of the Nolty Bolt Corporation for $52 on January 2, 2014. The Nolty Bolt Corporation reported net income of $54,000 and $60,000 for 2014, and 2015, respectively, and paid dividends of $20,000 and $24,000 on December 20 of 2014 and 2015, respectively. The accounting period is the calendar year. The market price of Nolty Bolt common stock was $58 on December 31, 2014, and $50 on December 31, 2015. This security is F. Sanderlin's only long-term portfolio investment.

Instructions

(a) For the investor's books, prepare all the necessary journal entries to record the foregoing events that occurred in 2014 and 2015, assuming the 2,000 shares represent 16% of the outstanding stock of the investee.

(b) For the investor's books, prepare all the necessary journal entries to record the foregoing events that occurred in 2014 and 2015, assuming the 2,000 shares represent 25% of the outstanding stock of the investee.

(c) Based on your entries in (a) and (b) above, complete the following:

	Situation (a) (Cost Method)	Situation (b) (Equity Method)
Dividend revenue or revenue from investment—2014	_____	_____
Balance of investment account— December 31, 2014	_____	_____
Carrying value of investment— December 31, 2014	_____	_____
Balance of Unrealized Gain (Loss)— Equity account—December 31, 2014	_____	_____
Dividend revenue or revenue from investment—2015	_____	_____
Balance of investment account— December 31, 2015	_____	_____
Carrying value of investment— December 31, 2015	_____	_____
Balance of Unrealized Gain (Loss)— Equity account—December 31, 2015	_____	_____

SOLUTION TO EXERCISE 12-5

(a)
2014
Jan. 2 Stock Investments   104,000
             Cash..   104,000
                  (To record purchase of 2,000 shares)

Dec. 20 Cash   3,200
             Dividend Revenue..   3,200
                  (To record receipt of $1.60 per share dividend)
                  ($20,000 X 16% = $3,200)
                  ($3,200 ÷ 2,000 shares = $1.60)

Dec. 31 Fair Value Adjustment—Non-Trading............................   12,000
             Unrealized Gain or Loss—Equity...........................   12,000

> **TIP:** At December 31, 2014, the market value of the non-trading securities (2,000 X $58 = $116,000) exceeds their cost ($104,000); hence, a valuation account with a $12,000 ($116,000 - $104,000 = $12,000) balance is necessary to report the securities at fair value on the balance sheet.

2015
Dec. 20 Cash   3,840
             Dividend Revenue...   3,840
                  (To record receipt of $1.92 per share dividend)
                  ($24,000 X 16% = $3,840)
                  ($3,840 ÷ 2,000 shares = $1.92)

Dec. 31	Unrealized Gain or Loss—Equity..	16,000	
	Fair Value Adjustment—Non-Trading......................		16,000
	(To record net unrealized loss on non-trading securities)		
	($50 market price X 2,000 shares = $100,000 market value)		
	($104,000 cost - $100,000 market = $4,000 debit balance needed in Fair Value Adjustment account)		
	($12,000 existing credit balance + $4,000 debit balance = $16,000 adjustment needed)		

(b)
<u>2014</u>

Jan. 2	Stock Investments	104,000	
	Cash		104,000
	(To record purchase of Nolty Bolt Common Stock)		
Dec. 20	Cash	5,000	
	Stock Investments		5,000
	(To record dividends received)		
	($20,000 X 25% = $5,000)		
Dec. 31	Stock Investments	13,500	
	Revenue from Stock Investments............................		13,500
	(To record 25% equity in Nolty Bolt's 2014 net income)		
	($54,000 X 25% = $13,500)		

<u>2015</u>

Dec. 20	Cash	6,000	
	Stock Investments		6,000
	(To record dividends received)		
	($24,000 X 25% = $6,000)		
Dec. 31	Stock Investments	15,000	
	Revenue from Stock Investments............................		15,000
	(To record 25% equity in Nolty Bolt's 2015 net income)		
	($60,000 x 25% = $15,000)		

(c)

	Situation (a) (Cost Method)	Situation (b) (Equity Method)
Dividend revenue or revenue from investment—2014	$ 3,200	$ 13,500
Balance of investment account—December 31, 2014	104,000	112,500
Carrying value of investment—December 31, 2014	116,000	112,500
Balance of Unrealized Gain (Loss)—Equity account—December 31, 2014	12,000	Not applicable
Dividend revenue or revenue from investment—2015	3,840	15,000
Balance of investment account—December 31, 2015	104,000	121,500
Carrying value of investment—December 31, 2015	100,000	121,500
Balance of Unrealized Gain (Loss)—Equity account—December 31, 2015	(4,000)	Not applicable

Approach and Explanation for Situation (b): Draw T-accounts for the investment and the investment revenue accounts. Enter the amounts as they would be posted to those accounts from the entries in (b) above.

Stock Investments					Revenue from Stock Investments		
1/2/14	104,000	12/20/14	5,000			12/31/14	13,500
12/31/14	13,500				12/31/14		
Bal.					Closing	13,500	
12/31/14	112,500					13,500	13,500
		12/20/15	6,000			12/31/15	15,000
12/31/15	15,000				12/31/15		
Bal.					Closing	15,000	
12/31/15	121,500					15,000	15,000

Explanation: When an investor has significant influence over an investee, the investor should use the equity method of accounting for the investment. When an investor does not have significant influence, the investor should use the cost method. When an investor owns 20% or more of the outstanding common stock of the investee, it is presumed that the investor has significant influence unless there is evidence to the contrary. (When one corporation owns more than 50% of another corporation, consolidated financial statements are usually prepared.)

Under the **cost method,** the investment in common stock is initially recorded at cost. The investor (1) makes no entry for net income or net loss reported by the investee and (2) credits cash dividends received to the Dividend Revenue account. Dividend revenue is reported in the Other Revenues and Gains section of a multiple-step income statement.

Under the **equity method,** the investment in common stock is initially recorded at cost, and the investment account is adjusted annually to reflect the investor's share of the investee's owners' equity. Each year, the investor (1) debits the investment account and credits revenue for the share of the investee's net income (or conversely, the investor debits a loss account and credits the investment account for its share of the investee's net loss) and (2) records dividends received by a credit to the investment account. The investment account is increased by the investor's share of investee's earnings and decreased by the investor's share of the investee's dividend distributions because the investor's investment account is to reflect the investor's share of the investee's net assets. As the investee's net assets (total stockholders' equity) balance changes, the investor's share of that change is reflected in its investment account.

TIP: The market value of the shares at the balance sheet date is **not** relevant for part (b) because the investment is **not** reported at fair value when the equity method is in use.

---

*EXERCISE 12-6

Purpose: (L.O. 7) This exercise will review the content of a worksheet for a consolidated balance sheet when the cost of the acquiring company's investment exceeds the book value of the underlying net assets of the investee.

On January 1, 2014, Eisner Corporation acquires 100% of Green Inc., for $645,000 in cash. The condensed balance sheets of the two corporations immediately following the acquisition are as follows:

	Eisner Corporation	Green Inc.
Current assets	$ 135,000	$120,000
Investment in Green Inc. common stock	645,000	
Plant and equipment (net)	900,000	630,000
	$1,680,000	$750,000
Current liabilities	$ 540,000	$150,000
Common stock	675,000	225,000
Retained earnings	465,000	375,000
	$1,680,000	$750,000

Instructions
Prepare a worksheet for a consolidated balance sheet.

SOLUTION TO EXERCISE 12-6

Eisner Corporation and Subsidiary
Worksheet—Consolidated Balance Sheet
January 1, 2014

	Eisner Corporation	Green Inc.	Eliminations Dr.	Eliminations Cr.	Consolidated Data
Assets					
Current assets	135,000	120,000			255,000
Investment in Green Inc. common stock	645,000			645,000	-0-
Plant and equipment (net)	900,000	630,000			1,530,000
Excess of cost over book value of subsidiary			45,000		45,000
Totals	1,680,000	750,000			1,830,000
Liabilities and stockholders' equity					
Current liabilities	540,000	150,000			690,000
Common stock— Eisner Corp.	675,000				675,000
Common stock— Green, Inc.		225,000	225,000		-0-
Retained earnings— Eisner Corporation	465,000				465,000
Retained earnings— Green, Inc.		375,000	375,000		-0-
Totals	1,680,000	750,000	645,000	645,000	1,830,000

TIP: When a company owns more than 50% of the common stock of another company, consolidated financial statements are usually prepared; that is, the investor and the investee report their assets, liabilities, revenues, and expenses as one company.

TIP: The cost of acquiring the common stock of another company may be above or below its book value. The management of the parent company may pay more than book value because it believes (1) the fair market values of identifiable assets such as land, buildings, and equipment are higher than their recorded book values or (2) the subsidiary's future earnings prospects warrant a payment for goodwill. The reason Eisner paid more than book value for Green's stock is unclear from the data given; thus, a payment for goodwill is assumed.

TIP: Consolidated balance sheets are prepared from the individual balance sheets of the affiliated companies. They are not prepared from ledger accounts kept by the consolidated entity because only the separate legal entities maintain accounting records.

All items in the individual balance sheets are included in the consolidated balance sheet except amounts that pertain to transactions between the affiliated companies. Transactions between the affiliated companies are identified as intercompany transactions. The process of excluding these transactions in preparing consolidated statements is referred to as **intercompany eliminations.** These eliminations are necessary to avoid overstating assets, liabilities, and stockholders' equity in the consolidated balance sheet. For example, amounts owed by a subsidiary to a parent company and the related receivable reported by the parent company would be eliminated. The objective in a consolidated balance sheet is to show only obligations to and receivables from parties who are not part of the affiliated group of companies.

The Investment in Green Company Common Stock that appears on the balance sheet of Eisner Company represents an interest in the net assets of Green Company. Thus, in this exercise, the investment on Eisner's books is eliminated against the stockholders' equity of the subsidiary because the investor's investment in the subsidiary (Green Company) is replaced by the individual assets and liabilities (net assets) of the investee in which the investor has an interest. The $45,000 excess of Eisner's cost of acquiring Green's stock in excess of the share of Green's recorded stockholders' equity represented by that stock appears as a component of assets on the consolidated balance sheet.

TIP: A worksheet is a tool. The preparation of consolidated financial statements is facilitated by the use of a worksheet. **It is important to note that intercompany eliminations are made solely on the worksheet to present correct consolidated data. They are not journalized or posted by either of the affiliated companies and therefore do not affect the ledger accounts.** The parent company's investment account and the subsidiary company's common stock and retained earnings accounts are reported by the separate entities in preparing their own individual financial statements.

EXERCISE 12-7

Purpose: (L.O. 1 thru 7) This exercise will quiz you about terminology used in this chapter.

A list of accounting terms with which you should be familiar appears below:

Consolidated financial statements
Controlling interest
Cost method
Debt investments
Equity method
Fair value
Fair value
Held-for-collection securities
*Intercompany eliminations

*Intercompany transactions
Investment portfolio
Long-term investments
Non-trading securities
Parent company
Short-term investments
Stock investments
Subsidiary (affiliated) company
Trading securities

*These items appear in the Appendix 12A in the text.

Instructions
For each item below, enter in the blank the term that is described.

1. _____ Investments that are readily marketable and intended to be converted into cash within the next year or operating cycle, whichever is longer.

2. _____ Investments that are **not** readily marketable or that management does not intend to convert into cash within the next year or operating cycle, whichever is longer.

3. _____ A group of stocks and bonds of different corporations held for investment purposes.

4. _____Investments in government and corporation bonds.

5. _____ Investments in the capital stock of corporations.

6. _____ An accounting method in which the investment in common stock is recorded at cost and revenue is recognized only when cash dividends are received.

7. _____ An accounting method in which the investment in common stock is initially recorded at cost, and the investment account is then adjusted annually to show the investor's equity in the investee.

8. _____ A company that owns more than 50% of the common stock of another entity.

9. _____ A company in which more than 50% of its stock is owned by another company.

10. _____ Financial statements that present the assets and liabilities controlled by the parent company and the aggregate profitability of the affiliated companies.

11. _____ Ownership of more than 50% of the common stock of another entity.

12. _____Securities bought and held primarily for sale in the near term to generate income on short-term price differences.

13. _____Stock investments that are held with the intent of selling them sometime in the future.

14. _____Debt securities which the investor has the intent and ability to hold to their maturity date.

15. _____Amount for which a security could be sold in a normal market.

16. _____Transactions between affiliated companies.

17. _____Eliminations made to exclude the effects of intercompany transactions in preparing consolidated statements.

SOLUTION TO EXERCISE 12-7

1.	Short-term investments	10.	Consolidated financial statements
2.	Long-term investments	11.	Controlling interest
3.	Investment portfolio	12.	Trading securities
4.	Debt investments	13.	Non-trading securities
5.	Stock investments	14.	Held-for-collection securities
6.	Cost method	15.	Fair value
7.	Equity method	16.	Intercompany transactions
8.	Parent company	17.	Intercompany eliminations
9.	Subsidiary (affiliated) company		

ANALYSIS OF MULTIPLE-CHOICE TYPE QUESTIONS

1.   **Question**
   (L.O. 2) When an investor's accounting period ends on a date that does **not** coincide with an interest receipt date for bonds held as an investment, the investor must:
   a.   make an adjusting entry to debit Interest Receivable and to credit Interest Revenue for the amount of interest accrued since the last interest receipt date.
   b.   notify the issuer and request that a special payment be made for the appropriate portion of the interest period.
   c.   make an adjusting entry to debit Interest Receivable and to credit Interest Revenue for the total amount of interest to be received at the next interest receipt date.
   d.   do nothing special and ignore the fact that the accounting period does not coincide with the bond's interest period.

Approach: Think of the requirements of the accrual basis of accounting: revenues are to be recognized when they are earned and expenses are to be recognized (recorded and reported) when they are incurred. Interest is earned by the passage of time and is usually collected after the time period for which it pertains. Thus, to comply with the revenue recognition principle, an adjusting entry is necessary to record the accrued revenue (revenue earned but not yet received). (Solution = a.)

2. **Question**
    (L.O. 5) At December 31, 2013, Bithlo Corporation reported the following for its portfolio of investments in marketable equity securities:

Investments in stocks, at cost	$400,000
Less fair value adjustment	39,000
Investments in stocks, at fair value	$361,000

    At December 31, 2014 the market value of the portfolio was $389,000. The cost of the portfolio remained at $400,000. Under what circumstances would Bithlo report a $28,000 credit on its income statement for 2014 as a result of the increase in the market price of the investments in 2014?
    a. When the security is classified in the trading category.
    b. When the security is classified in the non-trading category.
    c. When the security is classified in the held-for-collection category.
    d. No circumstances would call for such a credit of $28,000 on the 2014 income statement.

    Approach and Explanation: Quickly review the guidelines in accounting for an investment in equity securities; they are:
    > **Trading category:** Report at fair value on the balance sheet. Changes in fair value are reported on the income statement.
    > **Non-trading category:** Report at fair value on the balance sheet. Changes in fair value are reflected in a separate component of stockholders' equity rather than as a component of income.

    There is no held-for-collection category for equity securities; that is a name for a category of debt securities held as an investment.
    (Solution = a.)

3. **Question**
    (L.O. 5) The market value of Security A exceeds its cost, and the market value of Security B is less than its cost at a balance sheet date. Both securities are held as investments in equity securities; Security A is classified as trading and Security B is classified as non-trading. How should each of these assets be reported on the balance sheet?

	Security A	Security B
a.	Market value	Market value
b.	Cost	Cost
c.	Cost	Market value
d.	Market value	Cost

    Approach and Explanation: Mentally review the accounting requirements for non-trading equity securities. They are summarized in **Illustration 12-1.** Investments in equity securities classified as trading or non-trading are to be reported at fair value. Market value, if one is available, is used as a measure of fair value. (Solution = a.)

4.   **Question**
(L.O. 3) During 2013, Colquitt Company purchased 4,000 shares of Eichner Corp. common stock for $63,000 as a non-trading equity investment. The fair value of these shares was $60,000 at December 31, 2013. Colquitt sold all of the Eichner stock for $17 per share on December 31, 2014, incurring $2,800 in brokerage commissions. Colquitt Company should report a realized gain on the sale of stock in 2014 of:
a. $8,000.
b. $5,200.
c. $5,000.
d. $2,200.

Explanation: The gain is computed as follows:

Selling price ($17 X 4,000 shares)	$68,000
Cost of sale—commissions	(2,800)
Net proceeds (or net selling price)	65,200
Cost	63,000
Realized gain on sale	$ 2,200 (Solution = d.)

TIP: The valuation account balance existing at the end of 2013 would have no effect on this computation.

---

5.   **Question**
(L.O. 5) On its December 31, 2013 balance sheet, Simpson Company appropriately reported a $4,000 credit balance in its Fair Value Adjustment—Non-Trading account. There was no change during 2014 in the composition of Simpson's portfolio of marketable equity securities held as non-trading securities. The following information pertains to that portfolio:

Security	Cost	Fair value at 12/31/14
A	$ 50,000	$ 65,000
B	40,000	38,000
C	70,000	50,000
	$160,000	$153,000

What amount of unrealized loss on these securities should be included in Simpson's shareholders' equity section of the balance sheet at December 31, 2014?
a. $0
b. $3,000
c. $4,000
d. $7,000

Explanation: The Fair Value Adjustment—Non-Trading account would be increased by $3,000 to a $7,000 credit balance; hence the Unrealized Gain or Loss—Equity account would be also adjusted to a $7,000 debit balance. The Unrealized Gain or Loss—Equity account is reported as a separate line item in stockholders' equity; it reflects the net unrealized loss of $7,000 on this portfolio ($160,000 - $153,000 fair value = $7,000); it is a negative component of stockholders' equity in this case. (Solution = d.)

6. **Question**

    (L.O. 3) An investor has a long-term investment in stocks. Cash dividends received by the investor are recorded as:

Cost Method	**Equity Method**
a. Revenue	Revenue
b. A reduction of the investment account	A reduction of the investment account
c. Revenue	A reduction of the investment account
d. A reduction of the investment account	Revenue

    Approach and Explanation: Write down the journal entry to record the receipt of cash dividends under both the cost and equity methods. Observe the effects of the entries. Find the answer selection that correctly describes those effects.

Cost Method			**Equity Method**		
Cash	XXX		Cash	XXX	
Dividend Revenue		XXX	Stock Investments		XXX

    (Solution = c.)

7. **Question**

    (L.O. 3) The Suncom Corporation purchased 40,000 shares of common stock of the Flagship Corporation for $60 per share on January 2, 2014. The Flagship Corporation had 100,000 shares of common stock outstanding during 2014. Flagship paid cash dividends of $200,000 during 2014 and reported net income of $600,000 for 2014. The Suncom Corporation should report Revenue from Investment in Flagship in its 2014 income statement in the amount of:

    a. $80,000.
    b. $160,000.
    c. $240,000.
    d. $320,000.

    Explanation: Because the Suncom Corporation owns 40% (40,000 ÷ 100,000 = 40%) of the outstanding common stock shares of the investee, it is assumed that the investor can exercise significant influence over the financing and operating policies of the investee and must therefore use the equity method to account for the investment. Using the equity method, the investor will report investment income equal to the investor's proportionate share of the investee's earnings for the period regardless of the amount of cash dividends declared and paid by the investee. (40% X $600,000 = $240,000). (Solution = c.)

8. **Question**

    (L.O. 3) Refer to the facts in **Question 7** above. At the end of 2014, the carrying value of the investment on the investor's balance sheet should be:

    a. $2,640,000.
    b. $2,560,000.
    c. $2,400,000.
    d. $2,080,000.

    Approach and Explanation: Determine if the equity method is appropriate or not. Draw T-accounts and enter the amounts that would be reflected therein.

Stock Investments			
Acquisition cost	2,400,000		
Investor's share of investee's 2014 Earnings	240,000^a	Investor's share of dividends paid by investee	80,000^b
Balance, 12/31/14	2,560,000		

Revenue from Stock Investments	
	240,000^a
	Bal. 12/31/14 240,000

^{a}\$600,000 X 40% = \$240,000.
^{b}\$200,000 X 40% = \$80,000.

(Solution = b.)

TIP:	Under the equity method, the investment is originally recorded at cost and then subsequently adjusted by the investor's proportionate share of the investee's earnings and dividend payments. Income earned by the investee results in an increase in the investment account on the books of the investor. An investee's net loss or dividend payment reduces the balance of the investment account.

9. **Question**
    (L.O. 3) The Higgins Corporation purchased 6,000 shares of common stock of the Barnett Corporation for \$40 per share on January 2, 2014. The Barnett Corporation had 60,000 shares of common stock outstanding during 2014, paid cash dividends of \$30,000 during 2014, and reported net income of \$120,000 for 2014. The Higgins Corporation should report revenue from investment for 2014 in the amount of:
    a. \$3,000.
    b. \$9,000.
    c. \$12,000.
    d. \$15,000.

    Explanation: Because the Higgins Corporation owns only 10% of the outstanding common stock of the investee, it is assumed that Higgins Corporation cannot exercise significant influence over the financing and operating policies of the investee and must therefore use the cost method to account for the investment. Using the cost method, the investor will report dividend revenue equal to the amount of cash dividends received during the period. (\$30,000 X 10% = \$3,000). (Solution = a.)

10. Question

(L.O. 3) When the equity method is used to account for an investment in common stock of another corporation, the journal entry on the investor's books to record the receipt of cash dividends from the investee will:

a. include a debit to Cash and a credit to Dividend Revenue.
b. reduce the carrying value of the investment.
c. increase the carrying value of the investment.
d. be the same journal entry that would be recorded if the cost method were used to account for the investment.

Explanation: The journal entry will be a debit to Cash and a credit to Stock Investments. The credit portion of this entry reduces the balance of the investment account and, therefore, it reduces the carrying value (book value) of the investment. (Solution = b.)

*11. Question

(L.O. 7) A parent company purchases 100% of the stock of a subsidiary for cash. Goodwill will appear on the consolidated balance sheet when the:

a. cost of the parent's investment exceeds the book value of the parent's net assets.
b. cost of the parent's investment exceeds the fair market value of the investee's net assets.
c. fair market value of the investee's net assets exceeds the cost of the parent's investment.
d. book value of the parent's net assets exceeds the cost of the parent's investment.

Explanation: The cost of acquiring the common stock of another company may be above or below its book value. The management of the parent company may pay more than book value because it believes (1) the fair market values of identifiable assets such as land, buildings, and equipment are higher than their recorded book values, or (2) the subsidiary's future earnings prospects warrant a payment for goodwill. When a payment is made for goodwill, the cost of the investment exceeds the fair value of the investor's share of the investee's identifiable net assets. (Solution = b.)

*12. Question

(L.O. 7) Which statement is true regarding elimination entries made in preparing consolidated financial statements?

a. The entries are recorded in the consolidated general journal and are posted to the consolidated general ledger.
b. Each entry contains either debits or credits, but not both.
c. The entries are made to record sales and loans between affiliated companies.
d. The entries appear only on the consolidated worksheet.

Explanation: Elimination entries are made solely on the worksheet used to prepare consolidated financial statements. Elimination entries are made for all intercompany transactions. They are not journalized or posted by either of the affiliated companies and therefore do not affect the ledger accounts. (Solution = d.)

CHAPTER 13

STATEMENT OF CASH FLOWS

OVERVIEW

In previous chapters we have discussed the income statement (which reports on the results of operations for a period of time), the retained earnings statement (which reports on the reasons for changes in retained earnings for a period of time), and the balance sheet (which reports on the financial position of an entity at a point in time). Although a comparison of a balance sheet at the end of a period with a balance sheet at the beginning of the same period will disclose many changes (such as increases or decreases in certain assets, increases or decreases in certain liabilities, and increases or decreases in certain stockholders' equity items), none of the three financial statements discussed thus far discloses how an entity obtains cash and what it does with that cash during its financial reporting period. Thus, a fourth general purpose financial statement is required—the statement of cash flows. The primary purpose of this statement is to provide relevant information about the cash receipts and cash payments of an enterprise during a time period.

SUMMARY OF LEARNING OBJECTIVES

1. **Indicate the usefulness of the statement of cash flows.** The statement of cash flows provides information about the cash receipts, cash payments, and net change in cash resulting from the operating, investing, and financing activities of a company during the period.

2. **Distinguish among operating, investing, and financing activities.** Operating activities include the cash effects of transactions that enter into the determination of net income. Investing activities involve cash flows resulting from changes in investments and long-term asset items. Financing activities involve cash flows resulting from changes in long-term liability and stockholders' equity items.

3. **Prepare a statement of cash flows using the indirect method**. The preparation of a statement of cash flows involves three major steps. (1) Determine net cash provided/used by operating activities by converting net income from an accrual basis to a cash basis. (2) Analyze changes in noncurrent asset and liability accounts and report as investing and financing activities, or disclose as significant noncash transactions. (3) Compare the net change in cash on the statement of cash flows with the change in the Cash account reported on the balance sheet to make sure the amounts agree.

4. **Analyze the statement of cash flows.** Free cash flow indicates the amount of cash a company generated during the current year that is available for the payment of additional dividends or for expansion.

*5. **Explain how to use a worksheet to prepare the statement of cash flows using the indirect method.** When there are numerous adjustments, a worksheet can be a helpful tool in preparing the statement of cash flows. Key guidelines for using a worksheet are: (1) List accounts with debit balances separately from those with credit balances; (2) In the reconciling columns in the bottom portion of the worksheet, show cash inflows as debits and cash outflows as credits; (3) Do not enter reconciling items in any journal or account but use them only to help prepare the statement of cash flows.

The steps in preparing the worksheet are: (1) Enter beginning and ending balances of balance sheet accounts; (2) Enter debits and credits in reconciling columns; and (3) Enter the increase or decrease in cash in two places as a balancing amount.

6. Prepare a statement of cash flows using the direct method. The preparation of the statement of cash flows involves three major steps: (1) Determine net cash provided/used by operating activities by converting net income from an accrual basis to a cash basis. (2) Analyze changes in noncurrent asset and liability accounts and report as investing and financing activities, or disclose as significant noncash transactions. (3) Compare the net change in cash on the statement of cash flows with the change in the cash account reported on the balance sheet to make sure the amounts agree. The direct method reports cash receipts from operations less cash payments from operations to arrive at net cash provided by operating activities. Cash receipts and cash payments from operations are derived from converting the individual components of net income from an accrual basis to a cash basis.

*This material is contained in **Appendix 13A** in the text.
This material is contained in **Appendix 13B in the text.

TIPS ON CHAPTER TOPICS

TIP: Every transaction affecting the Cash account is to be reflected either as an inflow (receipt) or outflow (payment) on the statement of cash flows. Furthermore, the receipts and payments are to be classified by activity. The three activity classifications are: (1) operating, (2) investing, and (3) financing.

TIP: In determining if a cash transaction is related to an operating activity, investing activity, or financing activity, first see if it meets the definition of investing activities. If not, see if it meets the definition of financing activities. If not, then it is an operating activity. (Refer to **Illustration 13-1** for these definitions and examples.)

TIP: In determining if a cash transaction is an operating activity, investing activity, or financing activity, it is usually helpful to reconstruct the journal entry used to record the transaction. The following observations are also helpful:
1. The journal entry to record a transaction that is an investing activity which results in a cash flow will generally involve: (1) Cash and (2) an asset account other than Cash, such as Investment (short-term or long-term), Land, Building, Equipment, Patent, Franchise, etc.
2. The journal entry to record a transaction that is a financing activity which results in a cash flow will generally involve: (1) Cash and (2) a liability account or an owners' equity account such as Bonds Payable, Notes Payable, Dividends Payable, Common Stock, Paid-in Capital in Excess of Par Value, Treasury Stock, etc.
3. The journal entry to record a transaction that is an operating activity which results in a cash flow will generally involve: (1) Cash and (2) a revenue account or an expense account or a prepaid expense or an unearned revenue or a receivable or a payable account.

TIP: The statement of cash flows emphasizes reporting gross cash receipts and payments. Thus, if long-term debt is issued for $2,000,000 and payments of $300,000 on long-term debt occur during the same period, it is **not** permissible to just show the net inflow of $1,700,000. Rather, the inflow of $2,000,000 and the outflow of $300,000 must be separately shown in the financing activity section of the statement of cash flows. Similarly, if acquisitions and disposals of plant assets occur in the same period, the gross cash effects must be reported; they are not to be netted.

TIP: Homework and examination problems related to the subject of the statement of cash flows very often involve comparative balance sheet data. Although sometimes the older year's information is listed first so that the data is in chronological order, it is a common practice to list the current year's data first. Before beginning to work a problem, carefully note the order of the data so that you properly interpret the changes in accounts as being increases or decreases. These comparative balance sheets are often accompanied by additional information. If no additional information is given about an account, but the account balance has changed, assume that (1) only one transaction is responsible for the change in the balance, (2) the most common transaction occurred to change that particular account balance, and (3) cash was involved in the transaction.

TIP: In studying this chapter on the statement of cash flows and preparing homework assignments, you will encounter transactions for which you may not recall the proper accounting procedures. One of the challenging aspects about this chapter is that it draws on your knowledge of **all** of the chapters that precede it. Use this opportunity to look up the items you don't recall and refresh your memory. The procedures you review in this manner will be easier to recall the next time you need to use them.

TIP: A business enterprise that provides a set of financial statements that reports both financial position and results of operations is also required to provide a statement of cash flows for each period for which results of operations are provided. The information provided in a statement of cash flows, if used with related disclosures and information in the other financial statements, should help investors, creditors, and others to (a) assess the enterprise's ability to generate future cash flows; (b) assess the enterprise's ability to pay dividends and meet its obligations; (c) assess the reasons for differences between net income and net cash flow from operating activities; and (d) assess the effects on an enterprise's financial position of both its cash and noncash investing and financing transactions during the period.

ILLUSTRATION 13-1
OPERATING, INVESTING, AND
FINANCING ACTIVITIES (L.O. 2)

Definitions:

Operating activities—include all transactions and other events that are not defined as investing or financing. Operating activities generally involve producing and delivering goods and providing services. Cash flows from operating activities are generally the cash effects of transactions and other events that ultimately create revenues and expenses and thus enter into the determination of net income.

Investing activities—include (a) acquiring and disposing of investments in debt and equity instruments of other entities, (b) acquiring and disposing of property, plant, and equipment and other productive long-lived assets, and (c) lending money and collecting the loans.

Financing activities—include (a) borrowing money and repaying the amounts borrowed, or otherwise settling the obligation, and (b) obtaining resources from owners and providing them with a return on and a return of their investment.

Examples:

Operating activities:

Cash inflows

From sales of goods or services (includes cash sales and collections on account).

From returns on loans (interest received) and on equity securities (dividends received).

Cash outflows

To suppliers for inventory and other goods and services.

To employees for services.

To government for taxes.

To lenders for interest.

To others for other expenses.

Investing activities:

Cash inflows

From disposal of plant assets.

From sale of debt or equity securities of other entities.

From collection of principal on loans to other entities.

Cash outflows

To purchase property, plant, and equipment.

To purchase debt or equity securities of other entities.

To make loans to other entities.

Financing activities:

Cash inflows

From sale of equity securities (company's own stock).

From issuance of debt instruments (bonds and notes).

Cash outflows

To stockholders as dividends.

To reacquire capital stock.

To pay debt (long-term and certain short-term).

EXERCISE 13-1

Purpose: (L.O. 2) This exercise enables you to practice identifying investing and financing activities.

Instructions
Place the appropriate code in the blanks to identify each of the following transactions as giving rise to an:

Code
II   inflow of cash due to an investing activity, or
IO   outflow of cash due to an investing activity, or
FI   inflow of cash due to a financing activity, or
FO   outflow of cash due to a financing activity

_____ 1.   Sell common stock to new stockholders.

_____ 2.   Purchase treasury stock.

_____ 3.   Borrow money from bank by issuance of short-term note.

_____ 4.   Repay money borrowed from bank.

_____ 5.   Purchase bonds as an investment.

_____ 6.   Sell investment in real estate.

_____ 7.   Loan money to an affiliate.

_____ 8.   Collect on loan to affiliate.

_____ 9.   Buy equipment.

_____ 10.   Sell a plant asset.

_____ 11.   Pay cash dividends to stockholders.

SOLUTION TO EXERCISE 13-1

1. FI	4. FO	7. IO	10. II
2. FO	5. IO	8. II	11. FO
3. FI	6. II	9. IO	

Approach:
1.   Reconstruct journal entries for the transactions. Examine each entry to identify if there is an inflow of cash (debit to Cash) or an outflow of cash (credit to Cash).

2.   Write down the definitions for investing activities and financing activities (see below). Analyze each transaction to see if it fits one of these definitions.

a)   **Investing activities**—include (1) acquiring and disposing of investments in debt and equity instruments, (2) acquiring and disposing of property, plant, and equipment and other productive assets, and (3) making and collecting loans.

b)   **Financing activities**—include (1) borrowing money from creditors and repaying the amounts borrowed or otherwise settling the obligation, and (2) obtaining resources from owners and providing them with a return on and a return of their investment.

3.   Assume purchases and sales of items are for cash, unless otherwise indicated.

> **TIP:** The journal entry to record a transaction that is an investing activity which results in a cash flow will involve: (1) Cash and (2) an asset account other than Cash, such as Investments (short-term or long-term), Land, Building, Equipment, Patent, etc.
>
> **TIP:** The journal entry to record a transaction that is a financing activity which results in a cash flow will involve: (1) Cash and (2) a liability account or an owners' equity account, such as Bonds Payable, Note Payable, Dividends Payable, Common Stock, Paid-in Capital in Excess of Par Value, Treasury Stock, etc.

EXERCISE 13-2

Purpose: (L.O. 2) This exercise will give you practice in classifying transactions by activity.

The Wolfson Corporation had the following transactions during 2014:

1.   Issued $100,000 par value common stock in exchange for cash.
2.   Issued $22,000 par value common stock in exchange for equipment.
3.   Sold services for $52,000 cash.
4.   Purchased an investment for $18,000 cash.
5.   Collected $9,000 of accounts receivable.
6.   Paid $14,000 of accounts payable.
7.   Declared and paid a cash dividend of $12,000.
8.   Sold a long-term investment with a cost of $18,000 for $18,000 cash.
9.   Purchased a machine for $35,000 by giving a long-term note in exchange.
10.   Exchanged land costing $20,000 for equipment costing $20,000.
11.   Paid salaries of $6,000.
12.   Paid $1,000 for advertising services.
13.   Paid $8,000 for insurance coverage for a future period.
14.   Borrowed $31,000 cash from the bank.
15.   Paid $11,000 interest.
16.   Paid $31,000 cash to the bank to repay loan principal.
17.   Issued $40,000 par value common stock upon conversion of bonds payable having a face value of $40,000.
18.   Paid utilities of $4,000.
19.   Loaned a vendor $6,000 cash.
20.   Collected interest of $2,000.
21.   Collected $6,000 loan principal from borrower.
22.   Purchased treasury stock for $4,000.
23.   Sold treasury stock for $6,000 (cost was $4,000).
24.   Paid taxes of $20,000.

Instructions

Analyze each transaction above and indicate whether it resulted in a(n):
(a)	inflow of cash from operating activities.
(b)	outflow of cash from operating activities.
(c)	inflow of cash from investing activities.
(d)	outflow of cash from investing activities.
(e)	inflow of cash from financing activities.
(f)	outflow of cash from financing activities, or
(g)	noncash investing and/or financing activity.

SOLUTION TO EXERCISE 13-2

1.	e	6.	b	11.	b	16.	f	21.	c
2.	g	7.	f	12.	b	17.	g	22.	f
3.	a	8.	c	13.	b	18.	b	23.	e
4.	d	9.	g	14.	e	19.	d	24.	b
5.	a	10.	g	15.	b	20.	a		

Approach: Write down the definitions for investing activities, financing activities, and operating activities. (These definitions can be found in **Illustration 13-1**.) Analyze each transaction to see in which classification the transaction would be included. Watch for any transactions that do not result in a cash flow; they are noncash items.

Explanation:
1.	Issuance of stock for cash results in a cash inflow from financing activities.
2.	Issuance of stock in exchange for plant assets does **not** involve any flow of cash; the issuance of stock is a financing activity and the acquisition of plant assets is an investing activity. The transaction is a noncash financing and investing activity.
3.	The sale of services is a revenue transaction. The sale of services for cash results in an inflow of cash from operating activities.
4.	The purchase of an investment for cash results in an outflow of cash from investing activities.
5.	The collection of accounts receivable constitutes a cash inflow from a customer for a prior revenue transaction. A collection of cash from a customer is an inflow of cash from operating activities.
6.	The payment of accounts payable constitutes a payment to a supplier for inventory or other goods or services. There will be a related expense transaction either before the cash payment or after the time of cash payment. A payment to a vendor is an outflow of cash from operating activities.
7.	The payment of cash dividends to stockholders is an outflow of cash from financing activities.
8.	The sale of an investment constitutes an inflow of cash from investing activities.
9.	The acquisition of a plant asset is an investing activity. The issuance of a debt instrument is a financing activity. The purchase of a plant asset by issuance of a note payable does **not** involve a cash flow. Hence, the transaction is a noncash financing and investing activity.
10.	The acquisition of land (a plant asset) is an investing activity. The sale (disposal) of equipment (plant asset) is an investing activity. The exchange of one plant asset for another plant asset does **not** involve any flow of cash; the transaction is a noncash investing activity.
11.	The payment of salaries is a payment to employees for services rendered; it results from an expense transaction. The payment to employees for services is a cash outflow from operating activities.

12. The payment for advertising services is an example of a payment to suppliers of goods and services used in operations; it is a cash outflow from operating activities.

13. The payment for insurance coverage is an example of a payment to suppliers of goods and services used in operations. There will be an expense recognized in a future period. It does not matter in what period the expense recognition takes place; the cash flow occurred in the current period and results in a cash outflow from operating activities.

14. The borrowing of cash from a bank causes an issuance of a debt instrument (i.e., note payable). The borrowing of cash is a cash inflow from financing activities.

15. The payment to lenders for interest will cause an expense to be recognized on the income statement in the period the interest is incurred. The payment of interest is a cash outflow for operating activities in the period the cash is paid.

16. The payment of a loan (debt) is a cash outflow from financing activities.

17. The issuance of common stock is a financing activity and the liquidation (redemption) of bonds payable is a financing activity. However, the redemption of bonds by issuance of stock is a **noncash** financing activity because no cash is received or given in the exchange.

18. The payment of utilities is a payment to a supplier for a service used in operations. The related expense will appear on the income statement in the period the services are consumed. The payment will appear on a statement of cash flows as an outflow of cash from operating activities in the period the cash payment is made.

19. The payment of cash to another entity in the form of a loan to that other entity is a cash outflow from investing activities.

20. The collection of cash for interest is a cash inflow from operating activities.

21. The collection of cash for the principal on a loan to another entity is a cash inflow from investing activities.

22. The cash payment to reacquire a company's own capital stock (treasury stock) is a cash outflow from financing activities.

23. The sale of treasury stock for cash results in a cash inflow from financing activities.

24. The payment of cash to the government for taxes is a cash outflow from operating activities.

TIP: In determining if a cash transaction is an operating activity, investing activity, or financing activity, it is usually helpful to reconstruct the journal entry used to record the transaction. The following observations are also helpful:

1. The journal entry to record a transaction that is an investing activity which results in a cash flow will generally involve: (1) Cash and (2) an asset account other than Cash, such as Investment (short-term or long-term), Land, Building, Equipment, Patent, etc.

2. The journal entry to record a transaction that is a financing activity which results in a cash flow will generally involve: (1) Cash and (2) a liability account or an owners' equity account such as Bonds Payable, Notes Payable, Dividends Payable, Common Stock, Paid-in Capital in Excess of Par, Treasury Stock, etc.

3. The journal entry to record a transaction that is an operating activity which results in a cash flow will generally involve: (1) Cash and (2) a revenue account or an expense account; or, a prepaid expense or an unearned revenue; or, a receivable or a payable account.

EXERCISE 13-3

Purpose: (L.O. 3) This exercise will enable you to practice reconciling net income with net cash provided by operating activities.

The following data relate to the L. Heckenmueller Co. for 2014.

Net income	$ 75,000
Increase in accounts receivable	7,000
Decrease in prepaid expenses	3,200
Increase in accounts payable	5,000
Decrease in taxes payable	900
Gain on sale of investment	1,700
Depreciation	3,500
Loss on disposal of plant assets	600

Instructions
Compute the net cash provided by operating activities for 2014.

SOLUTION TO EXERCISE 13-3

Net income	$ 75,000
Increase in accounts receivable	(7,000)
Decrease in prepaid expenses	3,200
Increase in accounts payable	5,000
Decrease in taxes payable	(900)
Gain on sale of investment	(1,700)
Depreciation	3,500
Loss on sale of equipment	600
Net cash provided by operating activities	$ 77,700

Explanation:
1.   Net income is a summary of all revenues earned, all expenses incurred, and all gains and losses recognized for a period. Most revenues earned during the year result in a cash inflow during the same period but there may be some cash and/or revenue flows that do not correspond. Most expenses incurred during the year result in a cash outflow during the same period but there may be some cash and/or expense flows that do not correspond.

2.   An increase in accounts receivable indicates that revenues earned exceed cash collected from customers and, therefore, net income exceeds net cash provided by operating activities.

3.   A decrease in prepaid expenses indicates that expenses incurred exceed cash paid and, therefore, net income is less than net cash provided by operating activities.

4.   An increase in accounts payable indicates that expenses incurred exceed cash paid and, therefore, net income is less than net cash provided by operating activities.

5.   A decrease in taxes payable indicates expenses incurred are less than the cash paid, and, therefore, net income is greater than net cash provided by operating activities.

6. When an investment is sold, the entire proceeds are to be displayed as an investing activity on the statement of cash flows. The gain included in net income must, therefore, be deducted from net income to arrive at the net cash provided by operating activities. If this adjustment was not made, there would be double counting for the gain amount. For example: An investment with a carrying value of $4,000 is sold for $7,000. The entire $7,000 proceeds is an investing inflow; the $7,000 includes the gain of $3,000 and a recovery of the investment's $4,000 carrying value; the $3,000 gain will be deducted from net income to arrive at the net cash from operating activities figure.

7. Depreciation is a noncash charge (debit) against income. It must be added to net income to arrive at the amount of net cash provided by operating activities.

8. A loss on the sale of equipment does not cause a cash outlay so it is added back to net income to arrive at the amount of net cash provided by operating activities. The cash proceeds from the sale of equipment are shown as a cash inflow from an investing activity.

> **TIP:** Refer to the last two pages of **Illustration 13-2** for guidance in reconciling net income with net cash provided by operating activities.

EXERCISE 13-4

Purpose: (L.O. 3, 4) This exercise will provide you with an opportunity to prepare a statement of cash flows.

A comparative balance sheet for Hernan Perez Pictures appears below:

	December 31		
Assets	**2014**	**2013**	**Change**
Cash	$ 81,000	$ 35,000	$ 46,000
Accounts receivable	65,000	50,000	15,000
Inventory	155,000	96,000	59,000
Investments	100,000	70,000	30,000
Equipment	170,000	100,000	70,000
Accumulated depreciation	(31,000)	(20,000)	(11,000)
	$540,000	$331,000	$209,000
Liabilities and Stockholders' Equity			
Accounts payable	$ 31,000	$ 40,000	$ (9,000)
Long-term note payable	72,000	60,000	12,000
Bonds payable	100,000	0	100,000
Common stock, no par	250,000	200,000	50,000
Retained earnings	87,000	31,000	56,000
	$540,000	$331,000	$209,000

Additional information:
1. New equipment costing $80,000 was purchased for cash.
2. Old equipment was sold at a loss of $4,500.
3. Bonds were issued for cash.
4. An investment costing $30,000 was acquired by issuing a long-term note payable.
5. Cash dividends of $14,000 were declared and paid during the year.
6. Depreciation expense for 2014 was $15,000.
7. Accounts Payable relate to operating expenses.
8. Stock investments are classified as available-for-sale securities.
9. Net sales for 2014 were $80,000.

Instructions
(a)   Prepare a statement of cash flows for 2014 using the indirect method.
(b)   Compute the amount of free cash flow for 2014.

TIP: In this exercise, you must analyze the changes in the Retained Earnings account balance to determine the net income figure for 2014.

SOLUTION TO EXERCISE 13-4

(a)

HERNAN PEREZ PICTURES
Statement of Cash Flows
For the Year Ending December 31, 2014

Cash flows from operating activities		
Net income		$ 70,000
Adjustments to reconcile net income to net cash provided		
by operating activities:		
Increase in accounts receivable	$ (15,000)	
Increase in inventory	(59,000)	
Depreciation expense	15,000	
Loss on sale of equipment	4,500	
Decrease in accounts payable	(9,000)	(63,500)
Net cash provided by operating activities		6,500
Cash flows from investing activities		
Purchase of equipment	(80,000)	
Disposal of plant assets	1,500	
Net cash used by investing activities		(78,500)
Cash flows from financing activities		
Payment on long-term note payable	(18,000)	
Issuance of bonds	100,000	
Issuance of stock	50,000	
Payment of dividends	(14,000)	
Net cash provided by financing activities		118,000
Net increase in cash		46,000
Cash at beginning of period		35,000
Cash at end of period		$ 81,000
Noncash investing and financing activities		
Acquisition of investment in stock by issuance of long-term debt		$ 30,000

TIP:	Examine the statement and notice the major reasons for inflows and outflows of cash during the period.

Approach: Glance through the balance sheet data and additional information to get a feel for the facts given. Set up the format for the statement of cash flows by placing the major headings for the three activity classifications approximately where they go. Leave space to fill in the details later (allow about one-fourth page for investing activities, about one-fourth page for financing activities, and approximately one-half page for the operating activities section). Then take each fact in order and process it by placing it where it belongs on the statement of cash flows.

1. Find the net change in cash by comparing the balance of Cash at the end of the period with the balance of Cash at the beginning of the period. Use the net change in cash to reconcile beginning and ending cash balances.
2. Analyze every change in every balance sheet account other than Cash. Reconstruct the journal entries for the transactions that caused the balance sheet accounts to change. Examine each entry to identify if (a) there is an inflow of cash (debit to Cash) or an outflow of cash (credit to Cash) or no effect on cash; (b) if the transaction involves an operating, investing, or financing activity, and (c) where it goes on the statement of cash flows.
3. To help identify the activity classification for each transaction, write down the definitions for investing activities, financing activities, and operating activities. Analyze each transaction to see if it meets one of these definitions. (Refer to **Illustration 13-1** for these definitions.)
4. To help identify investing activities, recall that transactions involving investing activities typically cause changes in noncurrent asset accounts (or changes in current asset accounts such as short-term investments and nontrade receivables).
5. To help identify financing activities, recall that transactions involving financing activities typically cause changes in noncurrent liability accounts or stockholders' equity accounts (or changes in current liability accounts such as short-term nontrade notes payable).
6. To help identify transactions involving operating activities, recall that operating activities typically result in recording revenues or expenses in some period of time. Thus, the journal entry to record the transaction either involves revenue earned, expense incurred, a receivable, a prepaid expense, a payable or an unearned revenue. When the indirect method is used, the net income figure is used as a starting point for the calculation of "net cash flows provided by operating activities." The net income figure must then be converted from the accrual basis to a cash basis amount. To help identify the transactions requiring an adjustment to net income, find the transactions whose journal entries involve an income statement account and a balance sheet account other than Cash (such as depreciation or amortization of a prepaid expense) or that involve Cash and accruals or deferrals of revenues or expenses (such as the entry to record the payment of expense in advance of its incurrence).
7. If the reasons for changes in balance sheet accounts are not fully explained in the additional information, assume the most common reason for a change. Assume purchases and sales of assets are for cash unless otherwise indicated.
8. When more than one transaction accounts for the net change in an account balance, it is wise to draw a T-account for the account in question and reflect all transactions occurring during the period.

Explanation:
1. There was an increase of $46,000 in the Cash account. The net change goes near the bottom of the statement and reconciles the $35,000 beginning cash balance with the $81,000 ending cash balance.

2. The journal entry to record the increase in Accounts Receivable is reconstructed as follows:
   Accounts Receivable.. 15,000
       Sales   15,000

Net income is increased but Cash is not increased; thus, using the indirect method, this increase in receivables is deducted from net income to arrive at the net cash provided by operating activities. An increase in accounts receivable indicates that sales revenue for the period exceeds the cash collections from customers during the period; therefore, net income is greater than the net cash provided by operating activities.

3. The journal entry to record the increase in Inventory is reconstructed as follows:

Inventory..	59,000	
Cash...		59,000

Payments to suppliers are an operating outflow. This outflow is not reflected in the net income figure so, using the indirect method, the increase in inventory is deducted from net income to arrive at net cash provided by operating activities. An increase in inventory indicates that cost of goods sold expense is less than cash payments to suppliers; therefore, net income is greater than net cash provided by operating activities.

4. The journal entry to record the increase in Investments is reconstructed as follows:

Investments...	30,000	
Long-term Note Payable..		30,000

The acquisition of an investment is an investing activity, and the issuance of debt is a financing activity; however, there is no effect on cash. This noncash investing and financing activity must be reported on a separate schedule to accompany the statement of cash flows. It is **not** to be reported in the body of the statement of cash flows.

5. The T-accounts for Equipment, Accumulated Depreciation, and Loss on the Disposal of Plant Assets would appear as follows:

Equipment

Jan. 1, 2014 Balance	100,000	Unexplained transaction	
Acquisition during 2014	80,000	during 2014	10,000
Dec. 31, 2014 Balance	170,000		

Accumulated Depreciation

Unexplained transaction		Jan. 1, 2014 Balance	20,000
during 2014	4,000	Depreciation for 2014	15,000
		Dec. 31, 2014 Balance	31,000

Loss on Disposal of Plant Assets

Sale of equipment during 2014	4,500

The problem states that Equipment costing $80,000 was purchased. Depreciation expense amounted to $15,000, and old equipment was sold at a loss of $4,500. We can solve for the missing data—an unexplained credit of $10,000 to Equipment and an unexplained debit of $4,000 to Accumulated Depreciation. The most common reason for a credit to the Equipment account is the disposal of an asset. That transaction also explains the $4,000 reduction in the Accumulated Depreciation account and the recording of a $4,500 loss. Thus, it appears that an asset with a cost of $10,000 and a book value of $6,000 ($10,000 - $4,000 = $6,000) was sold at a loss of $4,500. This means the cash proceeds amounted to $1,500 ($6,000 book value - $4,500 loss = $1,500 proceeds).

The journal entries to record the transactions mentioned above would be reconstructed as follows:

Equipment	80,000	
Cash		80,000

Cash decreased. The purchase of plant assets is an investing activity. Therefore, an outflow is reported in the investing section.

Depreciation Expense	15,000	
Accumulated Depreciation		15,000

There is no effect on Cash but net income was reduced. Using the indirect method, depreciation is added to net income to compute the net cash provided by operating activities.

Cash	1,500	
Loss on Disposal of Plant Assets..................................	4,500	
Accumulated Depreciation	4,000	
Equipment		10,000

There is an inflow of $1,500 cash due to the disposal of plant assets which is an investing activity. When the indirect method is used, the loss must be added to net income; there was no corresponding outflow of cash.

6. The journal entry to record the decrease in Accounts Payable is reconstructed as follows:

Accounts Payable	9,000	
Cash		9,000

Payments to suppliers for goods and services consumed in operations is an operating activity. Using the indirect method, this decrease in Accounts Payable must be deducted from net income because a decrease in Accounts Payable indicates expenses incurred were less than cash payments to suppliers; hence, net income was more than the cash provided by operating activities.

7. The T-account for Long-term Note Payable would appear as follows:

<table>
<tr><td colspan="4" align="center">Long-term Note Payable</td></tr>
<tr><td>Unexplained transaction</td><td></td><td>Jan. 1, 2014 Balance</td><td>60,000</td></tr>
<tr><td>during 2014</td><td>18,000</td><td>Issued for investment in 2014</td><td>30,000</td></tr>
<tr><td></td><td></td><td>Dec. 31, 2014 Balance</td><td>72,000</td></tr>
</table>

The most common reason for a debit to a liability account is a payment. The journal entries for the transactions affecting this account are reconstructed as follows:

Investments...	30,000	
Long-term Note Payable		30,000

This transaction was analyzed and handled in point #4 above.

Long-term Note Payable	18,000	
Cash		18,000

This represents an $18,000 cash outflow due to the payment of a nontrade note payable which is a financing activity.

8. The journal entry to record the increase in Bonds Payable is reconstructed as follows:

Cash 100,000		
Bonds Payable		100,000

This is a cash inflow of $100,000 due to borrowing which is a financing activity.

9. The most common reason for an increase in the Common Stock account is the issuance of stock for cash. The journal entry to record that transaction is reconstructed as follows:

Cash	50,000	
Common Stock—No Par		50,000

This is an inflow of cash due to the issuance of stock which is a financing activity.

10. The Retained Earnings T-account would appear as follows:

Retained Earnings			
Declaration of Cash Dividends during 2014	14,000	Jan. 1, 2014 Balance	31,000
		Unexplained transaction during 2014	70,000
		Dec. 31, 2014 Balance	87,000

The most common reason for having a credit to Retained Earnings is net income. Because the indirect method is used, the net income figure is needed as the starting point for the computation of net cash provided by operating activities.

The journal entries to record the declaration and payment of cash dividends are reconstructed as follows:

Retained Earnings	14,000	
Dividends Payable		14,000
Dividends Payable	14,000	
Cash		14,000

Cash decreases by $14,000. Providing owners with a return on their investment constitutes a financing activity. The declaration of dividends has no effect on cash. The payment of a previously declared dividend reduces cash. The payment of cash dividends is to be reported as a financing outflow.

> **TIP:** The last step in the preparation of the statement of cash flows is to subtotal each of the three activity classifications. Inflows are shown as positive amounts; outflows are shown as negative amounts. An excess of inflows over outflows in a category results in a net inflow; an excess of outflows over inflows is captioned as a net outflow. The subtotals of the three activities are then summarized to determine the net change in cash during the year. This net change must agree with your analysis of the change in the Cash account balance (Step 1); otherwise, one or more errors exist and must be corrected to make the statement balance.

(b) (1)

Net cash provided by operating activities (from part (a) above)	$ 6,500
Capital expenditures	(80,000)
Dividends paid	(14,000)
Free cash flow	(87,500)

The company shows a negative free cash flow for the year ending December 31, 2014.

EXERCISE 13-5

Purpose: (L.O. 4) This exercise will help you to understand how to calculate a company's free cash flow.

Instructions
Using the data given in the following table, determine if the free cash flow for Exxon Mobil CP has increased/decreased during 2014 versus 2013. Figures given in the table are in billions.

Year ending	December 31, 2014	December 31, 2013
Cash Provided by Operating Activities	$52.0	$49.3
Capital Expenditures	$15.4	$15.5
Payment of Dividends	$ 7.9	$ 7.9

SOLUTION TO EXERCISE 13-5

Free cash flow is determined by subtracting Capital Expenditures and the Payment of Dividends from the Cash Provided by Operating Activities.

For the Year ending 12/31/2014 the free cash flow for Exxon Mobil CP was ($52.0B - $15.4B - $7.9B) = $28.7B.

For the Year ending 12/31/2013 the free cash flow for Exxon Mobil CP was ($49.3B - $15.5B - $7.9B) = $25.9B.

Exxon Mobil CP's free cash flow increased by $2.8B ($28.7B - $25.9B). The increase was due to the increase from the Cash Provided by Operating Activities since the Capital Expenditures and the Payment of Dividends essentially remained constant.

EXERCISE 13-6

Purpose: (L.O. 4) This exercise will help you to understand how the free cash flow can vary from one company to the next even though the companies are in the same industry.

Instructions
Using the data below (in billions), compute free cash flow for each company and compare.

Year ending December 31, 2014	Ford Motor Co.	General Motors Corp.
Cash Provided by Operating Activities	$17.10	$7.73
Capital Expenditures	$ 6.02	$7.5
Payment of Dividends	$ 0	$0.57

SOLUTION TO EXERCISE 13-6

Free cash flow is determined by subtracting Capital Expenditures and the Payment of Dividends from the Cash Provided by Operating Activities.

The free cash flow for the Ford Motor Co. was ($17.10B - $6.02B - $0) = $11.08B.

The free cash flow for General Motors Corp. was ($7.73B - $7.50B - $0.57B) = ($0.34B)

General Motors Corp. had a negative free cash flow for 2014 whereas Ford Motor Co. had a positive free cash flow. In fact, its free cash flow exceeded General Motor's Cash Provided by Operating Activities.

EXERCISE 13-7

Purpose: (L.O. 5) This exercise will prepare you to use a worksheet in helping you prepare the data for the statement of cash flows.

Jennifer & Dana Designs Inc.
Comparative Balance Sheets
December 31
(All numbers in millions)

Assets	2014	2013
Cash	$98,700	$ 47,250
Accounts Receivable	87,800	56,000
Inventories	121,900	103,650
Investments	81,500	87,000
Plant Assets	250,000	205,000
Accumulated Depreciation	(49,500)	(40,000)
Total	$590,400	$458,900

Liabilities and Stockholders' Equity		
Accounts Payable	$57,700	$48,280
Accrued Expenses Payable	12,100	18,830
Bonds Payable	100,000	80,000
Common Stock	250,000	200,000
Retained Earnings	170,600	111,790
Total	$590,400	$458,900

Jennifer & Dana Designs Inc.
Income Statement
For the Year Ended December 31, 2014

Sales		$312,500
Gain on sale of plant assets		8,750
		321,250
Less:		
Cost of goods sold	$99,460	
Operating expenses (excluding depreciation expense)	14,670	
Depreciation expense	49,700	
Income taxes	7,270	
Interest expense	2,940	174,040
Net income		$147,210

Additional information:
1. New plant assets costing $92,000 were purchased for cash during the year.
2. Investments were sold at cost.
3. Plant assets costing $47,000 were sold for $15,550 and resulted in a gain of $8,750.
4. A cash dividend of $88,400 was declared and paid during the year.

Instructions
Prepare a worksheet for a statement of cash flows. Enter the reconciling items directly in the work sheet columns, identifying the debit and credit amounts alphabetically.

Analysis:
a. Increase in receivables reduces cash inflow-credit.
b. Increase in inventories increases cash outflow-credit.
c. Increase in accounts payable reduces cash outflow-debit.
d. Decrease in accrued expenses payable increases cash outflow-credit.
e. Sale of investments increases cash inflow-debit.
f. Purchase of plant assets increases cash outflow-credit
g. Depreciation expense is a noncash charge to income-debit.
h. Sale of plant assets increases cash inflow-debit.
i. Issue of bonds increases cash inflow-debit.
j. Issue of common stock increases cash inflow-debit.
k. Net income increases cash inflow-debit.
l. Payment of dividends increases cash outflow-credit.
r. Increase in cash balance.

SOLUTION TO EXERCISE 13-7

Jennifer and Dana Designs Inc.
Work Sheet—Statement of Cash Flows
For the Year Ended December 31, 2014

Balance Sheet Accounts	Balance 12/31/13		Reconciling Items			Balance 12/31/14
Debits			Debit	Credit		
Cash	47,250	(r)	51,450			98,700
Accounts receivable	56,000	(a)	31,800			87, 800
Inventories	103,650	(b)	18,250			121,900
Investments	87,000			5,500	(e)	81,500
Plant assets	205,000	(f)	92,000	47,000	(h)	250,000
Totals	498,900					639,900
Credits						
Accounts payable	48,280			9,420	(c)	57,700
Accrued expenses payable	18,830	(d)	6,730			12,100
Bonds payable	80,000			20,000	(i)	100,000
Accumulated depreciation—						
plant assets	40,000	(h)	40,200	49,700	(g)	49,500
Common stock	200,000			50,000	(j)	250,000
Retained earnings	111,790	(i)	88,400	147,210	(k)	170,600
Totals	498,900					639,900

Statement of Cash Flow Effects

Operating activities

Net income	(k)	147,210			
Increase in accounts receivable			31,800	(a)	
Increase in inventories			18,250	(b)	
Increase in accounts payable	(c)	9,420			
Decrease in accrued expenses payable			6,730	(d)	
Depreciation expense	(g)	49,700			
Gain on sale of plant assets			8,750	(h)	

Investing activities

Sale of investments	(e)	5,500			
Sale of plant assets	(h)	15,550			
Purchase of plant assets			92,000	(f)	

Financing activities

Sale of common stock	(j)	50,000			
Issuance of bonds	(i)	20,000			
Payment of dividends			88,400	(l)	
Totals		626,210	574,760		
Increase in cash			51,450	(r)	
Totals		626,210	626,210		

TIP: When preparing a statement of cash flows, companies may need to make numerous adjustments of net income. A worksheet is often used to assemble and classify the data that will appear on the statement. The steps in preparing the worksheet are: (1) Enter in the balance sheet accounts section the balance sheet accounts and their beginning and ending balances. (2) Enter in the reconciling columns of the worksheet the data that explain the changes in the balance sheet accounts other than cash and their effects on the statement of cash flows. (3) Enter on the cash line and at the bottom of the worksheet the increase or decrease in cash. This entry should enable the totals of the reconciling columns to be in agreement.

ILLUSTRATION 13-2
CONVERSION FROM ACCRUAL BASIS
TO CASH BASIS (L.O. 3, **6)

Accrual Basis	**Cash Basis**
Revenues Earned	Cash In from Customers
- Expenses Incurred	- Cash Out for Operations
= Net Income	= Net Cash Provided by Operating Activities

INDIRECT METHOD

To Compute Net Cash Provided by Operating Activities:

Net income
Add noncash charges (such as depreciation expense and amortization of intangibles)
Add losses on sale of assets
Add (deduct) decrease (increase) in accounts receivable
Add (deduct) decrease (increase) in accrued receivables
Add (deduct) decrease (increase) in inventories
Add (deduct) decrease (increase) in prepaid expenses
Add (deduct) increase (decrease) in accounts payable
Add (deduct) increase (decrease) in accrued payables
Add (deduct) increase (decrease) in unearned revenues
Deduct noncash credits (such as amortization of premium on bonds payable and income recognized under equity method in excess of dividends received)
Deduct gains on sale of assets

= Net cash provided by operating activities

Explanation: Noncash charges (such as depreciation and amortization) are **added** to net income because they are expense items that do not require an outlay of cash. Losses (or gains) from the sale of assets or settlement of debt are **added** to (or **deducted** from) net income because they relate to transactions for which the related cash flows are to be classified as investing or financing activities. An increase in receivables indicates that revenues earned **exceed** cash inflows; therefore, net income **exceeds** net cash provided by operating activities. An increase in inventories or prepaid expenses indicates that expenses are **less** than cash outflows; hence, net income is **more** than net cash provided by operating activities. Increases in accounts receivable, accrued receivables, inventories, and prepaid expenses must therefore be **deducted** from net income to obtain the amount of cash generated by operations. On the other hand, an increase in accounts payable or accrued payables indicates that expenses incurred **exceed** the amount of cash paid for merchandise inventory and operating expenses. An increase in unearned revenues indicates that revenue earned is **less** than the cash received and net income is **less** than net cash generated by operations. Therefore, increases in accounts payable, accrued payables, and unearned revenues must be **added** to net income to compute the amount of cash generated by operations. Noncash credits (such as the recognition of income using the equity method) are **deducted** from net income because they increase net income without having a corresponding cash inflow.

The following material is contained in **Appendix 13B in the text.

DIRECT METHOD

To Compute Net Cash Provided by Operating Activities:

    Cash Received From Customers

+ Interest and Dividends Received

- Cash Paid for Merchandise Inventory and Operating Expenses

- Interest Paid

- Income Taxes Paid

- Other Operating Cash Payments

= Net Cash Provided by Operating Activities

Explanation: The major classes of cash receipts and cash payments from operating activities (for which the computations are shown below) are listed and summarized on the face of the statement of cash flows when the **direct method** is used.

To Convert Revenues Earned to Cash Received:

    Revenues Earned

- Increase in Accounts Receivable

+ <u>Increase in Unearned Revenues</u>

= Cash Received from Customers

Explanation: An increase in accounts receivable from one balance sheet date to the next indicates that revenues earned exceed cash collections from customers, hence, subtract the increase in receivables from revenues earned to obtain the amount of cash received from customers. (A decrease in receivables would indicate cash collections exceed revenues earned and would be added to revenues earned to compute cash collections.) An increase in unearned revenues indicates that revenues earned are less than cash collections; hence, add the increase in unearned revenues to revenues earned to obtain the amount of cash received from customers. (A decrease in unearned revenue indicates opposite relationships.)

OR

    Revenues Earned

+ Beginning Accounts Receivable

- Ending Accounts Receivable

- Beginning Unearned Revenues

+ <u>Ending Unearned Revenues</u>

= Cash Received From Customers

Explanation: The balance of accounts receivable at the beginning of the period represents revenues earned in a prior period that are collected in the current period; ending accounts receivable stem from revenues earned in the current period that are not yet collected. Beginning unearned revenues represent cash collections in a prior period (not the current period) that are revenues earned in the current period. Ending unearned revenues come from collections during the current period that are not yet recognized as earned revenues.

To Convert Cost of Goods Sold to Cash Paid:

	Cost of Goods Sold Expense
+	Increase in Inventory
=	Purchases
-	Increase in Accounts Payable
=	Cash Paid for Merchandise Inventory

Explanation: An increase in inventory means purchases for the period exceed cost of goods sold. An increase in accounts payable indicates purchases exceed cash payments for merchandise. (Decreases indicate opposite relationships.)

OR

	Cost of Goods Sold Expense
-	Beginning Inventory
+	Ending Inventory
=	Purchases
+	Beginning Accounts Payable (for purchases of merchandise)
-	Ending Accounts Payable (for purchases of merchandise)
=	Cash Paid for Merchandise Inventory

Explanation: Beginning inventory represents items purchased in a prior period that were consumed (sold) in the current year. Ending inventory represents items purchased in the current period that are not reported in the cost of goods sold expense (because they are on hand at the balance sheet date). Beginning accounts payable come from purchases of a prior period (as opposed to purchases of the current period) that require cash payment during the current period. The ending accounts payable balance stems from purchases in the current period that are not paid for in the current period.

To Convert Operating Expenses to Cash Paid:

	Operating Expenses Incurred **(Excluding Depreciation, Amortization, and Bad Debt Expense)**
+	Increase in Prepaids
-	Increase in Accrued Payables
=	Cash Paid for Operating Expenses

Explanation: An increase in a prepaid expense indicates expenses incurred are less than cash payments for those items. Therefore, the increase in the prepaid is added to the expense total to obtain the amount of related cash payments. An increase in accrued payables indicates the expense total exceeds the cash payments for these items; hence, the increase in accrued payables is deducted from the expense balance to arrive at cash payments. (A decrease is handled in the opposite manner.)

OR

Operating Expenses Incurred (**Excluding Depreciation, Amortization, and Bad Debt Expense**)
- Beginning Prepaids
+ Ending Prepaids
+ Beginning Accrued Payables
- Ending Accrued Payables
= Cash Paid for Operating Expenses

Explanation: Beginning prepaids represent an amount recognized as expense in the current period for which a cash payment is not made in the current period (the cash payment occurred in a prior period). Ending prepaids stem from cash payments in the current period for expenses not recognized in the current period (the expense recognition is being deferred to a future period). Beginning accrued payables come from expenses recognized in a prior period (not the current year) that require cash payments during the current period. Ending accrued payables stem from expenses recognized during the current year that have not yet been paid.

To Convert Interest Expense to Interest Paid:

Interest Expense
- Increase in Interest Payable
- Amortization of Discount on Debt
+ Amortization of Premium on Debt
= Interest Paid

Explanation: An increase in a payable indicates that expense exceeds the related cash payments. (A decrease in a payable would indicate the opposite relationship—that expense is less than cash payments.) The amortization of discount on a debt increases total interest expense but does not cause a cash outlay; the amortization of premium on a debt instrument decreases total interest expense but does not reduce the cash outlay required for the interest.

OR

Interest Expense
+ Beginning Interest Payable
- Ending Interest Payable
- Amortization of Discount on Debt
+ Amortization of Premium on Debt
= Interest Paid

Explanation: The balance of Interest Payable at the beginning of the period comes from interest expense accrued in a prior period. Therefore, that amount requires a cash outlay in the current period but relates to an expense of a prior period. The ending balance of Interest Payable comes from interest accrued in the current period. Therefore, this amount is part of the total interest expense for the current period but it is not part of the interest paid this period. The amortization of discount on a debt instrument increases total interest expense but does not cause a cash outlay; the amortization of premium on a debt instrument decreases total interest expense but does not decrease the corresponding cash outflow.

To Convert Income Tax Expense to Income Taxes Paid:

   Income Tax Expense
- Increase in Income Taxes Payable
= Income Taxes Paid

Explanation: An increase in Income Taxes Payable indicates that the amount of income tax expense for the period exceeds the amount paid for income taxes during the period.

OR

   Income Tax Expense
+ Beginning Income Taxes Payable
- Ending Income Taxes Payable
= Income Taxes Paid

Explanation: The beginning balance of Income Taxes Payable is an amount of taxes expensed in a prior period that is paid in the current period. The ending balance of Income Taxes Payable is an amount of taxes expensed in the current period that is to be paid in the next period.

TIP: For all of the items above, a **decrease** in an account balance will be handled in a manner **opposite** of the way an **increase** is to be treated.

SUMMARY OF TREATMENT FOR ACCRUALS AND DEFERRALS

The treatment of increases during the period for unearned (deferred) revenues, prepaid (deferred) expenses, accrued expenses, and accrued revenues can be summarized for both the direct method and the indirect method as follows:

	Indirect Method Net Income	**Direct Method** Revenues	Expenses
Increase in Unearned Revenues	+	+	
Increase in Prepaid Expenses	-		+
Increase in Payables	+		-
Increase in Receivables	-	-	
	Net Cash Provided by Operating Activities	**Cash Received From Operations**	**Cash Paid For Operations**

TIP: In examining the summary above, notice the mathematical signs are the **same** for both the direct method and indirect method for handling a change in unearned revenues or a change in receivables. The reasons for this are (1) changes in unearned revenues and receivables are items which explain the difference between revenues earned during a period and cash received from customers, and (2) revenues earned are a **positive** component of net income, and cash received from customers is a **positive** component of net cash provided by operating activities.

Also notice that the mathematical signs are **different** for the direct method and the indirect method for handling a change in prepaid expenses and payables. The reasons for this are (1) changes in prepaid expenses and payables are items which explain the difference between expenses incurred during a period and cash paid for operations, and (2) expenses incurred are a **negative** component of net income, and cash paid out for operations is a **negative** component of net cash provided by operating activities.

TIP: "Cash provided by operating activities" (or "cash provided by operations") is another name for "net income on a cash basis."

**EXERCISE 13-8

Purpose: (L.O. 6) This exercise will allow you to practice identifying how to classify transactions on a statement of cash flows using the direct method.

The J & M Salter Corporation uses the direct method for preparing the statement of cash flows. The following summarized transactions took place in 2014:

Collected cash from customers on account	$ 75,000
Paid interest on debt	3,000
Paid principal of note payable	30,000
Sold services for cash	19,000
Paid salaries and wages	27,000
Paid other operating expenses	41,000
Recorded depreciation expense	7,000
Paid dividends	6,000
Purchased machinery	60,000
Sold equipment for book value	12,000
Issued common stock in exchange for cash	45,000
Issued long-term debt	52,000
Amortized patents	1,000
Purchased treasury stock	4,000
Accrued salaries	800
Purchased an investment	38,200
Acquired a computer in exchange for J & M Salter common stock	10,000
Received dividends from investee	700
Paid income taxes	6,500
Sold an investment (and recognized a gain of $3,300)	24,000

Instructions
(a)   Compute the following:
   (1)   Net cash provided (used) by operating activities.
   (2)   Net cash provided (used) by investing activities.
   (3)   Net cash provided (used) by financing activities.
   (4)   Net increase (decrease) in cash for the period.
(b)   If any transactions are **not** used in the required computations in (a), explain why.
(c)   Based on the information given, prepare a statement of cash flows using the direct method. Assume the cash balance at the beginning of the year was $23,000.

SOLUTION TO EXERCISE 13-8

(a) (1) Collected cash from customers on account	$75,000
Sold services for cash	19,000
Received dividends from investee	700
Paid interest on debt	(3,000)
Paid salaries and wages	(27,000)
Paid other operating expenses	(41,000)
Paid income taxes	(6,500)
Net cash provided by operations	$17,200

(2)	Purchased machinery		$(60,000)
	Sold equipment for book value		12,000
	Purchased an investment		(38,200)
	Sold an investment		24,000
	Net cash used by investing activities		$(62,200)

(3)	Paid principal of note payable		$(30,000)
	Paid dividends		(6,000)
	Issued common stock		45,000
	Issued long-term debt		52,000
	Purchased treasury stock		(4,000)
	Net cash provided by financing activities		$57,000

(4)	Net cash provided by operating activities		$17,200
	Net cash used by investing activities		(62,200)
	Net cash provided by financing activities		57,000
	Net increase in cash		$12,000

(b) (1) Recorded depreciation expense, $7,000, was not used because it is a noncash charge to income. It is an expense which did not require a cash payment. (The cash outlay occurs at the date that payment is made for the related depreciable assets.)

(2) Amortized patents, $1,000, was not used because it is a noncash charge against income. It is an expense which did not require a cash outlay this period. (The cash outlay occurs at the date that cash payment is made for the related intangible assets.)

(3) Accrued salaries, $800, was not used because it relates to an expense recognized this period for which the related cash payment is being deferred until next period.

(4) Acquired a computer in exchange for stock, $10,000, was not used because this is a noncash financing and investing activity.

TIP: If the indirect method was used: (1) the depreciation of $7,000 and the amortization of $1,000 would be added to net income, (2) an increase in the Salaries Payable account of $800 (due to the accrued salaries) would also be added to net income, and (3) the $3,300 gain on sale of investment would be deducted from net income in the process of reconciling net income to net cash provided from operations.

(c)

J & M SALTER CORPORATION
Statement of Cash Flows
For the Year Ending December 31, 2014
(Direct Method)

Cash flows from operating activities		
Cash receipts from customers	$94,000[a]	
Dividends received from investee	700	
Interest paid	(3,000)	
Cash paid to employees	(27,000)	
Cash paid for operating expenses	(41,000)	
Income taxes paid	(6,500)	
Net cash provided by operating activities		$17,200
Cash flows from investing activities		
Purchase of machinery	(60,000)	
Sale of equipment	12,000	
Purchase of investment	(38,200)	
Sale of investment	24,000	
Net cash used by investing activities		(62,200)
Cash flows from financing activities		
Payment of note payable	(30,000)	
Payment of dividends	(6,000)	
Issuance of common stock	45,000	
Issuance of long-term debt	52,000	
Purchase of treasury stock	(4,000)	
Net cash provided by financing activities		57,000
Net increase in cash		12,000
Cash at beginning of period		23,000
Cash at end of period		$35,000[b]

Noncash investing and financing activities

Acquired a computer in exchange for common stock	$10,000

[a]$75,000 + $19,000 = $94,000.
[b]$12,000 net increase in cash + $23,000 beginning cash balance = $35,000 ending cash balance.

> **TIP:** An additional schedule reconciling net income to net cash provided by operating activities should be presented as part of the statement of cash flows when using the direct method. The information with this exercise is insufficient to prepare that complete schedule.

**EXERCISE 13-9

Purpose: (L. O. 6) This exercise will test your ability to convert accrual basis information to cash basis information.

The Tom Fuller Corporation reported the following on its income statement for 2014:

Sales revenue	$600,000
Cost of goods sold	400,000
Salaries expense	42,000
Insurance expense	3,000
Depreciation expense	50,000
Other operating expenses	60,000
Income tax expense	18,000
Net income	27,000

The comparative balance sheets reported the following selected information:

	12/31/14	12/31/13	Increase (Decrease)
Cash	$26,000	$12,000	$14,000
Accounts Receivable	37,000	41,000	(4,000)
Inventory	76,000	74,000	2,000
Prepaid Insurance	4,380	4,200	180
Accounts Payable	27,100	24,200	2,900
Salaries Payable	500	800	(300)
Income Taxes Payable	18,000	12,500	5,500

All of the operating expenses reflected in the "other operating expenses" category were paid in cash during 2014. Accounts payable relate to purchases of merchandise inventory.

Instructions

Compute the following amounts for 2014:
(a)   Cash collections from customers.
(b)   Cash payments for merchandise.
(c)   Cash payments to employees.
(d)   Cash payments for insurance.
(e)   Cash payments for income taxes.
(f)   Net cash provided by operating activities.

SOLUTION TO EXERCISE 13-9

(a)
Sales revenue	$600,000
Decrease in accounts receivable	4,000
Cash collections from customers	$604,000

OR

Sales revenue	$600,000
Beginning accounts receivable	41,000
Ending accounts receivable	(37,000)
Cash collections from customers	$604,000

(b)
Cost of goods sold expense	$400,000
Increase in inventory	2,000
Purchases	402,000
Increase in accounts payable	(2,900)
Cash payments for merchandise	$399,100

OR

Cost of goods sold expense	$400,000
Beginning inventory	(74,000)
Ending inventory	76,000
Purchases	402,000
Beginning accounts payable	24,200
Ending accounts payable	(27,100)
Cash payments for merchandise	$399,100

(c)
Salaries expense	$42,000
Decrease in salaries payable	300
Cash payments to employees	$42,300

OR

Salaries expense	$42,000
Beginning salaries payable	800
Ending salaries payable	(500)
Cash payments to employees	$42,300

(d)
Insurance expense	$3,000
Increase in prepaid insurance	180
Cash payments for insurance	$3,180

OR

Insurance expense	$3,000
Beginning prepaid insurance	(4,200)
Ending prepaid insurance	4,380
Cash payments for insurance	$3,180

(e)
Income tax expense	$18,000
Increase in income taxes payable	(5,500)
Cash payments for income taxes	$12,500

OR

Income tax expense	$18,000
Beginning income taxes payable	12,500
Ending income taxes payable	(18,000)
Cash payments for income taxes	$12,500

(f)	Cash received from customers	$604,000
	Cash payments for merchandise	(399,100)
	Cash payments to employees	(42,300)
	Cash payments for insurance	(3,180)
	Cash payments for income taxes	(12,500)
	Cash payments for other operating expenses	(60,000)
	Net cash provided by operating activities	$ 86,920

TIP: The change in the cash balance ($14,000 increase) had no effect on the computations requested. The net cash provided (used) by each of the three activity classifications (operating, investing and financing) should net to this $14,000 increase.

TIP: Refer to **Illustration 13-2** for explanations to the above computations.

EXERCISE 13-10

Purpose: (L.O. 1 thru 6) This exercise will quiz you about terminology used in this chapter.

A list of accounting terms with which you should be familiar appears below:

Direct method	Investing activities
Financing activities	Operating activities
Free cash flow	Statement of cash flows
Indirect method	

Instructions

For each item below, enter in the blank the term that is described.

1. _____A financial statement that provides information about the cash receipts and cash payments of an entity during a period, classified as operating, investing, and financing activities, in a format that reconciles the beginning and ending cash balances.

2. _____Cash flow activities that include (a) acquiring and disposing of investments and productive long-lived assets and (b) lending money and collecting on those loans.

3. _____Cash flow activities that include (a) obtaining cash from issuing debt and repaying the amounts borrowed and (b) obtaining cash from stockholders, repurchasing shares, and paying dividends.

4. _____Cash flow activities that include the cash effects of transactions that create revenues and expenses and thus enter into the determination of net income.

5. _____A method of preparing a statement of cash flows in which net income is adjusted for items that did not affect cash, to determine net cash provided by operating activities.

6. _____A method of determining the "net cash provided by operating activities" by adjusting each item in the income statement from the accrual basis to the cash basis and which shows operating cash receipts and payments.

7. _____Cash flow provided by operating activities adjusted for capital expenditures and dividends paid.

SOLUTION TO EXERCISE 13-10

1. Statement of cash flows	5.	Indirect method
2. Investing activities	6.	Direct method
3. Financing activities	7.	Free cash flow
4. Operating activities		

ANALYSIS OF MULTIPLE-CHOICE TYPE QUESTIONS

1. (L.O. 2) Which of the following would **not** produce an inflow of cash?
   a. Issuance of stock.
   b. Issuance of debt.
   c. Sale of plant assets at a price equal to 50% of book value.
   d. Purchase of an investment.

   Approach and Explanation: Prepare the journal entry for each transaction listed. Find the one without a debit to Cash. The journal entries for the transactions are constructed as follows:

   a. Cash   XX
           Common Stock   XX

   b. Cash   XX
           Debt   XX

   c. Cash   XX
       Loss   XX
       Accumulated Depreciation...   XX
           Plant Assets..   XX

   d. Investments   XX
           Cash   XX

   (Solution = d.)

2. (L.O. 2) Which of the following is an investing activity?
   a. Receipt of interest on bonds held as an investment.
   b. Sale of common stock.
   c. Sale of treasury stock.
   d. Collection of a loan receivable.

Approach and Explanation: Write down the definition of investing activities. Compare the answer selections with your definition. Investing activities include (a) acquiring and disposing of investments (short-term and long-term) and productive long-lived assets and (b) lending money and collecting the loans. Collection of interest is an operating activity. Both the sale of common stock and the sale of treasury stock are financing activities. The collection of a loan receivable is an investing activity. (Solution = d.)

3. (L.O. 2) An example of a cash flow from an operating activity is:
    a. payment to employees for services.
    b. payment of dividends to stockholders.
    c. receipt of proceeds from the sale of an investment.
    d. receipt of proceeds from the sale of common stock to stockholders.

    Explanation: Operating activities include the cash effects of transactions that ultimately create revenues and expenses and thus enter into the determination of net income. Operating activities include collections from customers, collections of interest and dividends, payments for merchandise and other goods and services, and payments for interest and taxes. The payment of dividends is a financing activity. The sale of an investment is an investing activity. The sale of common stock is a financing activity. (Solution = a.)

4. (L.O. 2) Which of the following would be classified as a financing activity on a statement of cash flows?
    a. Declaration and distribution of a stock dividend.
    b. Purchase of treasury stock.
    c. Sale of equipment.
    d. Payment of interest to a creditor.

    Approach and Explanation: Write down the definitions for investing, financing, and operating activities. Take each of the transactions and see if it meets the definition for a financing activity. Declaration and distribution of a stock dividend does not meet any of the definitions. It is an example of an item that is not reported anywhere on a statement of cash flows or in supplementary disclosures related to that statement. The purchase of treasury stock is a financing activity. The sale of equipment is an investing activity and the payment of interest to a creditor is an operating activity. (Solution = b.)

5. (L.O. 2) An example of a cash flow from an investing activity is:
    a. receipt of cash from an owner upon the issuance of stock.
    b. payment of cash to an owner to repurchase outstanding common stock.
    c. receipt of cash from the issuance of bonds payable.
    d. payment of cash to purchase bonds payable of another corporation.

    Approach and Explanation: Write down the definition of investing activities. Compare the answer selections with your definition. Investing activities include (a) acquiring and disposing of investments (short-term and long-term) and productive long-lived assets and (b) lending money and collecting the loans. The purchase of bonds of another corporation is the acquisition of an investment, hence, an investing activity. The receipt of cash from an owner upon the issuance of stock and the payment of cash to an owner to repurchase outstanding common stock (treasury stock) are financing activities. The receipt of cash from the issuance of bonds payable is also a financing activity. (Solution = d.)

6.   (L.O. 3) Net cash flow from operating activities for 2014 for Graham Corporation was $75,000. The following items are reported on the financial statements for 2014:

Depreciation and amortization	5,000
Cash dividends paid on common stock	3,000
Increase in accrued receivables	6,000

Based only on the information above, Graham's net income for 2014 was:
a. $64,000.
b. $66,000.
c. $74,000.
d. $76,000.
e.   None of the above.

Approach and Explanation: Write down the format for the reconciliation of net income to net cash flow from operating activities. Fill in the information given. Solve for the unknown.

Net income	$ X
Depreciation and amortization	5,000
Increase in accrued receivables	(6,000)
Net cash flow from operating activities	$75,000

Solving for X, net income = $76,000. Cash dividends paid on common stock have no effect on this computation because cash dividends paid is not a component of net income and not an operating activity. Cash dividends paid is classified as a financing activity. (Solution = d.)

7.   (L.O. 3) Which of the following items require(s) an amount to be **added to** net income to arrive at the amount of net cash provided by operating activities?
            1.   Amortization of patents.
            2.   Payment of salaries.
            3.   Accrual of salaries.
            4.   Payment of interest.
a.   Only items 1 and 3.
b.   Only items 1, 2, and 3.
c.   Only item 1.
d.   All four items.

Explanation: The amortization of patents reduces net income but does not affect cash. The accrual of salaries reduces net income but does not require a cash outflow. Both the payment of salaries and the payment of interest reduce net income and cash by the same amount. Therefore, only the amortization of patents and the accrual of salaries are added to net income to determine the amount of net cash provided by operating activities. (Solution = a.)

8.   (L.O. 3, 4) If the balance of a long-term liability account increases from one balance sheet date to the next, this normally indicates that long-term:
   a.   assets were purchased and an investing outflow should be reported on the statement of cash flows.
   b.   debt was paid and a financing outflow should be reported on the statement of cash flows.
   c.   debt was issued and a financing inflow should be reported on the statement of cash flows.
   d.   debt was issued and a financing outflow should be reported on the statement of cash flows.

Explanation: The most common reason for an increase in a long-term liability account is the issuance of a debt instrument to borrow cash. Borrowing money increases cash and is a financing activity. (Solution = c.)

9.   (L.O. 4) Free cash flow for a period is the amount of net cash provided by operations for the period reduced by
   a.   dividends paid.
   b.   investments purchased.
   c.   capital expenditures.
   d.   capital expenditures and dividends paid.

Explanation: Free cash flow is calculated to provide information regarding the company's cash generating ability. In the statement of cash flows, cash provided by operating activities is intended to indicate the cash-generating capability of the company. However, the cash provided by operating activities fails to take into account that the company must invest in new fixed assets and to at least maintain dividends at current levels. **Free cash flow** describes the cash remaining from operations after adjustment for capital expenditures and the payment of dividends. **Free Cash Flow = Cash Provided by Operating Activities – Capital Expenditures – Cash Dividends.** (Solution = d.)

*10.   (L.O. 5) In a worksheet for the statement of cash flows, a decrease in prepaid expenses is entered in the reconciling columns as a credit to Prepaid Expense and a debit in the:
   a.   operating activities section.
   b.   investing activities section.
   c.   financing activities section.
   d.   none of the above.

Explanation: A decrease in prepaid expenses means that expenses deducted in determining net income are greater than expenses that were paid in cash. Thus the decrease must be added to net income in determining net cash provided by operating activities. (Solution = a.)

11. (L.O. 6) Selected information for 2014 for the Truly Green Company follows:

Total operating expenses (accrual basis)	$200,000
(includes depreciation and amortization)	
Beginning prepaid expenses	10,000
Ending prepaid expenses	12,000
Beginning accrued liabilities	16,000
Ending accrued liabilities	19,000
Depreciation of plant assets	28,000
Amortization of intangible assets	7,500
Payment of cash dividends	5,000

The amount of cash payments made during 2014 for operating expenses is:
a. $234,500.
b. $165,500.
c. $163,500.
d. $160,500.
e.   None of these.

Approach and Explanation: Use one of the relevant formats in **Illustration 13-2** to convert operating expenses to cash paid.

Total operating expenses (accrual basis)	$200,000	
Increase in prepaid expenses	2,000	
Increase in accrued liabilities	(3,000)	
Depreciation of plant assets	(28,000)	
Amortization of intangibles	(7,500)	
Cash paid for operating expenses	$163,500	(Solution = c.)

TIP:	Notice that the amount given in the question for "total operating expenses" includes depreciation and amortization whereas the format calls for exclusion of these items. Depreciation and amortization are both expense items that do **not** require a cash outlay at the time the expense is recorded. Thus, they are deducted from the operating expense total to arrive at the amount of cash paid for operating expense items this period.
TIP:	Dividends paid are neither an operating expense nor an operating activity. Payment of dividends is a financing activity (outflow). The receipt of dividends from an investee is an operating activity (inflow).

**12. (L.O. 6) Donnegan Company reported salaries expense of $95,000 for 2014. The following data were extracted from the company's financial records:

	12/31/13	12/31/14
Prepaid Salaries	$20,000	$23,000
Salaries Payable	$70,000	$85,000

On a statement of cash flows for 2014, using the direct method, cash payments for salaries should be:
a. $77,000.
b. $83,000.
c. $107,000.
d. $113,000.

Approach and Explanation: Think of the relationship between salaries expense and cash payments for salaries when there is (1) an increase in prepaid salaries, and (2) an increase in salaries payable. Convert the expense amount to a cash paid figure.

Salaries Expense	$95,000
Increase in prepaid salaries	3,000
Increase in salaries payable	(15,000)
Cash payments for salaries	$83,000 (Solution = b.)

**13. (L.O. 6) The following data relate to the Greg Norman Corporation:

Beginning inventory	$14,000
Ending inventory	12,000
Beginning accounts payable (for merchandise)	2,200
Ending accounts payable (for merchandise)	1,600
Cost of goods sold (accrual basis)	92,000

The amount of cash payments to suppliers for merchandise during the period is:
a. $94,600.
b. $93,400.
c. $90,600.
d. $89,400.

Approach: Determine the change in the Inventory account and the change in the Accounts Payable account. Use the change in Inventory to convert cost of goods sold expense to purchases. Use the change in Accounts Payable to convert purchases to cash payments for merchandise.

Explanation:

Cost of goods sold	$92,000
Decrease in Inventory	(2,000)
Purchases	90,000
Decrease in Accounts Payable	600
Cash payments for merchandise inventory	$90,600 (Solution = c.)

**14. Question

(L.O. 6) The Shak Attack Corporation reported sales revenue (accrual basis) of $52,000 for 2014. The accounts receivable balance was $5,500 and $4,900 at January 1, 2014 and December 31, 2014, respectively. The amount of cash collected from customers during 2014 was:

a. $52,600.
b. $52,000.
c. $51,400.
d. $47,300.

Approach and Explanation: Set up the format for the computation requested. (See **Illustration 13-2.**) Plug in the data given and solve for the unknown.

Sales revenue	$52,000
Beginning accounts receivable	5,500
Ending accounts receivable	(4,900)
Cash collected from customers	$52,600

(Solution = a.)

CHAPTER 14

. . . .

*F*INANCIAL STATEMENT ANALYSIS

OVERVIEW

The significance of a single absolute dollar amount reported in the general purpose financial statements for an entity is difficult to assess. To determine the meaningfulness of one amount, we must consider the relative significance of the amount when compared with other relevant information. Various techniques can be used to perform this analysis of the financial statement data. Ratios developed for a particular company may be compared to industry averages to judge the solvency, strength, earning power, and growth potential of the company. Basic ratio analysis is discussed in this chapter. Also discussed is the use of horizontal analysis and vertical analysis.

When irregular items are included in an income statement, they must be properly reported or "earning power" may be misrepresented. The reporting guidelines for irregular items are included in this chapter.

SUMMARY OF LEARNING OBJECTIVES

1. **Discuss the need for comparative analysis.** There are three bases of comparison: (1) Intracompany, which compares an item or financial relationship with other data within a company. (2) Industry, which compares company data with industry averages. (3) Intercompany, which compares an item or financial relationship of a company with data of one or more competing companies.

2. **Identify the tools of financial statement analysis.** Financial statements may be analyzed horizontally, vertically, and with ratios.

3. **Explain and apply horizontal analysis.** Horizontal analysis is a technique for evaluating a series of data over a period of time to determine the increase or decrease that has taken place, expressed as either an amount or a percentage.

4. **Describe and apply vertical analysis.** Vertical analysis is a technique that expresses each item within a financial statement in terms of a percentage of a relevant total or a base amount.

5. **Identify and compute ratios and describe their purpose and use in analyzing a firm's liquidity, profitability, and solvency.** The formula and purpose of each ratio is presented in **Illustration 14-1** in this book.

6. **Understand the concept of earning power, and indicate how material items not typical of regular operations are presented.** Earning power refers to a company's ability to sustain its profits from operations. "Irregular items"—discontinued operations, and extraordinary items—are presented net of tax below income from continuing operations to highlight their unusual nature.

7. **Understand the concept of quality of earnings.** A high quality of earnings provides full and transparent information that will not confuse or mislead users of the financial statements. Issues related to quality of earnings are (1) alternative accounting methods, (2) pro forma income, and (3) improper recognition.

TIPS ON CHAPTER TOPICS

TIP: A company's financial statements may be compared to its own historical results. This is called an **intracompany** analysis. Additional information may be gained by comparing the company's results to **industry averages** or compare it to other companies who are their **competitors**.

TIP: The three basic techniques used for evaluating financial statements are (1) horizontal analysis, (2) vertical analysis, and (3) ratio analysis.

TIP: **Horizontal analysis** involves the expression of dollar amounts of financial statement items in percentage terms of the dollar amounts for the same items in a prior year. There may be two or more years involved in the analysis. **Trend analysis** is a type of horizontal analysis that is prepared for more than two years.

TIP: In **vertical analysis** (or the development of **common-size financial statements**), the relative importance of various items on a single financial statement is indicated by the relationships of these various items to some key figure on the same statement.

TIP: When you are analyzing comparative data, carefully notice which is for prior years and which is for the current year. On a comparative balance sheet, the current year data is typically placed in the first (inside) column. In some situations, however, the reverse may be found.

TIP: Financial statements can be analyzed in percentage terms by using one of two basic approaches: horizontal analysis or vertical analysis.

TIP: In horizontal analysis, a base year (usually the earliest year being analyzed) is selected. Each dollar item on the statements is then divided by the dollar amount reported in the base year for the same item. For instance if sales were $33,000 in Year 1, $46,000 in Year 2 and $50,000 in Year 3, horizontal analysis would yield percentages of 100% for Year 1, 139% for Year 2, and 152% for Year 3. The trend for sales is more clearly determined when expressed in percentage terms.

TIP: The key figure used for vertical analysis on the income statement is generally net sales so every other item in the same statement for the same year is expressed in percentage terms of the key figure. This is accomplished by **dividing** every dollar item reported on the income statement by the dollar amount of net sales for the year to obtain the percentages.

TIP: The key figure (the 100% figure) used for vertical analysis of the balance sheet is generally the company's total assets. Each item on the balance sheet is then described as a percentage of the total asset figure.

TIP: A **ratio** is an expression of the relationship of one item (or group of items) to a second item (or group of items). It is determined by dividing the first item (amount) by the second item (amount). The relationship may be expressed either as a percentage, a rate, or a simple proportion.

For example: If A is $100,000 and B is $25,000, the ratio of A to B can be expressed in several ways, such as the following:

A:B	A/B
4:1	4.00
4 to 1	$4.00
4 times	400%

The way in which the ratio is expressed depends on the particular ratio. If it is the current ratio or acid-test ratio, it would likely be expressed as a proportion (4:1 or 4 to 1) or as a rate (4 times). If it is the debt to stockholders' equity ratio, it would likely be expressed as a percentage (400%).

TIP: The **average collection period** which is the average number of days required to collect an account receivable (365 days divided by the receivables turnover) is not very meaningful until it is compared with the company's credit terms.

TIP: The numerator of the current ratio includes total current assets; the numerator of the acid-test ratio includes only cash, marketable securities, and net receivables.

TIP: The denominator of a turnover ratio (such as for receivables, inventory, or total assets) always involves an **average** balance. That average can be determined by adding the balance at the end of the period to the balance at the beginning of the period and dividing by 2. However, if seasonal variances are significant, the annual average should be determined by adding together the balances at the end of each month and dividing by 12.

TIP: If the rate of return on common stockholders' equity is greater than the rate of return on total assets, the interest rate on debt is less than the average rate of return on total assets; hence, the entity is **favorably trading on the equity.** However, if the cost of debt exceeds the rate of return on total assets, the rate of return on common stockholders' equity will be less than the rate of return on total assets; hence, the entity will be **unfavorably trading on the equity.**

TIP: Many enterprises have a small profit margin on sales and a high inventory turnover (grocery and discount stores); whereas, other enterprises have a relatively high profit margin but a low inventory turnover (jewelry and furniture stores).

TIP: A given piece of financial information which is reported on the financial statements may not be significant to a reader if the only information available is a given dollar amount. When an item for the current year is compared with the same item for the same company of the prior year (to determine the direction, dollar amount, and percent of change) or with other items on the same statement for the same year (to develop component percentages which may be compared to industry averages), the resulting relationship(s) may be more useful in determining the meaningfulness of the information being reported.

TIP: For ease of comparison companies need to prepare statements on a basis consistent with the preceding period. If there is an allowable change in an accounting principle, companies report both the current period and previous periods using the new principle.

TIP: Many analysts are concerned about the number of items that bypass the income statement. Now, in addition to reporting net income, a company must also report **comprehensive income** which includes all changes in stockholders' equity during a period except those resulting from investments by stockholders and distributions to stockholders.

TIP: The quality of a company's earnings is extremely important to analysts. A company that has a high **quality of earnings** provides full and transparent information that will not confuse or mislead users of the financial statements. Factors that affect the quality of earnings are alternative accounting methods, pro forma income, and improper recognition.

ILLUSTRATION 14-1
RATIOS: FORMULAS FOR COMPUTATIONS AND PURPOSES (L.O. 5)

Ratio	Formula for Computation	Purpose and/or Comments
Liquidity Ratios		
1. Current ratio	$\dfrac{\text{Current assets}}{\text{Current liabilities}}$	This ratio measures short-term debt-paying ability; it is an indication of a company's ability to meet its current liabilities with the cash flow that will result from its current assets. It is often called the **working capital ratio.** The higher the ratio, the greater the short-term solvency.
2. Acid-test (quick) ratio	$\dfrac{\text{Cash + Short-term investments + Receivables (net)}}{\text{Current liabilities}}$	This ratio measures immediate short-term liquidity. "Quick" assets are cash, short-term investments (marketable securities), and net receivables. The acid-test ratio (sometimes called the **quick ratio)** is a more severe test of short-run solvency than the current ratio. A large amount of inventory will cause an entity's acid-test ratio to be less than its current ratio.
3. Receivables turnover	$\dfrac{\text{Net credit sales}}{\text{Average net receivables}}$	This ratio measures liquidity of receivables. Unless seasonal factors are significant, average receivables outstanding can be computed from the beginning and ending balance of net trade receivables. This ratio is another figure frequently used to measure the quality of the receivables and the efficiency and safety of a company's credit-granting activity. The higher the turnover, the shorter the time period necessary to collect the average account receivable. The receivables turnover is converted into an **average collection period** by dividing 365 days by the receivables turnover.

| 4. | Inventory turnover | Cost of goods sold / Average inventory | This ratio measures liquidity of inventory; it measures how quickly inventory is sold. Dividing 365 days by the inventory turnover indicates the **average** number of **days** it takes **to sell the inventory** (or average number of days sales for which inventory is on hand). This ratio is an indication of the efficiency of management in dealing with inventories. The greater the inventory turnover, the more liquid it is, and the lower the costs of storage, property taxes, maintenance costs, and so forth. The lower the turnover, the greater the chance of loss through obsolescence. |

Profitability Ratios

5.	Profit margin	Net income / Net sales	This ratio measures net income generated by each dollar of sales. Because the ratio measures the profit on each sales dollar received, it provides some indication of the buffer available in case of higher costs or lower sales in the future.
6.	Asset turnover	Net sales / Average total assets	This ratio measures how efficiently assets are used to generate sales. If the asset turnover ratio is high, the implication is that the company is using its assets effectively to generate sales. If the turnover is low, the company either needs to use its assets more efficiently or dispose of them.
7.	Return on assets	Net income / Average total assets	The ratio measures overall profitability of assets used. Thus, this ratio measures the rate earned on each dollar invested in assets.
8.	Return on common stockholders' equity	Net income minus preferred dividends / Average common stockholders' equity	This ratio measures profitability of the owners' investment. If this ratio is greater than the rate of return on total assets ratio, the company is using creditor sources and is favorably trading on the equity. Trading on the equity increases the company's financial risk, but it enhances residual earnings whenever the rate of return on assets exceeds the cost of debt.
9.	Earnings per share (EPS)	Net income minus preferred dividends / Weighted average common shares outstanding	This ratio measures net income earned on each share of common stock. The EPS figure is one of the most important ratios used by investment analysts, yet it is one of the most deceptive.

10. Price-earnings ratio (P-E)	Market price per share of stock / Earnings per share	This ratio measures the ratio of the market price per share to earnings per share. The P-E ratio is an oft-quoted statistic used by analysts in discussing the investment possibility of a given enterprise. The higher the market's perception of the company's growth potential, the higher the P-E ratio is likely to be.
11. Payout ratio	Cash dividends / Net income	This ratio measures the percentage of earnings distributed in the form of cash dividends. Growth companies are characterized by low payout ratios because they reinvest most of their earnings. Another closely related ratio that is often used is the dividend yield—the cash dividend per share divided by the market price of the stock.

Solvency Ratios

12. Debt to total assets	Total debt / Total assets	This ratio measures the percentage of total assets provided by creditors. This ratio provides creditors with some idea of the corporation's ability to withstand losses without impairing the interest of creditors. From a creditor's point of view, a low ratio of debt to total assets is desirable; the lower the ratio the more "buffer" there is available to creditors before the corporation becomes insolvent. This ratio has a very definite effect on the company's ability to obtain additional financing.
13. Times interest earned	Income before income taxes and interest expense / Interest expense	This ratio measures the ability of an enterprise to meet interest payments as they come due. This ratio stresses the importance of a company being able to cover all interest charges.

EXERCISE 14-1

Purpose: (L.O. 3, 4) This exercise will provide you with an example of horizontal and vertical analyses.

The comparative income statements of The McAllister Wealth Builder Corporation are shown below:

THE MCALLISTER WEALTH BUILDER CORPORATION
Condensed Income Statement
For the Years Ended December 31

	2014	**2013**
Net sales	$150,000	$120,000
Cost of goods sold	81,000	66,000
Gross profit	69,000	54,000
Operating expenses	42,000	30,000
Income before income taxes	27,000	24,000
Income tax expense	10,800	9,600
Net income	$ 16,200	$ 14,400

Instructions
Round all percentage computations to the nearest tenth of one percent.
(a)   Prepare a horizontal analysis of the income statement data for The McAllister Wealth Builder Corporation using 2013 as a base. (Show the amount of increase or decrease and the percentage change.)
(b)   Prepare a vertical analysis of the income statement data for The McAllister Wealth Builder Corporation in columnar form for both years.
(c)   Briefly comment on the progress of the company as indicated by your comparative analyses.

SOLUTION TO EXERCISE 14-1

(a)   **THE MCALLISTER WEALTH BUILDER CORPORATION**

Condensed Income Statement
For the Years Ended December 31

	2014	**2013**	**Increase (Decrease)**	**Percentage Change From 2013**
Net sales	$150,000	$120,000	$30,000	25.0%
Cost of goods sold	81,000	66,000	15,000	22.7%
Gross profit	69,000	54,000	15,000	27.8%
Operating expenses	42,000	30,000	12,000	40.0%
Income before income taxes	27,000	24,000	3,000	12.5%
Income tax expense	10,800	9,600	1,200	12.5%
Net income	$ 16,200	$ 14,400	$ 1,800	12.5%

(b)
THE MCALLISTER WEALTH BUILDER CORPORATION
Condensed Income Statement
For the Years Ended December 31

	2014		2013	
	$	**Percent**	**$**	**Percent**
Net sales	$150,000	100.0%	$120,000	100.0%
Cost of goods sold	81,000	54.0%	66,000	55.0%
Gross profit	69,000	46.0%	54,000	45.0%
Operating expenses	42,000	28.0%	30,000	25.0%
Income before tax	27,000	18.0%	24,000	20.0%
Income tax expense	10,800	7.2%	9,600	8.0%
Net income	$ 16,200	10.8%	$ 14,400	12.0%

(c)   Although the dollar amounts for sales, gross profit, and net income showed improvement from 2013 to 2014, the vertical analysis shows that improvements were not made in all areas. The cost of goods sold as a percentage of sales improved as it declined from 55% to 54%. This is probably favorable unless there was a cut in the quality of goods (to get a lower cost per unit) or an increase in the unit sales price which may prove later to work in favor of competition. In light of the significant increase in total sales, the cutback in the cost of goods sold percentage is most likely from favorable reasons. A significant area that worsened from 2013 to 2014 is the operating expenses. They were 25% of sales in 2013 and increased to 28% of sales in 2014. Further investigation in this area would be warranted to determine if corrective action could be taken to reduce this cost percentage. Taxes are a lesser percentage of sales in 2014 because of the lower percentage of income subject to tax in 2014. The net income as a percent of sales was lower in 2014 because the higher operating expense percentage more than offset the lower cost of goods sold percentage. (The horizontal analysis confirms these observations.)

EXERCISE 14-2

Purpose: (L.O. 5) This exercise will give you practice in developing key ratios.

The balance sheets at December 31, 2014 and December 31, 2013 and the income statement and statement of cash flows for 2014 for the M.F. Specie Corporation are presented below:

M.F. SPECIE CORPORATION
Balance Sheet
December 31

Assets

	2014	2013
Cash	$ 40,000	$ 50,000
Marketable securities	35,000	20,000
Accounts receivable (net)	85,000	60,000
Inventory	170,000	150,000
Plant and equipment (net)	470,000	500,000
Total assets	$800,000	$780,000

Liabilities and stockholders' equity

	2014	2013
Accounts payable	$ 95,000	$130,000
Accrued liabilities	8,000	10,000
6% bonds payable	100,000	100,000
Common stock, $10 par	300,000	300,000
Retained earnings	297,000	240,000
Total liabilities and stockholders' equity	$800,000	$780,000

M.F. SPECIE CORPORATION
Income Statement
For the Year Ending December 31, 2014

Net sales		$900,000
Cost of goods sold		
Inventory, January 1	$150,000	
Purchases	570,000	
Goods available for sale	720,000	
Inventory, December 31	170,000	550,000
Gross profit		350,000
Operating expenses		
Depreciation	30,000	
Other	194,000	224,000
Income from operations		126,000
Bond interest expense		6,000
Income before income taxes		120,000
Income tax expense		48,000
Net income		$ 72,000

M.F. SPECIE CORPORATION
Statement of Cash Flows
For the Year Ending December 31, 2014

Cash flows from operating activities		
Net income		$72,000
Adjustments to reconcile net income to net cash		
provided by operating activities:		
Increase in net accounts receivable	$(25,000)	
Increase in inventory	(20,000)	
Depreciation expense	30,000	
Decrease in accounts payable	(35,000)	
Decrease in accrued liabilities	(2,000)	(52,000)
Net cash provided by operating activities		20,000
Cash flows from investing activities		
Purchase of marketable securities	(15,000)	
Net cash used by investing activities		(15,000)
Cash flows from financing activities		
Payment of cash dividends	(15,000)	
Net cash used by financing activities		(15,000)
Net decrease in cash		(10,000)
Cash at beginning of period		50,000
Cash at end of period		$ 40,000

Additional information: Dividends of $.50 per share were paid in 2014 to common stockholders. All sales during 2014 were on credit. The market value per share of common stock was $30 at December 31, 2014. The marketable securities are classified as available-for-sale securities. No disposals of plant assets occurred during the year.

Instructions

(a) Fill in the blanks below with the appropriate amounts to develop ratios for the M.F. Specie Corporation (you do not have to compute the ratios, but a full solution is provided if you choose to do so):

1. The current ratio at the end of 2014 would be computed by dividing
$_____ by $_____.
2. The acid-test (quick) ratio at the end of 2014 would be computed by dividing
$_____ by $_____.
3. The ratio of debt to total assets at the end of 2014 would be computed by dividing
$_____ by $_____.
4. The return on common stockholders' equity for 2014 would be computed by dividing
$_____ by $_____.
5. The asset turnover for 2014 would be computed by dividing
$_____ by $_____.
6. The number of times bond interest earned ratio for 2014 would be computed by dividing $_____ by $_____.
7. The profit margin on sales for 2014 would be computed by dividing
$_____ by $_____.

8. The return on assets for 2014 would be computed by dividing
    $_____ by $_____.
9. The payout ratio for 2014 would be computed by dividing
    $_____ by $_____.
10. The receivables turnover for 2014 would be determined by dividing
    $_____ by $_____.
    The average number of days required to collect from a customer for a credit sale would be determined by dividing
    _____ by _____.
11. The inventory turnover for 2014 would be determined by dividing
    $_____ by $_____.
    The average number of days sales included in inventory would be computed by dividing
    _____ by _____.
12. Earnings per share for 2014 would be determined by dividing
    $_____ by $_____.
13. The price-earnings ratio at the end of 2014 would be computed by dividing
    $_____ by $_____.

(b) Which of the ratios in part (a) above would be used to evaluate the company's financial strength and future solvency? Indicate your answers by use of appropriate numbers.
(c) Which of the ratios in part (a) above would be used to evaluate the company's earning power and growth potential? Indicate your answers by use of the appropriate numbers.

SOLUTION TO EXERCISE 14-2

(a) 1. 330,000; 103,000   9. 15,000; 72,000
    2. 160,000; 103,000   10. 900,000; 72,500; 365 days; 12.41
    3. 203,000; 800,000   11. 550,000; 160,000; 365 days; 3.44
    4. 72,000; 568,500   12. 72,000; 30,000
    5. 900,000; 790,000   13. 30; 2.40
    6. 126,000; 6,000
    7. 72,000; 900,000
    8. 72,000; 790,000

Approach: Write down the components of each ratio to be computed. (Refer to **Illustration 14-1** when needed.) Extract the pertinent data from the financial statements and additional information.

Explanation:

1. **Current ratio:** $\dfrac{\text{Current assets}}{\text{Current liabilities}} = \dfrac{\$40,000 + \$35,000 + \$85,000 + \$170,000}{\$95,000 + \$8,000} = 3.20 \text{ times}$

2. **Acid-test (quick) ratio:** $\dfrac{\text{Quick assets}}{\text{Current liabilities}} = \dfrac{\$40,000 + \$35,000 + \$85,000}{\$95,000 + \$8,000} = 1.55 \text{ times}$

3. **Debt to total assets:** $\dfrac{\text{Total liabilities}}{\text{Total assets}} = \dfrac{\$95,000 + \$8,000 + \$100,000}{\$800,000} = 25.38\%$

4. **Return on common stockholders' equity:**

   $\dfrac{\text{Net income minus preferred dividends}}{\text{Average common stockholders' equity}} = \dfrac{\$72,000 - \$0}{1/2(\$597,000^* + \$540,000)} = 12.66\%$

   *Total stockholders' equity is the sum of paid-in capital (common stock in this case) and retained earnings.

5. **Asset turnover:** $\dfrac{\text{Net sales}}{\text{Average total assets}} = \dfrac{\$900,000}{1/2(\$800,000 + \$780,000)} = 1.14 \text{ times}$

6. **Times interest earned:**

   $\dfrac{\text{Net income} + \text{income taxes} + \text{interest expense}}{\text{Interest expense}} = \dfrac{\$72,000 + \$48,000 + \$6,000}{\$6,000} = 21 \text{ times}$

7. **Profit margin:** $\dfrac{\text{Net income}}{\text{Net sales}} = \dfrac{\$72,000}{\$900,000} = 8.0\%$

8. **Return on assets:** $\dfrac{\text{Net income}}{\text{Average total assets}} = \dfrac{\$72,000}{1/2(\$800,000 + \$780,000)} = 9.11\%$

9. **Payout ratio:** $\dfrac{\text{Cash dividends}}{\text{Net income}} = \dfrac{\$.50(30,000 \text{ shares}^{**})}{\$72,000} = 20.83\%$

   **Common Stock account balance of $300,000 ÷ $10 par per share = 30,000 shares issued; there are no treasury shares so 30,000 shares are outstanding.

10. **Receivables turnover:**

    $\dfrac{\text{Net credit sales}}{\text{Average net receivables}} = \dfrac{\$900,000}{1/2(\$85,000 + \$60,000)} = 12.41 \text{ times}$

    Average number of days to collect an account receivable:

    $\dfrac{365 \text{ days}}{\text{Receivables turnover}} = \dfrac{365 \text{ days}}{12.41 \text{ times}} = 29.41 \text{ days}$

11. **Inventory turnover:** $\dfrac{\text{Cost of goods sold}}{\text{Average inventory}} = \dfrac{\$550,000}{1/2(\$170,000 + \$150,000)} = 3.44 \text{ times}$

Average number of days' sales in inventory:

$$\frac{365 \text{ days}}{\text{Inventory turnover}} = \frac{365 \text{ days}}{3.44 \text{ times}} = 106.10 \text{ days}$$

12. **Earnings per share:** $\dfrac{\text{Net income minus preferred dividends}}{\text{Weighted average shares outstanding}} = \dfrac{\$72,000 - \$0}{30,000} = \$2.40$

13. **Price-earnings ratio:** $\dfrac{\text{Market price per share of stock}}{\text{Earnings per share}} = \dfrac{\$30.00}{\$2.40} = 12.5 \text{ times}$

(b) 1, 2, 3, 6, 10, 11, 14, and 16.

(c) 4, 5, 7, 8, 9, 12, 13, and 15.

EXERCISE 14-3

Purpose: (L.O. 5) This exercise points out the effects of various transactions on selected computations and ratios.

The following list of transactions relate to the Huseman Corporation for 2014. You are to analyze the transactions assuming that on the date when each of the transactions occurred, the corporation's accounts showed only common stock (80,000 shares, $100 par) outstanding, a current ratio of 3.1 to 1 and a substantial net income for the year to date (before giving effect to the transaction concerned). Each numbered transaction is to be considered completely independent of the others, and its related answer should be based on the effect(s) of that transaction alone. Assume all amounts are material and all transactions were recorded in accordance with generally accepted accounting principles.

Instructions

For each of the transactions, indicate the effect (increase, decrease or no effect) on each of the following:
(a) The corporation's net income for 2014.
(b) The corporation's current ratio.

Transaction	Effect On Net income 2014	Current Ratio
1. The corporation declared a cash dividend of $1.00 per share	_____	_____
2. The corporation paid the cash dividend which had been recorded in the accounts at the time of declaration.	_____	_____
3. The corporation purchased 100 shares of treasury stock for $150 per share.	_____	_____

Transaction	Net income 2014	Current Ratio
4. The corporation sold 100 shares of treasury stock for $145 per share; the shares cost $150 per share.	_____	_____
5. Huseman sold a plot of land previously used in operations. The carrying value was $60,000 and the sales price was $50,000.	_____	_____
6. The corporation purchased equipment for $40,000 on account.	_____	_____
7. The corporation collected $25,000 from a customer on account.	_____	_____
8. Huseman purchased short-term debt investments for $29,000.	_____	_____
9. Huseman had cash sales of $400,000.	_____	_____
10. Huseman purchased $15,000 of inventory on account.	_____	_____

SOLUTION TO EXERCISE 14-3

	(a)	(b)		(a)	(b)
1.	No Effect	Decrease	6.	No Effect	Decrease
2.	No Effect	Increase	7.	No Effect	No Effect
3.	No Effect	Decrease	8.	No Effect	No Effect
4.	No Effect	Increase	9.	Increase	Increase
5.	Decrease	Increase	10.	No Effect	Decrease

Approach: Write down the components of net income and the current ratio computations. Prepare the journal entry for each transaction. Analyze the accounts in each entry for their effects on the various components of the computations in question.

$$\text{Revenues - Expenses = Net income}$$

$$\frac{\text{Current assets}}{\text{Current liabilities}} = \text{Current ratio}$$

Explanation:
1. Retained Earnings 80,000
       Dividends Payable.. 80,000
   (a) Dividends are not a determinant of income; they are a distribution of income.
   (b) Current liabilities are increased so the current ratio is decreased.

2. Dividends Payable   80,000
       Cash   80,000
    (a) There is no income statement element affected by this transaction.
    (b) Anytime the current ratio is greater than 1 to 1, a decrease in current liabilities, even when accompanied by a decrease in current assets of the same magnitude, will cause the current ratio to increase.

3. Treasury Stock   15,000
       Cash   15,000
    (a) There is no effect on net income.
    (b) There is a reduction in current assets; hence, the current ratio is reduced.

4. Cash   14,500
    Retained Earnings   500
       Treasury Stock   15,000
    (a) There is no accounting gain or loss. This is a capital transaction.
    (b) Current assets are increased; thus, the current ratio is increased.

5. Cash   50,000
    Loss on Sale of Land   10,000
       Land   60,000
    (a) Net income is decreased because of the loss.
    (b) Current assets are increased; thus, the current ratio is increased.

6. Equipment   40,000
       Accounts Payable   40,000
    (a) There are no income statement accounts involved.
    (b) The current ratio is reduced because of the increase in current liabilities.

7. Cash   25,000
       Accounts Receivable   25,000
    (a) There are no income statement accounts involved.
    (b) There is no net change in current assets and no effect on the current ratio.

8. Debt Investments (Short-term)   29,000
       Cash   29,000
    (a) There are no income statement accounts involved.
    (b) There is no net change in current assets and no effect on the current ratio.

9. Cash   400,000
       Sales Revenue   400,000
    (a) Net income is increased due to the revenue recognized.
    (b) Current assets are increased so the current ratio is increased.

10. Inventory   15,000
       Accounts Payable   15,000
    (a) There is no effect on net income.
    (b) Current liabilities are increased. Even though current assets increase by the same amount, the current ratio will decrease. Anytime the current ratio is greater than 1 to 1, an increase in current liabilities, even when accompanied by an increase in current assets of the same magnitude, will cause a decrease in the current ratio.

EXERCISE 14-4

Purpose: (L.O. 6) This exercise will test your knowledge of the elements and arrangement of the major sections of the income statement.

Instructions

The following list represents captions that would appear on an income statement (single-step format) for a company reporting an extraordinary gain and a loss from discontinued operations, as well as the results of continuing operations for the period. You are to "unscramble" the list and prepare a skeleton income statement using the captions given. If you do not wish to write out each caption above, you may still test your knowledge by listing the appropriate letters in the correct order.

(a)   Income before extraordinary item.
(b)   Revenues.
(c)   Income from continuing operations.
(d)   Income tax expense.
(e)   Discontinued operations.
(f)   Extraordinary gain (net of tax).
(g)   Expenses.
(h)   Loss from disposal of assets of discontinued segment of business (net of tax).
(i)   Net income.
(j)   Income before income taxes.
(k)   Loss from operations of discontinued segment of business (net of tax).

SOLUTION TO EXERCISE 14-4

COMPANY NAME
Income Statement
For the Year Ended December 31, 20XX

(b)   Revenues
(g)   <u>Expenses</u>
(j)   Income before income taxes
(d)   <u>Income tax expense</u>
(c)   Income from continuing operations
(e)   Discontinued operations:
(k)   Loss from operations of discontinued segment of business (net of tax)
(h)   <u>Loss from disposal of assets of discontinued segment of business (net of tax)</u>
(a)   Income before extraordinary item
(f)   <u>Extraordinary gain (net of tax)</u>
(i)   Net income

TIP:	Income taxes should be associated with the item that affects the taxes. Thus, the income tax consequences of all items appearing above the line "Income before income taxes" are summarized in the line "Income tax expense." Revenues cause an increase in income taxes and expenses cause a decrease in income taxes. The income tax consequences of items appearing below the "Income from continuing operations" line are included with the items (hence, these items are reported "net of tax").
TIP:	An extraordinary item is reported "net of tax" by deducting the tax effect from the related gain or loss. For example, if the tax rate is 30%, an extraordinary gain of $400,000 will be reported at $280,000 net of tax. Likewise, an extraordinary loss of $400,000 will be reported at $280,000 net of tax. The gain situation increases net income whereas the loss reduces it.

EXERCISE 14-5

Purpose: (L.O. 5, 6) This exercise will enable you practice identifying the proper classification for items on an income statement. It will also give you an example of how the tax effects of various items are reflected in the income statement.

Eliason Inc. reported income from continuing operations before income taxes for 2014 of $700,000. The income tax rate on all items was 30%. Additional transactions occurring in 2014 but not considered in the $700,000 are as follows:

1.   The corporation experienced an uninsured flood loss in the amount of $80,000 during the year. A flood is a very rare event in the area where the corporation is located.

2.   The corporation disposed of its recreational division at a loss of $150,000 before the related tax effect. This transaction meets the criteria for being classified as discontinued operations. The income from operations for this division was $60,000 (before taxes) for 2014.

Instructions
Prepare a part of the income statement for the year 2014 starting with "Income before income taxes."

SOLUTION TO EXERCISE 14-5

Eliason Inc.
Partial Income Statement
For the Year Ended December 31, 2014

Income before income taxes...		$700,000
Income tax expense...		210,000
Income from continuing operations..		490,000
Discontinued operations		
Income from operations of recreational division, net of		
$18,000 income taxes	$ 42,000	
Loss from disposal of recreational division, net of		
$45,000 income tax saving..	105,000	63,000
Income before extraordinary item		427,000
Extraordinary item		
Flood loss, net of $24,000 income tax saving		56,000
Net income..		$371,000

TIP: A discontinued segment of business can have either a positive (income from operations or gain on disposal) or a negative (loss from operations or loss on disposal) effect on net income. Extraordinary gains increase net income, whereas extraordinary losses decrease net income. In the income statement for Eliason Inc. which appears above, the $56,000 flood loss was deducted in arriving at net income.

TIP: Material items not typical of operations are reported in separate sections of the income statement, net of related income taxes. Study this solution as an illustration of the sequencing of such items and the labeling of amounts.

TIP: All data presented in determining income before income taxes on a corporation's income statement is the same as for an unincorporated company.

EXERCISE 14-6

Purpose: (L.O. 1 thru 7) This exercise will quiz you about terminology used in this chapter.

A list of accounting terms with which you should be familiar appears below:

Acid-test (quick) ratio	Price-earnings (P-E) ratio
Asset turnover	Profit margin
Change in accounting principle	Profitability ratios
Comprehensive income	Pro forma income
Current ratio	Quality of earnings
Debt to total assets ratio	Ratio
Discontinued operations	Ratio analysis
Earnings per share (EPS)	Receivables turnover
Extraordinary items	Return on assets
Horizontal analysis	Return on common stockholders' equity
Inventory turnover	Solvency ratios
Leveraging	Times interest earned
Liquidity ratios	Trading on the equity (leverage)
Payout ratio	Vertical analysis

Instructions
For each item below, enter in the blank the term that is described.

1. _____ A technique for evaluating financial statement data that expresses each item within a financial statement in terms of a percent of a base amount; often called common-size analysis.

2. _____ A technique for evaluating a series of financial statement data over a period of time to determine the increase (decrease) that has taken place, expressed as either an amount or a percentage; often called trend analysis.

3. _____ An expression of the mathematical relationship between one quantity and another. The relationship may be expressed either as a percentage, a rate, or a simple proportion.

4. _____ Measures of the short-term ability of the enterprise to pay its maturing obligations and to meet unexpected needs for cash.

5. _____ Measures of the income or operating success of an enterprise for a given period of time.

6. _____ Measures of the ability of the enterprise to survive over a long period of time.

7. _____ A measure used to evaluate a company's liquidity and short-term debt-paying ability, computed by dividing current assets by current liabilities.

8. _____ A measure of a company's immediate short-term liquidity, computed by dividing the sum of cash, short-term investments and (net) receivables by current liabilities.

9. _____ A measure of the liquidity of receivables, computed by dividing net credit sales by average net receivables.

10. _____ A measure of the liquidity of inventory, computed by dividing cost of goods sold by average inventory.

11. _____ Measures the percentage of each dollar of sales that results in net income, computed by dividing net income by net sales.

12. _____ A measure of how efficiently a company uses its assets to generate sales, computed by dividing net sales by average total assets.

13. _____ An overall measure of profitability, computed by dividing net income by average total assets.

14. _____ Measures the dollars of net income earned for each dollar invested by the owners, computed by dividing net income by average common stockholders' equity.

15. _____ The net income earned by each share of common stock, computed by dividing net income by the weighted average common shares outstanding.

16. _____ Measures the ratio of the market price of each share of common stock to the earnings per share, computed by dividing the market price of the stock by earnings per share.

17. _____ Measures the percentage of earnings distributed in the form of cash dividends, computed by dividing cash dividends by net income.

18. _____ Measures the percentage of total assets provided by creditors, computed by dividing total debt by total assets.

19. _____ Measures a company's ability to meet interest payments as they come due, computed by dividing income before interest expense and income taxes by interest expense.

20. _____ Borrowing money at a lower rate of interest than can be earned by using the borrowed money.

21. _____ A technique for evaluating financial statements that expresses the relationship between selected financial statement data.

22. _____ The disposal of a significant segment of a business.

23. _____ Events and transactions that meet two conditions: (1) unusual in nature, and (2) infrequent in occurrence.

24. _____ Use of an accounting principle in the current year that is different from the one used in the preceding year.

25. _____ Includes all changes in stockholders' equity during a period except those resulting from investments by stockholders and distributions to stockholders.

26. _____ Another name for trading on the equity.

27. _____ Indicates the level of full and transparent information provided to users of the financial statements.

28. _____ A measure of income that usually **excludes** items that a company thinks are unusual or nonrecurring.

SOLUTION TO EXERCISE 14-6

1. Vertical analysis
2. Horizontal analysis
3. Ratio
4. Liquidity ratios
5. Profitability ratios
6. Solvency ratios
7. Current ratio
8. Acid-test (quick) ratio
9. Receivables turnover
10. Inventory turnover
11. Profit margin
12. Asset turnover
13. Return on assets
14. Return on common stockholders' equity

15. Earnings per share (EPS)
16. Price-earnings ratio
17. Payout ratio
18. Debt to total assets ratio
19. Times interest earned
20. Trading on the equity (leverage)
21. Ratio analysis
22. Discontinued operations
23. Extraordinary items
24. Change in accounting practice
25. Comprehensive income
26. Leveraging
27. Quality of earnings
28. Pro forma income

ANALYSIS OF MULTIPLE-CHOICE TYPE QUESTIONS

1. **Question**
    (L.O. 3) The Goodings Corporation reported sales of $80,000 in 2012, $96,000 in 2013, and $112,000 in 2014. In a trend analysis for these years, where 2012 is used as the base year, the respective sales percentages would be:
    a.   100%; 120%; 137%.
    b.   100%; 120%; 117%.
    c.   100%; 120%; 140%.
    d.   80%; 96%; 112%.

    Explanation: Trend analysis is a type of horizontal analysis that is prepared for more than two years. In horizontal analysis, a base year (2012 in this case) is selected. Each item being analyzed is then divided by the amount reported for the base year for the same item. Thus, $80,000 is the 100% figure, $96,000 divided by $80,000 = 120%, and $112,000 divided by $80,000 = 140%. (Solution = c.)

2. **Question**
    (L.O. 4) An analyst is examining an income statement that shows only percentages; all items are expressed in terms of a percentage of net sales. This type of analysis is often called:
    a.   common-size analysis.
    b.   horizontal analysis.
    c.   comparative analysis.
    d.   multiple-step analysis.

    Explanation: Vertical analysis, sometimes referred to as **common-size analysis**, is a technique for evaluating financial statement data that expresses each item within a financial statement in terms of a percent of a base amount. For an income statement, net sales is used as the base amount. (Solution = a.)

3. **Question**
    (L.O. 4) The base figure used for vertical analysis of the income statement is:
    a.   net income.
    b.   gross profit.
    c.   income before income taxes.
    d.   net sales revenue.

    Explanation: On an income statement, net sales is the base amount for vertical analysis. All other items are then expressed as a percentage of that base amount. (Solution = d.)

4. **Question**
    (L.O. 4) The base figure used for vertical analysis of a corporate balance sheet is:
    a.   total assets.
    b.   current assets.
    c.   property, plant, and equipment.
    d.   stockholders' equity.

Explanation: In performing a vertical analysis of the balance sheet, total assets is the base figure. All other amounts are then expressed as a percentage of the total assets amount. (Solution = a.)

5. **Question**
   (L.O. 5) The current ratio is calculated by dividing:
   a. current assets by total liabilities.
   b. current assets by current liabilities.
   c. quick assets by current liabilities.
   d. total assets by total liabilities.

   Approach and Explanation: Write down the formula for the current ratio **before** you read the answer selections. Choose the answer that matches the formula.

   $$\text{Current ratio} = \frac{\text{Current assets}}{\text{Current liabilities}}$$

   (Solution = b.)

6. **Question**
   (L.O. 5) Which of the following items would **not** be used in calculating the working capital ratio?
   a. Accounts payable.
   b. Inventory.
   c. Accounts receivable.
   d. Furniture purchased during the current period.

   Approach and Explanation: Think about the working capital ratio and write down the formula to compute it. Then read the answer selections and determine which selection does not fit into the formula. The **working capital ratio** is another name for the **current ratio.** The current ratio is determined by dividing total current assets by total current liabilities at a point in time. Answer selection "d" would be classified under the property, plant, and equipment classification and would therefore not be included in the calculation of the working capital ratio. (Solution = d.)

7. **Question**
   (L.O. 5) Which of the following will **increase** the amount of working capital?
   a. Collection of accounts receivable.
   b. Sale of a long-term investment at book value.
   c. Purchase of inventory on account.
   d. Payment of a short-term note payable.

   Approach: Write down the formula for determining working capital. Write down the journal entry for each transaction mentioned. Analyze each account in each entry to determine its affect on the elements of the working capital computation.

Working Capital = Current Assets - Current Liabilities

Explanation:

a. Cash..   XX
        Accounts Receivable..   XX
    There is no net effect on total current assets (Cash increases by the same amount that Accounts Receivable decreases) and no effect on current liabilities; hence, there is no effect on working capital.

b. Cash..   XX
        Long-term Investment..   XX
    There is an increase in Cash (a current asset) and no effect on any other component of working capital; hence, working capital increases.

c. Inventory..   XX
        Accounts Payable..   XX
    Current assets increase (Inventory increases) by the same amount that current liabilities increase (Accounts Payable increases); therefore, there is no net effect on working capital.

d. Short-term Note Payable   XX
        Cash   XX
    Current liabilities decrease by the same amount that current assets decrease; hence, there is no net effect on working capital.

(Solution = b.)

8. **Question**
    (L.O. 5) Which of the following items would **not** be used in computing the quick ratio?
    a. Accounts receivable.
    b. Short-term investments.
    c. Inventory.
    d. Accounts payable.

    Approach and Explanation: Write down the formula for the quick ratio. Check each answer selection to see if it is used in this formula. The quick ratio is another name for the acid-test ratio.

    $$\text{Quick ratio} = \frac{\text{Cash + Short-term investments + receivables (net)}}{\text{Current liabilities}}$$

    Accounts receivable and short-term investments would both go in the numerator. Accounts payable is a current liability; hence, it goes in the denominator. Inventory is a current asset that is not included in "quick assets." (Solution = c.)

9. **Question**
    (L.O. 5) The current ratio at any given date for a particular company is:
    a. usually equal to the acid-test ratio at the same date.
    b. usually smaller than the acid-test ratio at the same date.
    c. usually larger than the acid-test ratio at the same date.
    d. computed by dividing current liabilities by current assets.

Approach and Explanation: Write down the formulas for both the current ratio and the acid-test ratio. Notice what is similar and what is different about them. Think about how the difference will affect the relative results. The current ratio is calculated by dividing total current assets by total current liabilities; whereas, the acid-test ratio is calculated by dividing cash plus current receivables plus short-term investments by total current liabilities. Current assets other than cash and short-term receivables and short-term investments would normally include inventory and prepaid expenses. Because the current ratio would normally have a larger numerator but the same denominator as the acid-test ratio, the current ratio would be larger than the acid-test ratio. (Solution = c.)

10. **Question**
(L.O. 5) A company has a current ratio of 2:1 at December 31, 2014. Which of the following transactions would increase this ratio?
a.   Purchase of merchandise on account.
b.   Sale of bonds payable at a discount.
c.   Payment of a 60-day note payable.
d.   Receipt of payment of an account receivable.
e.   Both b. and c.

Approach: Set up an example of the situation described; assume current assets are $8,000 and current liabilities are $4,000. Prepare the journal entry for each of the transactions (assume the amount involved is $2,000) and analyze the effect of the entry on the components of the current ratio.

Explanation:
a.   Inventory...   2,000
         Accounts Payable...   2,000
Current assets and current liabilities both increase by the same amount ($2,000); therefore, the current ratio will decrease. (The new ratio will be $10,000/$6,000 or 1.67:1 in this example.)

b.   Cash   2,000
         Discount on Bonds Payable..   200
         Bonds Payable   2,200
Current assets increase with no change in current liabilities; therefore, the current ratio will increase (The new ratio will be $10,000/$4,000 or 2.5:1 in this example.)

c.   Short-term Note Payable   2,000
         Cash...   2,000
Current assets and current liabilities both decrease by the same amount; therefore, the current ratio will increase because the ratio was greater than 1:1 before the transaction. (The new ratio will be $6,000/$2,000 or 3:1 in this example.)

d.   Cash   2,000
         Accounts Receivable..   2,000
Total current assets and total current liabilities both remain unchanged; therefore, there is no change in the current ratio.

e.   Both "b" and "c" cause an increase in the current ratio.

(Solution = e.)

11. **Question**
(L.O. 5) A company has a current ratio of 2:1 at December 31, 2014. Which of the following transactions will **not** cause a change in the current ratio?
a.   Declaration of a 10% stock dividend.
b.   Purchase of short-term investments for cash.
c.   Payment of a long-term liability.
d.   Declaration of a cash dividend.
e.   Both a. and b.
f.   Both a. and d.

Approach: Set up an example of the situation described; assume current assets are $8,000 and current liabilities are $4,000. Prepare the journal entry for each of the transactions (assume the amount involved is $2,000) and analyze the effect of the entry on the components of the current ratio.

Explanation:
a.   Retained Earnings   2,000
         Common Stock Dividends Distributable   500
         Paid-in Capital in Excess of Par Value   1,500
     There is no effect on current assets, current liabilities, or the current ratio. (The par value of the dividend shares is an assumed amount here.)

b.   Short-term Investments   2,000
         Cash   2,000
     There is no effect on total current assets, current liabilities, or the current ratio.

c.   Long-term Liability   2,000
         Cash   2,000
     Current assets are reduced and, therefore, the current ratio is decreased. Total current liabilities remain unchanged. (The new ratio in this example is $6,000/$4,000 or 1.5:1.)

d.   Retained Earnings   2,000
         Dividends Payable...   2,000
     Current liabilities are increased and, therefore, the current ratio is decreased. (The new ratio in this example is $8,000/$6,000 or 1.33:1.)

e.   Both "a" and "b" have no effect on the current ratio.

f.   Although "a" has no effect on the current ratio, "d" causes a decrease in the current ratio.

(Solution = e.)

12. **Question**
(L.O. 5) A company has a current ratio of 3:1 at December 31, 2014. Which of the following transactions would **decrease** this ratio?
a.   Pay an account payable.
b.   Sell bonds at a discount.
c.   Borrow cash by issuing a 90-day note payable.
d.   Issue stock for cash.

Approach: Set up an example of the situation described: assume current assets are $300,000 and current liabilities are $100,000. Prepare the journal entry for each of the transactions (assume the amount involved in the entry is $50,000) and analyze the effect of the entry on the components of the current ratio.

Explanation:
a.   Accounts Payable 50,000
      Cash 50,000
Current assets and current liabilities both decrease by the same amount ($50,000); therefore, the current ratio will increase. (The new ratio will be $250,000/$50,000 or 5:1 in this example.)

b.   Cash 50,000
Discount on Bonds Payable 5,000
      Bonds Payable 55,000
Current assets will increase with no change in current liabilities; therefore, the current ratio will increase. (The new ratio will be $350,000/$100,000 or 3.5:1 in this example.)

c.   Cash 50,000
      Short-term Note Payable 50,000
Current assets and current liabilities both increase by the same amount; therefore, the current ratio will decrease (the ratio was greater than 1:1 before the transaction). (The new ratio will be $350,000/$150,000 or 2.33:1 in this example.)

d.   Cash 50,000
      Common Stock 50,000
Current assets increase and current liabilities remain unchanged; therefore, the current ratio increases. (The new ratio will be $350,000/$100,000 or 3.5:1 in this example.)

(Solution = c.)

13. **Question**
(L.O. 5) Which of the following is the formula for the debt to total assets ratio?
a.   Current liabilities divided by current assets.
b.   Current liabilities divided by total assets.
c.   Long-term liabilities divided by total assets.
d.   Total liabilities divided by total assets.

Explanation: The debt to total assets ratio is an expression of the relationship between total debt and total assets. (Solution = d.)

14. **Question**
(L.O. 5) A corporation has two classes of stock outstanding. The return on common stockholders' equity is computed by dividing net income:
a.   minus preferred dividends by the number of common stock shares outstanding at the balance sheet date.
b.   plus interest expense by the average amount of total assets.
c.   by the number of common stock shares outstanding at the balance sheet date.
d.   minus preferred dividends by the average amount of common stockholders' equity during the period.

Explanation: The return on common stockholders' equity is computed by dividing the amount of earnings applicable to the common stockholders' interest in the company by the average amount of common stockholders' equity during the period. The amount of earnings applicable to the common stockholders is the amount of net income for the period less the dividends declared on preferred stock during the period. (Solution = d.)

15. **Question**
(L.O. 6) A loss from the disposal of a segment of business should be reported in the income statement:
a.   after extraordinary items.
b.   before extraordinary items.
c.   as an extraordinary gain.
d.   as an extraordinary loss.

Explanation: The correct order on an income statement of the items involved in the question is as follows:
   (1) **D**iscontinued operations
   (2) **E**xtraordinary items
Discontinued operations refers to the disposal of a significant component of a business. The income (loss) from discontinued operations consists of two parts: the income (loss) from operations and the gain (loss) on disposition of a segment. The results for the period from discontinued operations is reported separately from the results of continuing operations. (Solution = b.)

16. **Question**
(L.O. 6) A material loss should be presented separately as a component of income from continuing operations when it is:
a.   unusual in nature and infrequent in occurrence.
b.   unusual in nature but not infrequent in occurrence.
c.   an extraordinary loss.
d.   a cumulative effect of a change in accounting principle.

Approach: Visualize an income statement and mentally identify the section that reports income from continuing operations. Read one answer at a time and determine if it correctly describes how the statement in the question stem can be completed.

Explanation: A material loss that is (1) unusual in nature and (2) infrequent in occurrence should be reported as an extraordinary item. A loss that meets one of the criteria for being classified as extraordinary, but not both, should be separately disclosed as a component of income from continuing operations. An extraordinary item and a cumulative effect of a change in accounting principle are to be reported after (and not part of) income from continuing operations. (Solution = b.)

17. **Question**
(L.O. 6) During the year ended December 31, 2014, Schmelya Corporation incurred the following infrequent losses:

1.   A factory was shutdown during a major strike by employees; costs were $120,000.
2.   A loss of $50,000 was incurred on the abandonment of computer equipment used in the business.
3.   A loss of $82,000 was incurred as a result of flood damage to a warehouse.

How much total loss should Schmelya report in the extraordinary item section of its 2014 income statement?
a. $82,000.
b. $120,000.
c. $202,000.
d. $252,000.

Explanation: To be classified as extraordinary, an item needs to be unusual in nature and infrequent in occurrence. Examples of items to be classified as extraordinary gains or losses on the income statement include the following:
1. Effects of major casualties (acts of God), if rare in the area.
2. Expropriation (takeover) of property by a foreign government.
3. Effects of a newly enacted law or regulation such as a condemnation action on company property by a governmental agency.

There are certain items that do not constitute extraordinary items. A listing of these include:
1. Effects of major casualties (acts of God), not uncommon in the area.
2. Write-down of inventories or write-off of receivables.
3. Losses attributable to labor strikes.
4. Gains or losses from sales of property, plant, or equipment.

Approach: Review the lists of items above until you can readily recognize items that appear in the lists. In the question at hand, the first two items are on the list of items that are not extraordinary. Therefore, the only possible one being extraordinary is the loss from flood damage. A flood would be considered infrequent in some locations but not others. Because there is no answer selection of $0, the flood is apparently deemed infrequent for Schmelya. (Solution = a.)

18. **Question**
    (L.O. 6) If a transaction gives rise to an extraordinary loss of $100,000 and the company is subject to a tax rate of 40%, the transaction should be reported in the income statement at the net-of-tax amount of:
    a. $140,000.
    b. $100,000.
    c. $60,000.
    d. $40,000.

    Explanation: $100,000 X 40% = $40,000 tax saving.
    $100,000 loss - $40,000 tax saving = $60,000 loss net of tax.
    (Solution = c.)

19. **Question**
    (L.O. 5) Peter Wong Corporation had net income reported for 2014 of $880,000. During 2014, dividends of $120,000 were declared on preferred stock and dividends of $200,000 were declared on common stock. There were no changes in the 200,000 shares of common stock or the 40,000 shares of preferred stock outstanding during 2014. The earnings per share to be reported for 2014 is:
    a. $4.40.
    b. $3.80.
    c. $3.67.
    d. $2.80.

Approach and Explanation: Write down the formula to compute EPS. Solve using the data in this question.

$$\frac{\text{Net income - Preferred Dividends}}{\text{Weighted Average Number of Common Shares Outstanding}}$$

$$\frac{\$880,000 - \$120,000}{200,000} = \$3.80$$

(Solution = b.)

TIP:	EPS is only computed and presented for common stock.
TIP:	Dividends on common stock do **not** affect the EPS computation.

---

20. **Question**
    (L.O. 5) Clampitt Corporation had 60,000 shares of common stock outstanding on January 1, 2014. On April 1, 2014, an additional 40,000 shares were issued for cash. No other changes took place in the number of shares outstanding. The weighted average number of shares outstanding for purposes of earnings per share computations is:
    a. 70,000.
    b. 80,000.
    c. 90,000.
    d. 92,667.

Approach and Explanation: Think about how shares are to be weighted according to the length of time they are outstanding in relation to the period of time for which EPS is being computed. The computation is:

$$
\begin{array}{ll}
60,000 \times 12/12 = & 60,000 \\
40,000 \times 9/12 = & \underline{30,000} \\
& \underline{\underline{90,000}}
\end{array}
$$

The fraction of 12/12 is used for the initial 60,000 shares because they are outstanding all 12 of the 12 months in the period (year). The fraction 9/12 is used for the additional shares issued on April 1 because those shares are outstanding 9 months (from April 1 through December 31) of the 12-month period for which the computation is being made. (Solution = c.)

*T*IME VALUE OF MONEY

OVERVIEW

Due to the time value of money, a certain sum today is not equal to the same sum at a future point in time. We must consider the compound interest factor for the time between two given dates in order to determine what amount in the future is equivalent to a given sum today or what amount today is equivalent to a given sum in the future. We compound the dollar amount forward in time in the former case and discount the dollar amount from the future to the present time in the latter case. In this appendix we discuss the procedures for computing the future value and present value of a single sum and/or an ordinary annuity.

Future value and present value tables appear at the end of this appendix.

SUMMARY OF LEARNING OBJECTIVES

1. **Distinguish between simple interest and compound interest.** Simple interest is computed on the principal only, while compound interest is computed on the principal and any interest earned that has not been withdrawn.

2. **Solve for the future value of a single amount.** Prepare a time diagram of the problem. Identify the principal amount, the number of compounding periods, and the interest rate. Using the future value of 1 table, multiply the principal amount by the future value factor specified at the intersection of the number of periods and the interest rate.

3. **Solve for the future value of an annuity.** Prepare a time diagram of the problem. Identify the amount of the periodic payments (receipts), the number of payments (receipts), and the interest rate. Using the future value of an annuity of 1 table, multiply the amount of the payments by the future value factor specified at the intersection of the number of periods and the interest rate.

4. **Identify the variables fundamental to solving present value problems.** The following three variables are fundamental to solving present value problems: (1) the future amount, (2) the number of periods, and (3) the interest rate (the discount rate).

5. **Solve for the present value of a single amount.** Prepare a time diagram of the problem. Identify the future amount, the number of discounting periods, and the discount (interest) rate. Using the present value of 1 table, multiply the future amount by the present value factor specified at the intersection of the number of periods and the discount rate.

6. **Solve for the present value of an annuity.** Prepare a time diagram of the problem. Identify the amount of future periodic receipts or payments (annuities), the number of payments (receipts), and the discount (interest) rate. Using the present value of an annuity of 1 table, multiply the amount of the annuity by the present value factor specified at the intersection of the number of periods and the interest rate.

7. **Compute the present value of notes and bonds.** Determine the present value of the principal amount: Multiply the principal amount (a single future amount) by the present value factor (from the present value of 1 table) intersecting at the number of periods (number of interest payments) and the discount rate. Determine the present value of the series of interest payments: Multiply the amount of the interest payment by the present value factor (from the present value of an annuity of 1 table) intersecting at the number of periods (number of interest payments) and the discount rate. Add the present value of the principal amount to the present value of the interest payments to arrive at the present value of the note or bond.

8. **Use a financial calculator to solve time value of money problems**. Financial calculators can be used to solve the same and additional problems as those solved with time value of money tables. Enter into the financial calculator the amounts for all of the known elements of a time value of money problem (periods, interest rate, payments, future or present value) and it solves for the unknown element. Particularly useful situations involve interest rates and compounding periods not presented in the tables.

TIPS ON APPENDIX TOPICS

TIP: **Simple interest** is computed on the principal amount only. It is the return on the principal for one period. Simple interest is usually expressed as:

$$I(interest) = P(principal) \times R(rate) \times T(time)$$

TIP: **Compound interest** is computed on the principal and any interest earned that has not been paid or received. It is the return on the principal for two or more periods. Compound interest uses the accumulated balance (principal plus interest to date) at the end of each period to compute interest in the following period.

TIP: The **present value** of a single amount is the current worth of a future amount. **Future value** of a single amount is the future value of an amount to be put on deposit today (a present value figure).

TIP: The present value of a single amount is based on three variables: (1) the dollar amount to be received (future value), (2) the length of time until the amount is received (number of periods), and (3) the interest rate (the discount rate). The process of determining the present value is referred to as discounting the future value (i.e. future amount). The relationship of these fundamental variables is depicted in the following diagram.

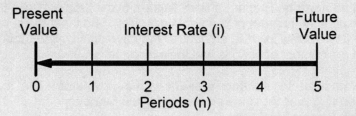

Unless otherwise indicated, an interest rate is stated on an annual basis. To convert an annual interest rate into a compounding period interest rate, divide the annual rate by the number of compounding periods per year. The total number of periods is determined by multiplying the number of years by the number of compounding periods per year.

TIP: The tip above can be reworded so that it applies to an amount to be paid in the future rather than received. Thus, present value concepts can be applied to situations where cash is to be received or paid in the future.

TIP: The **future value of 1** (a single amount) is sometimes referred to as the **future amount of 1**, and the **future value of an annuity** is sometimes called the **future amount of an annuity.**

TIP: The factor for the future value of an annuity of 1 for $n = 3$, $i = 6\%$ reflects interest for two periods on the first rent, interest for one period on the second rent, and no interest on the third rent.

TIP: An **annuity** is a series of equal periodic receipts or payments equally spaced. Unless otherwise indicated, the annuity is assumed to be an **ordinary annuity** in which the first receipt or payment is to be made at the **end** of the first interest period involved. Another type of annuity (called an **annuity in advance**) is one in which the first receipt or payment is to be made at the **beginning** of the first interest period involved. This latter type of annuity is **not** discussed in this book.

TIP: The factor for the present value of an (ordinary) annuity of 1 for n periods is the sum of factors for the present value of 1 for each of the n periods. For example, the factor for the present value of an annuity of 1 for $n = 3$, $i = 8\%$ (which is 2.57710) is equal to sum of the factors from the 8% column of the Present Value of 1 Table for $n = 1$, $n = 2$, $n= 3$ (.92593 + .85734 + .79383 = 2.57710).

TIP: One payment (or receipt) involved in an annuity is often called a **rent.**

TIP: Anytime you have a present value or a future value problem to solve, it is wise to draw a time diagram (often called a time line). This picture will help you to determine:
  (1)   if you are given present value or future value data or both.
  (2)   if you are dealing with a single amount or an annuity situation.
  (3)   what you are to solve for—present value or future value or n (number of periods) or i (interest rate*)* or rent.

TIP: Any present value or future value problem is an application (or variation) of one or more of the following formulas: (parentheses indicate multiplication)
        Future Value of an Amount = Present Value (Future Value of 1 Factor)
        Present Value of an Amount = Future Amount (Present Value of 1 Factor)
        Future Value of an Annuity = Rent (Future Value of an Annuity of 1 Factor)
        Present Value of an Annuity = Rent (Present Value of an Annuity of 1 Factor)
Each present value factor has two components—n and i, time period and interest rate.

TIP: The **interest rate** is often referred to as the **discount rate** in computing present value.

TIP: The higher the discount rate (interest rate) is, the lower the present value will be.

TIP: Tables of future value and present value factors are included at the end of this appendix. Each of these tables is described below:

  1. **Future Value of 1 Table.** Contains the amount to which $1 will accumulate if deposited now at a specified rate of interest and left for a specified number of periods (Table 1).
  2. **Future Value of an Annuity of 1 Table.** Contains the amount to which periodic rents of $1 will accumulate if the payments (rents) are invested at the **end** of each period at a specified rate of interest for a specified number of periods (Table 2).
  3. **Present Value of 1 Table.** Contains the amount that must be deposited now at a specified rate of interest to equal $1 at the end of a specified number of periods (Table 3).
  4. **Present Value of an Annuity of 1 Table.** Contains the amount that must be deposited now at a specified rate of interest to permit withdrawals of $1 at the **end** of regular periodic intervals for the specified number of periods (Table 4).

ILLUSTRATION D-1
STEPS IN SOLVING FUTURE VALUE AND
PRESENT VALUE PROBLEMS (L.O.2, 3, 4, 5, 6)

1. Classify the problem into one of four types:
    (1)   Future value of a single amount.
    (2)   Future value of an annuity.
    (3)   Present value of a single amount.
    (4)   Present value of an annuity.

2. Determine *n*, the number of compounding periods, and *i*, the interest rate per period.
    a.   Draw a time diagram. This is helpful when the number of periods or number of rents must be figured out from the dates given in the problem.
    b.   If interest is compounded more than once a year:
        (1)   to find *n*: **multiply** the number of years by the number of compounding periods per year.
        (2)   to find *i*: **divide** the annual interest rate by the number of compounding periods per year.
3. Use *n* and *i* (if known) to choose the proper interest factor from the interest table indicated in Step 1.
4. Solve for the missing quantity. A summary of the possibilities appears below in **Illustration D-2.** Abbreviations used in this summary are explained at the end of the summary.

ILLUSTRATION D-2
SUMMARY OF FOUR TYPES OF FUTURE VALUE AND PRESENT VALUE PROBLEMS (L.O. 2, 3, 5, 6)

1. **Future Value of a Single Amount**
   a. Future Value   =   Principal X FV Factor

   b. FV Factor   = $\dfrac{\text{Future Value}}{\text{Principal}}$

       (1) i unknown and n known or   Trace solved factor to Table 1.
       (2) n unknown and i known   Trace solved factor to Table 1.

2. **Future Value of an (Ordinary) Annuity**
   a. Future Value of an Ordinary Annuity   =   Rent X FVOA Factor

   b. Rent   = $\dfrac{\text{Future Value of an Ordinary Annuity}}{\text{FVOA Factor}}$

   c. FVOA Factor   = $\dfrac{\text{Future Value of An Ordinary Annuity}}{\text{Rent}}$

       (1) i unknown and n known, or   Trace solved factor to Table 2.
       (2) n unknown and i known   Trace solved factor to Table 2.

3. **Present Value of a Single Amount**
   a. Present Value   =   Future Amount X PV Factor

   b. PV Factor   = $\dfrac{\text{Present Value}}{\text{Future Value}}$

       (1) i unknown and n known, or   Trace solved factor to Table 3.
       (2) n unknown and i known   Trace solved factor to Table 3.

4. **Present Value of an (Ordinary) Annuity**
   a. Present Value of an Ordinary Annuity   =   Rent X PVOA Factor

   b. Rent   = $\dfrac{\text{Present Value of an Ordinary Annuity}}{\text{PVOA Factor}}$

   c. PVOA Factor   = $\dfrac{\text{Present Value of an Ordinary Annuity}}{\text{Rent}}$

       (1) i unknown and n known, or   Trace solved factor to Table 4.
       (2) n unknown and i known   Trace solved factor to Table 4.

ILLUSTRATION D-2 (Continued)

Abbreviations:

FV Factor	=	Future Value of 1 Factor
PV Factor	=	Present Value of 1 Factor
i	=	Interest Rate
n	=	Number of Periods or Rents
FVOA	=	Future Value of an (Ordinary) Annuity of 1 Factor
PVOA Factor	=	Present Value of an (Ordinary) Annuity of 1 Factor

TIP: "Principal" can be replaced by "Present value" in the formula for item 1 above. "Future value" and "future amount" are synonymous in items 1, 2, and 3 above.

ILLUSTRATION D-3
STEPS IN SOLVING FUTURE VALUE AND PRESENT VALUE PROBLEMS ILLUSTRATED (L.O. 2, 3, 4, 5, 6)

The steps in solving future value and present value problems (listed in **Illustration D-1**) are illustrated below and on the following pages:

Problem	**Solution**
1. If $10,000 is deposited in the bank today at 6% interest compounded annually, what will be the balance in 5 years?	**Step 1:** This is a future value of a single amount problem.
	Step 2: $n = 5$; $i = 6\%$

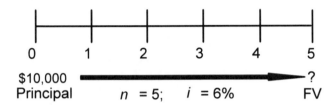

Step 3: The interest factor from Table 1 is 1.33823.

Step 4: Future Value = Principal X FV Factor
Future Value = $10,000 X 1.33823
Future Value = $13,382.30

2. A company needs $100,000 to retire debt when it matures two years from now. What amount must be deposited on Jan. 1, 2012 at 8% interest compounded semiannually in order to accumulate the desired sum by Jan. 1, 2014?

Step 1: This is a present value of a single amount problem.

Step 2: It is 2 years from 1/1/12 to 1/1/14. The annual interest rate is 8%. $n = 2 \times 2 = 4$; $i = 8\% \div 2 = 4\%$.

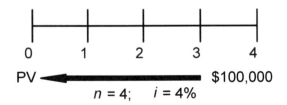

Step 3: The interest factor from Table 3 is .85480.

Step 4: Present Value = Future Amount X PV Factor
Present Value = $100,000 X .85480
Present Value = $85,480.00

3. If $71,178 can be invested now, what annual interest rate must be earned in order to accumulate $100,000 three years from now?

Step 1: This can be solved either as a future value or as a present value of a single amount problem. This solution illustrates the present value approach.

Step 2: $n = 3$; i must be solved for.

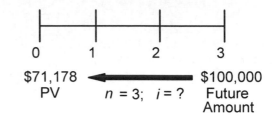

0   1   2   3

$71,178 ←——————— $100,000
PV $n = 3$; $i = ?$ Future
                              Amount

Step 3: i must be solved for.

Step 4: Present Value = Future Amount
                          X PV Factor
$71,178 = $100,000 X PV Factor
$71,178 ÷ $100,000 = PV Factor
.71178 = PV Factor
Refer to Table 3 in the 3 period row.
$\underline{i = 12\%}$.

4. If $1,000 is deposited into an account at the end of every year for six years, what will be the balance in the account after the sixth deposit if all amounts on deposit earn 6% interest?

Step 1: This a future value of an annuity problem.
Step 2: $n = 6$; $i = 6\%$

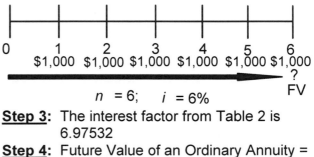

0   1   2   3   4   5   6
    $1,000 $1,000 $1,000 $1,000 $1,000 $1,000
                                                ?
                $n = 6$; $i = 6\%$ FV

Step 3: The interest factor from Table 2 is 6.97532
Step 4: Future Value of an Ordinary Annuity = Rent X FVOA Factor
Future Value of an Ordinary Annuity = $1,000 X 6.97532
Future Value of an Ordinary Annuity = $\underline{\$6,975.32}$

5. What amount was needed to be deposited at 10% in an account on Jan. 1, 2012 if it was desired to make equal annual withdrawals of $10,000 each, beginning on Jan. 1, 2013, and ending on Jan. 1, 2016?

Step: 1: This is a present value of an annuity problem.

Step: 2: The time diagram shows 4 withdrawals. $n = 4$; $i = 10\%$.

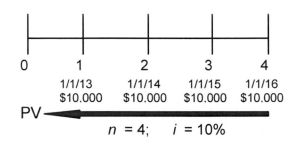

Step 3: The interest factor from Table 4 is 3.16986.

Step 4: Present Value of an Ordinary Annuity = Rent X PVOA Factor
Present Value of an Ordinary Annuity = $10,000 X 3.16986
Present Value of Ordinary Annuity = $31,698.60

6. What amount must be deposited at the end of each year in an account paying 6% interest if it is desired to have $10,000 at the end of the fifth year?

Step 1: This is a future value of an annuity problem.

Step 2: $n = 5$; $i = 6\%$.

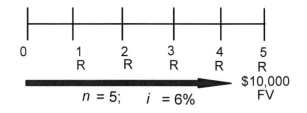

Step 3: The interest factor from Table 2 is 5.63709.

Step 4: Future Value of an Ordinary Annuity = Rent X FVOA Factor
$10,000 = Rent X 5.63709
$10,000 ÷ 5.63709 = Rent
Rent = $1,773.96

TIP: You can prove this solution by:
$1,773.96 X 5.63709 = $9,999.97
The difference of $.03 is due to rounding.

EXERCISE D-1

Purpose: (L.O. 2, 4, 5) This exercise will illustrate some key concepts such as (1) the more frequently interest is compounded, the more interest will accumulate and the lower the present value will be, and (2) the greater the interest rate, the lower the present value will be.

There are a wide variety of situations in which present value concepts must be applied. A few of them are illustrated in the questions that follow.

1.   If $1,000 is put on deposit today to earn 8% interest, how much will be on deposit at the end of 10 years if interest is compounded annually?

2.   If $1,000 is put on deposit today to earn 8% interest, how much will be on deposit at the end of 10 years if interest is compounded semiannually?

3.   In comparing questions 1 and 2, which answer would you expect to be the larger? Why?

4.   What is the value today of $1,000 due 10 years in the future if the time value of money is 8% and interest is compounded annually?

5.   What is the value today of $1,000 due 10 years in the future if the time value of money is 8% and interest is compounded semiannually?

6.   In comparing questions 4 and 5, which answer would you expect to be the larger? Why?

7.   What is the present value of $1,000 due in 10 years if interest is compounded annually at 10%?

8.   What is the present value of $1,000 due in 10 years if interest is compounded annually at 6%?

9.   In comparing questions 7 and 8, which answer would you expect to be the larger? Why?

Instructions
Answer each of the questions above. Interest tables are included at the end of this appendix. Use the appropriate factors where needed.

SOLUTION TO EXERCISE D-1

1.   (1)   This is a future value of a single amount problem.
     (2) $n = 10; i = 8\%$.

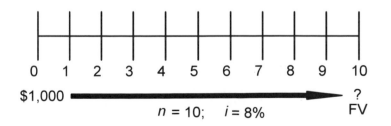

     (3)   The interest factor from Table 1 is 2.15892.
     (4)   Future Value = Principal X FV Factor
           Future Value = $1,000 X 2.15892
           Future Value = $2,158.92

2. (1) This is a future value of a single amount problem.
    (2) $n = 10 \times 2 = 20$; $i = 8\% \div 2 = 4\%$

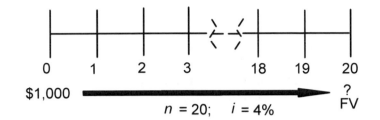

    (3) The interest factor from Table 1 is 2.19112.
    (4) Future Value = Principal X FV Factor
         Future Value = $1,000 X 2.19112
         Future Value = <u>$2,191.12</u>

3. We would expect the answer to question 2 to be a
    little larger than the answer to question 1 because
    the interest is compounded more frequently in
    question 2 which means there will be a larger
    amount of accumulated interest by the end of year
    10 in this scenario.

4. (1) This is a present value of a single amount problem.
    (2) $n = 10$; $i = 8\%$.

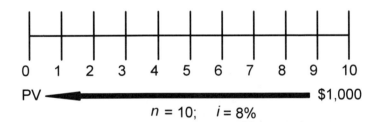

    (3) The interest factor from Table 3 is .46319.
    (4) Present Value = Future Amount X PV Factor
         Present Value = $1,000 X .46319
         Present Value = <u>$463.19</u>

5. (1) This is a present value of a single amount problem.
    (2) $n = 2 \times 10 = 20$; $i = 8\% \div 2 = 4\%$.

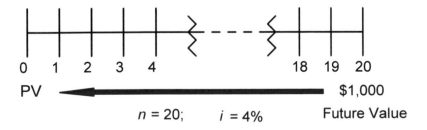

(3) The interest factor from Table 3 is .45639.
(4) Present Value = Future Amount X PV Factor
Present Value = $1,000 X .45639
Present Value = $456.39

6. We would expect the answer to question 4 to be the larger because the more frequently that interest is compounded, the more the total interest will be. The greater the interest, the less the present value. Thus, the answer to question 5 has more interest reflected and a lesser present value figure.

7. (1) This is a present value of a single amount problem.
    (2) $n = 10$; $i = 10\%$.

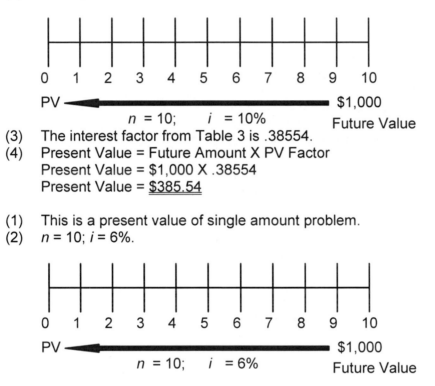

(3) The interest factor from Table 3 is .38554.
(4) Present Value = Future Amount X PV Factor
Present Value = $1,000 X .38554
Present Value = $385.54

8. (1) This is a present value of single amount problem.
    (2) $n = 10$; $i = 6\%$.

0   1   2   3   4   5   6   7   8   9   10

PV ◄━━━━━━━━━━━━━━━━━━━━━━━ $1,000
$n = 10$; $i = 6\%$ Future Value

(3) The interest factor from Table 3 is .55839.
(4) Present Value = Future Amount X PV Factor
Present Value = $1,000 X .55839
Present Value = $558.39

9. We would expect the answer to question 8 to be the larger because the smaller the discount rate, the larger the present value. This is the case because the interest amount is smaller. The less the interest, the greater the present value figure.

EXERCISE D-2

Purpose: (L.O. 7) This exercise will illustrate a situation that involves the present value of an annuity along with the present value of a single amount.

Bonds are being issued and the following facts are relevant:

1. Amount due at maturity $7,500,000
2. Interest payments are computed at a stated rate
    of 8% and are due semiannually $ 300,000
3. Effective rate of interest (discount rate) on an
    annual basis   12%
4. Term of the bonds   10 years

Instructions
Compute the present value of all of the promises embodied in the bond (maturity value of $7,500,000 plus semiannual interest payments of $300,000 each for 10 years).

SOLUTION TO EXERCISE D-2

Time diagram:

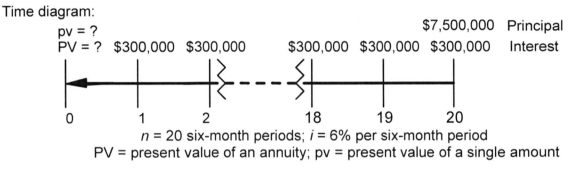

n = 20 six-month periods; i = 6% per six-month period
PV = present value of an annuity; pv = present value of a single amount

Present value of the principal = $7,500,000 X .31180 $2,338,500
Present value of the interest payments = $300,000 X 11.46992   3,440,976
Total present value of the bond liability $5,779,476

Approach: The present value of the bond liability is determined by discounting all of the future cash flows related to the bond issue back to the present date using the current market rate of interest (6% per six-month interest period). The face amount of the bonds ($7,500,000) is a single amount due in 10 years (20 semiannual periods). The interest payments constitute an ordinary annuity for twenty semiannual periods. Each $300,000 interest payment is computed by multiplying the stated rate (4% per interest period) by the face amount of the bonds ($7,500,000).

TIP:	The 8% stated rate must be expressed as 4% per six-month period before calculating the periodic $300,000 interest payment. Likewise, the 12% current market rate of interest (the effective rate) must be expressed on a per interest period basis (6%) before performing the present value computations.
TIP:	The amount described as Principal is a future amount in this context; this is **not** to be confused with a situation where the term "principal" refers to a present value figure as was demonstrated early in this appendix.
TIP:	The term principal, as it is used here, refers to the face value (face amount) of the bonds.

EXERCISE D-3

Purpose: (L.O. 2, 3, 5) This exercise will illustrate how to solve present value problems that require the computation of the rent in an annuity or the number of periods or the interest rate.

Instructions
Using the appropriate interest table, provide the solution to each of the following three questions by computing the unknowns.

(a)   Jimmy Gunshanan has $5,000 to invest today at 5% to pay a debt of $7,387. How many years will it take him to accumulate enough to liquidate the debt if interest is compounded once annually?

(b)   Jimmy's friend Nathan has a $6,312.40 debt that he wishes to repay four years from today. He intends to invest $5,000.00 for four years and use the accumulated funds to liquidate the debt. What rate of interest will he need to earn annually in order to accumulate enough to pay the debt if interest is compounded annually?

(c)   Jason Zahner wishes to accumulate $35,000 to use for a trip around the world. He plans to gather the designated sum by depositing payments into an account at Sun Bank which pays 4% interest, compounded annually. What is the amount of each payment that Jason must make at the end of each of six years to accumulate a fund balance of $35,000 by the end of the sixth year?

TIP: Calculated factors may not exactly match those on the interest tables. Use the closest match.

SOLUTION TO EXERCISE D-3

(a)   Time diagram:

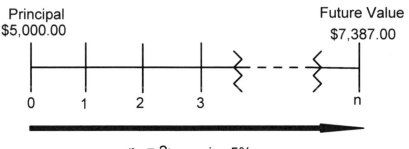

$$n = ?; \quad i = 5\%$$

Future Value Approach	**OR**	*Present Value Approach*
Future value = Principal X FV factor		Present value = Future value X PV factor
$7,387.00 = $5,000.00 X FV factor		$5,000.00 = $7,387.00 X PV factor
1.4774 = FV factor for i = 5%, n = ?		.67686 = PV factor for i = 5%, n = ?
By reference to Table 1, 1.47746 is		By reference to Table 3, .67684 is
the FV factor for i = 5%, n = 8		the PV factor for i = 5%, n = 8
n = <u>8 years</u>		n = <u>8 years</u>

(b)   Time diagram:

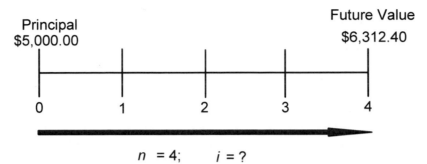

Principal
$5,000.00

Future Value
$6,312.40

0   1   2   3   4

$n = 4; \quad i = ?$

Future Value Approach
Future value = Principal X FV factor
$6,312.40 = $5,000.00 X FV factor
1.26248 = FV factor for $n = 4$, $i = ?$
By reference to Table 1, 1.26248 is
  the FV factor for $n = 4$, $i = 6\%$.
$i = \underline{6\%}$

OR   *Present Value Approach*
Present value = Future value X PV factor
$5,000.00 = $6,312.40 X PV factor
.79209 = PV factor for $n = 4$, $i = ?$
By reference to Table 3, .79209 is the
  PV factor for $n = 4$, $i = 6\%$
$i = \underline{6\%}$

(c)   Time diagram:

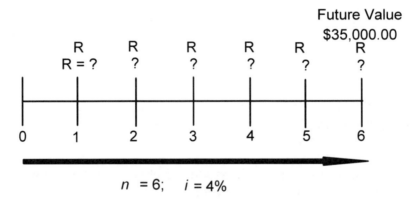

Future Value
$35,000.00

R   R   R   R   R   R
R = ?   ?   ?   ?   ?   ?

0   1   2   3   4   5   6

$n = 6; \quad i = 4\%$

R = rent

Future Value = Rent X FVOA Factor
By reference to Table 2, 6.63298 is the FVOA factor for $n = 6$, $i = 4\%$.
$35,000.00 = Rent X 6.63298
$35,000.00 ÷ 6.63298 = Rent
$\underline{\$5,276.66}$ = Rent

*ILLUSTRATION D-4
USING FINANCIAL CALCULATORS (L.O. 8)

Once you have mastered the underlying concepts in this chapter, you will find it extremely beneficial to learn how to solve time value of money problems by using a financial calculator. A business professional uses a financial calculator rather than the tables used in this chapter because most business applications involve an interest rate or time periods not provided in the interest tables. For example, most real life problems involve interest compounded monthly or daily. Thus a 6% annual rate compounded monthly for 5 years requires our calculations to use a .5% rate (not provided in the tables) for 60 periods (not provided in the tables). The most common keys used to solve time value of money problems are:

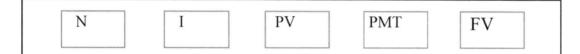

where

N	=	number of periods
I	=	interest rate per period (some calculators use I/YR or i)
PV	=	present value (occurs at the beginning of the first period)
PMT	=	payment (all payments are equal, and none are skipped)
FV	=	future value (occurs at the end of the last period)

On many calculators, these keys are actual buttons on the face of the calculator, on others, they appear on the display after the user accesses a present value menu.

In solving time value of money problems, you generally know (or are given) three of four variables and will solve for the remaining variable. The fifth key (the key not used) is given a value of zero to ensure that this variable is not used in the computation.

To illustrate the use of a financial calculator, let's assume that you want to know the future value of $10,000 invested to earn 8%, compounded annually for 5 years.

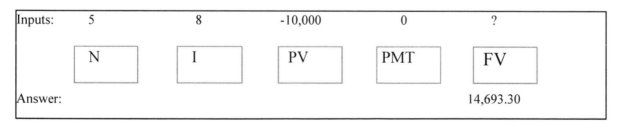

The diagram shows you the information (inputs) to enter into the calculator, N = 5, I = 8, PV = -10,000, and PMT is not used (or PMT = 0) because a series of payments did not occur in the problem. You press FV for the answer and the future value is $14,693.30. This is the same answer you would get using compound interest tables ($10,000 X 1.46933 = $14693.30).

The use of plus and minus signs in time value of money problems with a financial calculator can be confusing. Most financial calculators are programmed so that the positive and negative cash flows in any problem offset each other. In the future value problem above, we identified the $10,000 initial investment as a negative (outflow); the answer 14,693.30 was shown as a positive, reflecting a cash inflow. If the 10,000 were entered as a positive, then the final answer would have been reported as a negative (-14,693.30) If you understand what is required in a problem, you should be able to interpret a positive or negative amount in determining the solution to a problem.

In the problem above, we assumed that compounding occurs once a year. Some financial calculators have a default setting, which assumes that compounding occurs 12 times a year. You must determine what default period has been programmed into your calculator and change it as necessary to arrive at the proper compounding period.

Most financial calculators store and calculate using 12 decimal places. As a result, because compound interest tables generally have factors only up to 5 decimal places, a slight difference in the final answer can result. In most time value of money problems, the final answer will not include more than two decimal points.

To illustrate the future value of an ordinary annuity, assume that you are asked to determine the future value of five $1,000 deposits made at the end of each of the next 6 years, each of which earns interest at 6%, compounded annually. The setup is as follows:

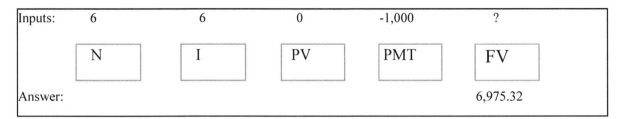

Inputs:	6	6	0	-1,000	?
	N	I	PV	PMT	FV
Answer:					6,975.32

In this case, you enter N = 6, I = 6, PV = 0, PMT = -1,000, and then press FV to arrive at the answer 6,975.32. The $1,000 payments are shown as negatives because the deposits represent cash outflows that will accumulate with interest to the amount to be received (cash inflow) at the end of 6 years.

Recall that in any annuity problem you must determine whether the periodic payments occur at the beginning or the end of the period. If the first payment occurs at the beginning of the period, most financial calculators have a key marked "Begin" (or "Due") that you press to switch from the end-of-period payment mode (for an ordinary annuity) to beginning-of-period payment mode (for an annuity due). For most calculators, the word BEGIN is displayed to indicate that the calculator is set for an annuity due problem. (Some calculators use DUE).

With a financial calculator you can solve for any interest rate or for any number of periods in a time value of money problem. For example, assume you are financing a car with a 3-year loan. The loan has a 9.5% nominal annual interest rate, compounded monthly. The price of the car is $6,000, and you want to determine the monthly payments, assuming that the payments start one month after the purchase.

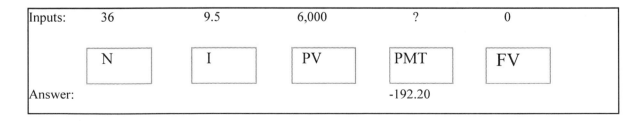

Inputs:	36	9.5	6,000	?	0
	N	I	PV	PMT	FV
Answer:				-192.20	

By entering N = 36 (12 x 3), I = 9.5, PV = 6,000, FV = 0, and then pressing PMT, you can determine that the monthly payments will be $192.20. Note that the payment key is usually programmed for 12 payments per year. Thus, you must change the default (compounding period) if the payments are different than monthly.

EXERCISE D-4

Purpose: (L.O. 8) This exercise will give you practice in using a financial calculator to solve problems involving the time value of money.

Interest is the cost of using the money of another entity. Each of the following two situations calls for you to compute the interest rate inherent in a set of facts.

a. Jacob Dobrofsky wishes to invest $19,000 on July 1, 2014, and have it accumulate to $49,000 by July 1, 2024.

   Instructions:
   Use a financial calculator to determine at what exact annual rate of interest Jacob must invest the $19,000.

b. On July 17, 2013, Elizabeth Dobrofsky borrowed $42,000 from her grandfather to open a clothing store. Starting July 17, 2014, Elizabeth has to make ten equal annual payments of $6,500 to repay the loan.

   Instructions:
   Use a financial calculator to determine what interest rate Elizabeth is paying.

SOLUTION TO EXERCISE D-4

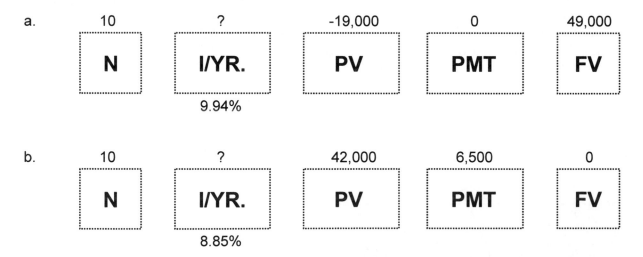

a.

| 10 | ? | -19,000 | 0 | 49,000 |
| N | I/YR. | PV | PMT | FV |

9.94%

b.

| 10 | ? | 42,000 | 6,500 | 0 |
| N | I/YR. | PV | PMT | FV |

8.85%

EXERCISE D-5

Purpose: (L.O. 1 thru 7) This exercise will quiz you about terminology used in this appendix.

At list of accounting terms with which you should be familiar appears below:

Annuity	Interest
Compound interest	Present value
Discounting the future amount(s)	Present value of an annuity
Future value of a single amount	Principal
Future value of an annuity	Simple interest

Instructions
For each item below, enter in the blank the term that is described.

1. _____The amount borrowed or invested.

2. _____A series of equal dollar amounts to be paid or received at evenly spaced time intervals (periodically).

3. _____Payment for the use of another's money.

4. _____The interest computed on the principal only.

5. _____The value at a future date of a given amount invested assuming compound interest.

6. _____The sum of all the rents (payments or receipts) plus the compound interest on them.

7. _____The value now of a given amount to be invested or received in the future assuming compound interest.

8. _____A series of future receipts or payments discounted to their value now (today) assuming compound interest.

9. _____The process of determining present value.

10. _____The interest computed on the principal and any interest earned that has not been paid or received.

SOLUTION TO EXERCISE D-5

1. Principal
2. Annuity
3. Interest
4. Simple interest
5. Future value of a single amount
6. Future value of an annuity
7. Present value
8. Present value of an annuity
9. Discounting the future amount(s)
10. Compound interest

ANALYSIS OF MULTIPLE-CHOICE TYPE QUESTIONS

1.   **Question**
     (L.O. 6) A grandfather wishes to set up a fund today that will allow his grandson to withdraw $5,000 from the fund at the end of each year for four years to pay for college expenses. The first withdrawal is to occur one year from today. How should grandpa compute the required investment if the fund is to earn 6% interest compounded annually and the fund is to be exhausted by the grandson's last withdrawal?
     a. $5,000 multiplied by the factor for the present value of 1 where $n = 4$, $i = 6\%$.
     b. $5,000 divided by the factor for the present value of 1 where $n = 4$, $i = 6\%$.
     c. $5,000 multiplied by the factor for the present value of an annuity of 1 where $n = 4$, $i = 6\%$.
     d. $5,000 divided by the factor for the present value of 1 where $n = 4$, $i = 6\%$.

     Approach and Explanation: Follow the steps in solving present value problems:

     1.   This is a present value of an annuity problem.
     2.   Time diagram:

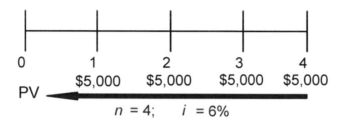

     3.   The factor for present value of an annuity of 1 for $n = 4$, $i = 6\%$ would be derived from Table 4.
     4.   Present Value of an Annuity = Rent X Present Value of an Annuity Factor

     Therefore, the present value of the annuity in question equals $5,000 multiplied by the factor for present value of annuity for $n = 4$, $i = 6\%$. (Solution = c.)

Questions 2 and 3 use the following present value table. Given below are the present value factors for $1.00 discounted at 9% for one to five periods.

	Present value of $1
Periods	**$i = 9\%$**
1	.91743
2	.84168
3	.77218
4	.70843
5	.64993

2.   **Question**
     (L.O. 5) What amount should be deposited in a bank account today if a balance of $1,000 is desired four years from today?
     a. $1,000 X .91743 X 4.
     b. $1,000 X .70843.
     c. $1,000 ÷ .70843.
     d. $1,000 X (.91743 + .84168 + .77218 + .70843).

     Approach and Explanation: Follow the steps in solving present value problems:
     1.   This is a present value of a single amount problem.
     2.   Time diagram:

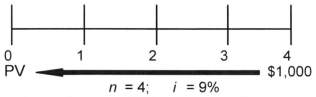

$n = 4; \quad i = 9\%$

3. The present value factor is .70843 for $n = 4$, $i = 9\%$.
4. Present Value = Future Amount X PV Factor
   Present Value = $1,000 X .70843 (Solution = b.)

3.   Question
(L.O. 2) If $1,000 is deposited today to earn 9% interest compounded annually, how much will be on deposit at the end of three years?
a. $1,000 X .77218.
b. $1,000 ÷ .77218.
c.   ($1,000 ÷ .91743) X 3.
d.   ($1,000 ÷ .77218) X 3.

Explanation:
1. This is a future value of a single amount problem.
2. Time diagram:

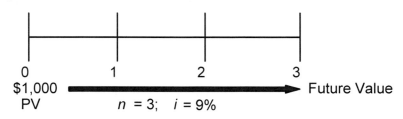

$n = 3; \quad i = 9\%$

3. The future value factor is not given in this question; however, for a single amount, the future value can be determined by using a present value factor as follows:

Present Value = Future Value X PV Factor

$$\frac{\text{Present Value}}{\text{PV Factor}} = \text{Future Value}$$

$$\frac{\$1,000}{.77218} = \text{Future Value}$$

(Solution = b.)

TIP: By looking at the time diagram, you can reason out that the amount on deposit at the end of three years should be greater than $1,000 but less than $1,500 (three years of 9% simple interest would give a balance of $1,270 and the compounding process would yield a little higher figure). In looking at the alternative answers, you can see that selection "a" will yield a result that is less than $1,000; selection "b" will give a result close to $1,300; selection "c" will give a result close to $3,300; and selection "d" will yield a result that is close to $3,900. Therefore, a reasonableness test would show that answer selection "b" must be the correct choice.

4. **Question**

(L.O. 2, 3, 5, 6) In the time diagram below, which concept is being depicted?

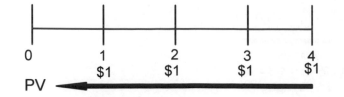

a. Present value of a single amount.
b. Present value of an annuity.
c. Future value of a single amount.
d. Future value of an annuity.

Explanation: It is an annuity since there is a series of equal periodic payments or receipts. The arrow is drawn so that it is headed back to the present rather than forward to the future. Thus, we have a present value problem. (Solution = b.)

5. **Question**

(L.O. 3, 6) A grandmother is setting up a savings account to help fund her granddaughter's college expenses. She is putting $40,000 in an account today that will earn 6% interest compounded annually. How much may Josey, the granddaughter, withdraw at the beginning of each of four years of college if her first withdrawal is to be one year from today and her last withdrawal is to exhaust the fund? The answer would be determined by which one of the following?

a. $40,000 multiplied by the factor for the present value of an annuity of 1 where
$n = 4, i = 6\%$.
b. $40,000 divided by the factor for the present value of an annuity of 1 where
$n = 4, i = 6\%$.
c. $40,000 multiplied by the factor for the future amount of an annuity of 1 where
$n = 4, i = 6\%$.
d. $40,000 divided by the factor for the future amount of an annuity of 1 where
$n = 4, i = 6\%$.

Approach and Explanation: Follow the steps in solving future value and present value problems.

1. This is a present value of an annuity problem. There are four rents and the first one is to be received a year from today.
2. Time diagram:

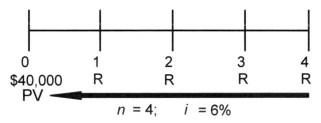

3. The factor for present value of an ordinary annuity for $n = 4, i = 6\%$ would be obtained from Table 4.
4. Present Value of an Ordinary Annuity = Rent X Present Value of an Ordinary Annuity Factor. The Rent would be determined by dividing both sides of the equation by the factor. Therefore, the rent would equal the $40,000 divided by the factor for the present value of an ordinary annuity of 1. (Solution = b.)

6.   **Question**
(L.O. 2) On May 1, 2014, a company purchased a new machine that it does not have to pay for until May 1, 2016. The total payment on May 1, 2016 will include both principal and accumulated interest. Assuming interest is computed at a 10% rate compounded annually, the total payment due will be the price of the machine multiplied by what time value of money factor?
a.   Future value of 1.
b.   Future value of an annuity of 1.
c.   Present value of 1.
d.   Present value of an annuity of 1.

Explanation: The total payment due will be the price today (present value) plus the interest that will accumulate in two years. In computing the future value of a given amount today, the given amount is multiplied by a future value of 1 factor. (Solution = a.)

7.   **Question**
(L.O. 2, 5) Which of the following statements is **true**?
a.   The higher the discount rate, the higher the present value.
b.   The process of accumulating interest on interest is referred to as discounting.
c.   If money is worth 10% compounded annually, $1,100 due one year from today is equivalent to $1,000 today.
d.   If a single amount is due on December 31, 2016, the present value of that amount decreases as the date draws closer to December 31, 2016.

Explanation: Selection "a" is false because the higher the discount rate the lower the present value. Selection "b" is false because the process of accumulating interest on interest is referred to as compounding; discounting refers to the process of computing present value. Selection "d" is false because the present value of a single amount increases over time due to the time value of money (accumulation of interest). Selection "c" is correct because 10% of $1,000 is $100 interest; $1,000 today plus interest of $100 for one year means $1,100 one year from today is equivalent to $1,000 today if money is worth 10%. (Solution = c.)

Table 1 FUTURE VALUE OF 1 (FUTURE VALUE OF A SINGLE AMOUNT)

TABLE 1 FUTURE VALUE OF 1 (FUTURE VALUE OF A SINGLE AMOUNT)									
(n) Periods	**4%**	**5%**	**6%**	**8%**	**9%**	**10%**	**11%**	**12%**	**15%**
1	1.04000	1.05000	1.06000	1.08000	1.09000	1.10000	1.11000	1.12000	1.15000
2	1.08160	1.10250	1.12360	1.16640	1.18810	1.21000	1.23210	1.25440	1.32250
3	1.12486	1.15763	1.19102	1.25971	1.29503	1.33100	1.36763	1.40493	1.52088
4	1.16986	1.21551	1.26248	1.36049	1.41158	1.46410	1.51807	1.57352	1.74901
5	1.21665	1.27628	1.33823	1.46933	1.53862	1.61051	1.68506	1.76234	2.01136
6	1.26532	1.34010	1.41852	1.58687	1.67710	1.77156	1.87041	1.97382	2.31306
7	1.31593	1.40710	1.50363	1.71382	1.82804	1.94872	2.07616	2.21068	2.66002
8	1.36857	1.47746	1.59385	1.85093	1.99256	2.14359	2.30454	2.47596	3.05902
9	1.42331	1.55133	1.68948	1.99900	2.17189	2.35795	2.55803	2.77308	3.51788
10	1.48024	1.62889	1.79085	2.15892	2.36736	2.59374	2.83942	3.10585	4.04556
11	1.53945	1.71034	1.89830	2.33164	2.58043	2.85312	3.15176	3.47855	4.65239
12	1.60103	1.79586	2.01220	2.51817	2.81267	3.13843	3.49845	3.89598	5.35025
13	1.66507	1.88565	2.13293	2.71962	3.06581	3.45227	3.88328	4.36349	6.15279
14	1.73168	1.97993	2.26090	2.93719	3.34173	3.79750	4.31044	4.88711	7.07571
15	1.80094	2.07893	2.39656	3.17217	3.64248	4.17725	4.78459	5.47357	8.13706
16	1.87298	2.18287	2.54035	3.42594	3.97031	4.59497	5.31089	6.13039	9.35762
17	1.94790	2.29202	2.69277	3.70002	4.32763	5.05447	5.89509	6.86604	10.76126
18	2.02582	2.40662	2.85434	3.99602	4.71712	5.55992	6.54355	7.68997	12.37545
19	2.10685	2.52695	3.02560	4.31570	5.14166	6.11591	7.26334	8.61276	14.23177
20	2.19112	2.65330	3.20714	4.66096	5.60441	6.72750	8.06231	9.64629	16.36654

–

Appendix D: Time Value of Money **D-25**

Table 2 FUTURE VALUE OF AN ANNUITY OF 1

TABLE 2
FUTURE VALUE OF AN ANNUITY OF 1

(n) Periods	4%	5%	6%	8%	9%	10%	11%	12%	15%
1	1.00000	1.00000	1.00000	1.00000	1.00000	1.00000	1.00000	1.00000	1.00000
2	2.04000	2.05000	2.06000	2.08000	2.09000	2.10000	2.11000	2.12000	2.15000
3	3.12160	3.15250	3.18360	3.24640	3.27810	3.31000	3.34210	3.37440	3.47250
4	4.24646	4.31013	4.37462	4.50611	4.57313	4.64100	4.70973	4.77933	4.99338
5	5.41632	5.52563	5.63709	5.86660	5.98471	6.10510	6.22780	6.35285	6.74238
6	6.63298	6.80191	6.97532	7.33592	7.52334	7.71561	7.91286	8.11519	8.75374
7	7.89829	8.14201	8.39384	8.92280	9.20044	9.48717	9.78327	10.08901	11.06680
8	9.21423	9.54911	9.89747	10.63663	11.02847	11.43589	11.85943	12.29969	13.72682
9	10.58280	11.02656	11.49132	12.48756	13.02104	13.57948	14.16397	14.77566	16.78584
10	12.00611	12.57789	13.18079	14.48656	15.19293	15.93743	16.72201	17.54874	20.30372
11	13.48635	14.20679	14.97164	16.64549	17.56029	18.53117	19.56143	20.65458	24.34928
12	15.02581	15.91713	16.86994	18.97713	20.14072	21.38428	22.71319	24.13313	29.00167
13	16.62684	17.71298	18.88214	21.49530	22.95339	24.52271	26.21164	28.02911	34.35192
14	18.29191	19.59863	21.01507	24.21492	26.01919	27.97498	30.09492	32.39260	40.50471
15	20.02359	21.57856	23.27597	27.15211	29.36092	31.77248	34.40536	37.27972	47.58041
16	21.82453	23.65749	25.67253	30.32428	33.00340	35.94973	39.18995	42.75328	55.71747
17	23.69751	25.84037	28.21288	33.75023	36.97371	40.54470	44.50084	48.88367	65.07509
18	25.64541	28.13238	30.90565	37.45024	41.30134	45.59917	50.39593	55.74972	75.83636
19	27.67123	30.53900	33.75999	41.44626	46.01846	51.15909	56.93949	63.43968	88.21181
20	29.77808	33.06595	36.78559	45.76196	51.16012	57.27500	64.20283	72.05244	102.44358

—

Table 3 PRESENT VALUE OF 1 (PRESENT VALUE OF A SINGLE AMOUNT)

(n) Periods	4%	5%	6%	8%	9%	10%	11%	12%	15%
	TABLE 3 **PRESENT VALUE OF 1 (PRESENT VALUE OF A SINGLE AMOUNT)**								
1	.96154	.95238	.94340	.92593	.91743	.90909	.90090	.89286	.86957
2	.92456	.90703	.89000	.85734	.84168	.82645	.81162	.79719	.75614
3	.88900	.86384	.83962	.79383	.77218	.75132	.73119	.71178	.65752
4	.85480	.82270	.79209	.73503	.70843	.68301	.65873	.63552	.57175
5	.82193	.78353	.74726	.68058	.64993	.62092	.59345	.56743	.49718
6	.79031	.74622	.70496	.63017	.59627	.56447	.53464	.50663	.43233
7	.75992	.71068	.66506	.58349	.54703	.51316	.48166	.45235	.37594
8	.73069	.67684	.62741	.54027	.50187	.46651	.43393	.40388	.32690
9	.70259	.64461	.59190	.50025	.46043	.42410	.39092	.36061	.28426
10	.67556	.61391	.55839	.46319	.42241	.38554	.35218	.32197	.24719
11	.64958	.58468	.52679	.42888	.38753	.35049	.31728	.28748	.21494
12	.62460	.55684	.49697	.39711	.35554	.31863	.28584	.25668	.18691
13	.60057	.53032	.46884	.36770	.32618	.28966	.25751	.22917	.16253
14	.57748	.50507	.44230	.34046	.29925	.26333	.23199	.20462	.14133
15	.55526	.48102	.41727	.31524	.27454	.23939	.20900	.18270	.12289
16	.53391	.45811	.39365	.29189	.25187	.21763	.18829	.16312	.10687
17	.51337	.43630	.37136	.27027	.23107	.19785	.16963	.14564	.09293
18	.49363	.41552	.35034	.25025	.21199	.17986	.15282	.13004	.08081
19	.47464	.39573	.33051	.23171	.19449	.16351	.13768	.11611	.07027
20	.45639	.37689	.31180	.21455	.17843	.14864	.12403	.10367	.06110

–

Table 4 PRESENT VALUE OF AN ANNUITY OF 1

(n) Periods	4%	5%	6%	8%	9%	10%	11%	12%	15%
				TABLE 4					
			PRESENT VALUE OF AN ANNUITY OF 1						
1	.96154	.95238	.94340	.92593	.91743	.90909	.90090	.89286	.86957
2	1.88609	1.85941	1.83339	1.78326	1.75911	1.73554	1.71252	1.69005	1.62571
3	2.77509	2.72325	2.67301	2.57710	2.53130	2.48685	2.44371	2.40183	2.28323
4	3.62990	3.54595	3.46511	3.31213	3.23972	3.16986	3.10245	3.03735	2.85498
5	4.45182	4.32948	4.21236	3.99271	3.88965	3.79079	3.69590	3.60478	3.35216
6	5.24214	5.07569	4.91732	4.62288	4.48592	4.35526	4.23054	4.11141	3.78448
7	6.00205	5.78637	5.58238	5.20637	5.03295	4.86842	4.71220	4.56376	4.16042
8	6.73274	6.46321	6.20979	5.74664	5.53482	5.33493	5.14612	4.96764	4.48732
9	7.43533	7.10782	6.80169	6.24689	5.99525	5.75902	5.53705	5.32825	4.77158
10	8.11090	7.72173	7.36009	6.71008	6.41766	6.14457	5.88923	5.65022	5.01877
11	8.76048	8.30641	7.88687	7.13896	6.80519	6.49506	6.20652	5.93770	5.23371
12	9.38507	8.86325	8.38384	7.53608	7.16073	6.81369	6.49236	6.19437	5.42062
13	9.98565	9.39357	8.85268	7.90378	7.48690	7.10336	6.74987	6.42355	5.58315
14	10.56312	9.89864	9.29498	8.24424	7.78615	7.36669	6.98187	6.62817	5.72448
15	11.11839	10.37966	9.71225	8.55948	8.06069	7.60608	7.19087	6.81086	5.84737
16	11.65230	10.83777	10.10590	8.85137	8.31256	7.82371	7.37916	6.97399	5.95424
17	12.16567	11.27407	10.47726	9.12164	8.54363	8.02155	7.54879	7.11963	6.04716
18	12.65930	11.68959	10.82760	9.37189	8.75563	8.20141	7.70162	7.24967	6.12797
19	13.13394	12.08532	11.15812	9.60360	8.95012	8.36492	7.83929	7.36578	6.19823
20	13.59033	12.46221	11.46992	9.81815	9.12855	8.51356	7.96333	7.46944	6.25933

–

APPENDIX E

. . . .

*P*AYROLL ACCOUNTING

OVERVIEW

Payroll and related fringe benefits often constitute a substantial percentage of current liabilities. In addition, employee compensation is often the most significant expense that a company incurs.

The proper accounting and control of payroll are very important to a business. Payroll accounting involves more than paying employees' salaries and wages. Companies are required by law to maintain payroll records for each employee, file and pay payroll taxes, and comply with numerous state and federal tax laws applicable to employee compensation. Accounting for payroll has become much more complex as a result of these regulations.

SUMMARY OF LEARNING OBJECTIVES

1. **Compute and record the payroll for a pay period.** The computation of the payroll involves gross earnings, payroll deductions, and net pay. In recording the payroll, Salaries and Wages Expense is debited for gross earnings, individual tax and other liability accounts are credited for payroll deductions, and Salaries and Wages Payable is credited for net pay. When the payroll is paid, Salaries and Wages Payable is debited, and Cash is credited.

2. **Describe and record employer payroll taxes.** Employer payroll taxes consist of FICA, federal unemployment taxes, and state unemployment taxes. The taxes are usually accrued at the time the payroll is recorded by debiting Payroll Tax Expense and crediting separate liability accounts for each type of tax.

3. **Discuss the objectives of internal control for payroll.** The objectives of internal control for payroll are (1) to safeguard company assets against unauthorized payments of payrolls, and (2) to ensure the accuracy and reliability of the accounting records pertaining to payrolls.

EXERCISE E-1

Purpose: (L.O. 1, 2) This exercise will review the computations and journal entries relating to payroll accounting.

Hunt Enterprises has six salaried office employees who get paid on the last day of each month. Information about employee earnings for the current month (December 2014) and cumulative earnings for the first eleven months of 2014 appear on the next page. Data on federal income tax withholdings and health insurance withholdings is also provided.

The tax rates in effect are as follows:

FICA: 8% on gross earnings of up to $50,000
Federal unemployment taxes: 0.8% on gross earnings of up to $7,000
State unemployment taxes: 5.4% on gross earnings of up to $7,000

Instructions
(a)   Compute the following items for December 2014 for each employee listed and fill in your answers on the schedule provided.
   1.   Employee FICA tax.
   2.   Employee's take-home pay.
   3.   Employer FICA tax.
   4.   Federal unemployment tax.
   5.   State unemployment tax.
(b)   Prepare the journal entries to record:
   1.   The December 31, 2014 payroll.
   2.   The payroll tax expense associated with the December 31, 2014 payroll.
   3.   The payment of the December 31, 2014 payroll.
(c)   Explain how the balances of the payable accounts will be reported on the financial statements.

TIP: Fixed amounts of compensation paid per week, month, or even per year, regardless of the number of hours worked during the designated period, are referred to as **salaries**. When an employee is paid a certain amount per hour, per day, or per unit, the compensation is referred to as **wages.** The wage rate multiplied by actual employee activity equals the amount of an employee's earnings for the period.

(a)

EMPLOYEE	Cumulative Earnings for Year up to Current Period	Earnings for Current Period (Mo. of Dec.)	Federal Income Tax Withheld This Period	Health Insurance Premiums Withheld This Period	(1) Employee FICA Tax	(2) Employee Take-home Pay	(3) Employer FICA Tax	(4) Federal Unemploy-ment Tax	(5) State Unemploy-ment Tax
James	$55,000.00	$ 5,000.00	$1,500.00	$100.00					
Mary Ann	8,800.00	800.00	140.00	50.00					
Ryan	1,500.00	500.00	100.00	50.00					
Cathy	2,100.00	700.00	80.00	100.00					
Margaret	16,500.00	1,500.00	200.00	100.00					
Diane	48,400.00	4,400.00	1,320.00	100.00					
Totals		$12,900.00	$3,340.00	500.00					

SOLUTION TO EXERCISE E-1

(a)

EMPLOYEE	Cumulative Earnings for Year up to Current Period	Earnings for Current Period (Mo. of Dec.)	Federal Income Tax Withheld This Period	Health Insurance Premiums Withheld This Period	(1) Employee FICA Tax	(2) Employee Take-home Pay	(3) Employer FICA Tax	(4) Federal Unemployment Tax	(5) State Unemployment Tax
James	$55,000.00	$5,000.00	$1,500.00	$100.00	$ 0[a]	$3,400.00	$ 0[a]	$ 0[b]	$ 0[b]
Mary Ann	8,800.00	800.00	140.00	50.00	64.00	546.00	64.00	0[b]	0[b]
Ryan	1,500.00	500.00	100.00	50.00	40.00[c]	310.00[d]	40.00[c]	4.00[e]	27.00[f]
Cathy	2,100.00	700.00	80.00	100.00	56.00	464.00	56.00	5.60	37.80
Margaret	16,500.00	1,500.00	200.00	100.00	120.00	1,080.00	120.00	0[b]	0[b]
Diane	48,400.00	4,400.00	1,320.00	100.00	128.00[g]	2,852.00	128.00[g]	0[b]	0[b]
Totals		$12,900.00	$3,340.00	500.00	408.00	8,652.00	408.00	9.60	64.80

[a]Cumulative earnings this year exceed $50,000.00 limit.
[b]Cumulative earnings this year exceed $7,000.00 limit.
[c]$500.00 X 8% = $40.00
[d]$500.00 - $100.00 - $50.00 - $40.00 = $310.00
[e]$500.00 X .8% = $4.00

[f]$500.00 X 5.4% = $27.00
[g]$50,000.00 - $48,400.00 = $1,600.00
$1,600.00 X 8% = $128.00

(b) 1. Dec. 31 Salaries and Wages Expense............................... 12,900.00
            Federal Income Tax Withholdings Payable.......   3,340.00
            Health Insurance Payable...............................   500.00
            FICA Taxes Payable 408.00
            Salaries and Wages Payable..........................   8,652.00
            (To record payroll for the month ending
            December 31)

    2. Dec. 31 Payroll Tax Expense 482.40
            FICA Taxes Payable 408.00
            Federal Unemployment Taxes Payable 9.60
            State Unemployment Taxes Payable...............   64.80
            (To record employer's payroll taxes on
            December 31 payroll)

    3. Dec. 31 Salaries and Wages Payable................................ 8,652.00
            Cash...   8,652.00
            (To record payment of payroll)

(c) At December 31, 2014, the balances in Federal Income Tax Withholdings Payable, Health Insurance Payable, FICA Taxes Payable, Federal Unemployment Taxes Payable, and Statement Unemployment Taxes Payable will be classified in the current liability section of the balance sheet because they are all obligations that become due shortly after the balance sheet date and will require the use of current assets to liquidate them.

Explanation:
* An amount equal to 8% of an employee's gross earnings is withheld from the employee's paycheck and is remitted to the federal government for FICA taxes. This represents the employee's share of the FICA tax.

* An employee's **net pay** (or **take-home pay**) is calculated by the following:
            Employee's gross earnings for the current period
        - Federal income tax withholdings
        - FICA tax withholdings
        - Withholdings for voluntary deductions such as for charitable contributions, group health and life insurance premiums, savings, retirement fund contributions, and loan repayments
        = Net (or take-home) pay

* The employer must also bear a portion of the FICA tax. The FICA tax applies on earnings up to a certain level ($50,000 in this exercise). The employee James had surpassed this level prior to December so no FICA taxes are due on him for December. The employee Diane has only $1,600 ($50,000 - $48,400) of her December pay subject to the FICA tax because her December earnings put her cumulative earnings over the $50,000 threshold.

* The employer must bear the federal unemployment tax which is .8% on the employee's first $7,000 of gross earnings from that employer for the current year. Only Ryan and Cathy are still subject to that tax in this exercise.

* The employer must bear the state unemployment tax which is 5.4% on the employee's first $7,000 of gross earnings from that employer for the current year. Only the earnings of Ryan and Cathy are still subject to that tax in this exercise.

TIP:	State income tax withholdings are treated in the same manner as the federal income tax withholdings. Voluntary deductions for union dues, charitable contributions, and the like are handled in the same manner as the health insurance premiums above.
TIP:	The tax rate and earnings base for the FICA tax that are used in this exercise do not represent what is currently in effect. The rate and base for this tax changes so frequently that an assumed rate and base are used here for simplicity. The same can be said for the tax rate and earnings base for the unemployment taxes. The Medicare portion of the FICA tax typically has a higher earnings base than the Social Security portion; that has been ignored in this exercise.

EXERCISE E-2

Purpose: (L.O. 1 thru 3) This exercise will quiz you about terminology used in this chapter.

A list of accounting terms with which you should be familiar appears below:

Bonus
Employee earnings record
Employee's Withholding Allowance Certificate (Form ?
Federal unemployment taxes
Fees
FICA taxes
Gross earnings
Net pay

Payroll deductions
Payroll register
Salaries
Statement of earnings
State unemployment taxes
Wage and Tax Statement (Form W-2)
Wages

Instructions
For each item below, enter in the blank the term that is described.

1. _____Specified amounts per month or per year paid to executive and administrative personnel.

2. _____Amounts paid to employees based on a rate per hour or on a piece-work basis.

3. _____Compensation to management personnel and other employees based on factors such as increased sales or the amount of net income.

4. _____Total compensation earned by an employee. Sometimes called **gross pay.**

5. _____Deductions from gross earnings to determine the amount of a paycheck.

6. _____A payroll record that accumulates the gross earnings, deductions, and net pay by employee for each pay period.

7. _____Gross earnings less payroll deductions. Sometimes called **take-home pay.**

8. _____An Internal Revenue Service form on which the employee indicates the number of allowances claimed for withholding of federal income taxes.

9. _____Taxes imposed on the employer that provides benefits for a limited time period to employees who lose their jobs through no fault of their own; the taxing authority is the federal government.

10. _____Taxes designed to provide workers with supplemental retirement, employment disability, and medical benefits.

11. _____A cumulative record of each employee's gross earnings, deductions, and net pay during the year.

12. _____Taxes imposed on the employer that provides benefits to employees who lose their jobs; the taxing authority is a state government.

13. _____A form showing gross earnings, FICA taxes withheld, and income taxes withheld which is prepared annually by an employer for each employee.

14. _____A document attached to a paycheck that indicates the employee's gross earnings, payroll deductions, and net pay.

15. _____Payments made for the services of professionals.

SOLUTION TO EXERCISE E-2

1. Salaries
2. Wages
3. Bonus
4. Gross earnings
5. Payroll deductions
6. Payroll register
7. Net pay
8. Employee's Withholding Allowance Certificate (Form W-4)
9. Federal unemployment taxes
10. FICA taxes
11. Employee earnings record
12. State unemployment taxes
13. Wage and Tax Statement (Form W-2)
14. Statement of earnings
15. Fees

ANALYSIS OF MULTIPLE-CHOICE TYPE QUESTIONS

1. **Question**
   (L.O. 1) An employee's net pay is determined by gross earnings minus amounts for income tax withholdings,
   a.   employee's portion of FICA taxes, and unemployment taxes.
   b.   employee's and employer's portion of FICA taxes, and unemployment taxes.
   c.   employee's portion of FICA taxes, unemployment taxes, and any voluntary deductions.
   d.   employee's portion of FICA taxes, and any voluntary deductions.

   Approach and Explanation: Before you read the answer selections, write down the model for the net pay (take-home pay) computation. Then find the answer selection that agrees with your model.
        Employee's gross earnings for the current period
   -   Federal income tax withholdings
   -   FICA tax withholdings
   -   Withholdings for voluntary deductions such as for charitable contributions, group health and life insurance premiums, savings, retirement fund contributions, and loan repayments
   =   Net (or take-home) pay

   (Solution = d.)

2. **Question**
    (L.O. 2) Which group of items would be recorded in the Payroll Tax Expense account?
    a. Employer's share of FICA taxes, federal unemployment tax, state unemployment tax.
    b. Federal and state income tax withholdings, all FICA taxes, federal unemployment tax, state unemployment tax.
    c. Federal and state income tax withholdings, employer's share of FICA taxes, federal and state unemployment taxes, union dues.
    d. Employer's share of FICA taxes, federal and state unemployment taxes, union dues, insurance premiums, contributions to charitable organizations.

    Approach and Explanation: Think of the payroll taxes the employer must bear; they are the ones recorded in the Payroll Tax Expense account. Payroll taxes borne by the employer include the employer's share of FICA tax and all unemployment taxes (both federal and state). Taxes withheld from an employee's payroll check (employee's share of FICA and income tax withholdings) represent a portion of the employee's total earnings (gross pay); therefore, they are in effect charged (debited) to a wages and salaries expense account. (Solution = a.)

3. **Question**
    (L.O. 2) Which group of items represents a cost burden for the employer rather than the employee?
    a. Federal income tax withholdings, employer's portion of FICA tax, state unemployment tax.
    b. Employer's portion of FICA tax, state unemployment tax, federal unemployment tax.
    c. Employer's and employee's portions of FICA tax, federal unemployment tax, state unemployment tax.
    d. Federal income tax withholdings, state income tax withholdings, employer's share of FICA taxes, federal unemployment tax, state unemployment tax.

    Explanation: The items to be borne by the employer include the employer's share of FICA tax and all unemployment taxes (both state and federal). Items which must be borne by an employee include the employee's share of FICA tax, federal income tax withholdings, state income tax withholdings, city income tax withholdings, and voluntary deductions. (Solution = b.)

4. **Question**
    (L.O. 1) Deductions from an employee's earnings may include:
    a. withholdings for federal and state income tax.
    b. FICA tax.
    c. union dues.
    d. amounts for purchase of savings bonds for employee.
    e. all of the above.

    Explanation: See **Explanation to Question 3** above. (Solution = e.)

APPENDIX F

. . . .

SUBSIDIARY LEDGERS AND SPECIAL JOURNALS

OVERVIEW

As transactions increase in number, so do the recordings and postings required to account for business activities. To deal with the large quantity of transactions, the accountant employs (1) special journals to efficiently organize and expedite the recording and posting process for transactions which occur frequently and (2) subsidiary ledgers to free the general ledger of details. A business may have a computerized accounting system or it may rely on a manual system. The steps in the accounting cycle remain the same whether or not the system is automated.

SUMMARY OF LEARNING OBJECTIVES

1. **Describe the nature and purpose of a subsidiary ledger.** A subsidiary ledger is a group of accounts with a common characteristic. It facilitates the recording process by freeing the general ledger from details of individual balances.

2. **Explain how special journals are used in journalizing.** Companies use special journals to group similar types of transactions. In a special journal, generally only one line is used to record a complete transaction.

3. **Indicate how a columnar journal is posted.** In posting a multi-column journal:
   (a) Companies post all column totals except for the Other Accounts column once at the end of the month to the account title specified in the column heading.
   (b) Companies do not post the total of the Other Accounts column. Instead, the individual amounts comprising the total are posted separately to the general ledger accounts specified in the Account Credited (Debited) column.
   (c) The individual amounts in a column posted in total to a control account are posted daily to the subsidiary ledger accounts specified in the Account Credited (Debited) column.

TIPS ON CHAPTER TOPICS

TIP:	It is sometimes confusing for a beginning accounting student to differentiate between subsidiary ledgers and special journals. It may help to think about how **special journals** are used **to record similar transactions** in a common place (such as all sales on account are recorded in the sales journal); thus, special journals are used in the recording process. All transactions affect accounts. **Subsidiary ledgers** are used to **group similar accounts** in a common place (such as an account receivable for each customer is included in the accounts receivable ledger); thus, subsidiary ledgers are used in the posting process.
TIP:	The **cash payments journal** is often called the **cash disbursements journal.**

EXERCISE F-1

Purpose: (L.O. 1) This exercise will test your understanding of the postings that appear in a subsidiary ledger.

Presented below is the account for the vendor, Kitchen Plastics Company, as it appears in the accounts payable subsidiary ledger of Great Value Hardware.

KITCHEN PLASTICS COMPANY

Date		Ref.	Debit	Credit	Balance
2014					
Jan.	1				17,000
	3	P17		22,000	39,000
	8	P18		13,000	52,000
	9	CP25	17,000		35,000
	11	G5	5,000		30,000
	17	CP28	30,000		-0-

Instructions
Explain each amount reflected in this subsidiary ledger account.

SOLUTION TO EXERCISE F-1

Jan. 1   The account started the period with a beginning balance of $17,000. This balance was the result of unpaid purchases from the prior period.

Jan. 3   A posting of $22,000 from page 17 of the purchases journal (P17) indicates that purchases of $22,000 were made on credit.

Jan. 8   A posting of $13,000 from page 18 of the purchases journal (P18) indicates that purchases of $13,000 were made on credit.

Jan. 9   A posting of $17,000 from page 25 of the cash payments journal (CP25) indicates that a cash payment of $17,000 was made to Kitchen Plastics on account.

Jan. 11   A debit posting of $5,000 from page 5 of the general journal (G5) probably stems from a purchase return or allowance.

Jan. 17 A posting of $30,000 from page 28 of the cash payments journal (CP28) indicates that a cash payment of $30,000 was made to the vendor on account.

TIP:	Think about the normal balance of an account payable—credit balance. Think about common reasons for increases (credits) and for decreases (debits). Identify the source of each posting by the abbreviation in the Ref. column. The transactions being posted should then be fairly evident.
TIP:	In addition to having subsidiary ledgers for accounts receivable and accounts payable, it is not uncommon for a business to also use control accounts and subsidiary ledgers for other accounts such as inventory (when a perpetual system is used), equipment, and selling and administrative expenses.

EXERCISE F-2

Purpose: (L.O. 2) This exercise will help you identify the journal in which to record specific transactions.

A list of abbreviations and a list of transactions (in random order) follow:

Abbreviations
S = Two-Column Sales Journal
CR = Multiple-Column Cash Receipts Journal
P = Single-Column Purchases Journal
CP = Multiple-Column Cash Payments Journal
GJ = Two-Column General Journal

Instructions
For each transaction, indicate the journal in which it would be recorded.

Transactions

_____ 1. Sold merchandise for cash.

_____ 2. Purchased merchandise for cash.

_____ 3. Made an adjusting entry for accrued salaries.

_____ 4. Made collection on an accounts receivable.

_____ 5. Paid rent for the month.

_____ 6. Accepted a note receivable from a customer in settlement of an account receivable.

_____ 7. Paid salaries for the current period.

_____ 8. Wrote a check to buy treasury stock.

_____ 9. Returned merchandise to a supplier for credit.

_____ 10. Sold merchandise on account.

_____ 11. Purchased merchandise on account.

_____ 12. Purchased equipment for cash.

_____   13.   Purchased equipment on account.

_____   14.   Purchased office supplies for cash.

_____   15.   Purchased office supplies on account.

_____   16.   Recorded depreciation on equipment for the period.

_____   17.   Received return of merchandise from a customer who had purchased it on credit. Issued a credit memorandum.

_____   18.   Recorded an adjustment for supplies used.

_____   19.   Recorded an adjustment for insurance which had expired.

_____   20.   Paid freight bill on purchases of merchandise inventory.

_____   21.   Loaned money to an employee.

_____   22.   Paid for merchandise which had been purchased on account. Paid within the discount period.

_____   23.   Recorded accrued revenue.

_____   24.   Paid the utilities bill.

_____   25.   Closed the temporary accounts.

_____   26.   Removed merchandise inventory from shelf for owner's personal use.

_____   27.   Paid a creditor after the 2% discount period lapsed.

_____   28.   Gave a cash refund to a customer who returned merchandise.

_____   29.   Paid freight on goods shipped to a customer FOB destination.

_____   30.   Collected revenue in advance.

_____   31.   Paid for an insurance premium one year in advance.

_____   32.   Received an additional investment of cash from an owner.

_____   33.   Sold inventory on credit.

_____   34.   Purchased inventory on credit.

_____   35.   Received a cash refund from a supplier upon return of merchandise.

_____   36.   Collected interest from employee who borrowed money.

SOLUTION TO EXERCISE F-2

1.	CR	10.	S	19.	GJ	28.	CP
2.	CP	11.	P	20.	CP	29.	CP
3.	GJ	12.	CP	21.	CP	30.	CR
4.	CR	13.	GJ	22.	CP	31.	CP
5.	CP	14.	CP	23.	GJ	32.	CR
6.	GJ	15.	GJ	24.	CP	33.	S
7.	CP	16.	GJ	25.	GJ	34.	P
8.	CP	17.	GJ	26.	GJ	35.	CR
9.	GJ	18.	GJ	27.	CP	36.	CR

Approach and Explanation: Keep in mind that a special journal is used to record similar types of transactions, such as all sales of merchandise or all cash receipts. Write down a brief description of the types of transactions to be recorded in each of the journals used in this exercise. They are:

   Sales journal—all sales of merchandise on account.
   Cash receipts journal—all receipts of cash (including cash sales).
   Purchases journal—all purchases of merchandise on account.
   Cash payments journal—all payments of cash (including cash purchases).
   General journal—all transactions that do not appropriately fit in a special journal (including adjustments and closing entries).

Identify the transactions that involve sales of merchandise on credit (items 10 and 33). They go in the sales journal. Identify the transactions that involve purchases of merchandise on account (items 11 and 34). They go in the purchases journal. Identify the transactions that involve the receipt of cash (items 1, 4, 30, 32, 35, and 36). They are to be recorded in the cash receipts journal.

Identify the transactions that involve a cash payment (items 2, 5, 7, 8, 12, 14, 20, 21, 22, 24, 27, 28, 29, and 31). They go in the cash payments journal. Identify the transactions that do not fit those first four categories (items 3, 6, 9, 13, 15, 16, 17, 18, 19, 23, 25, and 26). They go in the general journal. (Notice that items 3, 16, 18, 19 and 23 are adjusting entries and item 25 involves closing entries.)

EXERCISE F-3

Purpose: (L.O. 2, 3) This exercise reviews general ledger accounts and postings to them from special journals.

A list of abbreviations and a list of postings to general ledger accounts (in random order) follow:

Abbreviations

S = Two-Column Sales Journal
CR = Multiple-Column Cash Receipts Journal
P = Single-Column Purchases Journal
CP = Multiple-Column Cash Payments Journal
GJ = Two-Column General Journal

Instructions
For each of the postings to general ledger accounts listed below, indicate the most common source of the posting. Use the appropriate abbreviations to indicate your answer for each. (Assume all purchases of merchandise inventory and sales are made on account. Assume a perpetual inventory system is in use.)

Postings to General Ledger Accounts

_____ 1. Debits to Merchandise Inventory	_____ 13. Debits to Prepaid Insurance
_____ 2. Credits to Sales	_____ 14. Credits to Prepaid Insurance
_____ 3. Debits to Accounts Payable	_____ 15. Debits to Office Supplies on Hand
_____ 4. Credits to Accounts Payable	_____ 16. Credits to Office Supplies on Hand
_____ 5. Debits to Cash	
_____ 6. Credits to Cash	_____ 17. Credits to Bank Loans Payable
_____ 7. Debits to Accounts Receivable	_____ 18. Credits to Unearned Revenue
_____ 8. Credits to Accounts Receivable	_____ 19. Debits to Unearned Revenue
_____ 9. Credits to Interest Payable	_____ 20. Credits to Wages and Salaries Expense
_____ 10. Debits to Postage Expense	
_____ 11. Debits to Wages and Salaries Expense	_____ 21. Debits to Repairs Expense
_____ 12. Debits to Depreciation Expense	_____ 22. Credits to Interest Revenue

SOLUTION TO EXERCISE F-3

1.	P	7.	S	13.	CP	19.	GJ
2.	S	8.	CR	14.	GJ	20.	GJ
3.	CP	9.	GJ	15.	CP	21.	CP
4.	P	10.	CP	16.	GJ	22.	CR
5.	CR	11.	CP	17.	CR		
6.	CP	12.	GJ	18.	CR		

Approach and Explanation: Briefly describe the columns typically found in each of the special journals listed. Match them up with the postings in this exercise. The remainder of the postings has to come from the general journal (items 9, 12, 14, 16, 19, and 20).

Sales journal: Debit to Accounts Receivable } one
                       Credit to Sales   } column

                       Debit to Cost of Goods Sold   } one
                       Credit to Merchandise Inventory } column

Cash receipts journal: Debit to Cash
                               Debit to Sales Discounts
                               Credit to Accounts Receivable
                               Credit to Sales
                               Credit to Other Accounts (such as Interest Revenue, Notes Receivable, and Investments)

Purchases journal: Debit to Merchandise Inventory } one
                          Credit to Accounts Payable   } column

Cash payments journal: Credit to Cash
                              Credit to Merchandise Inventory
                              Debit to Accounts Payable
                              Debit to Other Accounts (such as Prepaid Insurance,
                                  Merchandise Inventory, Treasury Stock, Dividends, and various
                                  expense accounts)

> **TIP:**   Keep in mind that posting to a given account describes one-half of the dual effect of one transaction. For example, a posting "Debits to Advertising Expense" describes an increase in advertising expense. The most common transaction increasing advertising expense is the payment for advertising services. All cash payments are recorded in the cash payments journal. Therefore, the most common source of the posting of debits to the Advertising Expense account is the cash payments journal. For a second example, a posting "Credits to Interest Revenue" describes an increase in interest revenue. Although the Interest Revenue account can be increased at the end of a period because of an adjusting entry in the general journal to record accrued interest (revenue that has been earned but not received), the most common reason for having an increase in Interest Revenue is the collection of interest during a period. All cash collections are recorded in the cash receipts journal.
>
> **TIP:**   Remember that all transactions involving a receipt of cash go in the cash receipts journal, and all transactions involving a payment of cash go in the cash payments journal.

EXERCISE F-4

Purpose: (L.O. 1, 2) This exercise will discuss why a business employs special journals and subsidiary ledgers.

Up until this point, we have assumed that all transactions are recorded in the general journal and posted to the general ledger. In this chapter, we find that even small businesses can expedite the recording process by the use of special journals and subsidiary ledgers.

Instructions
(a)   Explain the advantages of using special journals.
(b)   Explain the advantages of using subsidiary ledgers.

SOLUTION TO EXERCISE F-4

(a)   The main advantages of using special journals are that they:
   (1)   **Permit greater division of labor** by allowing several individuals to record entries in different journals at the same time. For example, one employee may be responsible for journalizing all cash receipts, and another for journalizing all credit sales.
   (2)   **Reduce the time necessary to record and post transactions** by eliminating the need to repeatedly write out account titles in the general journal and by dramatically cutting down on the number of postings required to the general ledger. Monthly postings to some accounts may be substituted for daily postings.

(b)   The advantages of using subsidiary ledgers are that they:
   (1)   **Show transactions affecting one customer or one creditor in a single account,** thus providing necessary up-to-date information on specific account balances.
   (2)   **Free the general ledger of excessive details.** As a result, a trial balance of the general ledger does not contain a vast number of individual account balances.

(3)   **Help locate errors in individual accounts** by reducing the number of accounts combined in one ledger and by using controlling accounts.

(4)   **Make possible a division of labor** in posting by having one employee post to the general ledger and a different employee(s) post to the subsidiary ledgers.

> **TIP:**   A company may employ any number of special journals. A special journal can be designed to record any type of transaction that occurs frequently. The four special journals typically found in a merchandising entity are discussed in this chapter: sales journal, cash receipts journal, single-column purchases journal, and the cash payments journal. If a company finds it frequently has a transaction that is not recorded in one of these journals, it can design another special journal. For example, frequent sales returns for credit against the customers' account receivable balances would indicate the usefulness of designing a two-column sales returns journal. Amounts in the one column would get posted as debits to Sales Returns and credits to Accounts Receivable. Each return would also be individually posted to the customer's account in the accounts receivable subsidiary ledger. Amounts in the second column would get posted as debits to Merchandise Inventory and credits to Cost of Goods Sold. Amounts in the first column are selling prices of merchandise returned; amounts in the second column represent the cost of merchandise returned.

EXERCISE F-5

Purpose: (L.O. 2) This exercise will allow you to practice recording transactions in the sales journal and the cash receipts journal.

PW Company's chart of accounts includes the following **selected** accounts:

101	Cash		401	Sales
111	Accounts Receivable		415	Sales Discounts
120	Merchandise Inventory		416	Sales Returns
211	Accounts Payable		511	Cost of Goods Sold
311	Common Stock		521	Utilities Expense

PW Company has four customers. The following balances appeared in PW Company's accounts receivable subsidiary ledger at July 1, 2014:

Charlie Calhoun	$170
Charlie Daly	0
Bill Jackson	0
Jan Larson	105
Total	$275

PW Company uses a perpetual inventory system. A list of selected transactions for July 2014 for PW Company follows. The sales journal and the cash receipts journal follow that list.

Transactions

July	3	Sold merchandise to Charlie Daly for $100 on account; terms 2/10, n/30, Invoice No. 240. The cost of the merchandise sold was $60.
	5	Sold merchandise to Charlie Calhoun for $150 cash. Cost was $90.
	6	Sold merchandise to Jan Larson for $80 on account; terms n/30, Invoice No. 241. Cost was $60.
	10	Sold merchandise to Charlie Daly for $50 cash. Cost was $30.
	11	Sold merchandise to Bill Jackson for $200 on account; terms 2/10, n/30, Invoice No. 242. Cost was $140
	12	Collected $98 from Charlie Daly for the July 3 transaction.
	13	Sold merchandise to Jan Larson for $630 on credit; terms n/30, Invoice No. 243. Cost was $315
	14	Sold merchandise to Bill Jackson for $350 on account; terms 2/10, n/30, Invoice No. 244. Cost was $210.
	15	Sold merchandise to Charlie Daly for $600 on account; terms 2/10, n/30, Invoice No. 245. Cost was $300.

July 18   Collected $105 from Jan Larson on account for a credit sale made in June, no sales discount taken.

19   Collected $170 from Charlie Calhoun on account, no sales discount taken.

20   Collected $80 from Jan Larson on account.

20   Collected $196 from Bill Jackson for the sale on July 11.

23   Collected $343 from Bill Jackson for the sale on July 14.

25   Sold merchandise to Charlie Calhoun for $1,420 on credit; terms 2/10, n/30, Invoice No. 246. Cost was $980.

28   Sold common stock to John Purdy; deposited the proceeds of $800 cash into the company's bank account.

29   Received a $200 cash refund from a vendor for defective merchandise which was returned.

30   Received a $50 cash refund from the utility company because of an error in last month's billing. PW had paid the bill before the error was detected.

PW COMPANY
Sales Journal

S5

Date	Account Debited	Invoice No.	Ref.	Accounts Receivable Dr. Sales Cr.	Cost of Goods Sold Dr. Merchandise Inventory Cr.

PW COMPANY
Cash Receipts Journal

CR7

Date	Account Credited	Ref.	Cash Dr.	Sales Discounts Dr.	Accounts Receivable Cr.	Sales Cr.	Other Accounts Cr.	Cost of Goods Sold Dr. Mdse. Inv. Cr.

Instructions
(a) Journalize the transactions above in the sales journal and the multiple-column cash receipts journal.
(b) Foot and cross-foot the two journals at July 31, 2014.

SOLUTION TO EXERCISE F-5

(a)

PW COMPANY
Sales Journal

S5

Date		Account Debited	Invoice No.	Ref.	Accounts Receivable Dr. Sales Cr.	Cost of Goods Sold Dr. Merchandise Inv. Cr.
2014						
July	3	Charlie Daly	240		100	60
	6	Jan Larson	241		80	60
	11	Bill Jackson	242		200	140
	13	Jan Larson	243		630	315
	14	Bill Jackson	244		350	210
	15	Charlie Daly	245		600	300
	25	Charlie Calhoun	246		1,420	980
					3,380	2,065

PW COMPANY
Cash Receipts Journal

CR7

Date	Account Credited	Ref.	Cash Dr.	Sales Discounts Dr.	Accounts Receivable Cr.	Sales Cr.	Other Accounts Cr.	Cost of Goods Sold Dr. Mdse. Inv. Cr.
2014								
July 5			150			150		90
10			50			50		30
12	Charlie Daly		98	2	100			
18	Jan Larson		105		105			
19	Charlie Calhoun		170		170			
20	Jan Larson		80		80			
20	Bill Jackson		196	4	200			
23	Bill Jackson		343	7	350			
28	Common Stock		800				800	
29	Mdse. Inventory		200				200	
30	Utilities Expense		50				50	
			2,242	13	1,005	200	1,050	120

TIP: Purchase returns for cash are recorded in the cash receipts journal. Returns to suppliers on credit are recorded in the general journal unless a special journal for credit returns is established.

TIP: Nothing appears in the reference column in this solution because no instructions were given regarding postings. Recall, however, that amounts are usually posted to the subsidiary ledger daily. Postings will be illustrated in the next exercise.

TIP: When a periodic (rather than perpetual) inventory system is used, the sales journal will have only a single column (for Accounts Receivable Dr. and Sales Cr.)

(b)   **To foot** a journal means to sum each column in the journal. Thus, adding the amounts in the two columns in the sales journal constitutes footing the journal. There are six individual columns of figures to be added to foot the cash receipts journal. **To cross-foot** a journal means to prove the equality of the debits and credits recorded therein. Because each of the two columns in the sales journal has a total that gets posted both as a debit and a credit, there is nothing to cross-foot. In the cash receipts journal, the totals of the debit columns are added together ($2,242 + $13 = $2,255) and are compared to the sum of the totals of the credit columns ($1,005 + $200 + $1,050 = $2,255). Because the two grand totals equal, the journal is said to cross-foot. (The cost of good sold column total gets posted as both a debit and a credit so it does not enter into the cross-footing process.)

EXERCISE F-6

Purpose: (L.O. 1, 3) This exercise illustrates the relationship of the accounts receivable subsidiary ledger to the Accounts Receivable control account in the general ledger.

PW Company has four customer accounts in its accounts receivable ledger. The following balances appeared in that subsidiary ledger at July 1, 2014:

Charlie Calhoun	$170
Charlie Daly	0
Bill Jackson	0
Jan Larson	105
Total	$275

The cash receipts journal and the sales journal for July are reproduced below (from the **Solution to Exercise F-5).**

The accounts receivable subsidiary ledger and **selected** accounts from the general ledger appear below. Some accounts have a balance at July 1, 2014 as shown.

Instructions
(a)   Post the transactions to both the general ledger and the subsidiary ledger accounts. (Show the appropriate cross references in both the journals and the ledgers.)
(b)   Prove the agreement of the subsidiary ledger and its control account.
(c)   Explain how an accountant unfamiliar with a company could examine your work and determine the following:
   1.   What accounts are to receive postings from the sales journal?
   2.   Have the postings been completed to the general ledger accounts?
   3.   Have the postings been completed to the subsidiary ledger accounts?
   4.   What was the source of the $50 credit to the Utilities Expense account on July 30?

> **TIP:**   If you wish to more closely simulate a real life situation, you will post the transactions in chronological order. If you post all of the transactions in the sales journal before you post the transactions in the cash receipts journal, you should end up with the correct ending balances, but your postings will appear in an order different than the order shown in the solution presented below.
>
> **TIP:**   All credit sales are recorded in the sales journal, and all cash sales are recorded in the cash receipts journal so all sales transactions for July have been entered in the appropriate journals. However, a number of other transactions are not reflected in this exercise because they appear in the purchases journal, the cash payments journal, and the general journal and are, therefore, not included in this exercise.

(a)

PW COMPANY
Sales Journal

S5

Date		Account Debited	Invoice No.	Ref.	Accounts Receivable Dr. Sales Cr.	Cost of Goods Sold Dr. Merchandise Inv. Cr.
2014						
July	3	Charlie Daly	240		100	60
	6	Jan Larson	241		80	60
	11	Bill Jackson	242		200	140
	13	Jan Larson	243		630	315
	14	Bill Jackson	244		350	210
	15	Charlie Daly	245		600	300
	25	Charlie Calhoun	246		1,420	980
					3,380	2,065

PW COMPANY
Cash Receipts Journal

CR7

Date		Account Credited	Ref.	Cash Dr.	Sales Discounts Dr.	Accounts Receivable Cr.	Sales Cr.	Other Accounts Cr.	Cost of Goods Sold Dr. Mdse. Inv. Cr.
2014									
July	5			150			150		90
	10			50			50		30
	12	Charlie Daly		98	2	100			
	18	Jan Larson		105		105			
	19	Charlie Calhoun		170		170			
	20	Jan Larson		80		80			
	20	Bill Jackson		196	4	200			
	23	Bill Jackson		343	7	350			
	28	Common Stock		800				800	
	29	Mdse. Inventory		200				200	
	30	Utilities Expense		50				50	
				2,242	13	1,005	200	1,050	120

ACCOUNTS RECEIVABLE SUBSIDIARY LEDGER

Charlie Calhoun

Date	Explanation	Ref.	Debit	Credit	Balance
July 1	Balance	√			170

Charlie Daly

Date	Explanation	Ref.	Debit	Credit	Balance
July 1	Balance	√			0

Bill Jackson

Date	Explanation	Ref.	Debit	Credit	Balance
July 1	Balance	√			0

Jan Larson

Date	Explanation	Ref.	Debit	Credit	Balance
July 1	Balance	√			105

GENERAL LEDGER

Cash   No. 101

Date	Explanation	Ref.	Debit	Credit	Balance
July 1	Balance	√			1,400

Accounts Receivable   No. 111

Date	Explanation	Ref.	Debit	Credit	Balance
July 1	Balance	√			275

Merchandise Inventory   No. 120

Date	Explanation	Ref.	Debit	Credit	Balance
July 1	Balance	√			4,800

Common Stock   No. 311

Date	Explanation	Ref.	Debit	Credit	Balance
July 1	Balance	√			5,000

Sales   No. 401

Date	Explanation	Ref.	Debit	Credit	Balance
July 1	Balance	√			54,000

Sales Discounts   No. 415

Date	Explanation	Ref.	Debit	Credit	Balance
July 1	Balance	√			100

Cost of Goods Sold — No. 511

Date	Explanation	Ref.	Debit	Credit	Balance
July 1	Balance	√			30,000

Utilities Expense — No. 521

Date	Explanation	Ref.	Debit	Credit	Balance
July 1	Balance	√			1,300

SOLUTION TO EXERCISE F-6

(a)

PW COMPANY
Sales Journal

S5

Date	Account Debited	Invoice No.	Ref.	Accounts Receivable Dr. Sales Cr.	Cost of Goods Sold Dr. Merchandise Inv. Cr.
2014					
July 3	Charlie Daly	240	√	100	60
6	Jan Larson	241	√	80	60
11	Bill Jackson	242	√	200	140
13	Jan Larson	243	√	630	315
14	Bill Jackson	244	√	350	210
15	Charlie Daly	245	√	600	300
25	Charlie Calhoun	246	√	1,420	980
			√	3,380	2,065
				(111) (401)	(511) (120)

TIP: Practically all states and cities require a sales tax be charged on items sold, which the company must remit to the state or city. In this case, it is desirable to add an additional credit column to the sales journal for Sales Tax Payable. Sales Tax Payable is posted in total at the end of the month, similar to sales. Accounting for sales taxes is **not** illustrated in this exercise.

PW COMPANY
Cash Receipts Journal

CR7

Date	Account Credited	Ref.	Cash Dr.	Sales Discounts Dr.	Accounts Receivable Cr.	Sales Cr.	Other Accounts Cr.	Cost of Goods Sold Dr. Mdse. Inv. Cr.
2014								
July 5			150			150		90
10			50			50		30
12	Charlie Daly	√	98	2	100			
18	Jan Larson	√	105		105			
19	Charlie Calhoun	√	170		170			
20	Jan Larson	√	80		80			
20	Bill Jackson	√	196	4	200			
23	Bill Jackson	√	343	7	350			
28	Common Stock	311	800				800	
29	Mdse. Inventory	120	200				200	
30	Utilities Expense	521	50				50	
			2,242	13	1,005	200	1,050	120
			(101)	(415)	(111)	(401)	(X)	(511) (120)

ACCOUNTS RECEIVABLE SUBSIDIARY LEDGER

Charlie Calhoun

Date	Explanation	Ref.	Debit	Credit	Balance
July 1	Balance	√			170
19		CR7		170	0
25		S5	1,420		1,420

Charlie Daly

Date	Explanation	Ref.	Debit	Credit	Balance
July 1	Balance	√			0
3		S5	100		100
12		CR7		100	0
15		S5	600		600

Bill Jackson

Date	Explanation	Ref.	Debit	Credit	Balance
July 1	Balance	√			0
11		S5	200		200
14		S5	350		550
20		CR7		200	350
23		CR7		350	0

Jan Larson

Date	Explanation	Ref.	Debit	Credit	Balance
July 1	Balance	√			105
6		S5	80		185
13		S5	630		815
18		CR7		105	710
20		CR7		80	630

GENERAL LEDGER

Cash   No. 101

Date	Explanation	Ref.	Debit	Credit	Balance
July 1	Balance	√			1,400
31		CR7	2,242		3,642

Accounts Receivable   No. 111

Date	Explanation	Ref.	Debit	Credit	Balance
July 1	Balance	√			275
31		S5	3,380		3,655
31		CR7		1,005	2,650

Merchandise Inventory   No. 120

Date	Explanation	Ref.	Debit	Credit	Balance
July 1	Balance	√			4,800
29		CR7		200	4,600
31		S5		2,065	2,535
31		CR7		120	2,415

Common Stock   No. 311

Date	Explanation	Ref.	Debit	Credit	Balance
July 1	Balance	√			5,000
28		CR7		800	5,800

Sales   No. 401

Date	Explanation	Ref.	Debit	Credit	Balance
July 1	Balance	√			54,000
31		S5		3,380	57,380
31		CR7		200	57,580

Sales Discounts   No. 415

Date		Explanation	Ref.	Debit	Credit	Balance
July	1	Balance	√			100
	31		CR7	13		113

Cost of Goods Sold   No. `511

Date		Explanation	Ref.	Debit	Credit	Balance
July	1	Balance	√			30,000
	31		S5	2,065		32,065
	31		CR7	120		32,185

Utilities Expense   No. 521

Date		Explanation	Ref.	Debit	Credit	Balance
July	1	Balance	√			1,300
	30		CR7		50	1,250

TIP: The accounts listed above all have a single balance column. Therefore, the balance is assumed to be a normal balance for that type of account (debit versus credit) unless the balance is in brackets ( ) or is circled or is printed in red ink, in which case the balance is an abnormal one.

TIP: Total debits do not equal total credits in the general ledger accounts shown because only **selected** accounts are being illustrated in this exercise. The Merchandise Inventory account does not reflect any purchases made during July because the Purchases Journal is not illustrated in this exercise.

TIP: Examine the "Account Credited" column of the cash receipts journal. Notice that a subsidiary ledger account title is entered in that column whenever the entry involves an account receivable. Whereas, a general ledger account title is entered in that column whenever the entry involves an account that is not the subject of a special column (and an amount is entered in the "Other Accounts" column). No account title is entered in the "Account Credited" column if neither of the foregoing applies.

(b)   **Accounts Receivable Subsidiary Ledger**

Charlie Calhoun	$1,420
Charlie Daly	600
Bill Jackson	0
Jan Larson	630
	$2,650

Balance at July 31 per the Accounts Receivable account in the general ledger $2,650

(c)   1.   The accounts to receive postings from the sales journal can be determined by reading the single money column heading in that journal—Accounts Receivable Dr. and Sales Cr.

2.   An independent reviewer can readily see that the postings have been completed to the general ledger accounts because the relevant general ledger account numbers appear in parentheses below the totals of the money columns in the special journals. For example, the account numbers 111 (Accounts Receivable) and 401 (Sales) appear below the total of the first money column in the sales journal because that total was posted to both the Accounts Receivable account and the Sales account in the general ledger. The account number 101 (Cash) appears below the "Cash" column of the cash receipts journal, and so forth.

The transactions recorded in the cash receipts journal which affect accounts **other** than the accounts for which there are special money columns have been posted to those other accounts as can be determined by the relevant account numbers appearing in the Ref. column (311 for Common Stock, 120 for Merchandise Inventory and 521 for Utilities Expense).

3.   The completion of a posting to a subsidiary account is indicated by a "√" in the Ref. column of a special journal. All postings have been completed from the sales journal because there is a √ in the Ref. column on every used line. All postings have been completed from the cash receipts journal because a "√" appears in the Ref. column on every line that contains a **subsidiary ledger account title** in the Account Credited column.

4.   The source of the $50 credit to the Utilities Expense account on July 30 can be determined by looking in the Ref. column in the general ledger account for Utilities Expense. The posting for $50 on July 30 came from CR7 which stands for page 7 of the cash receipts journal.

TIP: A **control** account in the general ledger is often referred to as the **controlling** account for the related subsidiary ledger. Thus, the Accounts Receivable account is a controlling account for the accounts receivable subsidiary ledger.

TIP: Regardless of the journal in which it is recorded, a transaction involving a subsidiary ledger account must be posted to that subsidiary ledger account as well as to the control account in the general ledger.

TIP: The process of reconciling or proving a control account and its related subsidiary ledger consists of three steps:
(a)   Compute the balance of each account in the subsidiary ledger.
(b)   Add up (total) the balances of the subsidiary accounts.
(c)   Compare this total with the control account balance.

Any differences between the control account and the subsidiary ledger must be found and corrected.

TIP: Typically, postings from the special journals are made **daily** to the subsidiary ledgers; postings from the special journals are made **monthly** to the general ledger. For example, postings from the sales journal are made daily to the individual accounts receivable in the accounts receivable subsidiary ledger and monthly to the control account in the general ledger. For a second example, postings from the cash payments journal are made daily to the individual accounts payable in the accounts payable subsidiary ledger and monthly to the Accounts Payable control account in the general journal.

EXERCISE F-7

Purpose: (L.O. 2) This exercise will allow you to practice recording transactions in the purchases journal and the cash payments journal.

E & Y Company's chart of accounts includes the following selected accounts:

101	Cash	401	Sales
111	Accounts Receivable	415	Sales Discounts
120	Merchandise Inventory	416	Sales Returns
131	Prepaid Insurance	511	Cost of Goods Sold
140	Supplies	521	Utilities Expense
150	Equipment	522	Advertising Expense
211	Accounts Payable	523	Rent Expense
311	Ray Groves, Capital		

A list of selected transactions for June 2014 for E & Y Company (a sole proprietorship) appears below. The purchases journal and the cash payments journal follow that list.

Transactions

June	1	Purchased merchandise, check no. 103, $800.
	3	Purchased merchandise on account from Ed Hastings, Inc., invoice no. 1272, terms 2/10, n/30, $1,800.
	4	Purchased equipment on credit from Val Edmonds, Inc., $3,000.
	5	Purchased supplies on account from PV Roddy, $300.
	6	Purchased merchandise on account from Earl Elbert, invoice no. 1521, terms 2/10, n/30, $1,500.
	7	Purchased merchandise, check no. 104, $1,200.
	10	Purchased merchandise on account from Ed Hastings, Inc., invoice no. 1490, terms 2/10, n/30, $2,000.
	12	Paid Ed Hastings, Inc. for invoice no. 1272, $1,800 less 2% discount, check no. 105, $1,764.
	13	Paid Val Edmonds, Inc., $3,000 on account, check no. 106.
	14	Paid an advertising agency for ads to appear in June, check no. 107, $400.
	15	Purchased merchandise on account from Earl Elbert, invoice no. 1706, terms 2/10, n/30, $1,300.
	16	Paid premium due on a one-year insurance policy, check no. 108, $600.
	17	Paid PV Roddy on account, $300, check no. 109.
	18	Issued check no. 110 for $1,500 to Earl Elbert for payment on account.
	19	Paid Ed Hastings, Inc., in full for invoice no. 1490, $1,960, check no. 111.
	20	Purchased merchandise on account, from Earl Elbert, invoice no. 1811, terms 2/10, n/30, $1,400.
	21	Paid $75 for utilities, check no. 112.
	22	Paid $400 for rent for June, check no. 113.
	23	Purchased supplies on account from PV Roddy, $420.
	24	Paid Earl Elbert for invoice no. 1706, $1,300 less 2% discount, check no. 114, $1,274.
	26	Purchased supplies for cash, check no. 115, $100.
	27	Purchased merchandise for cash, $200, check no. 116.

Purchases Journal

P1

Date	Account Credited	Terms	Ref.	Merchandise Inventory Dr. Accounts Payable Cr.

Cash Payments Journal

CP1

Date	Ck. No.	Account Debited	Ref.	Other Accounts Dr.	Accounts Payable Dr.	Merchandise Inventory Cr.	Cash. Cr.

Instructions

(a) Journalize the transactions above in the single-column purchases journal and multi-column cash payments journal provided.

(b) Identify any transactions which must be recorded in a journal other than these two special journals.

(c) Foot and cross-foot the two special journals at June 30, 2014.

SOLUTION TO EXERCISE F-7

Purchases Journal

P1

Date		Account Credited	Terms	Ref.	Merchandise Inventory Dr. Accounts Payable Cr.
2014					
June	3	Ed Hastings, Inc.	2/10, n/30		1,800
	6	Earl Elbert	2/10, n/30		1,500
	10	Ed Hastings, Inc.	2/10, n/30		2,000
	15	Earl Elbert	2/10, n/30		1,300
	20	Earl Elbert	2/10, n/30		1,400
					8,000

Cash Payments Journal

CP1

Date		Ck. No.	Account Debited	Ref.	Other Accounts Dr.	Accounts Payable Dr.	Merchandise Inventory Cr.	Cash Cr.
2014								
June	1	103	Mdse. Inventory		800			800
	7	104	Mdse. Inventory		1,200			1,200
	12	105	Ed Hastings, Inc.			1,800	36	1,764
	13	106	Val Edmonds, Inc.			3,000		3,000
	14	107	Advertising Exp.		400			400
	16	108	Prepaid Ins.		600			600
	17	109	PV Roddy			300		300
	18	110	Earl Elbert			1,500		1,500
	19	111	Ed Hastings, Inc.			2,000	40	1,960
	21	112	Utilities Exp.		75			75
	22	113	Rent Exp.		400			400
	24	114	Earl Elbert			1,300	26	1,274
	26	115	Supplies		100			100
	27	116	Mdse. Inventory		200			200
					3,775	9,900	102	13,573

TIP: The **cash payments journal** is often called the **cash disbursements journal.**

(b)   Transactions which must be recorded in other journals are:

		Transactions	Journal
June	4	Purchased equipment on credit, $3,000	General Journal
	5	Purchased supplies on account, $300	General Journal
	23	Purchased supplies on account, $420	General Journal

> **TIP:** Some companies expand the purchases journal to include all types of purchases on account. Instead of one column for purchases of merchandise on credit (requiring postings to both Merchandise Inventory and Accounts Payable), a multiple-column format is used. The multiple-column format usually includes a credit column for accounts payable and debit columns for purchases of merchandise, purchases of office supplies, purchases of store supplies, and other accounts. A special column can be added for purchases of equipment if the activity warrants it.
>
> **TIP:** The general journal is used to record transactions that do not occur with enough frequency to warrant the creation of a special journal.

(c)   Footing is accomplished by adding the amounts of each column and inserting the totals at the bottom of the respective columns. There is nothing to cross-foot in a single-column journal because there is only one column. The cash payments journal is cross-footed by summing the totals of the debit columns ($3,775 +$9,900 = $13,675) and comparing that sum with the sum of the totals of the credit columns ($102 + $13,573 = $13,675). The two sums are equal so the journal cross-foots. This means the equality of the debits and credits entered in that journal has been proven.

EXERCISE F-8

Purpose: (L.O. 1 thru 3) This exercise will quiz you about terminology used in this chapter.

A list of accounting terms with which you should be familiar appear below.

Accounts payable (creditors') subsidiary ledger   Purchases journal
Accounts receivable (customers') subsidiary ledger   Sales journal
Cash payments (disbursements) journal   Special journal
Cash receipts journal   Subsidiary ledger
Control account

Instructions
For each item below, enter in the blank the term that is described.

1.   _____A journal that is used to record similar types of transactions such as all credit sales.

2.   _____A special journal used to record all sales of merchandise on account (on credit).

3.   _____A special journal used to record all cash received.

4.   _____A special journal used to record all purchases of merchandise on account (on credit).

5.   _____A special journal used to record all cash paid.

6.   _____A group of accounts with a common characteristic.

7.   _____A subsidiary ledger that contains accounts with individual creditors.

8. _____A subsidiary ledger that contains individual customer accounts.

9. _____An account in the general ledger that controls a subsidiary ledger.

SOLUTION TO EXERCISE F-8

1. Special journal
2. Sales journal
3. Cash receipts journal
4. Purchases journal
5. Cash payments (disbursements) journal
6. Subsidiary ledger
7. Accounts payable (creditors') subsidiary ledger
8. Accounts receivable (customers') subsidiary ledger
9. Control account

ANALYSIS OF MULTIPLE-CHOICE TYPE QUESTIONS

1. **Question**
   (L.O. 1) A general ledger account which summarizes the collection of related accounts appearing in a subsidiary ledger is called a:
   a.   contra account.
   b.   control account.
   c.   summary account.
   d.   subsidiary ledger account.

   Explanation: The subsidiary ledger reduces the number of accounts that otherwise would appear in the general ledger. The details about an item (such as accounts receivable or accounts payable or equipment, for example) are removed from the general ledger and are replaced by a single account (control account) which summarizes the detail. The details are then grouped and called a subsidiary ledger. A control account is often called the controlling account. (Solution = b.)

2. **Question**
   (L.O. 2) Each of the following likely appears as a column heading in the cash receipts journal **except:**
   a.   Accounts Receivable Cr.
   b.   Sales Dr.
   c.   Sales Discounts Dr.
   d.   Other Accounts Cr.

   Approach and Explanation: Think about the purpose of the cash receipts journal—to record all transactions involving a receipt of cash. A receipt of cash is recorded by a debit to Cash; therefore, the rest of the entry involves a credit to a noncash account. The credit is (1) to Sales for a cash sale of merchandise, or (2) to Accounts Receivable for a collection on a customer's account, or (3) to some other account (such as Equipment for a sale of equipment or Interest Revenue for interest earned on money loaned to others).

   If a merchandiser offers a cash discount on sales for timely payment of the customer's account, the collection of the account receivable within the discount period results in recording a debit to Sales Discounts (a contra sales account). Thus, a special column in the cash receipts journal for Sales Discounts Dr. is needed to accommodate the recording of this frequent transaction. Debits are made to the Sales account only to (1) correct erroneous credit entries to the same account, and (2) close the balance of the Sales account to Income Summary at the end of the period. Therefore, "Sales Dr." does not appear as a column heading in any special journal. (Solution = b.)

3. **Question**
    (L.O. 3) A checkmark entered in the "Ref." column of a single-column purchases journal indicates that the entry:
    a.   is not to be posted to any ledger.
    b.   has been posted to the general ledger.
    c.   has been posted to the appropriate subsidiary ledger.
    d.   has been posted to the general ledger and to the appropriate subsidiary ledger.

    Explanation: Answer selection "a" is incorrect because all transactions recorded in any journal must be posted to the general ledger and all transactions recorded in a single-column purchases journal must also be posted to a subsidiary ledger—the accounts payable ledger. Answer selection "b" is incorrect because the transactions recorded in the single-column purchases journal are posted to the general ledger in total at the end of the month, and the completion of that posting is indicated by placing the general ledger account numbers for Merchandise Inventory and Accounts Payable beneath the total of the single-money column. Answer selection "d" is incorrect because a checkmark appears by an individual transaction, and purchases are not posted individually to the general ledger. A checkmark is placed in the Ref. column when the posting has been made to the suppliers' (accounts payable) subsidiary ledger. Postings are to be made to the subsidiary ledger on a daily basis. (Solution = c.)

4. **Question**
    (L.O. 2) When special journals are used, the return of merchandise to a supplier for credit is usually recorded in the:
    a.   Sales journal.
    b.   Purchases journal.
    c.   Cash receipts journal.
    d.   Cash payments journal.
    e.   General journal.

    Approach and Explanation: List the four special journals discussed in this chapter and briefly describe their function. Also describe the general journal's function.
    1.   **Sales journal**—all sales of merchandise on account.
    2.   **Cash receipts journal**—all receipts of cash (including cash sales).
    3.   **Purchases journal**—all purchases of merchandise on account.
    4.   **Cash payments journal**—all payments of cash (including cash purchases).
    5.   **General journal**—all transactions that do not appropriately fit in a special journal (including adjustments and closing entries).
    The transaction described does not fit the description of any of the four special journals. Thus, it goes into the general journal. (Solution = e.)

5. **Question**
    (L.O. 2) When special journals are used, the payment to a supplier for merchandise which had previously been purchased on account is usually recorded in the:
    a.   Sales journal.
    b.   Purchases journal.
    c.   Cash receipts journal.
    d.   Cash disbursements journal.
    e.   General journal.

    Approach and Explanation: Mentally review the types of journals and their functions. All cash payments are recorded in the cash payments journal which is often called the cash disbursements journal. (Solution = d.)

6.   **Question**
(L.O. 2) When special journals are used, the most likely source of a debit posting to the Accounts Receivable account in the general ledger is the:
a.   Sales journal.
b.   Purchases journal.
c.   Cash receipts journal.
d.   Cash payments journal.
e.   General journal.

Approach and Explanation: Identify the most common reason for debits to Accounts Receivable—sales on account (on credit). Mentally review the special journals and the transactions recorded therein. All sales on account are recorded in the sales journal. (Solution = a.)

7.   **Question**
(L.O. 2) When special journals are used, the most likely source of a credit posting to an expense account in the general ledger is the:
a.   Sales journal.
b.   Purchases journal.
c.   Cash receipts journal.
d.   Cash payments journal.
e.   General journal.

Explanation: The most common reason for a credit to an expense account is a closing entry at the end of the period or possibly from an adjusting entry or a correction. All of these items are recorded in the general journal. (A cash refund for an item previously recorded as an expense would cause a credit posting and would be recorded in the cash receipts journal; however, this would not be as common as adjusting or closing entries.) (Solution = e.)

APPENDIX G

. . . .

OTHER SIGNIFICANT LIABILITIES

OVERVIEW

In addition to the various current and long-term liabilities discussed in Chapter 11, several other types of liabilities may exist that could have a significant impact on a company's financial position and future cash flows. These other significant liabilities have been classified in this appendix as (a) contingent liabilities, (b) lease liabilities, and (c) additional liabilities for employee fringe benefits (paid absences and post-retirement benefits).

SUMMARY OF LEARNING OBJECTIVES

1. **Describe the accounting and disclosure requirements for contingent liabilities.** If it is probable that the contingency will happen (if it is likely to occur) and the amount can be reasonably estimated, the liability should be recorded in the accounts. If the contingency is only reasonably possible (it could occur), then it should be disclosed only in the notes to the financial statements. If the possibility that the contingency will happen is remote (unlikely to occur), it need not be recorded or disclosed.

2. **Contrast the accounting for operating and capital leases.** For an operating lease, lease (or rental) payments are recorded as an expense by the lessee (renter). For a capital lease, the lessee records the asset and related obligation at the present value of the future lease payments.

3. **Identify additional fringe benefits associated with employee compensation.** Additional fringe benefits associated with wages are paid absences (paid vacations, sick pay benefits, and paid holidays), postretirement health care and life insurance, and pensions. The two most common types of pension arrangements are a defined-contribution plan and a defined-benefit plan.

EXERCISE G-1

Purpose: (L.O. 1) This exercise will test your ability to properly account for situations involving contingent liabilities.

As the accountant for the Blow-Dry Manufacturing Company you are to analyze the following situations in preparing the balance sheet at December 31, 2014:

1. The Blow-Dry Manufacturing Company grants a six-month warranty on each of the hair dryers it sells. Based on past experience, it is estimated that 3% of all hair dryers sold are returned; it costs the company an average of $4.40 to satisfy the warranty obligation for each unit returned. The company sold 77,000 hair dryers in the last half of 2014 and has spent $3,000 for warranty work on those units.

2. The Speedy-Dry Manufacturing Company has filed a lawsuit for $100,000 in damages against the Blow-Dry Manufacturing Company for infringement of patent rights. Legal counsel for Blow-Dry states that it is reasonably possible, but not likely, that there will be an unfavorable outcome of the case because the Blow-Dry Company has good evidence to support its position.

3. The Internal Revenue Service is currently auditing a tax return of the Blow-Dry Company for a prior year. It is remotely possible that the IRS may disallow a deduction of $4,200 on the tax return.

4. The Blow-Dry Company is a defendant in a lawsuit. A former executive filed suit on November 7, 2014 based on his claim that the Blow-Dry Company did not comply with a written promise to pay him a $50,000 bonus for 2013. The company did not make the bonus payment because the executive resigned the last week of December 2013. Legal counsel for the company states that the written agreement will probably be held to apply even though the executive resigned. The suit is expected to be settled early in 2015.

Instructions
Explain how to account for each of the situations. Should a liability be included in the body of the balance sheet at December 31, 2014 or should there only be disclosure in the notes accompanying the financial statements or should the item not be recorded or disclosed? Justify your answer.

SOLUTION TO EXERCISE G-1

1. Blow-Dry Manufacturing should **include** an estimated warranty **liability in the** current liability section of the **balance sheet** for $7,164 [(77,000 X 3% X $4.40) - $3,000]. Based on past experience, it is probable the company will have to expend goods and services to satisfy the warranty and the cost to do so is estimable.

2. Blow-Dry Manufacturing should **only disclose** this contingent liability **by a note** to accompany the financial statements. It is only reasonably possible that a liability exists at the balance sheet date due to the patent infringement lawsuit.

3. Blow-Dry Manufacturing Company **need not disclose** the IRS audit in the notes or include it in the body of the statements. It is only remotely possible that Blow-Dry will owe tax for the deduction in question.

4. Blow-Dry Company should **include** a $50,000 **liability in the** current liability section of the **balance sheet.** It appears probable that Blow-Dry will lose the suit and the amount is estimable. A journal entry should be made to accrue the loss to the current period (2014). The entry will include a debit to Loss from Lawsuit and a credit to Lawsuit Payable for $50,000.

Approach: Think about the definition of a contingent liability and how to account for one. A **contingent liability** is a potential liability that may become an actual liability in the future based on the outcome of some future event. The following guidelines apply:

1. If it is **probable** (likely) that a liability has been incurred and the amount is estimable, the liability should be recorded in the accounts. (The corresponding debit goes to an income statement account—expense or loss).

2. If it is only **reasonably possible** (less than likely and more than remote) that a liability exists, the potential liability should simply be disclosed in the notes that accompany the financial statements. That is, the potential liability will not appear in the body of the financial statements.

3. If it is only **remotely possible** (unlikely) that the future event will occur to substantiate a liability, the situation can be ignored. No liability is to be included in the balance sheet, and no note disclosure is required.

EXERCISE G-2

Purpose: (L.O. 1) This exercise will provide an example of how to account for the sale of a product that includes a warranty.

Colleen Mahla Company sells portable tables to be used for massage therapy. Each table has a built-in stereo system and carries a one-year warranty contract that requires the company to replace defective parts and to provide the necessary repair labor. During 2014, the company sold 300 tables at a unit price of $2,500. Sales occurred evenly throughout the year. The one-year warranty costs to repair defective tables are estimated to average $110 for parts and $130 for labor per unit. Approximately 10% of the tables sold are estimated to require warranty service. During 2014, the company's first year of operations, 11 units were submitted for warranty work at a total cost of $2,750.

Instructions
(a) Record the adjusting journal entry at the end of 2014 to accrue the estimated warranty costs on the 2014 sales.
(b) Prepare the entry to record repair costs incurred in 2014 to honor warranty contracts on 2014 sales.
(c) Explain how all of the relevant amounts would be reflected on the financial statements prepared at the end of 2014.
(d) Why are warranty costs accrued in the period of sale? Explain.

SOLUTION TO EXERCISE G-2

(a) 2014   Warranty Expense..   7,200
    Dec. 31   Estimated Warranty Liability....................................   7,200
                    (To accrue estimated warranty costs)
                    (300 X 10% X [$110 + $130] = $7,200)

(b) 2014   Estimated Warranty Liability...   2,750
    Jan. 1-   Repair Parts/Wages Payable   2,750
    Dec. 31   (To record honoring of 11 warranty contracts
                    on 2013 sales)

TIP: The entry in part (b) is shown in summary form. Throughout the year, customers will bring in units for warranty service and an entry to record the performance of the warranty work will be recorded at that time. The entry in part (a) is made only once a period, in the adjusting process at the end of the period, so the entry(s) in (b) is actually recorded chronologically before the entry illustrated in (a).

(c)   Warranty expense of $7,200 is reported in the selling expense classification (which is part of operating expenses) in the income statement for the year ending December 31, 2014. The balance of $4,450 ($7,200 - $2,750) in the Estimated Warranty Liability account is to be classified as a current liability on the balance sheet at December 31, 2014.

(d)   The accounting for warranty costs is based on the matching principle. To comply with this principle, the estimated cost of honoring product warranty contracts should be recognized as an expense in the period in which the sale occurs.

EXERCISE G-3

Purpose: (L.O. 2) This exercise reviews the characteristics and accounting aspects of the two types of leases.

A lease is a contractual arrangement between the lessor (owner of the property) and a lessee (renter of the property) that grants the lessee the right to use specific property for a period of time in return for cash payments. Some lease agreements are in substance installment purchases of assets by the lessees (and, thus, installment sales of the assets by the lessors), although their legal form is that of a lease.

The specific provisions of a lease contract may vary from other similar lease agreements. Generally accepted accounting principles require that each lease be properly classified as either a capital lease or an operating lease.

Instructions
Indicate whether each item below is most likely related to an operating lease or to a capital lease by using the appropriate code letters.

O = Operating Lease
C = Capital Lease

_____   1.   The lease is merely a short-term rental agreement for use of property.

_____   2.   The owner retains ownership of the leased property after the term of the lease and the property has substantial economic value after the lease has expired.

_____   3.   The lease is essentially an installment purchase of property by the lessee.

_____   4.   Rent expense appears on the lessee's financial statements in the periods in which it is incurred.

_____   5.   Interest expense is reported on the books of the lessee.

_____   6.   Rental payments are considered to be an installment of the asset's purchase price on the lessee's books.

_____   7.   Depreciation expense for the leased asset is recognized on the lessee's books.

_____   8.   Depreciation expense for the leased asset is **not** recognized on the lessee's books.

_____   9.   The lease contract is recorded by a debit to an asset account and a credit to a liability account on the lessee's books.

_____   10.   The leased asset appears on the books of the lessee.

_____ 11. The lessee uses up the total serviceability of the leased asset during the term of the lease.

_____ 12. The lessee has the right to buy the asset at the end of the lease term for a nominal purchase price.

_____ 13. The leased asset does **not** appear on the books of the lessee.

_____ 14. Present value of the minimum lease payments at the beginning of the lease term exceeds 90% of the fair value of the leased property at the inception of the lease.

_____ 15. End-of-the-period adjustments are made on the lessee's books for any accrued rent not yet paid or any rent paid in advance.

_____ 16. The lease is considered to be a purchase of the leased asset by the lessee and a sale of the leased asset by the lessor.

_____ 17. The lease transfers ownership of the property to the lessee by the end of the lease term.

SOLUTION TO EXERCISE G-3

1. O	6. C	11. C	16. C
2. O	7. C	12. C	17. C
3. C	8. O	13. O	
4. O	9. C	14. C	
5. C	10. C	15. O	

Explanation: If a lease meets any one of the following criteria, it is classified as a **capital lease:**

1. **The lease transfers ownership of the property to the lessee.** _Rationale:_ If during the lease term, the lessee receives ownership of the asset, the leased asset should be reported as an asset on the lessee's books.

2. **The lease contains a bargain purchase option.** _Rationale:_ If during the term of the lease, the lessee can purchase the asset at a price substantially below its fair market value, the lessee will obviously exercise this option. Thus, the leased asset should be reported on the lessee's books.

3. **The lease term is equal to 75% or more of the economic life of the leased property.** _Rationale:_ If the lease term is for much of the asset's useful life, the asset should be recorded on the lessee's books.

4. **The present value of the lease payments equals or exceeds 90% of the fair market value of the leased property.** _Rationale:_ If the present value of the lease payments is equal to or almost equal to the fair market value of the asset, the lessee has essentially purchased the asset. As a result, the leased asset should be recorded on the books of the lessee.

A **capital lease** is recorded on the books of the lessee by the following journal entry:

```
Leased Asset              XXX
      Lease Liability            XXX
```

The leased asset is reported on the balance sheet in the property, plant and equipment section and is depreciated in the same manner as other plant assets. The lease liability is reported as a liability on the balance sheet. The portion of the lease liability expected to be paid within the year that immediately follows the balance sheet date is classified as a current liability. The remainder is classified as a long-term liability. The portion of lease payments made during the current year that represents interest on the outstanding lease liability balance is reported under the other expense section in the income statement.

An **operating lease** is accounted for as a pure rental situation. Thus, the asset remains on the lessor's balance sheet and is depreciated by the lessor. Rent revenue is recognized by the lessor in the time period it is earned. The lessee reports rent (lease) expense in the time period it is incurred.

EXERCISE G-4

Purpose: (L.O. 1 thru 3) This exercise will quiz you about terminology used in this appendix.

A list of accounting terms with which you should be familiar appears below:

Capital lease	Operating lease
Contingent liability	Pension plan
Defined-benefit plan	Postretirement benefits
Defined-contribution plan	

Instructions
For each item below, enter in the blank the term that is described.

1. _____A potential liability that may become an actual liability in the future.

2. _____A contractual arrangement giving the lessee temporary use of the property with continued ownership of the property by the lessor.

3. _____A contractual arrangement that transfers substantially all the benefits and risks of ownership to the lessee so that the lease is in effect a purchase of the property.

4. _____Payments by employers to retired employees for health care, life insurance, and pensions.

5. _____An agreement whereby an employer provides benefits to employees after they retire.

6. _____A pension plan in which the employer's contribution to the plan is defined by the terms of the plan.

7. _____A pension plan in which the benefits that the employee will receive at retirement are defined by the terms of the plan.

SOLUTION TO EXERCISE G-4

1. Contingent liability
2. Operating lease
3. Capital lease
4. Postretirement benefits

5. Pension plan
6. Defined-contribution plan
7. Defined-benefit plan

ANALYSIS OF MULTIPLE CHOICE TYPE QUESTIONS

1. **Question**
   (L.O. 1) A company has a contingency. If it is probable that an actual liability exists at the balance sheet date, but the amount is **not** reasonably estimable, the contingent liability should be:
   a. ignored and not disclosed.
   b. reported on the face of the balance sheet without an amount.
   c. disclosed only in the notes accompanying the financial statements.
   d. reported only in the following period.

   Approach and Explanation: Briefly review in your mind the guidelines for reporting contingent liabilities:

   > If it is **probable** that a loss will occur and the amount is estimable, accrue the loss and report the liability on the face of the balance sheet.

   > If it is only **reasonably possible** a loss will occur, or if it is probable but not estimable, disclose only in the notes.

   > If the loss is **remotely possible,** it need not be disclosed or accrued.

   (Solution = c.)

TIP: In the context of accounting for contingencies, **probable** means "likely;" **remotely possible** means "not likely"; **reasonably possible** means "less than likely and more than remote."

---

2. **Question**
   (L.O. 1) An example of a contingent liability is:
   a. Sales taxes payable.
   b. Accrued salaries.
   c. Property taxes payable.
   d. A pending lawsuit.

   Approach and Explanation: Mentally define contingent liability and think of examples before you read the alternative answer selections. A **contingent liability** is a situation involving uncertainty as to possible loss or expense that will ultimately be resolved when one or more future events occur or fail to occur. Examples are pending or threatened lawsuits, pending IRS audits, and product warranties. Accrued salaries result in an actual liability. Sales taxes payable and property taxes payable are both actual liabilities if they exist at a balance sheet date. (Solution = d.)

3. **Question**
   (L.O. 1) Warranty costs are accrued in the period of sale to comply with the:
   a. matching principle.
   b. revenue recognition principle.
   c. cost principle.
   d. concept of conservatism.

Explanation: Revenues are recognized in the period they are earned to comply with the revenue recognition principle. Then the matching principle dictates that all costs incurred in generating the revenue recognized should be reported in the same time period as the revenue. Therefore, warranty costs are to be matched with the revenue from the sale of the product under warranty. (Solution = a.)

4. **Question**
   (L.O. 1) A contingent loss which is judged to be reasonably possible and estimable should be:

	Accrued	**Disclosed**
a.	Yes	Yes
b.	Yes	No
c.	No	Yes
d.	No	No

   Explanation: A contingent loss that is probable and estimable is to be accrued. A contingent loss that is reasonably possible should be disclosed, but it should not be accrued. A contingent loss that is remotely possible can be ignored. (Solution = c.)

5. **Question**
   (L.O. 1) D. Scott Corporation provides a two-year warranty with the sale of its product. Scott estimates that warranty costs will equal 4% of the selling price the first year after sale and 6% of the selling price the second year after the sale. The following data are available:

	2013	**2014**
Sales	$400,000	$500,000
Actual warranty expenditures	10,000	38,000

   The balance of the warranty liability at December 31, 2014 should be:
   a. $12,000.
   b. $42.000.
   c. $44,000.
   d. $50,000.

   Approach and Explanation: Draw a T-account for the liability and enter the amounts that would be reflected in the account and determine its balance.

	Estimated Warranty Liability		
(2) Expenditures in 2013	10,000	(1) Expense for 2013	40,000
(4) Expenditures in 2014	38,000	(3) Expense for 2014	50,000
		12/31/14 Balance	42,000

   (1) $400,000 X (4% + 6%) = $40,000 expense for 2013.
       The total warranty cost related to the products sold during 2013 should be recognized in the period of sale (matching principle).
   (2) Given data. Actual expenditures during 2013.
   (3) $500,000 X (4% + 6%) = $50,000 expense for 2014.
   (4) Given data. Actual expenditures during 2014.

   (Solution = b.)

TIP: Because some items are sold near the end of the year and the warranty is for two years, a portion of the warranty liability should be classified as a current liability (the amount pertaining to the actual expenditures estimated to occur in 2015) and the remainder as a long-term liability.

6.   **Question**
(L.O. 2) Which of the following statements is **false** regarding the proper accounting for equipment acquired by a lessee through a capital lease?:
a.   The equipment will be reported on the lessee's balance sheet.
b.   A lease liability will be reported as a long-term liability on the lessee's balance sheet.
c.   Interest expense will be reported on the lessee's income statement.
d.   The entire amount of lease payments made during the period will be reported on the lessee's income statement as Lease Expense.

Explanation: Each lease payment is viewed as an installment loan payment; thus, a portion of each payment is recorded as interest expense and the remainder is recorded as a reduction of the lease liability. Answer selection "d" describes an operating lease. (Solution = d.)

7.   **Question**
(L.O. 2) A lease meeting certain criteria should be capitalized (recorded as an asset) for financial reporting purposes. A capitalized lease will result in reporting items on financial statements that differ from the items that are reported when accounting for an operating lease. Which of the following groups represents items that will be reported by a lessee of equipment subject to a capital lease?
a.   Rent expense and prepaid rent.
b.   Interest expense and prepaid rent.
c.   Depreciation expense and interest expense.
d.   Depreciation expense and rent expense.

Approach and Explanation: Write down the entry to record the inception of a capital lease. That entry is

Leased Asset—Equipment..	XX	
Lease Liability...		XX

Think about what this will lead to as the lease period begins to progress. The asset will be depreciated (thus resulting in depreciation expense) and the liability will incur interest expense with the passage of time. Thus answer "c" is correct. An operating lease will give rise to recording prepaid rent when the rent is paid in advance and rent expense as the lease period passes. (Solution = c.)

8.   **Question**
(L.O. 2) Tom Hanks Co. has an operating lease. Rents are a constant amount each year. Rent payments made in 2014 that pertain to use of the leased asset in 2015 should be reported as:
a.   rent expense in 2014.
b.   accrued rent on the December 31, 2014 balance sheet.
c.   prepaid rent on the December 31, 2014 balance sheet.
d.   rent payable on the December 31, 2014 balance sheet.

Explanation: Rent expense paid in advance represents an asset at the December 31, 2014 balance sheet date. Rent expense paid in advance is often called prepaid rent expense or deferred rent expense. (Solution = c.)

Lightning Source UK Ltd.
Milton Keynes UK
UKOW010313150812

197528UK00002B/3/P